World War II Singapore

World War II Singapore

The Chōsabu Reports on Syonan

Translated and Edited by
Gregg Huff and Shinobu Majima

NUS PRESS
SINGAPORE

Published by:

NUS Press
National University of Singapore
AS3-01-02, 3 Arts Link
Singapore 117569

Fax: (65) 6774-0652
E-mail: nusbooks@nus.edu.sg
Website: http://nuspress.nus.edu.sg

ISBN 978-981-4722-62-9 (case)

National Library Board, Singapore Cataloguing in Publication Data

Name(s): Huff, Gregg, editor, translator. | Majima, Shinobu, editor, translator.
Title: World War II Singapore: the Chōsabu reports on Syonan / translated and edited by Gregg Huff and Shinobu Majima.
Description: Singapore: NUS Press, National University of Singapore, [2018]
Identifier(s): OCN 992984696 | ISBN 978-981-47-2262-9 (hardcover)
Subject(s): LCSH: Singapore—History—Japanese occupation, 1942–1945. | Singapore—Economic conditions—20th century. | Singapore—Social conditions—20th century.
Classification: DDC 959.5703—dc23

Typeset by: Ogma Solutions Pvt Ltd
Printed by: Mainland Press Pte Ltd

Contents

List of Tables

List of Figures

Weights and Measures

1 picul = 133.3lb = 60.478982kg = 16.8 long tons (2,240lb) in the United Kingdom, British-controlled Southeast Asia and Hong Kong.

In Japan and Taiwan, 1 picul = 60kg.

1 gantang = 6 catties, 3.6kg of rice. For rice the conversion rate of one gantang = 6 catties was the standard used by the British colonial government (*Straits Times*, 16 Aug. 1921, p. 10).

1 metric ton = 1,000kg = 2,205lb = 0.9844 long ton.

1 long ton (British ton) = 2,240lb = 1,016.0469088kg.

1kg = 1,000g = 2.205lb.

One catty (kati) = 1.33lb = 1/100 picul.

1 kin or catty = 0.6048kg in Singapore = 0.6kg or 600g in Taiwan.

A useful benchmark in assessing rations and food availability is that 12 kins = 240g.

1kg = 1.66666666667 catty or 0.00110231131092 ton (short, US).

1 sen = 1/100 yen = 1 cent = 1/100 dollar. Nominally, $1 equalled one Japanese yen and one Thai baht. The dollar was divided into 100 cents and the yen into 100 sen.

Notes

We do not attempt to change numbers if, as happens sometimes in the tables, they do not appear to add up to totals. Additionally, in the manuscripts some numbers are illegible. Where possible we have tried to fill in the gaps. Even so, column totals may not always add up to what, in the case of partial illegibility, appear to be their components. When reading the reports it is important to remember that they were produced under considerable pressure and with the added impediment that only poor-quality paper was available.

In the reports the term 'pre-war' refers to dates before 15 February 1942, when the Japanese occupied Singapore. 'The war' is used to indicate the period beginning 15 February 1942 and lasting until the end of World War II in the authors' introductions, but in the reports 'the war' indicates the period between December 1941 and February 1942, when the British and the Japanese engaged in actual combat. 'The present' denotes the time at which a given report was written.

Foreign words that are not readily translatable are put in italics.

In a number of places, square brackets ([ ]) are used to indicate passages we have written to try to amplify or explain the meaning or context of the original Japanese text.

All footnotes beginning in chapter 3 are notes written by the editors to provide additional explanation or amplify the Japanese text.

Translation

The manuscripts of the Chōsabu reports are stored in two archives in Tokyo: the whole surviving set, April 1943–January 1944, in Hitotsubashi University Library; and another, partial set, April 1943–October 1943, in the National Institute for Defense Studies. The originals are often mimeographed on crumbling paper and are in old, pre-1945 handwritten Japanese. Translation was not a straightforward matter. It first required a team of translators to decipher the script and then numerous English versions to arrive at a final translation. The aim was to remain faithful to the meaning and spirit of the Japanese original and to render this in the clear, educated English equivalent to these same characteristics of the Japanese original. Shiori Hijikata, Shinobu Majima, Gregg Huff and Gillian Huff worked on the translation through several early versions, comparing the initial translation and modified versions on the same page. All statistical tables and numbers in the text were then checked with the originals. Gregg Huff, Gillian Huff and Shinobu Majima worked on the final versions through multiple drafts to arrive at a final text.

Acknowledgements

Earlier versions of chapter 2 were presented at two seminars at Gakushuin University in March 2015 and one each at the University of Tokyo in April 2016 and Hitotsubashi University in April 2017. Our thanks go to the seminar participants and two anonymous referees for many helpful comments. We also owe a debt of gratitude for extensive and detailed comments to Yōji Akashi, Yoshiki Enatsu, Yumiko Himemoto, Tsutomu Hirayama, Brad Horton, Yukinobu Kitamura, Paul Kratoska, Bryan Lim, Sandra Manickam, Takao Matsumura, Tamotsu Nishizawa, Kōnosuke Odaka, Takashi Ōba, Osamu Saito, Masuyo Takahashi, Fiona Tan and Shun'ichi Teranishi. Shiori Hijikata and Gillian Huff worked tirelessly on the translation. Jason Lim was particularly helpful with difficult Singapore-Chinese translations in rendering characters in the original into dialect names. Shingo Kakino provided outstanding research assistance. Mike Shand drew the maps.

Shinobu Majima gratefully acknowledges support and funding from the Gakushuin University Research Institute for Oriental Cultures (Collaborative Research Grant, 2014–16) and from the Institute of Economic Research, Hitotsubashi University (Part-time Research Fellowship, 2016–17). We would not have published without the grant from the Institute of Oriental Cultures and particularly the overall support and the fellowship from the Institute of Economic Research. Majima would also like to thank Hitotsubashi University for special access to the wartime photographs, and she is also grateful to Hitotsubashi College History Archive for special consultation of this private archival collection.

Gregg Huff gratefully acknowledges support and funding from an ESRC grant (RES-062-23-1392). A Leverhulme Fellowship provided support and funding at a critical juncture which is gratefully acknowledged. Without financial support from the Leverhulme Trust, this book could not have been completed.

Part I

Singapore and the Chōsabu

CHAPTER 1

The Chōsabu Reports and the Occupation of Singapore

Gregg Huff

Singapore was fundamental to Japan's plans for control of Southeast Asia and its realization of a Greater East Asia Co-Prosperity Sphere. Of even greater worth than its status as one of the half-dozen largest cities in Southeast Asia, Singapore was strategically central to the region and its most important port. Although in preparing for war Japanese leaders were fully aware of the value of the city, plans for the effective management of an occupied Singapore remained sketchy. And yet three principal problems that would be encountered in Singapore must have been apparent even before the start of the Pacific War that began with the 7 December 1941 attack on Pearl Harbor.[1] One problem was Singapore's predominantly Chinese population and overwhelmingly Chinese character. Second, the city relied heavily on importing food from relatively distant areas. Third, weak pre-war industrialization and a predominantly unskilled labour force precluded local production from making a significant contribution either to the support of the city or to the supply of industrial goods needed for the Japanese war effort. Together, these problems made the difficulties of managing Singapore once it was in Japanese hands probably the most formidable of any of Southeast Asia's major cities.

At the end of 1942, a large number of Japanese academics and civil servants were sent to Southeast Asia as members of the Chōsabu (Department of Research), which was to report on Southeast Asian economies and societies and give Japan's administrators a better understanding of the region. Although clearly this research was intended to contribute to the military struggle, it was probably also meant to help achieve wider and longer-term aims in the enlargement of

[1] The Japanese attacked the Malay Peninsula about half an hour before Pearl Harbor. However, by itself that would probably not have caused the United States to declare war.

a Japanese empire in East Asia. Even as late as the end of 1942, and certainly during pre-war and early wartime planning, it seemed possible that Japan, as part of an enhanced empire, would control a large part of Southeast Asia for the foreseeable future.

By late 1943, when the Chōsabu first began to issue reports on Syonan (the renamed city of Singapore) and Syonan-to (Singapore Island), nearly two years of war and military occupation had considerably intensified the known pre-war problems of managing the city and its economy. The main aim of this chapter is to analyze the Chōsabu reports on Syonan in light of the policies instituted by Japanese administrators. Syonan remained under Japanese administration throughout the war, and for the whole of this time the war effort was the overriding objective of the military and Japanese administrators. The Southeast Asian civilian population came a distant second. As Japanese Finance Minister Kaya Okinori explained in November 1941, 'We will have to pursue [in occupied Southeast Asia] a so-called policy of exploitation'. He added Japan must 'adopt a policy of self-sufficiency in the South [and] keep the shipment of materials from Japan to that area to the minimum amount necessary to maintain order and to utilize labour forces there'.[2]

The combined Japanese unwillingness and, to a substantial extent, inability to ensure adequate supplies of basic foodstuffs and consumer goods for wartime Singapore meant that it was never possible effectively to manage the city either to benefit Japan's war effort or to avoid for Singaporeans chronic shortages of food and consumer goods. By the late stages of the war, malnutrition was widespread in Singapore. The city was too globally oriented, too Chinese, and too much a product of individual enterprise for the Japanese approach of restriction, regulation and self-sufficiency to work. Even by the war's early stages the complexities of managing Syonan had considerably increased, because as Japanese troops advanced southwards down the Malay Peninsula, large numbers of refugees fled south towards Singapore. By the time Singapore became Syonan the island's population had risen to perhaps 900,000, compared to 727,600 in 1939, and the problem of food supply had grown accordingly. To begin with, rice stockpiled by the British could be distributed as rations and used to feed the population.[3] Furthermore, the initial near-total Japanese hegemony in Southeast Asia, and the latter's role as the world's main exporting region, suggested that food sufficient to maintain Syonan's population at a functioning level would not

[2] Japan, Imperial Headquarters, Nampō Senryōchi Gyōsei Jisshi Yōkō, presented at the Imperial Conference, 5 November 1941, in Kishi Collection B1-224. Kaya repeated these same policies at the Imperial Conference on 1 December when Japan took the formal decision for war.

[3] National Archives, Kew (hereafter NA, Kew), CO852/327/9, 'Food Supplies: Malaya' details the pre-war build-up of stocks of rice and other foodstuffs.

be a stumbling block. Before long, however, a lack of transport and misguided Japanese attempts at control led to increasingly severe food shortages. By mid-1943, low nutritional levels among employees made it difficult to secure adequate work effort even in Japanese factories.

At first, Chōsabu members were primarily observers, reporters and advisers. Although the Chōsabu bore no responsibility for early events in Syonan, after January 1944, as explained in chapter 2, members of the Chōsabu began to be called upon to formulate policies and strategies to try to deal with serious and mounting problems in the city and apparently had some role in its day-to-day running. It is unclear, however, to what extent, if any, the Chōsabu had any major policy impact. By the time the researchers began to assess Syonan's economy and society, official policies had long been in place and would have been hard to reverse. Furthermore, both the Chōsabu's advice and its researchers apparently were often distrusted by the military.

The Chōsabu reports, translated here for the first time, afford some of the only extant Japanese-language records of wartime Syonan, since near the end of the war or just after, on orders from Tokyo, most records on Southeast Asia were destroyed. A strongly empirical approach runs throughout the work of the Chōsabu. That makes its reports, written between October 1943 and October 1944, especially valuable in helping to understand what happened in Singapore during Japan's occupation.

The Chōsabu reports on Syonan are the book's subject, but these were part of a much wider Japanese research agenda that encompassed most of Southeast Asia. Branches of the Chōsabu in Indonesia, North Borneo and the Philippines were all supervised by the Syonan and Malaya Chōsabu. In Burma and Sumatra, Chōsabu research was carried out under the auspices of the Manchurian Railways Company. Researchers were not sent to Thailand and Indochina because in both countries pre-war governments continued to operate.

This chapter analyzes the extent and nature of Chōsabu research on Syonan. In the next chapter discussion focuses on the men of the Chōsabu, their research interests, their place in Japanese economic and social thought, and their careers after the war.

Pre-war Singapore

Singapore was even more of a Chinese city than Bangkok or Saigon-Cholon. In 1939, Chinese comprised in excess of three-quarters of the over half a million residents of Singapore municipality and a similar share of the 727,600 inhabitants of Singapore Island as a whole. Because the peopling of Singapore had depended on large immigrant inflows from southeastern China, most Chinese, even when not recently arrived immigrants, looked to China and felt an allegiance towards it akin to nationalism. Identification with China and, furthermore, implacable opposition to Japan strengthened after the outbreak of the Sino-Japanese War in July 1937. Singapore Chinese business, almost wholly the preserve of the so-called China-Chinese as contrasted with a comparatively small English-educated contingent, quickly mounted effective boycotts of Japanese goods. These were stiffened by strong patriotism and peer pressure, and further enforced by measures such as severing one or both ears of transgressors.[4] Neither the roughly 10 per cent of those in Singapore who were Indians nor a similarly sized Malay population afforded any real counterweight to Chinese dominance. For occupied Singapore to function even partially, Japan had to achieve, through some combination of compulsion and incentives, at least tacit cooperation from a substantial section of the Chinese community.

The problem of supplying Syonan with enough food—in effect rice, the staple on which nearly all its residents relied—was formidable. Other large Southeast Asian cities were either contiguous to their great rice-growing regions (Rangoon, Bangkok and Saigon-Cholon) or not too far from rice-growing areas (Manila was near Central Luzon and Jakarta in rice-producing West Java). By contrast, Singapore, an island of just 225 square miles at the tip of the Malay Peninsula, grew little of its own food. Moreover, the Malay Peninsula's extreme specialization in producing tin and rubber for export left it, too, chiefly reliant on rice imports. In 1931, rice cultivation in Malaya (Singapore plus the Malay Peninsula and Penang) totalled 670,000 acres, or about a fifth of rubber acreage. The country harvested 173,000 tons of clean rice annually and imported 550,000 to 600,000 tons.[5]

Rice reached Singapore principally from Thailand, where Bangkok Chinese controlled exports as millers and traders and had close links with their Singapore Chinese counterparts. However, benefiting from its geographical location, Singapore also distributed rice from Burma and Indochina. Trade was often two-sided. Just as imports from Thailand gave rise to return cargoes of dried fish, sugar and cotton piece goods, commerce in rice with Southeast Asia's other main producers was bound up with trade in non-rice foodstuffs including Chinese vegetables and dried fish and also the transport of Chinese immigrants. These commercial interlinkages enabled Singapore to draw freely and at low prices on rice supplies throughout Southeast Asia. In the early 1930s some 18 firms organized as the Singapore Rice Traders' Association were the rice trade's market makers, buying from importers and reselling to distributors in the city. For the

---

[4] National Archives of Singapore (hereafter NAS), Oral History interview 000283/2, Ng Seng Yong.

[5] Federated Malay States, *Report of the Rice Cultivation Committee*, 2 vols, Vol. 1 (Kuala Lumpur: Government Press, 1931), pp. 17–8.

trade in rice from Thailand, the Rice Traders' Association was dominated, until this changed during the war, by men from the Teochew dialect group; Teochew was the language spoken around the port of Swatow (Shantou) in China. Within the association, there were almost certainly trading rules that were generally understood, although probably not extensively formalized in writing. As one of the association's members explained: 'we form our own little parties and tender for the rice.'[6]

Singapore developed as what can be called a staple port: an urban economy devoted above all to handling staples, in this instance rubber and tin produced in the Malay Peninsula and outer islands of Indonesia and selling to these regions return flows of imported food, above all rice, and simple manufactures. Overwhelmingly a service provider, Singapore manufactured little itself: urbanization could be seen as driven by industrialization only in the secondary sense that manufacturing in the West created a demand for the rubber and tin that Singapore handled. Singapore relied on imports for almost all of its supply of textiles and basic consumer goods such as thread, matches, light bulbs and essential medicines. It is unclear how the Chōsabu report *Countermeasures for Prices* defined consumer goods, but its estimation that before the war Singapore imported 75 per cent of these was probably about right. Even when a few goods such as matches and soap had been produced locally, this depended on importing some raw or manufactured materials necessary for production. Nevertheless, Singapore was by far Malaya's main industrial centre. Penang had a municipal population of 149,000 and Kuala Lumpur one of 111,400, and so markets too small to support much consumer-based manufacturing industry. Once Japan occupied Singapore, nearly all foreign trade ceased. The supply of consumer goods for Syonan and Malaya as a whole became almost entirely reliant on a combination of drawing down pre-war stocks and devising substitutes.

The lack of industry in Singapore accorded poorly with Japanese occupation policy, which decreed that Southeast Asian countries, and by the late stages of the war even regions or subregions, become self-sufficient in food and basic manufactures. Local manufacturing was expected additionally to contribute to Japan's war effort. Singapore had engineering and metal production enterprises linked to the tin and rubber industries and facilities for ship repair. Otherwise, however, the city could make only a small contribution to Japan's military needs. Nor with a few exceptions, notably a factory to make acetylene needed for the repair of airplanes, did the Japanese set up new industries.

---

[6] Straits Settlements, *Report of the Commission to Enquire into and Report on the Trade of the Colony*, 5 vols, Vol. 2 (Singapore: Government Printing Office, 1934), p. 636; Gregg Huff, *The Economic Growth of Singapore: Trade and Development in the Twentieth Century* (Cambridge: Cambridge University Press, 1994), pp. 102–6, 155.

Singapore Becomes Syonan

The speed with which, after the attack on Pearl Harbor, the Japanese military swept through Southeast Asia gave little opportunity to consider how to overcome the problems of managing Singapore. The city fell on 15 February 1942, a little over two months after Japanese troops had first landed in northern Malaya. Singapore became Syonan (or Shōnan translated from Japanese as *Shō* meaning 'radiant', as in the ruling dynasty Shōwa, and *Nan* meaning 'south'. Syonan is, however, often rendered in English as 'Light of the South').[7] By May 1942, Japan controlled all Southeast Asia's main countries of Burma, Thailand, Malaya, Indonesia, Indochina and the Philippines. The geographical extent of Southeast Asia (1.7 million square miles) and its large population (145 million, about twice that of Japan) badly stretched Japanese administrative resources and ensured, especially in the early stages of occupation, a limited civilian presence to temper military control.

Colonel Watanabe Wataru, characterized as the architect of military administration in Malaya, was a principal figure during the start and early phase of the occupation of Syonan. Watanabe's administrative approach was shaped by his previous tenure with the Tokumu Kikan (Special Service Agency) in occupied China and the unquestioning acquiescence of a coterie of lieutenants, like Watanabe all from the Japanese prefecture of Okayama. Draconian social control methods were apparently formulated on high authority. They are believed to have been masterminded by Colonel Tsuji Masanobu and were ordered by Yamashita Tomoyuki, who had led the invasion of Singapore and after the war was executed for his part in the Rape of Manila. Repressive measures applied upon occupying Syonan emphasized violence and the aim of 'spiritual cleansing'. The latter had its fullest expression in the slaughter of perhaps 23,000 (estimates vary from 5,000 to upwards of 40,000) Syonan Chinese soon after occupation.[8]

Japanese bureaucrats who arrived to administer Malaya disapproved of Watanabe's hard line and of his cronies. The latter were systematically transferred from Malaya, although Watanabe did not depart until March 1943. By then, continued strong repression had fed a combination of widespread, deep Syonan Chinese resentment, often hatred, towards the Japanese and a real fear of them. Understandably, most of those in Syonan opted for caution and discretion.

---

[7] Tessa Morris-Suzuki, *Shōwa: An Inside History of Hirohito's Japan* (London: Athlone Press, 1984), p. 99.

[8] Akashi Yoji, 'Colonel Watanabe Wataru: The Architect of the Malayan Military Administration, December 1941–March 1943', in *New Perspectives on the Japanese Occupation in Malaya and Singapore, 1941–1945*, ed. Akashi Yoji and Yoshimura Mako (Singapore: NUS Press, 2008), pp. 33–64; Akashi Yoji, 'Japanese Policy towards the Malayan Chinese 1941–1945', *Journal of Southeast Asian Studies* 1, 2 (1970): 61–89; Yuma Totani, *The Tokyo War Crimes Trial: The Pursuit of Justice in the Wake of World War II* (Cambridge: Harvard University Asia Center, 2008), pp. 163–4.

Although underground resistance emerged, particularly in the Malay Peninsula—where the Chinese-dominated, mainly Communist Malayan People's Anti-Japanese Army operated—in Syonan organized opposition to the Japanese did not develop. As Virginia Thompson has observed, the strictness of Japanese rule seems to have eliminated any possibility of strikes.[9] For the most part, people got on with life as best they could under increasingly difficult circumstances.

Transport soon became a bottleneck to supplying Syonan with rice and other foodstuffs, and by mid-1943 increasingly serious Japanese merchant shipping shortages put severe pressure on food supplies. In December 1941 Japan's merchant fleet was already too small to meet the needs of the home economy and the logistic requirements of her forces in the Pacific.[10] Despite this, Japanese war planners assumed that shipping losses would be relatively small and could be made good by the construction of new ships. Merchant ships were, however, inadequately protected against Allied air and, especially, submarine attack, because they were not organized in a convoy system and because they were poorly deployed. Serviceable Japanese merchant tonnage contracted from 5.4 million tons in December 1941 to 4.2 million tons in December 1943 and 2 million tons a year later. By the time Japan surrendered in August 1945 it had just a million tons of merchant shipping.[11]

According to the report written by the Department of Police Administration on *Economic Security* (chapter 8), the original intention was to draw on rice in Burma to feed Syonan. The logic was probably that Burma was the world's largest rice exporter and that its supply of Syonan and Malaya would allow Thailand to export chiefly to Japan and Japanese troops in China. It soon became apparent that rice could not be moved from Burma for want of shipping and because the Allies increasingly wrested control of the seas from Japan and Japanese ships faced almost constant danger from Allied air and submarine attack.

By 1944 the Japanese Home Islands were badly in need of food imports. Although during the first two years of the war Japan obtained large quantities of rice from Thailand and Indochina, thereafter supplies fell sharply as a result of the losses sustained by Japan's merchant fleet and the reassignment of vessels to military use. Instead of Burma, Japanese officials had to turn to Thailand to supply rice to Syonan and Malaya. While Thailand was not far from Syonan, obtaining rice through officially designated channels proved difficult. Syonan

---

[9] Virginia Thompson, *Labor Problems in Southeast Asia* (New Haven: Yale University Press, 1947), p. 12.

[10] United States Strategic Bombing Survey, *The Effects of Strategic Bombing on Japan's War Economy* (Washington, DC: Overall Economic Effects Division, United States Strategic Bombing Survey, 1946), p. 41.

[11] United States Strategic Bombing Survey, *The War against Japanese Transportation 1941–1945* (Washington, DC: Transportation Division, United States Strategic Bombing Survey, 1947), p. 116.

officials had instead to look to supplies brought, under permit, to the city by private Chinese traders and also to a large black market to feed the city even at subsistence levels.

Occupation Comparisons

Although military occupation in Syonan had its own distinct features, little or nothing was unique in the city's experience. Probably greater differences existed between Syonan and either Rangoon or Saigon-Cholon than between Syonan and Athens. The Greek capital, with a 1940 census population of 956,800, was comparable in size to the three Southeast Asian cities; and common to Athens and the cities in Southeast Asia was a non-industrial character that limited their contribution to the German and Japanese war efforts.[12] While all four cities had predominantly agricultural hinterlands, what divided them was access to food. While Rangoon and Saigon-Cholon were located in two of the world's great food-surplus regions, Syonan and Athens were surrounded by food-deficit areas. Greece imported 45 per cent of all consumed cereals, a proportion that, although less than Malaya's, was nevertheless substantial.[13] Nor did either Malaya or Greece specialize in producing raw materials of any great use to their occupiers; Malayan rubber and tin were of almost no value to the Japanese. A report on food supply in Greece emphasized the role of the black market and concluded that: 'If all the Greeks based their hopes of being fed solely on the efforts of the government, no one would remain alive for this report.'[14] Syonan, unlike Rangoon and Saigon-Cholon but in common with Athens, suffered acute wartime food shortages, received net inflows of people from rural districts hoping to find food and work, and had a population for whom recourse to the black market was essential for survival.

In Syonan and Athens alike, the principal characteristics that allowed rampant black markets were a chronic lack of goods and governments too weak to implement effective price controls over extensive urban areas. In Syonan, for example, the report on *Economic Security* (chapter 7) recorded some 1,971 rice retailers, including 548 who dealt in 1–15 sacks per month and many larger distributors. Both cities experienced runaway inflation and then hyperinflation as a result of wholesale money creation to shift the costs of occupation onto the occupied. In each city the scarcity of food along with the lack of goods helped to push up prices more than might have been expected from monetary expansion

[12] V.G. Valaoras, 'Some Effects of Famine on the Population of Greece', *Milbank Memorial Fund Quarterly* 24, 3 (1946): 215.

[13] Violetta Hionidou, 'The Demography of a Greek Famine: Mykonos, 1941–1942', *Continuity and Change* 10, 2 (1995): 296.

[14] Mark Mazower, *Inside Hitler's Greece: The Experience of Occupation, 1941–44* (New Haven: Yale University Press, 1993), p. 53. Mazower was quoting Marcel Junod of the Red Cross.

alone. Syonan and Athens alike were partially cut off from surrounding regions and so hampered in bringing in supplies from pre-war sources. Isolation was a greater hardship for Syonan than Athens because before the war it had relied on imports, mostly from the West, for such a high proportion of basic consumer items.

While among Greeks inflation led to the use of olive oil and quinine tablets as a money substitute, in Syonan Japanese-issued military scrip continued to serve as a medium of exchange. The divergence is probably largely explained by much higher Greek than Malayan inflation. Between July 1939 and 1944, Greek note circulation increased by 312,421,900 per cent; notes issued in November 1944 were at a rate of one new drachma for 50,000 million old drachma.[15] An additional reason for the Greek use of money substitutes is probably that while the incidence of malaria increased in both cities, the distribution in Greece of quinine tablets by the Red Cross appears to have made them more available than in Syonan. There may also have been a greater fear of malaria in Greece than in Syonan, and this would have enhanced the 'moneyness' of the tablets by making them more readily exchangeable.[16] By the later stages of the war, malnutrition was evident in both cities although more widespread in Syonan. However, unlike Greece, neither Syonan nor Malaya experienced mass famine.

Terror functioned as a means of social control in both Syonan and Athens. In Syonan, however, after the early massacre of Chinese, this seems to have continued at a lower intensity than in Athens, where arbitrary round-ups and executions became routine in response to a widespread and organized resistance. Insofar as the underground network of resistance to the Nazis that emerged in the Greek city had a counterpart, it operated chiefly in the Malay Peninsula.

A crucial determinant of the eventual social and economic costs of occupation is the extent to which armed conflict takes place during occupation or liberation. In January 1942 General Douglas MacArthur decided not to try to defend Manila, and, apart from some destruction of strategic facilities by departing American forces, the Japanese took over a more or less intact city. By contrast, in February 1945 the Japanese determined that Manila must be defended to the last building and man. During a lengthy battle, Manila, once the 'Pearl of the Orient', became the scene of some of World War II's most extreme atrocities. It was second only to Warsaw as the most damaged city in countries occupied during World War II. According to Shinozaki Mamoru, if the Allies had invaded Syonan the 'loss of lives and damage to property would probably have been greater than in Manila. In Singapore, the Japanese were better armed and had enough rice to last them

---

15 League of Nations, *World Economic Survey, 1942/44* (Geneva: League of Nations, 1945), pp. 201–2, 209.

16 Mazower, *Inside Hitler's Greece*, pp. 65, 203–4; Violetta Hionidou, *Famine and Death in Occupied Greece, 1941–1944* (Cambridge: Cambridge University Press, 2006), p. 94.

a year.'[17] Japanese troops would, as their training demanded, have fought to the death. Even Chōsabu members, as noted in chapter 2, attended drills in the use of suicide bombs to blow up tanks.

As events transpired, occupation in Syonan ended rather quietly. There was, of course, a degree of civil disorder and retributions until the Allies began to arrive about a month after the sudden Japanese surrender on 15 August 1945. Athens, by contrast, experienced extreme disorder. The Greek resistance, which had struggled against the Nazis, then fought, in brutal and protracted conflict, Greek rightists and, in December 1944, British troops for control of Athens. Syonan was lucky to be spared a violent and destructive end to war in the city and during the aftermath of liberation. It was, of course, just luck. But for the citizens of Syonan, that had been lacking during three and a half years of occupation.

Population, Labour Supply and Industrial Production

Chapter 3: Population by Occupation in Syonan Municipality. Surveyed by Odabashi Sadatoshi and Ōmura Junzaburō, December 1943

Chapter 4: Reorganizing Commercial Businesses in Syonan Municipality. Higuchi Gorō and Nagamori Masaji, September 1944

Chapter 5: A Study of the Labour Situation in Syonan Municipality, Focusing on Factories Managed by Japanese. Surveyed by Civilian Administrator Izawa Kozō and Civilian Associate Ōmura Junzaburō, October 1944

Chapter 6: An Overview of Important Industrial Factories in Syonan Municipality. Military Administration, Department of General Affairs, Research Office, March 1943

Population

In late 1943, as well as a remarkably racially and ethnically varied population, Syonan had many more people than before the war. The most recent census was in 1931, although British officials had estimated the island's 1939 population. A main purpose of the Chōsabu report *The Population of Syonan* was, as a complement to a 1943 Japanese police census, to establish who the people in Syonan were, where they lived and what they did. Census information was part of attempts to achieve effective rationing, to gauge the need to supply food and other goods, and to try to make efficient use of labour in Syonan.

In 1943 the Japanese enumerated 855,700 people living on Syonan Island compared to the 727,600 estimated by the British in 1939, an annual average growth rate of 4.1 per cent. Such rapid increase can only have reflected

[17] Shinozaki Mamoru, *Syonan, My Story: The Japanese Occupation of Singapore* (Singapore: Times Books International, 1975), p. 94.

substantial inward migration.[18] Contrary to the suggestion that during the war in a number of Southeast Asia's large cities many people evacuated to rural areas to begin subsistence cultivation, Syonan experienced net inflows of people from surrounding areas.[19]

Table 1.1 Syonan population by race and ethnic group, 1931 and 1943

		1931	%	1943	%
Chinese		421,821	76.4	675,726	78.8
	Hokkien	181,287	32.8	253,547	29.6
	Teochew	82,516	14.9	119,702	14.0
	Cantonese	95,114	17.2	121,274	14.1
	Hakka	19,716	3.6	22,981	2.7
	Hainanese	20,040	3.6	34,739	4.1
	Others	23,148	4.2	123,483	14.4
Indians		51,019	9.2	78,213	9.1
Malays		71,177	12.9	91,509	10.7
Others		8,352	1.5	12,225	1.4
Total		552,369	100.0	857,673	100.0

Note: For both 1931 and 1943 population by race does not add up to total population and percentages may be slightly inaccurate. In 1943 the high percentage of 'other Chinese' is almost certainly due to a failure to classify a number of Chinese according to ethnic group.

Source: Vlieland, Malaya 1931 census, pp. 180–1; chapter 3, table 3.1.

Between 1931 and 1943, the increase in Syonan's population by just under 300,000 was accompanied by some modification in its racial and ethnic composition (table 1.1). Syonan became, if anything, more of a Chinese city. In 1931 Chinese comprised 76.4 per cent of the population, but by 1943 this figure had increased to 78.8 per cent. The relative importance of Chinese dialect groups appears to have stayed more or less constant, although the large number

[18] The police census in the spring of 1943 showed a population of 863,700.

[19] For the argument of a wartime urban exodus in large cities including Syonan, see D.W. Fryer, 'The "Million City" in Southeast Asia', *Geographical Review* 43, 4 (1953): 491; James C. Scott, 'An Approach to the Problems of Food Supply in Southeast Asia during World War Two', in *Food Supply in the Second World War*, ed. Bernd Martin and Alan S. Milward (Ostfildern: Scripta Mercaturae, 1985), p. 271; Lizzie Collingham, *The Taste of War: World War II and the Battle for Food* (London: Allen Lane, 2011), p. 335.

of Chinese unclassified by the Chōsabu survey and listed as 'others' makes it impossible to be certain. Between 1931 and 1943, while the share of Indians in the population did not alter significantly there was a noticeable fall in the Malay presence. That may have been because Malays, as the racial group most likely to have family or kinship ties in the peninsula, would have had the best chance of leaving Syonan if they wished. Syonan Malays may also have been more willing to retreat to the peninsula to engage in agriculture. Few people in Syonan had either relatives up-country or, more important, any farming experience.[20] Both these considerations were, however, probably less true of Malays than other races.[21] Many Malays lived on the fringes of the city or outside it and engaged in at least some agricultural activity.

Labour

The bulk of Syonan Chinese were either Hokkiens (the dialect pronunciation of the Southeastern Chinese province of Fukien (Fujian) from where they came) or Teochews who originated from that part of Kwangtung (Guangdong) province near the port of Swatow (Shantou) and adjacent to the Fukien border. Although these two groups spoke mutually intelligible dialects, other Chinese ethnic groups conversed in their own dialects that were different from both Hokkien and Teochew. Malays and Indians had their own languages, which among the latter varied depending on geographical origin in India. As part of the effort to integrate Syonan into the Co-Prosperity Sphere, the Japanese tried to teach their own language, Nippon-Go. Its general use could, however, have been achieved only over a long period. Japanese-language textbooks and teachers did not arrive in Syonan until July 1942, and even after that Japanese songs and the national anthem comprised a significant part of the language curriculum in schools. During the occupation, English afforded the only possible lingua franca.

For Japanese researchers the structure of employment in Syonan was possibly one of the most unexpected, and troubling, findings of the *Population of Syonan*. Most of the Chōsabu reports are concerned with problems of labour mobilization and the difficulties of feeding the population. Table 1.2 helps to grasp the dimensions of these issues and provides some historical perspective on them. During the 1930s an equalization of the sex ratio, already under way for some decades, continued; and, associated with this, birth rates rose. Mainly as a result of these demographic changes there was a sharp increase in Syonan's

---

20 Shinozaki, *Syonan, My Story*, p. 80.

21 Although 'race' is not a strictly correct term, it is sanctioned by Malayan usage. It regards Chinese, Indians and Malays as the three main races. Chinese dialect groups or 'tribes' are denoted as ethnic groups. See C.A. Vlieland, *British Malaya, A Report on the 1931 Census* (Singapore: Government Printing Office, 1932), p. 73.

Table 1.2 Syonan labour force by employed and unemployed, 1931 and 1943

	1931	1943
Employed males	256,277	307,454
Unemployed males	10,991	27,091
Male labour force	267,268	334,545
% of males employed	95.9	91.9
Employed females	18,027	33,819
Unemployed females	109,007	162,578
Female labour force	127,034	196,397
% of females employed	14.2	17.2
Total labour force employed	274,304	341,273
Total labour force	394,302	530,942
% of total labour force employed	69.6	64.3
Total population	567,453	855,679
Labour force as % of total population	69.5	62.0

Note: In 1943 labour force is defined as the population aged 15 to 50. For 1931 it is the total of those employed by industry, and the total labour force is those aged 15 to 54.

Source: Malaya 1931 census, pp. 120–1, 180, 232–3, 252–5; Huff, *Economic Growth of Singapore*, pp. 407–11; chapter 3, table 3.2.

dependency ratio.[22] A ratio of 30.5 per cent in 1931 had, by 1943, risen to close to 40 per cent. Furthermore, although between 1931 and 1943 the proportion of working women increased, the female labour force participation rate remained low, at just 17.2 per cent in 1943. While the number of working-age women rose by over 69,000, the number of employed women increased by less than 16,000. The *Population* report, translated as chapter 3, repeatedly emphasizes two aspects of Syonan's labour force. One is how few women in Syonan worked, and the consequent economic burden of feeding a large non-working contingent of working-age females; the other the desirability of mobilizing labour and

[22] The dependency ratio is the population ages 0–14 and 55 and over as a proportion of the remainder of the population, defined here as the labour force and inclusive of everyone aged 15–54.

shifting it into more productive pursuits. At the end of December 1944 the Japanese enforced regulations that directed men aged 15 to 40 to work in essential activities, defined as agriculture, war establishments, and the production of needed consumer goods and manufactured materials.[23]

The Chōsabu report's surprise at low female labour force participation in Syonan is understandable: it might have been thought that where food and other resources had become as scarce as they had, all possible sources of income, including paid employment, would be exploited by women as well as men. One possibility is that no jobs existed; however, the Japanese researchers appear to have believed that they did, and in keeping with their assessment, it seems likely that in fact there were many unfilled jobs. In that case, were women engaged in activities that were more advantageous than paid employment? If so, the explanation must be that unfilled jobs were unattractive either because people did not want to work for the Japanese or because total remuneration from taking available jobs was no more, or even less, than rations plus income from other possible pursuits such as hawking, queue-standing, scavenging, supporting the home economy, or casual employment including occasional prostitution. Any of these activities might yield higher returns than employment in available jobs if these were far from the place of residence, as for example agricultural work, and if this work hindered the ability to queue from the early hours of morning for rations. The progressive wartime loss of public transport was a serious impediment to labour mobility. For most Syonanese, an available job outside central Syonan's densely packed centre would require travel and this might be difficult and would entail expense. Travel away from home might also compromise the chance of obtaining rations, which might suddenly become available and for which queuing for long periods became increasingly necessary.

The Japanese wartime problem of supporting a larger population than in 1931 and one with proportionately fewer workers is, however, likely somewhat overstated by the data in table 1.2. One reason for this is merely statistical: in 1931 the labour force included the population aged 15 to 54 but (following Japanese practice) in 1943 only those aged 15 to 50. That discrepancy is, however, of only minor significance. Probably more important is that, apart from the known increase in open unemployment, the economic effects of the wartime Japanese military occupation also pushed more workers into the informal sector and casual employment. Some of these individuals were probably not included in the Chōsabu population census. Among the informal workers and the partially employed who may not have been recorded as in employment, but who in fact would not have been supported by those classified as working, could have been the city's many minor black market brokers and information gatherers. Much

[23] Paul H. Kratoska, *The Japanese Occupation of Malaya: A Social and Economic History* (London: Hurst & Company, 1998), p. 188.

larger groups among those who in fact worked during the occupation, but were almost certainly not all enumerated as working, were hawkers and prostitutes. There was an upsurge in both of these occupations during the war.[24] The difficulty of recording these people was increased by the fact that some of them were almost certainly part-time or occasional workers.

While hawking and prostitution were well-established pursuits, queue-standing appeared as a new wartime occupation and one that could easily have been missed. As the Chōsabu report on the *Labour Situation* (chapter 5) notes, people began to queue for rationed goods from 2am onwards. For many unemployed, older or less able-bodied people, chronic shortages of goods and a large black market made queue-standing a recognized 'profession'. In urban Malaya, for those lacking other work, queuing and the sale of rationed goods at enhanced prices was 'always a possible source of livelihood'.[25]

Syonan was not, of course, unique in the responses of many of its citizens to arbitrage opportunities and a low cost of time. Black marketeers in early post-war Japan 'would get waifs and strays to sit in the queue for them, and then they would sell the [railway] tickets at some vastly inflated price'.[26] In Syonan, a number of those who queued for a living probably worked, as in Japan, for someone else and were financed by them. For most of those who queued professionally in Syonan, the opportunity cost of alternative employment is likely to have been low while the rewards from queuing could be high: when successful, 'the proceeds of the long wait could be disposed of at ten times the sum paid'.[27]

The Japanese occupation soon destroyed Syonan's economy, and with this the social order also broke down as food became increasingly scarce and unemployment and, probably even more, underemployment became widespread. The Japanese employed about 70,000 persons, more than a fifth of the labour force. Some people, although subject to accusations of being sympathizers, were happy to work for the Japanese.[28] Others were not. Nor could employment by the Japanese possibly take up all the slack of a primarily commercial economy where

---

[24] Chin Kee Onn, *Malaya Upside Down* (Singapore: Jitts & Co., 1946), p. 69. Similarly, in Jakarta in response to wartime unemployment 'many Chinese found themselves running small stalls' described as a 'new and flourishing trade'. Twang Peck Yang, *The Chinese Business Elite in Indonesia and the Transition to Independence* (Kuala Lumpur: Oxford University Press, 1998), p. 101.

[25] M.V. Del Tufo, *Malaya, A Report on the 1947 Census of Population* (London: Crown Agents, 1949), p. 34.

[26] Tessa Morris-Suzuki, *Shōwa: An Inside History of Hirohito's Japan* (London: Athlone Press, 1984), p. 200.

[27] N.I. Low, *When Singapore Was Syonan-to* (Singapore: Eastern Universities Press, 1973), p. 63; N.I. Low and H.M. Cheng, *This Singapore (Our City of Dreadful Night)* (Singapore: Ngai Seong Press, 1946), pp. 127–8.

[28] NAS, Oral History interviews 000021, Chan Chee Seng, and 000007, Wong Lau Eng.

pre-war commerce had effectively ceased and the labour supply was swollen by inwards migration. As discussed above, and as the Chōsabu reports make clear, many Syonanese turned to hawking or other self-employment occupations with minimal entry barriers.

To some extent an increase in self-employed traders and hawkers reflected a wartime climate of imperfect information, risk, fear and a burgeoning black market. Information deficiencies gave rise to new classes of brokers who, often as part of complex networks, facilitated the discovery of scarce goods. Chin describes those in the upper echelons of an informal economy that grew up as part of a wartime distributive system: '[T]he highest class of brokers were the "arm-chair brokers" [who each] had a corps of co-operatives. Chief among these were "lieutenant brokers"' who specialized in one type of goods or another. Lieutenants alone had the right to approach the chief and directed 'field brokers.' These latter went about the city nosing for contacts and relied on a yet larger group of brokers, the so-called nondescripts. Such men were the first point of contact between buyer and seller. Like packs of reporters, they haunted the coffee shops, hotels, restaurants and lodging houses and roved the country in search of goods.[29] In the report on *Economic Security* (chapter 8), it was recommended that Syonan's brokers be shut down. That appears, however, never to have happened.

At the bottom of Syonan's new wartime informal economy, hawkers had an important distributive role. Uniquely, they had informational advantages that derived from an area-specific knowledge and a known clientele. In Syonan, retail black market distribution of basic goods like food was generally through coffee shops and hawkers. One reason for this was that most 'wholesale' distributors assessed contact with the public as too risky.[30] For a great number of people, however, hawking appears to have been a residual occupation. The Chōsabu *Population* census explained that: 'groups such as street vendors have no choice about their work. If they are able to find a better job, they will willingly change their occupation. But in present conditions they cannot find satisfactory work and are compelled to do what they can to buy food.'

Although the Japanese researchers seem to have thought the overspill of street vendors a new phenomenon, hawking had always had this function in Singapore at times of economic downturn like the slump at the beginning of the 1930s. In an analysis much like that in the *Population* census, the 1932 Hawkers Enquiry Commission found that 'the "out-of-work" have taken to hawking in considerable numbers as the only means of earning even a small pittance'.[31] The burgeoning number of 1930s 'slump hawkers' resulted in a lack of street discipline, pavement

---

[29] Chin, *Malaya Upside Down*, pp. 42–3.

[30] Kratoska, *Japanese Occupation*, p. 169.

[31] Straits Settlements, 'Committee to Investigate the Hawker Question', *Straits Settlements Legislative Council Proceedings 1932*, p. C12; see also p. C70.

obstruction, and encouragement to corruption through bribes to the lower ranks of the police and municipal servants. In 1930 the Singapore Police Force dealt with over 22,000 cases of unlicensed hawkers and the obstruction of streets and five-foot ways with goods stalls, etc.[32]

The wartime overspill of hawkers onto the streets of Syonan was, however, probably even more extreme than in the 1930s because the economic downturn was more severe and because the 'safety valve' for unemployment and underemployment of returning to China that had previously operated in Singapore was now unavailable. Chōsabu reports, like British reports before them, frequently point to the need to restrict hawkers to specified areas with fixed shelters for these traders. According to Chin Kee Onn, during the war 'hawkers increased by the thousands, and they glutted highways and byways; perambulating-stalls and semi-permanent stalls were everywhere; five-foot ways became open-air cafes'.[33] Likewise, after the war the British apparently were unable to confine hawking to so-called shelter hawkers (i.e., hawkers operating from a shelter rather than simply being on the street). One of the most visible aspects of immediately post-war central Singapore was the very great number of unregulated street sellers.[34]

Concerns over labour supply, as well as being a theme that runs throughout the Chōsabu reports discussed in this section, appear in much other Research Bureau work. The allocation of labour concerned the Chōsabu for two main reasons. One was that by the time its researchers began to examine Syonan's economy, the Japanese were encountering labour shortages. It is not known, however, to what extent, if at all, Chōsabu recommendations influenced the December 1944 policy, indicated above, that workers should move from jobs that did not contribute to the war effort in favour of work in agriculture, in war establishments, or in the production of essentials like soap and paper.

A second, related concern was that despite a perceived lack of workers, there appeared to the Chōsabu to be a considerable reservoir of labour available if it could be moved out of seemingly low-productivity occupations. Accordingly, the Chōsabu suggested that Syonan's many marginal workers could be mobilized to more productive pursuits. Hawkers were among the clearest examples and were accused of being unproductive and 'at the root of the problems concerning food rationing and price controls' (*Reorganizing Commercial Businesses*, chapter 4).

Agriculture was one occupation to which Chōsabu analysis suggests that apparently surplus labour could be mobilized. Japanese officials, as advocated in the report on *Lowest Levels of Living* (chapter 12), had to try to provide food to maintain all of Syonan's population at a subsistence level, and movement

32 'Report on the Straits Settlements Police Force and on the State of Crime', *Straits Settlements Annual Reports 1930* (Singapore: Government Printing Office, 1931), p. 498.

33 Chin, *Malaya Upside Down*, p. 69.

34 O.W. Gilmour, *With Freedom to Singapore* (London: Ernest Benn, 1950), pp. 112, 157.

into agriculture would help to meet that goal. The argument was that rather than eating food produced by others on the island or which came as imports, a proportion of those in Syonan's oversupplied informal economy could move out of the city centre to farm in the island's rural districts or, better, in the Malay Peninsula. Labour reallocation would furnish workers needed for a threefold increase in land under cultivation recommended in the Chōsabu report *Methods of Increasing Food Production* (chapter 9).

Chōsabu recommendations for a relocation of labour from Syonan were not new. In August 1943, when the population of Syonan was estimated to be a million, the Japanese military set an evacuation target of 300,000 with transport to be provided by the army. There was, however, never any major evacuation; the largest organized resettlement programme was the Chinese settlement of Endau, 136 miles from Syonan in northeastern Johore, which after its first year had about 12,000 settlers. A parallel attempt to resettle Syonan Eurasians and Catholics in Negeri Sembilan was a dismal failure. Even to sustain Endau, the Japanese had to send rice to support the population.[35] No significant resettlement of Syonan's population appears to have been possible, at least under Japanese direction.

Two main considerations told heavily against the likely success of achieving any substantial reallocation of Syonan's population into agricultural pursuits in the Malay Peninsula. One was that by the 1940s Syonan had a growing, if still relatively small, middle class for whom agriculture was unattractive or impossible. Second, while Syonan could offer labour and Malaya abundant land, the Japanese were not in a position to supply other complementary inputs such as credit, tools and technical knowledge fundamental to successful subsistence agriculture.

Apart from agriculture, the other main area in which the Chōsabu researchers considered that labour could be better allocated was a shift of workers to Japanese undertakings. Here, however, low human capital seems to have been an obstacle. In 1940, recent immigrants from China still made up a large proportion of Syonan's workforce. Partly because most Chinese immigrants came as young men and had received minimal, if any, education in China, illiteracy levels among Syonan Chinese were high. The Chōsabu report *A Study of the Labour Situation* cites the high proportion of unskilled workers in Syonan's labour force and the city's lack of an industrial heritage (part of the explanation for low skills) as barriers to staffing Japanese enterprises. Just after the war, as was observed of Malaya, the proportion of the labour force with skills was low and these were almost exclusively adapted to the tin and rubber industries.[36] Inadequate nutrition was a further serious obstacle to efficient use of labour. By 1944, as discussed below, hunger debilitated many workers and resulted in

---

[35] Shinozaki, *Syonan, My Story*, pp. 79–92.

[36] Thompson, *Labor Problems*, p. 10.

chronic absenteeism. An unwillingness to work for the Japanese and exploitation associated with a contractor (mandore) system, particularly when overseen by Japanese, were further reasons for difficulty in securing labour. Chinese worked harder than other racial groups and, the Chōsabu emphasized, were best managed by other Chinese.

The Chōsabu considered that part of the explanation for an over-large Syonan commercial sector was that for Chinese even petty commercial pursuits seemed to offer a chance of fulfilling their 'overriding aim' (*Reorganizing Commercial Businesses*) of becoming successful merchants. Wages may, however, afford an alternative explanation. Money wages in Japanese factories appear to have been low, since, on Chōsabu evidence, in 1943 and 1944 despite high inflation they were often not greatly above pre-war levels and as little as a third of wages in non-Japanese enterprises. While low nominal wages may help to explain labour shortages encountered by the Japanese factories, their practice of giving priority rations, a part of which could be sold on the black market, must often have helped considerably to make up for a low money component of wages and probably offered a number of workers a higher income than they could achieve outside the Japanese sector.

Industrial Factories

The Japanese military took over many of Malaya's industrial facilities intact.[37] Despite this head start and Japanese claims of new industrialization, factories in Syonan seem, from a Japanese perspective, to have done disappointingly little to meet either military requirements or the needs of Syonan consumers. An important factor restricting potential industrialization was the relatively limited amount of pre-war industry in Syonan. There was, for example, no chemical industry before the war; and although a Ford factory had assembled automobiles in Singapore, all the parts for assembly and repair were imported from Britain and the United States.[38]

With a few exceptions, the Chōsabu report on *Important Industrial Factories* (chapter 6) found that, rather than starting new factories, the Japanese had taken over and now managed established enterprises. The Chōsabu list may, however, have excluded Japanese enterprises that followed the military to Syonan. The city became the Japanese regional supply base, and because of this many Japanese firms opened branches to supply the military quickly. It is unclear, though, how far they manufactured in Syonan or were merely agents for whatever imports came from Japan.

[37] Office of Strategic Services (hereafter OSS), *Industrial Facilities in Malaya* (Washington, DC: Research and Analysis Branch, Office of Strategic Services, May 1944), p. 1.

[38] Ibid., p. 3.

For the military, one of the most useful of Syonan's pre-war enterprises was United Engineers. Before the war it had extensive facilities and manufactured a variety of engineering goods for the rubber and tin industries.[39] Under Japanese control United Engineers converted to a munitions factory. The Singapore Gas Works was restarted and supplied gas lighting in the city. In March 1943, however, this public good component of the standard of living remained restricted and just 840 of some 4,050 gaslights in Syonan were operative. Electricity generation for the city was similarly curtailed.

A major new Japanese enterprise was the attempt to build wooden boats. Although ultimately this was a failure because the boats proved unusable, the industry employed about 1,000 people and absorbed substantial resources, including imported wood. Early in 1943 this was intended to be teak from Burma, but shipping difficulties soon forced a reliance on local wood. The Japanese appear to have started an enterprise to make steel drums as well as a carbolic acid gas factory and in 1943 planned to build a bottle-making plant. A restarting of the production lines of the pre-war Malayan Breweries and Archipelago Breweries was no doubt welcomed by Japanese military and civilian personnel. Mamoru Shinozaki recalled 'the reasonably-priced and very tasty Kirin beer ... brewed by the Kirin Beer Kaisha on the premises of Tiger Brewery, off Alexandra Road'.[40]

In March 1943, pre-war stocks of raw material imports still kept a number of industrial concerns operating, but for others the wartime unavailability of imported inputs, for example caustic soda to manufacture soap, forced adaptation and the use of substitutes. Some of these, detailed in *Important Industrial Factories* (chapter 6), were effected only through highly labour-intensive processes, such as the use of rice paper for the manufacture of cigarettes; the recycling of paper, described as resembling a handicraft; and the separation by hand of pineapple fibres from plant leaves as a substitute for cotton.

Little effort appears to have gone into the production of consumer goods, with the exception of soap. By contrast, the Japanese attempted to start the manufacture of a variety of basic consumer goods in Indonesia, including in the Outer Islands.[41] In Syonan, as also happened in Vietnam, Indonesia and elsewhere in Southeast Asia, shortages of basic goods were to some extent alleviated by substitutes devised by local entrepreneurs. Small firms, often Chinese, cropped up in the city to make replacement goods for items no longer available.[42] Lee Kuan Yew describes how he, along with a friend and the families of both men,

---

[39] Huff, *Economic Growth of Singapore*, pp. 216–7.

[40] Shinozaki, *Syonan, My Story*, p. 57.

[41] Anon., 'The Industries of the Indies since the Japanese Capitulation', *Economic Review of Indonesia* 1, 2 (1947): 21, 24.

[42] David G. Marr, *Vietnam: State, War and Revolution* (1945–1946) (Berkeley: University of California Press, 2013), p. 318; Anon., 'The Industries of the Indies'.

manufactured stationery gum in their homes. Branded as 'Stikfas', the gum was brewed from a mixture of tapioca, carbolic acid and palm oil.[43]

Prices, Inflation and Rationing

Chapter 7: Countermeasures for Prices for Syonan Municipality. Compiled for the Committee for the Problem of Prices, data compilation by Kirita Naosaku, March 1944

Chapter 8: Conditions of Economic Security in Syonan Municipality and Johore. Department of Police Administration, March 1943

Japanese finance for occupation was predominantly through monetary creation, which inevitably led to high and accelerating inflation. This section looks first at the methods of finance used by Japan. It then considers rationing of food and goods as a response to both acute shortages and chronic inflationary problems. Shortages sharply worsened. By March 1944, a Chōsabu analyst had been driven to the stark position that: 'For the local population in receipt of priority rations, the minimum standard of living should be at the level at which the labour force can just be maintained; for those on general rations, it should be the level at which death from starvation can just be avoided' (*Countermeasures for Prices*, chapter 7).

War Finance and Prices

War can be financed by selling bonds to banks or to the public, through taxation, and by printing money. This last, as well as printing in the literal sense of currency rolling off presses, includes indirect creation of money in the form of bank deposits, matched by holdings of bonds in the banks' balance sheets. Indirect money was, however, unimportant in Syonan and the rest of Malaya. All the main banks, including the three great British banks—Hongkong and Shanghai; the Chartered Bank of India, Australia and China; and the Mercantile Bank of India—were taken over by the Japanese and eventually liquidated. A number of Syonan's local Chinese banks were, however, allowed to reopen. Although the Chōsabu report *Countermeasures for Prices* (chapter 7), written in March 1944, suggests that these banks be required to buy bonds to help absorb excess liquidity, this probably did not happen. Even if it did, the contribution of the Chinese banks would have been slight, since in pre-war Singapore they were small in banking terms and, furthermore, did relatively little business during the occupation.

---

[43] Lee Kuan Yew, *The Singapore Story: Memoirs of Lee Kuan Yew* (Singapore: Times Editions, 1998), p. 67.

While the destruction of the pre-war European banking system effectively ruled out bonds as a way for the Japanese to finance occupation, taxation remained a possibility. That was difficult, however, because pre-war export specialization in Malaya in rubber and tin was in response to a global, predominantly American, market. Japan, no more than partially industrialized before the war and consuming just 5 per cent of world rubber and less than 4 per cent of world tin production, could use only a fraction of Malayan output of the two commodities. Once the occupation cut off Syonan and the rest of Malaya from global, chiefly Western, markets, their economies collapsed and, with this, so too did their tax bases. In reporting on *Important Industrial Factories* the Department of General Affairs Research Office put pre-war rubber consumption in Malaya at a minuscule 1,000 tons annually. That compared with Malayan exports of well over half a million tons annually before the war. Large rubber and tin stockpiles built up, even though the output of both commodities plummeted.

To try to mobilize finance, Japanese administrators initiated savings campaigns including compulsory post office saving. Additionally, as the *Countermeasures* report makes clear, numerous new taxes were introduced in an attempt to retain pre-war tax arrangements and milk them as much as possible. Chinese businessmen were an easy target for new taxation, and, in the words of the report, 'Donations from the overseas Chinese have, under Imperial Army occupation, been considerable'. Probably the most notorious of these donations was a 'voluntary' $50 million gift from Chinese businessmen. No doubt in part it aimed to limit inflation by taking currency out of circulation, but the donation must also have been partly intended to cow influential Chinese opposition to occupation.[44]

Over the course of the war, the Japanese administration instituted lotteries and encouraged gambling as ways to tax. Gambling was farmed out, and the Shaw brothers, leading figures in post-war Singapore society, are said to have become prosperous by virtue of gaining a licence to run gambling farms.[45] Chōsabu analysis draws particular attention to the Southern Dream Lottery (Konan Lottery) and recommends variations in timing and prizes to promote a sense of anticipation. Japanese officials also levied taxes on amusement parks, including Great World and New World, and on cinemas, hawkers, dogs and fishing licences. Prostitutes were taxed to try to generate revenue from the great wartime spread of prostitution, as were waitresses, restaurants and coffee shops.[46] But taxes, like savings, raised only relatively small amounts of finance.

---

[44] Tan Yeok Seong, *The Extortion by the Japanese Military Administration of $50,000,000 from the Chinese in Malaya* (Singapore: Nanyang Book Co., 1947).

[45] Lee, *Singapore Story*, p. 76.

[46] Chin, *Malaya Upside Down*, pp. 54, 192.

Despite energetic and sometimes inventive ways to tax devised by the Japanese and their use of other non-financial methods such as price controls and direct confiscation to obtain resources in Syonan, the occupation had, almost inevitably, to be paid for mainly by the taxation of printing money. Money, like any commodity, can be taxed, and governments can finance themselves, perhaps even chiefly, through monetary expansion and therefore seigniorage, defined as the revenue that governments realize from their right to issue money. Seigniorage is the difference between the cost of printing money and what it will buy. Such taxation continues and remains a viable source of government revenue so long as the public is willing to hold, or can be forced to hold, a substantial proportion of its wealth as money. That depends, possibly along with coercion, on inflation being judged as not too high and on money's usefulness as a medium of exchange, if not as a store of value. As shown by Syonan during the Japanese occupation, even when high inflation almost daily destroys the value of money, it is not easily replaced for the transactional purposes of everyday use.

In Syonan, the Japanese promoted the use of the money they issued by paying wages and collecting taxes in it. At the same time, they prohibited, and enforced with strong sanctions, the use of other monies, including the pre-war Straits dollar. The population of Syonan continued to hold Japanese money because, apart from some clandestine use of pre-war currency, almost no other money was available and Japanese money was useful in, and generally necessary for, everyday transactions such as to buy goods, including rationed items, and to pay for lottery tickets and at amusement parks.

Money to finance the occupation of Syonan and Malaya was not difficult for the Japanese to create. Military scrip, unbacked paper money, could be printed at will and at minimal cost while the nominal spending power generated was the face value of the notes. The Japanese therefore transferred resources to themselves simply by printing as scrip the required amount of currency. Scrip—printed expressly for Syonan and Malaya—was, as before the war, denominated in Straits dollars. Now, however, currency carried new, 'appropriate' pictures. Banana plants featured on the Malayan $10 note. Before long, as Japanese scrip continuously lost value, it became known derisively as 'banana money'.[47] However, as the war turned against Japan and the need for finance increased, scrip was issued in such large quantities that it continuously lost value, and the Japanese had to print ever greater quantities of notes to try to achieve the same real (actual) transfer of resources to themselves as previously. Monetary promiscuity led to extremely high inflation in Syonan and finally, during the last stages of the war, hyperinflation. Inflation was further exacerbated by acute shortages of most

[47] Paul H. Kratoska, 'Banana Money: Consequences of the Demonetization of Wartime Japanese Currency in British Malaya', *Journal of Southeast Asian Studies* 23, 1 (1992): 322–45.

essential goods, especially rice, the preferred staple of almost everyone in Syonan and basic to the standard of living.

Prices in Syonan doubled between February and June 1942, were double again in June 1943, and doubled a further time by January 1944. In March 1944, when the Chōsabu reported on measures to control prices, they were rising at some 25 per cent a month, consistent with a yearly increase of around 1,355 per cent. Unsurprisingly, most Syonanese became continuously more unwilling to hold Japanese banana money, and as the speed at which it changed hands (its velocity of circulation) accelerated so, too, did inflation. Between February 1942 and July 1945, while money supply rose 15-fold prices increased by a factor of 150 (figure 1.1).

Figure 1.1 Syonan money supply and prices, February 1942–July 1945

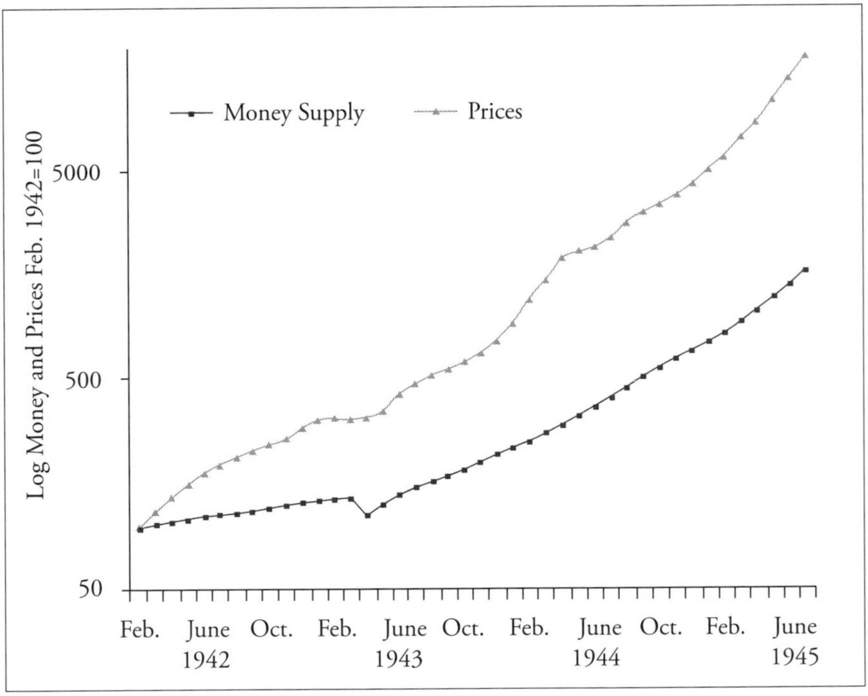

By 1944 the store of value motive for holding money had disintegrated. Although money remained a unit of account to measure prices and was used as a medium of exchange for everyday transactions, people held goods where possible. In Thailand, Chinese traders who supplied rice to Syonan wanted goods such as petrol, rubber oil, cloth and basic consumer items in exchange. The Chōsabu reports accord considerable attention to the availability of these latter and refer to them as collateral goods (or as exchange goods).

While the Chōsabu report *Countermeasures for Prices* (chapter 7) recognizes the excessive printing of money as a contributory factor in rapid price escalation in Syonan, it does not acknowledge money creation as the main reason. It appears that the report's author was unaware of the role of printing money as the principal cause of very high inflation, perhaps partly because the report predates Philip Cagan's conclusive demonstration of this.[48] Possibly, the report's author also exercised a degree of diplomacy in attributing Syonan inflation chiefly to shortages of goods and transport. It might be that the military administration did not welcome reference to excessive monetary expansion or that the report's author recognized that because Japan had little choice in financing occupation except to print money, discussion of the monetary origins of inflation had little point.

Countermeasures argues that price rises stemmed from four main causes, all on the supply side of the economy and all of which modern economists would recognize as aggravating and intensifying Syonan's wartime inflation. One was Syonan's high dependence on imported food, assessed by the Chōsabu at two-thirds of total supplies. A second, closely related, cause was a shortage of transport. The problem of a lack of shipping to bring food to Singapore from Malaya and elsewhere in Southeast Asia was never satisfactorily resolved, and, as shown by *Malayan Rice Imports* (chapter 11), even its partial resolution required a considerable reliance on private Chinese boatbuilding. Although shipping probably posed the most significant difficulty in regard to transporting food supplies, overland transport on the island itself and from nearby areas was also lacking. Public transport in the city so deteriorated that, as *A Study of the Labour Situation* (chapter 5) records, by the latter half of 1944 only a third of trams and buses were in service. With motorized vehicles hardly available and petrol scarce, Singaporeans increasingly turned to rickshaws, bullock carts and horse carriages for transport.[49] *Countermeasures* recommends (and the report repeats four times) a greater use of oxcarts to improve transport and so combat inflation.

Chōsabu analysis, in its identification of the third and fourth causes of inflation, returned to themes familiar throughout the Research Bureau's reports on Syonan: a lack of sufficient local food production and the perfidious and devious Chinese mercantile class. In developing this latter argument, reasoning begins

---

48 Philip Cagan, 'The Monetary Dynamics of Hyperinflation', in *Studies in the Quantity Theory of Money*, ed. Milton Friedman (Chicago: University of Chicago Press, 1956), pp. 25–117.

49 National Archives of Singapore, *Reflections and Memories of War, Vol. 2: Syonan Years 1942–1945: Living beneath the Rising Sun* (Singapore: National Archives of Singapore, 2009), pp. 220–1.

with what the report calls a 'stock economy' that existed because occupation had, apart for some inventive but generally rather imperfect substitutes, prevented any significant addition to the region's stock of consumer goods after 1941. The progressive depletion of pre-war stocks, and the ever-rising prices of those still in the hands of Chinese merchants, allowed these men to accumulate large amounts of liquidity and so, it was argued, contribute to inflation by unrealistically bidding up prices.

Local food production, in the view of the Chōsabu, had increased much less during occupation than it should have. A consequent greater than necessary dependence on imported food pushed up prices. While a number of other Chōsabu reports, such as *Methods of Increasing Food Production* (chapter 9), on Syonan Island focus mainly on measures to increase land under cultivation, to grow more root crops and to improve the efficiency with which agricultural land was cultivated, *Countermeasures* is more concerned with a large, apparently unproductive, sector of Syonan's labour force in activities like hawking. The report emphasizes that workers like these would be better utilized in agriculture and ideally should be shifted out of the city to start farming in Malaya. Two reports that more fully develop these ideas are *Reorganizing Commercial Businesses* (chapter 4) and *A Study of the Labour Situation* (chapter 5).

While wholesale money creation continued, any possible countermeasures against price rises could never have staved off the high inflation, and ultimately hyperinflation, that Syonan experienced. Nevertheless, the analysis in *Countermeasures for Prices* of possible inflation palliatives reveals much about shortages, markets and distributive systems in the city. A theme, not always acknowledged, that runs through the report is the importance of incentives in securing food, recruiting labour and explaining the presence of a large black market in Syonan. *Countermeasures* and *Malayan Rice Imports* consider the use of collateral goods, notably soap, tobacco, cloth or other basic materials, as an inducement to those in possession of rice to sell it. As in other occupied economies, for example those of the Third Reich, meant to contribute to a war effort, Syonan's Japanese authorities used priority food rations to secure labour and to try to make workers more productive.[50] By the time *Countermeasures* was written, fish prices in Syonan, despite high inflation, had been fixed for nearly two years. A disincentive to sell fish through official channels but strong incentives to resell it at an unregulated price was obvious and helps to account for Syonan's burgeoning black market. Official rice prices were similarly far outdistanced by those on the black market. Two further stimuli to a large black market were, as noted in *Methods of Increasing Food Production* (chapter 9), that the military paid food producers just 10 per cent to 30 per cent of market prices and that, as

[50] Adam Tooze, *The Wages of Destruction: The Making and Breaking of the Nazi Economy* (London: Allen Lane, 2006), pp. 528–51.

detailed in the report *Conditions of Economic Security* (chapter 8), rice prices were held below prices of substitute foods.

The meagre amounts of officially available food, indicated in the numerous tables that accompany the *Countermeasures* text, suggest that the city's black market must have had a substantial role in sustaining Syonan's population, if often at low levels. To try to counter the upper end of the black market the Chōsabu suggested, possibly partly with the Chinese mercantile class in mind, establishing a luxury department store to absorb excess purchasing power. The idea is reminiscent of anti-inflation and revenue-enhancing measures in the former Soviet Eastern Bloc. So too is the corruption of Japanese officials in the distribution of food and consumer goods. The local population was, however, largely shut out of the most luxurious bars and restaurants. Even if the general population had been permitted entry, few could have afforded to eat and drink in these establishments.[51]

Rationing

For the distribution of goods in Syonan, the Japanese authorities adopted a consumption policy analogous to that in Britain and the Soviet Union during World War II.[52] Basic items including rice, salt, sugar and cloth were rationed and sold at frozen, or only slowly adjusted, prices, while the prices of other goods were left free to rise on the open market. The fundamental principle behind this rationing system, in which rice was easily the most important item, was to provide a minimum standard of living to those in Syonan. Initially the Japanese authorities used registers kept by retailers to control amounts given as rations, as had the British colonial government after the outbreak of war. But from August 1942 rationing was through cards issued to individuals.[53] Possession of a card entitled the bearer to purchase a specified amount of rationed goods at controlled prices.

While the aim remained to guarantee at least a subsistence level of essential foods, rationed amounts increasingly fell short of this target. Food available for rations decreased because pre-occupation stocks were soon depleted; because of a continuously widening gap between controlled and black market prices; and because of a shortage of transport both to bring food to Syonan and to distribute it within the island. Immediately after occupation, in March 1942, rice rations were 12,066 grams per person per month (397 grams per day, equivalent to about 1,421 calories). That was not egregiously adrift of an estimate, reproduced in an

[51] Shinozaki, *Syonan, My Story*, p. 58.

[52] On a consumption policy of rationing, see Alan S. Milward, *War, Economy and Society, 1939–1945* (London: Allen Lane, 1977), p. 239.

[53] NA, WO 852/327/9, 'Food Supplies Malaya', p. 2.

official British report, of daily pre-war rice consumption in Malaya of 499 grams (1,786 calories) per capita, but far below the *Conditions of Economic Security* (chapter 8) estimate of 660 grams per capita.[54] By February 1944, however, monthly rice rations had fallen to 158 grams (566 calories) per day for men and 119 grams (426 calories) for women, although small amounts of tapioca noodles and tapioca bread flour were also available through official channels.[55] Since the basal metabolic rate (the level at which no surplus for physical activity exists) is 1,080 calories for women aged 18 to 30 and 1,450 for men aged 18 to 60, Syonanese had clearly to find energy sources alternative to rice. Even when food was available it could not always reach consumers. In late 1944, when 30 lorries should have been available to bring food from collection points in Malaya, the actual fleet was only 11 and three of these had broken down. Some perishable foods were left to rot for lack of transport (*Methods of Increasing Food Production*, chapter 9).

As official rations dwindled and even these became more difficult to obtain in practice, Syonan's black market grew proportionately. By mid-1943, most Syonanese probably had to rely for food on both constituents of a parallel structure of controlled and black markets. The gap between prices at which rations were sold and black market prices increasingly widened.

In late 1943 the Chōsabu began to research prices, rationing and living standards. The bureau's concern was not to alter established rationing principles but to make existing arrangements work better. 'The fundamental goals of price measures,' as stated in *Countermeasures for Prices*, 'are to sustain minimum standards of living for the local people, to secure the supply of materials and labour for the military in preparation for the Imperial Army's final battle, and to maintain public order by safeguarding the lives of the population. Measures should thus focus on the general population, especially on those who engage in productive work.'

To realize these objectives the Chōsabu stressed the close interrelations between local food availability, prices and rationing. Larger food supplies would bring down prices, ease pressures on rationing and help guarantee minimum living standards. Both the reports on the *Conditions for Economic Security*, not authored by Chōsabu members, and, even more, on *Countermeasures for Prices*, emphasize the need for better regulation, the elimination of corruption, and an adjustment of amounts rationed to accord more closely with the military goals of labour supply and production. In *Countermeasures for Prices*, Chōsabu researchers draw attention to the need to increase the amenity, efficiency and organization

[54] Malaysia, Arkib Negara (hereafter AN) 1957/0575131 Intelligence 506/30, 'Appreciation of the Economic Position of Malaya under the Japanese', p. 3.

[55] NA, WO 203/4499, 'Rice—S.E.A.C. Territories', pp. 54–5; WO 203/2647, 'Summary of Economic Intelligence No. 130, 15 Oct., 1945', p. 5.

of transport for food from Malaya and on Syonan island itself. Perishable foods sometimes spoiled for want of transport. Tellingly, neither of the two reports analyzes the role that higher prices or a freer market might have had in easing price and rationing problems.

Rationing schemes sometimes address and succeed in reducing social inequalities, as for example happened in World War II Britain. Evidence in the Chōsabu reports, discussed elsewhere in this chapter, suggests that, if anything, inequalities in Syonan widened during the war because, as rations fell and black market prices rose, low earners, often with the disadvantage of relatively inflexible nominal wages, found it increasingly difficult to get adequate food. Chōsabu evidence, discussed in connection with the report *Lowest Levels of Living* (chapter 12), suggests a probably greater gulf than before the war between better-off and poorer groups. Among the latter, Malays and Indian estate workers were especially prominent.

An important respect in which rationing altered income distribution was through generous priority rations for those employed by the military or by Japanese firms. By tying rationing for these workers to a concept of real wages, priority rations may well have provided a significant number of Syonanese with a quantity of rice as large as, or perhaps even larger than, before the war. The attempt to maintain real wages was, of course, badly undermined by a lack of goods to buy, possibly with the proceeds of selling priority rations, and by high prices. Nevertheless, priority rationing probably left many of those working for the Japanese better off than a number of their counterparts employed in non-Japanese-run sectors of the economy. That Japanese firms had to offer this inducement to recruit labour would provide support for an argument that although large numbers of Syonanese were willing to accept employment in Japanese undertakings, many others were not. Along with a tendency to substitute labour for capital and so extreme labour intensity in some Japanese undertakings, this unwillingness to work for the Japanese would help to account for the labour shortages experienced by the Japanese after about mid-1943.

Successful rationing depends on general acceptance of a rationing system by the public and so a willingness to comply with the rationing system, combined with an availability of sufficient goods to avoid straining compliance beyond breaking point. In Syonan, neither of these constituents existed. Even had there been a greater supply of goods, the spectacle of the British colonial rulers being routed followed by the pressures of occupation would probably still have caused the social order to disintegrate to an extent that rationing and price control could never be more than partially effective. During the war, the black market became a way of life. People in Syonan begin to think of it as normal, and 'when the stage arrived at which the public was compelled to pay black market prices for such things as bus-tickets, railway-tickets, cinema-tickets, cloth-coupons and even newspapers, the situation was beyond redemption'.[56] Encumbered by the wartime legacies of a pervasive black economy, social breakdown, and severe shortages of food and consumer goods, the post-war British Military Administration became popularly known as the Black Market Administration.

Rice and Food Supplies

Chapter 9: Methods of Increasing Food Production on Syonan Island. Yamada Isamu, October 1944

Chapter 10: Food Problems and Cultivation of the Sweet Potato. Unknown author, c. early 1943

Chapter 11: Rice Imports to Malaya, with Special Reference to Syonan Municipality. Matsu'ura Shigeharu, surveys by Kirita Naosaku and Nagamori Masaji, September 1944

Rice, as the staple food favoured by almost everyone in Syonan, was basic to Japanese policies to feed the city's population. It also set price levels for most other commodities. In common with many other parts of Southeast Asia, a rise in rice prices signalled an increase in all other prices. As a 1920 Straits Settlements commission on inflation and wages explained, rice served as 'the pecunia of the East'.[57] The failure of the Japanese government to provide and adequately supply rice to the Malayan population was, according to Chin Kee Onn, the 'fundamental cause of all the economic ills of the country'.[58] This section first considers attempts by the Japanese and those in Syonan to substitute for the lack of rice. The latter part of the section looks at how by 1944 the Japanese authorities were forced to try to reorganize the import of rice and to offer greater incentives for Chinese rice traders in order to increase supplies to Syonan.

Food Self-sufficiency

The report on *Rice Imports to Malaya* (chapter 11) provides new information on how during 1944 the Japanese authorities reacted to a critical shortage of rice in Syonan. One response, illustrated by the reports in this section, was to try to expand the extent of cultivated acreage and encourage Syonan's population to grow substitute crops, especially tapioca and sweet potatoes. Japanese administrators

---

[56] Chin, *Malaya Upside Down*, p. 37.

[57] Straits Settlements, 'Commission on Profiteering, Straits Settlements (Second Interim Report)', *Straits Settlements Legislative Council Proceedings*, 1920 (Singapore: Government Printing Office), p. C273.

[58] Chin, *Malaya Upside Down*, p. 55; on rice as a leading indicator of prices, see p. 59.

strongly promoted grow-your-own food campaigns and the dissemination of information on the preparation of unfamiliar foodstuffs. At times, Japanese plans suggesting that food self-sufficiency could be easily achieved and may indeed be just around the corner assumed an air of fantasy. The best example is *Food Problems and Cultivation of the Sweet Potato* (chapter 10). It argues, in a seemingly logical but altogether fanciful way, that sweet potatoes could fill the food gap by everyone finding spare land to grow enough potatoes for their own needs. The joint goals of an end to food shortages and self-sufficiency could be realized, almost magically, by an inexorable spread of the sweet potato across Syonan, Malaya and Indonesia.

The song in *Food Problems and Cultivation of the Sweet Potato* was meant to encourage at least some greater cultivation of potatoes. Any effect may, however, have been limited if comprehension in Syonan was similar to that in Sarawak, where in organized language classes 'children and adults alike picked up some Japanese words and phrases [and] sang a few songs with little understanding of the lyrics'.[59] In reality, as food scarcity worsened and hunger left an increasingly debilitated people, urban gardening became a necessity. In the words of a Japanese observer, food shortages changed 'the appearance of the city as much as that of the people. Tapioca and sweet potato plants replaced flowering plants in practically every garden, every patch of available land'.[60]

Even so, central Syonan was exceptionally densely populated and offered limited scope for cultivation: in 1947 an area of 2,285 acres that made up the inner city wards amounted to 11 per cent of the municipality but accommodated just under half its population.[61] Where land was available, some municipal residents kept chickens and ducks that they fed on the city's two-inch cockroaches trapped in the sewers at night.[62] Additionally, the area of Syonan island under market gardens expanded from 1,500 acres to 7,000 acres. That was, however, just 0.021 of an acre for each of the 263,600 additions to the city's population between 1938 and 1944.[63] Cats and dogs afforded an obvious source of high protein. These animals disappeared in sufficiently great numbers to qualify as endangered species.[64]

59 Ooi Keat Gin, 'The Japanese Occupation and the Peoples of Sarawak', in *Southeast Asian Minorities in the Wartime Japanese Empire*, ed. Paul H. Kratoska (London: Routledge, 2002), p. 146.

60 Shinozaki, *Syonan, My Story*, p. 59.

61 Singapore Department of Social Welfare, *A Social Survey of Singapore* (Singapore: Department of Social Welfare, 1947), p. 24.

62 NAS, Oral History interview 000265, Lee Tian Soo.

63 AN, 1957/0572056 CA (MPU) War Office M.G.D. AGM/22, O.W. Gilmour, 'Assessment of War Damage', 15 Apr. 1944, p. 5.

64 He Wen-Lit, *Syonan Interlude* (Singapore: Mandarin Paperbacks, 1991), p. 156.

Rice Imports and Chinese Traders

The lack of land in Syonan and large rice deficit in the Malay Peninsula left the Japanese authorities no alternative but to feed the population through large imports of rice from elsewhere in Southeast Asia.[65] Although rice was plentifully available in Thailand, traditionally Singapore's main supplier and also under Japanese control, *Rice Imports to Malaya* (chapter 11) demonstrates why the authorities in Syonan were nevertheless unable to access it in sufficient quantities to maintain anything close to pre-war living standards, and the policy compromises necessary to secure even inadequate supplies. The Japanese were forced to abandon an attempt at tight controls over rice imports in favour of a partial free market. They had to rely, both tacitly and openly, on Chinese rice importers who, as part of a trade stretching over much of Asia, had always been instrumental in feeding the city.

Between 1942 and 1944, rice, largely from Thailand, reached Syonan through two main channels. One was official, regulated imports by the Japanese for the military and distribution as rations. The Japanese trading companies Mitsubishi and Mitsui were designated suppliers. For distribution within Syonan, the Japanese relied chiefly on Chinese and directed Tan Keng Kow, the managing director of Tan Guan Lee & Co. and president of the Thailand Traders Association, to form a Syonan Rice and Paddy Distributing Association.[66] The other import channel was a large, and growing, trade in unregulated or smuggled rice conducted by Syonan Chinese traders. Karimun-Balai, previously an obscure fishing island, functioned as an unofficial trade centre for Malaya, Sumatra and Java. Known as Little Syonan and just 28 nautical miles from its Syonan namesake, Karimun became home to over 100 firms, the port for a flotilla of small vessels, and a hub of smuggling and black marketeering. Although well known to the Japanese military command, a blind eye was turned to Karimun, partly in the interest of food supplies for Syonan.[67]

During the course of the occupation, the Japanese found it increasingly difficult to import rice. One reason for this was that as inflation and so black market rice prices increasingly outdistanced official prices paid by the Japanese, sales to them became unattractive. Second, a growing trade imbalance with Thailand, due substantially to the demand for Thai rice, made Chinese traders in Thailand more unwilling to accept cash for rice. Although initially set at parity, by early 1944 the Straits dollar had depreciated by two-thirds against the Thai baht. Due to the falling Straits dollar and an acute shortage of goods throughout

---

[65] For a history of pre-1944 Japanese control of rice and food distribution, see NA, Kew, WO203/4499, 'Rice—S.E.A.C. Territories', pp. 49–57; and Kratoska, *Japanese Occupation*, pp. 247–83.

[66] Kratoska, *Japanese Occupation*, p. 250.

[67] Twang, *Chinese Business Elite*, pp. 94–6.

Southeast Asia, Thai traders wanted to barter their rice. In this, however, Japanese buyers were not as flexible as Syonan Chinese both because they were less agile in a market where prices shifted rapidly and because in many instances they had less access to barter goods.

Barter items, termed collateral (or exchange) goods by the Chōsabu, included clothing, towels, thread, rubber oil, matches, soap, candles and other daily necessities. Chin, writing immediately after occupation ended, observed that Thai traders did not want Japanese scrip: 'They wanted gold, diamonds, jewellery, Straits Currency, American dollars, or substantial commodities such as machinery, lorry-tyres, engineering goods, tin, and oil.'[68] Collateral goods were highly desirable in the inflationary war environment of wartime Southeast Asia because they offered Thai rice suppliers (and Syonan Chinese) a hedge against inflation. Furthermore, Syonan and Thai traders could realize a profit both when selling the goods and through the sale of rice, as had been pre-war practice in the two-sided produce exchange trade discussed above.[69]

On 20 March 1944, *Rice Imports to Malaya* (chapter 11) recounts, Japanese officials suddenly reacted to Mitsubishi's difficulty of obtaining rice in competition with private purchasers in Thailand and the depreciation of the Straits dollar. In an attempt to exercise control over rice supplies, they banned private imports. The measure was, however, short-lived. Within a month, on 13 April 1944, Japanese authorities turned to Syonan Chinese enterprise to arrange for the supply of rice and just over a month later set up the Syonan Rice Import Association, which involved a large body of Syonan Chinese traders, and liberalized the rice trade. Along with levy or tax rice to be delivered to the military administration, these traders were entitled to sell unregulated or freedom rice on the open market.[70] As *Rice Imports to Malaya* emphasized in regard to the new association: 'A successful operation requires the support of overseas Chinese, which would be difficult to gain without the prospect of adequate economic profits.'

Much of the report explains how beginning in May 1944 three main rice importers operated under the authority of the Japanese. One was Mitsubishi and a second the Nami Institute, which was run by the military but charged with importing rice for civilians and in consequence given access to collateral goods as a counterpart to this import trade. The third was a newly formed Syonan Import Association, which, with 181 members, appears to have incorporated, along with various Japanese officials, almost all of the main Syonan Chinese rice importers. The majority of these men were from the Hokkien dialect group, who,

68 Chin, *Malaya Upside Down*, p. 59.

69 Huff, *Economic Growth of Singapore*, pp. 92–102.

70 According to NA, Kew, WO203/4499, 'Rice—S.E.A.C. Territories', p. 60, all private imports of rice by civilians using their own junks were utilized by the Food Control Department; but other evidence indicates that this was not the case.

for reasons that remain unclear, during the war apparently supplanted pre-war Teochew dominance in the rice trade with Thailand.[71] As well as the Import Association, the Japanese sponsored Ban Hong and Co., a trading organization set up in Thailand to buy rice in Bangkok and deliver it to Songkhla.

The Import Association constituted in May 1944 was an admission that Syonan Chinese were indispensable and that the Japanese had no choice but to rely on them. But in addition, it represented an attempt to regularize import arrangements and exercise some control over rice imports. A long list of formal rules, set out in the appendix of chapter 11, was drawn up for the Import Association, although how far these operated in practice is not known. The partial freeing of rice sales in Syonan was sufficiently successful that before long the association took over the import of rice by the Nami Institute, which was wound up on 6 August 1944.

Once the Japanese liberalized trade in rice and the Songkhla route opened, Syonan Chinese began furiously to build boats to carry back rice from Thailand. According to Ng Seng Yong, speaking much later but calling on what were apparently vivid memories, 'Most of us were doing boat construction and everyone was rushing to get this rice'.[72] The traders organized themselves into cooperative groups. An essential component of any group was a 'leg man', almost certainly with Japanese connections, to secure various official permits. Another person or persons financed the venture. Finance included funds to build a ship of about 35 tons and pay for an engine as well as petrol to run it. Permits were also required to get engines and petrol. These may not have been easy to acquire without some official connections.

Those with permits also had to have finance to buy collateral goods and to hire four men as ship's crew, since the families of these men had to be supplied with rations for a month while the men were away, and to buy rubber oil as a collateral good to take to Thailand. Although rubber oil (known among Syonanese by the nickname *chew ni yu*) was easily available on the Syonan open market, rice suppliers in Southern Thailand demanded it because of fuel shortages there. During the month-long round trip to Thailand, so long as the syndicate could engage the services of an experienced navigator, the main danger was Allied bombing.

No man would work for wages on the ships bringing rice from Thailand, but labour was readily available with a sharecropping arrangement of payment of

[71] However, Cheah credits the Teochew with a major role in the wartime rice trade with Thailand. Cheah Boon Kheng, *Red Star over Malaya: Resistance and Conflict during and after the Japanese Occupation, 1941–1946*, 3rd ed. (Singapore: Singapore University Press, 2003), pp. 47–8.

[72] NAS, Oral History interview 000283, Ng Seng Yong.

part of the rice cargo on return to Syonan. When the rice got to Syonan, it was immediately sold by the bag ex vessel to wholesalers who met returning ships, usually at Crawford Bridge. There a free market operated: Chinese who imported the better grades of rice set their own prices. That traders' ability to specify prices was an important incentive in securing private supplies of rice cannot be doubted. Wartime possession of a junk in which rice could be transported was 'like owning six ships during the peace time'.[73]

When reading *Rice Imports to Malaya* one wonders why the Japanese were unable simply to decree that rice be supplied to Syonan and organize imports themselves. Price and incentives are prominent explanatory reasons. Just as the Japanese found it difficult to secure rice without recognizing the power of the market for a commercially oriented overseas Chinese population, neither could the British after the war buy rice from Chinese in Thailand without paying market prices. The British post-war settlement with Thailand, which in 1942 had allied itself with Japan, stipulated the delivery without payment of 1.5 million tons of rice for distribution in Malaya, Singapore, Burma and India. Chinese who controlled Thailand's rice trade were, however, unwilling to hand over supplies to the British or to sell to the Thai government. They sold, instead, on the black market. In May 1946 the British relented and offered to pay for Thai rice, although only at reduced prices. Finally, in December 1946 the British, somewhat like the Japanese authorities in wartime Syonan, had to acknowledge the power of Thai Chinese traders and the importance of market prices in eliciting the supply of rice. Rice from Thailand was forthcoming once the British agreed to pay Bangkok Chinese world market prices.[74]

Living Standards

Chapter 12: A Study of Lowest Levels of Living by Ethnic Group in Syonan Municipality: Price, Quantity and the Relative Importance of Daily Necessities, by Ethnic Group. Surveyed by Yamada Isamu and Kawai Mikio, October 1943

Japanese expectations for the living standards of Southeast Asians during occupation were never high. Finance Minister Kaya's November 1941 statement said as much in asserting that it would be relatively easy to maintain the livelihoods of those in Southeast Asia because of the region's rich natural resources and since

[73] NAS, Oral History interview 000362, Jack Kim Boon Ng.

[74] Nicholas Tarling, '"An Attempt to Fly in the Face of the Ordinary Laws of Supply and Demand": The British and Siamese Rice 1945–7', *Journal of the Siam Society* 75 (1987): 179–81; Jan M. Pluvier, *South-East Asia from Colonialism to Independence* (Kuala Lumpur: Oxford University Press, 1974), pp. 406–7.

'the culture of the inhabitants is low'.[75] Nevertheless, it was considered that in Syonan a minimum standard needed to be maintained for purposes of public order, and that for some groups higher levels had to be offered to be consistent with the Japanese aim that Southeast Asians must contribute to war production.

Evidence from the Chōsabu reports *Lowest Levels of Living* and *Economic Security* (chapters 12 and 8) shows that as early as October 1943 living standards in Syonan had, for many, already fallen quite low, although levels varied considerably between Chinese, Indians and Malays and, as discussed above, depended partly on a willingness to work for the Japanese. Between the October 1943 report *Lowest Levels of Living* and the end of the war in August 1945, living conditions in Syonan greatly worsened. They probably fell further than even Japanese authorities ever envisaged. The final part of this section uses wartime and post-war data to give some indication of living standards during the occupation as a whole, and of differences between Syonan's main ethnic groups.

Lowest Levels of Living helps to understand Japan's policy, set out by Finance Minister Kaya in November 1941, that only a minimum standard of living consistent with ensuring public order and utilizing the labour force needed to be maintained. Applying these principles to Syonan, the report argued that 'considerable hardship' for the people of Syonan after less than two years of occupation had put at risk the three main objectives of military administration: acquiring resources for the military, realizing self-sufficiency, and keeping public order. Starvation, the report observed, was likely to foster public unrest, already to some extent in evidence. The 1944 report *A Study of the Labour Situation* (chapter 5) found that in Syonan hunger and a lack of public transport reduced production and seriously impeded the war effort through contributing to sickness and absenteeism. A lack of nutrition left many workers unable to work hard, while others were physically drained from time spent on transport. Starvation would, by definition, also be inconsistent with self-sufficiency. While recognizing current problems and probable future ones, *Lowest Levels of Living* tries mainly to establish facts on living standards. A number of the recommendations on living standards are contained in the 1943 *Economic Security* report.

Because of Syonan's racially varied population, *Lowest Levels* compiled lists of budgets and of food and clothing necessities for a few representative households in each of Syonan's three main races of Chinese, Indians and Malays. While the smallness of the samples limits the usefulness of these lists, the researchers' more general observations are illuminating in two respects. One is to show the great extent to which for many of the worst-off living standards had fallen by late 1943. The other is to reveal already quite substantial variations between racial groups.

[75] Japan, Imperial Headquarters, Nampō Senryōchi Gyōsei Jisshi Yōkō, presented at the Imperial Conference, 5 Nov. 1941.

A combination of high inflation, generally rather rigid money wages or low returns from self-employment, and acute shortages of even basic goods was important in accounting for a sharp drop in living standards. According to *Countermeasures for Prices* (chapter 7 and table 7.8), although in early 1944 the ration target was 1,400 calories per day only 905 calories were being provided. Since the latter figure is less than required for survival, it may help to explain the report's finding that consumption of staple foods was 32 per cent of pre-war levels, while for vegetables and fruit the percentage was 29 per cent and for fish and meat 59 per cent. On the basis of the estimated figure for pre-war rice consumption of 499 grams per person per day, this Chōsabu finding for staple foods suggests that by the latter stages of the war Syonan residents may on average have been able to consume something like 160 grams (573 calories) of rice daily, and that for people to survive rice must have been supplemented by a substantial amount of other foods like tapioca and sweet potatoes and extensive recourse to the black market.

Average figures reported by the Chōsabu masked considerable inequality in food availability. By October 1943, in-depth Chōsabu research established that in Syonan many people, although preferring rice, no longer ate it. Since the *Conditions of Economic Security* report recorded that in late 1943 rations still provided 280 grams of rice a day (so long as the distributing system functioned as intended), many of these people, as indicated above, must have sold their rations on the black market to be able to buy adequate quantities of cheaper foods and non-food necessities.

The about 70,000 people who worked for the Japanese were almost certainly better able to protect their living standards than most others in the city through being given priority rations. Together with normal rations these yielded a total of 460 grams (1,647 calories) of rice daily. Although meant to provide enough food to secure workers and maintain their productiveness, priority rations, in the view of both the *Economic Security* and *Lowest Levels* reports, were more generous than necessary. Many people appear routinely to have sold a proportion of their priority rations on the black market. The resale of rations may have been a significant source of black market supply and, if so, played an important part in redistributing official Japanese food supplies towards wealthier, middle-class Syonan residents.

Wartime living standards were badly impacted by Syonan's extreme dependence on imported consumer goods and its lack of local manufacturing. Rations in 1944 of one yard of cloth per person per year were, as *Countermeasures for Prices* (chapter 7) observed, too little to be of much use. Even in 1943, however, cloth and clothing were apparently largely unavailable. *Lowest Levels of Living* found that no one surveyed had been able to buy new clothes since the start of the occupation. A 'desperate' state of affairs with regard to clothing was 'becoming the norm'. Soap to wash clothes and, more important, underwear was in scarce supply. Washing had often to be only in water or with ash as a soap substitute.

For Chinese, the lowest standard of living existed among those crammed into the two densely packed Chinatowns (referred to by Chōsabu researchers as the old town) on either side of the Singapore River. Here the large majority of Syonan's low-paid factory workers, coolies, hawkers and rickshaw-pullers were housed. All of these occupational groups were badly affected by inflation and had particularly low living standards. Malays, however, located on the fringes of the city, were found to live 'in far lower conditions' than the 'overseas Chinese' who dominated Syonan's Chinatowns. Tamils were the poorest Indians and, because they accounted for the great bulk of Syonan Indians, probably placed last in terms of wartime living standards. Rubber coolies, whose wages seem to have remained largely static between 1941 and 1943, were especially adversely affected. They 'live desperate lives at bare subsistence levels' (*Lowest Levels of Living*, chapter 12).

The Chōsabu was not set up to deal with those on the fringes of society and outside the rationing system and established social networks. Indonesians brought to Syonan by the Japanese, probably from Java and for work on military bases, were an egregiously deprived group. Many of those workers who deserted Japanese employment found their way to Orchard Road. There they were on their own without food and had to rely on 'whatever they can grab—banana skin, pineapple skin—they just grab and eat. And most of them got swollen legs [you would see them] Everyday. Outside the old Orchard Road market, you can get about 50/60 at a time. Some were lying dead due to maybe hunger or sickness ... This is a very regular occurrence.'[76] The life chances of Indonesians transported to Syonan do not appear to have been good whether or not they remained working for the Japanese. A Javanese civilian provided the Tokyo War Crimes Tribunal with an affidavit that he was made to work at Kampong Barrow in Syonan, where 'only 1,000 among 2,000 coolies were physically able to work' and '4 to 6 died everyday'.[77]

Post-war Urban Health and Nutrition

Wartime statistics on death rates and infant mortality for Syonan tend to confirm Chōsabu findings both of a sharp drop in living standards and of the differing impact of occupation on the city's three main races. By the end of the war, almost no one in Syonan had escaped significant nutritional deprivation and associated impairments to health. The returning British found 'a very large percentage

[76] NAS, Oral History interview 000152, Heng Chiang Ki.

[77] Totani, *Tokyo War Crimes Trial*, p. 180.

of the population was suffering from serious under-nourishment'.[78] Between about two-fifths and two-thirds of Singapore schoolchildren were malnourished by pre-war standards.[79] Most children showed stunted growth and very poor musculature.[80]

In Syonan, as in much of Japanese-occupied Southeast Asia, health services and anti-malarial work were progressively abandoned. Death rates surged due to declining health services, reduced availability of clean water and inadequate diets, this last evidenced, for example, by a much higher incidence of beriberi (dietary deficiency associated with an overload of carbohydrates) and infantile convulsions. The latter figure, indicative of malnutrition among infants under one year old, was high because poorly fed women were unable to suckle their infants and could not obtain milk.[81] Between 1941 and 1944, Syonan's crude death rate more than doubled. Birth rates fell more slowly than death rates rose, but by 1945 the crude birth rate of 27.5 per thousand was not much above half its 1940/41 average and far below crude deaths of 39.8 (table 1.3).

Infant mortality is a good indicator of health trends and, in particular, a usual measure of access to clean water. In Syonan the infant death rate rose markedly during the Japanese occupation (table 1.3). Between 1940 and 1942, an 86 per cent rise in Syonan's infant death rate compares with a 40 per cent increase in occupied Europe's over a similar period and indicates how quickly and how greatly conditions deteriorated.[82] Between 1942 and 1945, infant deaths accounted for a quarter of total deaths but for a much higher share of the increase in deaths. In comparison to 1940, between 1942 and 1945, while average annual deaths excluding infants increased by 56 per cent, infant deaths rose by 256 per cent.

In 1940, a much higher Malay than either Chinese or Indian infant death rate points to pre-war deprivation compared to the other races. During the war, however, Indians were more adversely affected than Malays. A wartime explosion of Indian infant mortality provides clear evidence for the collapse in Indian living

---

78 Singapore, *Annual Report of the Medical Department 1946* (Singapore: Government Printing Office, 1947), p. 13; see also Singapore Department of Social Welfare, *First Report of the Singapore Department of Social Welfare, June to December 1946* (Singapore: G.H. Kiatt, 1947), p. 15; National Institute for Defense Studies, Military History Research Centre, Tokyo, Shochoshi Dai 35 Go, *Syonan Tokubetsu Shi wo Chushin to seru Bukka Taisaku* [Countermeasures for Prices], pp. 315–6.

79 Geoffrey H. Bourne, 'Nutrition Work in Malaya under the British Military Administration', *International Review of Vitamin Research* 21 (1949): 286.

80 AK, BMA Dept/1/3 pt. II, British Military Administration, 'Final Report Nutrition Unit' (Apr. 1946), Appx. A(i); see also Bourne, 'Nutrition Work', pp. 286–7.

81 Singapore, *Report of Medical Department 1946*, p. 2.

82 League of Nations, *World Economic Survey, 1941/42* (Geneva: League of Nations, 1942), p. 18.

standards that the Chōsabu identified. Substantially because of the high 1940 pre-war Malay starting point, between then and 1944 the percentage increase in Malay infant deaths (61.4 per cent) was considerably less than for Chinese infants (100 per cent). However, both races were far outdistanced by an increase of 166.7 per cent for Indian infants. Between 1940 and 1944, while infant death rates for Singapore as a whole doubled, they were 2.7 times higher among Indians (table 1.3).

Table 1.3 Singapore and Kuala Lumpur crude birth and death rates, 1940–47

(births and deaths per 1,000 population)

		Singapore		Kuala Lumpur		Jakarta Municipality	
		Births	Deaths	Births	Deaths	Births	Deaths
1939		45.0	20.9			28.0	16.0
1940							
1941		44.8	20.8	48.6			
1942		34.6	37.3	21.5			
1943		37.7	26.4			29.0	18.0
1944		36.9	49.7	25.8	20.7		
1944	(1)					22.0	19.0
1944	(2)					17.0	23.0
1945		27.5	39.8			15.0	28.0
1946		42.3	16.7	42.9	16.3		
1947		45.8	13.3	50.9			

Note:
1. For 1946 for Kuala Lumpur, births are estimated using the census population figure for 1947.
2. Death rates, in particular, may be understated for Singapore and Kuala Lumpur due to non-reporting.
3. Data for Jakarta Municipality for 1944 refer to the first and second halves of the year.
4. Jakarta Municipality includes a substantial area around the city. Statistics for it are therefore not entirely comparable with Singapore and Kuala Lumpur, but still point to likely trends in urban Jakarta.

Source: Singapore, *Annual Report on the Registration of Births and Deaths for the Years 1940–47* by E.J. Phillips (Singapore: Government Printing Office, 1948), pp. 6, 8, 12; AK 1957/0292046. RC Selangor 269/1947 *Report of the Kuala Lumpur Town Board, 1946*, p. 22 and 1957/0294190, Selangor Secretariat 554/1948 *Report of the Kuala Lumpur Town Board, 1947*, p. 17; Netherlands, Centraal Bureau voor de Statistiek, 'De economische toestand', p. 127.

Conclusion

The Chōsabu reports, written between October 1943 and October 1944, are valuable because they are the first-hand observations of trained social scientists who had at their disposal a staff of assistants. Taken together, the reports provide considerable new data and information on wartime Syonan. Economic and social conditions continuously deteriorated as the war worsened for the Japanese, although, unlike in wartime Jakarta and Hanoi, famine was avoided in Syonan, apart from a few unfortunates like the imported Indonesian labourers described above. Nevertheless, by the end of the war most Syonan residents had experienced serious hardship. In the face of social and economic dislocation, the overwhelming impression one gets from reading the Chōsabu reports is of a group of academic researchers looking to resolve problems for which, given the policies of occupation and their inherent contradictions, no solutions existed. At best, only palliatives were possible; and even where these were recommended, for example in policy adjustments in regard to labour, agriculture and the allocation of rations, the Chōsabu may have had limited influence.

Even though the Chōsabu probably often failed to shape policy, their reports give insight into the occupation period as among its few surviving Japanese-language documents. As such, the reports help in understanding what Japanese officials regarded as the important problems in Syonan and how these might be addressed. The Japanese approach was inevitably determined by the overriding need to maximize the war effort. Because this required the city's effective management and mobilization of its population, the Chōsabu reports extend to issues touching on aspects of society. It is striking, especially since Syonan presented a society so different from Japan's, that Chōsabu researchers do not seem to have had particularly open or flexible approaches in recommending solutions to the problems that they encountered. They appear seldom to have recognized the role of incentives in a commercial society like pre-war Singapore or that Syonanese could not be expected to display the deference to authority that existed in Japan.

In Syonan, Japanese officials favoured rigid controls and tight economic management. Such an approach was effective in the Japanese Home Islands. There, neighbourhood associations kept the population under constant surveillance, large quantities of 'voluntary' saving could be forced from the citizenry, strict rationing was successfully implemented, and business became subservient to the government and followed its lead. However, similar controls and collectivism had little chance of success in Syonan. Its population was not culturally Japanese, did not share Japan's tradition of centralized control, and had been strongly biased against the Japanese by a reign of terror at the outset of occupation. The ethos of pre-war Syonan was strongly free market and gave maximum scope to individual freedom and initiative.

As the war continued, local transport to move food and other civilian supplies became increasingly unavailable. Japanese in Syonan, as throughout Southeast Asia, requisitioned large numbers of ships and most automobiles and lorries for military purposes and their own use. An acute shortage of petrol and lack of spare parts hindered the use of transport still permitted to civilians. In Syonan, a combination of transport shortages and low, fixed prices for rice threatened to turn food crisis into famine. The Chōsabu reports show that by late 1943 many people in Syonan no longer ate rice. Insofar as poorer people received rationed rice it was apparently sold on the black market and the proceeds used to buy cheaper and more affordable foods such as tapioca and sweet potatoes. Even such substitution typically seems to have yielded inadequate quantities of food. The Chōsabu reports reveal, however, a few instances where Japanese administrative flexibility was not entirely lacking. In mid-1944, when food shortages in Syonan had become critical, a relaxation of controls over the import and distribution of rice enabled Chinese importers to bring rice from Thailand and sell on an effectively free market in Syonan. It seems likely that without this change in policy wartime nutritional deprivation in Syonan would have been much worse.

The already large pre-war number of hawkers and petty traders in Syonan was increased yet further by unemployment after the collapse of Syonan's pre-war export economy and by its new, complex structure of parallel black, free and grey markets. No doubt a considerable part of this burgeoning informal sector represented an 'overspill' of labour, but it also performed a real economic function in a wartime environment of uncertain information, where only the very closest friends might be trusted. Large amounts of apparently 'unproductive' labour in Syonan became a focus for Chōsabu analysis, since by 1944 Japanese enterprise and the military needed more local workers to contribute to the war economy. Street vendors in particular were categorized by the *Population Survey of Syonan* as 'in a surplus occupation'. Low female labour force participation, shown by the employment census, is a striking finding of the bureau's research and for the Chōsabu became part of a focus on how to mobilize labour in Syonan. However, attempts at mobilization appear largely to have failed.

Although, as the Chōsabu reports describe, Japanese administrators made numerous efforts to finance occupation through various direct and indirect taxes and so avoid wholesale money creation as a means of paying for the war, these provided limited amounts of revenue. Large arbitrary levies were imposed on the Chinese business community. In general, however, most taxes were petty in nature and highly regressive, since they consisted of lotteries or applied to everyday transactions and amusements of the poorest classes of Syonan's population. Ultimately, to pay for the cost of occupying Syonan and the rest of Malaya the Japanese administration had to rely primarily on taxation through printing military scrip.

Data collected by the Chōsabu establish that many ordinary people in Syonan worked for the Japanese, including the some 45,000 estimated by *A Study of the Labour Situation* as employed in Japanese-managed factories. Chōsabu reports document how rice rations were much increased to secure this factory labour, with a consequent fillip to the black market from the sale of at least part of these incentive rations. The black market hardly needed this further stimulus from the sale of preferential rations. A wartime economy of serious and growing shortages, price controls on over 200 items, and the organization of most business into Japanese-granted monopolies ensured a large and, as the occupation continued, growing black market in virtually all essential goods.

While it has been suggested that in some parts of wartime Southeast Asia Japanese firms and the military initiated substantial new import substitution industrialization, they did not do so in Singapore. The Chōsabu reports provide detailed discussion of the Japanese industrial effort and point out that it consisted almost entirely of the takeover of pre-war British and Chinese firms. However, it frequently proved difficult to keep even this industrial base operative owing to lack of raw material inputs and spare parts.

The Chōsabu reports make apparent, although seldom explicitly state, how difficult it was for the Japanese to try to run Syonan. Although able successfully to repress open dissent, and indeed persuade many Chinese to work for them, the Japanese never had adequate resources effectively to administer Syonan and provide for the welfare of its people. By the end of 1942, when the Chōsabu arrived in Syonan, the war had already turned, probably decisively, against Japan. Much of Syonan's pre-war economy had already ground to a halt and been replaced by a makeshift informal economy, in part supported by the city's huge black market. The Japanese themselves depended on this not just to prevent a total collapse of Syonan but also for a number of their own needs. Perhaps as much as anything so pervasive can, Singapore's black market and the dire shortages of food and consumer goods that created it, encapsulates the breakdown of the economy, and with this also society, in wartime Syonan.

Figure 2.1 A view of part of Singapore and the harbour taken from behind the YMCA sports ground, 7 February 1942

Source: 'The War in Malaya: Latest Scenes and Side-Lights on Events in the Malay Peninsula and Singapore; of Fighting, Defences, and of the Evacuation of Refugees.' *Illustrated London News*, 7 Feb. 1942: 174.

CHAPTER 2

The Chōsabu Members and the Chōsabu Reports[1]

Shinobu Majima

A photograph published by the *Illustrated London News* on 7 February 1942 shows the principal buildings and sites of Singapore. The Raffles Hotel is on the left and the Supreme Court on the right, with the harbour and sea in the background. It was taken from the top of the YMCA building near Fort Canning, and a week or so later everything shown in the photograph was occupied by the Japanese army. The Department of Research (Chōsabu) of the Southern Military Administration Superintendent General's Office (Nanpō Gunsei Sōkanbu), one of the research teams dispatched by the Japanese government to Southeast Asia, used the Raffles Hotel, Supreme Court and Fort Canning during its members' stay in Singapore.[2] The Chōsabu was entrusted to supervise other research teams in Malaya and Sumatra (initially as one entity by Manchurian Railway Co.), Java (Institute for East Asian Affairs, Planning Board of Japan), North Borneo (Pacific Association), the Philippines (Mitsubishi Economic Research Institute) and Burma (again by Manchurian Railway Co.). While the Chōsabu's main interest was in newly occupied Singapore, it also produced research reports to cover the

[1] This chapter is based on an earlier article, 'The Japanese Military Administration Department of Research Reports on Singapore's Wartime Economy', *Journal of Asian Cultures* 18 (Mar. 2016), substantially revised and updated for this book.

[2] The Southern Military Administration was first headquartered in the Fullerton Building, the Syonan Municipal Administration was located in City Hall, and the YMCA building was used by a branch of the Syonan Military Police. Fort Canning served as the headquarters of the Military Police and later also housed, in addition to the Chōsabu, many other departments and offices of the Military Administration, such as the Department of Finance and the Office of Tokugawa Yoshichika. Gaus Mahjudin, *M. Gaus Kaisō Roku* [Memoir of M. Gaus] (Tokyo: Waseda University Asia Pacific Research Centre, 2012).

Southern Regions in general.[3] With a staff of 56 Japanese and 67 Singaporeans, the Chōsabu became involved in both surveying and running the economy of Singapore from the end of 1942. After changes in role allotment, the Chōsabu assumed a similar role in the Malayan economy beginning in 1944.[4]

The wartime activities of the Chōsabu researchers in Singapore have so far attracted little academic attention. The limited number of articles and chapters written in English and Japanese on the Chōsabu give a general picture of the team's time in occupied Singapore and/or discuss in greater detail the involvement of its two prominent researchers—Akamatsu Kaname (1896–1974),[5] the director of the Chōsabu, and his right-hand man, Itagaki Yoichi (1908–2003)[6]—in

[3] Akashi Yōji, 'Japanese Research Activities in Occupied Malaya/Syonan, 1943–45', in *New Perspectives on the Japanese Occupation in Malaya and Singapore, 1941–1945*, ed. Akashi Yōji and Yoshimura Mako (Singapore: NUS Press, 2008); Tokyo Daigaku Kyōyō Gakubu Kokusai Kankeiron Kenkyūshitsu, ed., *Interview Kiroku D – Nihon no Gunsei 6* [Interview Record D: Japanese Military Administration 6] (Tokyo: Tokyo Daigaku Kyōyō Gakubu Kokusai Kankei Ron Kenkyūshitsu, 1981); Fukami Sumio, 'Tōnan Asia ni okeru Nihon Gunsei no Chōsa' [Research by the Southern Military Administration in Southeast Asia], *Nan'yō Bunka* 15 (Nov. 1988): 119–41; Nippon no Eiryō Malaya/Singapore Senryō Shiryō Chōsa Forum, ed., *Interview Kiroku – Nippon no Eiryō Malaya/Singapore Senryō 1941–1945* [Interview Records: Japan's Occupation of British Malaya and Singapore 1941–45] (Tokyo: Ryūkei Shosha, 1998); Akashi Yōji, ed., *Sakakibara-ke Shozō Nanpōgun Gunsei Sōkanbu Kankei Bunsho* [Documents of Sakakibara Family Related to Southern Military Administration Superintendent General's Office], Vol. 7 (Tokyo: Ryūkei Shosha, 2004); Akashi Yōji, ed., *Nanpōgun Gunsei Sōkanbu Chōsabu, Malaya Gunsei Kanbu Chōsabu Hōkokusho* [Research Reports by the Southern Military Administration Chōsabu and the Malayan Military Administration Chōsabu], 1943–45, Vol. 1 (Tokyo: Ryūkei Shosha, 2006), pp. 7–17.

[4] See Appendix A.1 List of Chōsabu Members.

[5] Kojima Kiyoshi, ed., *Akamatsu Kaname Hakase Kanreki Kinen Ronshū: Keizai Seisaku to Kokusai Bōeki* [Anthology Commemorating the Sixtieth Birthday of Dr. Akamatsu Kaname: Economic Policy and International Trade] (Tokyo: Shunjyūsha, 1958); Ikeo Aiko, *Hyōden Nihon no Keizaishisō: Akamatsu Kaname* [Biographies of Japanese Economic Thoughts: Akamatsu Kaname] (Tokyo: Nihon Keizai Hyōron Sha, 2008).

[6] The political movement of Kesatuan Rakyat Indonesia Semenanjung (KRIS, Indonesian Peninsular People Union), led by Ibrahim Yaacob of the former Kesatuan Melayu Muda (KMM, Young Malay Union), was supported by Itagaki and Akamatsu. Cheah Boon Kheng, 'The Japanese Occupation of Malaya, 1941–1945: Ibrahim Yaacob and the Struggle for Indonesia Raya', *Indonesia* 28 (Oct. 1979); Cheah Boon Kheng, *Red Star over Malaya: Resistance and Conflict during and after the Japanese Occupation, 1941–1946*, 3rd ed. (Singapore: Singapore University Press, 2003), pp. 11–3, 19–20, 52, 101–8, 299 and index for KMM; Itagaki Yoichi, *Asia to no Taiwa* [Conversation with Asia] (Tokyo: Ronsōsha, 1988); Itagaki Yoichi, 'Malaya Fukugō Shakai ni Okeru Nationalism no Hatten' [The Development of Nationalism in Malayan Plural Society], *Hitotsubashi University Research Annual: Economic Research*, Departmental Bulletin Paper No. 6, Mar. 1962; Chōsa Forum, ed., *Interview Records*, pp. 19–57; Karashima Masato, *Teikoku Nihon no Asia Kenkyū* [Research on Asia by Imperial Japan] (Tokyo: Akashi Shoten, 2015).

political activities associated with an unsuccessful attempt to gain independence for a Malay-dominated state towards the end of the war after their roles in research enterprise of the Military Administration terminated. No substantial work investigates the socio-economic content of the research reports themselves; these were mostly handwritten and mimeographed due to the circumstances of occupation and economic collapse. This chapter provides an analysis of the Chōsabu reports that concentrate on wartime economic matters. It reveals an alternative picture of the researchers' presence in Singapore and differs from the stories focused on the failed independence movement instigated by Japanese officials in the final few months of the war.[7]

The Chōsabu members were mainly economists from the Institute of East Asian Economies at the Tokyo University of Commerce (Tokyo Shōka Daigaku, also translated as Tokyo College of Commerce), which was the forerunner of the Institute of Economic Research at Hitotsubashi University, the Japanese equivalent to the London School of Economics and Political Science. When the researchers were first put up at the Raffles Hotel they were thrilled by the music bands, the tropical fruits and the genteel colonial culture of Singapore. Although the propaganda of the military state denounced what it considered as Western decadence, 'the Japanese in fact enjoy modern Western products, living like white men and conquerors in Malaya'.[8] During the Chōsabu's assignment in Singapore and Malaya, 84 reports were printed and circulated to be read by the superintendent general and other high-ranking officers and advisers to the Southern and Malayan Military Administrations and Syonan Municipality staff.[9] These included Marquis Tokugawa Yoshichika (1886–1976), a friend of Sultan Ibrahim I of Johore, fluent in Bahasa Melayu, who was known to have struggled to save Singapore's Raffles Museum and Botanic Gardens to make Singapore the academic core of the Southern Region,[10] and Shinozaki Mamoru (1908–91), who had been attached to the Foreign Office before the war and is sometimes

[7] Kheng, 'The Japanese Occupation of Malaya'; Chōsa Forum, ed., *Interview Records*, pp. 49–57.

[8] Su Fang Ng, 'Chin Kee Onn's Ma-rai-ee and the Narration of the Malayan Nationalist Subject in the Aftermath of the Pacific War', *Journal of Commonwealth Literature* 34, 1 (1999): 87.

[9] See Appendix A.2 List of Chōsabu Reports and Chōsabu News. Altogether 84 reports were written, or planned to be written, out of which 48 survived. Many of the reports written after December 1944 are missing.

[10] Edred John Corner, *The Marquis: A Tale of Syonan-to* (Singapore: Heinemann Asia, 1981); Louis Allen, 'Japan as Occupying Power: The Revision of History', in *Rethinking Japan: Social Sciences, Ideology and Thought*, ed. Adriana Boscaro, Franco Gatti and Massimo Raveri (London: Routledge, 1995); Tokugawa Yoshichika, *Saigo no Tonosama* [The Last Samurai Lord] (Tokyo: Kodansha, 1973); Odabe Yūji, *Tokugawa Yoshichika no Jūgonen Sensō* [Tokugawa Yoshichika's 15-Year War] (Tokyo: Aoki Shoten, 1988).

credited with 'saving a considerable number of Chinese from ill-treatment' at the beginning of the occupation.[11]

The Chōsabu team was led by Akamatsu Kaname, a professor of economic policy at the Tokyo University of Commerce, who had been specially recruited to head the Institute of East Asian Economies in 1941. The flying geese pattern of economic development (in which less-developed economies catch up with more advanced ones), for which Akamatsu became well-known later in the 1960s,[12] was first formulated in the 1930s from his observation of the Japanese textile industry's growing competitiveness with its British counterpart in world trade.[13] Because of Akamatsu's pre-war and post-war academic interest, we might expect to find a policy application of the flying geese idea in the wartime reports on Singapore written by Akamatsu's team.[14] A synergy of Akamatsu's own economic theory with those economic policies to build the Greater East Asia Co-prosperity Sphere drafted by government officials, such as the Planning Board, the Ministry of Commerce and Industry, the army and the navy, might also be expected from the reports.[15] However, such a dimension of Japan-led industrial development of Asia, which appeared in the title of Akamatsu's seminar talk before his departure from Japan, was absent from the Chōsabu reports.[16] Why was his catching-up

---

[11] Paul Kratoska, *The Japanese Occupation of Malaya 1941–1945* (London: Hurst & Co., 1998), p. 97; Shinozaki Mamoru, *Syonan, My Story: The Japanese Occupation of Singapore* (Singapore: Times Books International, 1975); Shinozaki Mamoru, *Singapore Senryō Hiwa: Sensō to sono Ningenzō* [Secret Stories of the Occupation of Singapore] (Tokyo: Hara Shobō, 1976).

[12] Akamatsu Kaname, 'A Theory of Unbalanced Growth in the World Economy', *Welwirtschaftliches Archiv* 86, 2 (1961): 192–215; Akamatsu Kaname, 'A Historical Pattern of Economic Growth in Developing Countries', *Developing Economies* 1 (1962): 1–23.

[13] Akamatsu Kaname, 'Wagakuni Yōmō Kōgyōhin no Sūsei' [Trend of Japan's Woollen Goods Industry], *Shōgyō Keizai Ronsō* 13 (1935): 129–212.

[14] Kojima Kiyoshi, 'Bōeki Seisaku, Keizai Kaihatsu Ron' [Trade Policy and Economic Development], in *Hitotsubashi Daigaku Gakumonshi* [Intellectual History of Hitotsubashi], ed. Hitotsubashi Daigaku Gakuenshi Kankō Iinkai (Tokyo: Hitotsubashi Daigaku Gakuenshi Kankō Iinkai, 1986). Kojima provides a consistent story of intellectual development from Ueda Teijirō, through Akamatsu Kaname and Itagaki Yoichi to Kojima himself, as an inheritor of Akamatsu's catching-up theory.

[15] Adachi Hiroaki, 'Dai Tōa Kyōei Ken' no Keizai Kōsō: Ikinai Sangyō to Dai Tōa Kensetsu Shingikai [Economic Design of the 'Greater East Asia Co-prosperity Sphere': Intra-sphere Industrial Development and the Council for the Greater East Asia Co-prosperity Sphere] (Tokyo: Yoshikawa Kobunkan, 2013); Yamamoto Yūzō, 'Dai Tōa Kyōei Ken' no Keizai Shi [An Economic History of the Greater East Asia Co-prosperity Sphere] (Nagoya: Nagoya University Press, 2011).

[16] Institute of East Asian Economies, *Tokyo Sangyō Daigaku Tōa Kenkyūjo Gaiyō* [A Summary of the Institute of East Asian Economies at Tokyo University of Industry] (Tokyo: Tokyo Sangyō Daigaku Tōa Kenkyūjo, 1943). The title of Akamatsu's seminar talk in August 1942 was 'Building Great East Asia'.

theory, or a modified version of it, not central to the work of his team, and what else characterizes the unique collection of economic research reports in its absence? The reason may be, as suggested by the brief given to the Chōsabu by the military, that Singapore and the Southern Regions in general were not seen as potential competitors to Japan but as a complement to it. The reports are characterized by the Chōsabu members' ambiguously affirmative attitudes towards *laissez-faire* colonialism and a wartime controlled economy, the latter typically justified by the theory of wartime social policy in the 1940s.[17]

The Tokyo University of Commerce was given the official offer to form a team of researchers as the Chōsabu on 30 June 1942. Its mission was laid out on 16 August by a secret order from the army, and its members were sent to Singapore in December, a year after the outbreak of a war that many suspected Japan could not win.[18] They were ordered to conduct research on how best to extract the natural resources essential to national defence, to ensure economic stability in the occupied areas and to give guidance to the various ethnic communities in the region. The reports were written broadly within these categories, but the individual research themes were chosen by the researchers themselves. The Chōsabu men recalled in their memoirs that they thought they were doing 'research for research's sake only' and on that basis decided to collaborate with the army. In reality, however, they became involved in policy implementation during the occupation.[19]

Because Akamatsu was second in rank only to the superintendent general of the Southern Military Administration, the Chōsabu were given almost complete

---

17 Ōkōchi Kazuo gave a talk on wartime social policy at the Japan Economic Policy Association 1940 Conference, which was published as *Senji Shakai Seisaku* [The Theory of Wartime Social Policy] (Tokyo: Jichō Sha, 1940). The Brentano-inspired reformist policy of Ōkōchi (1905–84) is known to have served as a justification for intellectuals to collaborate with the military. See Matsumura Takao, *'ABC' Mondai wa Kaiketsu dekirunoka* [Can We Solve the 'ABC' Problem?] (Tokyo: ABC Kikaku Iinkai, 2014), p. 43, for criticism of Ōkōchi's theory, which Matsumura regards as an affirmation of wartime labour mobilization in Korea, China and other occupied territories. At the same conference, Sugimoto Ei'ichi read a paper criticizing the current state of economic control in Japan, and advocated an ideal control system that would secure short-term monetary liquidity and increase effective aggregate demand. Sugimoto Ei'ichi, 'Keizai Tōsei to Ryūdōsei Genri' [Economic Control and the Principle of Liquidity], *Ikkyō Ronsō* 6, 1 (1940).

18 'Nanpō Gunsei Chōsa Keikaku An [Southern Military Administration Research Plan], 16 August 1942', based on Riku-a-mitsu [Riku = Army, A = Asia, Mitsu = Secret] Order No. 2772, in *Documents of Sakakibara Family*, Vol. 7, ed. Akashi (1942).

19 Ko Yamada Isamu Sensei Tsuitō Bunshū Kankō Sewanin Kai, *Riron to Keiryō ni Tesshite: Yamada Isamu Sensei Tsuitō Bunshū* [Devoted to Theory and Quantification: Anthology in Memory of Professor Yamada Isamu] (Tokyo: Ronsōsha, 1987); *Interview Record D, Japanese Military Administration 6*, p. 119.

autonomy on what they could express in the reports—they were free to give 'verdicts' or recommendations on the policies of the Military Administration, although these were often completely ignored by those high-ranking policymakers.[20] The verdicts were concisely summarized at the beginning of each report and gave recommended solutions to administrative problems, based on their academic, rational judgement. However, their verdicts were given to each element of policy at particular stages of Japan's occupation, not on the final outcome of the war economy: they had to halt their research, and produced no more reports after May 1945. Other descriptions of the war economy can be found in Chin Kee Onn's frequently cited *Malaya Upside Down*, praised by the Malayan colonial official Victor Purcell and published in 1946.[21] The Chōsabu's and Chin's perceptions of the socio-economic problems resonate with each other on a number of themes. This book as a compilation of selected reports focuses on those socio-economic themes, such as the black market, inflation and rice rations. In these reports, one can see the varying roles adopted by the Chōsabu researchers. These range from a detached observation of the Japanese Military Administration to dissent and criticism of its policies.

The first section of this chapter briefly discusses how the reports should be read and evaluated, and considers the role played by the Chōsabu team in the Southern Military Administration. The second section puts the authors of the Chōsabu reports in a wider academic context, focusing particularly on two junior

[20] More than half the Chōsabu reports have a 'verdict' section at the beginning; others start with a 'summary' or an 'introduction'. 'Verdict' often meant 'conclusion' in Japanese military language. The Chōsabu reports were almost never acknowledged by those at the Department of Industry who made and implemented economic mobilization policies. Iwatake Teruhiko, *Nanpō Gunsei-ka no Keizai Shisaku: Malaya, Sumatra, Java no Kiroku* [Economic Policy under the Southern Military Administration: Report on Malaya, Sumatra and Java] (Tokyo: Ryukei Shosha, 1995); Iwatake Teruhiko, *Nanpō Gunsei Ronshū* [Essays on Southern Military Administration] (Tokyo: Gannandō Shoten, 1989).

[21] Chin Kee Onn, *Malaya Upside Down* (Singapore: Jitts & Co. Ltd., 1946). Chin's book was praised for its 'most complete and illuminating account of Malaya under the Japanese' in Colonel Victor Purcell's foreword written November 1945. Chin's own wartime involvement is documented in the Japanese translation of his book. Chin Kee Onn, *Bushidō ni Naku: Nihon Saiken wo Kigansuru Ichi Gaijin yori* [Crying for Samurai Spirit: By a Foreigner Who Prays for Reconstruction in Japan] (Tokyo: Shintai Sha, 1949). It is notable that the foreword by Shinozaki, who was the copyright holder in Japan, was omitted due to 'convenience of the publisher'. Chin worked 'under the supervision of Mr H. Hitomi of the Perak State Cultural Economic Research Institute in Ipoh' during the Japanese occupation.

economists, Yamada Isamu (1909–86)[22] and Higuchi Gorō (1906–71), who produced more reports than Akamatsu or Itagaki. Sections 3 to 6 trace how the Chōsabu came to be involved in carrying out various policies to ameliorate the adverse effects of the worsening war situation and an increasing military monopoly. Discussion of this evolution of the Chōsabu's role starts by evaluating the reports written not by the Chōsabu (Department of Research) but by the Departments of Police Administration and General Affairs in the spring of 1943 (section 3),[23] then the survey reports written in response by the Chōsabu in the autumn of 1943 (section 4),[24] the Chōsabu's renewed policy recommendations made in the spring of 1944 (section 5),[25] and finally the action reports put

[22] There were three Yamadas associated with the Chōsabu and the Institute of East Asian Economies, and they should not be confused. One was Yamada Isamu (1909–86), who is discussed in detail in this chapter. A second was Professor Yamada Yūzō (1902–96), who was sent to Beijing in February 1943 to set up the North China Chōsashitsu as a branch office of the institute. He was another pupil of Fukuda and had studied at the University of Vienna under the supervision of Osker Morgenstern in 1935–37. Finally there was Yamada Hideo (1917–2002), who was a Chōsabu member, joining the research expedition as a research associate only a few years after his graduation. He was a pupil of Takashima Zenya (1904–90), who was supervised by Ōtsuka Kin'nosuke. Promoted to an associate professor in 1944, Yamada Hideo authored *Chōsabu Report No. 53: Syonan-tō Kakyō Yasai Nōka Jittai Chōsa Hōkoku* [A Study of Overseas Chinese Vegetable Farmers on Syonan Island] with research associate Ōno Seizaburō (1918–2005), which was due to be published in March 1945 but is now missing. After the war, Yamada Hideo and Ōno Seizaburō resigned from the institute together with other researchers but were then re-employed as office clerks of the institute. Later they both became professors and served as directors of the Institute of Economic Research in the late 1960s and early 1970s; they received emeritus professorship on their retirement in the early 1980s.

[23] NIDS, Nansei Gunsei 29, *Syonan Tokubetsushi Jūyō Kōjō Genjō Gaikyō* [Important Industrial Factories in Syonan Municipality] (Singapore: Southern Military Administration, Department of General Affairs, Research Office, Mar. 1943); NIDS, Nansei Gunsei 29, *Keizai Hoan ni kansuru Jōkyō Shirabe, Syonan Tokubetsushi oyobi Johore-shū* [Conditions of Economic Security in Syonan Municipality and Johore] (Singapore: Southern Military Administration, Department of Police Administration, Mar. 1943).

[24] NIDS, Nansei Gunsei 16, *Chōsabu Report No. 12: Syonan-shi ni okeru Minzoku-betsu Saitei Seikatsu Jittai Chōsa: Minzoku-betsu Jūyō Seikatsu Hitsujuhin ni kansuru Kakaku, Sūryō oyobi Hitsuju no Teido no Chōsa wo chūshin to shite* [A Study of Lowest Levels of Living by Ethnic Group in Syonan Municipality: Price, Quantity and the Relative Importance of Daily Necessities, by Ethnic Group] (Singapore: Southern Military Administration Chōsabu, Oct. 1943).

[25] NIDS, Nansei Gunsei 18, *Chōsabu Report No. 35: Syonan Tokubetsushi wo chūshin to seru Bukka Taisaku* [Countermeasures for Prices for Syonan Municipality] (Singapore: Southern Military Administration Chōsabu, Mar. 1944). There was a change in administrative location of the military from Singapore to Taiping in January 1944, and the Chōsabu followed suit, reorganized and relocated to the peninsula (see section 5).

together by the Chōsabu in the autumn of 1944 (section 6).[26] Section 7 tells the afterstory of how the Chōsabu members returned to endure in post-war Japan the psychological burden of cooperating with the Military Administration.

The Chōsabu Researchers' Reports

The 84 Chōsabu researchers' reports, listed in Appendix A.2, may be grouped into three periods: from April 1943 to September 1943, when the Chōsabu was still searching for its role within the Military Administration and wrote on the Southern Regions in general (nos. 1–10); from October 1943 to October 1944, when the Chōsabu rose to a position of confidently reporting on Singapore (nos. 11–51); and from November 1944 to April 1945, from which period most of the reports did not survive (nos. 52–84). The 48 surviving reports were written and mimeographed between the spring of 1943 and the winter of 1944 and cover a diverse range of topics.[27] Those recruited to supplement the team of economists—including a bio-scientist, a medical doctor, and researchers on religion and education—wrote on their preferred subjects. The political economists, such as Itagaki, developed ethno-political interests and translated reference materials on Muslim religious conventions.[28] Just over half of the surviving reports (26 of the 48) focus on the economic themes of labour, mining and manufacturing, commerce, transport, money, and finance. The depth of the arguments and complexity of the analyses indicate that food, commerce and money were priority themes, stemming from the problems caused by the war and the cessation of international trade—namely, the issues of rationing, in-migration

[26] IER, Azb: 8, *Chōsabu Report No. 51: Malaya tokuni Syonan Tokubetsushi ni okeru Beikoku Yu'nyū ni tsuite* [Rice Imports to Malaya, with Special Reference to Syonan Municipality] (Taiping: Malayan Military Administration Chōsabu, Oct. 1944); IER, Azb: 3, *Chōsabu Report No. 44: Syonan Tōnai Shokuryō Zōsan Saku ni tsuite* [Methods of Increasing Food Production on Syonan Island] (Taiping: Malayan Military Administration Chōsabu, Oct. 1944); IER, Azb: 4, *Chōsabu Report No. 45: Syonan Tokubetsushi Syōgyō Seibi ni tsuite* [Reorganizing Commercial Businesses in Syonan Municipality] (Taiping: Malayan Military Administration Chōsabu, Sept. 1944); IER, Azb: 5, *Chōsabu Report No. 47: Syonan Tokubetsushi Rōmu Jijō Chōsa: Hōjin Keiei Kōgyō wo chūshin to shite* [A Study of the Labour Situation in Syonan Municipality, Focusing on Factories Managed by Japanese] (Taiping: Malayan Military Administration Chōsabu, Oct. 1944).

[27] For a list of all the report titles, see Appendix A.2 List of Chōsabu Reports and Chōsabu News.

[28] Japanese National Institute for Defense Studies, Military Archives Collection [hereafter NIDS], Nansei Gunsei 47, 'Perak Dokō Jijō ni tsuite' [Matters Related to the Sultan of Perak], *Chōsabu News* 4 (21 June 1944): 3–6; NIDS, Nansei Gunsei 18, *Chōsabu Report No. 41: Dokō Kankei Shūkyō Gyōsei Sankō Shiryō* [Reference Materials on Sultan's Religious Administration] (Singapore: Southern Military Administration Chōsabu, July 1944).

and inflation, which affected the everyday life of Singaporeans. Research and development relating to the manufacturing industry, especially on utilization of available resources in the Southern Regions, was not part of the Chōsabu's remit.[29] The Chōsabu reports rarely discussed primary commodities but allocated more space to a discussion of distributive issues related to ordinary Singaporeans as consumers and workers during the Japanese occupation. The reports reveal the progression of the Chōsabu researchers' thoughts, attitudes and actions during the course of a deepening adverse military and economic situation.

The surviving reports, written between the spring of 1943 and the winter of 1944, cover two rounds of an annual plan-action-evaluation cycle—the first under the Southern Military Administration from spring 1943 in Singapore, and the next under the Malayan Military Administration from the spring of 1944. Reports start around the time of the annual allocation of food rations at the beginning of the fiscal year in April. The researchers were initially involved substantively not in planning, but in evaluating policy outcomes. Many of the reports were submitted and mimeographed in the autumn months—12 of the 26 reports from 1943, and 10 of the 22 reports from 1944 were dated September, October and November. Conferences for all the heads of research in the Southern Regions, held in spring and autumn, provided important occasions to set the overall research agenda and to showcase the Chōsabu team's research outcomes to senior officials of the Military Administration.

The Chōsabu was also responsible for coordination of surveys and research conducted by other departments of the Military Administration and by Syonan Municipality. Team members instructed departments and research offices in other parts of the Southern Regions to produce reports on the state of economy and industry at the beginning of 1943—so mainly at a time before they settled down to start their own research. The Chōsabu researchers strongly emphasized at the beginning of their assignment the importance of using standard survey research methods for all the southern research teams and offices, probably having been struck by the lack of empiricism and the arbitrariness in the format of reports written by the other offices in Singapore.[30] Not all research bodies adhered to the empirical methods recommended by the Tokyo University of Commerce academics, but some provided raw data on price, population and rations for the

[29] The Committee for Resource Utilization, established at the beginning of 1943 with representatives from the military and private businesses, discussed the possibility of industrialization in the Southern Regions. From the Chōsabu, only one representative (and not Akamatsu) was accepted in as a mere observer. Kawai Juntarō, a chemist and a lecturer of commodity studies, attended the meeting at the beginning, but after he left for Japan together with Sugimoto and others, Taniyama Seizō, a researcher on agriculture and forestry, took over the role of an observer in this committee.

[30] See later section on 'Spring 1943: Examples of Infeasible Industrial Plans'.

Chōsabu researchers. The latter were then able to compile and critically analyze the data and give their own verdicts on the war economy.[31] However, before venturing a detailed deciphering of the reports themselves, this chapter first investigates the research methods used by the Chōsabu researchers in their socio-economic surveys, and the intellectual standpoints of these men before and after their arrival in Singapore. The background of the academic training in Japan of Chōsabu researchers throws important light on these issues.

The Chōsabu Team[32]

The idea of sending a group of researchers to the south started at the Tokyo University of Commerce with President Ueda Teijirō's (1879–1940) trip to China in 1939.[33] His tour of cities of Asia—including Seoul, Dalian and Beijing—was sponsored by Kagami Kenkichi (1869–1939), the president of Tokyo Fire and Marine Insurance Co., an internationally known businessman who was once on the cover of *Time* magazine.[34] Both Ueda and Kagami were proponents of free trade in the inter-war period. Ueda was a student of Fukuda Tokuzō (1874–1930), who despite never holding the post of president of the Tokyo University of Commerce is considered the most influential figure in the university's history, guiding its rise from a former commercial school (Tokyo Higher Commercial School, Tokyo Kōtō Shōgyō Gakkō) to a university. Fukuda was influenced by Lujo Brentano during his time studying in Munich between 1897 and 1900,[35] and used Alfred Marshall's *Principles of Economics* (for which

---

[31] Hitotsubashi University, Institute of Economic Research Library [hereafter IER], Azb: 48, 'Syonan Seikatsu Hitsujuhin Kouri Kakaku Shirabe [Survey of Retail Prices of Everyday Necessities in Singapore], April 1943–April 1944', *Chōsabu News* 2 (25 May 1944); NIDS, Nansei Malaya/Java 412, *Syonan Seikatsu Hitsujuhin Kouri Kakaku Gaikyō* [Summary Report on Retail Prices of Everyday Necessities in Singapore] (Singapore: Southern Military Administration, June 1944).

[32] For the relationship among the Tokyo University of Commerce academics, see Appendix A.1 List of Chōsabu Members.

[33] Hitotsubashi Daigaku Gakuenshi Hensan Jigyō Iinkai, ed., *Dainiji Taisen to Hitotsubashi* [World War II and Hitotsubashi] (Tokyo: Hitotsubashi Daigaku Gakuenshi Hensan Jigyō Iinkai, 1983), p. 20.

[34] Ueda was introduced to Kagami through Murata Shōzō (1878–57), the president of Osaka Steamship Company and a peer, who became the special adviser to the Japanese Military Administration in the Philippines, bringing in a team of scholars, in addition to Mitsubishi Economic Research Institute, which produced *Hishima Chōsa Hōkokusho* [Philippines Research Reports], Vols 1–4, Sept. 1943 (reprint published by Ryūkei Shosha, 1993). Ueda Teijirō, *Ueda Teijirō Nikki* [Diary of Ueda Teijirō] (Tokyo: Keiō Tsūshin, 1963), p. 315.

[35] Nishizawa Tamotsu, 'Fukuda Tokuzō no Keizai Shisō: Kōsei Keizai, Shakai Seisaku wo chūshin ni' [Economic Ideas of Fukuda Tokuzō: On Welfare Economics and Social Policy], *Ikkyō Ronsō* 132, 4 (2004): 357–85.

Brentano wrote the introduction to the German translation) as a textbook, having had it translated by his student Ōtsuka Kin'nosuke (1892–1977). Ōtsuka later became the central figure responsible for reforming the Institute of East Asian Economies after World War II. Akamatsu, Nakayama Ichiro (1898–1980)—known as the Japanese Schumpeter—and Sugimoto Ei'ichi (1901–52), who most probably masterminded the Chōsabu research agenda for Singapore and the Southern Regions in general, were also students of Fukuda and represented the diverse range of economics subjects studied and taught in Japanese universities. Later, in the 1920s, Fukuda showed an inclination towards economists from Oxford and the London School of Economics such as John A. Hobson, Edwin Cannan and William Beveridge, whose empiricism and reformist policies influenced the socio-political overtone of the Chōsabu Reports.[36]

Ueda, the founder of the Institute of East Asian Economies, had a more practical inclination, having picked it up in England, where he was initially influenced by William Ashley, the founder of the Faculty of Commerce at the University of Birmingham, but then moved to Manchester to attend lectures by Sydney Chapman, author of *The Lancashire Cotton Industry*.[37] He was influenced also by Seki Hajime (1873–1935), a colleague of Fukuda who became the mayor of Osaka, 'Manchester of the Orient', in Fukuda's absence from the college. Ueda also toured Germany and the United States, visiting Wall Street and the Harvard Business School before returning to Japan.[38] A few decades later Akamatsu, who had learned case study methodology at Harvard and opened the Industrial Research Laboratory at Nagoya Higher Commercial School, was invited by Ueda to lead the institute from April 1941.[39] A move away from Marshallian economics characterized none other than Ōtsuka, who went to Berlin to study under the supervision of Werner Sombart. By the outbreak of the war he was no longer at the Tokyo University of Commerce, having been arrested by the Special Higher Police in 1933 for writing a chapter of the *History of the Development*

---

[36] Nishizawa Tamotsu, 'Fukuda Tokuzō no Keizai Shisō: Kōsei Keizai, Shakai Seisaku wo chūshin ni' [Economic Ideas of Fukuda Tokuzō: On Welfare Economics and Social Policy], *Hitotsubashi Forum* 21, no. 59, a public lecture delivered on 28 June 2005, available at http://jfn.josuikai.net.

[37] Sydney J. Chapman, *The Lancashire Cotton Industry: A Study in Economic Development*, Reprint (Clifton: A.M. Kelley, 1973).

[38] Ueda Teijirō, *Diary of Ueda Teijirō*, pp. 126–206, 388; Nishizawa Tamotsu, 'Ueda Teijirō no Keizai Shisō: Shakaikaizō to Kigyōsha wo chūshin ni' [Economic Ideas of Ueda Teijirō: On Social Reform and Entrepreneurship], in *Kindai Nihon to Igirisu Shisō* [Modern Japan and British Philosophy], ed. Sugihara Shirō (Tokyo: Nihon Keizai Hyōron Sha, 1995), pp. 152–3.

[39] Akamatsu Kaname, 'Ueda Sensei to Shōdai Tōa Keizai Kenkyūjo' [Professor Ueda and the Research Institute for East Asian Economies at Tokyo University of Commerce], *Hitotsubashi Ronsō* 7, 1 (1941): 112.

of Capitalism in Japan and charged with political subversion.[40] Succeeding to Ōtsuka's teaching position in the socialist-leaning principles of economics—in parallel to Nakayama's lecture course on the principles of modern economics—was Sugimoto, who had just returned from Germany via the United States. He had studied at the Institute for the World Economy (Institut für Weltwirtschaft) at the University of Kiel, where he became acquainted with Wassily Leontief. An expert on quantitative economics, Sugimoto joined the Chōsabu for half a year and laid the foundations for the standard empirical survey methods.

The generation of junior researchers of the Chōsabu did not have the privilege of studying abroad like their seniors but were influenced by the disciples of Fukuda Tokuzō, including Ueda, Akamatsu, Ōtsuka, Nakayama and Sugimoto. Before and during the war, Sugimoto focused on introducing methods to estimate demand and supply of rice using statistical data collected by the Ministry of Agriculture, and was also involved in setting up a survey of household expenditure at the Cabinet Statistical Office, employing Yamada Isamu for the actual data work.[41] Yamada was educated at the Nagoya Higher Commercial School and worked at the Industrial Physics Laboratory, offering physical testing of fibre contents, before moving to Yokohama Higher Commercial School, where he was discovered by Nakayama and invited to join the Institute of East Asian Economies.[42] Yamada's main research focus was statistics and standards of living. Before coming to Singapore he had produced a series of agricultural production indices for Japan, Taiwan and Korea, which were published as the first—and the last, because of the war—monograph of the institute.[43] Yamada's research showed that, unlike Japan and Taiwan, where an increase in rice production led to a reduction in other grain crops, Korea saw a parallel increase in production of both rice and other grains.[44] This is evidence of the harsh reality of Korea's rice exports to Japan, which left local residents partly reliant on other grains despite rice being a staple of the Korean diet. Yamada was a dedicated empirical researcher

---

40 Ōtsuka Kin'nosuke, *Ōtsuka Kin'nosuke Chosaku Shū* [Writings of Ōtsuka Kin'nosuke], Vol. 1 (Tokyo: Iwanami Shoten, 1980), p. 423.

41 Sugumoto Ei'ichi, *Beikoku Juyō Hōsoku no Kenkyū* [A Study of Patterns of Rice Demand] (Tokyo: Iwanami Shoten, 1925); Japan Statistical Office of the General Administrative Agency of the Cabinet, *Kakei Chōsa Kekka no Gaiyō* [Summary of Household Expenditure Survey], October 1941–September 1942 (Tokyo: Statistical Office of the General Administrative Agency of the Cabinet, 1977); Isono Osamu and Emi Kōichi, 'Tōkeigaku, Keiryō Keizaigaku' [Statistics and Quantitative Economics], in *Hitotsubashi Daigaku Gakumonshi.*

42 Sewanin Kai, *Devoted to Theory and Quantification*, p. 16.

43 Yamada Isamu, *Tōa Nōgyō Seisan Shisū no Kenkyū: Naichi, Chōsen, Taiwan no bu* [A Study of East Asian Agricultural Production Indices], Institute of East Asian Economies Monograph No. 1 (Tokyo: Nihon Hyōron Sha, 1942).

44 Odaka Kōnosuke, 'Senji-ka no Gakumon to Kenkyū' [Scholarship and Education during the War], Josuikai Forum: 7/8, uploaded on 1 Apr. 2008, available at https://www.josuikai.net.

who quietly gathered hard evidence to present as criticism of the military state. He was sent by Sugimoto to work on the household expenditure survey while still in Japan in 1941, and he was particularly involved in understanding the lowest levels of living among labourers and peasants.[45]

Unlike other junior researchers, Yamada refused to take up the position of 'civil administrator' of the army but insisted on joining the Chōsabu team as an academic researcher. Senior researchers who already had tenured posts at the Tokyo University of Commerce also joined the southern expedition in their capacity as academics. Other younger scholars received increased earnings and a special promotion of two ranks for becoming army officers, but Yamada was instead promoted nominally within the university to the post of assistant professor when he left for Singapore.[46] Itagaki did not accept a position as a civil administrator, either, having been an assistant professor for a year and teaching 'colonial policy' at the time of his departure.[47] His early wartime experience was quite different from the rest of the younger scholars, having been privately funded to travel to Indonesia, meeting the nationalist Ernest Douwes Dekker before his arrest, and given public talks on colonialism before setting off for Singapore.[48]

Higuchi Gorō was one of those Chōsabu junior staff who became civil administrators and about whom not much is known. He was a student of Naitō Akira (1883–1949) and probably influenced by Yamaguchi Shigeru (1893–1974),[49] who after Naitō's retirement before the war led the commercial scientists in money and banking at the Tokyo University of Commerce. They were both students of the first president of the university, Sano Zensaku (1873–1952), whose academic inclination derived from the tradition of the former commercial school—another strand separate from Fukuda's line of modern economics. Sano was the headmaster of the commercial school when he was endorsed by the Western-educated Fukuda and Ueda to be the first president of

---

[45] Japan Cabinet Statistical Office, *Kakei Chōsa Kekka no Gaiyō* [A Summary of Household Expenditure Survey Results], October 1941–September 1942 (Tokyo: Cabinet Statistical Office, 1977).

[46] Southern Military Administration Superintendent General's Office, 'Shōkō-ren Meibo Kōtōkan-ren Meibo [List of Officers' Names, List of Higher Civil Administrators' Names] 21 March 1943', in *Documents of Sakakibara Family*, Vol. 7, ed. Akashi. Akamatsu was on grade 2-5, Higuchi on grade 6-8 as a civil administrator, and Yamada on grade 7-6 (grade 7 was the lowest rank). See Appendix A.1 List of Chōsabu Members.

[47] Odaka, 'Scholarship and Education during the War'.

[48] Itagaki, *Conversation with Asia*, p. 145; Karashima, *Research on Asia*, pp. 67–75.

[49] Hitotsubashi Daigaku Gakuenshi Hensan Jigyō Iinkai, Hitotsubashi no Seminar [Seminars at Hitotsubashi] (Tokyo: Hitotsubashi Daigaku Gakuenshi Hensan Jigyō Iinkai, 1983); Yamashita Kunio, 'Kin'yū Ron [Money Theory]', in *Hitotsubashi Daigaku Gakumonshi*; Yamaguchi Shigeru and Higuchi Gorō, *Nihon Inflation no Bunseki* [Analysis of Inflation in Japan], Monographs in Modern Economics No. 12 (Tokyo: Tōyō Keizai Shinpō Sha, 1948).

the university, which Fukuda had struggled to establish with Seki. The fourth president, Takase Sōtarō (1892–1966), who held the position throughout the war, also derived from Sano's group of scholars. Takase made the decision to collaborate with the army, sent Yamaguchi and a few other commercial scientists to investigate the extremely high inflation in Shanghai, and dispatched the rest of the institute to Singapore, while he himself paid short visits to Shanghai in 1942 and Singapore in 1943.[50]

The Tokyo University of Commerce had started responding to the call for cooperation in the agenda of Japanese nationalists and tilted towards the eventual war after the Second Sino-Japanese War erupted. Having set up the institute in April 1940, funded by Kagami's bequest, Ueda suddenly passed away in May, and Takase took over the presidency of the university and the directorship of the institute. The university sent students to Shanghai as the 'Building Asia' Student Voluntary Work Force and allowed drills to be held on campus in order to protect the students and academic autonomy as much as possible. On 8 December 1941, with the outbreak of the Pacific War, there was a long discussion among the researchers of the institute where Sugimoto, according to Akamatsu, led an enthusiastic argument to turn this opportunity of war to their advantage.[51] The university and the institute offered their services to the army section of the Imperial Headquarters through a brother of Takase who worked in the Department of the General Staff.[52] A series of in-house weekly seminars at which members of the institute presented their preparatory research began in April 1942, with Akamatsu presenting first on 'the pattern of industrial development in the developing countries', followed by Yamada—in second place although a junior member of the institute—on the 'measurement of economic self-sufficiency'. Yamaguchi presented on 'Asian characters in currency' in May and Sugimoto on 'the heterogeneous character of the East Asian economy' in June, followed by junior scholars such as Higuchi. While giving an oral presentation in July on the topic of 'financing the Co-prosperity Sphere',[53] Higuchi did not contribute to the annual report of the Institute of

---

50 Takase Sōtarō Sensei Kinen Jigyōkai, ed., *Takase Sōtarō* (Tokyo: Takase Sōtarō Sensei Kinen Jigyōkai, 1970), pp. 552–85.

51 Hara Yōnosuke, 'Hitotsubashi Daigaku no Asia-gaku: Akamatsu Kaname no Asia Keizairon wo chushin toshite' [Asian Studies at Hitotsubashi: Theory of Asian Economics by Akamatsu Kaname], *Japanese Asian Studies: Booklet Series Middle East within Japan*, No. 8, Mar. 2011, available at http://www2.econ.hit-u.ac.jp.

52 Hitotsubashi, *World War II and Hitotsubashi*, p. 21.

53 Institute of East Asian Economies, *A Summary of the Institute of East Asian Economies at Tokyo University of Industry*. The Tokyo University of Commerce was renamed Tokyo University of Industry during the war because trade and commerce were seen as unnecessary occupations in military-governed Japan.

East Asian Economies as Akamatsu as other senior professors did,[54] nor did he produce a monograph like Yamada's.[55]

These topics demonstrate specific research interests of the scholars of the institute. Obliged to comply with the national effort, both Yamaguchi and Higuchi tended to argue that inflation in China, and to a lesser extent in the Southern Regions, was the result not of an issue of excess currency but of a growing demand for material goods. Although the increased issue of military scrip was a fundamental cause of price increases, Yamaguchi and Higuchi were not overtly critical of the printing of money, focusing more on the fact that wartime inflation was exacerbated by acute shortages of goods. For some reason the topic of colonial ethnic policy with a pro-trade *laissez-faire* overtone that Itagaki had been propagating elsewhere, such as at Dai Nippon Colonial Studies, was missing on these occasions.[56] On 17 August 1942 Akamatsu gave a seminar talk on 'building Greater East Asia', right after receiving the Chōsabu research plan as a Secret Order from the army. From surviving records, it is not possible to know how far Akamatsu discussed the plan with staff members. Nevertheless, it is significant that the title of his seminar talk omitted the phrase 'Co-prosperity Sphere'. The Chōsabu research reports produced later in Singapore never even repeated the phrase 'building Asia' nor emphasized the need for a Japan-led industrialization of Asia.[57]

---

[54] Institute of East Asian Economies, *Tōa Keizai Nenpō* [Annual Report on East Asian Economy], Vol. 1 (Tokyo: Nihon Hyōron Sha, 1942).

[55] Yamada, *East Asian Agricultural Indices*.

[56] Hara Kakuten, *Gendai Asia Kenkyū Seiritsushi Ron* [A Study of the History of Modern Asian Studies] (Tokyo: Keisō Shōbō, 1984), p. 57.

[57] Okazaki Tetsuji, 'Development and Management of the Manchurian Economy under Japan's Empire', in *Economies under Occupation: The Hegemony of Nazi Germany and Imperial Japan*, ed. Marcel Boldorf and Tetsuji Okazaki (London: Routledge, 2015). The Chōsabu never advocated the applicability of the development model of the Manchurian economy in Singapore and Malaya. An analysis of the effectiveness of a wartime controlled economy can be found in Hirayama Tsutomu, 'Kokusaku Gaisha ni okeru Shain Dantai no Bunseki: Mantetsu no Middle Management wo megutte [An Analysis of an Employee Association in a Statutory Corporation: On the Middle Management of Manchurian Railway]', *Journal of Oriental Cultures* 18 (Mar. 2016): 67–104.

Spring 1943: Examples of Infeasible Industrial Plans

In February 1943, a month after the Chōsabu's boat journey to the south with the other research teams, a meeting for all heads of research in the Southern Regions was held in Singapore.[58] 'Research on minimum standards of living' and 'research on how to set up a trade and finance system in the Co-prosperity Sphere' became the two top priorities for all the research teams attached to each regional military administration.[59] In other words, having arrived in Singapore, the Chōsabu's interest in restoring the former British monetary and trade policies in the sterling area countries in Asia seemed more appropriate than building a new Asia under a socio-economic development plan. Takase on his brief visit to Singapore confided to his former student stationed there his vision of developing the occupied areas through industrialization, which was not taken up by Akamatsu's team.[60] Nor was a guideline handout prepared in February 1943 by the academics under Akamatsu's command well received by the other commercial and/or governmental research teams elsewhere in Asia. Researchers in Jakarta, for example, refused to be convinced by Yamada, who flew over to convey his passion for organizing household expenditure surveys in Java and elsewhere in parallel with the one in Singapore. Individual teams each ended up working on their own account in different parts of Southeast Asia.

As noted earlier, Akamatsu, an expert on patterns of industrialization, did not author any reports himself, and the Chōsabu did not leave any substantial

58 The Chōsabu and other research organizations of the Southern Regions travelled together on a boat in late December 1942, while the Mantetsu team as an advance team flew in by air in late November. The Mantetsu team and the Chōsabu initially had a somehow overlapping place and position of assignment, but the Mantetsu team moved to Sumatra and Burma after April 1943. Some of its members were later assigned to the Chōsabu as contract researchers. See Appendix A.1 List of Chōsabu Members.

59 NIDS, Nansei Gunsei 27, *Showa 19 nendo Malaya-chiku Chōsa Keikaku* [A (Draft) Research Plan for the Malaya Region in 1943] (Singapore: Southern Military Administration, Chōsabu, June 1943); Southern Military Administration Superintendent General's Office, 'Gunsei Sōkanbu Sōmu-buchō Kōen Yōshi [Summary of a Speech by the Director of General Affairs Department, Southern Military Administration Superintendent General's Office], 8 February 1943, by Lieutenant General Takahashi Tan', in *Documents of Sakakibara Family*, Vol. 6, ed. Akashi. The short-term visiting academics, such as Sugimoto Ei'ichi and Takahashi Taizō (1905–89), were influential in setting up the two top priorities for the Chōsabu. Takahashi, a scholar of finance and money, later attempted to make an estimate of the wartime national income in the Southern Region. Yamamoto, *An Economic History of the Greater East Asia Co-prosperity Sphere*, chapter 9. Sugimoto, Takahashi and two other tenured lecturers stayed only for six months before returning to the university to teach. See Appendix A.1 List of Chōsabu Members.

60 *Takase Sōtarō*, p. 586. For a discussion on the industrialization model, see Okazaki, 'Development of the Manchurian Economy', p. 183.

research results on the issues of industrialization. However, the report prepared by the Research Office of the Southern Military Administration Department of General Affairs, which was probably in charge of research activities before the arrival of the Tokyo University of Commerce researchers, gives information about the state of the industrial sector in Singapore at the beginning of 1943. Written as reference material for the Committee for Resource Utilization, the Research Office's report titled *Important Industrial Factories in Syonan Municipality* (chapter 6)[61] gives details of representative factories in Singapore, ranging from an electric power plant to an opium factory. A detailed description of these factories, including their organization and how the state-of-the-art machinery confiscated from the enemy companies worked, is provided in this brief report. Almost all the factories had been owned by British or foreign nationals before the war and were transferred to Japanese management except the wine and soap factories—'soap production was one of those lucrative ventures' set up by the Singaporeans[62]—and were showcased to visitors such as Takase, who also toured a wooden boat factory.[63]

Characteristic of the *Important Industrial Factories* report, written by 'the elite of the elites among the bureaucrats drafted from Ministry of Internal Affairs',[64] is an overtly optimistic account of industrial capacity. In Malaya fibre resources, for example, were in short supply. While there were programmes to plant cotton trees (kapok trees), sisal hemp, Manila hemp and other plants suitable for producing fibre, the Japanese also began to experiment with pineapple fibres, which were collected manually from pineapple leaves, as *Important Industrial Factories* reveals.[65] In May 1943 hand-spinning of pineapple fibre became possible using small wooden spinning wheels. The report offers a calculation of pineapple fibre output: '2g of fibre can be made from a pineapple leaf [...] Daily production per female worker is 4–5 ounces. At present daily production of pineapple fibre is 12–13 pounds, and over the whole peninsula

---

61 NIDS, Nansei Gunsei 29, *Important Industrial Factories in Syonan Municipality*, by General Affairs Research Office.

62 Chin, *Malaya Upside Down*, p. 184.

63 *Takase Sōtarō*, p. 574.

64 Akashi Yōji, 'Colonel Watanabe Wataru: The Architect of the Malayan Military Administration, December 1941–March 1943', in *New Perspectives on the Japanese Occupation in Malaya and Singapore, 1941–1945*, ed. Akashi Yōji and Yoshimura Mako (Singapore: NUS Press, 2008), p. 46; and Akashi, 'Japanese Research Activities in Occupied Malaya/Singapore', p. 158.

65 Utilization of pineapple fibre was also attempted by the British, for example in North Borneo. 'Pineapple Fibre', *British North Borneo Herald and Official Gazette* (16 Apr. 1898): 125. This article, based on a report by the United States Department of Agriculture, explains the history of this fibre, which goes back to 1600. Singapore traded pineapple fibre, whose quality and strength were generally higher than flax.

it is possible to produce 2,000 tons.'[66] Increasing yearly production to this level would require at least 36,000 female workers and approximately 250,000 pineapples a day. This rather unrealistic expectation of macro-level output echoes the 18 million square yard target output of textiles set for Malaya for 1943 in the *Five-Year Plan of Local Self-sufficient Economy*, requiring a few thousand tons or more of fibre, depending on the thickness of the textiles. This shows just one example of the barely feasible less-than-five-year plan laid out by the Southern Military Administration in September 1943 for 1943–46.[67]

Another report produced by the Department of Police Administration in spring 1943, titled *Conditions of Economic Security in Syonan Municipality and Johore* (chapter 8), also reveals unwarranted optimism in regard to a planned economy. At the basic level of Singaporean life, bare-bones subsistence was narrowly managed, as the former department administrators recalled after the war. To try to achieve this, Syonan Municipality placed priority on ensuring that rationing was 'efficient and effective'.[68] The approach followed was to adjust the number of traders given permits to trade in controlled goods at the discretion of the administrators. Taking rice as an example, rice rationing was initially through 50 wholesale dealers and 1,971 retailers in Syonan Municipality in March 1943. The author of *Conditions of Economic Security* noted that among these, 'there were 548 small-scale retailers who only deal in 1–15 sacks of rice per month. Because the handling charge is set so low per sack of rice, it is not surprising that misconduct occurs.'[69] The number of rice distribution stations was subsequently reduced to 1,007 retailers by March 1944.

Proper control of the rationing system was seen as the most crucial policy in stabilizing the economy and gaining approval from the local people under Japanese occupation. 'Rice was the fulcrum upon which inflation and cost of living see-sawed.'[70] The Food Division of the Department of Industry, which adhered to the rules of the former British administration, and the Department of Police Administration, which took a more robust approach, were together instrumental in overseeing the whole rationing operation. Later, as seen with tapioca bread and tapioca noodle rationing, the coverage of influence of the

---

[66] NIDS, Nansei Gunsei 29, *Important Industrial Factories in Syonan Municipality*, by General Affairs Research Office, p. 28.

[67] IER, Bn: 4, *Gench Jikatsu Gokanen Keikaku (An)* [A (Draft) Five-Year Plan for a Local Self-sufficient Economy] (Singapore: Southern Military Administration, Department of General Staff, September 1943).

[68] Singapore Shisei Kai, ed., *Syonan Tokubetsushi Shi: Senji chū no Singapore* [History of Syonan Municipality: Singapore during the War] (Tokyo: Nihon Singapore Kyōkai, 1987), p. 220.

[69] NIDS, Nansei Gunsei 29, *Conditions of Economic Security in Syonan Municipality and Johore*, by Police Administration.

[70] Chin, *Malaya Upside Down*, p. 59.

Department of Police Administration extended through the Auxiliary Police Assistants Organization. This was set up by local leaders, collaborating with the Japanese, who were appointed as auxiliary police assistants to supervise local affairs. A total of 196,082 households (as of June 1944) were gathered into 5,101 teams, with 30–40 households per team.[71] The auxiliary police assistants issued and updated census cards for the population in each team, organized night watches, and promoted general peace and welfare, including the administration of rationing.[72] The recommendations laid out in *Conditions of Economic Security* and implemented over the course of 1943–44 included (1) reducing rations for rural residents, (2) reducing the number of ration stations, and (3) unifying the policing power of the Food Controller and the Department of Police Administration (and letting the latter take control).

The Chōsabu worked alongside the Department of Police Administration—for example, they used the census card records collected by the police assistants in their analyses and reports—and whenever possible in their subsequent reports, they also tried to correct incorrect assumptions made by the police administrators—for example, as discussed below, regarding the custom of rice eating. While the Chōsabu researchers did not collaborate with resource utilization in the industry sector, they did try to expand their influence over the rationing operations because researchers such as Yamada, for example, were concerned about the lives of the local people and because issues of inflation and cost of living were their areas of expertise.

Autumn 1943: The Chōsabu's Response

Standard of Living

On 11–12 October the Heads of Research Conference was held in Singapore, for which the Chōsabu members prepared a number of reports. The report titled *The Lowest Level of Living* (chapter 12) is particularly notable among those published in autumn 1943, as it was a direct response to the research priority set by the Chōsabu in February 1943. It also corrected the impression wrongly created by a comment of an administrative officer of the Department of Police Administration on his visit to Terengganu, as cited in *Conditions of Economic Security*: 'it is incorrect to consider the entire Malayan population as rice eaters; at present many of the lower classes do not eat rice.' This official assumed that

[71] IER, Azb: 48, 'Syonan Tokubetsushi Shuyō Shokuryō Haikyū Kikō ni tsuite' [Syonan Municipality Major Food Rationing Organizations], *Chōsabu News* 6 (20 July 1944): 7.

[72] Shisei Kai, *History of Syonan Municipality*, pp. 220–1.

'they keep back the rationed rice and sell it on the black market'.[73] In response to this, however, Yamada, the principal author of *The Lowest Levels of Living*, clearly stated that 'the main food of Malays is white rice'.[74] Intending to provide accurate information on necessary consumption items for the subsequent full-scale household expenditure survey, he also emphasized that the same was true for the Chinese and Indians and that everybody was entitled to a 'fair' share of essential rice rations.

Chin bitterly but probably not correctly remarks: 'The rice-consuming populace of Malaya revealed too openly that they could not live without rice, and the Japanese made full use of that fact.'[75] The lure of special rice allocations to labourers, which often disrupted the 'fair' distribution, concerned Yamada's co-author, who cited the request made by all ethnic groups for an increase in white rice rations, while noting that a coolie who received 14 catties (8.4kg) of rice every month and meals every day at the workplace still considered the ration 'insufficient'. Surveying the people at the lowest level of living, Yamada—who took over again from the second author when writing the conclusion—tried hard to present an accurate judgement. At the time of the survey in April–July 1943, the level of rations and the state of the economy were still showing a relatively stable outlook. Compared to pre-war conditions, nominal wages had risen for most of the surveyed households except for Chinese rubber company coolies and Indian and Malay rubber plantation coolies. Yamada was eager to include them as respondent households in the survey of lowest levels of living, being particularly sympathetic to the plight of plantation workers after the cessation of rubber exports. In general, nominal wages rose much less rapidly than inflation and so almost certainly increased the cost of living at that time. Already in the first half of 1943 the repercussions of high prices were felt, for example, by the Indians who struggled to obtain imported spices.

Population by Occupation

Another response from the Chōsabu researchers to the work done by the Department of Police Administration can be seen in their use of census cards as a data source for their analysis in *Population by Occupation in Syonan Municipality*

[73] NIDS, Nansei Gunsei 29, *Conditions of Economic Security in Syonan Municipality and Johore*, by Police Administration.

[74] NIDS, Nansei Gunsei 16, *Chōsabu Report No. 12: The Lowest Levels of Living by Ethnic Group*.

[75] Chin, *Malaya Upside Down*, p. 60.

(chapter 3).[76] On the face of it, this report only provides descriptive statistics, showing the number of people in each occupational category, broad and narrow, by ethnic group and by gender. However, reading between the lines and from inserted sentences on a piece of paper stuck over one page, it is clear that the Chōsabu members became worried about the outcome of their analysis if it were used against groups of people such as the Chinese in commercial occupations. By the time of the publication of this report in December 1943, plans to utilize the underemployed and unemployed workforce in important industries had been drawn up and Syonan Municipality had already facilitated the movement of Chinese migrants to a resettlement town in Johore, known as Endau.[77] The inserted note in *Population by Occupation in Syonan Municipality* tries to explain why population numbers in other occupations apart from commerce might be underestimates. It states that 'consequently, adding these numbers and merging the numerous coolies with those in mining and manufacturing reduces the share of commerce in the employed population'. This insertion was probably made to lessen the impact of the comment below it on the likelihood of an excessive number of people in commerce: 'in view of the present state of mining and manufacturing in Syonan Municipality, it is not per se unlikely that there are an excessive number of people in commerce.'[78] The Chōsabu authors were, however, worried about this conclusion and were careful not to overemphasize the figure.

At the end of 1943 the Chōsabu researchers were not yet of one opinion. Some, such as Yamada, had a more independent approach than many Chōsabu members and were not afraid of appearing overtly critical; others stayed quieter and were more careful. But in 1944, for the second round of the plan-action-evaluation cycle, more reports had been written with fewer apparent inconsistencies among them. The October 1943 Heads of Research Conference, followed by the Conference of Science Institutions, outwardly propagated this change while inwardly consolidating the more liberal faction within the Military Administration. One reason why the idea of 'building Asia' was retracted by the Chōsabu is revealed in the closing speech by Lieutenant General Takahashi Tan, director of the General Affairs Department, on 12 October. He not only mentioned the difficult war situation from Burma to New Guinea, urging the heads of research to prepare for a decisive war, but also openly denounced the idea of building the Greater East Asia Co-prosperity Sphere that was propagated at the beginning of the war. He then emphasized the importance of more basic

[76] IER, Azb: 50, *Chōsabu Report No. 26: Syonan Tokubetsushi no Shokugyō betsu Jinkō* [Syonan Municipality Population by Occupation] (Singapore: Southern Military Administration Chōsabu, Dec. 1943).

[77] Shinozaki, *Secret Stories of the Occupation of Singapore*, p. 98.

[78] IER, Azb: 50, *Chōsabu Report No. 26: Population by Occupation in Syonan Municipality*, p. 14.

academic research, i.e., research on fauna and flora of the tropics and ethno-cultural lifestyles, in comparison to practical, short-term measures, as for example a concentration on 'new industries' to produce wartime substitutes for consumer and other manufactured goods. This might well mean that Takahashi was sympathetic to the vision of Marquis Tokugawa, who acknowledged the collapse of the economy on his departure from Singapore.[79]

In this, the interest of the Chōsabu researchers did not contradict and so did not curb the Imperial Army Headquarters' emphasis, which had turned away from the initial optimistic vision of building Asia through the Co-prosperity Sphere and now focused on establishing a new framework to fight the decisive war until the end. The new emphasis of the Military Administration was placed more upon gaining hearts and minds of the people in preparation for the final battle, which in effect meant giving more economic autonomy to the collaborative Singaporeans.

Spring 1944: The Chōsabu Comes to Be Invited in Policymaking

In January 1944, in a comprehensive redeployment of army force allocation in the Southern Regions with the movement of the Southern General Army to Manila, the Malayan Military Administration located itself in Kuala Lumpur and the 29th Army Headquarters in Taipin. The Chōsabu's office also transferred. The Malayan Military Administration had Colonel Hamada Hiroshi as director of the General Affairs Department; he realized that the Chōsabu might be useful and allowed its role to expand. It now not only wrote descriptive research reports but was also involved in actual implementation of policy administration.[80] Singapore continued to accommodate numerous army units of the Southern Army, now renamed the Seventh Area Army, with Lieutenant General Takahashi in the General Staff's Office. The island of Singapore was governed more or less autonomously by Syonan Municipality, which had local staff from the previous British administration, including a few British engineers and Japanese staff with knowledge of pre-war Singapore. The latter included Shinozaki Mamoru, who now served as director of the Department of Welfare. When the main office

[79] IER Azb: 27A, *Chōsakikan Shunin Kaidō Hōkokusho* [Report on the Heads of Research Conference], 11–12 Oct. 1943 (Singapore: Military Administration Chōsabu, 1943). Research on fauna and flora included the development of military technology using luminescent bacteria at the Southern Department of Epidemic Prevention and Water Purification (Bōeki Kyūsui bu).

[80] Akashi Yōji, 'Japanese Research Activities in Occupied Malaya/Singapore', in *New Perspectives on the Japanese Occupation in Malaya and Singapore, 1941–1945*, ed. Akashi Yōji and Yoshimura Mako (Singapore: NUS Press, 2008).

of the Chōsabu was relocated in peninsular Malaya, a small branch office including Yamada and his team of local statistical officers was left behind under Shinozaki's direction.[81]

By the end of the fiscal year 1943–44, when the Chōsabu wrote their planning recommendation for the coming year, the situation with food imports had worsened. The Japanese defeat in the Battle of Imphal terminated rice imports from Burma, which Singapore had partly relied upon before the Japanese occupation. The report titled *Countermeasures for Prices for Syonan Municipality* (chapter 7) described measures to tackle the five-fold increase in prices seen over the previous year.[82] The content and format of the report resembled *Conditions of Economic Security*, but while the 1943 report only covered rice, salt and sugar as controlled goods, the 1944 version also explained the state of control and rationing for rice, vegetables, fruit, meat and fish and attempted to calculate the actual and recommended caloric intake for starch and protein. The report's argument centred on how the revised level of rations, which was imposed in February 1944, could not sustain a minimum standard of living for the people in Singapore.[83] Reduced rations meant that for an adult male general monthly rice rations were 8 catties (160g, 544kcal daily), supplementary food rations 4 catties (80g, 273kcal of mainly tapioca and sweet potatoes), and vegetables 3 catties (36kcal), which at 905kcal amounted to less than a life-sustaining level for an adult male. Those who worked in essential factories or in the port received a further 180g of special rations (612kcal), making the total 1,517kcal.

The Chōsabu's report recommended a higher level of rations to allow a minimum standard of living: for an adult male rice rations of 12 catties (240g, 816kcal daily), supplementary food rations 8 catties (160g, 547kcal), vegetables 4.5 catties (90g, 54kcal), and fish and meat 2.6 catties (52g, 52kcal). In total, the daily calorific intake for adult males just on general rations should be at least 1,469kcal and on special rations 2,081kcal.[84] To tackle the problem of food shortages, the report then laid out a set of policy recommendations, which were regarded as effective countermeasures for rapidly rising prices through increasing food production, streamlining freight collection, prioritizing rations, encouraging out-migration, and increasing both controlled and uncontrolled imports of rice by local traders. What the Chōsabu researchers recommended in March 1944 became what they in fact helped to implement during the following

81 Shinozaki, *Secret Stories of the Occupation of Singapore*, p. 100.

82 NIDS, Nansei Gunsei 18, *Chōsabu Report No. 35: Countermeasures for Prices for Syonan Municipality*.

83 Kratoska, *Japanese Occupation*, p. 253.

84 NIDS, Nansei Gunsei 18, *Chōsabu Report No. 35: Countermeasures for Prices for Syonan Municipality*. The total of 1,469kcal is a barely life-sustaining level of calorific intake for a man of 1m 42cm with a BMI of 22.

months. Their activity provided the basis of the subsequent research reports published in September and October 1944, which put forward the requirement to crack down on harmful practices of military monopoly and to respect local businesspeople in order to secure enough food for Syonan's population of close to a million, including numerous prisoners of war and captured foreign civilians on the island. The prisoners of war were then given 460g rice rations for heavy-duty labour until 9 March 1945.[85] This was just a little more than the recommended level of 420g rations for the local civilians on heavy duty.[86]

Autumn 1944: The Chōsabu's Action Reports

Asking Overseas Chinese Businesses for Help

After the October 1943 transfer of the northern rice-producing region of Kedah to Thailand, restrictions on retail rice prices were lifted and the market price of rice rose. This situation became of major concern to the Military Administration when severe flooding in Kedah in November, and conversion of rice paddies into experimental fields for agro-industry (for fibre and munitions), followed by less than usual rainfall in spring 1944, added to the existing scarcity of rice, putting further upward pressure on prices.[87] There was a sharp increase in Japanese government dollars sent to Alor Setar, Kedah, which led to the sudden announcement of the prohibition of unregulated rice imports on 20 March 1944. Mitsubishi and other Japanese trading companies were directed to monopolize the collection of rice, but their purchasing price was too low to obtain much rice. A large proportion of rice continued to be sold on the black market, and Alor Setar prices shot up even further.

Scarcity of Kedah rice and a reduction in general rations from February 1944 onwards led to public discontent, which Director of General Affairs Hamada took seriously; he allowed the Chōsabu and Syonan Municipality to improvise a policy allowing direct import of rice from Bangkok by overseas Chinese businesses in Singapore. A preparatory committee for the Syonan Rice Import Association was inaugurated on 13 April, followed by the Padi Dealings Enactment of 3 May 1944, which allowed Chinese businesses to deal directly with rice mills.[88] In Singapore, the Syonan Rice Import Association was established on 16 May

[85] Harold Atcherley, *Prisoners of Japan* (Cirencester: Memoirs, 2012), p. 275.

[86] NIDS, Nansei Gunsei 18, *Chōsabu Report No. 35: Countermeasures for Prices for Syonan Municipality*.

[87] IER, Azb: 8, *Chōsabu Report No. 51: Rice Imports to Malaya, with Special Reference to Syonan Municipality*.

[88] Paul Kratoska, 'Malayan Food Shortages and the Kedah Rice Industry', in *Food Supplies and the Japanese Occupation in Southeast Asia*, ed. Paul Kratoska (Basingstoke: Macmillan, 1998), p. 115.

by Tan Ken Kow of Tan Guan Lee Co. and other prominent Chinese leaders. In Penang, the young Chinese leaders of the Eppōsho (reading room),[89] opened by the Chōsabu on 4 June, created the Penang Rice Import Public Bureau on 20 June 1944. A problem was that the Nami Kikan, the army's secret intelligence agency, also declared on 16 May its involvement in rice imports via the east coast Singgora route.[90] The Nami Kikan began dealing in padi to give work to junk boat owners in return for their loyalty to the secret agency. The junk boats had been anchored in the nearby islands after the prohibition of unregulated imports on 20 March, and they were susceptible to being used by Allied commandos. The Chōsabu report *Rice Imports to Malaya, with Special Reference to Syonan Municipality* (chapter 11)[91] elaborates how the Nami Kikan's activities impeded the initiative of the Chinese business leaders of the Syonan Rice Import Association, and how they managed to persuade the Nami Kikan to suspend selling rice in the city on 6 August. From 17 August, rice imported by private traders appointed by the Syonan Rice Import Association and the Penang Rice Import Public Office also supplied other states in Malaya.

Between the end of June and the end of August 1944, the Penang Rice Import Bureau imported through Alor Setar more than 60,000 piculs (3,600 tons) of uncontrolled rice. While at that time much of the imported rice also came via Sumatra and Saigon by Mitsubishi-run cargo ships, in about four months by mid-October 1944, the Syonan Rice Import Association managed to import 123,461 piculs (7,470 tons), which together with the seized cargoes from the Nami Kikan amounted to 221,672 piculs (13,411 tons).[92] It is hard to judge how effective these rice import operations were, but one ex-Chōsabu member stated that it required constant hard work for him and his team to gain economic cooperation from the overseas Chinese at a level which, in the end, was capable of mobilizing large quantities of food, labour and even sufficient money to build an airport.[93] Having generated a flurry of activity, the Military Administration gave a formal approval of 'controlled' private import in October

---

89 Akashi Yōji, 'Japanese Policy towards the Malayan Chinese, 1941–1945', *Journal of Southeast Asian Studies* 1, 2 (1970): 61–89; IER, Azb: 48, 'Penang Eppōsho no Kaisetsu' [Establishment of a Reading Room in Penang], *Chōsabu News* 4 (20 June 1944): 19.

90 The Nami Kikan was established in late 1943, after the Allied bombing of seven navy ships in Seletar Island; Ibaragi Kikan of the 7th Area Army—in charge of special manoeuvres—and Shio Kikan of the navy—also in charge of marine intelligence—were set up at the same time (Shinozaki, *Secret Stories of the Occupation of Singapore*, p. 97).

91 IER, Azb: 8, *Chōsabu Report No. 51: Rice Imports to Malaya, with Special Reference to Syonan Municipality*.

92 IER, Azb: 8, *Chōsabu Report No. 51*; NIDS, Nansei Malaya/Java 412, *Malaya Tōkei* [Malayan Statistics], *No. 3 Penang* (Penang: Penang State Government, Jan.–June 1944).

93 Akashi, *Interview Record D: Japanese Military Administration 6*, pp. 115–67.

1944, just when the Chōsabu report on rice imports was published and reported all this activity.[94] At the end of the war, as of 31 August 1945, the Syonan Municipality stock of rice was a little more than the one-month reserve at 5,641 tons, of which more than a third comprised private importers' rice.[95]

Inflation as a Reflection of Material Shortage

From May to August 1944 Singapore's food price index more or less stabilized, possibly due partly to the increased supply of rice brought in by the Syonan Import Association and others. Among the Chōsabu researchers, Higuchi worked on the problem of high prices.[96] He was sent to set up the Monetary Forum in Kuala Kangsar and Kuala Lumpur from 30 May.[97] As described in the report *Conditions of Economic Security* prepared by the Police Administration Department, inconsistent rules to control prices and a lack of cooperation among the municipality, the Military Administration and the motley collection of military units stationed in Singapore had created an economic hazard that required a comprehensive and cooperative solution. Higuchi already felt helpless in face of the pressure of high prices, despite his tougher line of argument in his earlier report titled *Withdrawal of Local Currency*. He concluded in a short article in the *Chōsabu News* that 'all countries at war are facing the same problem' and that they could not do any more apart from following the standard measures of tightening rationing and price controls and absorbing any excess currency in circulation.[98]

---

[94] Kratoska, *Japanese Occupation*, p. 252; IER, Azb: 8, *Chōsabu Report No. 51: Rice Imports to Malaya, with Special Reference to Syonan Municipality*.

[95] United Kingdom National Archives [hereafter NA], WO203/4499, 'Rice—S.E.A.C. [South East Asia Command] Territories', p. 58. The author would like to thank her co-author, Gregg Huff, for sharing a copy of this document.

[96] Other reports written by Higuchi were: IER, Azb: 50, *Chōsabu Report No. 23: Zairai Tsūka Kaishū Mondai ni tsuite* [On Issues Related to Withdrawal of Local Currency] (Singapore: Southern Military Administration Chōsabu, Dec. 1943); IER, Azb: 1, *Chōsabu Report No. 36: Malaya ni okeru Inflation no Jōkyō to Sono Taisaku* [Inflationary Situation in Malaya and Its Countermeasures] (Taiping: Malayan Military Administration Chōsabu, Apr. 1944); IER, Azb: 10, *Chōsabu Report No. 55: Malacca Shū Shokuryō Tōsei Mondai tokuni Kōtei Kakaku Sei Haishi ni tsuite* [On the Issue of Food Control in Malacca Region, Particularly the Repeal of the System of Official Pricing] (Taiping: Malayan Military Administration Chōsabu, Nov. 1944); and IER, Azb: 13, *Chōsabu Report No. 61: Malaya ni okeru Seisen Shokuhin Tōsei Hōshiki to Nijū Kakaku-sei Mondai ni tsuite* [On the System of Controlling Perishable Foods and the Issue of Double Pricing in Malaya] (Taiping: Malayan Military Administration Chōsabu, Jan. 1945).

[97] IER, Azb: 48, 'Chōsabu Nisshi' [Chōsabu Diary], *Chōsabu News* 3 (5 June 1944): 35–6.

[98] IER, Azb: 48, 'Malaya ni okeru inflation no Jōkyō to Taisaku' [Inflationary Situation in Malaya and Its Countermeasures], *Chōsabu News* 2 (25 May 1944): 23.

The extent to which tight rationing, combined with the effort to increase food supplies, was effective in stabilizing price increases can be checked by the data on Syonan retail prices collected by the Chōsabu from April 1943 to January 1945 or later.[99] Here it should be noted that the three components of the food price index—the ration prices, controlled prices and black market prices—were simply averaged and not properly weighted.[100] The concept of a 'shopping basket' was not employed. Soaring black market prices affected the daily lives of Singaporeans, who required more food than allowed in rations, but they also probably affected expensive Japanese restaurants. In March 1944, new official prices for fresh fish and salted fish were set 11 times higher than pre-war prices. Higuchi wrote that fish prices tended to rise fast because Japanese restaurants were willing to pay a premium for high-quality fish. The same was true of meat. In response to this situation, the Military Administration introduced the experiment of abolishing official prices in May 1944 in order to lower the market prices of fish, meat and vegetables, in response to the request by the leaders of overseas Chinese businesses who strongly opposed the 'associationism' introduced by the Japanese administration.[101] 'As soon as an Association (*Kumiai*) for any particular commodity was founded, the commodity soon disappeared from the market.'[102] The flattening of the price index from April to July 1944 may have resulted partly from this reversal measure.

Higuchi anticipated, however, that the abolition of official prices would 'only have a temporary effect'. As he pointed out in his report, it was not only the scarcity of food and raw materials that was driving up prices but also military defeats, which lowered the credibility of Japanese military scrip.[103] The prices of perishable foods in the peninsula were also rising quickly since the purchasing power of Singapore transmitted itself to the producing areas. Higuchi seems to have been in two minds about the situation in Malacca and

99 IER, Azb: 48, 'Survey of Prices in Singapore', *Chōsabu News* 2; NIDS, Nansei Malaya/Java 412, *Summary of Prices in Singapore*.

100 IER, Azb: 48, *Syonan Seikatsu Hitsujyuhin Kourikakaku Gaiyō* [Summary of Retail Prices of Daily Necessities in Singapore], May 1944 (Taiping: Malaya Military Administration Chōsabu, June 1944), p. 2. Household expenditure survey results could theoretically provide the weights for the retail price indices, but the expenditure survey results were in practice not used for this purpose at this stage. The report on the survey results was published belatedly in October 1944 (see 'IER, Azb: 7, *Chōsabu Report no. 50: Malaya-chiku Kakei Chōsa Hōkoku* [A Report on the Household Expenditure Survey in Malaya] [Taiping: Malayan Military Administration Chōsabu, Oct. 1944]).

101 IER, Azb: 48, 'Syonan Bukka no Dōkō [Movement of Prices in Singapore], June 1944', *Chōsabu News* 6 (20 July 1944): 15–8.

102 Kratoska, *Japanese Occupation*, p. 166; Chin, *Malaya Upside Down*, p. 88.

103 IER, Azb: 10, *Chōsabu Report No. 55: Repeal of the System of Official Prices in Malacca*; IER, Azb: 13, *Chōsabu Report No. 61: Control of Perishable Foods and Double Pricing*.

Kuala Lumpur. On one hand, he thought that removing all the restrictions on vegetables, fish and meat was inevitable; but on the other he was worried that 'star-marked automobiles of the military units and their appointed agents come from the south to smuggle pork and vegetables out of the state without permission from the state council'.[104] The state council in Malacca abolished official prices, following Singapore, but the state of Selangor introduced two levels of prices for perishables to prevent them from disappearing from the state's official channels. Higuchi endorsed this halfway solution, which, in response to the needs of the Japanese (and the Singaporeans employed by the state) whose wages were pegged to the value of military scrip, secured meat, fish and vegetables at official prices (implying a combination of contract delivery and licensing). This, he believed, also provided incentives to producers and eased the inflow of perishable foods into the city, in order to allow ordinary citizens 'whose incomes were not fixed' to get access to the available food at unrestricted prices.[105]

Managing the Population in Commerce and Industry

Apart from his work on money, Higuchi authored the report titled *Reorganizing Commercial Businesses in Syonan Municipality* (chapter 4).[106] This report led on from *Population by Occupation in Syonan Municipality*, which counted the number of people working in commercial businesses, although the Chōsabu authors were careful not to exaggerate the share of commercial population in the total population. Higuchi and his colleague Nagamori Masaji were now given the task of choosing which businesses to close down, and by doing so they stepped in to prevent the Military Administration from choosing these at random. Many pages and tables in this report are allocated to the 'resilience test' of commercial businesses, based on the number of years in business and the amount of capital. The report avoids giving one single recommendation but leaves multiple simulations as a result of the resilience test, so that the final decision was not made by the authors themselves. Families in commercial businesses were expected to migrate outside Singapore to new settlements like

---

[104] IER, Azb: 10, *Chōsabu Report No. 55: Repeal of the System of Official Prices in Malacca*, p. 20.

[105] IER, Azb: 48, 'Syonan Haikyū Kikō' [Rationing Organization in Singapore], *Chōsabu News* 6 (20 July 1944): 1–7; IER, Azb: 13, *Chōsabu Report No. 61: Control of Perishable Foods and Double Pricing*, pp. 60–1.

[106] IER, Azb: 4, *Chōsabu Report No. 45: Reorganizing Commercial Businesses*.

in Endau, which was self-governed by the Overseas Chinese Association.[107] Employees of commercial businesses were expected to become wage-earning industrial workers, for many factories run by Japanese companies suffered from a lack of new recruits and a high labour turnover rate. Three months later the Restriction of Male Employment Ordinance was passed in order to bolster recruitment into the farming settlements and factories.[108]

The only report the Chōsabu itself produced on the topic of industrial factories was concerned with the working conditions in the factories. The author of the report observed that workers in factories run by local business people were much happier and did not tend to quit their jobs so readily. *A Study of the Labour Situation in Syonan Municipality* (chapter 5) recommends that Japanese factories focus on retaining the existing workforce by giving them better pay in kind—particularly rice and tobacco—more holidays, better transport to work, and better welfare facilities such as in-house clinics. The style of writing is remarkably different from *Important Industrial Factories in Syonan Municipality*, written by the Department of General Affairs over a year earlier, in which optimistic calculations for future increases in output had been made. The Chōsabu's analysis of industrial factories was far more cautious: it recommended that religious holidays should be respected and expressed reservations about the suggestion of recruiting young female workers, which the Military Administration was pressing. The author stressed that 'in view of the intellectual level, physical strength, ethnic divisions and religious barriers of local women, in addition to the population composition of Syonan Municipality (the female population was 70 per cent that of the male), female labour force ratios are to some extent as high as they can be'.[109] The author of chapter 3, *Population by Occupation in Syonan Municipality*, also noticed how women were respected in local communities, that 'women are not just stay-at-home housewives and stand on an equal footing to the employed members of the family'.[110]

Although the civilian-run Japanese factories were cautiously urged to change their traditional ways and start taking in more women, they were also urged to

---

[107] Some memoirs state that the whole resettlement programme was one of Shinozaki's ingenious ideas, but Shinozaki himself recalls it as being a response to *Operation Command No. 1: Evacuation of the Locals*. This was sent directly from Tokyo headquarters after the bombing of seven ships in September 1943, and set the goal of evacuating 300,000 people from Syonan. By the end of the war 1,200–1,700 families, promised complete freedom from the Japanese army, had been sent to Endau settlement to cultivate new land and build their own new village.

[108] Chin, *Malaya Upside Down*, p. 49.

[109] IER, Azb: 5, *Chōsabu Report No. 47: A Study of the Labour Situation in Syonan Municipality*, p. 26.

[110] Chapter 3, 5-(3) Occupations of other household members where head of household works.

improve working conditions to prevent workers from moving to the military sector, which paid much higher wages. The need for better transport to work was an issue that required urgent attention. The number of days on which work transport was provided decreased, while only one-third of public transport was in service because of shortages of spare parts and tyres. The author of chapter 5 worried that this resulted in severe crowding and left workers physically drained. By surveying and drawing up a map of work transport provided by the sample factories and plotting the residential areas of workers of different ethnicities, the author implicitly recommended sharing of vehicles among factories on the same thoroughfares, such as Bukit Timah Road, while being careful not to raise interracial tensions. The report also recommended that a centralized department for labour management for both civilian and military sectors should be created in order to stop competition for new recruits. It urged the setting up of an institution to give educational guidance, training and labour exchange services for the local people, part of which idea materialized in the form of the Guidance and Counselling Office, opened in May 1945, where most of the Chōsabu members ended up after the termination of research activities.

Taste of Tapioca

The struggle against the economic monopoly of the military sector was the most pressing concern for Yamada, who was preoccupied by the issue of food allocation in Singapore. The Syonan Municipality staff did everything in their power to keep food supplies for local Singaporeans at least at subsistence level. In the difficult situation towards the end of the war, the Japanese Syonan Municipality staff even went about purchasing meat and vegetables directly from producers in other states so as not to be outdone by the military units.[111] Much of their effort, however, went into cultivating and processing tapioca, which, with a shorter growing period, could provide a more immediate bulk solution to food shortages than rice. Sweet potatoes and tapioca were rationed in the raw, or as processed food, cooked, dried and pounded into powder because of their tendency to rot in the heat. There were 18 tapioca bread factories; bread was rationed through 1,007 ration stations at one loaf per day for a household of three people and two loaves or more for larger families. The bread tasted just 'like rubber' or 'like our eraser', according to a Singapore resident.[112] There were also 29 tapioca noodle factories, whose products were rationed by auxiliary police assistants and their sub-organizations, at 600g per family every three days.[113]

---

111 Singapore Shisei Kai, *History of Syonan Municipality*, p. 175.

112 Kratoska, *Japanese Occupation*, p. 264.

113 IER, Azb: 48, 'Syonan Rationing Organizations', *Chōsabu News* 6: 7.

With the possibility of total cessation of food imports in the event of an Allied landing, it became apparent that the level of local food production required was much higher and the acreage of land required for cultivation thus much larger.[114] The Military Administration set the target acreage of land to be cultivated in order to achieve self-sufficiency on Syonan Island at 15,000 acres, on which daily 200 tons of vegetables, sweet potatoes and tapioca were to be produced. Yamada was set the task of calculating how feasible this target may be. The most significant aspect of his writing in *Methods of Increasing Food Production on Syonan Island* (chapter 9) was his strong recommendation that farmland under military management be transferred to Syonan Municipality for civilian use.[115] Yamada saw that many military-managed farms were inefficient and unproductive owing to a lack of fertilizers and bad subcontracting agents, who treated local farmers in such a way that they were left with no incentive or strength to work. He recommended that of the existing 7,000 acres of military farmland, 3,000 should be transferred to civilian use and a further 7,740 acres should be newly cultivated for sweet potatoes and tapioca, in addition to 4,260 acres of existing farmland under civilian management. It was estimated that this land could produce 2.5 tons of tapioca and 6 tons of vegetables per acre per year. That level of output would yield 90g of tapioca and 96g of vegetables per person per day for the 850,000 people in Singapore. Yamada concluded that this targeted production would result in 66.7 per cent more sweet potatoes and tapioca, and 45.5 per cent more green vegetables than the level achieved in autumn 1944, when the report was written. The total 186g was also higher than the pre-war sum of 142g per person, but not enough to sustain life if rice imports ceased altogether.

It is difficult to know whether Yamada's assumptions about potential production levels were realistic or whether he was making an over-optimistic estimate. He used the average productivity levels of the selected military farms as the basis for his calculation of civilian tapioca production. These were comparable to the reliable productivity level figures for Syonan farmers surveyed by his younger colleagues. These two colleagues stated that for professional farmers, average annual productivity levels for tapioca and vegetables were 5 and 12 tons per acre respectively—that is, double the calculated output informing

[114] In view of the prospect around the same time, Lieutenant Takahashi of Changi Prison told the prisoners of war on 10 September that the supply of vegetables by the army would cease sooner or later, and that they should try cultivating more. Atcherley, *Prisoners of Japan*, p. 211.
[115] IER, Azb: 3, *Chōsabu Report No. 44: Methods of Increasing Food Production on Syonan Island.*

Yamada's recommendation.[116] A different report written by a research officer in Medan, Sumatra, uses an average annual productivity level of tapioca as high as 16.2 tons per acre, to make a grand estimate that a community of 5 million residents could be fed by 20,000 professional farmers.[117] Yamada carefully used much lower estimates, taking into account the poor soil condition of the newly cultivated land and the low skill levels of newly recruited farmers. His calculations indicated that, realistically, if the military did not hand over half of its good farmland, which was then poorly managed, significant difficulty would be caused to the local population and Japanese municipality staff alike. This was a stark criticism of the inefficiency of management and the wasted acreage of land under military control.

There was also an unresolved dilemma in Yamada's recommendation that could result in determining the number of necessary workers on farms and thus compelling resettlement of the local people, such as those who worked in commerce, as mentioned in chapters 3 and 4. To cultivate 7,260 acres of existing farmland, including 3,000 acres returned from the military, and 7,740 acres of additional land, 6,130 farming families, comprising at least 18,390 able workers, were required, according to Yamada's calculation. And to cultivate the would-be-reduced military-managed farmland of 4,000 acres, an additional 14,629 coolies who could perform intensive farming were required. The number of necessary workers depended on which productivity level Yamada chose. His numbers can be compared to the results of the resilience test in chapter 4 which calculated out about three-fourths of 8,025 trading families and three-fourths of 21,683 employees of traders as subject to change of occupations. Yamada may have carefully calculated 6,130 necessary families, using the labour productivity rate of 1 acre per family for existing farmland and 2 acres per family for newly cultivated land for the civilian farms, and consciously chosen the productivity level of 5 coolies per acre to calculate 14,629 workers for the military-managed farms. While relocation in general would have been resisted by the local residents, resettling within the island of Singapore may have appeared less troublesome than moving to Endau.

Around the same time that Yamada was frantically calculating the productivity level and the reallocation of the necessary farmland, he also had his co-author write up the results of the household expenditure survey of Malaya. The results

---

116 IER, Azb: 48, 'Syonan-tō Hatasaku Nōka Jittai Chōsa Kanken' [A Survey of Syonan Island's Vegetable Farmers], *Chōsabu News* 6 (20 July 1944): 8–11. The authors of this short article, Yamada Hideo and Ōno Seizaburō, also wrote a report criticizing the use of Taiwanese double-cropping rice in Krian, Perak. Yamada Hideo is not related to Yamada Isamu.

117 NIDS, Nansei Gunsei 30, *Shokuryō Mondai to Kansho Saibai* [Food Problems and Cultivation of the Sweet Potato] (Publication place unknown [probably Medan, Sumatra]; n.d. [probably spring 1943]).

of the cost of living survey were expected to reveal how the living standards of Singaporeans declined since the pilot survey in 1943, and whether the actions taken by the Chōsabu to crack down on harmful practices of military monopoly and to respect the livelihoods of local people had really had any effect. Yamada and his co-author could thus provide their own verdict on the two years of Chōsabu work. Based on a mixed sample of what seemed to be average-level ordinary households—teachers and officers as well as coolies and street hawkers—the household spending records, which cover half a year from November 1943 to April 1944, reveal the effect of reduced rations in February 1944 as well as the effect of ongoing high inflation. Expenditure survey results in monetary terms show that many of the items bought by ordinary families were either price controlled or rationed, so that families' expenditure may have risen less rapidly than overall prices.

The survey results of quantities consumed show that an apparently slower rise of household spending was also a manifestation of reduced rations. The combined amounts of daily carbohydrates—including rice, sweet potatoes and tapioca—were: Malays 282g, Indians 386g and Chinese 375g in February–April 1944, when ration reductions affected the actual intake of carbohydrates. The combined amounts of protein (mostly fish) were: Malays 70g, Indians 55g and Chinese 75g, which saw 10–20 per cent reductions compared to November 1943–January 1944.[118] Many households received special rations of tapioca bread, sugar and coconut oil and supplemented their diets with food bought outside rations—a large amount of vegetables, beans and coconuts from street hawkers. The levels of their caloric intake were below the bare subsistence level for able-bodied workers that the Chōsabu recommended in March 1944 at: Malays 1,470kcal, Indians 1,956kcal and Chinese 1,826kcal.

Yamada and his co-author seem to have conducted the second round of the household expenditure survey from May 1944 and intended to report the findings, but somehow only the first round of the survey was published belatedly in October 1944. Had the second survey results been published, they might have provided a more incisive verdict on their efforts over half a year to increase

---

[118] IER, Azb: 7, *Chōsabu Report No. 50: Malaya-chiku Kakei Chōsa Hōkoku* [A Report on the Household Expenditure Survey in Malaya] (Taiping: Malayan Military Administration Chōsabu, Oct. 1944). The amounts of staple foods consumed in the Chōsabu survey results are lower than those recommended by C.L. Dunn and D.D. Pandya, *Indian Hygiene and Public Health* (Calcutta: Butterworth & Co., 1925), showing as the bare subsistence level the amount of starch at 213g (873kcal), protein at 60g (246kcal) and fat at 21g (198kcal) daily (p. 138). The Chōsabu also used much lower conversion rates into caloric values than Dunn and Pandya—closer to those found on USDA's National Nutrient Database for Standard Reference.

food supply in Singapore.[119] The statement of actual monthly supplies to Syonan Municipality, which was seized by the British Military Administration, tells us that on average 4,572 tons of rice (5.4kg per person for the population of 850,000) were received and distributed as rations every month between May and December 1944. The situation worsened in February and March 1945 with severe Allied bombing, but recovered towards the end of the war.[120]

The Chōsabu research activities were terminated and the members dismissed at the end of April 1945. They were reorganized and dispatched to each of the Malay Peninsula states to set up a Guidance and Counselling Office. Higuchi was sent to the state of Perak together with another colleague who also specialized in money and finance. Akamatsu and Itagaki were in Taipin, and their Central Guidance and Counselling Office, which was modelled on Eppōsho in Penang, eventually helped facilitate a Malay independence movement. Among those who stayed in Singapore, Yamada—while also attending compulsory drills to blow up tanks with suicide bombs wrapped in blankets—was working frantically to push through an evacuation project in the municipality. The project, which started with the Endau settlement, had been expanded to other locations and had now been swamped with applicants. The Japanese thought that the British would occupy Pulau Ubin by July and start bombing Singapore. Evacuees were given rice, salt, sugar and military scrip and sent to the peninsula by train, or to Java or Sumatra by boat. All the survey research officers of the various ethnic groups, which numbered 33 at the end of 1944, helped Yamada to send people out. On 13 August, as the final boatload of 300 people left Keppel Harbour, they wished it a safe arrival in Jakarta. Had it not arrived safely, they could have been accused of war crimes for unnecessarily risking the lives of Singaporeans.

After the Japanese Surrender

The announcement of surrender on 15 August 1945 was calmly accepted by the Chōsabu members and Japanese civilian administrators, who had been prepared to die in Singapore. The town was kept under control until the British arrived on 6 September. None of Yamada's multiracial team of survey officers at Syonan Municipality was accused of helping the Japanese occupation.[121] After the arrival of the British, the Japanese in Singapore voluntarily constructed a concentration camp in Jurong—in the area with poor soil conditions mentioned in the farmland survey, where the Japanese established good relationships with

---

119 See Appendix A.2 List of Chōsabu Reports and Chōsabu News. Yamada did not author any report after *No. 50: A Report on the Household Expenditure Survey in Malaya.*

120 NA, WO203/4499, 'Rice—S.E.A.C. Territories', p. 57; Atcherley, *Prisoners of Japan.*

121 Sewanin Kai, *Devoted to Theory and Quantification*, p. 43.

local farmers helped by an overseas Chinese agent. Yamada lived there for half a year, in company with other Japanese civilians, growing vegetables and farming fish in the pond. A one-year supply of rice, miso and soy sauce was brought in from the Syonan Municipality storage, and eventually the British started to provide rations, including chocolate.[122] Until he was allowed to board ship for Japan on 13 April 1946, Yamada translated documents for the British.

In March 1946, when some of the Chōsabu members were back in Japan, the Institute of East Asian Economies was renamed the Institute of Economic Research. The membership list of the new institute tells us that although its name was changed, its members and structure remained the same: University President Takase was the director of the institute; Akamatsu, Itagaki and a few others were described as 'on a research expedition in the south'. In August 1946, a new university president was elected and a Purge Qualification Committee was set up at the Tokyo University of Commerce, following a decree from General Headquarters of the Supreme Commander of the Allied Powers.[123] Sugimoto, who had gone to the south with Akamatsu, although only for six months, was selected as a member of the committee. As in many organizations in Japan, those who were seen to have fascist ideas were purged while those who had liberal ideas and had been made redundant during the war came back to their offices. Three people were purged by the Tokyo University of Commerce. One of them had written an essay called 'The Historical Inevitability of the Great East Asia Co-prosperity Sphere' in the *Annual Report on East Asian Economy*.

In the same volume, Akamatsu contributed a paper titled 'Historical Patterns of East Asian Trade', which comprised tables on Japanese and Chinese world trade statistics from the late 19th century to the early 20th.[124] Akamatsu's catching-up theory was a story of export-oriented industrialization. It drew on the example of Japan's textile industry and a Japanese late 19th- and early 20th-century development pattern that depended on open markets and free trade. Akamatsu's vision was not central to the Chōsabu's work in Singapore and Malaya because it was predicated on a different, open economic regime than those either of the Co-prosperity Sphere or the local self-sufficient economy created by the Japanese military. Having a pro-free trade emphasis in their research, Akamatsu

---

[122] Singapore Shisei Kai, *History of Syonan Municipality*, p. 254.

[123] Hitotsubashi Daigaku Gakuseishi Senmon Iinkai, *Hitotsubashi Daigaku Gakusei Shi Shiryō* [Historical Material on the Academic Organization of Hitotsubashi University], Vol. 8 (Tokyo: Hitotsubashi Daigaku Gakuen Shi Henshū Iinkai, 1986), p. 101.

[124] Kaneko Takanosuke, 'Dai Tōa Kensetsu no Rekishiteki Hitsuzensei' [Historical Inevitability of the Greater East Asia Co-prosperity Sphere], *Tōa Keizai Kenkyūjo Nenpō*, Vol. 1 (Tokyo: Nihon Hyōron Sha, 1942); Akamatsu Kaname, 'Dai Tōa Bōeki no Rekishiteki Ruikei' [Historical Patterns of Great East Asian Trade], *Tōa Keizai Kenkyūjo Nenpō*, Vol. 1 (Tokyo: Nihon Hyōron Sha, 1942).

and all the other researchers who were sent to the south survived the purge.[125] Yamaguchi, who had been sent to Shanghai, was said to have shed tears when seeing one of the purged professors leaving the university.[126]

Ōtsuka, who was not employed by the university during the war, was allowed to come back to the university and was asked to become the new director of the institute by its younger members in September 1946. A Reconstruction Committee for the Institute was set up in November 1946 with Ōtsuka, Akamatsu, Nakayama and Sugimoto as elected tenured professors, and eight elected younger members, including Yamada and Higuchi. At the end of 1947, all the members submitted their resignations in response to the demand for a complete overhaul from liberal-minded students and younger members of the university, and in January1948 Ōtsuka chose who would remain at the institute and himself prepared to resign. Only Yamada Isamu and Tsuru Shigeto (1912–2006) were asked to stay, with the latter nominated as the new director.[127] Tsuru had come back from the United States, where he had studied in the company of Paul Samuelson and John Kenneth Galbraith and had been awarded a PhD in Economics from Harvard University in 1940. He had started teaching at Harvard immediately before the war but had to quit, and he joined the Institute of East Asian Economies after his return to Japan. Tsuru became the director of the institute, and Nakayama became president of the now renamed Hitotsubashi University in May 1949.

Higuchi published *Analysis of Inflation in Japan* with Yamaguchi in 1948.[128] They criticized the payment of a large sum of money (1,000 yen per person) to the few million civilian returnees from Korea, Taiwan, China and other occupied areas as the cause of high inflation and the divergence between 'effective demand' and industrial production in the course of reconstruction in Japan. In the world of free speech after the war, they vocally argued that printing a large quantity of paper money could not stimulate production in post-war Japan. Higuchi put forward this argument as a researcher at the Tokyo University of Commerce's

[125] Akamatasu notes that his PhD dissertation 'Keizai Shin Chitsujo no Keisei Genri' [Theory of the Formation of a New Economic Order], which was accepted in 1944 after changing the words and 'eliminating the elements of democracy', and the book *Kokubō Keizai Ron* [The Economics of National Defence] by Akamatsu and Nakayama could have been a reason to purge Akamatsu from the university, but he survived and returned to teach. Kojima, ed., *Akamatsu Kaname*, p. 49; Akamatsu Kaname, *Keizai Shin Chitsujo no Keisei Genri* [Theory of the Formation of New Economic Order] (Tokyo: Risōsha, 1944); Akamatsu Kaname, Nakayama Ichirō and Ōkuma Nobuyuki, *Kokubō Keizai Sōron* [Theory of National Defence Economy] (Tokyo: Ganshōdō, 1942).

[126] Odaka, 'Scholarship and Education during the War'.

[127] Sewanin Kai, *Devoted to Theory and Quantification*, p. 55.

[128] Yamaguchi and Higuchi, *Analysis of Inflation in Japan*.

Institute of Economic Research. Later he found a tenured post in Yokohama City University.[129] He took early retirement from the university in 1970 aged 64, before he died of illness the following year. He never wrote or spoke publicly about his wartime experience.

Yamada translated his Malayan household expenditure surveys while he was a visiting scholar in the early 1960s at the University of Malaya, where he left a copy.[130] He also wrote articles titled 'Measuring Changes in Economic Structure with Special Reference to the Industrial Population in Malaya' and 'Input-Output Model of a Dual Economy' for the newly established *Kajian Ekonomi Malaysia: Journal of the Malaysian Economic Association*, in its first and third issues in the 1960s. He also wrote, in English, *Theory and Application of Interindustry Analysis* (1961), reflecting his wartime interest in Leontief's concept of input-output tables.[131] He taught at Hitotsubashi University until his retirement and also served as the president of the Japanese Statistical Society between 1976 and 1978. He had an edited book in English dedicated to him on his retirement: *Technology, Organization and Economic Structure: Essays in Honour of Prof. Isamu Yamada*.[132] Yamada's friend and colleague Itagaki wrote publicly on his pre-war visits to Java and wartime experience in Malaya. He became instrumental in establishing the Institute of Developing Economies and emerged as a pillar of Asian research in Japan. Yamada never talked about his wartime existence even to his family until his death in 1986. He left a bundle of handwritten memoirs on his desk to be found by his family after his death.[133]

---

129 Higuchi Gorō, *Sengo Zaisei Seisaku to Kokumin Keizai Kanjō* [Post-war Financial Policy and National Income Calculation] (Tokyo: Tōyō Keizai Shinpō Sha, 1950); Higuchi Gorō, *Ginkō Riron* [Theory of Banking] (Tokyo: Tōyō Keizai Shinpō Sha, 1963); Higuchi Gorō, *Kin'yū Shinron* [New Theory of Finance] (Tokyo: Kin'yū Journal Sha, 1964); Higuchi Gorō, *Kokusai Kin'yū Ron* [International Monetary Theory] (Tokyo: Tōyō Keizai Shinpō Sha, 1967); Higuchi Gorō, 'Kikeika shita Nihon no Kin'yū Seisaku' [Deformation of Japan's Monetary Policy], *Keizai Ōrai* 20, 3 (Mar. 1968): 42–51.

130 This is one of the reasons why Chōsabu Report No. 50 was not included in this translated book. However, at present the author has not identified the location of the translated report.

131 'Measuring Changes in Economic Structure with Special Reference to the Industrial Population in Malaya', *Kajian Ekonomi Malaysia: Journal of the Malaysian Economic Association* 1, 1 (June 1964): 59–69; 'Input-Output Model of a Dual Economy', *Kajian Ekonomi Malaysia: Journal of the Malaysian Economic Association* 3, 2 (Dec. 1966): 59–70; *Theory and Application of Interindustry Analysis*, Economic Research Series No. 4, Institute of Economic Research, Hitotsubashi University (Tokyo: Kinokuniya, 1961).

132 Ryūzō Satō and Martin J. Beckmann, eds, *Technology, Organization and Economic Structure: Essays in Honour of Prof. Isamu Yamada*, Lecture notes in economics and mathematical systems (New York: Springer-Verlag, 1983).

133 Sewanin Kai, *Devoted to Theory and Quantification*.

Conclusion

This chapter shows that the Chōsabu men from the Institute of East Asian Economies of the Tokyo University of Commerce became involved in running the economy of Singapore during the course of war. They were ordinary academics, well established in their professions, who initially viewed the opportunity of going to the south as a chance to continue research projects of their own preferences without being conscripted into the war effort. Before and during the war, methods of data collection and data analysis were being modernized and standardized within the government and academic institutes. The Japanese Military Administration in Singapore recognized the importance of accurate measurement of the economy and thought that the research of the Chōsabu men could be used to stabilize the economy. Within a limited time and in adverse circumstances, the Chōsabu managed to produce a large number of original reports, giving an insightful picture of wartime economy seen through their own eyes. If they had had more time and manpower, a more comprehensive research programme such as comparative surveys across different occupied areas within the Southern Regions might have been possible. Nevertheless, in terms of the economy of Singapore alone, the reports written during the occupation provide a useful guide while also accounting for the dilemma that the members had to cope with, torn between their sympathy towards the local populace and the demands of the military.

The Chōsabu members had to hide their regrets in being constrained in helping the local population and being unable to do more to promote modern socio-economic survey research in Singapore and Malaya. After the war, they could not but feel quietly ashamed of their association with the army during the Japanese occupation. In post-war Japanese society, many of them—apart from Itagaki and Akamatsu—found it difficult to give an adequate explanation of their struggle during the war.

The reason neither Akamatsu's development theory nor Itagaki's colonialism became central to or even noticeable in the Chōsabu's research reports may be partly due to their extreme care not to leave any suspicious written documents that carried their names. Other reasons may be, as noted already, that their visions of development and colonialism were more closely linked to a world of open free trade than the controlled economy. They realized on their arrival in Singapore that any form of 'building Asia' had already become unrealistic. The war economy was led by the optimistic research and planning activities of other departments and by private companies that had taken over mining and manufacturing activities in the Southern Region before the Chōsabu's arrival. The reports of the Chōsabu were regarded as only sometimes useful in controlling the military units, which acted in a lordly manner, and the Japanese companies and agents attached to them. Thus, Akamatsu, Itagaki and a few others may have decided rather than restricting themselves to academic research to become active behind the scenes of the Military Administration in 'gaining hearts and minds of the people'—for example, by setting up the Eppōsho in Penang or by helping Ibrahim Yaacob to start up the independence movement.[134] Further research is, however, necessary before forming firm conclusions about their actual wartime involvement.

The Chōsabu reports and other related documents were left untouched for decades in the library of the Institute of Economic Research at Hitotsubashi University.[135] Despite devoted efforts during the occupation years, the contributors and named authors of the Chōsabu reports—namely, the junior scholars—tended to stay silent throughout their lives. Ōtsuka, who had been the interim director of the institute after the war, had a poem published in the 1970s before his death:[136]

> At age 22 / purged from office / sodden with drink / you were a victim of militarism
>
> In Singapore / protected by bayonets / could such 'research' / bring a plus to you?

This poem might not have been about any particular individual researcher, but it seems to capture the sense of helplessness and guilt shared by the young researchers who were co-opted by the military. Yamada's memoir was only found posthumously and was privately printed by his colleague and friend Itagaki in the 1980s. A careful reading of the Chōsabu reports reveals that, despite their association with the army and with the failed attempt at instigating Malayan independence, the experience of each Chōsabu member was far more complicated and full of dilemmas.

The individual Chōsabu members' experiences and the ways they reacted during their assignments in Singapore and Malaya differed widely. As the surviving reports reveal, Akamatsu and Itagaki's pre-war agendas were not pronounced, while Higuchi and Yamada appeared to possess different ideas to one another and different attitudes towards the Military Administration. Many of their activities were governed by fear. Despite their inability to prevent socio-economic turmoil and mass malnutrition, the Chōsabu men openly

---

134 *Interview Record D: Japanese Military Administration 6*, pp. 117–70.

135 Makoto Ikema, Yoshio Inoue, Tamotsu Nishizawa and Susumu Yamauchi, eds, *Hitotsubashi University, 1875–2000: A Hundred and Twenty-five Years of Higher Education in Japan* (London: Palgrave, 2000); Odaka, 'Scholarship and Education during the War'.

136 The poem was published in the poetry journal *Do [or Dray Horse]* 9 (Nov. 1970) and collated in Ōtsuka Kin'nosuke, *Ōtsuka Kin'nosuke Chosaku Shū* [Writings of Ōtsuka Kin'nosuke], Vol. 9 (Tokyo: Iwanami Shoten, 1980), p. 350. The second line of this poem is cited also in Matsumura, *'ABC' Mondai wa Kaiketsu dekirunoka*, p. 63.

disputed the military factions and reserved their right to make judgements on the policies of the Military Administration. Their opinions came to matter more towards the end of the war in the Military Administration's attempt to prevent local hostility. They may have made at least some contribution in helping to prevent an even more severe food crisis in Singapore, comparable to the mass famines in northern Vietnam and Java.[137] The titles of the reports that were to be written in the final few months of their research activity, nonetheless, only reveal an air of resignation and their inability to refuse research missions placed upon them.[138]

---

137 Kratoska, *Japanese Occupation*, p. 255; Aiko Kurasawa, 'Senjiki Malaya Singapore ni okeru Beikoku Haikyū Seido' [Rice Rationing System in Wartime Malaya and Singapore], *Mita Gakkai Zasshi* 104, 4 (Jan. 2012): 623–49. Aiko Kurasawa, 'Transportation and Rice Distribution in South-East Asia during the Second World War'; Shigeru Satō, 'Oppression and Romanticism: The Food Supply of Java during the Japanese Occupation'; Furuta Moto'o, 'A Survey of Village Conditions during the 1945 Famine in Vietnam', in *Food Supply and the Japanese Occupation*, ed. Kratoska.

138 See Appendix A.2 List of Chōsabu Reports and Chōsabu News.

Appendices

A.1 List of Chōsabu Members

Table A.2.1 List of Chōsabu members

(1) Rank 1943	*(2) Title*	*(3) Name*	*(4) Sections within Chōsabu*	*(5) Birth–Death*	*(6) Chōsabu Report*	*(7) Pre-war Affiliation*	*(8) Affiliation as of July 1945*	*(9) Post-war Affiliation*
2-5	Professor	Akamatsu Kaname	General affairs	1896–1974	No. 80	Tokyo University of Commerce	Taipin, Central G&C Office	Hitotsubashi University
2-6	Professor	Sugimoto Ei'ichi	(Short-term visit)	1901–52	none	Tokyo University of Commerce	Returned to Japan	Hitotsubashi University
3-3	Professor	Kawai Juntarō	(Short-term visit) Mining and manufacturing, Southern Region in general	1893–n.d.	No. 13, 30, 31, 32	Tokyo University of Commerce, Professional College	Returned to Japan	(-n.d.)** Tokyo Keizai University
3-4	Civilian Administrator	Chiba Tamatsu	General affairs	1893–n.d.	n/a	Institute of East Asian Economies (clerk)	Returned to Japan	(clerk, -n.d.)** unknown
4-6	Professor	Yamanaka Tokutarō	(Short-term visit) Southern Region in general	1901–81	No. 5	Tokyo University of Commerce	Returned to Japan	Hitotsubashi University

(cont'd overleaf)

Table A.2.1 (cont'd)

(1) Rank 1943	*(2) Title*	*(3) Name*	*(4) Sections within Chōsabu*	*(5) Birth–Death*	*(6) Chōsabu Report*	*(7) Pre-war Affiliation*	*(8) Affiliation as of July 1945*	*(9) Post-war Affiliation*
4-7	Professor	Ishida Ryujirō	General affairs, geography, farming economy	1904–79	No. 7, 16, 48, 75	Tokyo University of Commerce, Preparatory School	Syonan Municipality Office	Hitotsubashi University
4-7	Assistant Professor	Takahashi Taizō	(Short-term visit) Finance and money, Southern Region in general	1905–89	No. 8	Tokyo University of Commerce	Returned to Japan	Hitotsubashi University
5-7	Professor	Odabashi Sadatoshi	Labour management, population, farming economy	1904–84	No. 16, 26, 57, 59	Tokyo University of Commerce	Syonan Municipality Office	Hitotsubashi University
6-5	Assistant Professor	Uchida Naosaku	Overseas Chinese, commerce, trade, ration, mining and manufacturing	1905–87	No. 9, 68, 79, 84	Tokyo University of Commerce	Kuala Lumpur, Central G&C Branch Office	(–1949)** Seijō University
6-7	Assistant Professor	Itagaki Yoichi	Muslim administration, Sultan question, Southern Region in general	1908–2003	No. 5, 78	Tokyo University of Commerce	Taipin, Central G&C Office	Hitotsubashi University

Table A.2.1 (cont'd)

(1) Rank 1943	*(2) Title*	*(3) Name*	*(4) Sections within Chōsabu*	*(5) Birth–Death*	*(6) Chōsabu Report*	*(7) Pre-war Affiliation*	*(8) Affiliation as of July 1945*	*(9) Post-war Affiliation*
6-7	Civilian Administrator	Kirita Naosaku	Agriculture and forestry, finance and money, Southern Region in general	1902–n.d.	No. 21, 35	Institute of East Asian Economies	Penang G&C Office	(–n.d.)** Ibaraki University
6-8	Civilian Administrator	Higuchi Gorō	Finance and money, commerce, trade, ration, household budget and price	1906–71	No. 6, 23, 36, 45, 55, 61, 76, 82	Institute of East Asian Economies	Perak G&C Office	(–n.d.)** Yokohama City University
7-6	Assistant Professor	Yamada Isamu	Statistical office, household budget and price, agriculture and forestry	1909–86	No. 12, 44, 50	Tokyo University of Commerce	Syonan Municipality Office	Hitotsubashi University / IER (professor)
7-8	Civilian Administrator	Taniyama Seizō	Agriculture and forestry, farming economy, Southern Region in general	1918–n.d.	No. 10, 24, 52, 81	Institute of East Asian Economies	Johore G&C Office	(–n.d.)** Meiji Gakuin University
-	Research Assistant	Yamada Hideo	Agriculture and forestry, customs and public sentiment, land institutions	1917–2002	No. 46, 53	Tokyo University of Commerce (later assistant professor)	Selangor G&C Office	Hitotsubashi University / IER (clerk>professor)

(cont'd overleaf)

Table A.2.1 (cont'd)

(1) Rank 1943	*(2) Title*	*(3) Name*	*(4) Sections within Chōsabu*	*(5) Birth–Death*	*(6) Chōsabu Report*	*(7) Pre-war Affiliation*	*(8) Affiliation as of July 1945*	*(9) Post-war Affiliation*
-	Civilian Associate	Ōno Seizaburō	Agriculture and forestry, farming economy, Southern Region in general	1918–2005	No. 11, 46, 53	Institute of East Asian Economies (research assistant)	Taipin, Central G&C Office	Hitotsubashi University / IER (clerk>professor)
-	Civilian Associate	Utsugi Tadashi	Mining and manufacturing, farming economy	n.d.	No. 75	Institute of East Asian Economies (research assistant)	Pahang G&C Office	Hitotsubashi University / IER (clerk>lecturer)
-	Civilian Associate	Kawai Mikio	Statistical office, household budget and price	1915–n.d.	No. 12, 50	Institute of East Asian Economies	Kuala Lumpur, Central G&C Office	(–1949)** unknown
-	Civilian Associate	Hayakawa Yasumasa	Finance and money, Southern Region in general	1918–n.d. (BA 1941)	No. 8, 15	Institute of East Asian Economies	Returned to Japan	University of Hokkaido
-	Civilian Associate	Mizuno Takeshi	-	1917–2004	none	Institute of East Asian Economies (joined later)	unknown	Kobe University
-	Civilian Administrator	Izawa Kōzō	Labour management, mining and manufacturing, transport	1903–n.d. (BA 1942)	No. 47, 72	Tokyo University of Commerce, Teacher Training School	Taipin, Central G&C Office	(clerk, –n.d.)** unknown

Table A.2.1 (cont'd)

(1) Rank 1943	*(2) Title*	*(3) Name*	*(4) Sections within Chōsabu*	*(5) Birth–Death*	*(6) Chōsabu Report*	*(7) Pre-war Affiliation*	*(8) Affiliation as of July 1945*	*(9) Post-war Affiliation*
-	Civilian Associate	Ōmura Junzaburō	Labour management, population	n.d. (BA 1946)	No. 26, 47	Tokyo University of Commerce, Teacher Training School	Syonan Municipality Office	unknown
-	Civilian Associate	Kubomura Ryūsuke	Mining and manufacturing, labour management, household budget and price	1914–n.d. (BA 1946)	No. 66	Tokyo University of Commerce, Teacher Training School	Negeri Sembilan G&C Office	Yokohama National University
-	Civilian Associate	Koga Minoru	Ethnic administration, Sultan question	n.d.	none	Tokyo University of Commerce, Teacher Training School	unknown	unknown
-	Civilian Associate	Saji Kōji	Mining and manufacturing, labour management, Southern Region in general	n.d.	No. 20, 30, 31, 32, 54	Tokyo University of Commerce, Teacher Training School	unknown	Saji Trading Company
-	Civilian Associate	Tanaka Mitsuo	Statistical office, commerce, trade, ration	n.d. (BA 1946)	none	Tokyo University of Commerce, Teacher Training School	Selangor G&C Office	unknown

(cont'd overleaf)

Table A.2.1 (cont'd)

(1) Rank 1943	*(2) Title*	*(3) Name*	*(4) Sections within Chōsabu*	*(5) Birth–Death*	*(6) Chōsabu Report*	*(7) Pre-war Affiliation*	*(8) Affiliation as of July 1945*	*(9) Post-war Affiliation*
-	Civilian Associate	Nagamori Masaji	Agriculture and forestry, commerce, trade, ration	n.d. (BA 1946)	No. 18, 45, 63, 74	Tokyo University of Commerce, Teacher Training School	Penang G&C Office	University of Toyama
-	Civilian Associate	Nagaya Yūji	Religion and education, Muslim administration	n.d.	No. 4, 28, 40	Tokyo University of Commerce, Teacher Training School	Johore G&C Office	unknown
-	Civilian Associate	Hoshino Susumu	Customs and public sentiment, Muslim administration, bureaucracy, population	n.d. (BA 1946)	No. 37, 67, 69, 70, 71	Tokyo University of Commerce, Teacher Training School	Taipin, Central G&C Office	unknown
-	Civilian Associate	Matsu'ura Shigeharu	Overseas Chinese, bureaucracy, transport, commerce, trade, ration	1913–n.d. (BA 1946)	No. 51	Tokyo University of Commerce, Teacher Training School	Taipin, Central G&C Office	Oita University
-	Civilian Associate	Yamagata Tomoaki	Finance and money, commerce, trade, ration	n.d. (BA 1947)	No. 22	Tokyo University of Commerce, Teacher Training School	Perak G&C Office	unknown

Table A.2.1 (cont'd)

(1) *Rank 1943*	(2) *Title*	(3) *Name*	(4) *Sections within Chōsabu*	(5) *Birth–Death*	(6) *Chōsabu Report*	(7) *Pre-war Affiliation*	(8) *Affiliation as of July 1945*	(9) *Post-war Affiliation*
-	Contract Researcher	Azuma Akio	Mining and manufacturing	n.d.	No. 33	Manchurian Railway (Mantetsu) Chōsabu	Returned to Japan	unknown
-	Contract Researcher	Imanishi Gorō	Transport	n.d.	none	Manchurian Railway (Mantetsu) Chōsabu	Maritime Bureau	unknown
-	Contract Researcher	Ogawa Takao	Labour management	n.d.	No. 17, 29	Keio University	Syonan Municipality Office	unknown
-	Contract Researcher	Kabuki Keizō	Clerical office, commerce, trade, ration	n.d.	none	Army (full-time contract researcher)	Malacca G&C Office	unknown
-	Contract Researcher	Gotō Yūji	Customs and public sentiment, land institutions	n.d.	No. 14	Manchurian Railway (Mantetsu) Chōsabu	Returned to Japan	unknown
-	Contract Researcher	Saitō Isamu	Transport	n.d.	No. 19, 25, 38	Manchurian Railway (Mantetsu) Chōsabu	Returned to Japan	unknown

(cont'd overleaf)

Table A.2.1 (cont'd)

(1) Rank 1943	*(2) Title*	*(3) Name*	*(4) Sections within Chōsabu*	*(5) Birth–Death*	*(6) Chōsabu Report*	*(7) Pre-war Affiliation*	*(8) Affiliation as of July 1945*	*(9) Post-war Affiliation*
-	Contract Researcher	Narimatsu Yoshikiyo	Transport	n.d.	No. 34	Manchurian Railway (Mantetsu) Chōsabu	Returned to Japan	unknown
-	Assistant Professor	Nomura Torajirō	Transport, Southern Region in general	n.d.	No. 27, 39	Kobe University of Commerce	Returned to Japan	unknown
-	Contract Researcher	Haebaru Shūichi	Household budget and price	n.d.	none	Army (part-time contract researcher)	Syonan Municipality Office	unknown
-	Contract Researcher	Hashima Susumu	Public health	1901–72	No. 17, 29	Keio University	Returned to Japan	Keio University
-	Professor	Mukai Umeji	Customs and public sentiment, Muslim administration, land institutions, commerce, trade	1907–86	No. 37, 49, 56, 58, 60, 62, 65, 77	Takaoka Higher Commercial School	Taipin, Central G&C Office	University of Toyama
-	Civilian Administrator	Suzuki Tomohide	Customs and public sentiment, Muslim administration	n.d.	No. 78	Institute of Islamic World	Taipin, Central G&C Office	University of Hokkaido

Table A.2.1 (cont'd)

(1) Rank 1943	*(2) Title*	*(3) Name*	*(4) Sections within Chōsabu*	*(5) Birth–Death*	*(6) Chōsabu Report*	*(7) Pre-war Affiliation*	*(8) Affiliation as of July 1945*	*(9) Post-war Affiliation*
-	Civilian Administrator	Yamashita Kakutarō	Finance and money	n.d.	none	Kobe University of Commerce	Kuala Lumpur, Central G&C Office	Hiroshima University
-	Civilian Administrator	Watanabe Umeo	Religion and education	1893–1978	No. 40, 83	Ministry of Education (full-time contract researcher)	Pahang G&C Office	Tsurumi University
-	Secretary	Asō Fukumaru	Document office	1907–74	n/a	Institute of East Asian Economies (clerk)	Syonan Municipality Office	Hitotsubashi Univ. Library (clerk)
-	Civilian Associate	Ozaki Kenji	Clerical office	n.d.	n/a	Institute of East Asian Economies (clerk)	Taipin, Central G&C Office	unknown
-	Civilian Associate	Tsuchiya Sadayuki	Clerical office	1918–n.d.	n/a	Tokyo University of Commerce, Teacher Training School	Syonan Municipality Office	unknown
-	-	Hoshi Nobuko	Clerical office	1926–n.d.	n/a	Institute of East Asian Economies (clerk)	Taipin, Central G&C Office	unknown

(cont'd overleaf)

Table A.2.1 (cont'd)

(1) Rank 1943	*(2) Title*	*(3) Name*	*(4) Sections within Chōsabu*	*(5) Birth–Death*	*(6) Chōsabu Report*	*(7) Pre-war Affiliation*	*(8) Affiliation as of July 1945*	*(9) Post-war Affiliation*
-	-	Saeki Satako	Clerical office	1921–n.d.	n/a	Institute of East Asian Economies (clerk)	Kuala Lumpur, Central G&C Office	unknown
-	-	Saitō Nobuko	Clerical office	1925–n.d.	n/a	Institute of East Asian Economies (typist)	Taipin, Central G&C Office	unknown
-	-	Tori'i Kin	Clerical office	1923–n.d.	n/a	Institute of East Asian Economies (typist)	Taipin, Central G&C Office	unknown
-	-	Mōri Sawako	Clerical office	n.d.	n/a	Institute of East Asian Economies (typist)	Kuala Lumpur, Central G&C Office	Hitotsubashi University/IER (clerk)
-	-	Kawakami Kume	Clerical office	n.d.	n/a	Institute of East Asian Economies (clerk)	Returned to Japan	unknown
-	-	Mogi Ren	Clerical office	n.d.	n/a	Institute of East Asian Economies (clerk)	Returned to Japan	unknown
-	-	Sudō Kaichi	Clerical office	n.d.	n/a	(driver)	unknown	unknown

Notes:

The total number of Chōsabu members was 123, including 56 Japanese members, as above, and 67 local members, as below.

Local members of the Chōsabu, as of December 1944

- Kuala Lumpur Chōsabu Main Office:
  Special duty research officer, 0
  Ordinary research officers, 4
  Clerical workers, 12
  Other workers, 5
- Syonan Chōsabu Branch Office:
  Special duty research officer, 1
  Ordinary research officers, 32
  Clerical workers, 10
  Other workers, 3

Nine items of information related to the 56 Japanese Chōsabu members are as below:

(1) *Rank 1943*: The official rank within the Army. Akamatsu was on the second rank after the superintendent general of the Southern Military Administration.

(2) *Title*: The established academics of Tokyo University of Commerce retained their academic title. The younger researchers took the military post of civil administrator or civilian associate.

(3) *Name*: Name of the researcher or the clerical staff

(4) *Sections within Chōsabu*: Role allocation and sections within the Chōsabu changed a few times over the three years. Here we note all the section names relevant to the individual researcher.

(5) *Birth–Death*: The years of birth and death of the researcher if they are known. For younger scholars, the year of receiving a bachelor's degree is shown.

(6) *Chōsabu Report*: Here we note the research report number that each researcher authored, as listed in Appendix 2.1.

(7) *Pre-war Affiliation*: Affiliation of the researcher and the clerical staff before World War II. The junior members of the Chōsabu included a dozen students affiliated to the Teacher Training School, which was an additional institution to the Commerce Professional College within the university. After the enactment of the wartime emergency measure on education in October 1943, their position in the Teacher Training School protected them from being conscripted to the frontline. These 'special education students' had graduated from either the Commerce Professional College or from any other higher commercial school, and taught for at least two years before applying for the special course in this school. Takase envisaged this course as also being used at the Japan Institute of Commercial Education, which he set up, rather secretly, during the war with donations from alumni. This special course required 'research' as a mandatory subject.

(8) *Affiliation as of July 1945*: Affiliation of the researcher and the clerical staff right before the end of World War II, as noted in *Memoranda on Guidance and Counselling Office*. 'G&C Office' denotes 'Guidance and Counselling Office', where the Chōsabu members, after being dismissed from their initial research duty, were re-employed to establish offices in Taipin, Kuala Lumpur and other states at the end of May 1945, to give guidance and counselling to local residents in Singapore and the Malay Peninsula. The former Chōsabu members were called guidance counsellors and were divided into three groups to accommodate Chinese, Malay and Indian visitors to the office. The aim

of this enterprise was to facilitate a smooth running of the Military Administration by promptly responding to claims and opinions from local residents, and to help organize the Malay nationalist anti-colonial independence movement in the event of Indonesian independence.

(9) *Post-war Affiliation*: Affiliation of the researchers after World War II. '**' denotes mid-career retirement from Hitotsubashi University. Year of retirement is provided in brackets where that is known. The year of retirement as 'n.d.' refers to the immediate post-war years before 1949. 'IER' denotes the Institute of Economic Research, which is the successor to the Institute of East Asian Economies, re-established in May 1949.

Sources:

1. Southern Military Administration Superintendent General's Office, *Shōkō-ren Meibo Kōtōkan-ren Meibo* [List of Officers' Names, List of Higher Civil Administrators' Names] *21 March 1943*, in *Documents of Sakakibara Family*, Vol. 7, ed. Akashi.

2. *Ikkyō Shimbun* [Ikkyō Newspapers], 25 Jan. 1939.

3. Hitotsubashi University, College History Archive, *Malaya Gunsei Kanbu Chōsabu Kankōshiryhō Mokuroku* [List of Publications, Malayan Military Administration Department of Research], handwritten by Hoshino Susumu, July 1946.

4. CHA, 'Malaya Minzoku Keizai Kankei Shiryō Mokuroku' [List of Publications Related to Ethnic and Economic Issues in Malaya], as of December 1944, *Chōsabu News* 21 (8 Dec. 1944).

5. CHA, 'Malaya Minzoku Keizai Kankei Shiryō Mokuroku' [List of Publications Related to Ethnic and Economic Issues in Malaya], as of April 1945, *Chōsabu News* 41 (1 May 1945).

6. CHA, *Genjūmin Chūō Hodōsho Kankōbutsu* [List of Publications, Central Guidance and Counselling Office], handwritten by Hoshino Susumu, July 1946.

7. CHA, 'Malaya Gunsei Kanbu Chōsabu Shokitei' [Rules and Regulations, Malay Military Administration Department of Research], as of April 1944, *Chōsabu News* 1 (1 May 1945).

8. CHA, 'Malaya Gunsei Kanbu Chōsabu Shokitei' [Rules and Regulations, Malay Military Administration Department of Research], as of December 1944, *Chōsabu News* 21 (8 Dec. 1944).

9. CHA, *Genjūmin Hodōsho Oboegaki* [Memoranda on Guidance and Counselling Office], handwritten by Hoshino Susumu, July 1946.

A.2 List of Chōsabu Reports and Chōsabu News

The Chōsabu Reports

No. 1: Mines in Western Malaya, April 1943

No. 2: Academic Institutions in Malaya, May 1943

No. 3: Inflation in Malaya, June 1943

No. 4: Education and Training in Malaya, surveyed by Nagaya Yūji, June 1943

No. 5: Living Conditions of Ethnic Groups in Java, surveyed by Yamanaka Tokutarō and Itagaki Yoichi, July 1943

No. 6: Problems of Inflation in East Coast Residency, Sumatra, surveyed by Higuchi Gorō, June 1943

No. 7: Comparison of Climate Condition in Thailand and Malaya, reported by Ishida Ryūjirō, July 1943

No. 8: Currency in Java, by Takahashi Taizō and Hayakawa Yasumasa, July 1943

No. 9: Problems of Rice Rationing in Malaya, reported by Uchida Naosaku, Sept. 1943

No. 10: Palm Oil Production Capacity in Sumatra, surveyed by Taniyama Seizō, Sept. 1943

No. 11: Rice Cultivation in Java, surveyed by Ōno Seizaburō, Oct. 1943

No. 12: A Study of Lowest Levels of Living by Ethnic Group in Syonan Municipality: Price, Quantity and the Relative Importance of Daily Necessities, by Ethnic Group, surveyed by Yamada Isamu and Kawai Mikio, Oct. 1943 [see chapter 12]

No. 13: Bauxite on Bintan Island, by Kawai Juntarō, Oct. 1943

No. 14: Matrilineal Native Communities in Negeri Sembilan and 'Adat', surveyed by Gotō Yūji, Oct. 1943

No. 15: Currency and Finance in Malaya, surveyed by Hayakawa Yasumasa, Oct. 1943

No. 16: The Real State of Agricultural Life in Malaya (interim report), surveyed by Professor Ishida *et al.* and reported by Professor Odabashi, Oct. 1943

No. 17: Medical Research on Labour Force in the Southern Region, by Harashima Susumu and Ogawa Takao, Nov. 1943

No. 18: Copra Production Capacity in Malaya and Its Collection Policy, surveyed by Nagamori Masaji, Dec. 1943

No. 19: Prospects of Malayan Automobile Industry, surveyed by Saitō Isamu, Oct. 1943

No. 20: Rare Elementary Minerals in Malaya: A Summary, surveyed by Saji Kōji, Nov. 1943

No. 21: Trade between French Indochina and Thailand, by Civilian Administrator Kirita Naosaku, Dec. 1943*

No. 22: Overseas Chinese Remittance to Mainland China, surveyed by Yamagata Tomoaki, Nov. 1943

No. 23: Withdrawal of Local Money from Circulation, by Higuchi Gorō, Dec. 1943

No. 24: Palm Oil Production Capacity and Its Bottleneck in Malaya, written by Taniyama Seizō, Dec. 1943

No. 25: Enhancement Plan for Automobile Repairs, surveyed by Saitō Isamu, Dec. 1943

No. 26: Population by Occupation in Syonan Municipality, surveyed by Odabashi Sadatoshi and Ōmura Junzaburō, Dec. 1943 [see chapter 3]

No. 27: Transportation of Prime Cargoes in Malaya, by Assistant Professor Nomura Torajirō, Dec. 1943

No. 28: Primary School Education in Malaya after the Start of Occupation, surveyed by Nagaya Yūji, Dec. 1943

No. 29: Physical Characteristics of Southern Ethnic Groups, by Harashima Susumu and Ogawa Takao, Jan. 1944

No. 30: Industries in Indochina: Vol. 1, Agriculture, Forestry and Fishery, by Professor Kawai Juntarō and Civilian Associate Saji Kōji, Feb. 1944*

No. 31: Industries in Indochina: Vol. 2, Mining, by Professor Kawai Juntarō and Civilian Associate Saji Kōji, Feb. 1944*

No. 32: Industries in Indochina: Vol. 3, Manufacturing, by Professor Kawai Juntarō and Civilian Associate Saji Kōji, Feb. 1944*

No. 33: Technical Capability of Local Inhabitants in the Malay Region, surveyed by Azuma Akio, Feb. 1944

No. 34: Composition of Railway Network in the Southern Region, by Contract Researcher Narimatsu Yoshikiyo, Jan. 1944*

No. 35: Countermeasures for Prices for Syonan Municipality, compiled for the Committee for the Problem of Prices, data compilation by Civilian Administrator Kirita Naosaku, Mar. 1944 [see chapter 7]

No. 36: Inflationary Situation in Malaya and Its Countermeasures, by Civilian Administrator Higuchi Gorō, April 1944

No. 37: 'Queue Riots' and 'Pahang Disturbances', translated by Hoshino Susumu and revised by Mukai Umeji, May 1944

No. 38: Issues Related to Increasing Vehicle Transportation Capacity in Malaya, written by Saitō Isamu, May 1944

No. 39: Transportation of Prime Cargoes in Java, surveyed by Nomura Torajirō, June 1944

No. 40: Changes in Religious Policies under the Military Administration, surveyed by Army Civilian Administrator Watanabe Umeo, assisted by Nagaya Yūji, July 1944

No. 41: Reference Materials on Sultan's Religious Administration, translated by Itagaki Yoichi, July 1944

No. 42: Agrarian Institutions in Malaya and Overseas Chinese, by Yamada Hideo, Oct. 1944

No. 43: Issues Related to Guidance and Utilization of Religious Customs under the Military Administration, surveyed by Army Civilian Administrator Watanabe Umeo, assisted by Nagaya Yūji, Aug. 1944

No. 44: Methods of Increasing Food Production on Syonan Island, surveyed by Yamada Isamu, Oct. 1944 [see chapter 9]

No. 45: Reorganizing Commercial Businesses in Syonan Municipality, by Army Civilian Administrators Higuchi Gorō and Nagamori Masaji, Sept. 1944 [see chapter 4]

No. 46: A Study of Agricultural Villages in Negeri Sembilan: Land Compositions of Malayan Kampongs, Assistant Professor Yamada Hideo and Research Assistant Ōno Seizaburō, Mar. 1945

No. 47: A Study of the Labour Situation in Syonan Municipality, Focusing on Factories Managed by Japanese, surveyed by Civilian Administrator Izawa Kozō and Civilian Associate Ōmura Junzaburō, Oct. 1944 [see chapter 5]

No. 48: A Study of Agricultural Villages in Kerian District: A Summary Report, surveyed by Ishida Ryūjirō *et al.*, Sept. 1944

No. 49: Religious Administrative Organizations in the States of Negeri Sembilan and Malacca, by Mukai Umeji, Nov. 1944

No. 50: Household Expenditure Survey: A Report, surveyed by Yamada Isamu and written by Kawai Mikio, Oct. 1944

No. 51: Rice Imports to Malaya, with Special Reference to Syōnan Municipality, by Matsu'ura Shigeharu, surveys by Kirita Naosaku and Nagamori Masaji, Oct. 1944 [see chapter 11]

No. 52: Limits of Food Securement in Syonan Municipality, by Civil Administrator Taniyama Seizō, Jan. 1945*

No. 53: A Study of Overseas Chinese Vegetable Farmers on Syonan Island, by Assistant Professor Yamada Hideo and Research Assistant Ōno Seizaburō, Mar. 1945*

No. 54: Distribution of Groups of Workers along the Cross-Country Malayan Railroad, surveyed by Saji Kōji, Nov. 1944

No. 55: Problems of Food Control, Especially the Abolition of Official Prices, surveyed by Higuchi Gorō, Nov. 1944

No. 56: Lineage of Overseas Chinese in Perak, by Professor Mukai Umeji, Dec. 1944*

No. 57: Chinese Workers in Federated Malay States: Vol. 1, by Professor Odabashi Sadatoshi, Mar. 1944*

No. 58: Palm Oil Industry in Malaya, by Mukai Umeji, Dec. 1944

No. 59: Population Compositions of Malaya, Professor Odabashi Sadatoshi, Feb. 1945*

No. 60: Lim Boon Keng's Theory of Overseas Chinese, by Professor Mukai Umeji, Feb. 1945*

No. 61: Control of Perishable Foods in Malaya and Double Pricing, by Higuchi Gorō, Jan. 1945

No. 62: Policies and Policy Makers towards Overseas Chinese before and after the Outbreak of War, by Professor Mukai Umeji, forthcoming*

No. 63: Abolition of Rationing and Collection Control in Syonan Municipality and Its Consequences, by Civilian Administrator Nagamori Masaji, Feb. 1945*

No. 64: Opinions of Local Residents on Official Prices and Associational Controls, by the Second Section of the Chōsabu, Feb. 1945*

No. 65: A History of the Overseas Chinese Secret Society, by Professor Mukai Umeji, Mar. 1945*

No. 66: Manufacturing of Daily Necessities and Its Reorganization in Malaya, by Civilian Associate Kubomura Ryūsuke, Mar. 1945

No. 67: A History of Malayan Migration: Malayan, Indian, Chinese and British Incomers, by Civilian Associate Hoshino Susumu, Mar. 1945*

No. 68: Reorganizing Penang Palm Oil Industry, by Assistant Professor Uchida Naosaku, forthcoming*

No. 69: Rules Related to Pre-war Bureaucracy: Documents on Malayan Bureaucracy, by Civilian Associate Hoshino Susumu, Apr. 1945*

No. 70: Statistical Tables Related to Pre-war Bureaucracy: Documents on Malayan Bureaucracy No. 2, by Civilian Associate Hoshino Susumu, Apr. 1945*

No. 71: Commentary on Pre-war Bureaucracy: Documents on Malayan Bureaucracy No. 3, by Civilian Associate Hoshino Susumu, Apr. 1945*

No. 72: A Study of the Labour Situation in Factories Managed by Japanese in Malaya and Their Problems, by Civilian Administrator Izawa Kōzō, forthcoming*

No. 73: Productivity of Machine Factories Run by Local Managers, by Civilian Associate Kubomura Ryūsuke, forthcoming*

No. 74: Conditions after the Abolition of Control Prices in the State of Malacca and Its Consequences for Consumers, by Civilian Administrator Nagamori Masaji, forthcoming*

No. 75: Periodic Market in Kerian, by Professor Ishida and Civilian Associate Utsugi Tadashi, forthcoming*

No. 76: Conditions of Prices in Malaya and Rollback Measures, by Civilian Associate Higuchi Gorō, Apr. 1944*

No. 77: Measures to Stabilize Public Sentiment under Increasing Severity of Bombing: Special Research No. 4 Commissioned by the Superintendent of Military Administration, by Professor Mukai Umeji, Apr. 1945*

No. 78: Human Development Measures for Malays and Indians: Special Research No. 3 Commissioned by the Superintendent of Military Administration, by Assistant Professor Itagaki Yoichi and Civilian Administrator Suzuki Tomohide, Apr. 1945*

No. 79: What Enterprise May Be Most Suitable for Employing Overseas Chinese: Special Research No. 2 Commissioned by the Superintendent of Military Administration, by Assistant Professor Uchida Naosaku, Apr. 1945*

No. 80: Our Opinion in Response to Overseas Chinese Central Joint Council Report, Chōsabu Director Akamatsu Kaname, Apr. 1945*

No. 81: Limits to Increasing Production Capacity in Coconut Plantations, by Civilian Administrator Taniyama Seizō, forthcoming*

No. 82: Dual Economy in Malaya and the Dual Price System, by Civilian Administrator Higuchi Gorō, forthcoming*

No. 83: Primary Daoist Gods in Malayan Overseas Chinese Temples and Places of Worship, by Civilian Administrator Watanabe Umeo, forthcoming*

No. 84: Thai Rice Imports and Utilization of Overseas Chinese Private Vessels, by Assistant Professor Uchida Naosaku, forthcoming*

The Chōsabu News

No. 1, 1 May 1944	No. 23, 20 Dec. 1944
No. 2, 25 May 1944	No. 24, 30 Dec. 1944
No. 3, 5 June 1944	No. 25, 5 Jan. 1945
No. 4, 20 June 1944	No. 26, 10 Jan. 1945
No. 5, 5 July 1944	No. 27, 15 Jan. 1945
No. 6, 20 July 1944	No. 28, 25 Jan. 1945
No. 7, 5 Aug. 1944	No. 29, 1 Feb. 1945
No. 8, 20 Aug. 1944	No. 30, 8 Feb. 1945
No. 9, 5 Sept. 1944	No. 31, 15 Feb. 1945
No. 10, 20 Sept. 1944	No. 32, 25 Feb. 1945
No. 11, 5 Oct. 1944	No. 33, 5 Mar. 1945
No. 12, 15 Oct. 1944	No. 34, 15 Mar. 1945
No. 13, 20 Oct. 1944	No. 35, 20 Mar. 1945
No. 14, 25 Oct. 1944	No. 36, 23 Mar. 1945
No. 15, 1 Nov. 1944	No. 37, 3 Apr. 1945
No. 16, 8 Nov. 1944	No. 38, 10 Apr. 1945
No. 17, 15 Nov. 1944	No. 39, 18 Apr. 1945
No. 18, 20 Nov. 1944	No. 40, 25 Apr. 1945
No. 19, 25 Nov. 1944	No. 41, 1 May 1945
No. 20, 1 Dec. 1944	No. 42, 8 May 1945
No. 21, 8 Dec. 1944	No. 43, 15 May 1945
No. 22, 15 Dec. 1944	No. 44, 25 May 1945

Note: * = missing; forthcoming = in press as of April 1945.

Sources:

1. CHA, 'List of Publications', as of December 1944, *Chōsabu News* 21 (8 Dec. 1944).
2. CHA, 'List of Publications', as of April 1945, *Chōsabu News* 41 (1 May 1945).

2.3 The Institute going South: Photographs of Chōsabu Members, September 1943

Figure A.2.1 (a) The Institute going South

Source: *Tokyo Shōka Daigaku Sotsugyō Kinen Shashin Chō* [Tokyo University of Commerce Graduation Album] (Tokyo: Kawamura Shashinkan, Sept. 1943), p. 272.

Figure A.2.1 (b) Sultan of Selangor (Malaya)

Source: Tokyo University of Commerce Graduation Album, Sept. 1943, p. 272.

Figure A.2.1 (c) After playing badminton (Professors Ishida, Yamanaka and Takahashi)

Source: Tokyo University of Commerce Graduation Album, Sept. 1943, p. 272.

Figure A.2.1 (d) In front of XX headquarters*

Source: Tokyo University of Commerce Graduation Album, Sept. 1943, p. 272.

* The original photo caption contained turned letters which are denoted as 'XX' here. The letters were concealed possibly due to wartime censorship.

Figure A.2.1 (e) Director (Professor Akamatsu)

Source: Tokyo University of Commerce Graduation Album, Sept. 1943, p. 272.

Figure A.2.1 (f) In front of staff accommodation (Professors Yamanaka and Ishida)

Source: Tokyo University of Commerce Graduation Album, Sept. 1943, p. 273.

Figure A.2.1 (g) Coconut-harvesting monkey (Malaya)

Source: Tokyo University of Commerce Graduation Album, Sept. 1943, p. 273.

Figure A.2.1 (h) Chōsabu girls army

Source: Tokyo University of Commerce Graduation Album, Sept. 1943, p. 273.

Figure A.2.1 (i) Under a parasol (Professor Yamanaka)

Source: Tokyo University of Commerce Graduation Album, Sept. 1943, p. 232.

Figure A.2.1 (j) A high-ranking officer in Johore

Source: Tokyo University of Commerce Graduation Album, Sept. 1943, p. 273.

Figure A.2.1 (k) The dashing researchers of the institute

Source: Tokyo University of Commerce Graduation Album, Sept. 1943, p. 274.

Figure A.2.1 (l) Malay school in Kg Pilah (Malaya)

Source: Tokyo University of Commerce Graduation Album, Sept. 1943, p. 274.

Figure A.2.1 (m) Professor Itagaki

Source: Tokyo University of Commerce Graduation Album, Sept. 1943, p. 274.

Figure A.2.1 (n) Professor Itagaki and a publicity vehicle (Malaya)

Source: Tokyo University of Commerce Graduation Album, Sept. 1943, p. 275.

Figure A.2.1 (o) Minangkabau people (Malaya)

Source: Tokyo University of Commerce Graduation Album, Sept. 1943, p. 275.

Figure A.2.1 (p) Professor Akamatsu and the women of the institute

Source: Tokyo University of Commerce Graduation Album, Sept. 1943, p. 275.

2.4 Photographs of Singapore under Japanese Occupation, September 1944

Figure A.2.2 (a) A rickshaw puller on the right, and assistant soldiers in a sidecar on the left.
A sidecar is usually attached to the front, side or back of a bicycle.

Source: HERMES-IR: Special Collection, Pre-World War II Asia in Photos, Reference code: 2587. Photo courtesy of Hitotsubashi University Library. Photo previously owned by the Japanese Army Accounting School, stamped Oka Field Supply Regiment, Sept. 1944.

Figure A.2.2 (b) Syonan Municipality farm training centre*

Source: HERMES-IR: WWII Asia, 2619. Oka Supply Regiment, Sept. 1944.

* In the photograph, the nameplate on the gatepost says: 'Collective Farming Training Facility: Municipality No. 1 Farm'.

Figure A.2.2 (c) Tapioca-cultivating farm in Malaya, February 1944
Censored by the Bureau of Information.

Source: HERMES-IR: Special Collection, Pre-World War II Asia in Photos, Reference code: 2622. Photo courtesy of Hitotsubashi University Library. Photo previously owned by the Japanese Army Accounting School, stamped *Dōmei Tsūshin Sha* [Federated News Agency of the Empire of Japan], Feb. 1944.

Figure A.2.2 (d) Tapioca, the main food of local inhabitants

Source: HERMES-IR: WWII Asia, 2624. Oka Supply Regiment, Sept. 1944.

Figure A.2.2 (e) Supply of bread
The bread baked at the Southern Army Field Supply Regiment includes 30 per cent tapioca starch and is supplied to critically ill patients.

Source: HERMES-IR: WWII Asia, 2678. Oka Supply Regiment, Sept. 1944.

Figure A.2.2 (f) Geylang Lorong No. 1 Factory
Assembly work on a barge made of plywood.

Source: HERMES-IR: WWII Asia, 2666. Oka Supply Regiment, Sept. 1944.

Figure A.2.2 (g) Handlooms in a textile factory
There are three textile factories in this region, all of which are small and equipped with handlooms. The total number of XX hundred handlooms can altogether provide XX million metres of fabric per year using the confiscated cotton and the pineapple fibre produced in this region.*

Source: HERMES-IR: WWII Asia, 2677. Oka Supply Regiment, Sept. 1944.

* The original photo caption contained turned letters which are denoted as 'XX' here. The letters were concealed possibly because the anonymous writer at the Japanese Army Accounting School did not know the actual figures.

Figure A.2.2 (h) Brickwork

Within the Malayan region, the soil on Syonan Island is suitable for bricks. There are more than a dozen brickworks on Syonan Island, which produce 3 million bricks per month. The production method is the same as in Japan and requires wood or coal as fuel. Because Syonan obtains 90 per cent of its coal from outside the island, this creates a bottleneck for brick production.

Source: HERMES-IR: WWII Asia, 2697. Oka Supply Regiment, Sept. 1944.

Figure A.2.2 (i) Factory producing rubber coverings
Due to a lack of paper and dehydrated oils in this region, this factory produces thin rubber sheets as a covering substitute [for oil paper]. Annual production is XX thousand pieces. Additionally, protective clothing against poison gas attacks is now planned.*

Source: HERMES-IR: WWII Asia, 2719. Oka Supply Regiment, Sept. 1944.

* The original photo caption contained turned letters which are denoted as 'XX' here. The letters were concealed possibly because the anonymous writer at the Japanese Army Accounting School did not know the actual figures.

Figure A.2.2 (j) Street market, Syonan Chinatown
Many different kinds of second-hand clothes are collected and sold; also known as the Robbers' Market.

Source: HERMES-IR: WWII Asia, 2719. Oka Supply Regiment, Sept. 1944.

Figure A.2.2 (k) Street market 'Syonan'

Source: HERMES-IR: WWII Asia, 2720. Oka Supply Regiment, Sept. 1944.

Figure A.2.2 (l) Outside view of a Syonan market*

Source: HERMES-IR: WWII Asia, 2724. Oka Supply Regiment, Sept. 1944.

* In the photograph, the sign on the front wall says 'Changi Market 1938' in both English and Chinese.

Note for HERMES-IR: Special Collection, Pre-World War II Asia Photos:

This special collection of photographs encompasses the pre-World War II period.* The collection contains 3,705 photographs assembled by the Japanese Army Accounting School, showing landscapes, local manners and customs, ethnic groups and industries in the Asian and Pacific regions from the early Syowa period to the end of World War II. The photographs are categorized and enclosed in 330 envelopes by region and subject. There are also 1,289 uncategorized photographs.

Coverage: The actual dates of the photographs are mostly unknown. The dates written on the photo-mounts range from April 1915 to March 1944, but in most cases the dates are not recorded on the photo-mounts.† The dates on the envelopes range from September 1944 to March 1945. The regions covered by the collection range from: No. 1 North China (1,393 pieces) through to No. 53 Outer Pacific (2 pieces); including No. 15 Malaya (159 pieces) and No. 16 Syonan (7 pieces). Total: 330 envelopes, 3,705 pieces.

Historical note: The photograph collection was probably brought to Hitotsubashi University Library after World War II when books and documents of the Japanese Army Accounting School were transferred to the university. However, the exact reason for the transfer and circumstances of it are unknown. The photographs were likely collected and stored initially by the Army Accounting School according to the reference code number stamped on the back of the photo-mounts, and between 1944 and 1945 were reorganized and categorized by region and subject. The Japanese Army Accounting School was established in 1890 in order to 'provide the high-ranking officers of accounting and finance with the necessary knowledge of liberal arts' and continued teaching young officers until the end of World War II. The school had an in-house 'Department of Research' that conducted 'academic research and surveys on the subject of Army accounting and finance'.

Note for The Institute going South: Photographs of Chōsabu Members, 1943:

The special four-page feature 'Institute going South' appeared at the end of Tokyo University of Commerce Graduation Album, September 1943. The feature was after the photographs of individual students, lecturers and tutors, and placed in a section for sporting circles, reading circles, seminar groups and the like. The date of graduation was moved half an academic year earlier due to the wartime in order to shorten undergraduate courses. Many of the students in this album were sent to the front line as combatants. The special feature pages included photographs of the Chōsabu members and the places they visited in Singapore, Malaya, Thailand, Java and Madura. Photographs were taken and brought back to Japan by the short-term visiting lecturers in Singapore. Of the 33 snapshot photographs in the album, 16 were selected for reproduction in this book. Reproduction is by the special permission of Hitotsubashi University Library.

---

* The period before 15 August 1945 is sometimes referred to as 'pre-war' in Japanese history.

† Photographs of Malaya and Singapore without dates were taken by the Oka Supply Regiment ('Oka' was the codename for the Seventh Area Army) and probably between April 1944 and September 1944.

Part II The Chōsabu Reports

Population, Labour Supply and Industrial Production

CHAPTER 3

Population by Occupation in Syonan Municipality

Surveyed by Odabashi Sadatoshi and Ōmura Junzaburō, December 1943

Contents

[1] 'Verdict' refers to the summary recommendation made by the Chōsabu as the unique research and consultation organ for the superintendent general of the Military Administration.

5. **The Working Population by Household**
   (1) Average household size
   (2) Occupation of heads of household
   (3) Occupation of other household members where the head of household works
   (4) Employed household members where the head of household is unemployed
   (5) Occupational comparison between heads of household and other household members

6. **Employed and Unemployed Populations**
   (1) Rate of employment
   (2) Rates of employment by ethnic group

Appendices

A.1. Statistical Tables

Table A.3.1 Syonan Municipality police precinct population by ethnic group, November 1943[2]

Table A.3.2 Syonan Municipality ethnic group population by police precinct, April 1943

Table A.3.3 Syonan Municipality employed and unemployed population by ethnic group, November 1943

Table A.3.4 Syonan Municipality household population by occupation, November 1943

Table A.3.5 Syonan Municipality occupation by ethnic group, November 1943

Table A.3.6 Syonan Municipality occupation by ethnic group and gender, November 1943

Table A.3.7 Syonan Municipality occupational subgroups by ethnic group, November 1943

Table A.3.8 Syonan Municipality occupation by gender, 1931 and November 1943

[2] The eight police precincts were: A. Central South Bridge Road, B. Kandang Kerbau, C. Beach Road, D. Tanjong Pagar, E. Orchard Road, F. Joo Chiat, G. Paya Lebar and H. Adjacent Islands.

A.2. List of Occupations

Verdict

1. The population of Syonan Municipality, including the adjacent islands, is over one million. The present survey shows a population of 855,679, excluding Japanese, the adjacent islands, Seletar Naval Port, the police dormitory and the jail (2-(1) of this report).[3] The male population is estimated to be 510,000 and the female population 350,000. Males remain a disproportionately large part of the population (2-(3) of the report).
2. The largest ethnic group, Chinese, comprise 79 per cent of the population, followed by Malays at 11 per cent and Indians at 9 per cent (2-(2) of the report).
3. There are about 340,000 persons in the working population, amounting to 40 per cent of the total population.[4] Male workers comprise 60.3 per cent of the male population and female workers 9.6 per cent of the female population. Compared with Japan, the employment rate is low. The female employment rate is particularly low, being only half that in Japan (6-(1) of the report). Employment rates vary according to ethnic group, but a comparatively small proportion of females, old people and children in the ethnic population tends to improve rates. This is obvious, and we should not be deceived by the apparent employment rate by ethnic group (6-(2) of the report).
4. Analysis of the working population by occupation shows that the largest occupation is commerce, in which 29 per cent of the working population is classified. Coolies are the next largest occupational group, accounting for 20 per cent. The third-largest group is mining and manufacturing, which includes about 17 per cent. All three occupational groups are considerably larger than they were in 1931. The increase in commerce is particularly remarkable and accounts for 50 per cent of the total increase. The main increase in numbers within commerce is those employed as street vendors (16,000), goods sellers (10,000), store clerks and shop assistants (7,000) (3-(4) of the report).

---

[3] If these exclusions are included, Syonan's population was about 1,030,000.

[4] This corresponds to the Japanese word *yūgyōsha*: people with occupations, including employers, self-employed and employees. It should be noted that *yūgyōsha* also includes those who have an occupation and are looking for work but who are neither employed nor self-employed at the time of the survey. By contrast, *mugyōsha* is chiefly meant to include people who are not working and currently have no intention of looking for work, such as housewives and the elderly. However, probably also included in *mugyōsha* are a proportion of those who work as unpaid family members in a shop or other business. In the translation we use the terms 'working' and 'employed' interchangeably, although this does not strictly correspond to the Japanese word *yūgyōsha*.

5. Each ethnic group has its own particular occupation. Hokkien and Teochew work in commerce; Hainanese in domestic occupations and restaurants; Cantonese in mining and manufacturing; Malays in fisheries and as drivers and sailors; Indians as guards, police officers and coolies (4-(1) of the report).
6. The average family size is 4.37 persons, among whom an average of 1.74 are employed and support the family (5-(1) of the report). Heads of households' occupations are commerce, mining and manufacturing, and coolies, in that order. However, other household members work in commerce, as coolies, followed by mining and manufacturing. The importance of these occupational groups differs somewhat between heads of household and other household members (5-(5) of the report). For women the largest occupational group is 'other', which includes household servants (5-(2) to 5-(4) of the report).

Report

1. Methods of Data Collection

There have been no data on the population of Syonan Municipality by occupation since the last census in 1931 [by the British colonial government]. The census survey[5] conducted by the police stations [of Syonan Municipality] in April 1943 had a category that recorded occupation. Aggregating these numbers yields approximate recent population numbers and occupations in Syonan Municipality.

However, the census survey was not solely intended to gather information on the occupations of inhabitants. Its aim was to identify the circumstances among the population in regard to rationing and other matters. Thus, it is uncertain to what extent occupations were correctly declared. The survey asked questions in six areas: 1. name, 2. age, 3. sex, 4. family relationship, 5. nationality, 6. occupation. Inhabitants were required to fill out a form. The categories of name, age and sex are unambiguous, but it should be noted that the other categories are more subject to misstatement. For example, some inhabitants neglected to supply information on family relationships. For nationality, most Chinese responded with their home region but a few identified themselves only as Chinese. There was no consistency. The same is true of occupation. Some inhabitants gave details, but many answered only with general occupational categories. For example, some just responded with one character,

[5] The original called this a 'door-to-door population survey', probably because the Japanese word for census, *kokusei chōsa*, denotes a national-level survey.

shō.[6] Others replied with 'manager' or 'company executive'. Moreover, there was an insufficiently clear distinction between the categories of 'industry' and 'occupation'. For example, some replied 'xxxx machine company' and neglected to specify the workplace. However, as this current survey shows aggregate information on occupation, it is reasonable to say that these numbers can be regarded as the total statistics of occupation. Moreover, as it would take a long time to conduct a fresh survey, these statistics, although possibly inexact, will help to clarify the current situation.

Method of aggregation

(i) The census cards were first sorted into six ethnic groups: Chinese (Hokkien, Cantonese, Hakka, Teochew, Hainanese and other Chinese), Malay, Indian, Eurasian, European and other.

(ii) Householders in each group were then divided into employed [*yūgyōsha*] and unemployed.[7]

(iii) Unemployed householders [*mugyōsha*] were then divided according to whether within the family there were other members employed or all family members were unemployed.

Each census card, as indicated above, recorded the occupation of the employed by sex, while the unemployed aged 15 to 50 were simply counted by age and sex. (Although in Japan this age range is usually between 15 and 60, due to local conditions those aged over 50 must be regarded as old.) Those outside these age ranges were merely counted. Initial categorization of occupation gave 44 occupations. Ultimately, when the numbers had been aggregated, the number of occupations was reduced to 39. Further merging resulted in seven broad categories of occupation. Where there were a large number of inhabitants in a specific occupation, they formed a separate category. Examples are car drivers, carpenters and porters. Details of types of occupation are given in Appendix A.2 [List of Occupations].

Aggregation and analysis of the numbers was conducted in mid-November 1943. Because the census cards [lodged at the police stations and continuously updated to record any incoming and outgoing residents] reflect day-to-day fluctuations in the numbers, it is reasonable to say that the data relate to conditions in the middle of November 1943.

---

[6] Abbreviation of *shōgyō* (commerce) and *shōnin* (merchant).

[7] This corresponds to the Japanese word *mugyōsha*: people without occupations, including the retired, sick, wounded and/or unemployed, as well as housewives and other family members helping the family.

2. Population of Syonan Municipality

(1) Total population

The result of aggregation [as conducted by the Chōsabu in November 1943] shows the total population as 855,679 (see appendix 1, table A.3.1). This is slightly different from the count of the Department of Police Administration in the spring of 1943, which gave a total population of 863,715 (see table A.3.2). However, the total population in the spring of 1943 included 4,482 officers lodging in the police dormitory and 1,163 officers living elsewhere. These persons are excluded in the present count. Their exclusion from the total population in the spring of 1943 gives a total population of 858,070, so that the difference with the present count is only 2,500. This does not appear to be a large discrepancy.

However, when the results are compared at the police precinct level, there are still large gaps between the two population surveys.[8] It is not clear that these discrepancies arise from population movements between police precincts. For reference, we give details of population numbers.

Table 3.1 Syonan Municipality population by police precinct, April and November 1943

Police precinct	Apr. 1943	Nov. 1943	Difference
A	152,136	150,819	-1,317
B	136,887	138,981	+2,093
C	119,535	118,879	-656
D	116,231	116,288	+57
E	86,914	90,774	+3,883
F	126,086	128,039	+1,953
G	111,051	103,729	-7,332
M[9]	9,230	8,170	-1,060
Total	858,070	855,679	-2,391

[8] The translation uses the term 'precinct' to denote a geographical police area or region. Syonan Municipality had eight precincts, each of which was divided into seven or eight geographical sections. There were a total of 59 sections. At the level below sections, there were ten wards per section, ten teams per ward, and 30–40 households per team.

[9] In some reports, police precinct M is referred to as precinct H. Both M and H denote the police area that extended to some of the adjacent islands.

Table 3.1 shows that the population of Syonan Municipality is approximately 860,000. Both counts exclude the population in the adjacent islands [i.e., Bintan Island, etc.] (about 130,000) and in Seletar port, lodgers in the police dormitory, and prisoners (about 35,000). If all these groups are included in the total population, this figure is 1,030,000. Additionally, neither of the two counts includes Japanese inhabitants. Therefore, population size in Syonan Municipality is similar to that in the six largest cities in Japan, excluding Tokyo and Osaka.

Comparison with the 1931 census population of 567,453 gives a population increase of 460,000 if we take the population to be approximately 1,030,000. If the population is counted as 860,000, the increase is approximately 300,000. This rapid increase is remarkable. Analysis in this report takes the total population to be 855,679 as mentioned above.

(2) Population by ethnic group

When the population is divided into the six ethnic groups of Chinese, Indians, Malays, Eurasians, Europeans and other, the predominant group is Chinese. They make up 79 per cent of the population. Malays are 11 per cent of the population, Indians 9 per cent, Eurasians less than 1 per cent and Europeans only 0.05 per cent. Among the Chinese, Hokkien are the largest group. They number 250,000, almost half the total of the five largest home regions. Cantonese and Teochew are the next largest groups, with a population of 120,000 each. There are relatively few Hainanese and Hakkas, only 30,000 and 20,000 respectively. However, 'other Chinese' number 120,000. As already noted, many Chinese did not indicate their home region. Therefore, most of them should be allocated to one of the five largest Chinese home regions (tables A.3.1 and A.3.3).

Comparing this to the 1931 survey, the Chinese population increased by 250,000 and became 1.6 times larger, the Malay population 1.3 times larger, the Indian population 1.5 times larger, and the Eurasian 1.2 population times larger, while the Europeans and others declined remarkably. This is because enemy countrymen retreated during the war.

The rises and falls in Chinese population by home region and percentage of Chinese who did not fill in the form seem to correlate. So, we used estimates based on the ratios of the Chinese from the five largest home regions and found that there was not a large discrepancy. Although groups like the Hainanese, which used to be a relative minority in Syonan, saw an increase in their ratios, the growth in the actual number of Hokkien, Cantonese and Teochew is of course remarkable.

Table 3.2 Syonan Municipality population, 1931 and November 1943

	1931	Nov. 1943	Difference
Chinese	421,821	673,726	+253,905
Malays	72,177	91,509	+20,332
Indians	51,019	76,219	+25,200
Eurasians	6,937	8,124	+1,187
Europeans	8,147	324	-7,763
Other	8,352	3,717	-4,635
Total	567, 453	855,679	+288,226

Table 3.3 Syonan Municipality percentage of Chinese population by ethnic group, 1931 and November 1943

	1931	Nov. 1943
Hokkien	47.4	46.0
Cantonese	22.9	21.9
Hakka	4.7	4.1
Teochew	20.3	21.7
Hainanese	4.8	6.3
Total	100.0	100.0

(3) Population by age and gender

This survey was originally intended to categorize the population into the employed and unemployed. Therefore, we have extracted the age data only in terms of whether the unemployed were of working age or not. Similarly, we used the data on gender only for the employed population and those of working age. Therefore, analysis of the total population by gender requires some guesswork. While we will refer to the old and the juvenile later, here we try and provide an estimate of total population by gender.

There are 334,000 males in the labour force. This number includes the employed male population and also the unemployed male population aged 15 to 50. Using the same definitions of the labour force and the employed population, there are 196,000 females in the labour force (table A.3.3). Old people and children number 324,000. Extrapolating from the age and sex structure of old people and children in the 1931 census, we can estimate the current age and sex structure of those over 50 and under 15. For the category aged over 50 [in our estimate], 48,000 males and 32,000 females are unemployed. Below the age of 15 there are 126,000 males and 117,000 females. Adding these population groups to the employed group and comparing the sum with the population in 1931 produces the result in Table 3.4.

Table 3.4 Syonan Municipality population by gender, 1931 and November 1943

	1931	Nov. 1943	Difference
Total	567,453	855,679	+288,226
Male	357,691	509,032	+151,341
Female	209,762	346,647	+136,885

The increase in male population is apparent in table 3.4. The female population has, however, increased with particular rapidity. The female population has also tended to increase in Malaya as a whole, probably due to higher female immigration over the last ten years and rising birth rates in the peninsula.

3. Population by Occupation and Increase and Decrease in Occupations

(1) Total employed

The results gave the total employed as 340,000 (approximately 310,000 males and 30,000 females). This is about 40 per cent of the total population. An employed person is defined as a person who earns his or her income; therefore, pensioners and those who receive remittances are excluded. Those who live with families and only do housework or remain at home are also excluded. However, monks, nuns and unlicensed prostitutes are provisionally included.

The total number of unemployed is 510,000.[10] Within this group there are close to 190,000 persons of working age (15 to 50 years old), comprising of 27,091 males and 162,578 females.

Analyzing the population by household and whether or not household heads are employed, of the 195,824 heads of household, 170,000 are employed and about 25,000 unemployed. It is mainly female heads of household who

[10] This means those who do not have jobs or earn an income.

are unemployed. Of the 20,000 female heads of household, about 12,000 are unemployed and 8,361 employed.

(2) Population by occupation

Of the 340,000 employed population classified by occupation, the largest group is in commerce, which comprises 98,886 persons, or 29 per cent of the total employed population. The next largest group, around 70,000 (20 per cent), are coolies. Mining and manufacturing follow, with 58,000 persons (17 per cent). 'Other' includes 46,000 persons (13.5 per cent). Farming, fishing, transport, government and professions are a relatively small group, comprising less than 10 per cent of the employed population (table A.3.4).

Although comparison is made difficult by differences in methods of classification, a consideration of the working population of Tokyo in 1930 is useful. Here the percentage in mining and manufacturing was quite high, at 33 per cent; commerce comprised 30 per cent; government and professions constituted 14 per cent. The large share of commerce suggests a surplus of retailers, due to the depression [in Japan]. At the time of the census [of Tokyo], there was already concern among intellectuals about this unbalanced occupational structure. The occupational distribution of the population in present-day Syonan reflects the same conditions.

As already noted, police officers are not included in the group of civil servants and professionals; it is for this reason that the group is such a small percentage of the employed population. Neither are Japanese military officers and administrators included, with the same implications for occupational structure. Consequently, adding these numbers, and merging the numerous coolies who work in mining and manufacturing into the category of mining and manufacturing, reduces the share of commerce in the employed population.[11]

However, in view of the present state of mining and manufacturing in Syonan Municipality, it is not per se unlikely that there is an excessive number of people in commerce. When we allow a detailed consideration of commerce [as below], we might have to consider carefully various issues including the possibility that there are quite a few irregular street vendors.

---

[11] This paragraph (and the opening word 'However' in the next paragraph) was inserted later, written by a different author with different handwriting on a piece of paper pasted onto the page, starting with 'In view of'. This insertion was probably made in order to lessen the impact of the comment below on the likelihood of an excessive number of people in commerce. The same handwriting appears in the final paragraph of 3-(4), starting with 'However, it is therefore difficult to achieve a strict or accurate comparison'.

Table 3.5 Tokyo and Syonan Municipality population by occupation, 1930 and November 1943

(%)

	Tokyo (1930)	Syonan Municipality (1943)
Farming and fishing	7.0	9.1
Mining and manufacturing	33.0	17.2
Commerce	30.0	29.0
Transport	6.0	7.6
Government and professions	14.0	3.3
Coolies	0.0	20.3
Other	10.0	13.5

Occupational subcategories are now considered (table A.3.7). In farming and fishing, agriculture is clearly the larger occupational group. Farming includes fruit and vegetable growing, gardening and stock farming. There are 24,000 workers in agriculture, four times as many as in fishing.

In mining and manufacturing, there is almost nothing to note in mining (although this changes to a certain extent if Bintan Island is included). Most of this group are employed in manufacturing. The result shows that mechanics are the most numerous group, at 14,000. This is followed by carpenters, who number 12,000. These occupations comprise almost half those in mining and manufacturing. They are followed by tailors (5,000), builders (3,200), electrical machinery workers (2,800), painters (2,600), blacksmiths (2,400) and shoemakers (2,200). None of the subcategories of food manufacture operatives, printers and factory workers (not included in any other category) occupy as many as 2,000. In this count, the approximately 9,000 people in the 'other workers' subcategory were employed in household industries, such as textiles, dyeing, book making, hat making and paper box making.

Transport, which covers both marine and land transport, includes warehousemen. There are, however, only 247 warehousemen. The largest group in transport are the 9,400 rickshaw pullers. They are followed by drivers (7,750 persons). There are 7,700 boatmen and sailors. Land transport workers other than rickshaw men and car drivers number less than expected at just 800.

In commerce, the largest group are merchandise distributors. Within this group, street vendors, at 38,000 persons, are the biggest subcategory. There are 27,676 other merchandise distributors (mainly shopkeepers). Among other merchandise distributors, there are 2,000 restaurant owners. Salespeople and shop assistants hired by shopkeepers account for 25,000 persons. Moneylenders and brokers are small groups, the former numbering 1,800 and the latter 1,400. Commerce also includes approximately 3,000 barbers/hairdressers.

Government and professions are difficult to categorize. At over 3,800, the largest group is 'other professions', which includes artists, surveying engineers, translators, writers, monks and nuns. In the present count, 'medical and pharmaceutical professions' include not only doctors but also medical students, pharmacists, nurses, midwives and dentists. This subcategory, surprisingly, is numerous at 2,900. There are 2,400 government administrators but only 1,150 police officers. The explanation for this is that police officers living in the police dormitory are not included in this survey.

Within the large 'other' category, the biggest group are service providers, such as domestic workers and doorkeepers. The second biggest group are salaried workers, such as secretaries and clerks who are not included in the group of civil servants, traders and mechanics. The third biggest group are the wholly uncategorized. Among these, the most numerous, 21,576, are household servants. There are over 14,000 clerical workers. They are followed by 'other' workers (6,000 persons) and doorkeepers (4,000 persons).

(3) Working population by gender

As already mentioned, there are relatively few female workers. The overall occupational distribution therefore reflects the male distribution. Thirty-eight per cent of employed females are categorized as 'other' workers, including household servants. Ten thousand female workers, almost a third of all employed females, are household servants (table A.3.4). The next largest group are coolies; there are 6,000 of them, 20 per cent of total employment. Other principal groups of employed females are farmers, street vendors (3,300 of each), shop assistants (1,100) and tailors (900). Medicine and teaching are also relatively large groups, with 657 and 258 persons respectively. Government and professions, too, are comparatively large employments, comprising 5.2 per cent of employed females, compared with 3.1 per cent of males.

(4) Increase and decrease in occupations

It is difficult to make a rigorous comparison of the 1931 and 1943 populations. However, if the statistics collected in 1931 are reworked to correspond as closely as possible to those of 1943, the two censuses can be compared (table A.3.8).

The numbers show an increase of 67,000 in the total working population, which is low compared to the increase in total population. The employment rate is therefore also low. Occupations with increased numbers are those in commerce, coolies, and workers in manufacturing and mining, farming and fishing. Occupations where numbers have fallen are transport, government and professions, and others. The increased employment in commerce is particularly remarkable. It has grown by 34,000 and accounts for over half the total increase in employment.

Underlying the higher employment in agriculture and fishing is a fall by 800 in male workers and an increase of 1,300 in female workers,[12] resulting in a net increase of 500, which is quite small. However, more detailed examination of the figures shows that the number of farmers has fallen by 1,100 and the number of fishermen has increased by 1,600. Consequently, the size of the agricultural working population has, in fact, fallen. Overall, compared to 1931, the figures reflect the remarkable growth of commerce, industry and urbanization.

Falls in transport employment originate mainly in shipping and may reflect the fact that Syonan Island has lost its former status as an entrepot for world trade. These recent changes have led to unemployment.

As already noted, falls in the number of civil servants and professionals can be attributed to the exclusion from the survey of a large number of police officers and Japanese administrative personnel.

The increase in the number employed in commerce merits further consideration, because it is caused by rising numbers of street vendors, who have increased by 15,677; merchandise distributors, up by 10,945; and salespeople and shop assistants, with 7,090 more than in 1931. Over the three occupations, this is a total increase of around 34,000.

The higher number employed in mining and manufacturing arises from the development of factory manufacturing. There has been remarkable growth in the number of mechanics and electrical machinery workers and blacksmiths. The growth in the number of coolies is connected with these developments. In the 1931 census, those coolies who could not be included in other categories were counted as coolies. The present count included many who declared their occupation simply as 'coolies' without stating their workplace.[13] The classification of 'coolie' is therefore somewhat inconsistent. However, it should be borne in mind that the increase in the number of coolies is linked to the rapid development of mining and manufacturing. We might also consider

---

12 Here several words were deleted and replaced by a long arrow ——>.

13 Due to the design of the census, if coolies did not specify their place of work voluntarily they were just recorded as coolies.

that it derives from the appearance of unemployment, which resulted in a reserve of unattached labourers just after the beginning of the war.[14]

However, it is therefore difficult to achieve a strict or accurate comparison, owing to variations in methods of classification and inconsistent definitions. Table 3.6 compares the numbers employed in 1931 and 1943 where the category definitions are almost the same.

Table 3.6 Syonan Municipality population by occupation, 1931 and November 1943

	1931	Nov. 1943
Farmers	25,479	24,374
Blacksmiths	1,056	2,435
Mechanics	8,112	14,211
Electrical machinery workers	1,403	2,839
Tailors	4,147	5,026
Shoemakers	1,933	2,218
Carpenters	10,835	11,648
Painters	1,610	2,623
Automobile drivers	8,752	7,750
Street vendors	22,725	38,402
Rickshaw pullers	10,537	9,419
Traders (incl. restaurants)	16,131	27,676
Salesmen and shop assistants	18,220	25,319
Doctors	2,918	2,920
Teachers	1,890	1,083
Coolies	22,301	69,219
Domestic servants	24,134	21,576
Clerical workers	19,293	14,818

[14] There occurs here the change in handwriting and in the direction of argument away from discussion of the role of pull and push factors in the increase in factory workers.

4. Occupation and Ethnic Group

A correlation between occupation and ethnic group requires two sets of information. The first is the structure of occupation by ethnic group; the second the pattern of occupation in each ethnic group. In the South,[15] particular occupations tend to be dominated by ethnic groups or individuals originating from the same regions in China. Therefore, there is a close connection between occupation and ethnic group (tables A.3.5, A.3.6 and A.3.7).

(1) Occupations favoured by ethnic groups

(i) Chinese

The Chinese are the largest ethnic group in Syonan. Although they are found in all occupations, commerce, which employs about 85,000, is the most favoured. Commerce engages about one-third of the entire Chinese working population. The second largest occupation, mining and manufacturing, includes 48,000, or about 19 per cent of the total Chinese working population. The next group are coolies, of whom there are about 40,000. 'Others' number only 33,000. Agriculture, fishing and transport are relatively small sources of employment, and the government and professions are of very minor importance. However, the small number of Chinese in these categories arises from the fact that the workforces in these occupations are small rather than demonstrating any Chinese-specific occupational structure. Chinese, who are 76 per cent of the total working population, are the dominant group. Ninety per cent of workers in agriculture and fishing are Chinese, 86 per cent in commerce, and 82 per cent in mining and manufacturing. These are very high percentages. In transport and 'other' occupations, 70 per cent are Chinese. However, Chinese account for just 59 per cent of civil servants and professionals, and 57 per cent of coolies. The rest are other ethnic groups, which clearly shows that [non-Chinese] are often employed in these occupations.

Hokkien

Hokkien are known for their business ability. They often also become coolies. It is therefore in these two occupations that Hokkien concentrate. Twenty-eight thousand are employed in commerce and 16,000 as coolies. Agriculture and transport each employ 12,000. In view of the smallness of agricultural employment, the level of Hokkien employment in this sector is remarkably large, at 40 per cent of the entire agricultural workforce. A lower proportion of

[15] The Nanyang or South Seas.

Hokkien engage in mining and manufacturing, which employs only 8,000. The contrast with the high proportion of Cantonese in this workforce is striking.

Cantonese

As just noted, many Cantonese work in mining and manufacturing. This sector provides employment for about 40 per cent of Cantonese. Commerce is the second most important employment, with 22 per cent of Cantonese working in the sector, followed by 'others' and coolies. The high level of Cantonese employment in mining and manufacturing reflects the fact that Cantonese originally migrated to Malaya as mineworkers.

Hakkas

The Hakkas also migrated to Malaya principally as mineworkers. Twenty-seven per cent of Hakkas are employed in mining and manufacturing in Syonan. This, however, is less than the 35 per cent in commerce. 'Others' and coolies are also large groups of employment for Hakkas.

Teochew

The Teochew occupational structure is similar to the Hokkien. However, a higher percentage of Teochew are found in commerce, where over 40 per cent are employed. For reasons that will be described later, they are particularly concentrated in banking and finance and, in this respect, contrast with the Hokkien. About 15 per cent of Teochew are employed in agriculture and fishing, indicating their similarity to the Hokkien. However, it should be noted that a much larger proportion of Teochew than Hokkien work in fishing, while they are also numerous in farming.

Hainanese

Many Hainanese are employed in commerce, which is the occupational category of 38 per cent of all employed Hainanese. The characteristic feature of this group is that 20 per cent are classified in 'other' occupations, owing to the fact that they are higher-ranking domestic servants.

(ii) Malays

In general, many Malays in the peninsula are farmers. In Syonan, however, the largest percentage of Malays (about 30 per cent) are coolies followed, in order of importance, by those employed in transport, 'other' occupations, mining and manufacturing, commerce, and agriculture and fishing. The importance of the transport sector arises from the predominant Malay presence among automobile drivers and sailors. Most Malays in the agricultural and fishing sectors work in fisheries. This is the distinctive Malay occupational pattern.

(iii) *Indians*

Like Malays, most Indians are coolies, and 37 per cent of Indian workers are so employed. Commerce is the second most important occupational category, and 22 per cent of Indians are classified in this group. A large number of Indians are found in 'other' occupations and work as secretaries and guards. Many are also civil servants and professionals, including administrators and policemen. This is a distinctive occupational pattern, not seen among other ethnic groups.

(iv) *Eurasians*

Many Eurasians are employed in office jobs. Their largest occupation is 'other', which includes 31 per cent of Eurasians. This is followed, in order of importance, by mining and manufacturing, government, and professions.

(v) *Europeans and others*

The working population is very small for these groups. They are employed mainly as civil servants and in the professions and commerce. A relatively small number work in manufacturing.

(2) Ethnic groups associated with each occupation

(i) *Agriculture and fishing*

Within this category, Chinese are the largest ethnic group. They make up a remarkably high share (90 per cent) of employment in this category. Other sectors do not show such a high concentration of Chinese. However, as noted above, only a small number of people are actually employed in agriculture and fishing. As already indicated, ethnic trends are for Hokkien to concentrate in agriculture, and Malays and Teochew in fishing.

(ii) *Mining and manufacturing*

The Chinese dominate this category, comprising 82 per cent of its workforce. The second largest group, Indians, are 10 per cent of the workforce, the third, Malays, 6.5 per cent. Among the Chinese, Cantonese are the largest group, followed, in order of importance, by Hokkien, Teochew, Hakkas and Hainanese. Among mechanics, Cantonese are the most numerous Chinese group. Many Cantonese are employed as tailors, carpenters and printers. These occupational trends account for the high number of Cantonese in mining and manufacturing. However, many Indians and Malays also work as mechanics. This employment comprises 35 per cent of the Indian and Malay workforce in mining and manufacturing.

(iii) Transport

Chinese are by far the largest ethnic group in the transport sector. They account for 73 per cent of the workforce, a slight under-representation in terms of their share of the population. Seventeen per cent of the workforce is Malay and 9 per cent Indian. Malays therefore are disproportionately represented in the transport workforce. About half of all drivers, 3,238, are Malay. Many Malays are also sailors. Two thousand three hundred Indians are employed in transport, and of these, 1,450 are drivers, constituting 20 per cent of all drivers.

Hokkien are the largest Chinese group in this category. Of those who originate from the five Chinese regions, 77 per cent of drivers in the transport workforce are Hokkien. This is because of the large number of Hokkien rickshaw pullers. There are in total 9,419 rickshaw pullers, around two-thirds of whom are Hokkien. Among Hokkien, many are from Foochow and Hockchia. These latter in particular tend to be rickshaw pullers.

(iv) Commerce

At 86 per cent of those employed in commerce, Chinese are the largest ethnic group in this sector. Indians constitute 11 per cent of the workforce and are the second largest group. Of those Chinese who originate from the five Chinese ports of embarkation, the biggest group—41 per cent—are Hokkien. They are followed by the Teochew, at 29 per cent.

The ethnic patterns in commerce are more or less repeated in the subcategories. Street vendors, merchandise distributers, salesmen and shop assistants comprise the leading subcategories, and in them Hokkien are the largest ethnic group, followed in rank order of importance by Teochew and Cantonese. However, exceptionally, in business and banking, Teochew are the most numerous group, followed by Hokkien and Cantonese. Hokkien are the largest group among restaurant owners, followed by Hainanese, Teochew and Cantonese. Hairdressers/barbers are, in order of importance, Hokkien, Cantonese and Hainanese.

(v) Government and the professions

A large number of police officers and military officers are not included in the survey. But among the 11,298 workers in this category, the largest group is Chinese, at around 60 per cent of the total. This 60 per cent and the 57 per cent who are coolies indicate that there is generally a low proportion of Chinese in these categories. Indians and Malays, on the other hand, at 18 per cent and 16 per cent of the workforce, are disproportionately numerous. Among Chinese, the largest groups are, in order of importance, Hokkien, Cantonese and Teochew. This order reflects population shares.

Although the total number of police officers is not reported, the survey shows that Malays are the largest ethnic group, followed by Indians and then Chinese. There are 479 Malay police officers and 382 Indians. These two groups together constitute about 75 per cent of all police officers. On the other hand, at 261, the number of Chinese is very small, at less than 23 per cent of the total. Among administrators, although there is a slightly higher proportion of Chinese, the actual number is only 893. There are 654 Malay administrators and 635 Indian. These figures reveal no distinct ethnic pattern. Similarly, there are 584 Chinese, 224 Malay and 150 Indian teachers. Compared to Malay and Indian representation in the total population, they have a disproportionately large representation in these categories.

Among civil servants and professionals, 'medicine' and 'other professions' include a relatively large number of Chinese. Seventy per cent of each category are Chinese, followed by Indians and then Malays. The Indian share in medicine, at 14 per cent, is relatively high. Overall, in view of the large Chinese population, Chinese representation among civil servants and professionals is low.

(vi) Coolies

Although 57 per cent of this group are Chinese, compared to other occupations this proportion is not high. The Indian share of 26 per cent is large, in view of the proportion of Indians in the population. Over 17 per cent of coolies are Malay. After those employed in transport, coolies are therefore the largest Malay occupational category.

Among Chinese coolies originating from the five Chinese ports of embarkation, 48 per cent are Hokkien, who are the largest Chinese ethnic group in this category. Twenty-two per cent of Chinese coolies are Cantonese, 20 per cent are Teochew, 8 per cent are Hainanese, and 3 per cent are Hakkas. These proportions reflect those of the employed population.

(vii) Other

The survey shows that the largest ethnic group in this category are Chinese: they comprise 70 per cent of those so classified, followed by Indians at 19 per cent and Malays at 8.5 per cent.

Among domestic servants, Chinese are the largest group, followed by Malays and Indians. Of Chinese servants, Cantonese are the most numerous, followed in rank order by Hokkien, Hainanese and Teochew. Hainanese favour domestic service, and this occupation accounts for 20 per cent (2,800) of all Hainanese workers (14,000). Guards are overwhelmingly Indian. Of a total of 4,000 guards, 3,500, or 86 per cent, are Indian. Less than 10 per cent are Chinese. There are even fewer Malays.

In clerical employments, the largest group is Chinese, at 78 per cent, followed by Indians at 17 per cent. Among Chinese, the ethnic rank order is Hokkien, Teochew, Cantonese. This reflects relative population shares.

In general, Chinese form the largest group among 'other' employments, followed by Indians and Malays. But there is a relatively high proportion of Indians: the survey shows the Chinese share at 60 per cent and the Indian at about 20 per cent.

5. The Working Population by Household

(1) Average household size

This survey covers a total of 195,824 households. On average, there are 4.37 persons per household. Table 3.7 shows average household size for both employed and unemployed heads of household (see also tables A.3.9 and A.3.10).

Table 3.7 Syonan Municipality households by employment, November 1943

	Employed heads of household	Unemployed heads of household	Total
Number of households	170,874	24,950	195,824
Number of people in households	742,344	113,335	855,679
Number of employed people in households	311,883	29,390	341,273
Number of employed heads of household	170,874	0	170,874
Number of employed members of households	141,009	29,390	170,399
Average household size	4.34	4.54	4.37
Average number of employed people in the household	1.83	1.18	1.74
Average number of unemployed people in the household	2.51	3.36	2.63

In summary, average household size is larger in households where the head of household is employed than where the head is unemployed. But where heads of household are unemployed, other employed household members provide support, or the unemployed head of household has an income other than salary. Such households tend to be relatively wealthy and large. On the other hand, there are also many one-person households where the head of household is employed. This results in a low average number of people per household. The average number of employed household members is 1.83 in households headed by an employed person, and 1.18 in households headed by an unemployed person. This shows that other household members contribute to household income. Apart from households where the head of household has a non-salary income, in households headed by an unemployed person, 1.18 people have to maintain household outgoings for 4.54 people. By contrast, where the head of household is employed, 1.83 people maintain household outgoings for 4.34 people.

(2) Occupation of heads of household

The head of household is defined as the individual who has responsibility for household members, not the person who financially supports the household. As a rule, the income of the employed head of household tends to account for most of the household outgoings.

Occupational trends for heads of household are similar to those for the employed population. Commerce is the most important category followed, in order of importance, by mining and manufacturing, coolies, 'other', agriculture and fishing, transport, and government and the professions. Among the heads of household, there are fewer coolies than there are workers in mining and manufacturing. This is the reverse of the trend for the population as a whole, where the number of coolies exceeds the workforce in mining and manufacturing.

Gender analysis of heads of household shows that they are overwhelmingly male. Occupational patterns can therefore be taken as patterns for male heads of household. Female occupational patterns differ from male. 'Other occupations' is the largest category for females and includes 35 per cent of all employed female heads of household. The next most important category, with 24 per cent of female heads of household, is commerce. These two groups comprise 60 per cent of these females. In 'other occupations' there are 1,900 female domestic servants. Commerce includes 1,300 female street vendors; 1,600 females are coolies; and 900 females are employed in mining and manufacturing, of whom 380 are classified in 'other industries' and 300 as tailors.[16]

[...] women are not just stay-at-home housewives and stand on an equal footing to the employed members of the family.

---

[16] Here, one full page is missing from the original report. This page should be on '(3) Occupation of other household members where the head of household works'.

(4) Employed household members where the head of household is unemployed

When the head of household is unemployed, it might be thought that male household members provide household income. Consequently, occupational patterns are similar to those where the head of household is employed. This would lead to occupational categories being ranked in the following order: mining and manufacturing, commerce, coolies, and 'other occupations'. The first three occupations total 73 per cent of those employed. Only 22 per cent are coolies, although among the members in the household with employed heads of household, 27 per cent are in this group.

The largest group of females—38 per cent of the total—are classified in 'other occupations', while mining and manufacturing and coolies respectively account for 21.4 per cent and 20.6 per cent. These three occupations comprise 80 per cent of the whole group. Only 14.6 per cent are classified in commerce.

(5) Occupational comparison between heads of household and other household members

In each occupational category, as in all occupations mentioned above, the number of employed heads of household exceeds the number of other household members who are employed (whether or not the head is employed). The opposite pattern is found for females. There are fewer employed male heads of household than other employed household members only in the broad category of coolies. Within the broad category of mining and manufacturing, there are the subcategories of mechanics, shoemakers, food manufacturing workers and painters, with fewer employed male household heads than other employed household members. The same is true for rickshaw pullers, boatmen, and 'other surface transport', 'other marine transport', etc., in the broad category of transport. The difference is not, however, large. In commerce, it is only in the narrower category of salesmen and shop assistants that rather large discrepancies are found. One-third of salespeople and shop assistants are heads of household, while two-thirds are other household members. In general, the category of civil servants and professionals includes many heads of household. Female heads of household are outnumbered by other employed household members. Exceptions to this are guards and doorkeepers and 'other occupations', where there are more female heads of household than other household members. Even when the head of household has an occupation,[17] this does not necessarily indicate that he or she owns a business. Therefore, whether a small or large number of household heads have an occupation in a certain trade is unrelated to the size of the business

[17] That is to say, is a *yūgyōsha* (which is elsewhere translated as 'employed').

units in the trade. Heads of household are, however, employed in relatively high-earning occupations that can contribute enough income to support the household. Earnings in those occupations where females and other household members generally work can be regarded as supplementary contributions to household income.

6. Employed and Unemployed Populations

(1) Rate of employment

As already indicated in section 3, 340,000 people are employed, amounting to 40 per cent of the total population. There are 300,000 employed males, who account for 60 per cent of the total male population. About 34,000 females are employed, or 9.6 per cent of the female population. If these percentages are taken to be the rate of employment, the rate cannot necessarily be viewed as satisfactory. It should be noted that these employment rates were exceeded by Japan even in 1930, a time of profound trade depression. Furthermore, comparing these rates with those in Syonan in 1931, although employment rates are slightly higher for females, they are distinctly lower for males.

Table 3.8 Syonan Municipality and Japan employment by gender, 1930, 1931 and November 1943

Employment rate	Total	Males	Females
Syonan, 1943	39.9	60.3	9.6
Syonan, 1931	48.3	72.3	8.6
Japan, 1930	46.0	58.8	33.0
Urban areas in Japan	42.5	62.3	21.3
Tokyo	42.5	61.8	20.4

Syonan was originally a city in which a high percentage of the population was of working age. It is therefore unsurprising that the male employment rate was high in 1931. Since it is hard to believe that the proportion of old people and children has suddenly increased, there must be other explanations for the decreasing employment rate.

The fall in the male employment rate can be explained by misstatements in the questionnaire. Part of the problem, as previously noted, is due to the exclusion of people who should have been included in the category of civil servants and professionals. Furthermore, newcomers tend not to state their occupation on the census cards after their arrival.[18]

There seems to have been a slight improvement in the female employment rate. But this does not compensate for the decline in the employment rate as a whole. Previously unemployed females, for example, entered employment during the depression, often in commerce or as coolies. Nevertheless, the relatively low female employment rate in Syonan is marked, particularly in comparison with the situation in Japan.

Overall, even for the employed, earnings do not necessarily provide an adequate income. The fact cannot be ignored that even where people are employed, some are only partially so and therefore can be regarded as partially unemployed. For example, groups such as street vendors have no choice about their work. If they are able to find a better job, they will willingly change their occupation. But in present conditions they cannot find satisfactory work and are compelled to do what they can to buy food. If such people were included as unemployed, the unemployment rate would be far higher. The number of job seekers is, however, relatively small because they cannot, or prefer not to, engage in manual labour and no other acceptable jobs are available.

(2) Rates of employment by ethnic group

Employment rates by ethnic group are given in table 3.9.

Table 3.9 Syonan Municipality percentage employed by main population group, November 1943

Indians	62.6
Europeans	57.6
Chinese	38.2
Malays	34.5
Other	30.1
Eurasians	29.8

Among Chinese workers from the five Chinese ports of embarkation, Hainanese have the highest employment rate (43 per cent), followed by Cantonese (42.9 per cent), other Chinese (41.4 per cent), Teochew (37.8 per

[18] Census cards were kept at the local police stations, where the records of incoming and outgoing residents were updated. This functioned as a sort of resident register system.

cent) and Hakkas (36.9 per cent). None of these groups exceeds the Indian rate. Differences arise from the different sex and age structures of population groups. For example, if we look at the aggregate of employed and unemployed males of working age, the proportions are 84.6 per cent of Indians, 70.3 per cent of Hainanese, 61.6 per cent of other Chinese and 72.6 per cent of Teochew. Ethnic groups with a high male preponderance tend to have high employment rates. However, while only 55 per cent of both Europeans and Cantonese are males, each group has relatively good employment rates. This arises not from the sex ratio, but from the fact that neither of these two ethnic groups includes many old people or children. Moreover, when the number of employed and unemployed people in the working-age population of 15 to 50 is totalled and compared to the number of old people and children, Indians, with 26 per cent, have the lowest dependency ratio. They are followed by Europeans, with 33.7 per cent. The employment rate is favourable when there are small proportions of females, old people and children in the population. There is therefore no doubt that low employment rates among Malays, Hokkien, Hakkas, Eurasians and other groups reflect their balanced sex ratio and their inclusion of populations of old people and children.

Details of the employed population by sex and age are essential to understanding what proportion of each racial and ethnic group is employed or unemployed. However, the present count did not aggregate this data and so cannot contribute in this regard.[19] Table A.3.11 sets out the rates as stated above.

[19] See 'method of aggregation' in section 1 above. Counting over 170,000 census cards was a time-consuming job before the age of computers. As the cards were filled in at the household level, it was even more troublesome to count individual-level data for the household members.

Appendices

A.1. Statistical Tables

Table A.3.1 Syonan Municipality police precinct population by ethnic group, November 1943 (Census Cards aggregated in mid-November 1943)

		Police precinct[20]								
		A	B	C	D	E	F	G	H	Total
Chinese	Hokkien	32,627	32,637	30,848	46,066	34,803	41,940	34,459	167	253,547
	Cantonese	50,387	16,899	18,593	17,663	4,910	10,192	2,619	11	121,274
	Hakka	2,632	3,359	5,198	1,824	3,504	4,195	2,255	14	22,981
	Teochew	29,200	17,881	13,138	7,428	12,930	12,550	26,326	249	119,702
	Hainanese	1,679	6,154	5,867	2,556	6,498	6,874	5,097	14	34,739
	Others unknown	26,259	22,954	29,511	12,948	7,361	6,443	16,354	1,648	123,483
	Subtotal	142,784	99,884	103,155	83,485	70,006	82,199	87,110	2,103	675,726
Malay		1,811	13,072	8,564	11,443	13,518	31,363	6,306	5,432	91,509
Indian		5,929	21,909	6,071	15,620	6,653	10,226	9,197	614	76,219
Eurasian		130	3,035	416	486	309	2,699	1,028	21	8,124
European		41	37	95	22	135	42	12	–	384
Others		124	1,044	578	232	153	1,510	70	–	3,717
Total		150,819	132,981	118,879	116,288	90,774	123,039	103,723	8,170	855,679

[20] The eight police precincts were: A. Central South Bridge Road, B. Kandang Kerbau, C. Beach Road, D. Tanjong Pagar, E. Orchard Road, F. Joo Chiat, G. Paya Lebar and H. Adjacent Islands.

Table A.3.2 Syonan Municipality ethnic group population by police precinct, April 1943 (Census Cards aggregated in April 1943)

Police precinct	Chinese	Malay	Indian	Eurasian	Others	Male	Female	Number of households	Total
A	144,600	1,632	5,749	71	84	84,615	67,521	32,710	152,136
B	98,497	12,781	21,489	2,954	1,166	76,239	60,648	26,444	136,887
C	104,495	8,195	5,662	524	659	73,015	46,520	29,128	119,535
D	90,447	11,143	13,963	486	192	65,084	51,147	21,834	116,231
E	66,255	13,697	6,352	318	292	48,234	38,680	19,212	88,914
F	81,298	31,288	9,591	2,728	1,181	65,560	60,526	27,924	126,086
G	90,565	7,371	12,037	916	162	63,353	47,698	15,579	111,051
H	2,227	6,500	477	20	6	5,386	3,844	1,041	9,230
Subtotal	678,384	92,607	75,320	8,017	3,742	481,486	376,584	173,872	858,070
Police officers living-in	333	2,780	1,348	11	10	2,626	1,856	1,094	4,482
Police officers living-out	703	137	319	3	1	1,130	33	-	1,163
Total	679,420	95,524	76,987	8,031	3,753	485,242	378,473	174,966	863,715
%	78.8	11.1	8.9	0.9	0.4				

Table A.3.3 Syonan Municipality employed and unemployed population by ethnic group, November 1943[21]

		Employed population			Unemployed population				
		Males	Females	Total employed	Males aged 15–50	Females aged 15–50	Under 15 and over 50	Total unemployed	Total
	Hokkien	78,441	7,900	86,341	7,620	50,060	109,526	167,206	253,547
	Cantonese	40,110	11,891	52,001	3,592	23,802	41,879	69,273	121,274
	Hakka	7,485	1,004	8,489	690	4,376	9,426	14,492	22,981
Chinese	Teochew	41,520	3,758	45,278	3,094	23,078	48,252	74,424	119,702
	Hainanese	14,326	627	14,953	1,231	5,809	12,746	19,786	34,739
	Others	44,497	6,625	51,122	2,945	22,870	46,546	72,361	123,483
	Subtotal	226,870	31,805	258,184	15,172	129,995	268,375	417,542	675,726
Malay		30,780	809	31,599	3,224	21,139	35,547	59,910	91,509
Indian		47,235	491	47,726	3,953	8,805	15,733	28,493	76,219
Eurasian		1,959	465	2,424	546	1,719	3,435	5,700	8,124
European		151	70	221	8	58	97	163	384
Others		946	179	1,119	186	862	1,550	2,598	3,717
Total		307,454	33,819	341,273	27,091	162,578	324,737	514,406	855,679

[21] For an explanation of the employed (*yūgyōsha*) and unemployed population (*mugyōsha*), see p. 134n7.

(cont'd overleaf)

Table A.3.3 (cont'd)

		Employed population			Unemployed population				Total
		Males	Females	Total employed	Males aged 15–50	Females aged 15–50	Under 15 and over 50	Total unemployed	
(%)									
Chinese	Hokkien	31.0	3.1	34.1	3.0	19.7	43.2	65.9	100.0
	Cantonese	33.1	9.8	42.9	3.0	19.6	34.5	57.1	100.0
	Hakka	32.6	4.3	36.9	3.0	19.1	41.0	63.1	100.0
	Teochew	34.7	3.1	37.8	2.6	19.3	40.3	62.2	100.0
	Hainanese	41.2	1.8	43.0	3.6	16.7	36.7	57.0	100.0
	Others	36.0	5.4	41.4	2.4	18.5	37.7	58.6	100.0
	Subtotal	33.5	4.7	38.2	2.9	19.2	39.7	61.8	100.0
Malay		33.6	0.9	34.5	3.5	23.1	38.9	65.5	100.0
Indian		62.0	0.6	62.6	5.2	11.6	20.6	37.4	100.0
Eurasian		24.1	5.7	29.8	6.7	21.2	42.3	70.2	100.0
European		30.4	18.2	57.6	2.1	15.1	25.2	42.4	100.0
Others		25.3	4.8	30.1	5.0	23.2	44.7	69.9	100.0
Total		35.3	4.0	39.9	3.2	19.0	37.9	60.1	100.0

Table A.3.4 Syonan Municipality household population by occupation, November 1943

	Householders				Other household members				Total household members				Total population, male and female	
	Male		Female		Male		Female		Male		Female			
	Number	%	Number	%	Number	%	Number	%	Number	%	Number	%	Number	%
Farming and fishing	17,646	10.9	524	6.3	10,141	7.0	2,790	11.6	27,787	9.0	3,314	9.8	31,101	9.1
Mining and manufacturing	28,194	17.2	910	10.9	26,134	18.0	3,415	13.4	54,328	17.7	4,325	12.8	58,653	17.2
Commerce	53,800	33.1	1,974	23.6	39,611	27.3	3,501	13.7	93,411	30.4	5,475	16.2	98,886	29.0
Transport	14,047	8.6	2	-	11,827	8.2	15	0.1	25,874	8.4	17	0.1	25,891	7.6
Government and professions	5,839	3.6	432	5.2	3,744	2.6	1,333	5.2	9,583	3.1	1,765	5.2	11,945	3.3
Coolies	25,408	15.6	1,621	19.4	37,808	26.1	4,382	17.2	63,216	20.6	6,003	17.7	69,219	20.3
Other	17,579	10.3	2,898	34.6	15,676	10.8	10,022	39.4	33,255	10.8	12,920	38.2	46,175	13.5
Total	162,513	100.0	8,361	100.0	144,941	100.0	25,458	100.0	307,454	100.0	33,819	100.0	341,273	100.0

Table A.3.5 Syonan Municipality occupation by ethnic group, November 1943

Occupation	Chinese								Other ethnic groups					Total
	Hokkien	Cantonese	Hakka	Teochew	Hainanese	Sub-total	Other Chinese	Total Chinese	Malay	Indian	Eurasian	European	Others	
Farming and fishing	12,420	1,404	755	7,563	854	22,996	4,823	27,879	2,788	406	18	1	9	31,101
Mining and manufacturing	8,158	19,165	2,260	3,756	1,665	35,004	13,044	48,048	3,823	6,135	537	17	93	58,653
Transport	12,145	995	101	2,036	571	15,848	8,053	18,901	4,523	2,329	84	2	52	25,891
Commerce	27,618	12,105	2,899	19,717	5,682	68,021	16,811	84,832	2,886	10,401	238	49	480	98,886
Government and professions	1,806	1,551	446	1,173	324	5,300	1,433	6,733	1,809	2,025	488	125	168	11,348
Coolies	15,865	7,155	1,004	6,680	2,566	33,270	5,988	39,258	11,852	17,782	237	-	90	69,219
Other	8,329	9,626	1,024	4,353	3,291	26,623	5,910	32,533	3,918	8,648	822	27	227	46,175
Total	86,341	52,001	8,489	45,278	14,953	207,062	51,122	258,184	31,599	47,726	2,424	221	1,119	341,273

Table A.3.5 (cont'd)

Occupation	Chinese								Other ethnic groups					Total
	Hokkien	Cantonese	Hakka	Teochew	Hainanese	Sub-total	Other Chinese	Total Chinese	Malay	Indian	Eurasian	European	Others	
(%)														
Farming and fishing	39.93	4.51	2.43	24.32	2.75	73.94	15.70	89.64	8.96	1.31	0.06		0.03	100.00
Mining and manufacturing	13.91	32.68	3.85	6.40	2.84	59.68	22.24	81.92	6.52	10.46	0.91	0.03	0.16	100.00
Transport	46.91	3.84	0.39	7.86	2.21	61.21	11.79	73.00	17.47	9.00	0.32	0.01	0.20	100.00
Commerce	27.93	12.24	2.93	19.94	5.75	62.79	17.00	85.79	2.92	10.52	0.24	0.05	0.48	100.00
Government and professions	15.91	13.67	3.93	10.34	2.85	46.73	12.63	59.33	15.94	17.85	4.30	1.10	1.48	100.00
Coolies	22.92	10.34	1.45	9.65	3.71	48.07	8.65	56.72	17.12	25.63	0.34	-	0.13	100.00
Other	13.04	20.34	2.22	9.43	7.13	57.66	12.80	70.46	8.48	18.73	1.78	0.06	0.49	100.00
Total	25.30	15.23	2.49	13.27	4.38	60.67	14.98	75.65	9.26	13.92	0.71	0.07	0.33	100.00

Table A.3.6 Syonan Municipality occupation by ethnic group and gender, November 1943

	Chinese								Other ethnic groups					
	Males													
Occupation	Hokkien	Cantonese	Hakka	Teochew	Hainanese	Subtotal	Other Chinese	Total Chinese	Malay	Indian	Eurasian	European	Others	Total
Farming and fishing	11,097	1,062	582	6,894	806	20,441	4,173	24,614	2,750	395	18	1	9	27,787
Mining and manufacturing	7,479	17,275	2,141	3,592	1,622	32,109	11,740	43,849	3,757	6,122	506	17	77	54,328
Transport	12,143	994	99	2,034	571	15,841	3,045	18,886	4,522	2,329	84	2	51	25,874
Commerce	26,754	10,120	2,733	19,013	5,541	64,161	15,577	79,738	2,776	10,264	142	48	443	93,411
Government and professions	1,542	1,114	328	955	301	4,240	1,149	5,389	1,680	1,954	363	62	135	9,583
Coolies	14,095	4,785	919	6,246	2,437	28,482	4,963	33,445	11,733	17,720	236	-	82	63,216
Other	5,331	4,760	683	2,786	3,048	16,608	3,550	20,453	3,572	8,451	610	21	143	38,255
Total	78,441	40,110	7,485	41,520	14,326	181,832	44,437	226,379	30,790	47,235	1,959	151	940	307,454

Table A.3.6 (cont'd)

	Chinese								Other ethnic groups					
	Females													
Occupation	Hokkien	Cantonese	Hakka	Teochew	Hainanese	Subtotal	Other Chinese	Total Chinese	Malay	Indian	Eurasian	European	Others	Total
Farming and fishing	1,323	342	173	669	48	2,555	710	3,265	38	11	-	-	-	3,314
Mining and manufacturing	679	1,890	119	164	43	2,895	1,304	4,199	66	13	31	-	16	4,325
Transport	3	1	2	2	-	7	8	15	1	-	-	-	1	17
Commerce	864	1,985	166	704	141	3,860	1,234	5,094	110	137	96	1	37	5,475
Government and professions	264	437	118	218	23	1,066	284	1,344	129	71	125	63	38	1,765
Coolies	1,770	2,370	85	434	129	4,788	1,025	5,813	119	62	1	-	8	6,003
Other	2,998	866	341	1,567	243	10,015	2,060	12,075	346	197	212	6	84	12,920
Total	7,900	11,891	1,004	3,758	627	25,180	6,625	31,805	809	491	465	70	179	33,819

Table A.3.7 Syonan Municipality occupational subgroups by ethnic group, November 1943

			Chinese							Other ethnic groups					
			Hokkien	Cantonese	Hakka	Teochew	Hainanese	Other Chinese	Total Chinese	Malay	Indian	Eurasian	European	Other	Total
Farming and fishing	1	Farmers	11,066	1,344	743	5,679	541	4,163	23,536	439	381	10	1	7	24,374
	2	Fishermen	1,354	60	12	1,884	313	720	4,343	2,349	25	8	-	2	6,727
Mining and manufacturing	3	Miners	4	5	5	223	3	43	283	-	2	-	-	-	285
	4	Blacksmiths	205	922	480	121	36	486	2,250	57	123	2	-	3	2,435
	5	Mechanics	1,355	5,309	186	632	267	2,534	10,283	1,330	2,272	291	3	32	14,211
	6	Electricians	434	406	37	304	87	288	1,356	638	493	129	8	15	2,839
	7	Factory workers	526	241	52	101	106	300	1,326	417	104	27	1	1	1,876
	8	Tailors	348	2,264	385	131	88	1,036	4,266	82	649	12	2	15	5,020
	9	Shoemakers	166	665	433	137	46	626	2,073	68	73	-	-	4	2,218
	10	Makers of foodstuff	293	592	51	171	175	364	1,646	24	243	-	-	1	1,914
	11	Carpenters	1,846	4,503	278	390	295	3,563	11,075	218	348	2	-	5	11,648
	12	Building workers	627	943	93	153	24	605	2,445	22	750	20	1	-	3,238
	13	Printers	164	652	22	73	51	258	1,220	50	125	3	-	2	1,400
	14	Painters	542	849	28	306	29	638	2,392	30	200	-	-	1	2,623
	15	Other workers	1,648	1,814	210	794	458	2,309	7,233	887	753	51	2	14	8,940

Table A.3.7 (cont'd)

			Chinese							Other ethnic groups					
			Hokkien	Cantonese	Hakka	Teochew	Hainanese	Other Chinese	Total Chinese	Malay	Indian	Eurasian	European	Other	Total
Transport	16	Drivers	1,939	175	46	246	123	480	3,009	3,238	1,452	42	-	9	7,750
	17	Rickshaw pullers	6,446	525	24	1,067	15	1,243	9,320	21	35	8	-	35	9,419
	18	Boatmen	2,041	60	9	442	224	690	3,466	331	103	1	-	4	3,905
	19	Other workers in water transport	1,521	181	11	196	196	576	2,681	788	309	3	-	2	3,783
	20	Workers in land transport	153	36	10	57	12	42	310	124	341	11	1	-	787
	21	Warehousemen	45	18	1	28	1	22	115	21	89	19	1	2	247
Commerce	22	Goldsmiths	68	477	175	137	19	246	1,122	29	161	1	-	-	1,313
	23	Merchants	7,973	2,168	893	4,815	871	3,575	20,295	1,260	3,734	40	32	241	25,602
	24	Food and drink shopkeepers	678	138	37	226	342	387	1,808	22	221	15	-	8	2,074
	25	Salesmen and shop assistants	6,872	2,555	975	4,496	2,059	5,303	22,260	300	2,520	128	2	109	25,319
	26	Hawkers and stall keepers	10,402	5,978	610	9,270	2,076	6,500	34,837	1,091	2,418	13	-	43	38,402
	27	Moneylenders	430	158	95	523	66	181	1,463	70	240	13	7	43	1,836
	28	Brokers	449	142	37	167	47	124	966	89	210	23	6	32	1,406
	29	Barbers	745	489	77	83	202	485	2,081	25	817	5	2	4	2,934

(cont'd overleaf)

Table A.3.7 (cont'd)

			Chinese							Other ethnic groups					
			Hokkien	Cantonese	Hakka	Teochew	Hainanese	Other Chinese	Total Chinese	Malay	Indian	Eurasian	European	Other	Total
Government and professions	30	Police and army	75	14	8	39	10	115	261	479	382	15	1	12	1,150
	31	Government service	283	213	35	135	90	138	393	654	635	181	7	12	2,382
	32	Physicians	668	563	248	237	114	401	2,231	134	405	120	11	19	2,920
	33	Teachers	185	61	35	50	5	248	584	224	150	81	17	27	1,083
	34	Other professions	595	701	120	712	105	531	2,764	318	453	91	89	98	3,813
Coolies	35	Coolies	15,865	7,155	1,064	6,630	2,566	5,988	39,258	11,852	17,782	237	-	90	69,219
Other	36	Domestic servants	3,217	6,038	353	1,806	2,854	3,187	17,460	2,176	1,671	180	-	81	21,576
	37	Clerks	4,410	1,850	536	2,183	284	1,652	10,955	712	2,401	621	16	113	14,818
	38	Guards	76	101	13	85	10	53	341	255	3,457	4	-	10	4,067
	39	Other workers	623	1,637	97	269	133	1,015	3,777	775	1,119	17	3	23	5,714
		Total	86,341	52,001	8,489	45,278	14,953	51,122	258,184	31,599	47,726	2,424	221	1,119	341,273

Table A.3.8 Syonan Municipality occupation by gender, 1931 and November 1943

	Males				Females				Total			
	1931		November 1943		1931		November 1943		1931		November 1943	
	Number	%	Number	%	Number	%	Number	%	Number	%	Number	%
Farming and fishing	28,640	11.2	27,737	9	1,998	11.1	3,314	9.8	30,638	11.2	31,101	9.1
Mining and manufacturing	44,761	17.5	54328	17.7	2,447	13.6	4,325	12.8	47,208	17.2	58,653	17.2
Commerce	62,959	24.6	93,411	30.4	1,501	8.3	5,476	16.2	64,460	23.4	98,836	29
Drivers	40,231	15.7	25874	8.4	975	5.4	17	0.1	41,206	15	25,891	7.6
Government and professions	10,559	4.1	9583	3.1	1,723	9.6	1,765	5.2	12,282	4.5	11,348	3.3
Coolies	26,309	10.2	63,216	20.6	992	5.5	6,003	17.7	27,301	10	69,219	20.3
Other	42,828	16.7	33,255	10.8	8,391	46.5	12,920	38.2	51,209	18.7	46,175	13.5
Total	256,277	100.0	307,454	100.0	18,027	100.0	33,819	100.0	274,304	100.0	341,273	100.0

Table A.3.9 Syonan Municipality occupation of heads of household and other household members, November 1943

	Employed heads of household			Household members with employed household heads (A)			Household members with unemployed household heads (B)			Total household members (A+B)		
	Males	Females	Total	Males	Females	Total	Males	Females	Total	Males	Females	Total
Farming and fishing	17,646	524	18,170	9,409	2,734	12,133	732	66	798	10,141	2,790	12,931
Mining and manufacturing	28,194	910	29,104	19,789	2,124	21,913	6,345	1,291	7,636	26,134	3,415	29,549
Transport	14,047	2	14,049	10,402	11	10,413	1,425	4	1,429	11,827	15	11,842
Commerce	53,800	1,974	55,774	34,020	2,622	36,642	5,591	879	6,470	39,611	3,501	42,112
Government and professions	5,839	432	6,271	3,086	1,084	4,170	658	249	907	3,744	1,333	5,077
Coolies	25,408	1,621	27,029	32,693	3,142	35,841	5,109	1,240	6,349	37,808	4,382	42,190
Other	17,579	2,893	20,477	12,170	7,727	19,897	3,506	2,295	5,801	15,676	10,002	25,698
Total	162,513	8,361	170,874	121,575	19,434	141,009	23,366	6,024	29,390	144,941	25,459	170,399

Table A.3.9 (cont'd)

	Employed heads of household			Household members with employed household heads (A)			Household members with unemployed household heads (B)			Total household members (A+B)		
	Males	Females	Total	Males	Females	Total	Males	Females	Total	Males	Females	Total
(%)												
Farming and fishing	10.9	6.3	10.6	7.7	14.0	8.6	3.1	1.1	2.7	7.0	11.0	7.6
Mining and manufacturing	17.3	10.9	17.0	16.3	10.9	15.5	27.2	21.4	26.0	18.0	13.4	17.3
Transport	8.6	-	8.2	8.6	0.6	7.4	6.1	0.1	4.9	8.2	0.1	6.9
Commerce	33.1	23.6	32.6	28.0	13.5	26.0	23.9	14.6	22.0	27.3	13.8	25.3
Government and professions	3.6	5.2	3.7	2.5	5.6	3.0	2.8	4.1	3.1	2.6	5.2	3.0
Coolies	15.6	19.4	15.8	26.9	16.2	25.4	21.9	20.6	21.6	26.1	17.2	24.8
Other	10.8	34.7	12.0	10.0	39.8	14.1	15.0	38.1	19.7	10.8	39.3	15.1
Total	100.0	100.0	100.0	100.0	100.0	100.0	100.0	100.0	100.0	100.0	100.0	100.0

Table A.3.10 Syonan Municipality unemployed population by ethnic group, November 1943

		Chinese												
		Hokkien	Cantonese	Hakka	Teochew	Hainanese	Other	Subtotal	Malay	Indian	Eurasian	European	Other	Total
Unemployed heads of household	Males (15–50)	967	376	131	454	519	385	2632	664	994	167	4	37	4,498
	Females (15–50)	3,111	2,709	291	1,631	412	1,651	9,835	1,181	499	212	6	96	11,829
	Total (15–50)	4,078	3,085	422	2,085	761	2,036	12,467	1,845	1,493	379	10	133	16,327
	Total (under 15, over 50)	2,771	1,724	191	1,175	231	945	7,037	746	456	306	12	66	8,623
	Total	6,849	4,809	613	3,260	992	2,981	19,504	2,591	1,949	685	22	199	24,950
Household members with employed household heads	Males (15–50)	5,493	2,593	452	2,161	744	2,144	13,587	2,067	2,438	187	3	93	18,375
	Females (15–50)	41,851	17,846	3,737	19,426	4,996	19,613	107,483	18,164	7,375	1,054	41	606	134,723
	Total (15–50)	47,344	20,139	4,209	21,581	5,740	21,757	121,070	20,231	9,813	1,241	44	699	153,098
	Total (Under 15, over 50)	94,583	33,863	8,389	41,621	11,063	40,975	230,491	30,607	12,941	2,145	49	1127	277,363
	Total	141,927	54,302	12,598	68,203	16,803	62,732	351,561	30,838	22,754	3,386	93	1826	430,461

Table A.3.10 (cont'd)

		Chinese												
		Hokkien	Cantonese	Hakka	Teochew	Hainanese	Other	Subtotal	Malay	Indian	Eurasian	European	Other	Total
Household members with unemployed household heads	Males (15–50)	1,160	623	107	479	166	416	2953	496	528	192	1	56	4,218
	Females (15–50)	5,098	3,847	328	2,027	371	1,606	12,677	1,794	931	453	11	160	16,026
	Total (15–50)	6,258	3,870	435	2,506	539	2,022	15,630	2,287	1,454	645	12	216	20,244
	Total (Under 15, over 50)	12,172	6,292	846	5,456	1,452	4,626	30,844	4,194	2,336	984	36	357	38,751
	Total	184,430	10,162	1,281	7,962	1,991	6,648	46,474	6,481	3,790	1,629	48	573	58,995
Total	Males (15–50)	7,620	3,592	690	3,094	1,231	2,945	19,172	3,224	3,955	546	8	186	27,091
	Females (15–50)	50,060	23,802	4,376	23,078	5,809	22,870	129,995	21,139	8,805	1,719	58	862	162,578
	Total (15–50)	57,680	27,394	5,060	26,172	7,040	25,815	149,167	24,363	12,760	2,265	66	1048	189,669
	Total (Under 15, over 50)	109,526	41,879	9,426	48,252	12,746	46,546	268,375	35,547	15,733	3,435	97	1550	324,737
	Total	167,206	69,273	14,492	74,484	19,786	72,361	417,542	59,910	28,493	5,700	163	2598	514,406

Table A.3.11 Syonan Municipality percentage of employed and unemployed population by ethnic group, November 1943

		Population employed %	Population unemployed %	Males aged 15–50 as % of total population	Dependency ratio[22]
Chinese	Hokkien	34.1	65.9	59.8	76.0
	Cantonese	42.9	57.1	55.5	
	Hakka	30.9	63.1	56.2	
	Teochew	37.8	62.2	72.6	
	Hainanese	43.0	57.0	70.7	
	Other	41.4	58.6	61.7	
	Subtotal	38.2	61.8	60.3	
Malay		34.5	65.5	60.8	63.5
Indian		62.6	37.4	84.6	26.0
Eurasian		29.8	70.2	53.4	73.6
European		57.6	42.2	55.4	33.7
Other		30.1	69.9	52.0	71.5
Total		39.9	60.1	63.0	61.1

Notes:

1. Percentage of population employed = Number of population with employment ÷ Whole population x 100
2. Percentage of population unemployed = Number of population without employment ÷ Whole population x 100
3. Males aged 15–50 as % total population = Male population employed + Male unemployed aged 15 to 50 ÷ Total population x 100
4. Dependency ratio = Unemployed population aged 0–14 and over 50 ÷ Total employed population + Unemployed population ages 15 to 50

[22] This is a modified concept of the dependency ratio, which attempts to show more accurately the burden of the employed population in supporting those who were unemployed because they were either young or old (aged 0–14 or over 50). The concept is modified because it takes account of the young and old who were in fact employed.

A.2. List of Occupations

Figure A.3.1 List of occupations in English and Chinese

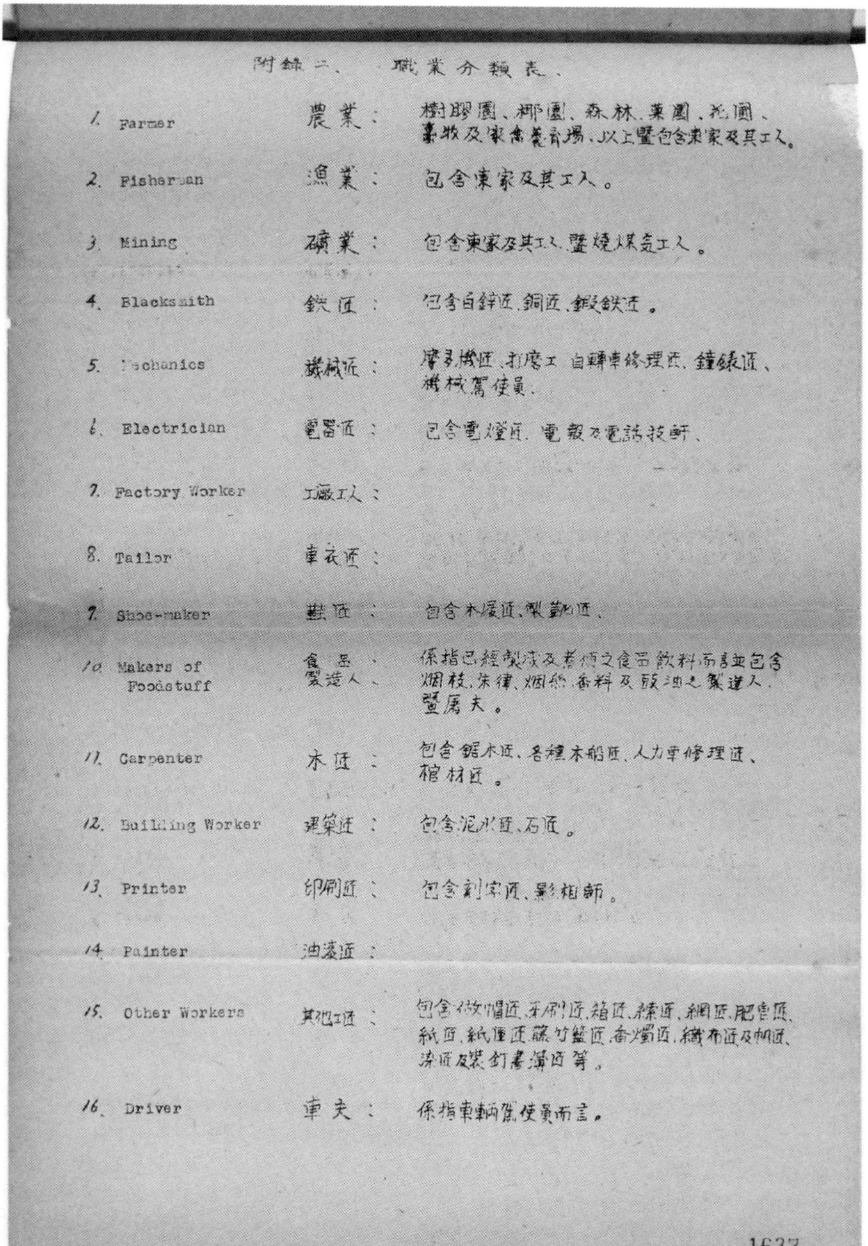

附錄二、 職業分類表、

1. Farmer	農業：	樹膠園、椰園、森林、菓園、花園、畜牧及家禽養育場、以上暨包含東家及其工人。
2. Fisherman	漁業：	包含東家及其工人。
3. Mining	礦業：	包含東家及其工人、暨燒煤炭工人。
4. Blacksmith	鉄匠：	包含白鉄匠、銅匠、鍜鉄匠。
5. Mechanics	機械匠：	摩多機匠、打磨工 自轉車修理匠、鐘錶匠、機械駕使員、
6. Electrician	電器匠：	包含電燈匠、電報及電話技師、
7. Factory Worker	工廠工人：	
8. Tailor	車衣匠：	
9. Shoe-maker	鞋匠：	包含木屐匠、製鞋匠、
10. Makers of Foodstuff	食品製造人：	係指已經製成及煮便之食品飲料而言並包含烟枝、朱律、烟絲、香料及豉油之製造人、暨屠夫。
11. Carpenter	木匠：	包含鋸木匠、各種木船匠、人力車修理匠、棺材匠。
12. Building Worker	建築匠：	包含泥水匠、石匠。
13. Printer	印刷匠：	包含刻字匠、影相師。
14. Painter	油漆匠：	
15. Other Workers	其他工匠：	包含做帽匠、牙刷匠、箱匠、藤匠、網匠、肥皂匠、紙匠、紙匣匠、藤竹籃匠、香燭匠、織布匠及帆匠、漆匠及裝釘書簿匠等。
16. Driver	車夫：	係指車輛駕使員而言。

1637

Figure A.3.1 (cont'd)

17. Rickshaw Puller	人力車夫：	包含東洋車及三輪車夫。
18. Boatman	艇夫：	係指舢舨夫、艍舡及駁船夫。
19. Other Workers in Water Transportation	其他水上運輸工人：	包含水手、船員、行船人、船務員。
20. Workers in Land Transportation	陸上運輸工人：	包含火車、電車、巴士車之工人、收票員、查票員、記時員、開車員等。
21. Warehouseman	貨倉管理員：	包含管棧員及包裝員。
22. Goldsmith	打金匠：	包含打銀匠。
23. Merchant	商家：	包含店東、商東、商人、包租人、舊貨商、生草药販。
24. Eating & Drinking Shop-Keeper	茶樓飯館商及經理：	係指食堂、咖啡店、飲料店、茶樓、菜館、客棧、旅館及飯店之東家及經理而言。
25 Salesman Shop-Assistant	推銷員及店員：	包含拍賣員、枱球記錄員、收銀員、男女招待員。
26. Hawker Stall-Keeper	過街小販及排攤人：	
27. Money-Lender Pawn-Broker Landlord	揭借業、当店東、屋主及地主：	包含銀行商及貨倉主並經理人。
28. Broker & Contractor	經紀及包工人：	包含掮客人及起落貨包工人。
29. Barber	剪髮匠：	
30. Police & Army	警察員及陸軍：	包含消防隊人員、軍補。
31. Government Service	政府職員：	包含協警。
32. Physician	醫師：	包含医生、医生助手、配药員、製药師、看護婦、接生婦及牙科医師。
33. Teacher	教員：	
34. Other Professions	其他專門職業人員：	包含繙譯員、美術家、戲劇員、音樂家、記者、著作人、律師、畫測師、尼姑、和尚、道士、相卜及講古事人。

1638

CHAPTER 4

Reorganizing Commercial Businesses in Syonan Municipality

Higuchi Gorō and Nagamori Masaji, September 1944

This report is part of the research report on Syonan Municipality by Higuchi Gorō and Nagamori Shōji of the Chōsabu. Statistical material on merchandise distribution derives from Merchandise Distributors Declaration Cards gathered by the Syonan Municipality Department of Commerce and Industry. Other information and survey assistance was offered by other departments of Syonan Municipality.

Contents[1]

1. **An Overview of the Commercial Population**[2]
2. **The Present State of Business and Its Reorganization**
    (1) Traders in staple foods (note 1)
    (2) Traders in supplementary foods (note 2)
    (3) General commerce (note 3)

[1] A list of contents does not appear in the original report but is inserted here for convenience and to conform with other Chōsabu reports.

[2] The category of commerce here includes both retailers and wholesalers, who in Japanese are called *shōnin* (merchant/tradesman) and who submitted Merchandise Distributors Declaration Cards. Other categories of distributive trades, such as restaurateurs, stallholders and hawkers, moneylenders, and barbers, are managed with different licences and are not the focus of this report.

(4) Restaurants
(5) Hawkers and street vendors

3. Important Information on Effecting Changes in Occupation

Supplementary Material: Summary of Merchandise Distributors Declaration Cards

1. Method of Aggregation

2. Number of Local Distributors of Merchandise

(1) Total number of traders

(2) Traders by trade

(3) Traders by area

(4) Traders by ethnic group

(5) Traders by length of time in trade

(6) Traders by capital

(7) Criteria of business resilience by trade: An experimental analysis

(8) Traders by sales and capital turnover in each trade[3]

(9) Number of family members and other employees[4]

3. Organization of Japanese Merchandise Distributors

(1) Total number of traders

(2) Traders by trade

(3) Traders by area

(4) Traders by length of time in trade

(5) Traders by capital size

(6) Traders by sales and capital turnover in each trade

(7) Number of family members and employees

Appendix Tables

---

[3] Capital turnover is defined as average sales divided by average capital.

[4] In this chapter, unless otherwise indicated, family members include the spouses, children, parents and relatives of traders, and also the traders themselves in the statistical tables. The overall category is 'persons in commerce' whether or not they actually work as family workers. Separate from this category, non-family employees are 'employees in commerce'.

1. An Overview of the Commercial Population

According to the census [of Syonan Municipality Department of Police Administration, using Resident Certificates as resident registry] compiled and aggregated in November 1943, the local population of Syonan Municipality (excluding Seletar and the islands) was 855,679. The employed population numbered 341,273, and those not in work 514,406 (see table 4.1).[5] Twenty-nine per cent (98,886) of the employed were in commercial occupations [i.e., in all distributive trades] (see table 4.2). A more detailed breakdown of employment in commercial occupations is given in table 4.3.

The Census of Distributive Trades [by Syonan Municipality Department of Commerce and Industry, using Merchandise Distributors Declaration Cards] compiled and aggregated in May 1944 showed 8,025 local traders [in the narrower category of commerce].[6] This number may have included some stallholders. The November 1943 census reported the number of persons who engaged in commerce as 26,915, excluding employees in commerce. As the note to table 4.3 indicates, the numbers calculated in the November 1943 census may be an overestimate.[7] Nevertheless, despite the difference in research dates, the data can be used to give an estimate of the number of family workers: that is, 26,915 – 8,025 = 18,890.

It can be assumed that most of these 18,890 who engage in commerce are registered as family workers. According to the May 1944 census of distributive trades, 53,855 family members, including the 8,025 traders themselves mentioned above [together with their spouses, children, parents and relatives], are in the category of commerce [whether or not they actually work as family workers].[8] These 53,855 are made up of 18,341 males, 15,381 females and 20,133 children. In May this year [1944], there were 21,683 employees in commerce, a figure very close to that in the November 1943 census.[9]

---

[5] *Yūgyōsha*, as defined in chapter 3.

[6] The 8,025 local traders consisted of 2,191 staple food traders, 627 supplementary food traders and 5,207 general traders (from tables 4.4–4.6).

[7] The authors appear to have been dissatisfied with the way the Department of Police Administration placed persons of unknown occupation in the category of commerce.

[8] The 53,855 family members consisted of 15,491 in staple foods, 4,242 in supplementary foods, and 34,122 in general trades (from tables 4.4–4.6).

[9] 21,684 in November 1943 (from table 4.3). From this estimate, we can assume the following numbers: traders 8,025; family workers of the traders 18,890; non-working family members 26,940; employees of the traders 21,683.

2. The Present State of Business and Its Reorganization

(1) Traders in staple foods

In May 1944 in the category of staple foods, there were 2,191 traders and 15,491 persons in trading families, including the traders themselves and family members [13,300], and 5,018 employees (table 4.4). We note here that the Food Supply Office of Syonan Municipality is the central rationing agency for rice, salt and sugar. More than 1,000 distributing stations have been set up as the last part of the rationing chain. The number of stations in each precinct has been determined by population distribution. However, as well as rice, salt and sugar, the distributing stations sell uncontrolled foods and sundry goods.[10] Rice, salt and sugar are not necessarily a large proportion of total sales at some of these distribution stations.

In the intermediate distribution stages there are 69 wholesalers, 42 for rice, 7 for salt and 20 for sugar. Their function has become only a warehousing one. Apart from them, to handle rationing to institutions and large customers, there are 22 specialist retailers for salt and 29 for sugar. There have been cuts in rations of salt and sugar allocated to institutions, making it difficult for the specialist retailers to carry on business.

Of the 2,191 grain merchants and grocers in table 4.4, 1,120 sell foodstuffs controlled by the Food Supply Office. This leaves 1,071 other traders selling only non-controlled foods such as grains other than rice.

The trade in staple foods poses two problems for the future. One is the reorganization of the 1,120 traders involved in distributing controlled foods. The other is reorganizing the distribution of uncontrolled foods, which involves 1,071 traders. The distribution of controlled foods should be reorganized as soon as possible, by ensuring that the size of businesses is reasonable and by trying to improve the efficiency of ration management. Uncontrolled food businesses should be integrated with controlled food businesses so that the distributing stations can trade in these foods on their premises.

---

[10] Table 4.4 shows that more than 90 per cent of staple food traders were general grocers, who sold both controlled and uncontrolled foods and sundry goods.

Table 4.1 Syonan Municipality population by employment status, November 1943

		Employed population			Non-employed population				
		Male	Female	Total	15–50 Male	15–50 Female	Over 51, under 15	Total	Total
Chinese	Hokkien	78,441	7,900	88,341	7,620	50,060	109,526	167,206	253,547
	Cantonese	40,110	11,891	52,001	3,592	23,802	41,879	69,273	121,274
	Hakka	7,485	1,004	8,489	690	4,376	9,426	14,492	22,981
	Teochew	41,520	3,758	45,278	3,094	23,078	48,252	74,424	119,702
	Hainanese	14,326	627	14,953	1,231	5,809	12,746	19,786	34,739
	Others	44,497	6,625	51,122	2,945	22,870	46,546	72,361	123,483
	Subtotal	226,379	31,805	258,184	19,172	129,995	268,375	417,542	675,726
	Malay	30,790	809	31,599	3,224	21,139	35,547	59,910	91,509
	Indian	47,235	491	47,726	3,955	8,805	15,733	28,493	76,219
	Eurasian	1,959	465	2,424	546	1,719	3,435	5,700	8,124
	European	151	78	221	8	58	97	163	384
	Others	94	179	1,119	186	863	1,550	2,598	3,717
	Total	307,454	33,819	341,273	27,091	162,578	324,737	514,406	855,679

Note: Excludes Seletar Naval Port.

Table 4.2 Syonan Municipality employed population, 1941 and November 1943[11]

	Male				Female				Total			
	1931		1943		1931		1943		1931		1943	
	Number	%	Number	%	Number	%	Number	%	Number	%	Number	%
Farming and fishing	28,640	11.2	27,737	9.0	1,998	11.1	3,314	9.8	30,638	11.2	31,101	9.1
Mining and manufacturing	44,761	17.5	54,328	17.7	2,447	13.6	4,325	12.8	47,208	17.2	58,653	17.2
Commerce	62,959	24.6	93,411	30.4	1,501	8.3	5,475	16.2	34,460	23.4	98,886	29.0
Transport	40,231	15.7	25,874	8.4	975	5.4	17	0.1	41,206	15.0	25,891	7.6
Government and professions	10,559	4.1	9,583	3.1	1,723	9.6	1,765	5.2	12,252	4.5	1,348	3.3
Others	42,818	16.7	33,255	10.8	8,391	46.5	12,920	36.2	51,209	18.7	46,175	13.5
Coolie	26,309	10.2	63,216	20.6	992	5.5	6,003	17.7	27,301	10.0	69,219	20.3
Total	256,277	100.0	307,454	100.0	18,027	100.0	33,819	100.0	274,304	100.0	341,273	100.0

[11] See chapter 3 for further details.

Table 4.3 Syonan Municipality commercial occupations, November 1943[12]

Trade	Number of traders
Commerce, business owners	26,915
Employees in commerce	21,684
Restaurant owners	2,074
Restaurant employees	3,635
Hawkers and street vendors	38,402
Moneylenders, pawnbrokers and landowners	1,836
Brokers and contractors	1,406
Barbers	2,934
Total	98,886

Note: Commerce includes workers who did not specify their occupation or cannot be classified. Therefore, the number of those who are in commerce may be overstated.

Table 4.4 Syonan Municipality local staple food traders, employees and family members, May 1944

Trade	Business owners	Employees	Family members (including business owners)			
			Males	Females	Children	Total
Rice and grain traders	85	453	237	270	270	777
General grocers	2,106	4,565	5,268	4,114	5,332	14,714
Total	2,191	5,018	5,505	4,384	5,602	15,491

Surveyed by Syonan Municipality Department of Commerce and Industry.

(2) Traders in supplementary foods [i.e., vegetables, fish, meat and oil]

According to the May census, there are 627 supplementary food traders, excluding hawkers and street vendors. There are 4,242 people in this group [of trading families], including the owners of businesses and their family members. Additionally, there are 794 employees.

---

[12] See chapter 3, table A.3.7 for details.

Table 4.5 Syonan Municipality local non-staple food traders, employees and family members, May 1944

Trade	Business owners	Employees	Family members (including business owners)			
			Males	Females	Children	Total
Greengrocers	159	262	329	266	424	1,019
Fishmongers	266	220	574	492	560	1,626
Butchers	107	80	201	196	329	726
Dried fish sellers	42	69	127	102	122	351
Cooking oil sellers	53	163	186	159	175	520
Total	627	794	1,417	1,215	1,610	4,242

Surveyed by Syonan Municipality Department of Commerce and Industry.

(i) Greengrocers

Twenty-five distributing stations in the markets have been appointed under the control of the Syonan Vegetable and Fruit Rationing Association, and 22 outside the markets, a total of 47. All 25 of the distributing stations inside the markets have set themselves up as companies [or guilds (*kong-si*)]. These companies have 556 members working for them as greengrocers in the markets. Those greengrocers [in companies] share the profits from sales of controlled vegetables and fruit within each company. At the same time, as individuals they sell uncontrolled vegetables and fruit produced on Syonan Island. In addition to these greengrocers, there are 2,746 hawkers and street vendors holding licences who sell greengroceries. As indicated above, they operate in the uncontrolled greengroceries sector.[13]

(ii) Fishmongers

There are 40 appointed distributors in the markets and 30 outside them, making a total of 70. All 40 of the distributors inside the markets take the form of companies (*kong-si*), from which 840 persons work in the market as fishmongers and are affiliated to one or other company. Profits from fish sales are divided between fishmongers, but individual shops have been closed. This is because fish distribution is wholly controlled, and it is impossible for individual shops to buy fish on the free market.

[13] The term 'market' refers to physical markets in Syonan. There were perhaps one or two markets in each police precinct.

(iii) Butchers

Thirty-nine distributing stations have been appointed in the markets and 27 outside them, a total of 66. In the markets, all 39 distributing stations are companies and have 253 butchers. Profits from meat sales are divided between butchers affiliated to each company. The position regarding individual shops is the same as for fishmongers, since meat rations are totally controlled.

(iv) Dried fish sellers

There are 42 appointed stations in the markets and 26 outside them, making a total of 68 appointed stations. All 42 distributing stations are companies, and 339 persons work for their affiliated companies inside the markets as dried fish sellers. They divide profits from dried fish sales. Their situation is the same as that of fishmongers, and the collection and distribution of fish is totally controlled.

(v) Cooking oil sellers

There are 39 appointed distributing stations in the market and 30 outside, making a total of 69. They engage in the distribution of controlled cooking oil. However, cooking oil from Riau Islands and Johore is not rationed or price-controlled.

As shown above, there are 320 distributors of the five supplementary foods. Most are distributors who were approved to continue businesses that they began before the outbreak of the war. For distributors outside the markets, we need to take into consideration the size of the local population in each precinct and convenient locations for serving it. There are quite a few former restaurants, coffee shops and grocers [outside the market] that have now been appointed as rationing stations for supplementary foods. In general, the number of distributors is appropriate. Therefore, the tasks that lie ahead relating to the sale of supplementary foods are confined to the following points.

Ideally, rationing of fruit and vegetables grown on Syonan Island should be handled by the 47 appointed distributing stations, which get their entire stock from the Syonan Vegetable and Fruit Rationing Association. But if this ideal is attempted immediately, it might destroy the existing complicated collection and distribution system, which is an intricate network, and create unease about food shortages. Consequently, to be effective, reform must be postponed until there is a higher yield of vegetables and fruit and greater quantities delivered, including supplies from outside the island.[14] Therefore, it seems better to allow

[14] See chapter 9.

the continued operation of greengrocers in the market, and of street hawkers who sell vegetables and fruit grown on Syonan Island.

The collection and distribution of fish, meat and dried fish are completely controlled, and employ a total of 1,432 persons in the markets. As already noted, the shops in the markets have assumed the form of companies and divide their profits. Some traders, except for those who also work as rationing clerks, may run their business outside the markets and also deal in the black market. In these cases, business permits should be revoked, and these individuals should be urged to change their occupations and become workers or farmers.

Traders who sell uncontrolled supplementary foods such as dried vegetables and grains other than rice still have to be reorganized into businesses of a reasonable size, and the effectiveness of rationing management must be improved.

(3) General commerce

As shown in table 4.6, the May census found 5,207 traders in general commerce apart from traders in staples and supplementary foods. (This number excludes licensed pharmacists and other traders and street hawkers who are licensed by company regulation bylaws.) Including traders themselves, a total of 34,122 members of trading families and 15,871 employees work in general commerce. About 52 per cent of traders entered their occupations after the outbreak of war. Data for the main businesses are as shown in table 4.6.

Table 4.6 Syonan Municipality local traders, employees and family members in general commerce, May 1944

	Business owners	Employees	Family members (incl. business owners)			
			Males	Females	Children	Total
Liquor sellers	254	770	731	753	910	2,394
Drapers	311	872	602	511	759	1,872
Building materials suppliers	103	1,373	319	345	464	1,128
China and earthenware sellers	95	378	265	218	349	832
Gramophone sellers and repairers	13	40	37	33	39	109
Cobblers	225	541	440	407	480	1,327

Table 4.6 (cont'd)

	Business owners	Employees	Family members (incl. business owners)			
			Males	Females	Children	Total
Engravers and printers	24	52	43	49	42	134
Stationers	125	917	386	383	549	1,318
Musical instrument sellers	15	30	41	40	61	142
Sanitary goods sellers	9	35	14	11	12	37
Antique dealers	15	30	29	25	33	87
Hatters and milliners	7	188	22	19	30	71
Tinware sellers	40	73	75	66	122	263
Fishing tool sellers	16	108	59	80	117	256
Tea traders	37	144	91	92	101	284
Tailors	260	531	472	446	641	1,559
Furniture sellers	135	469	300	247	356	903
Electrical appliance sellers and repairers	78	281	168	194	229	591
Florists	12	20	25	21	17	63
Leather goods sellers	170	459	393	294	285	972
Automobile part sellers and repairers	106	322	277	268	414	959
Book and magazine sellers	41	56	89	72	69	230
Camera sellers and repairers	13	24	20	28	38	86
Funeral directors	35	116	83	77	104	264
Mine and plantation suppliers	6	27	16	25	23	64

(cont'd overleaf)

Table 4.6 (cont'd)

	Business owners	Employees	Family members (incl. business owners)			
			Males	Females	Children	Total
Watch sellers and repairers	199	237	346	366	449	1,161
Sporting goods sellers	11	19	16	12	12	40
Confectioners	104	432	230	176	237	643
Haberdashers	796	2,106	1,624	1,244	1,650	4,518
Rattan goods traders	48	116	89	84	118	291
Machinery sellers and repairers	99	446	244	284	398	926
Glassware sellers	45	88	93	77	90	260
Wood and charcoal traders	138	215	330	296	373	999
Bicycle part sellers and repairers	256	434	473	406	543	1,422
Toy sellers	9	33	13	9	27	49
Jewellers	206	1,011	573	546	767	1,886
Rope traders	10	73	25	21	36	82
Livestock feed suppliers	92	181	242	175	287	704
Tobacco traders	687	867	1,256	630	734	2,620
Others	362	1,817	868	752	956	2,576
Total	5,207	15,871	11,419	9,782	12,921	34,122

Surveyed by Syonan Municipality Department of Commerce and Industry.

(i) Drapers

Drapers are doing almost no business because stocks are so low and few rationing tickets are distributed among the citizens. Their business comes to life only when they sell imports [from other parts of the Greater East Asia Co-prosperity Sphere] such as rayon, which is distributed from the Syonan Rationing Association through the Syonan Overseas Chinese Traders Association. There are, however, few trade goods. Sales are consequently very low compared with the capital of these traders, and they have severe financial problems.

Recently, some have been operating as drapers and at the same time selling everyday sundries such as tea and coffee. Some drapers have also started to rent a part of their shop to other traders to sell shoes, leather goods and cosmetics. A few drapers attempt to give the impression that they manage this entire business themselves, but in other cases multiple traders operate independently in one shop.

(ii) Tailors

Fabrics for clothing are usually sold by rationing tickets and then made up by tailors in their shops. But stocks of fabrics and threads are very low and there are also few tickets, so these tailors are doing almost no business. Their current situation is identical to that of drapers, in that some tailors also sell everyday sundries in their shops, or raise income by renting part of their shop to other traders.

(iii) Haberdashers

The stock of imported goods is becoming very low. Nor can further imports [from other parts of the Greater East Asia Co-prosperity Sphere] be expected. The sale of locally manufactured products is falling, because of shortages in raw materials. The current outlook is poor. In an attempt to make good losses, haberdashers sell everyday sundries, but this makes up only a little of the shortfall. Haberdashers are in a bad situation, and some have revealed a desire to change occupation to help increase food production.

Haberdashers, who number 796, are the largest group of local merchandise distributors. Sixty-three per cent of them opened their shops after the outbreak of war.

(iv) Cobblers and leather goods traders

It is becoming difficult to obtain raw materials and products. Eighty-four per cent of leather goods traders and 70 per cent of cobblers began their businesses after the outbreak of the war; most were previously clerks.

(v) Traders in alcohol

Some liquor traders are also tobacco traders or run taverns. They buy locally produced alcohol through 40 wholesale traders.[15]

(vi) Tobacco traders

Tobacco leaves are usually imported from Sumatra, but quantities are declining. Tobacco is purchased directly from manufacturers through the Tobacco

[15] See chapter 10.

Association. As with traders in alcohol, tobacco traders need to obtain a licence from the Syonan Municipality Department of Finance. There are quite a large number of tobacco traders, and they are the second largest group after haberdashers, numbering 687. Seventy per cent started their tobacco businesses after the outbreak of war.

(vii) Confectioners

Some confectioners run coffee shops at the same time. Sugar and coffee beans are bought on the black market and confectioneries purchased from confectionery manufacturers.

(viii) Sellers of watches, machinery, electrical appliances, automobiles and bicycle parts

With the decrease in imported stocks, the daily business of this group tends to be the repair rather than the sale of products. Some sellers buy second-hand items for repair and resale. But the shortage of parts is making it difficult even to repair items.

(ix) Jewellers, goldsmiths and silversmiths

These businesses usually serve customers who need to sell gold items they own for cash or because they do not need them anymore. They also recast gold and reset jewels for resale to customers. Most of the customers are Chinese women, and here the business relationship is of trust and long standing. There is little business in silver items. Sales of silver items are from pre-war stocks. But because of the lack of customers current conditions are bad.

Most stocks of imported goods such as raw materials and supplies for drapers, tailors, haberdashers, cobblers and leather goods sellers were bought before the war. The increasing shortage of stocks and almost complete cessation of imports has destroyed the complicated multi-layered relationships between importers, wholesalers and retailers. They are now replaced with what resembles a one-layered relationship with everyone being a retailer. Thus, retailers cannot buy retail goods from a wholesaler and inevitably buy from other retailers at retail prices. They then offer the goods for sale to customers at a higher price. In extreme cases, coolies are sent to buy up large quantities of goods for a retailer from other retailers. The goods are then offered for sale to customers. Buying and selling between retailers drives up prices. These practices work against rationing. Thorough reorganization would improve the rationing system.

For liquor, tobacco and confectionery traders, the purchase of raw materials and products is easier than for the drapers, tailors and others described above, but the amounts involved are very much less than before the war. Here also fundamental reorganization is necessary.

In view of the fall in imported stock, repair requirements have sharply increased among sellers of watches, machinery, electrical appliances, and automobile and bicycle parts. If there is to be reorganization, this point should be taken into careful consideration.

Overseas Chinese businesses have strong relationships with their employees because of ties of kinship and origin in the same district. Thus Hokkiens tend to be sellers of automobile and bicycle parts, Teochews sell china and earthenware and Hakkas tinware. The Hainanese are butchers, and those originating from Shanghai sell furniture. These are the largest groups for each occupation. Within each trade, however, merchants do not share capital or information because of origin in the same home regions. They run their individual businesses but have almost no relationship with each other. Reorganizing these trades systematically would not cause any trouble.

(4) Restaurants

In May 1944 the number of restaurants was as in table 4.7.

Table 4.7 Syonan Municipality restaurants, cafeterias and cold drink shops by ethnic group, May 1944

	Business owners	Japanese	Chinese	Indian	Malay	Others
Restaurants	1,382	44	1,150	168	17	3
Cafeterias	387	3	368	13	2	1
Cold drink shops	188	0	126	62	0	0
Total	1,957	47	1,644	243	19	4

Surveyed by Syonan Municipality Department of Public Security.

Securing food rations for households has reduced the allocation of staples and other foods to eateries. Restaurants, apart from rations, therefore have no option but to purchase expensive unrationed foods, or buy on the black market illicitly channelled rationed food intended for distribution to general households. Eateries also buy household rations from coolies and the like who resell their rations. Disruption in food rationing and price controls is caused by restaurants. Their main customers are upper- and middle-class salaried workers. The restaurants must therefore be thoroughly reorganized. The Restaurants Association should be strengthened, and all remaining restaurants should be brought under a policy of effective control.

(5) Hawkers and street vendors

In May 1944 the number of hawkers and street vendors was as in table 4.8.

Table 4.8 shows the number of licence holders. But in reality these figures probably represent only about 50 per cent of itinerant hawkers and 80 per cent of stall hawkers.

With regard to food hawkers and street vendors, it must be emphasized that this group does not get any food from rations of staples and other foods.[16]

Table 4.8 Syonan Municipality hawkers by trade, May 1944

	Itinerant hawkers	Stall hawkers	Shelter hawkers	Total
Cooked food	5,312	833	391	6,536
Vegetables and fruit	2,709	0	37	2,746
Second-hand goods	0	0	85	85
Sundries	2,409	82	278	2,769
Total	10,430	915	791	12,136

Surveyed by Syonan Municipality Department of Public Security.

Consequently, hawkers have no choice but to buy expensive foods outside the rationing system, or to pay black market prices for illicitly channelled rations meant for distribution to general households, or to buy household rations from coolies and the like. The hawkers are at the root of the problems concerning food rationing and price controls and have an effect similar to that of restaurants. However, their main customers are coolies or poorly paid workers. Although the current situation with hawkers should not be allowed to continue, some coolies do not cook food at home, and patronizing street stalls is their only way of eating. Therefore, simply removing these stalls from the street would not be a satisfactory solution. While it is necessary to bring all hawkers under control, a rationalization of businesses should be aimed for. This problem could be resolved by using public markets, deserted because of food rationing. To bring this about, there should be a relocation of street hawkers. Practical measures to facilitate their control should be put in place. The solution of relocation was attempted

[16] This means that hawkers are not given any food to sell.

under British rule for reasons of hygiene. This programme led to the emergence of shelter hawkers in the People's Park and other markets. The control of hawker food prices requires urgent action. Furthermore, there should be official methods for hawkers to purchase ingredients in order to make the management of this trade efficient. This could be accomplished by the implementation of policies such as the provision of meal tickets for coolies without cooking facilities at home and the direct distribution of foods to their chosen hawkers in exchange for meal tickets.

Means to deal with street hawkers of vegetables and fruit have already been proposed.[17]

In view of current social conditions, street hawkers of second-hand goods have to be allowed. However, there is no reason to allow street hawkers of sundries. Therefore, this group of street hawkers must change occupation.

3. Important Information on Effecting Changes in Occupation

(1) Chinese regard those who earn profits by nothing more than the sale and resale of goods as clever, but those who earn their living by labouring as fools. Accordingly, coolies who manage to accumulate a little capital and change their jobs to become traders or merchants are regarded as successful. Being successful has always been the overriding aim of migrants from China. This is why it is so difficult to make traders or merchants change occupation and become workers. Policies aimed at both cultural and economic considerations should be adopted to overcome this difficulty. Cultural attitudes should be tackled by promoting awareness of the value of labour and its significance to the prosecution of a holy war. The other need is to deal with economic concerns. Rationing should strongly favour shopkeepers who have changed their occupation, and rations should be cut for those who persist in their former occupation. Supervision of rationing and price control of businesses should be stepped up for those who do not change occupations. The Ordinance for the Control of Finance and Salaries (*Keiri Kyūyo Tōsei Rei*) should be rigorously enforced, and advance warning should be given that it may be necessary to require the collection of income tax and the deposit of company shares and government bonds into the community chest [under the control of the Legal Affairs Bureau]. These measures should be publicized in advance to warn local traders of the severe difficulties that their businesses might have to contend with in the near future. Furthermore, those traders [who are willing to obey the order] should not suffer from a change of occupation while others who are unwilling to make the required changes continue to reap large profits.

---

[17] See section (2) above.

Age restrictions on male workers should also be extended to prohibit those aged between 16 and 35 from working in commerce as employees. This policy should have the effect of restricting retail businesses.

(2) Some observations on the nature of these traders may be useful. Commercial employees, street hawkers, small shopkeepers and their families can relatively easily change their occupations to become workers. On the other hand, large traders, or shopkeepers of long standing, will be reluctant to change occupation to become workers. However, they might be more willing to become farmers.

(3) When determining the number who should remain in their original occupations, weight should be given to reallocation and reorganization according to the population in each precinct; the issue has already been resolved for traders in foods and daily necessities, where these factors were taken into account when distribution stations were established. In some other trades, theoretically the number should be determined by the level of current imports and local production in relation to the level of imports and local production before the war; in other words, account must be taken of the decline in the volume of trade. Realistically, however, one must allow for a necessary workforce and food supply [on Syonan Island], and also for the course of the war. With regard to changing occupation, in particular to farming, account should be taken of the preparedness of the farming organization in the farming area and the adequacy of transport to and from these areas. However, these decisions will have to be left to political judgement.

For the target number of those in each trade who may be allowed to remain in their current occupations, consideration should also be given to the size of their ethnic group in relation to other ethnic groups in the local population.

Care must also be taken, when determining the number of people remaining in trades concerned with repair and renewal, to make proper allowance for their location in relation to demand for their services.

(4) When the number of people remaining in their original occupations has been determined, the appointment of the individual traders should be based on their trustworthiness and business size. Supervision is difficult where traders are small and do not have specific shop premises, and they can easily become the centre of black market dealings. It is these circumstances that can bring about the entire breakdown of price control and rationing. But where large and highly trusted traders are concerned, such breakdown is relatively unlikely.

(5) The degree of trustworthiness and the size of a business should be measured by several factors such as the length of time an organization has been trading, its capital and sales, whether there has been an attitude of cooperation with the Japanese, and any violations of economic regulations.

(6) The level of technical difficulties and period of preparation required to change occupation will vary by trade, such as the differences that may appear when transforming street hawkers into workers, or jewellers and drapers into farmers. A start should therefore be made first with those trades where a change of occupation is easy to accomplish, and gradually move to cover all trades.

(7) Reorganization trade by trade should group similar trades together and treat them as a single trade, such as rice traders and grocers, drapers and tailors, cobblers and leather goods sellers.

(8) A business licence system should be applied to those remaining in their original occupations, first among groups that have been reorganized, and then, in stages, to all trades. This licence system is necessary to solve remaining problems: these may render the whole policy ineffective, because some traders, even if they give up their business, may take up other commercial activity, or even if they change their occupation they may subsequently return to their previous dealings.

Where business licences are issued, they should specify the trade and number of employees. Alterations in these details should be reflected in the licence system.

Street hawkers should be under strong and rigorous licence control. A fully effective licence system depends not merely on the issue of licences, but on a system in which licence holders can instantly be identified, such as by wearing an identification badge.

(9) The stock of traders who change their businesses should be purchased by those remaining in the trade. But to ensure that the price and conditions of sale are fair, an avenue to sell the stock to organizations such as Syonan Municipality or the Syonan Rationing Association should be opened for those wishing to change.

(10) In some instances, new companies might be formed between appointed traders remaining in their original trades, who would constitute the core members of the new company, and those who are changing occupation, who would still retain some position in the new company. In these cases, those who have changed occupations would not need to sell their stock for cash. Even after a change of occupation, they would retain the right to a share of the profits. Those remaining in the old occupation could be made responsible for looking after the house, furniture and household possessions on behalf of those who have changed occupation. This would make it easier for traders to change occupation.

(11) Those deciding to change occupation are to be redeployed as workers or farmers as appropriate, according to a predetermined plan. Also through these measures, we could avoid a situation in which traders live an idle life, wasting their past savings, or become black market dealers after disappearing from public view. In order to implement the predetermined plan, a list of the names of people who have changed their occupations should be made using the Merchandise

Distributors Declaration Cards, a copy of the licence issued by the Department of Public Security and the individual returns of the November census. Such a list should be prepared by the Labour Office [*Rōdō Jimukyoku*], which is to be the advising and mediating institution for those willing to change occupation. It would be useful to identify precisely who has changed occupation. Additionally, it would help to prevent giving rations to people who are unwilling to change their old occupations, and if necessary implement additional sanctions.

(12) Ethnic groups and trade associations should be encouraged to provide guidance and mediation to those who wish to change their occupations, while a dedicated organization should be established, such as a vocational training centre, to advise and help those who are thinking of changing their occupations to become workers.

(13) The above suggestions apply to local traders. But, as table 4.9 shows, the May census identified 95 Japanese distributors of merchandise. Seventy-nine of them began in this business after the outbreak of war. Many of them are actually ethnic Taiwanese-Japanese. There is little reason to allow these traders to continue, and they should be compelled to close their businesses and change occupation. The 16 Japanese traders who began their business before the outbreak of war should be required to relocate their shops so that they can regroup to create a few distribution stations within the city for the exclusive use of Japanese buyers. The authorities should also prohibit Japanese buyers from purchasing goods from local shops. This measure prevents another problem of price increases in Syonan, that of transit troops and other Japanese who do not know true local prices and buy at inflated prices.[18] Japanese traders should therefore purchase from the stock of local merchants who have changed occupation so as to ease shortages. Additionally, if necessary, one possibility would be to select local traders remaining in their original occupation who are trustworthy and to appoint them as Japanese-customer-only merchants. Such merchants already exist. One general rationing station and four stations for perishable foods have been appointed to sell only to Japanese. Japanese have already been prohibited from buying any controlled foods [rice, salt and sugar] from local shops.

[18] Although the authors appear to be critical of Japanese traders in general for monopolizing the lucrative trade with Japanese customers, here they are eager to allow a monopoly by the 16 Japanese traders. This is because the authors believed that military units were a social menace that drove up prices in the uncontrolled market.

Table 4.9 Syonan Municipality Japanese traders, employees and family members, May 1944

	Business owners	Employees	Family members (including business owners)			
			Male	Female	Child	Total
Greengrocers	2	39	7	2	4	13
Liquor sellers	7	54	11	3	4	18
Building material suppliers	3	134	1	-	-	1
China and earthenware sellers	1	4	-	-	-	-
Stationers	2	11	-	1	-	1
Antique dealers	4	30	3	-	-	3
Fishmongers	4	38	3	-	-	3
Cooking oil sellers	1	11	1	1	-	2
Furniture dealers	3	34	6	3	3	12
Electric tool sellers and repairs	1	16	-	-	-	-
Leather goods sellers	4	24	6	4	-	10
Book and magazine sellers	3	31	-	2	-	2
Camera sellers and repairers	1	16	1	1	-	2
Mine and plantation suppliers	1	7	2	-	-	2
Watch sellers and repairers	7	36	5	4	6	15
Confectioners	4	21	6	4	4	14
Haberdashers	7	66	5	2	5	12
Machinery sellers and repairers	2	34	1	-	-	1
General grocers	22	318	27	12	13	52
Livestock feed suppliers	1	-	-	-	-	-
Tobacco traders	1	1	1	-	-	1
Others	14	1,542	20	21	21	62
Total	95	2,467	106	60	60	226

Surveyed by Syonan Municipality Department of Commerce and Industry.

Supplementary Material: Summary of Merchandise Distributors Declaration Cards

1. Method of Aggregation

Aggregated data derive from Merchandise Distributors Declaration Cards issued by Syonan Municipality, Department of Commerce and Industry in May 1944. Occupations were first classified into 47 different trades and then aggregated in various groups and analyzed with regard to ethnic group, region, length of time in business, capital and sales. The number of members of trading families [including the traders themselves] (distinguishing males, females and children) and employees (distinguishing males and females) have also been aggregated. This will establish Syonan Municipality's current commercial structure, and it is anticipated that it will be useful as a basis for commercial reorganization.

When the data were aggregated from declaration cards as described above, steps were also taken to confirm the details of these written declaration cards for the main trades, and to make enquiries about other matters necessary for reorganization, in order to reach a true understanding of the current situation.

2. Number of Local Distributors of Merchandise

(1) *Total number of traders*

The declaration cards give the total number of traders as 8,025. Pharmacists, street hawkers, and restaurant owners holding special business licences and others with business permits provided by the Ordinance for the Control of Companies [*Kigyō Torishimari Rei*] were not required to submit a declaration card and are not included in this total. Some traders might not have submitted their cards. However, Syonan Municipality issued a specific public notification that traders who did not submit a declaration card would not be allowed to continue their businesses. Therefore, 8,025 may on the whole be regarded as a reliable total.

(2) *Traders by trade*

It is difficult to be precise in classifying traders by trade, because a relatively large number are simultaneously engaged in several businesses. Classification of the main trade relies on those administrators who were actually engaged in aggregating data. A few errors in the data must therefore be accepted. (For example, there is hardly any difference between a rice trader and a general grocer. Moreover, some trades are so closely related that it is almost impossible to put them in the correct category, such as cobblers and leather goods sellers, drapers and tailors. In particular, there is a recent tendency for these traders to deal in cosmetics and everyday sundries, and they have become similar to haberdashers.) The largest trade is that of grocers, who are about 26 per cent of the total. The other relatively large trades are set out in table 4.10; see also table 4.1.

Table 4.10 Various trades as a percentage of total trader numbers, May 1944

General grocers	26.00
Haberdashers	9.90
Tobacco traders	8.60
Drapers	3.90
Fishmongers	3.30
Tailors	3.24
Bicycle part sellers and repairers	3.19
Liquor traders	3.15
Cobblers	2.80
Jewellers	2.55
Watch sellers and repairers	2.50
Leather goods sellers	2.11

(3) Traders by area

Aggregation was conducted by police precinct and by wider area. At present we consider only the distribution pattern of traders by police precinct: the largest precinct is Beach Road Police Station, which has 2,360 traders (29.4 per cent), followed by South Bridge Road Central Police Station with 1,965 traders (24.4 per cent) and Kandang Kerbau Police Station with 1,382 traders (17.2 per cent). These three police precincts include about 71 per cent of traders (see appendix table A.4.1).

Turning to the size of the consumer population per trader, the November 1943 census showed that, on the basis of a total population of 847,509, there were 105 people per trader. Performing the same exercise in police precincts shows that the Beach Road Police Station precinct (population 18,879) has, with about 50 people per trader, the highest trader density. The densities per trader in other precincts are approximately as follows:

Central Police Station (population 150,819), 77 people;

Kandang Kerbau (population 138,981), 100 people;

Joo Chiat Police Station (population 128,039), 167 people;

Tanjong Pagar Police Station (population 116,288), 194 people;

Orchard Road Police Station (population 90,774), 199 people;

Paya Lebar Police Station (population 103,729), 210 people per trader.

Local trade densities are relatively similar in different areas for food traders, tobacco traders, tailors, and sellers of bicycle parts. But merchants selling goods such as textiles, alcohol, shoes, leather, confectionery and jewellery are highly concentrated in the Beach Road, Central and Kandang Kerbau Police Station precincts.

(4) Traders by ethnic group

Of all traders, 77 per cent (6,196) are Chinese, 20 per cent (1,680) Indian, and Malays and others only about 2 per cent (149). Trades in which Indian traders are relatively predominant are shown in table 4.11 (see also appendix table A.4.2).

Table 4.11 Percentage of Indian merchants in selected trades, May 1944

Sporting goods sellers	81.8
Tobacco traders	64.0
Glassware traders	55.5
Drapers	35.0
Haberdashers	35.0
Radio part sellers and repairers	31.0
Book and magazine sellers	34.0
General grocers	25.4
Jewellers	21.4

The distribution pattern for these Indian traders shows the largest concentration in the Kandang Kerbau Police Station precinct, especially Serangoon Road. The second largest concentration is in the Beach Road Police Station precinct.

Table 4.12 Percentage of Chinese ethnic groups in general commerce, May 1944

Hokkien	39.3
Teochew	28.3
Cantonese	16.1
Hakka	10.1
Hainanese	3.3
Shanghainese	2.0

Turning to the ethnic origin of the Chinese, the largest group, 39.3 per cent, are Hokkien. Table 4.12 gives percentages for other Chinese groups.

The notable point is that district of origin and trade are closely related, and these groups concentrate together in location and in trade. Tables 4.13 to 4.16 show the percentages of Chinese ethnic groups in various trades.

Table 4.13 Percentage of Hokkien in various trades

Bicycle part sellers and repairers	97.0
Automobile part sellers	92.0
Building material suppliers	88.0
Fishmongers	70.0
Tea traders	66.0
Liquor sellers	60.0
Cooking oil sellers	57.0
Book and magazine sellers	53.0
Livestock feed suppliers	52.0
Rice and grain traders/grocers	47.7
Drapers	41.0
Tobacco traders	41.0
Furniture dealers	35.5
Machinery sellers and repairers	35.0

Table 4.14 Percentage of Teochew in various trades

China and earthenware traders	73.0
Greengrocers	66.0
Wood and charcoal traders	64.0
Dried fish sellers	57.5
Funeral directors	51.0
Livestock feed suppliers	45.0
General grocers	37.1
Confectioners	36.4
Haberdashers	34.0
Leather goods sellers	34.0
Tobacco traders	31.0
Stationers	29.0
Fishmongers	27.0
Butchers	26.5

Table 4.15 Percentage of Cantonese in various trades

Watch sellers and repairers	65.0
Glassware traders	60.0
Tailors	48.0
Rattan goods sellers	45.6
Jewellers	37.0
Electrical appliance sellers	36.0
Butchers	34.0
Machine and tool sellers	30.0
Stationers	30.0
Leather goods sellers	29.0
Confectioners	27.0
Drapers	21.0
Tobacco traders	21.0

Table 4.16 Percentage of Hakka in various trades

Tinware sellers	82.5
Cobblers	50.0
Rattan goods sellers	39.1
Jewellers	30.0
Tailors	24.4
Haberdashers	23.5
Machine and tool sellers	21.0

In addition, Hainanese are predominant among butchers (26.5 per cent of the trade), and Chinese from Shanghai dominate among furniture sellers (20 per cent of the trade) (see appendix table A.4.2). It is quite clear that people originating from the same district in China tend to engage in the same trade, concentrate in one area and live together. But since the outbreak of war, because associations such as trade associations and public gatherings are banned, there is now almost no special relationship (such as the relationship between a master and his followers) or capital relationship but only a simple business-to-business relationship among traders in the same trade.

(5) Traders by length of time in trade

The strength of a business's foundations and its reliability are indicated by the length of time it has traded. Data gathered from the declaration cards submitted show that of 8,025 traders, about 52 per cent (4,184) started their business after the outbreak of war. A total of 20.4 per cent (1,641) had been in business for less than five years before the outbreak of war, 13.8 per cent (1,113) for between five and ten years before the outbreak of war, 9.1 per cent (738) for between 10 and 20 years, 2.5 per cent (205) for between 20 and 30 years before the outbreak of war, and 1.7 per cent (144) for over 30 years. A very large number of businesses are relatively new. Only 13.5 per cent of traders began their businesses more than ten years before the outbreak of war.

These figures suggest that conditions in general businesses are unstable. But they do not show the actual situation, since the date on which a business is said to have been established in the written declaration is not always the real date. Among traders who state that they began business after the outbreak of war, some were in business in the same trade before the outbreak of war. Relocation of shops or reorganization of ownership structure, such as from individual ownership to a cooperative or corporate ownership, might lead to the declaration of a later date of foundation. The written date of establishment given by many traders is often actually based on the date of relocation or of reorganization of ownership, so that the 52 per cent who give their date of establishment as after the outbreak of war may not reflect the real facts. Bearing this caveat in mind, the information supplied by traders who identified themselves as having started in business after the outbreak of war is recorded in table 4.17.

Table 4.17 Percentage of traders starting business after February 1942, May 1944

Leather goods sellers	84.0
Fishmongers	75.0
Cooking oil sellers	73.0
Cobblers	70.0
Tobacco traders	70.0
Confectioners	67.0
Haberdashers	63.0
Watch sellers and repairers	62.0
Dried fish sellers	62.0
Livestock feed suppliers	59.4
Butchers	56.0

The major groups in business before the outbreak of war are shown in table A.4.3.

Table 4.18 Percentage of traders starting business before February 1942, May 1944

Funeral directors	77.0
Tailors	74.6
Tinware traders	72.0
China and earthenware traders	67.0
Drapers	67.0
Stationers	66.0
Automobile part sellers and repairers	65.0
Machine and tool sellers	60.0
Tea traders	59.4

Table 4.18 (cont'd)

Rattan goods sellers	58.3
Jewellers	57.0
Rice and grain traders/grocers	56.0
Book and magazine sellers	56.0
Glassware traders	53.0

These two sets of data (tables 4.17 and 4.18) indicate that shoe, leather and haberdashery businesses (there has recently been an increase in locally produced goods) have relatively easy entry, allowing other traders to make these their second business.

(6) Traders by capital

Of the 8,025 traders, 80 per cent have capital of less than $5,000. This illustrates the dominance of small business. On the other hand, 9.5 per cent have capital of $5,000 to $10,000, 6.3 per cent capital of $10,000 to $30,000, 1.8 per cent capital of $30,000 to $50,000, 1.2 per cent capital of $50,000 to $100,000, and 0.3 per cent capital of $100,000 to $200,000. Only 13 traders have capital of over $200,000. The trades with an average capital of over $10,000 are given in tables 4.19 and 4.20. Traders listed in table 4.19 sell mainly intermediate goods, while those in table 4.20 sell consumer goods.

The three groups of traders with the smallest average capital—greengrocers, fishmongers and butchers—have businesses with particularly small capital. This may be explained by the fact that many of these traders work from market stalls (see table A.4.4).

Although Chinese traders generally have only small capital, they are resilient traders. This is because they organize their businesses in the form of small companies [*kong-si*] (usually they have fewer than five partners) and have close ties in a common place of origin and ethnic group, and also because they develop good commercial skills and have frugal lifestyles.

Table 4.19 Traders with capital of over $10,000, May 1944

Mine and plantation material suppliers	203,057
Rope traders	26,940
Fishing tool sellers	23,779
Machine and tool sellers	17,072
Building material suppliers	15, 856

Table 4.20 Traders with capital of over $10,000 selling consumer goods, May 1944

Drapers	23,841
Sporting goods sellers	13,337
Jewellers	13,163
Stationers	11,590
Automobile part sellers and repairers	11,662

Tables 4.21 to 4.23 show trades according to average capital, $10,000 and under.

Table 4.21 Traders with capital of $5,000 to $10,000, May 1944

Sanitary goods sellers	9,605
Tea traders	8,872
Musical instrument sellers	8,449
Radio sellers and repairers	8,226
Haberdashers	8,190
China and earthenware traders	6,637
Electrical appliance sellers	6,563
Camera sellers and repairers	6,284
Liquor sellers	6,256
Antique dealers	5,900
General grocers	5,598
Livestock feed suppliers	5,505
Funeral directors	5,135
Cooking oil sellers	5,085

Table 4.22 Traders with capital of $3,000 to $5,000, May 1944

Leather goods sellers	4,208
Furniture dealers	3,714
Bicycle part sellers and repairers	3,667
Cobblers	3,462
Dried fish sellers	3,393
Rattan goods sellers	3,117

Table 4.23 Traders with capital of under $3,000, May 1944

Hatters and milliners	2,885
Glassware traders	2,716
Book and magazine sellers	2,600
Tobacco traders	2,497
Wood and charcoal traders	2,444
Confectioners	2,380
Watch sellers and repairers	2,132
Tailors	1,682
Tinware traders	1,680
Greengrocers	1,448
Fishmongers	952
Butchers	658

(7) Criteria of business resilience by trade: An experimental analysis

The resilience of businesses is one of the yardsticks for reallocating surplus businesses from trades. In theory, this measure should be based on a combination of the criteria of management structure, the number of years the business has traded, its capital and its business acumen. For the present, the strength of businesses in each trade is defined primarily by the number of trading years and size of capital.[19] However, as explained below, we do not intend to argue here that when reorganization is actually carried out, it should be based on just one particular combination of measures from four possible combinations (i)–(iv) for uniform application to every sector. This is only an experimental analysis to establish whether such a measure would be technically useful or not (see table A.4.5).

(i) Resilient traders

Traders in business before the war with capital of over $5,000, and traders with capital of less than $5,000 who were in business for more than five years before the war [defined as resilient traders]: Among the total of 8,025 traders, 2,447 (30.5 per cent) fall into this category.

[19] This is because management structure and business acumen were considered difficult to quantify.

(ii) Resilient traders

There are 2,322 traders (28.9 per cent) with capital of over $10,000 who were in business before the war, or with capital of less than $10,000 but who were in business for more than five years before the war. The characteristics of this group are almost identical to group (i). Lists and details of trades are therefore omitted.

Table 4.24 Resilient traders: (i) with capital of over $5,000 or trading for over five years before the war, May 1944

Drapers	56.9
Radio sellers and repairers	53.8
Stationers	52.0
Musical instrument sellers	60.0
Tinware traders	50.0
Fishing tool sellers	68.8
Tea traders	51.4
Funeral directors	51.1
Mine and plantation material suppliers	50.0
Sporting goods sellers	54.0
China and earthenware traders	43.0
Greengrocers	32.0
Liquor sellers	34.3
Building material suppliers	35.0
Sanitary goods suppliers	33.0
Hatters and milliners	42.8
Tailors	46.5
Furniture dealers	37.0
Automobile part sellers and repairers	46.0
Camera sellers and repairers	46.0
Butchers	33.6
Machine and tool sellers	47.0
Glassware traders	33.0
Wood and charcoal traders	35.5
General grocers	34.0

Table 4.24 (cont'd)

Jewellers	41.0
Rope traders	30.0
Cobblers	17.0
Engravers and printers	12.5
Antique dealers	20.0
Fishmongers	13.0
Cooking oil sellers	21.0
Electrical appliance sellers	29.5
Florists	8.0
Leather goods sellers	9.5
Book and magazine sellers	29.0
Watch sellers and repairers	19.0
Dried fish sellers	28.6
Confectioners	18.0
Haberdashers	23.0
Rattan goods sellers	29.0
Bicycle part sellers and repairers	24.0
Livestock feed suppliers	15.0
Tobacco traders	11.0

(iii) Resilient traders

There are 1,551 traders (19.3 per cent) with capital of over $5,000 who were in business before the war, or with capital of less than $5,000 but who were in business for more than ten years before the war.

(iv) Resilient traders

There are 1,317 traders (16.4 per cent) with capital of over $10,000 who were in business before the war, or with capital of less than $10,000 but who were in business for more than ten years before the war.

Table 4.25 Resilient traders: (iii) with capital of over $5,000 or trading for over ten years before the war, May 1944

Drapers	46.9
China and earthenware traders	32.0
Radio sellers and repairers	38.5
Stationers	42.4
Musical instrument sellers	40.0
Fishing tool sellers	62.5
Tea traders	35.0
Automobile part sellers and repairers	34.0
Funeral directors	37.0
Mine and plantation material suppliers	50.0
Machine and tool sellers	40.0
Jewellers	30.6
Rope traders	30.0
Liquor sellers	22.8
Building material suppliers	24
Tinware traders	27.5
Cooking oil sellers	17.0
Tailors	23.0
Furniture dealers	21.5
Electrical appliance sellers	21.8
Book and magazine sellers	19.5
Camera sellers and repairers	23.0
Sporting goods sellers	27.0
Dried fish sellers	21.4
Haberdashers	17.0
Rattan goods sellers	22.9
Glassware traders	15.5
Wood and charcoal traders	15.9
General grocers	19.3
Greengrocers	13.8
Cobblers	9.8

Table 4.25 (cont'd)

Engravers and printers	8.3
Sanitary goods suppliers	1.0
Antique dealers	13.3
Fishmongers	5.6
Leather goods sellers	5.9
Watch sellers and repairers	10.5
Butchers	15.0
Confectioners	12.5
Bicycle part sellers and repairers	11.3
Livestock feed suppliers	8.7
Tobacco traders	5.4

Table 4.26 Resilient traders: (iv) with capital of over $10,000 or trading for over ten years before the war, May 1944

Liquor sellers	22
Drapers	39.5
China and earthenware traders	23.0
Radio sellers and repairers	30.7
Stationers	33.6
Musical instrument sellers	40.0
Tinware traders	27.5
Fishing tool sellers	62.5
Tea traders	32.4
Tailors	20.8
Automobile part sellers and repairers	23.6
Camera sellers and repairers	23.0
Funeral directors	31.4
Mine and plantation material suppliers	50.0
Sporting goods sellers	27.0
Machine and tool sellers	36.4
Jewellers	23.3
Rope traders	30.0

(cont'd overleaf)

Table 4.26 (cont'd)

Greengrocers	11.3
Building material suppliers	17.5
Sanitary goods suppliers	11.0
Antique dealers	13.0
Cooking oil sellers	15.0
Furniture dealers	18.5
Electrical appliance sellers	18.0
Book and magazine sellers	14.6
Watch sellers and repairers	10.0
Dried fish sellers	19.0
Butchers	15.0
Haberdashers	13.6
Rattan goods sellers	14.6
Glassware traders	13.3
Wood and charcoal traders	13.8
General grocers	16.8
Cobblers	9.3
Engravers and printers	8.3
Fishmongers	5.3
Leather goods sellers	4.0
Confectioners	8.7
Bicycle part sellers and repairers	9.0
Livestock feed suppliers	8.7
Tobacco traders	5.0

The resilience of a business as shown in the experimental analysis above and below is more clearly linked to the length of time the business has traded than to its capital. But there are a number of different ways in which length of time in trade and size of capital can be combined, not just the ways shown above. In reorganizing business structure, numerous other considerations must be taken into account, such as the nature of the trade, its social and economic functions, current importance, the size of its stock, future production capacity, average capital, average sales, and ethnic characteristics. These matters will have to be considered in each trade, to reach an appropriate combination of length of trading time and size of capital. The number of traders who are actually necessary and possess resilience can then be allowed to continue and be located appropriately.

(8) Traders by sales and capital turnover in each trade

There are sales data for just one month in 1944, April. It would be rash on this basis to estimate the state of a business and its sales capacity. Moreover, it is inappropriate to assess business conditions only by the value of sales. A comparison must at the same time be made of capital, the prices at which goods are sold, the rate at which prices have increased, and profit margins. However, there is insufficient data available to address the overall situation; so here we focus on the value of sales.

A total of 32.7 per cent of traders have monthly sales of under $1,000, and 33 per cent have monthly sales of $1,000 to $3,000. The available material shows that most traders have monthly sales of less than $3,000. On the other hand, 12.6 per cent of traders have monthly sales of $3,000 to $5,000, 10.7 per cent have sales of $5,000 to $10,000, 7.1 per cent have sales of $10,000 to $30,000, and 1.7 per cent have sales of $30,000 to $50,000. Just 1.8 per cent have monthly sales of over $50,000 (see table A.4.6).

Capital turnover ratios [average sales divided by average capital] for one month in April 1944 are shown in table 4.27. At present, the speed with which goods are sold immediately results in price increases. Owing to rapidly rising prices, capital turnover ratio is generally very high. Where capital turnover ratio is over 100 per cent in a month, this indicates a high level of activity in the trade, as in trades now discussed.

Trades with capital turnover of over 100 per cent are mainly in foods and non-essential items [i.e., discretionary items such as alcohol, tobacco and confectionery]. There are 21 trades in which the monthly capital turnover ratio is between 50 per cent and 100 per cent. Where trades have a monthly capital turnover ratio of less than 50 per cent, this is an indication that the businesses are in relatively bad condition. These businesses are probably experiencing difficulties owing to the sharp decline in stocks, since these consist of imports before the outbreak of war.

Table 4.27 Traders by capital turnover, April 1944

Greengrocers	415.5
Fishmongers	390.8
Butchers	307.0
Cooking oil sellers	255.0

(cont'd overleaf)

Table 4.27 (cont'd)

Livestock feed suppliers	249.0
Confectioners	236.0
Dried fish sellers	226.0
Liquor sellers	208.0
Hatters and milliners	201.0
General grocers	167.0
China and earthenware traders	151.5
Tobacco traders	134.0
Jewellers	121.0
Leather goods sellers	95.6
Furniture dealers	91.3
Rattan goods sellers	83.0
Machine and tool sellers	82.0
Glassware traders	80.0
Wood and charcoal traders	79.0
Tinware traders	77.7
Tea traders	77.7
Cobblers	75.4
Stationers	73.7
Building material suppliers	67.0
Funeral directors	66.0
Florists	64.0
Toy sellers	65.0
Watch sellers and repairers	60.0
Antique dealers	58.4
Tailors	55.9
Electrical appliance sellers	55.7
Bicycle part sellers and repairers	53.0
Book and magazine sellers	51.0
Engravers and printers	50.8
Fishing tool sellers	16.8
Sanitary goods suppliers	19.1

Table 4.27 (cont'd)

Sporting goods sellers	21.0
Drapers	21.5
Rope traders	22.0
Mining and plantation material suppliers	26.0
Tinware traders	29.0
Musical instrument sellers	33.1
Haberdashers	39.0
Automobile part sellers and repairers	41.4
Radio sellers and repairers	44.2

(9) Number of family members and other employees

Aggregating the declaration cards, there is a total (including traders themselves) of 18,341 males, 15,381 females and 20,133 children who are part of a trading family. This is a total of 53,855 people, and so an average of six or seven family members per business. In terms of family structure, 34 per cent of traders are in families of fewer than 3, 18 per cent in families of 4 or 5, 31 per cent in families of 6 to 10, 8.7 per cent in families of 11 to 15, 3 per cent in families of 16 to 20, and 3.7 per cent in families of over 21. Where there are three ore fewer members in a family, men are a dominant 69 per cent, women constitute 21 per cent of members, and children constitute only about 10 per cent. For families of four members or more, the ratio of men to women is almost even, but there are large numbers of children of both genders.

This is relevant because as a rule the gender balance of overseas Chinese in Malaya is remarkably uneven, and the large numbers of children indicate the potential for rapid Chinese population growth. Although some men apart from the owner of the business follow other occupations, the rest are mainly engaged in the family business. Most women perform housework and childcare. A change of occupation may of course pose various problems for traders with large families. However, large families also give merchandise traders the capacity to augment the labour force (see table A.4.7). The direction of reallocation of those who change occupations will have to take into account characteristics such as age, ability and previous social background. With these considerations in mind, candidates should be appropriately relocated to occupations where either they would help to increase food production or supply labour for industry.

Of the total number of employees in trades, there are 18,498 men and 3,185 women. The average for the total of 21,683 employed persons is 2.6 employees per trader. Among the traders, 79 per cent employ fewer than 3 people; 9 per cent employ 4 or 5; 7 per cent employ 6 to 10; 2 per cent employ 11 to 15; and 2 per cent employ 16 or more. Male employees form a majority of 85 per cent of total employees. Table 4.28 lists trades where the average number of employees is relatively large.

Many of the trades in table 4.28 are concerned with manufacturing and processing industries (see table A.4.7). The number of people employed is certainly lower than before the war. But research on actual conditions shows that a considerable number of employees who are unnecessary and parasitic on their employers can still be found. When these employees are reorganized they should become factory workers, since few of them have family encumbrances and many are of working age. In addition, the numbers of employees in shops who remain in their present trades should be controlled according to the scale and nature of the business. Furthermore, there should be a notification system [i.e., self-registration on a voluntary basis] implemented for the transfer of employees.

With few exceptions, the relationship between traders and employees is bound by rigid ties arising from their membership of the same ethnic group or origin in the same area, and the level of their mutual trust and paternalistic comradeship is extremely high.

Table 4.28 Trades by number of employees, May 1944

Hatters and milliners	26.8
Building material suppliers	12.7
Stationers	7.3
Rope traders	7.3
Fishing tool sellers	6.7
Jewellers	4.9
Machine and tool sellers	4.5
Confectioners	4.3
China and earthenware traders	4.0
Furniture dealers	3.5
Electrical appliance sellers	3.6
Automobile part sellers and repairers	3.0
Rattan goods sellers	2.4
Tea traders	3.9
Liquor sellers	3.0
Cooking oil sellers	3.1

Table 4.28 (cont'd)

Haberdashers	2.7
Leather sellers	2.5
Cobblers	2.4
Drapers	2.4
General grocers	2.2
Tailors	2.1

3. Organization of Japanese Merchandise Distributors

(1) Total number of traders

According to the declaration cards, there are 95 Japanese traders.

(2) Traders by trade

As table A.4.8 shows, the largest trade is that of grocers (22). Table 4.29 gives the other trades. The trades shown in table 4.29 are the main ones in which Japanese traders are found.

Table 4.29 Japanese traders by trade, May 1944

General grocers	22
Haberdashers	7
Liquor sellers	7
Watch sellers and repairers	7
Confectioners	4
Antique dealers	4
Fishmongers	4
Leather goods sellers	4
Building material suppliers	3
Furniture dealers	3
Second-hand book dealers	3

(3) Traders by area

Of the total 95 traders, 47, or about half, are located in the Central Police Station precinct, 24 in the Orchard Road Police Station precinct, and 15 in the Beach

Road Police Station precinct. Only nine traders are located in the Kandang Kerbau, Tanjong Pagar and Joo Chiat Police Station precincts.

(4) Traders by length of time in trade

The declaration cards show about 83 per cent (79) of traders declaring that their business started after the outbreak of war. There are 8 traders who began their businesses fewer than 5 years before the outbreak of war, 3 who began between 10 and 20 years before, 4 who started 20 to 30 years before, and 1 trader who began business over 30 years before the outbreak of war. Analysis by trade of traders who began business before the war shows three leather goods sellers and two fishmongers. The following trades have one trader each: liquor, china and earthenware, cooking oil, electrical appliances, books, watches and repairs, confectionery, haberdashery, groceries. In the 'other trades', there are two traders who began business before the war.

(5) Traders by capital size

Japanese traders have large capital compared to local traders. The biggest group (26 traders, 27 per cent of the total) have capital of between $10,000 and $30,000. The next biggest group (18 traders, 19 per cent of all traders) have capital of between $30,000 and $50,000. These two groups are followed by 17 traders (18 per cent of the total) with capital of between $5,000 and $10,000, 16 (16.8 per of the total) with capital of between $50,000 and $100,000, and 4 with capital of over $100,000. Only 14 (14.7 per cent) of traders have capital of under $5,000. Of the traders with capital of over $10,000, 15 are grocers and 4 are haberdashers. Three each are traders of liquor, building materials, leather, and watch sales and repairs. Two traders are in each of these trades: greengroceries, antiques, fishmongering, furniture selling, book dealing, confectionery selling and machine tools. There is one trader in each of the following trades: stationery, electrical appliances, mining and rubber plantation supplies, and livestock feed. 'Other trades' have a total of 13 traders with capital of over $10,000.

(6) Traders by sales and capital turnover in each trade

Among Japanese traders, 84 of the total 95 have stated the value of their sales. Taking monthly sales for April 1944, the largest group of traders—26.1 per cent of the 84 (22 traders)—had total sales of between $10,000 and $30,000; 15 had $50,000 to $100,000; 11 had $30,000 to $50,000; 10 had $5,000 to $10,000; 8 had $3,000 to $5,000; 7 had $1,000 to $3,000; 6 had over $100,000; and 5 had less than $1,000.

Next, we look at the monthly capital turnover ratio by each trade, indicating average monthly sales in April 1944 divided by average capital.

Table 4.30 Japanese traders by capital turnover

Cooking oil sellers	716.0
Liquor sellers	390.0
Stationers	313.0
Confectioners	226.0
Tobacco traders	130.0
Haberdashers	110.0
General grocers	106.0
Furniture dealers	71.0
China and earthenware traders	70.0
Fishmongers	58.0
Machine and tool sellers	54.0
Building material suppliers	49.0
Greengrocers	40.3
Electrical appliance sellers	33.7
Watch sellers and repairers	34.0
Antique dealers	19.0
Second-hand book dealers	18.0
Camera sellers and repairers	6.0

The figures in table 4.30 suggest that Japanese traders are not always prosperous.

(7) Number of family members and employees

An aggregation of the declaration cards shows the total number of family members of the 95 traders (excluding the traders themselves) as 106 men, 60 women and 60 children, a total of 226 persons. This averages about 2.4 family members per trader. Employees are 1,657 men and 810 women, a total of 2,467. This averages 25.9 employees per trader, which is much more than for local traders. Of the traders, 16.8 per cent (16) have fewer than 3 employees, 18.9 per cent (18) employ 4 or 5, 30.5 per cent (29) employ 6 to 10, 7.3 per cent (7) employ 11 to 15, 11.5 per cent (11) employ 16 to 20, and 15.8 per cent (14) employ over 20. The majority of employees (67 per cent) are male.

Table 4.31 shows the average number of employees per trader by trade for those with a large number of employees.

Table 4.31 Japanese traders by average number of employees

Building material suppliers	44.6
Electrical appliance sellers	16.0
Camera sellers and repairers	16.0
General grocers	14.4
Furniture dealers	11.3
Cooking oil sellers	11.0
Confectioners	10.5
Booksellers	10.3
Greengrocers	9.7
Fishmongers	9.5
Haberdashers	9.4

Appendix Tables

Table A.4.1 Syonan Municipality traders by trade, region and ethnic group, May 1944

	Number of traders by police precinct							Total	Ratio by trade %	Ratio by ethnic groups %		
	A	B	C	D	E	F	G			Chinese	Indian	Other
Rice and grain traders	37	-	7	-	36	5	-	85	1.05	91.8	5.9	2.4
Greengrocers	14	84	36	8	7	7	3	159	1.98	87.4	6.3	6.3
Liquor sellers	90	53	58	25	8	13	7	254	3.17	97.1	2.5	0.4
Drapers	126	8	156	3	10	5	3	311	3.88	62.7	35.0	2.3
Building material suppliers	15	24	34	3	3	11	13	103	1.28	99.0	1.0	-
China and earthenware sellers	27	7	44	8	1	2	6	95	1.18	97.9	1.0	1.0
Radio sellers and repairs	-	7	-	-	4	2	-	13	0.16	69.2	30.8	-
Cobblers	50	24	116	23	6	4	2	225	2.80	94.6	3.1	2.2
Engravers and printers	11	1	12	-	-	-	-	24	0.30	100.0	-	-
Stationers	76	3	38	3	1	3	1	125	1.56	85.6	13.6	0.8
Musical instrument sellers	5	5	5	-	-	-	-	15	0.19	86.7	6.7	6.7

(cont'd overleaf)

Table A.4.1 (cont'd)

	Number of traders by police precinct							Total	Ratio by trade %	Ratio by ethnic groups %		
	A	B	C	D	E	F	G			Chinese	Indian	Other
Sanitary goods sellers	1	1	6	-	-	1	-	9	0.11	100.0	-	-
Antique dealers	8	-	4	-	3	-	-	15	0.19	93.3	-	6.6
Hatters and milliners	2	-	4	1	-	-	-	7	0.08	85.7	-	14.3
Tinware sellers	8	4	14	4	1	4	5	40	0.50	100.0	-	-
Fishing tool sellers	5	-	10	-	-	1	-	16	0.20	100.0	-	-
Fishmongers	10	75	156	11	8	2	4	266	3.31	99.6	-	0.4
Cooking oil sellers	15	9	14	4	-	3	8	53	0.66	84.9	13.2	1.9
Tea traders	21	-	10	2	2	2	-	37	0.46	89.2	8.1	2.7
Tailors	51	51	77	23	26	18	14	260	3.24	85.0	14.2	0.8
Furniture sellers	13	26	75	-	4	16	1	135	1.68	100.0	-	-
Electrical appliance sellers	21	23	19	-	7	8	-	78	0.97	74.4	10.2	15.4
Florists	-	6	-	-	4	2	-	12	0.15	58.3	41.6	-
Leather goods sellers	72	22	47	14	1	12	2	170	2.12	82.9	12.4	4.7
Automobile part sellers and repairs	1	58	42	1	1	2	1	106	1.32	99.1	0.9	-

Table A.4.1 (cont'd)

	Number of traders by police precinct							Total	Ratio by trade %	Ratio by ethnic groups %		
	A	B	C	D	E	F	G			Chinese	Indian	Other
Book and magazine sellers	4	13	14	3	-	5	2	41	0.51	36.6	34.1	29.3
Camera sellers and repairs	5	5	2	-	-	-	1	13	0.16	92.3	7.7	-
Funeral directors	5	3	19	-	1	5	2	35	0.44	82.8	2.8	14.3
Mine and plantation suppliers	6	-	-	-	-	-	-	6	0.07	100.0	-	-
Watch sellers and repairs	57	36	67	13	7	13	6	199	2.48	91.9	4.0	4.0
Sporting goods sellers	8	1	2	-	-	-	-	11	0.14	18.2	81.8	-
Dried fish sellers	8	25	-	4	1	-	4	42	0.52	95.2	-	4.8
Butchers	18	16	41	4	22	3	3	107	1.33	91.6	4.7	3.7
Confectioners	26	17	29	16	2	7	8	104	1.30	81.7	13.4	4.9
Haberdashers	310	58	214	87	23	94	10	796	9.92	61.9	35.1	2.9
Rattan goods sellers	4	14	27	-	1	1	1	48	0.60	95.8	2.1	2.1
Machinery sellers	28	3	65	-	-	2	1	99	1.23	98.0	2.0	-
Glassware sellers	13	8	15	1	3	4	-	45	0.56	44.4	55.5	-

(cont'd overleaf)

Table A.4.1 (cont'd)

	Number of traders by police precinct							Total	Ratio by trade %	Ratio by ethnic groups %		
	A	B	C	D	E	F	G			Chinese	Indian	Other
Wood and charcoal traders	25	37	41	7	2	18	8	138	1.72	98.6	-	1.4
Bicycle part sellers and repairers	20	67	78	12	19	31	29	256	3.19	98.4	0.8	0.8
Toy sellers	2	6	-	1	-	-	-	9	0.11	100.0	-	-
General grocers	438	351	386	198	146	379	208	2,106	26.24	73.6	25.4	1.0
Jewellers	71	19	90	4	3	13	6	206	2.57	78.2	21.4	0.5
Rope traders	2	-	6	-	-	-	2	10	0.12	70.0	20.0	10.0
Livestock feed suppliers	12	14	17	1	15	2	31	92	1.15	96.7	3.3	-
Tobacco traders	130	148	194	87	25	37	66	687	8.56	35.3	63.8	0.9
Others	94	50	69	29	54	30	36	362	4.51	85.3	14.1	0.6
Total	1,965	1,382	2,360	600	457	767	494	8,025	100.00			

Note: Precincts were A. Central Police Station; B. Kandang Kerbau Police Station; C. Beach Road Police Station; D. Tanjong Pagar Police Station; E. Orchard Police Station; F. Joo Chiat Police Station; G Paya Lebar Police Station.

Table A.4.2 Syonan Municipality Chinese traders by trade and ethnic group, May 1944

	A	B	C	D	E	F	G	Total
Rice and grain traders	52	2	-	23	-	1	-	78
Greengrocers	39	5	1	92	-	2	-	139
Liquor sellers	149	23	9	47	1	17	-	246
Drapers	81	41	24	35	8	4	2	195
Building material suppliers	90	7	-	5	-	-	-	102
China and earthenware sellers	17	2	4	68	2	-	-	93
Radio sellers and repairers	3	1	-	4	-	1	-	9
Cobblers	19	60	106	11	5	8	4	213
Engravers and printers	4	4	7	7	1	1	-	24
Stationers	12	32	14	31	13	4	1	107
Musical instrument sellers	5	2	3	1	2	-	-	13
Sanitary goods sellers	3	3	2	-	-	1	-	9
Antique dealers	1	-	-	1	2	1	3	8
Hatters and milliners	-	1	2	-	-	3	-	6
Tinware sellers	3	-	33	4	-	-	-	40
Fishing tool sellers	2	1	-	12	1	-	-	16
Fishmongers	188	2	2	71	-	2	-	265
Cooking oil sellers	26	7	-	6	-	6	-	45
Tea traders	22	5	1	2	-	3	-	33
Tailors	25	106	54	13	13	10	-	221
Furniture sellers	48	29	-	27	28	3	-	135
Electrical appliance sellers	12	21	1	18	-	6	-	58
Florists	3	2	-	2	-	-	-	7
Leather goods sellers	10	41	26	48	11	2	-	141

(cont'd overleaf)

Table A.4.2 (cont'd)

	A	B	C	D	E	F	G	Total
Automobile part sellers and repairers	97	-	2	3	1	3	-	105
Book and magazine sellers	8	1	2	1	3	-	-	15
Camera sellers and repairers	-	6	1	5	-	-		12
Funeral directors	11	1	2	15	-	-	-	29
Mine and plantation suppliers	2	3	-	1	-	-	-	6
Watch sellers and repairers	25	118	8	26	1	5	-	183
Sporting goods sellers	1	-	-	-	-	-	1	2
Dried fish sellers	14	1	-	23	-	2	-	40
Butchers	11	34	1	26	-	26	-	98
Confectioners	18	23	4	31	-	9	-	85
Haberdashers	88	55	116	168	35	25	6	493
Rattan goods sellers	1	21	18	6	-	-	-	46
Machinery sellers	34	29	21	12	-	1	-	97
Glassware sellers	2	12	-	5	-	1	2	20
Wood and charcoal traders	43	-	5	87	1	-	-	136
Bicycle part sellers and repairers	246	1	-	5	-	-	-	252
Toy sellers	4	1	1	-	3	-	-	9
General grocers	726	138	63	581	3	39	-	1550
Jewellers	11	60	48	38	-	4	-	161
Rope traders	4	-	-	1	-	2	-	7
Livestock feed suppliers	47	1	-	40	-	1	-	89
Tobacco traders	100	51	13	76	-	3	-	243
Others	127	45	32	77	17	9	2	309
Total	2434	998	626	1755	151	205	21	6196

Table A.4.3 Syonan Municipality traders by trade and years in business, May 1944

	Began business after February 1942	Length of time in business before February 1942					Total
		Under 5 years since 1937–41	Between 5 and 10 years since 1932–36	Between 10 and 20 years since 1922–31	Between 20 and 30 years since 1912–21	Over 30 years since before 1911	
Rice and grain traders	31	16	15	17	5	1	85
Greengrocers	78	32	32	16	-	1	159
Liquor sellers	132	43	24	26	11	18	254
Drapers	102	66	61	50	17	15	311
Building material suppliers	56	19	15	7	15	1	113
China and earthenware sellers	31	30	15	16	-	3	95
Radio sellers and repairers	1	7	4	1	-	-	13
Cobblers	157	33	19	11	3	2	225
Engravers and printers	21	-	1	1	-	1	24
Stationers	42	29	23	19	5	7	125
Musical instrument sellers	2	4	4	3	1	1	15
Sanitary goods sellers	6	1	1	1	-	-	9
Antique dealers	10	2	3	-	-	-	15
Hatters and milliners	3	1	3	-	-	-	7
Tinware sellers	11	9	9	7	1	3	40
Fishing tool sellers	1	9	3	1	1	1	16

(cont'd overleaf)

Table A.4.3 (cont'd)

	Began business after February 1942	Length of time in business before February 1942					Total
		Under 5 years since 1937–41	Between 5 and 10 years since 1932–36	Between 10 and 20 years since 1922–31	Between 20 and 30 years since 1912–21	Over 30 years since before 1911	
Fishmongers	201	31	21	12	1	-	266
Cooking oil sellers	39	5	4	2	2	1	53
Tea traders	15	4	9	5	3	1	37
Tailors	66	75	66	37	13	3	260
Furniture sellers	50	40	22	13	8	2	135
Electrical appliance sellers	43	16	9	8	-	2	78
Florists	6	5	1	-	-	-	12
Leather goods sellers	143	14	7	4	2	-	170
Automobile part sellers and repairers	37	26	22	19	2	-	106
Book and magazine sellers	18	14	4	3	2	-	41
Camera sellers and repairers	6	1	3	3	-	-	13
Funeral directors	8	9	7	5	4	2	35
Mine and plantation suppliers	3	2	-	-	1	-	6
Watch sellers and repairers	125	38	17	13	3	3	199
Sporting goods sellers	4	1	4	1	1	-	11
Dried fish sellers	26	6	4	5	1	-	42

Table A.4.3 (cont'd)

	Began business after February 1942	Length of time in business before February 1942					Total
		Under 5 years since 1937–41	Between 5 and 10 years since 1932–36	Between 10 and 20 years since 1922–31	Between 20 and 30 years since 1912–21	Over 30 years since before 1911	
Butchers	60	11	20	14	2	-	107
Confectioners	70	18	7	8	1	-	104
Haberdashers	509	138	72	53	13	11	796
Rattan goods sellers	20	16	5	7	-	-	48
Machinery sellers	39	21	14	12	8	5	99
Glassware sellers	21	10	7	5	1	1	45
Wood and charcoal traders	65	25	29	15	2	2	138
Bicycle part sellers and repairers	132	66	40	11	4	3	256
Toy sellers	8	1	-	-	-	-	9
General grocers	931	500	359	223	56	37	2,106
Jewellers	88	47	39	19	7	6	206
Rope traders	7	-	-	2	1	-	10
Livestock feed suppliers	64	14	7	7	-	-	92
Tobacco traders	485	126	44	19	7	6	687
Others	211	60	38	37	11	5	362
Total	4,184	1,641	1,113	738	205	144	8,025

Table A.4.4 Syonan Municipality traders by trade and capital, May 1944

	Less than $5,000	Between $5,000 and $10,000	Between $10,000 and $30,000	Between $30,000 and $50,000	Between $50,000 and $100,000	Between $100,000 and $200,000	Over $200,000	Total	Average capital ($)
Rice and grain traders	44	7	23	5	4	-	2	85	28,602
Greengrocers	149	8	2	-	-	-	-	159	1,448
Liquor sellers	201	33	14	1	3	2	-	254	6,256
Drapers	151	58	44	31	15	9	3	311	23,841
Building material suppliers	56	26	11	3	5	1	1	103	15,856
China and earthenware sellers	68	16	6	4	1	-	-	95	6,637
Radio sellers and repairers	7	2	4	-	-	-	-	13	8,226
Cobblers	204	15	5	1	-	-	-	225	3,462
Engravers and printers	21	1	2	-	-	-	-	24	1,898
Stationers	72	21	24	3	3	2	-	125	11,590
Musical instrument sellers	12	-	2	-	1	-	-	15	8,449

Table A.4.4 (cont'd)

	Less than $5,000	Between $5,000 and $10,000	Between $10,000 and $30,000	Between $30,000 and $50,000	Between $50,000 and $100,000	Between $100,000 and $200,000	Over $200,000	Total	Average capital ($)
Sanitary goods sellers	7	-	1	1	-	-	-	9	9,605
Antique dealers	11	2	-	2	-	-	-	15	5,900
Hatters and milliners	7	-	-	-	-	-	-	7	2,885
Tinware sellers	38	2	-	-	-	-	-	40	1,680
Fishing tool sellers	7	-	3	5	1	-	-	16	23,779
Fishmongers	258	4	2	1	1	-	-	266	952
Cooking oil sellers	40	5	8	-	-	-	-	53	5,085
Tea traders	23	6	6	2	-	-	-	37	8,872
Tailors	248	12	-	-	-	-	-	260	1,682
Furniture sellers	114	14	5	2	-	-	-	135	3,714
Electrical appliance sellers	56	9	8	4	1	-	-	78	6,563
Florists	11	1	-	-	-	-	-	12	1,426
Leather goods sellers	141	20	7	2	-	-	-	170	4,208

(cont'd overleaf)

Table A.4.4 (cont'd)

	Less than $5,000	Between $5,000 and $10,000	Between $10,000 and $30,000	Between $30,000 and $50,000	Between $50,000 and $100,000	Between $100,000 and $200,000	Over $200,000	Total	Average capital ($)
Automobile part sellers and repairers	53	20	21	6	6	-	-	106	11,663
Book and magazine sellers	36	4	1	-	-	-	-	41	2,600
Camera sellers and repairers	11	-	2	-	-	-	-	13	6,284
Funeral directors	29	3	2	-	1	-	-	35	5,135
Mine and plantation suppliers	1	1	-	2	-	-	2	6	203,057
Watch sellers and repairers	182	13	4	-	-	-	-	199	2,132
Sporting goods sellers	7	-	1	2	1	-	-	11	13,337
Dried fish sellers	33	4	5	-	-	-	-	42	3,393
Butchers	105	2	-	-	-	-	-	107	658
Confectioners	95	8	1	-	-	-	-	104	2,380
Haberdashers	601	112	56	15	9	2	1	796	8,190
Rattan goods sellers	41	6	1	-	-	-	-	48	3,117

Table A.4.4 (cont'd)

	Less than $5,000	Between $5,000 and $10,000	Between $10,000 and $30,000	Between $30,000 and $50,000	Between $50,000 and $100,000	Between $100,000 and $200,000	Over $200,000	Total	Average capital ($)
Machinery sellers	55	14	16	6	5	3	-	99	17,072
Glassware sellers	39	4	2	-	-	-	-	45	2,716
Wood and charcoal traders	132	4	1	1	-	-	-	138	2,444
Bicycle part sellers and repairers	226	16	8	4	1	1	-	256	3,667
Toy sellers	9	-	-	-	-	-	-	9	1,722
General grocers	1727	185	129	30	30	2	3	2,106	5,598
Jewellers	130	31	29	5	8	2	1	206	13,163
Rope traders	7	1	1	-	-	-	1	10	26,940
Livestock feed suppliers	74	9	6	2	1	-	-	92	5,505
Tobacco traders	647	27	10	-	2	1	-	687	2,497
Others	272	42	39	6	1	2	-	362	-
Total	6,458	768	512	146	100	27	14	8,025	

Table A.4.5 Syonan Municipality resilient traders by trade, May 1944

	Total	(i) Traders with capital of over \$5,000 or in business for over 5 years before the war	(ii) Traders with capital of over \$10,000 or in business for over 5 years before the war	(iii) Traders with capital of over \$5,000 or in business for over 10 years before the war	(iv) Traders with capital of over \$10,000 or in business for over 5 years before the war
Rice and grain traders	85	44	43	37	28
Greengrocers	159	51	50	22	18
Liquor sellers	254	87	83	58	56
Drapers	311	177	163	146	123
Building materials suppliers	103	36	32	25	18
China and earthenware sellers	95	41	35	30	22
Radio sellers and repairers	13	7	6	5	4
Cobblers	225	39	38	22	21
Engravers and printers	24	3	3	2	2
Stationers	125	65	60	53	42
Musical instrument sellers	15	9	9	6	6
Sanitary goods sellers	9	3	3	1	1
Antique dealers	15	3	3	2	1
Hatters and milliners	7	3	3	0	0
Tinware sellers	40	20	20	11	11
Fishing tool sellers	16	11	11	10	10
Fishmongers	266	35	34	15	14
Cooking oil sellers	53	11	11	9	8
Tea traders	37	19	18	13	12
Tailors	260	121	119	60	54

Table A.4.5 (cont'd)

	Total	(i) Traders with capital of over $5,000 or in business for over 5 years before the war	(ii) Traders with capital of over $10,000 or in business for over 5 years before the war	(iii) Traders with capital of over $5,000 or in business for over 10 years before the war	(iv) Traders with capital of over $10,000 or in business for over 5 years before the war
Furniture sellers	135	50	47	29	25
Electrical appliance sellers	78	23	21	17	14
Florists	12	1	1	0	0
Leather goods sellers	170	16	14	10	7
Automobile part sellers and repairers	106	49	41	36	25
Book and magazine sellers	41	12	10	8	6
Camera sellers and repairers	13	6	6	3	3
Funeral directors	35	18	18	13	11
Mine and plantation suppliers	6	3	3	3	3
Watch sellers and repairers	199	38	37	21	20
Sporting goods sellers	11	6	6	3	3
Dried fish sellers	42	12	11	9	8
Butchers	107	36	36	16	16
Confectioners	104	19	16	13	9
Haberdashers	796	184	165	137	108
Rattan goods sellers	48	14	12	11	7
Machinery sellers	99	47	46	40	36
Glassware sellers	45	15	14	7	6

(cont'd overleaf)

Table A.4.5 (cont'd)

	Total	(i) Traders with capital of over $5,000 or in business for over 5 years before the war	(ii) Traders with capital of over $10,000 or in business for over 5 years before the war	(iii) Traders with capital of over $5,000 or in business for over 10 years before the war	(iv) Traders with capital of over $10,000 or in business for over 5 years before the war
Wood and charcoal traders	138	49	48	22	19
Bicycle part sellers and repairers	256	62	60	29	23
Toy sellers	9	0	0	0	0
General grocers	2,106	721	696	407	354
Jewellers	206	84	79	63	48
Rope traders	10	3	3	3	3
Livestock feed suppliers	92	14	14	8	8
Tobacco traders	687	78	76	37	34
Others	362	102	98	72	63
Total	8,025	2,447	2,322	1,544	1,310

Table A.4.6 Syonan Municipality traders by trade and sales, May 1944

	Less than $1,000	Between $1,000 and $3,000	Between $3,000 and $5,000	Between $5,000 and $10,000	Between $10,000 and $30,000	Between $30,000 and $50,000	Between $50,000 and $100,000	Over $100,000	Total	Average monthly sales ($, April 1944)
Rice and grain traders	12	26	14	12	8	4	7	2	85	13,845
Greengrocers	80	41	6	12	11	8	-	1	159	6,016
Liquor sellers	1	51	114	58	19	6	2	3	254	13,016
Drapers	111	71	40	54	34	1	-	-	311	5,116
Building material suppliers	20	19	15	17	22	6	4	-	103	10,622
China and earthenware sellers	12	22	11	17	24	8	1	-	95	10,053
Radio sellers and repairers	4	4	1	3	1	-	-	-	13	3,636
Cobblers	62	107	32	22	2	-	-	-	225	2,620
Engravers and printers	20	3	1	-	-	-	-	-	24	965
Stationers	22	30	19	23	25	2	4	-	125	8,540
Musical instrument sellers	5	4	4	1	1	-	-	-	15	2,797
Sanitary goods sellers	7	1	-	-	1	-	-	-	9	1,834

(cont'd overleaf)

Table A.4.6 (cont'd)

	Less than $1,000	Between $1,000 and $3,000	Between $3,000 and $5,000	Between $5,000 and $10,000	Between $10,000 and $30,000	Between $30,000 and $50,000	Between $50,000 and $100,000	Over $100,000	Total	Average monthly sales ($, April 1944)
Antique dealers	9	2	-	1	3	-	-	-	15	3,448
Hatters and milliners	5	1	-	-	-	1	-	-	7	5,788
Tinware sellers	27	10	1	2	-	-	-	-	40	1,306
Fishing tool sellers	3	7	1	4	1	-	-	-	16	4,003
Fishmongers	90	156	1	1	16	1	-	1	266	3,720
Cooking oil sellers	10	9	12	7	9	3	2	1	53	12,977
Tea traders	8	9	8	4	7	-	1	-	37	6,897
Tailors	219	30	8	3	-	-	-	-	260	940
Furniture sellers	39	51	17	18	10	-	-	-	135	3,390
Electrical appliance sellers	36	22	6	9	4	1	-	-	78	3,653
Florists	10	1	1	-	-	-	-	-	12	915
Leather goods sellers	31	69	30	31	8	1	-	-	170	4,022
Automobile part sellers and repairers	36	34	11	14	8	2	-	1	106	4,821
Book and magazine sellers	30	7	3	-	1	-	-	-	41	1,339

Table A.4.6 (cont'd)

	Less than $1,000	Between $1,000 and $3,000	Between $3,000 and $5,000	Between $5,000 and $10,000	Between $10,000 and $30,000	Between $30,000 and $50,000	Between $50,000 and $100,000	Over $100,000	Total	Average monthly sales ($, April 1944)
Camera sellers and repairers	8	3	-	2	-	-	-	-	13	1,820
Funeral directors	18	9	4	3	-	1	-	-	35	3,376
Mine and plantation suppliers	2	-	-	2	1	-	-	1	6	52,846
Watch sellers and repairers	137	41	13	6	2	-	-	-	199	1,269
Sporting goods sellers	4	3	3	-	1	-	-	-	11	2,843
Dried fish sellers	12	18	-	3	6	3	-	-	42	7,653
Butchers	54	39	4	6	4	-	-	-	107	2,017
Confectioners	39	15	14	15	16	4	1	-	104	5,601
Haberdashers	213	305	116	106	50	1	3	2	796	3,181
Rattan goods sellers	13	20	10	5	-	-	-	-	48	2,574
Machinery sellers	25	30	10	8	17	1	5	3	99	13,905
Glassware sellers	21	14	5	4	1	-	-	-	45	2,158
Wood and charcoal traders	40	83	7	5	3	-	-	-	138	1,935

(cont'd overleaf)

Table A.4.6 (cont'd)

	Less than $1,000	Between $1,000 and $3,000	Between $3,000 and $5,000	Between $5,000 and $10,000	Between $10,000 and $30,000	Between $30,000 and $50,000	Between $50,000 and $100,000	Over $100,000	Total	Average monthly sales ($, April 1944)
Bicycle part sellers and repairers	163	65	10	9	7	2	-	-	256	1,955
Toy sellers	4	5	-	-	-	-	-	-	9	1,123
General grocers	466	811	301	246	150	56	53	23	2,106	9,332
Jewellers	68	36	16	27	32	12	7	8	206	15,940
Rope traders	4	1	3	-	2	-	-	-	10	5,903
Livestock feed suppliers	14	27	16	17	9	2	5	2	92	13,731
Tobacco traders	287	228	76	47	32	8	6	3	687	3,340
Others	127	111	54	41	23	5	1	-	362	-
Total	2,628	2,651	1,018	865	571	139	102	51	8,025	

Table A.4.7 Syonan Municipality traders by number of family members and employees, May 1944

	Business owners	Family members (including business owners)				Employees		
		Male	Female	Child	Total	Male	Female	Total
Rice and grain traders	85	237	270	270	777	427	26	453
Greengrocers	159	329	266	424	1,019	252	10	262
Liquor sellers	254	731	753	910	2,394	611	159	770
Drapers	311	602	511	759	1,872	822	50	872
Building material suppliers	103	319	345	464	1,128	1,193	120	1,313
China and earthenware sellers	95	265	218	349	832	356	22	378
Radio sellers and repairers	13	37	33	39	109	39	1	40
Cobblers	225	440	407	480	1,327	428	113	541
Engravers and printers	24	43	49	42	134	42	10	52
Stationers	125	386	383	549	1,318	736	181	917
Musical instrument sellers	15	41	40	61	142	22	8	30
Sanitary goods sellers	9	14	11	12	37	28	7	35
Antique dealers	15	29	25	33	87	26	4	30
Hatters and milliners	7	22	19	30	71	62	126	188
Tinware sellers	40	75	66	122	263	71	2	73
Fishing tool sellers	16	59	80	117	256	102	6	108
Fishmongers	266	574	492	560	1,626	215	5	220
Cooking oil sellers	53	186	159	175	520	154	9	163
Tea traders	37	91	92	101	284	112	32	144
Tailors	260	472	446	641	1,559	466	65	531
Furniture sellers	135	300	247	356	903	415	54	469
Electrical appliance sellers	78	168	194	229	591	254	27	281
Florists	12	25	21	17	63	18	2	20
Leather goods sellers	170	393	294	285	972	293	166	459
Automobile part sellers and repairers	106	277	268	414	959	276	46	322
Book and magazine sellers	41	89	72	69	230	42	14	56
Camera sellers and repairers	13	20	28	38	86	21	3	24

(cont'd overleaf)

Table A.4.7 (cont'd)

	Business owners	Family members (including business owners)				Employees		
		Male	Female	Child	Total	Male	Female	Total
Funeral directors	35	83	77	104	264	108	8	116
Mine and plantation suppliers	6	16	25	23	64	27	-	27
Watch sellers and repairs	199	346	366	449	1,161	209	28	237
Sporting goods sellers	11	16	12	12	40	19	-	19
Dried fish sellers	42	127	102	122	351	67	2	69
Butchers	107	201	196	329	726	67	13	80
Confectioners	104	230	176	237	643	370	62	432
Haberdashers	796	1,624	1,244	1,650	4,518	1,496	610	2,106
Rattan goods sellers	48	89	84	118	291	90	26	116
Machinery sellers	99	244	284	398	926	415	31	446
Glassware sellers	45	93	77	90	260	74	14	88
Wood and charcoal traders	138	330	296	373	999	195	20	215
Bicycle part sellers and repairers	256	473	406	543	1,422	403	31	434
Toy sellers	9	13	9	27	49	20	13	33
General grocers	2,106	5,268	4,114	332	9,714	4,320	245	4,565
Jewellers	206	573	546	767	1,886	926	85	1,011
Rope traders	10	25	21	36	82	62	11	73
Livestock feed suppliers	92	242	175	287	704	177	4	181
Tobacco traders	687	1,256	630	734	2,620	711	156	867
Others	362	868	752	956	2,576	1,259	558	1,817
Total	8,025	18,341	15,381	15,133	53,855	18,498	3,185	21,683

CHAPTER 5

A Study of the Labour Situation in Syonan Municipality, Focusing on Factories Managed by Japanese

Surveyed by Civilian Administrator Izawa Kōzō and Civilian Associate Ōmura Junzaburō, October 1944

This report is written on the basis of research conducted by the civil administrator Izawa Kōzō and civilian associate Ōmura Junzaburō [both of whom are affiliated to the Chōsabu of the Malayan Military Administration]. Its relevance is not confined to Syonan Municipality. This report was mimeographed to be offered as a reference to those concerned.

Contents

(2) Industrial workers in Syonan Municipality
(3) Industrial workers by age in Syonan Municipality
(4) Workers in transport and communications

3. Demand and Supply of Workers

(1) Increasing demand for workers
(2) Turnover of labour
(3) Substitution of female for male labour
(4) Methods of new labour recruitment

4. Labour Conditions

(1) Wages
(2) Payments in kind
(3) Working hours
(4) Rate of absenteeism

5. Welfare Facilities

(1) Workers' housing
(2) Workers' transport
(3) Medical facilities and treatment of illness and injury
(4) Educational guidance and training of workers
(5) Labour organizations

6. Conclusion: Appropriate Action

1. Aim, Subject and Methods of the Research

(1) Aim

Local self-sufficiency in the supply of munitions, food and other necessities is an urgent and important military administration policy. The degree to which the policy of self-sufficiency is successful will have an enormous and direct impact on operations. Currently, there are numerous hindrances to the delivery of operations in various fields. One of these is the shortage of workers in manufacturing industries. Therefore, this survey focuses on labour management in factories in private ownership in the Malay Region [Malay Peninsula and Singapore] that are concentrated in Syonan Municipality and considers what policies would yield a sufficient supply of workers. Moreover, the research aims to propose how quality should compensate for quantity through studying how labour management might be improved to compensate for the lack of labour supply.

(2) Research subject: Sectors covered by the study

We chose, by industry, 20 Japanese-run civilian-owned factories in Syonan Municipality, together with some factories owned by locals in Syonan Municipality. Also selected were seaborne and land transport companies, together with communications companies in Syonan Municipality.

(i) Japanese private companies

Table 5.1 Syonan Municipality Japanese factories, a sample of 20 factories for this report

Industry	Factory
Metalworking	Osaka Steel Plate Co., Ltd. Syonan Factory [*A*]
	Sakaguchi Teikichi Trading Co., Ltd. Syonan Factory [*B*]
	Tokyo Shibaura Electric Co., Ltd. Syonan Factory [*C*]
Shipyards	Gokō Shipyard [*D*]
	Eifuku Industry Company Kojima Shipyard [*E*]
Ceramics	Kurosaki Ceramics Co., Ltd. Syonan Factory [*F*]
	Southern Regions Bricks Factory [*G*]
Chemicals	Japan Nitrogen Fertilizer Co., Ltd.[*H*]
	Yokohama Rubber Co. Syonan Factory [*I*]
	Dai-Nippon Paint Co. Ltd. [*J*]

(cont'd overleaf)

Table 5.1 (cont'd)

Industry	Factory
Woodworking	Nisshin Plywood Manufacturers Co., Ltd. Syonan Factory [*K*]
	Nozaki Wooden Barrel Manufacturers [*L*]
Electricity	Japan Electricity Generation and Transmission Co., Ltd. [*O*]
Civil engineering	Shimizu Construction Company [*P*]
	Tajima Construction Company [*Q*]
Food	Kirin Beer Co., Ltd. [*M*]
	Noda Soy Source Co., Ltd. [*N*]
Smelting	Mitsui Mining Co., Syonan Smeltmills [*R*]
Other industries	Mitsui Bussan Co., Ltd. Syonan Branch Thompson Factory [*S*]
	Syonan Used Textile Bleaching Factory [*T*]

Note: We only investigated the Tokyo Shibaura Electric Co. River Valley factory. Although the factory is expected to produce and repair electrical appliances, we classify it as a metalworking factory producing nails because its major product is nails. Sixty per cent of the workers engage in metal processing.[1]

(ii) Transport and communications

Table 5.2 Syonan Municipality transport and communications, a sample for this report

Transport	Land	Trains, buses	Syonan Municipality Department of Transport
			Tokyo Kyuko Electric Transportation Co. Ltd.
		Cars	Syonan Taxi Association
		Trains	Syonan Station and Engine Terminal
		Oxcarts	Syonan Oxcart Association
		Rickshaws	Syonan Rickshaw Association
		Tricycles	Syonan Kōsei Tricycle Association

[1] The River Valley factory was owned by Toshiba, which was the largest maker of electrical bulbs and home appliances in Tokyo.

Table 5.2 (cont'd)

	Sea	Malayan Maritime Association Southern Navigation Company
Loading / unloading	Land	Southern Regions Corporation
	Sea	Syonan Port Co., Ltd.
Communications	Central Post Office of Syonan Municipality	
	Syonan Central Telephone and Telegraph Exchange, Department of Postal Services and Telecommunications, Malayan Military Administration	

(3) Research methods

We drew up a questionnaire in advance and conducted an interview survey of the following at the 20 factories:

(i) The number of workers (by ethnic group, occupation and age)
(ii) Labour demand and supply
 a. Recruitment procedures
 b. Labour turnover
 c. Possibilities for substitution
(iii) Labour conditions (wages, working hours, days off and payments in kind)
(iv) Welfare facilities
 a. Accommodation
 b. Transport to and from work
 c. Medical facilities for the treatment of disease and injuries
 d. Concessions for female and juvenile workers
 e. Educational guidance and training of factory workers
 f. Medical equipment
(v) Workers' organizations
(vi) Barriers to increased rate of worker attendance

2. Size and Composition of the Workforce

(1) Overall size of the workforce in Syonan Municipality

Our Chōsabu aggregation of the door-to-door census of mid-November 1943 [conducted by the Department of Police Administration] showed the population of Syonan Municipality (excluding the Japanese population, the

Table 5.3 Syonan Municipality number of employed and manual workers[2]

		Employed population			Manual-worker population		
	Total	Number	% of population	% of the employed	Number	% of population	% of manual workers
Total population	855,679	341,273	39.9	100.0	210,507	24.6	100.0
Male	509,033	307,454	60.4	90.0	186,114	36.6	88.4
Female	346,647	33,819	9.8	10.0	24,393	7.0	12.6

Note 1: Japan, Manchuria, Germany, United States, Britain, France and Italy comparative international data for employed population (thousand persons).

	Japan	Manchuria	Germany	United States	Britain	France	Italy
Total population	64,450	35,800	65,218	122,775	44,795	41,228	41,177
Employed population	29,620	13,012	32,296	48,830	21,035	21,613	21,262
Employed as % of total population	46.0	26.2	49.5	39.8	47.0	52.4	41.9

Cabinet Statistical Office 1937, ed., 'An Outline of World Census', cited in Koyama Eizō, *Minzoku to Jinko no Riron* [The Theory of Ethnicity and Population] (Tokyo: Hata Shoten, 1941), p. 288.

Note 2: Japan, Manchuria, Germany, United States, Britain, France and Italy percentage of employed population (per cent).

	Japan	Manchuria	Germany	United States	Britain	France	Italy
Total	45.6	36.5	49.5	39.7	47	53.3	41.9
Male	59.1	61.6	65.7	61.3	68.9	70.2	66.3
Female	31.9	6.1	34.2	17.7	26.8	37.5	18.5

These data refer to the following years: Japan 1930, Manchuria 1936, Germany 1933, United States 1930, Britain 1931, France 1926 and Italy [n.d.]. Cited in Koyama Eizō, *Minzoku to Jinko no Riron*, p. 288.

---

[2] The Census/Resident Registry was kept by the Syonan Municipality Department of Police Administration and aggregated in November by the Chōsabu. The figures here are comparable to chapter 3 tables A.3.3 and A.3.8, but the number of manual workers here is probably the sum of 'mining and manufacturing (excl. Europeans)', 'transport (excl. Europeans and Eurasians)', 'government and professions (excl. Europeans, Eurasians, Others)', 'coolies', and 'other (excl. Europeans)' in table A.3.8.

adjacent islands, Seletar Navy port, police dormitory and jail) as 855,679.[3] The employed population[4] was 341,273 (39.7 per cent), and the population of manual workers was 210,507 (24.6 per cent). The male population was 509,033, of whom 307,454 (61.4 per cent) were employed. In the female population of 346,647, 33,819 (9.8 per cent) were employed. The male employment rate is almost the same as in leading pre-war countries in other parts of the world [table 5.3, note 1]. However, the female employment rate of 9.8 per cent is as low as in Manchuria.

The employment rate for the population as a whole is the same as in the wartime United States (see note 1). Among manual workers, 88.4 per cent are male and 11.6 per cent female, while for the employed population as a whole the ratios are 90 per cent for men and 10 per cent for women. However, the ratio of female manual workers is probably higher than indicated because there are quite a few female coolies (see table 5.3).

(A) Employed population by industry

The statistics given in table 5.4 (which excludes the Japanese population, the adjacent islands, Seletar Navy port, etc.) derive from data produced by the Labour Office [*Rōdō Jimukyoku*] of Syonan Municipality and the Chōsabu aggregation of the census of mid-November 1943.[5] 'Senji Keizai no Rinkaku' (Outline of the War Economy), *Ikkyō Ronsō* 1, 1 (1938): 16. For comparative purposes, we include data from Tokyo. However, slight differences in the classification system preclude strict comparison.

(B) Source of labour supply in Syonan Municipality (excluding the Japanese, the adjacent islands and the area of Seletar)

Sources of labour in Syonan Municipality are listed below. Appropriate measures should be taken to maintain the size of the available workforce from these sources to ensure that industrial production is able to respond to variations in demand.

(i) Number of male workers in inessential occupations (Aggregated result as of June 1944)[6]

---

[3] See chapter 3.

[4] This corresponds to the Japanese term *yūgyōsha*, meaning people with occupations.

[5] Labour Office and Labour Book—The Labour Book was used to try to control workers centrally. An article by Ueda Teijirō on how a war economy should be pursued is informative. He provides an extensive survey of British wartime mobilization policy and points out that the British did not use Labour Books but the Germans did in World War I, which explains why the British were not so efficient in conscripting and mobilizing labour for the war effort.

[6] See chapter 4.

Table 5.4 Syonan Municipality estimate of employed population by industry, May 1944, compared to Tokyo, 1930

	Syonan total	Syonan %	Tokyo %
Manufacturing (excl. factories under direct military control)	70,000	20.4	33.0
Commerce	95,000	27.7	30.0
Transport (incl. dockworkers)	23,000	6.8	6.0
Farming and fishing	31,000	9.0	7.0
Workers in factories/units under direct military control	83,000	24.2	n.d.
Domestic service	15,000	4.3	n.d.
Government and professions	11,000	3.2	14.0
Clerical	15,000	4.3	n.d.
Total	343,000	100.0	n.d.

Note 1: In manufacturing, there are 45,000 workers in Japanese-managed factories. (According to the Labour Office of Syonan Municipality, there are 43,000 factory workers. Our figure of 45,000 takes the upper bound of estimation.[7]) The workforce in locally managed factories is estimated at 25,000. (The Labour Office of Syonan Municipality's estimate is 20,000 for the number of factory workers in factories with more than five workers. We have increased this figure by 5,000.)

Note 2: Syonan Municipality employed population by selection of trades, November 1943[8]

Commerce	98,886
Transport	25,891
Farming and fishing	31,101
Domestic service	21,576
Government and professions	11,348
Clerical	14,818

Note: [In order to construct table 5.4] from the category of 'domestic service' [here as shown in note 2, and in chapter 3 table A.3.7], cooks who work at hotels or restaurants are moved to 'commerce', and cooks in the military are categorized as 'workers under direct military control'. Consequently the remaining 15,000 workers [in table 5.4] are counted in the 'domestic service' category.

[7] See table 5.7; 42,841 x 1.038 = 44,468.

[8] This list of 'employed population by trade' does not include 'mining and manufacturing', 'coolies' and 'other' as broad categories. 'Domestic service' and 'clerical' are narrow categories, which come under 'other' in chapter 3, table A.3.7.

Table 5.5 Syonan Municipality number of male workers in essential occupations, June 1944[9]

Business owners in commerce	26,915
Employees in commerce	21,684
Restaurant owners	2,074
Employees in restaurant industry	3,635
Street vendors, hawkers	38,402
Moneylenders, pawnbrokers, landowners	1,836
Brokers, contractors	1,406
Barbers	2,934
Total	98,886

(ii) Female non-working population (November 1943)

Table 5.6 Syonan Municipality female non-working population, November 1943[10]

Female occupied population	33,819
Female unoccupied population	312,828
Females of working age (15–50)	(162,578)
Females aged under 14 and over 51	(150,250)

(iii) Unemployed males of working age number 27,091.

(2) *Industrial workers in Syonan Municipality*

Data collected by the Labour Office of Syonan Municipality (see table 5.7) show that at the end of May 1944 Japanese-managed factories in Syonan Municipality had a total workforce of 42,841, of whom 32,215 (75.2 per cent) were male and 10,626 (24.8 per cent) female. Analysis of distribution by industry shows that over half of the workforce in Japanese companies (55.7 per cent) were employed

[9] These are in fact November 1943 figures. The total corresponds to 'commerce' as a broad category in chapter 3 table A.3.7, etc.

[10] The month of this table is illegible or perhaps intentionally wiped out, which makes it readable as January 1943, but these are November 1943 figures. These figures correspond to the numbers in chapter 3 tables A.3.3 and A.3.4.

in the civil engineering and construction sectors. Such a large proportion reflects the fact that the city is now being reconstructed by the Military Administration. In the food industry, the main activity under Japanese management is beer and soy sauce production. Since other food is produced mainly under local management, there are only a small number of workers in Japanese food manufacturing companies.

Among locally managed industries, the food industry employs the highest proportion of workers. The smallest proportion of workers is employed in the chemical industry. Gender analysis shows more female than male workers in the locally managed food industry. In miscellaneous industries, there are an equal number of males and females in both Japanese and local companies. These industries retain the character of cottage industries, which are suitable for female workers.

For comparative purposes, we have included in this table data on composition by sector and gender relating to Japan.

Of the factory workers included in this survey (see table 5.8), the number of female workers is 18.6 per cent that of male workers. Compared to the situation in Japan, there is still room for an increase in female labour force participation. By ethnic group, the largest proportion of the working population is Chinese, followed by Indians and Malays. This ethnic pattern can be seen in all industries. (See table A.3.5 of the November 1943 census.)

(3) Industrial workers by age in Syonan Municipality

There is insufficient data to calculate the age structure of workers in the entire sample surveyed. In this study, we therefore show the results of the age structure in 11 factories that reported the age structure. Among female workers, the under 14 and over 51 age groups as a proportion of their total is higher than for male workers. Although comparison with Japan is difficult because of differences in labour conditions, for purposes of reference, taking all male workers as 100, the percentage aged over 50 is 2.5 per cent for males and 1.2 per cent for females. (For those under 14 years of age, comparison with Japan is not possible because Japanese survey data for this group do not exist. Data from Labour Annual of 1940 [Japan].) There is little difference between male workers in Japan and Syonan, but the labour force participation rate is higher among older female workers in Syonan than in Japan. This may be due to the large number of female coolies.

Table 5.7 Syonan Municipality manufacturing workers by industrial sector and gender (based on data from the Labour Office of Syonan Municipality), unknown date[11]

	Japanese-managed industry							Locally managed industry							Total	%
	Male	%	Female	%	Male : female	Total	%	Male	%	Female	%	Male : female	Total	%		
Metalworking	4,490	14.4	411	3.5	91.6 : 8.4	4,901	11.4	3,537	25.4	343	6.6	91.2 : 8.8	3,880	20.3	8,781	16.5
Shipbuilding	2,504	8.0	65	0.6	97.5 : 2.5	2,569	6.0	305	2.2	0	0.0	100.0 : 0	305	1.6	2,874	5.4
Ceramics	1,132	3.6	203	1.9	84.8 : 15.2	1,335	3.1	979	7.0	126	2.4	79.6 : 11.4	1,105	5.8	2,440	4.6
Chemicals	2,230	7.1	2,050	17.6	52.1 : 47.9	4,280	10.0	156	1.1	80	1.5	66.1 : 33.9	236	1.2	4,516	8.5
Woodworking	1,411	4.5	217	2.0	86.7 : 13.3	1,628	3.8	2,032	14.6	77	1.5	96.3 : 3.7	2,109	11.0	3,737	6.1
Food	666	2.1	190	1.8	77.8 : 22.2	856	2.0	1,735	12.4	2,087	40.2	45.4 : 54.6	3,822	20.0	4,678	8.8
Electrical engineering	730	2.3	0	0.0	100.0 : 0	730	1.7	430	3.1	115	2.2	78.9 : 21.1	545	2.8	1,275	2.4
Civil engineering/ construction	16,554	53.0	7,318	62.9	69.3 : 30.7	32,876	55.7	2,893	20.8	595	11.5	82.9 : 17.1	3,488	18.2	27,360	36.1
Miscellaneous	1,488	4.8	1,182	10.2	55.7 : 44.7	2,670	6.2	1,869	13.4	1,765	34.0	51.4 : 48.6	3,634	19.0	6,304	11.8
Total	31,215	100.0	11,626	100.0	75.2 : 24.8	42,841	100.0	13,936	100.0	5,188	100.0	71.9 : 27.1	19,124	100.0	61,965	100.0

Based on data from the Labour Office of Syonan Municipality.

[11] The print quality of the original of this table is particularly poor. The illegible figures were reconstructed by calculation, using the characteristics of a cross-tabulation table. The rows that are particularly illegible are the fourth row for Japanese-managed 'chemicals' factories and the eighth row for Japanese-managed 'civil engineering/construction' companies. In the original table the entries for 'chemicals' were obliterated.

Note 1 [for table 5.7]: In the electrical industry, Japanese companies generate electricity while local companies produce electrical appliances and are different in character.

Note 2 [for table 5.7]: Japan manual workers by industry and females per 100 workers, 1939.

	Manual workers	% of employed population	Females per 100 workers
Spinning and weaving	976,953	30.4	81.2
Metalworking	377,398	11.7	8.6
Machinery	860,431	26.8	10.2
Ceramics	105,345	3.3	13.0
Chemicals	322,205	10.0	31.3
Woodworking	113,823	3.5	12.3
Printing and binding	63,568	2.0	14.2
Food	190,697	5.9	26.7
Gas and electricity	10,517	0.3	0.6
Other	194,484	6.1	54.4
Total	3,215,421	100.0	37.9

Note: Data from 1939.

Table 5.8 Syonan Municipality manufacturing workers by industrial sector, ethnic group and gender (for 20 factories surveyed for this report), May 1944

	Ethnic group (Male)					Ethnic group (Female)					Sex distribution of workforce (%)		Total	% of total industrial workforce
	Chinese	Malay	Indian	Other	Total	Chinese	Malay	Indian	Other	Total	Male	Female		
Metalworking	1,029	438	447	46	1,960	173	0	6	0	179	91.6	8.4	2,139	20.1
Shipbuilding	706	88	97	1	892	70	0	0	0	70	92.7	7.3	962	9.1
Ceramics	322	109	159	2	592	41	9	17	0	67	89.8	10.2	659	6.2
Chemicals	748	329	227	1	1305	424	50	2	0	476	73.3	26.7	1,781	16.8
Woodworking	297	152	30	0	479	163	0	0	0	163	74.6	25.4	642	6.1
Food	241	73	120	6	440	162	23	0	0	185	70.4	29.6	625	5.7
Electricity	141	170	495	11	817	0	0	0	0	0	100.0	0.0	817	7.7
Civil engineering and construction	1,120	0	480	0	1,600	400	0	0	0	400	80.9	20.0	2,000	19.9
Smelting	94	43	47	38	222	49	0	0	0	49	81.9	18.1	271	2.0
Spinning	136	0	5	0	141	300	0	0	0	300	32.0	68.0	441	4.2
Miscellaneous	140	29	12	0	181	81	0	0	0	81	69.1	30.9	262	2.5
Total	4,974	1,431	2,119	105	8,629	1,863	82	25	0	1,970	81.4	18.6	10,599	100.0

Note: Electricity indicates power supply.

Table 5.9 Syonan Municipality number and percentage of factory workers by age (11 factories), May 1944

	Under 14		15–50		Over 51		
	Number	%	Number	%	Number	%	Total
Male	139	3.7	3,571	93.7	73	1.9	3,783
Female	133	20.9	457	71.8	44	6.9	634
Total	272	6.2	4,028	91.2	117	2.6	4,417

(4) Workers in transport and communications

The distinctive points with regard to workers in the transport and communication sectors are as discussed below.

(i) Many Indian workers are employed in government enterprises (trains, buses and railways), as was true of the pre-war period (see table 5.10). As Syonan was under British rule, this is understandable.

(ii) There were almost no female workers in the transport and communications industry.

3. Demand and Supply of Workers

(1) Increasing demand for workers

The increase in working population by month in 25 Japanese-managed companies between September 1943 and April 1944 is shown in table 5.11 (compiled by the Labour Office).[12] The overall trend is an increase in numbers employed. But the data show a few instances of decreasing employment since January (those numbers are underlined in the table). The reasons for this trend are:

(i) Workers are attracted to newly expanding industries.

(ii) There is an increasing labour demand in the military sections, where working conditions are better. (Comparison of the working population at the end of last October and the end of this May shows an increase of about 36,000 labourers in these eight months [in the military sections].)

[12] The names of the companies are anonymized, but we assume that they correspond to those listed in tables 5.1 and 5.2. Overlaps are identifiable from the detailed characterization of the factories in the text.

Table 5.10 Syonan Municipality workers in transport and communications by ethnic group, May 1944

Industry			Ethnic group (male)				Total	Female	Total
			Chinese	Malay	Indian	Other			
Transport	Land	Trains and buses	278	157	558	17	1,010	0	1,010
		Automobiles	935	103	139	11	1,188	0	1,188
		Railways	Δ21	Δ21	Δ170	0	Δ212	0	Δ212
		Oxcarts	60	0	240	0	300	0	300
		Rickshaws	0	0	0	0	×4000	0	×4000
		Tricycles	0	0	0	0	×1920	0	×1920
	Sea		7,175	1,930	440	9	9,554	0	9,554
Loading and unloading	Land		216	0	0	0	216	0	216
	Sea		0	0	0	0	4,547	120	4,667
Communications			52	119	122	8	301	0	301
Total			8,737	2,330	1,669	45	23,248	120	23,368

Notes: 1. Δ Approximate number.
2. × No ethnic data.
3. A few females are included in communications and work as operators.
4. High-ranking employees in government enterprise are excluded.
5. High-ranking sailors in maritime transport are included.

Table 5.11 Syonan Municipality number of workers for 25 selected establishments by month, September 1943–April 1944 [compiled by the Labour Office][13]

	F Mining	N Iron Scrap	O Steel Plate	S Electricity	N Nitrogen	Y Rubber	M Shipbuilding	G Shipbuilding	N Plywood	K Co. Ltd	S Trading Company	K Beer	N Soy Sauce	D Beer	K Civil Engineering	O Construction	N Trading Company	T Construction	E Steel	T Express Train	M Trading Company	B Rationing Association	E Distribution	C Salvage Works Association
September 1943	1,451	985	1,199	231	303	876	298	179	377	254	127	308	115	246	104	208	369	119	183	324	525	185	190	-.
October	1,443	953	1,253	264	349	932	445	184	493	273	147	-.	109	232	105	262	345	246	184	324	527	-.	198	-.
November	1,483	1,032	1,314	268	350	1,030	531	215	528	299	160	341	276	258	110	235	902	253	244	323	529	-.	197	486
December	-.	859	1,329	251	-.	1,030	-.	-.	554	338	158	349	299	255	115	-.	1,397	284	262	-.	-.	-.	196	-.
January 1944	1,604	894	1,172	275	418	1,269	799	-.	528	281	220	-.	328	252	148	-.	1,223	338	241	-.	-.	456	-.	504
February	1,774	950	1,134	275	421	1,215	-.	-.	512	257	284	-.	397	268	159	-.	940	338	264	-.	555	610	199	525
March	1,883	855	1,179	-.	427	1,182	-.	305	510	384	312	333	410	262	163	133	938	360	-.	330	541	633	-.	544
April	-.	790	1,174	274	439	-.	1,458	297	510	-.	313	-.	404	-.	157	219	859	324	249	324	689	-.	-.	540

Note: Underlines indicate a decrease from the previous month.

[13] Company names are not given. Companies are identified by the initial letter of their name. Ten out of 20 selected companies, as in table 5.1, are identifiable: O=Osaka Steel Plates; S=Shibaura Electric; N=Nippon Nitrogen; Y=Yokohama Rubber; G=Goko Shipbuilding; N=Nisshin Plywood; K=Kurosaki Ceramics; K=Kirin Beer; N=Noda Soy Sauce; T=Tajima Construction. Also, one of the 12 transport and communications companies and organizations, as in table 5.2, is identifiable: T=Tokyo Kyuko Electric Transportation. Two of the 16 important factories, as in chapter 6, are identifiable: S=Shiraki Trading Company; D=Dai-nippon Beer. Other identifiable initials, not mentioned in other tables, are: F=Furukawa Mining; N=Nippon Steel Corporation; M=Mitsubishi Heavy Industry Shipyard; M=Mitsubishi Shoji Trading Company; B=Syonan (Busshi) Rationing Association.

However, as quite a few workers have not yet applied for their Labour Book, we suspect a disparity between the numbers reported to the Labour Office and the number actually employed. (A survey of labour conditions in a sample of five factories at the end of this April [1944] showed that although the total workforce reported to the Labour Office was 1,738, we calculated the number actually employed as 1,805. The difference between the two statistics is 67 workers, or 3.8 per cent of the total number reported to the Labour Office.)

We turn to the current new demand for labour (see table 5.12). Among the factories in this survey, 3,095 workers are needed, which is 47 per cent of the entire labour force [6,585] of the [15] factories that are currently recruiting new labour. It is difficult to establish the number needed in this sector as a whole by extrapolating from the evidence of these few factories. If, however, we apply the rate of 47 per cent, as above, to the approximately 45,000 workers employed by Japanese companies (see table 5.7), 21,100 more workers would have to be supplied.

This year's demand for labour in other sectors is now considered:

(i) Maritime workers: The number of sailors rose by 2,382 in the six months before April, an increase of 397 a month. If we extrapolate from these figures, in the next six months there will be a demand for 2,500 new workers.

(ii) Dock labourers: It is said that there is a shortage of about 2,000 labourers in this category. If in the future a shift system of working is introduced, the number of new labourers required will be over 5,000.

(iii) Land transport workers: The production of oxcarts and pushcarts has been increased to supplement lorries, which are in short supply. One coolie is required to operate an oxcart, while handcarts need two or three coolies. If 500 oxcarts and 500 handcarts can be produced by December, they will need about 2,000 coolies to work them.

When the labour force required to increase agricultural production is also taken into account, the number of workers needed in the near future is enormous. It is therefore extremely important to resolve labour shortages; we have to be able to supply enough workers to keep pace with demand at any given time.

Furthermore, the highest rate of demand for labour in the manufacturing industry is found in woodworking (93 per cent) followed by the smelting, chemical and metal-working industries. Although data for the following table has been collected from only a few factories, these data bear out our analysis.

Table 5.12 Syonan Municipality demand for new labour, selected factories, April 1944[14]

	Size of workforce (April 1944)	Extra labour requirement	%
Metalworking	1,685	900	54
Shipbuilding	298	40	13
Ceramics	452	60	13
Chemicals	1,903	1,045	55
Woodworking	648	600	93
Food	625	130	24
Smelting	271	200	22
Miscellaneous	793	100	14
Total	6,585	3095	47

Note: 'Smelting' includes other related production activities.

(2) Turnover of Labour

Of the 20 factories surveyed (see table 5.13), we exclude two ceramics factories that reported no change in labour force, one factory that supplied no data, and some factories that gave answers that were not clear. The remaining 14 factories had recruited 588 workers (9.2 per cent) and discharged 638 (10 per cent).

It is difficult to determine overall conditions from data relating to a single month. In general, however, it may be said that newly constructed factories have a high labour turnover. On the other hand, factories long-established in the pre-war period that have relatively large workforces experience low labour turnover. (Examples are factories D, F, G, O and Q.) These factories have in common that they are all family-owned firms. This is a significant point when taken with the finding of very low labour turnover in small, locally managed factories (see table 5.14).

[14] The aggregate figure for 'metalworking' is for Osaka Steel/Sakaguchi Trading/Tokyo Shibaura. 'Shipbuilding': Goko Shipbuilding. 'Ceramics': Kurosaki Ceramics. 'Chemicals': Nippon Nitrogen/Yokohama Rubber/Dai-Nippon Paint (though the total workforce for these is 1,858 in table 5.13). 'Woodworking': Nissin Plywood/Nozaki Barrel. 'Food': Kirin Beer/Noda Soy Sauce. 'Miscellaneous' includes two textile-related companies: Mitsui Bussan and Used Fabric Bleaching. The sample excludes companies in 'electrical engineering' and 'civil engineering and construction'. Table 5.8 shows the actual total number of workers at the end of May. Despite the labour requirement indicated by this table, only the 'metalworking' industry managed to recruit new labour; other industries failed to recruit enough new labour to fill vacancies.

Table 5.13 Syonan Municipality survey of recruitment and discharge of labour, April 1944 (20 factories)[15]

	Factory	Workers	Recruitment		Discharge		Note
			Number	%	Number	%	
A	[Osaka Steel]	1,179	127	10.8	132	11.2	
B	[Sakaguchi Trading]	232	87	37.5	59	25.4	New factory
C	[Tokyo Shibaura]	274	5	1.9	7	2.6	Convenient for transport
D	[Gokō Shipyard]	298	26	8.7	0	0	Private management
E	[Eifuku Industry]	664	21	3.2	59	8.8	
F	[Kurosaki Ceramics]	453	-	-	-	-	No change
G	[Southern Regions Bricks]	206	-	-	-	-	Low turnover of employees and private management
H	[Nippon Nitrogen]	427	36	8.3	24	5.6	
I	[Yokohama Rubber]	1,248	89	7.1	168	13.4	Partly newly constructed
J	[Dai-Nippon Paint]	183	23	12.6	7	3.8	
K	[Nisshin Plywood]	382	21	5.5	12	3.2	
L	[Nozaki Barrel]	266	35	13.2	20	7.5	New factory
M	[Kirin Beer]	198	15	7.6	17	8.6	

[15] Discharge refers to workers who leave employment in these factories. For example, the note 'convenient for transport' helps to explain the low discharge rate.

(cont'd overleaf)

Table 5.13 (cont'd)

	Factory	Workers	Recruitment		Discharge		Note
			Number	%	Number	%	
N	[Noda Soy Sauce]	427	60	14.1	76	17.8	New factory
O	[Japan Electric Generation]	817	-	-	-	-	Large turnover of employees
P	[Shimizu Construction]	2,000	-	-	-	-	Unknown
Q	[Tajima Construction]	353	1	0.3	8	2.3	Private management
R	[Mitsui Mining]	271	-	-	-	-	Large turnover of employees
S	[Mitsui Bussan]	441	-	-	-	-	Large turnover of employees
T	[Used Fabric Bleaching]	262	42	16.0	49	18.7	New factory
	Total	6,393	588	9.2	628	9.8	

Note: The results for factories F [no change], G [no change], O [no clear answer], P [no data], R [no clear answer] and S [no clear answer] are not included in the total.

Table 5.14 Syonan Municipality labour turnover in locally managed factories, June 1944 (12 local factories)

Factories	Workers	Recruitment	Discharge
A'	44	0	0
B'	44	0	0
C'	48	0	0
D'	4	0	0
E'	14	2	0
F'	18	0	0
G'	162	6	8
H'	43	0	0
I'	11	0	0
J'	7	0	0
K'	41	0	0
L'	37	0	4
Total	421	8 (1.7%)	12 (2.5%)

Factories with locational advantages (good transport connections, proximity to residential areas) also show low rates of labour turnover (for example, factory H on McPherson Road and factory C close to the River Valley area).

There are also gender differences in labour turnover (see table 5.15). The male recruitment rate is 7.5 per cent of the male labour force and the discharge rate 9.8 per cent. The female recruitment rate is 18.4 per cent of the female labour force and the rate of discharge 9.4 per cent. Female recruitment is higher than male because female workers are taken on to fill vacancies arising from male workers having left jobs, as well as in response to the absolute shortage of labour.

For reference purposes, we calculated the total number of workers taken on and discharged in eight factories for the last three months (February, March and April). The overall recruitment rate was 9.7 per cent and the discharge rate 9.2 per cent. From this we conclude that in the last three months these factories became more or less able to find the labour to fill vacancies (see table 5.16).

According to recent research by the Labour Office of Syonan Municipality, the average recruitment rate from January to June was 10.2 per cent and the discharge rate 6.1 per cent (see table 5.17).

Table 5.15 Syonan Municipality labour turnover by gender, April 1943 (10 factories [total 5,563 workers])

Male				Female			
Workers	Recruited	Discharged	Total turnover	Workers	Recruited	Discharged	Total turnover
4,585	342 (7.5%)	451 (9.8%)	793	978	180 (18.4%)	92 (9.4%)	272

Table 5.16 Syonan Municipality labour turnover by month February–April 1944 (8 factories)

February			March			April		
Workers	Recruited	Discharged	Workers	Recruited	Discharged	Workers	Recruited	Discharged
4,865	583 (12.0%)	469 (9.7%)	5,003	393 (7.9%)	383 (7.7%)	5,086	467 (9.2%)	530 (10.4%)

Note: The number of workers is the figure for the beginning of each month.

Table 5.17 Syonan Municipality manual worker recruitment and discharge rates, January–June 1944 (45 factories)

Month	% recruited	% discharged
January	17.2	11.2
February	11.0	5.1
March	6.9	6.0
April	9.8	7.7
May	9.3	5.5
June	7.1	4.2
Average	10.2	6.1

Notes:

Surveyed by the Labour Office in Syonan Municipality.

(1) Data from 45 Japanese-managed factories

(2) Average estimated by Chōsabu

(3) Substitution of female for male labour

The total workforce in 19 of the 20 factories that we surveyed (we excluded a construction subcontractor who did not record gender ratios) was 8,581. Of these, 1,597, or 18 per cent, were females.

When we asked what the upper limit of substitution of female for male labour could be, many answered that it should be more or less around 21–30 per cent (see table 5.18). Internationally, wartime female labour force ratios are 46 per cent in Britain,[16] 47 per cent in Germany, 50 per cent in Italy, 30 per cent in the United States and 50 per cent in the Soviet Union (data from *Diamond*).[17] Compared to these levels of females in the labour force, female ratios in Syonan are still too low.[18] But female labour force ratios are to some extent as high as they can be in view of the intellectual level, physical strength, ethnic divisions and religious barriers of local women as well as the population composition of Syonan Municipality (the female population is 70 per cent of the male). However, because of the urgency and importance of labour shortages, each factory should draw up plans to recruit more female workers. Even in those factories where the maximum possible number of females has been employed, the stated limit may not be the actual limit. (Our research, for example, found one factory that said its limit was only 3 per cent of the labour force but in the same industry another factory told us that the maximum female proportion of its labour force would be 50 per cent. See table 5.18, F and G [i.e., Kurosaki Ceramics and Southern Regions Bricks].)

If the female workforce could be increased to 30 per cent of the labour force [as in Japan], there would be 12 per cent more female workers. Therefore, the total of 45,000 industrial workers employed by Japanese-managed companies (see table 5.7) could be increased by about 5,400 additional female labourers. However, specific local conditions make impossible the substitution of female for male workers in the transport and communications industries.

---

[16] This number appears in a British source, too. See EMP.4.282 Standing Joint Committee of Women's Industrial Organization, The Position of Women after the War, p. 4.

[17] A weekly opinion magazine on economic issues aimed at a general readership.

[18] These figures may refer to World War I. The article is 'How to Use the Underutilized Workforce', *Diamond* 31, 18 (21 June 1943): 20–1. For a more accurate review of World War II female labour force participation rates, see Alan S. Milward, *War, Economy and Society 1939–1945*, London: Penguin, 1977, pp. 219–21.

Table 5.18 Syonan Municipality females as a percentage of the total labour force and new demand for female employment, April 1944

Factory	Total	Males	Females	% Female	New demand for female workers	Notes
A [Osaka Steel]	1,179	1,061	118	10	20%	Metalworking
B [Sakaguchi Trading]	232	210	22	10	None	Metalworking
C [Tokyo Shibaura]	274	260	14	5	12%	Metalworking
D [Gokō Shipyard]	298	237	61	20	None	Shipbuilding
E [Eifuku Industry]	664	655	9	1	None	Shipbuilding
F [Kurosaki Ceramics]	453	392	61	13	50%	Ceramics
G [Southern Regions Bricks]	206	200	6	3	None	Ceramics
H [Nippon Nitrogen]	427	411	16	4	15%	Chemicals
I [Yokohama Rubber]	1,248	788	460	38	50%	Chemicals
J [Dai-Nippon Paint]	183	160	23	13	None	Chemicals
K [Nisshin Plywood]	382	271	111	29	33%	Woodworking
L [Nozaki Barrel]	266	214	52	20	None	Woodworking
M [Kirin Beer]	198	113	85	42	None	Food
N [Noda Soy Sauce]	427	327	100	23	None	Food
O [Japan Electric Generation]	817	817	0	10	25%	Electrical
P [Shimizu Construction]	-	-	-	-	-	Civil engineering
Q [Tajima Construction]	353	324	29	6	12%	Civil engineering
R [Mitsui Mining]	271	222	49	18	None	Smelting
S [Mitsui Bussan]	441	141	300	68	None	Spinning
T [Used Fabric Bleaching]	262	181	81	31	None	Bleaching
Total	8,581	6,984	1,597	18		

(4) *Methods of new labour recruitment*

Of the 20 factories surveyed, 14 recruited labourers through personal connections, 3 used subcontractors, 1 replied that it left recruitment to an Indian manager, 1 replied that it used the Labour Office, and 1 replied that special locational conditions (Bukit Timah Road, Mile 7) made any recruitment policy unnecessary. It would therefore seem that labour recruitment policies are close to those under absolutely free market conditions. So long as this situation persists, imbalances between the demand and supply of labour will cause unauthorized [black market] payments or variations in wages and create unanticipated difficulties in labour administration.

Although almost none of the factories used the Labour Office of Syonan Municipality for labour recruitment, workers employed by the army are often hired through the office. The current situation [as detailed by the Labour Office] is set out in table 5.19.

Overall, the availability of temporary workers is adequate at present. But the severe imbalance in permanent employment between demand and supply makes urgent the development of a new source of labour (see tables 5.19 and 5.20).

Table 5.19 Syonan Municipality adequacy in the supply of temporary labourers, June 1944

Month	January	February	March	April	May	June
Demand	87,272	80,531	48,073	38,942	45,074	52,696
Supply	55,437	59,192	48,347	38,671	42,497	41,392
% Replenished	63.5	73.5	100.6	99.3	94.3	78.6

Surveyed by Labour Office, Syonan Municipality.

Table 5.20 Syonan Municipality adequacy in the supply of permanent labourers, June 1944

Month	January	February	March	April	May	June
Demand	1,920	1,142	2,149	1,786	5,506	3,436
Supply	373	1,028	658	522	773	443
% Replenished	19.0	90.0	31.0	29.0	14.0	18.0

Surveyed by Labour Office, Syonan Municipality.

4. Labour Conditions

(1) Wages

The average daily male wage is $1.79 and the female wage $1.07 (see table 5.21). The reason for the high female wage is that factory G [Southern Regions Bricks] pays $1.50, factory L [Nozaki Barrel] $1.52, and factory T [Syonan Textile Bleaching] $1.30. These factories' female wage rates are high. Excluding these special cases, the average female wage is 97 cents. At locally managed industrial factories, the average wage is $5.43 for males, $2.84 for females, $2 for girls and $1 for boys. (The figures are for the end of June. Although these figures are not strictly comparable with the averages of Japanese-managed factories in April 1944, they will help in understanding the overall pattern of wages.) Comparing locally managed factories with Japanese-managed factories, wages are about three times higher for males and double for females. (If female wages are 97 cents [excluding special cases] in Japanese-run factories, they are three times higher in locally managed factories.) Furthermore, taking into account payments in kind and other benefits at local factories, wage disparities are a serious problem (see table 5.24).

We do not have sufficient data from our survey to comment on wage increments. But a recent survey of three factories over five months (see table 5.22) indicates that there was not much difference in the daily nominal wage while real monthly income increased slightly. There are several special allowances, including family allowance (two factories), transport costs (two factories), attendance bonus (four factories), bonus for speaking Japanese (two factories), hazard pay, tool allowance (where workers use their own tools), hygiene allowance and holiday allowance ($1 is paid as drink money for employees who work during the four large festivals).

Table 5.21 Syonan Municipality labour conditions for selected 20 factories, April 1944[19]

	Male wages ($)	Female wages ($)	Allowances	Working hours	Overtime daily	Days off	Absenteeism (%)
A	2.10	1.50		8.00		Twice monthly	30
B	2.80	1.20		Daytime 8.00 Night 4.30		Day and night work on weekly shift	13
C	1.95	1.00	Family allowance	8.30	2.00	Every Sunday	35
D	Contract			8.30		None	5
E	2.60	1.10		8.00	2.00	Twice monthly	7
F	1.90	1.10	Tool, good attendance, holiday allowances	8.30		None	6
G	1.80	1.50		10.00		None	26
H	1.20	0.70	Commuting, night work, family, Japanese-speaking allowances	Daytime 8.00 Night 6.00		None	High
I	1.5	0.75	Good attendance allowance	9.00		Every Sunday	15
J	2.50	1.30	Good attendance allowance	8.00		None	22
K	1.90	0.80		8.00	2.00	Twice monthly	16
L	3.00	1.52	Hazard pay, hygiene allowance	7.00		Twice monthly	15

[19] Companies A–T are the same as in tables 5.1, 5.13 and 5.18.

(cont'd overleaf)

Table 5.21 (cont'd)

	Male wages ($)	Female wages ($)	Allowances	Working hours	Overtime daily	Days off	Absenteeism (%)
M	1.45	0.84		8.30		Every Sunday	8
N	1.30	0.90	Japanese-speaking, executive, good attendance allowances	8.00		Twice monthly	17
O	-		Commuting allowance	7.20	2.00	Twice monthly (optional)	25
P	Contract			8.00		None	-
Q	-			8.00		None	13
R	1.30–4.00	1.00		8.30	2.00	Every Sunday	17
S	1.00	0.85		8.00		None	High
T	1.60	Piecework		8.15		Part of every Sunday	10

Summary notes:

Allowances: The allowances paid in the surveyed companies include family allowance, allowance for good attendance, commuting allowance, Japanese-speaking allowance, hazard pay, tool allowance, hygiene allowance and holiday allowance.

Working hours: On average 8 hours 30 minutes.

Overtime: Five companies allow overtime work of two hours and provide overtime payment.

Holidays: Six companies provide days off twice monthly (including optional); four companies allow a day off every Sunday; eight companies allow no days off.

Absenteeism: On average 15%.Two factories replied 'high' but gave no clear figure; one factory provided no data.

Table 5.22 Syonan Municipality daily and monthly wage scales, January–May 1944, in three selected factories, in comparison to a transport company

				January	February	March	April	May
Beer	Chinese	Male	Nominal	-	1.14	1.22	1.15	-
			Real	-	32.00	34.56	33.38	-
		Female	Nominal	-	0.58	0.49	0.65	-
			Real	-	16.42	16.75	20.69	-
	Malay	Male	Nominal	-	0.95	0.95	1.07	-
			Real	-	23.98	20.88	34.75	-
		Female	Nominal	-	0.73	0.71	0.77	-
			Real	-	16.51	15.03	21.44	-
	Indian	Male	Nominal	-	1.35	1.36	1.63	-
			Real	-	43.35	41.56	52.27	-
Rubber	Malay	Male	Nominal	-	-	-	-	1.37
	(Hosepipe)		Real (daily)	1.48	1.55	1.64	1.72	1.65
	Chinese	Female	Nominal	-	-	-	-	0.80
	(Latex)		Real (daily)	0.85	0.89	0.93	0.98	0.91
Steel sheet	Factory total		Nominal	-	1.39	1.37	1.33	1.29
			Real	-	54.27	56.17	54.66	53.32
Transport	Chinese		Nominal	1.02	1.00	1.24	1.28	1.25
(lorry drivers)			Real	33.55	36.84	41.65	47.36	51.17
	Indian		Nominal	1.00	1.01	1.24	1.15	1.15
			Real	33.56	35.39	38.33	41.56	39.38
	Malay		Nominal	1.00	1.04	1.35	1.34	1.34
			Real	33.08	38.27	48.00	47.87	46.73

Note: Wages are daily wages for nominal wages and monthly wages for real wages, unless otherwise stated in brackets. In the rubber company, Malays, predominantly men, work in the hosepipe section, and Chinese, mostly women, work in the latex section.

Table 5.23 Syonan Municipality daily wage scales, June 1944

Industry	Maximum	Minimum	Average
Mining	3.50	1.60	-
Stone collecting	3.00	1.50	-
Metalworking industry	5.50	2.00	-
Shipbuilding	4.00	2.10	-
Chemical industry	5.00	1.00	-
Gas, electricity, waterworks	3.60	2.10	-
Nitrogen and quarrying	3.00	1.20	-
Spinning	-	-	-
Lumber and wood	3.50	1.50	-
Foods	3.50	1.30	-
Printing and bookbinding	5.00	1.00	-
Civil engineering and construction	3.50	1.20	-
Other industry	3.00	1.00	-
Agriculture and forestry	2.00	0.95	-
Fisheries	-	-	-
Transport	3.30	1.00	-
Miscellaneous	2.50	1.20	-
Commerce	2.50	1.00	-

Table 5.24 Syonan Municipality daily wage scales in small locally managed factories, June 1944 (12 factories)

Factory	Industry	Male wages ($)	Female wages ($)	Payments in kind	Note
A'	Glass	-		2 cigarettes (daily), three meals (daily) for adult males	
B'	Paper	21.00 (Boy 1.50)	4.00 (Girl 1.80)	5 catties of rice (monthly)	
C'	Tobacco		5.00	None	Female workers only
D'	Rattan furniture	60.00 monthly		3 meals (daily)	Male workers only
E'	Printing	2.30	1.50	2 cigarettes (daily) for men 5 catties of rice (monthly) for all	
F'	Leather	3.50		3 meals (daily)	Male workers only
G'	Iron	10.00	2.40	15 catties of rice (monthly)	Rice is supplied by the army.
H'	Machinery	5.00	2.00	2 cigarettes (daily) for males 5 catties of rice (monthly) for all	
I'	Printing	3.50		5 catties of rice (monthly)	Male workers only
J'	Rubber	4.00	3.00	3 meals (daily)	
K'	Palm plantation	1.80		9 catties of rice (monthly) 2 cigarettes (daily)	This is an Indian company. The workers are also all Indian.
L'	Soap	1.20 (Boy 0.50)	2.00 (Girl 1.20)	3 meals (daily) for men 5 catties of rice (monthly) for all	

Summary notes:
Average wages: Males 5.43, females 2.84, girls 2.00, boys 1.00.
Payment in kind: Five factories provide three meals daily, and four factories provide two cigarettes daily. As for rice, one factory provides 15 catties monthly, another nine catties monthly, and five factories five catties monthly.

It is widely known that wage systems such as those for subcontracted work and piecework systems stimulate the work efficiency of the local, particularly Chinese, labour force. A study of these wage systems should urgently be done, and subcontracted work and piecework systems should be introduced if possible. However, if factories are unable to secure good supervisors or instructors, these systems, rather than increasing profits, will only be a bad influence. Prizes and bonuses if applied skillfully have also proved to be effective in raising productivity. Their use should also be studied. There is a precedent provided by factory N that suggests pay-for-performance (paid when productivity exceeds a certain level) has some impact.

Wages in the transport sector are generally low (the average wage is $1.38 a day). Wages generally tend to be low especially for government undertakings (trains, railways, buses). However, trishaw and rickshaw drivers earn relatively high wages. (Trishaw drivers earn $10–20 daily. Because vehicle hire costs $2 daily, their actual income is thus $8–18 daily.) Overtime payments are made according to rules applying to factories (Ordinance of Finance and Salaries, Rule 2-[4]) in all the cases surveyed.

(2) Payments in kind

With the current fall in the value of money, payments in kind may be more important than cash wages. The situation for payment in kind in the 20 selected factories is shown in table 5.25.

The most important element in payments in kind is rice. Payment in rice is the surest method of securing a workforce under the present conditions of food shortage. Provision of rice has been the only reason that continues to prevent labour from migrating to locally managed factories. Differences in labour turnover between military sector workers and civilian sector workers are due also to the imbalance in rice distribution. Each factory distributes rice on a scale assigned by the Labour Office, which classifies work as heavy or light, and also according to each worker's employment record (see table 5.25). Monthly statistics compiled since the introduction of the priority rationing system in Syonan Municipality are shown in table 5.26.

Table 5.25 Syonan Municipality payments in kind for 20 selected factories, April 1944[20]

Factory	Rice monthly (catties)	Tobacco and other	Note
A	Males 9 Females 6	1 tobacco daily 1 soap for laundry	Half loaf of tapioca bread paid for overtime work
B	9 per person		Paid by rate of attendance
C	5 per person		Nail factory pays 5 catties extra from Special Rations provided by the armoury.
D	-	-	
E	9 for heavy workers 5 for light workers	Tobacco	3 catties of rice is distributed to clerks from company's own stock of rice. Some of the Special Rations rice is provided in the form of lunch.
F	Average 6–7		
G	9	Tobacco	
H	Average 8	Tobacco	
I	-		
J	Average 5–6		Special Rations are given to workers with good attendance records, and to workers in priority work and to those working overtime.
K	Average 12		Payment dependent on attendance.
L	Average 10		Payment dependent on attendance.

[20] Factories A–T refer to those in tables 5.1, 5.13, 5.18 and 5.21.

(cont'd overleaf)

Table 5.25 (cont'd)

Factory	Rice monthly (catties)	Tobacco and other	Note
M	Males 4 Females and children 2	1–2 coffee weekly	
N	10 for workers in heavy labour		Payment dependent on attendance.
O	5		
P	500 workers daily		Extra 20% ration for night work. Commuters get only 60% of ration.
Q	Average 10–12		
R	9 for workers in heavy labour 5 for workers in light labour	Tobacco on Special Rations	Rationed rice is cooked and distributed. Laundry soap, salted fish, fruit and garden vegetables are also provided
S	200 workers daily	Tobacco	
T	5		The ration is reduced for significantly poor attendance records.

Table 5.26 Syonan Municipality priority rations for manual workers, September 1943–May 1944

Month	Number of people receiving priority rations	Increase in rations per labourer (catties)	General public		
			Male	Female	Child
September 1943	19,329	5	12	12	12
October	26,056	5	12	12	12
November	28,794	5	12	9	6
December	32,842	5	12	9	6
January 1944	29,412	5	12	9	6
February	33,782	5	8	6	4
March	13,673	5	8	6	4
	32,429	9	8	6	4
April	27,311	5	8	6	4
	36,800	9	8	6	4
May	19,003	5	8	6	4
	38,482	9	8	6	4

Table 5.27 Syonan Municipality tobacco rations, October 1943–May 1944

Month	Number of people	Cigarettes for labourers, pieces	Cigarettes for others, pieces
October 1943	24,418	3,298,920	-
November	36,169	5,492,700	-
December	47,011	5,790,300	-
January 1944	46,771	4,481,880	-
February	46,929	4,496,340	22,601,250
March	46,972	4,491,660	31,515,950
April	48,496	4,499,560	16,406,730
May	48,874	4,500,540	9,744,440

Note: The rise in the number of labourers reflects an increase in the number of applications, not an increase in the absolute number of individuals. Assessed by Syonan Municipality, Labour Office.

(3) Working hours

(i) Working hours

The actual working day is 8 hours 30 minutes on average. Compared to the working day in Japan of about 10 hours (see note 1), this is short but has to be interpreted in light of climatic conditions and ethnic customs. It should be noted that although factory G [Southern Regions Bricks] responded that a working day was ten hours, its rate of absenteeism was also high (26 per cent). Where the food supply is adequate, some factories can add one or two hours of overtime (see table 5.21). Only five factories have begun to introduce overtime and have extended the working day by two hours. In the pre-war period, working hours were limited to nine (and in practice, eight hours were worked) (see note 2).

(ii) Days off

Sunday was reserved as a day off at four factories. However, six factories allowed a day off twice a month (including one factory that allowed ad hoc leave two or three times a month), while eight factories set no days off. We tried to establish whether there was a connection between days off and absenteeism, but within the confines of our research the relationship of the two elements proved elusive. However, it should be noted that when one factory operated Sunday working, the rate of absenteeism increased (see 4-[4]).

During the pre-war period a six-day week was the norm, but there was no standard practice with regard to days off set by law (see note 2). There is no reliable source on working hours and overtime in the transport sector.

In most small local factories eight hours are actually worked. (Among 12 factories, one had a working day of 9 hours, one a working day of 8 hours 20 minutes, one a working day of 8 hours 30 minutes, and the remainder of the factories a working day of 8 hours.) This has been customary since the period of British administration.

Note 1: Japan length of working days in factories

December 1941	January 1942	February	March	April	May
10 hrs 40 mins	10 hrs 34 mins	10 hrs 40 mins	10 hrs 34 mins	10 hrs 39 mins	10 hrs 32 mins

Note 2: For details, see Harold Butler, *Problems of Industry in the East: With Special Reference to India, French India, Ceylon, Malaya and the Netherlands Indies* (International Labour Office publication), trans. Eizō Sakai (Tokyo: Hanyōsha, 1942), p. 110.

Table 5.28 sets out data from the Labour Office of Syonan Municipality on the lengths of the working day in various industries.

Table 5.28 Syonan Municipality length of working day (hours and minutes)

Industry	Maximum working day	Minimum working day	Average
Mining	10.00	10.00	10.00
Stone quarrying	10.00	10.00	10.00
Metalworking	10.00	8.30	9.50
Shipbuilding	10.00	9.00	9.50
Gas, electricity, waterworks	9.00	9.00	9.00
Chemicals	10.00	9.00	9.20
Ceramics	10.00	10.00	10.00
Lumber and wood	10.00	9.00	9:30
Foods	10.00	8.30	9:40
Printing and bookbinding	10.00	8.30	9.10
Civil engineering and construction	10.00	9.00	9.30
Other manufacturing	10.00	8.30	9.00
Agriculture and forestry	10.00	10.00	10.00
Fisheries	10.00	9.00	9.50
Transport	10.00	9.00	9.40
Commerce	10.00	9.00	9.50
Miscellaneous	10.00	10.00	9.20

Surveyed by Syonan Municipality Labour Office.

Note: Within these working hours, 1–1.5 hours are allowed for breaks. Therefore, actual working hours are 1–1.5 hours less than the hours given above.

(4) Rate of absenteeism

We estimate that on average the absenteeism rate in April was 15 per cent (see table 5.21). There are large variations in absenteeism between factories because of differences in the way each factory treats and records absenteeism. (For example, some factories exclude from the report workers with particularly high absenteeism records.) While we regard the information provided by factories as reliable, when we surveyed the worker attendance of five companies in May we found an average attendance of 83.4 per cent (see table 5.29), giving an absenteeism rate of about 17 per cent. For gender differences in attendance, accuracy is difficult to achieve, as there is no survey providing gender-specific data [for all five companies]. Attendance of female workers at a woodworking factory [probably Nozaki Barrel] was 87.2 per cent and at a food factory [Noda Soy Sauce] 70 per cent. The average for both factories is about 79 per cent. This is a low level when compared with the male attendance at these two factories of 89 per cent.

We now show monthly average levels of absenteeism in a rubber company over the last year. The following figure is based on accurately calculated rates.

Figure 5.1 Fluctuation in absenteeism levels in a rubber company in Syonan Municipality

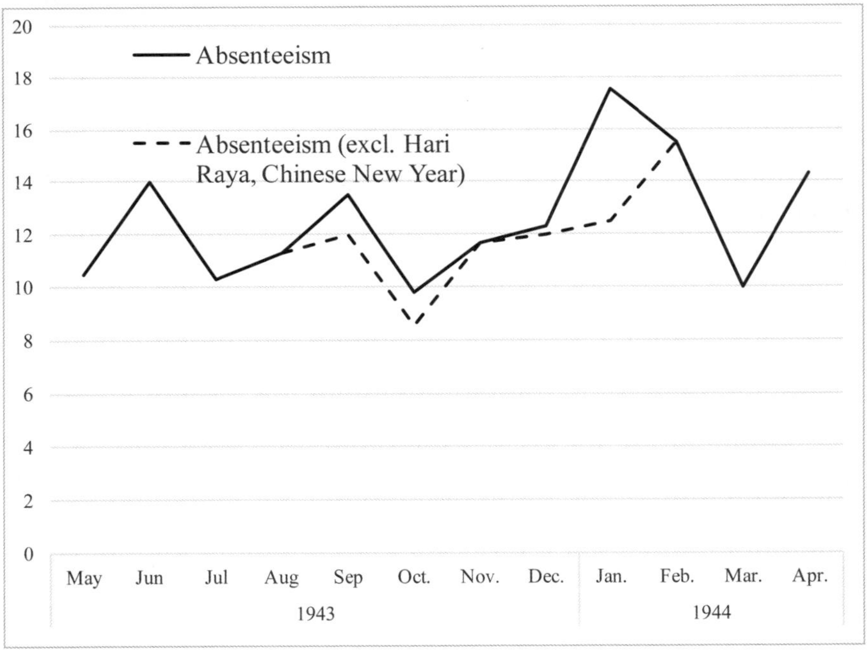

Note 1: 'Absenteeism' is defined here as the percentage of absent workers in the total workforce.

Note 2: The dotted line shows the average rate of absenteeism excluding the exceptionally high figures for 30 September and 1 October (just after the Puasa [Hari Raya Puasa]), and 25 and 26 January (Chinese New Year).

Table 5.29 Syonan Municipality attendance rates of workers, May 1944 (5 factories)

Day	Day of week	Woodwork [Nozaki Wooden Barrel]			Food [Noda Soy Sauce]					Metalwork [Osaka Steel Plate]	Rubber [Yokohama Rubber]	Transport [Southern Regions Co.]
		Male	Female	Total	Male	Boy	Female	Girl	Total			
1	Mon.	89.4	90.9	90.8	90.0	93.0	73.0	95.0	89.0	80.4	80.5	84.0
2	Tue.	77.4	88.3	78.9	96.0	95.0	84.0	100.0	95.0	73.5	83.4	84.0
3	Wed. (rainy)	81.4	85.9	82.4	96.0	85.0	52.0	95.0	88.0	83.4	86.7	86.0
4	Thur. (rainy)	87.1	87.8	87.2	97.0	95.0	77.0	100.0	94.0	78.8	84.8	85.0
5	Fri.	85.4	90.7	86.9	97.0	95.0	72.0	98.0	97.0	70.7	80.4	83.0
6	Sat.	85.5	87.5	86.2	99.0	95.0	84.0	100.0	96.0	73.9	83.9	85.0
7	Sun. (rainy)									20.3		80.0
8	Mon. (rainy)	78.3	88.6	80.6	97.0	83.0	58.0	88.0	87.0	73.7	78.2	78.0
9	Tue.	82.2	85.9	83.3	96.0	95.0	68.0	90.0	90.0	76.4	88.9	87.0
10	Wed.	84.2	91.1	86.2	95.0	95.0	72.0	98.0	92.0	76.6	89.6	90.0
11	Thur. (rainy)	86.8	87.5	87.9	89.0	89.0	68.0	100.0	88.0	74.7	87.8	89.0
12	Fri.	79.1	84.0	80.6	96.0	95.0	58.0	88.0	88.0	78.8	78.0	90.0
13	Sat.	77.2	79.2	77.8	98.0	95.0	68.0	95.0	92.0	73.7	77.9	88.0
14	Sun.	80.3	81.4	80.3								
15	Mon.	88.3	91.7	89.3	99.0	89.0	81.0	95.0	94.0	79.9	81.1	90.0
16	Tue.	83.7	81.8	83.2	96.0	83.0	58.0	93.0	88.0	67.1	80.2	89.0
17	Wed. (rainy)	70.7	80.6	80.2	90.0	77.0	72.0	93.0	86.0	71.0	82.3	89.0

(cont'd overleaf)

Table 5.29 (cont'd)

Day	Day of week	Woodwork [Nozaki Wooden Barrel]			Food [Noda Soy Sauce]					Metalwork [Osaka Steel Plate]	Rubber [Yokohama Rubber]	Transport [Southern Regions Co.]
		Male	Female	Total	Male	Boy	Female	Girl	Total			
18	Thur.	82.9	81.8	82.6	92.0	91.0	71.0	98.0	88.0	71.8	82.5	86.0
19	Fri.	83.1	86.4	84.9	92.0	95.0	84.0	82.0	91.0	74.1	89.5	85.0
20	Sat.	88.6	88.3	88.5	99.0	100.0	87.0	95.0	96.0	76.5	80.5	87.0
21	Sun.									25.5		85.0
22	Mon. (rainy)	82.9	87.1	84.2	95.0	100.0	56.0	93.0	89.0	76.1	82.5	87.0
23	Tue.	85.8	85.0	85.6	96.0	100.0	67.0	93.0	91.0	79.9	82.4	87.0
24	Wed.	77.5	89.3	81.3	95.0	95.0	71.0	98.0	92.0	74.2	84.4	82.0
25	Thur.	75.6	86.1	79.3	90.0	95.0	56.0	85.0	84.0	78.3	82.1	89.0
26	Fri.	76.4	92.5	81.7	98.0	100.0	77.0	95.0	94.0	74.9	84.0	88.0
27	Sat.	87.9	91.4	89.0	95.0	100.0	72.0	72.0	93.0	78.5	85.6	87.0
28	Sun.	78.2	95.4	83.9						58.2		84.0
29	Mon.	69.2	94.4	84.2	87.0	90.0	68.0	93.0	86.0	71.4	86.8	90.0
30	Tue.	82.0	90.3	84.6	90.0	100.0	77.0	93.0	90.0	79.1	86.0	82.0
31	Wed.	86.6	93.5	88.7	98.0	85.0	68.0	93.0	90.0	81.5	86.6	83.0
Average		82.7	87.6	84.1	95.0	93.0	70.0	94.0	91.0	71.5	83.6	86.0

Summary notes:
Average male attendance in the woodwork factory was 82.7%, and female attendance was 87.6%.
By contrast, in the food factory the average male attendance was 95% and female attendance was 70%.
The combined average for these two factories was 89% for males and 79% for females.

Table 5.30 Syonan Municipality welfare facilities and workers' organizations for 20 selected companies, April 1944[21]

Factory	Accommodation	Means of transport	Medical facilities	Labourers' organization	Labour training	Note
A	None	12 lorries	None	Leader – unit leader – mechanic – apprentice – coolie	Training only for 30 special mechanics	Steel plate
B	Planning	2 lorries	None	Manager – assistant manager – mechanic	None	Busheled iron
C	None	None	None	Japanese engineer – foreman – labourer	None	Electric/Nail making
D	None	Use of lorry after 7.30pm when it rains	None	Kepala – labourer	None	Shipbuilding
E	None	None	Appointed doctor	Group leader (coolie leader) – coolie	None	Shipbuilding
F	70 rooms for about 300 labourers	12 lorries	Simple medical facility but no doctor	Japanese manager – Indian manager – secretary – foreman – mechanic	Planning to train special mechanics	Ceramics
G	30 houses for 60–120 labourers	None	None	Coolie leader – coolie	None	Brickmaking
H	30 houses for 30 leading skilled workers and their families	None, but travel allowance is paid	None	Leader – assistant foreman – group leader – assistant group leader – unit leader	Plan suspended	Nitrogen

[21] Factories A–T refer to those in tables 5.1, 5.13, 5.18, 5.21 and 5.25.

(cont'd overleaf)

Table 5.30 (cont'd)

Factory	Accommodation	Means of transport	Medical facilities	Labourers' organization	Labour training	Note
I	Coolie lines	Lorry	Commissioned doctor (twice a week)	Leader – unit leader – engineer – coolie	None	Rubber
J	[Accommodation for] 5 skilled workers and their families	1 lorry	Appointed doctor	Leader – mechanic	Planning	Paint
K	5 Mandore families	None	None	Mandore – factory labourer	Planned but not yet realized	Plywood
L	5 houses for 15 families	2 lorries	None	Kepala – coolie leader – coolie	None	Wooden barrel making
M	Coolie lines for about 45 labourers	1 lorry	Medical room and an Indian assistant surgeon	Foreman – unit leader – mechanic	Japanese training (one hour per day)	Beer
N	None	3 lorries	None	Unit leader – labourer	Planned but not yet realized	Soy source
O	Coolie lines for 100 labourers	None, but travel allowance is paid	None	Foreman – mechanic – coolie leader – coolie	None	Electric engineering
P	None	Lorry	None	-	None	Construction
Q	None	3 lorries	None	Coolie leader – coolie	None	Construction
R	20 houses for 500 labourers	Lorry	Commissioned doctor (once a week)	Foreman – assistant – unit leader	None	Mining
S	None	Lorry	None	Coolie leader – coolie	None	Spinning
T	None	None	None	-	-	Textile bleaching

(i) High absenteeism in January and February, especially in January, was due to the absenteeism of Chinese labourers because of Chinese New Year on 25 and 26 January, which was an important factor. But the sharp rise in prices of daily necessities (the price index was 712 in October, 766 in November, 869 in December, 1069 in January and 1438 in February) must have also played a part in the high rate of absenteeism. Price rises caused considerable unease and led to a deterioration in diets and rising levels of exhaustion and disease.

(ii) High absenteeism on 30 September (42 per cent) and 1 October (42 per cent) resulted from these days being immediately after the Puasa [Hari Raya Puasa]. Similarly, the high absenteeism of 25 and 26 January (61 per cent and 60 per cent respectively) was occasioned by Chinese New Year. Such events reflect seasonal fluctuations arising from local customs.

5. Welfare Facilities

(1) Workers' housing

In terms of accommodation for workers, ten companies in our survey provide housing and ten do not (see table 5.30). Even among the companies that do provide housing, only four accommodate general labourers. Other companies house mainly supervisors, mechanics or engineers. The provision of housing is an urgent matter in improving attendance rates, avoiding labour turnover, increasing efficiency through the use of a shift system, and improving workers' welfare through guidance in recreation and hygiene. But the shortage of materials and labour in current conditions makes it difficult to provide sufficient accommodation.

(2) Workers' transport

Ten factories informed us that they use lorries to pick up and drop off labourers every day. One factory responded that it uses a lorry only after 7.30pm and during wet weather (see table 5.30, Factory D). Inadequate transport affects when work can start and is a major impediment to efficiency. The number of days on which lorry transport services are provided is decreasing, because of the shortage of spare parts and tyres. All the factories raised this problem with us. The state of repair of tram lines and city buses is also deteriorating to the extent that only one-third of trams and buses are in service (see table 5.31). The inevitable result is severe crowding at rush hours. It should be noted that without question these problems negatively affect workers: they spend too much time on transport and are physically drained.

Table 5.31 (A) Syonan Municipality operating trams, April 1943–March 1944

Date	Total number of trams	Number of trams in operation	Percentage of trams in operation
April 1943	63.0	49.9	79.2
May	63.4	53.5	84.7
June	63.1	46.8	74.2
July	63.0	40.1	63.6
August	63.0	29.5	46.8
September	63.0	26.0	41.3
October	63.0	31.1	49.4
November	63.0	19.1	29.5
December	63.0	15.6	24.7
January 1944	63.0	18.7	29.7
February	63.0	20.0	31.7
March	63.0	23.0	36.5

Surveyed by Syonan Municipality Department of Transport.

Table 5.31 (B) Syonan Municipality operating buses, April 1943–March 1944

Date	Total number of buses	Number of buses in operation	Percentage of buses in operation
April 1943	110.0	47.6	43.3
May	110.0	44.3	40.3
June	110.0	41.7	37.9
July	110.0	34.4	31.3
August	110.0	28.3	25.7
September	110.0	52.2	47.5
October	110.0	37.1	33.7
November	110.0	19.9	11.1
December	110.0	17.8	16.2
January 1944	110.0	27.8	25.3
February	109.8	26.3	24.0
March	109.0	23.0	21.3

Surveyed by Syonan Municipality Department of Transport.

Table 5.32 (A) illustrates the results of the lorry service survey for four factories on Bukit Timah Road and three in the Pasir Panjang area, which use lorries to pick up and drop off labourers.

Thus, for Bukit Timah Road factories six or seven vehicles are sent to New Bridge Road, Serangoon Road and Jalan Besar. A few vehicles are allocated around Serangoon Road and Tiong Bahru to serve factories at Pasir Panjang. The fact that the lorries go around Serangoon Road and Tiong Bahru shows that those areas are densely populated with labourers.

Table 5.32 (A) Syonan Municipality distribution of vehicles allocated for workers' transport, Bukit Timah Road factories

Location	Woodwork [Nozaki Barrels]	Battery [Kurosaki Ceramics]	Steel plate [Osaka Steel]	Soy sauce [Noda Soy Sauce]	Total
Tanjong Pagar New Bridge Road by Southern Sky Restaurant, Cross Street and Upper Cross Street	1	1	3	1	6
Serangoon Road, Jalan Besar by the Central Hospital, Bukit Timah 3 miles	1	2	3	2	8
Geylang Road		1	1		2
Paya Lebar		1	1		2
Bukit Timah 10 miles			3	3	6
Jurong Road 3 miles		1			1
Total	2	6	12	3	26

Notes:
A lorry for the woodworking factory goes around River Valley after Upper Cross Street.
A lorry for the steel plate factory stops by Bukit Timah 3 miles.
A lorry for the battery factory goes around Tanjong Pagar after Geylang Road.
The steel plate factory sends three small vehicles to Bukit Timah Road.

Table 5.32 (B) Syonan Municipality distribution of vehicles allocated for workers' transport, Pasir Panjang Road factories

Location	Bricks [Southern Regions Bricks]	Paints [Dai-Nippon Paint]	Rubber [Yokohama Rubber]	Total
Tanjong Pagar	1			1
New Bridge Road				
Southern Sky Restaurant, Cross Street and Upper Cross Street				
Serangoon Road	1		2	3
Jalan Besar, Central Hospital, Jalan Sultan, Middle Road				
Geylang Road		1		1
Alexandra Road, Tiong Bahru, Keppel Harbour			3	3
West Coast			1	1
Total	2	1	6	9

Note: A lorry for the brick factory goes around Tiong Bahru Street after Tanjong Pagar, and another goes around Orchard Road and Hill Street after Serangoon Road.

(3) Medical facilities and treatment of illness and injury

No factory has proper medical facilities. One factory has a medical room and an Indian doctor. Others have contracted doctors who come once or twice a week. Two factories have appointed doctors, and 15 factories have no policy whatsoever. Sick workers are sent to the Syonan Municipality Central Hospital or the Maternity Hospital.

All factories bear the medical costs of industrial injuries. But there is almost no provision for disease or injury that occurs outside work or among family members. Table 5.33 shows medical provisions in a rubber factory, which provides the best care of the factories surveyed.

The general rule for industrial injuries is that when a worker is injured in an accident for which he is not responsible, the factory pays the cost of medical treatment from a contracted or appointed doctor. An allowance equal to the worker's wage is also paid during his absence from work (Code of Workers Payment, Rule 13, of this factory).

Figure 5.2 Distribution of workers in Syonan Municipality

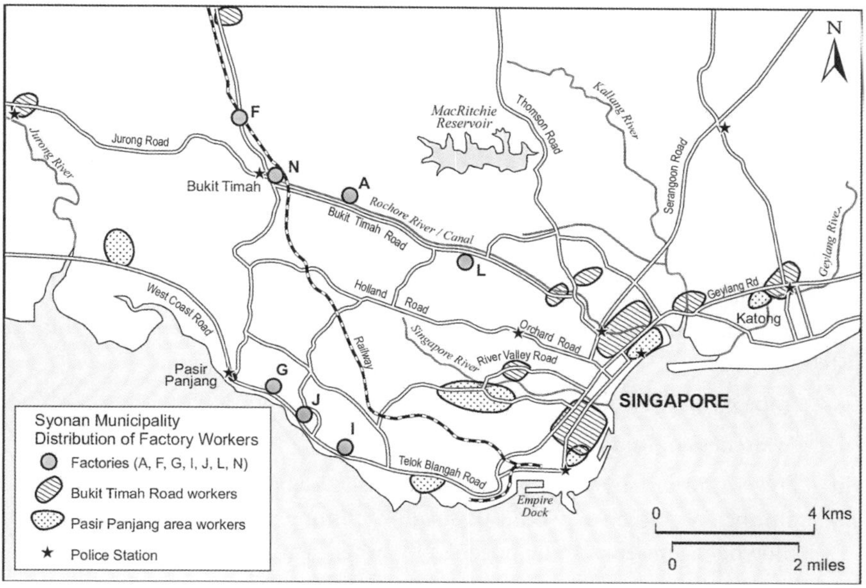

Table 5.33 sets out the scale of allowances for general injuries and illness.

Table 5.33 Injury and disease allowance for a rubber company

	Injury and disease	Medical subvention (%)
1.	The worker	
	(1) Malaria	100
	(2) Acute infectious disease	90
	(3) Other	50
2.	Family	
	(1) Malaria	50
	(2) Acute infectious disease	50
	(3) Other	20

Note: The worker's 10% (or 50% or 20%) share of medical expenses may vary depending on the case. In all cases, the subvention is paid only after examination by the doctor appointed or contracted by the company.

Simple medical facilities (with at least a nurse and appropriate medicine) should urgently be established at each factory to prevent absenteeism, retain the workforce and nurture the workers.

(4) Educational guidance and training of workers

Many companies insist that formal training institutions would be necessary to provide workers with educational guidance and training. Only two factories in the ceramics industry considered training/guidance institutions to be unnecessary.

A few factories are planning to establish a training institution, but it is difficult to realize the project because of the shortage of instructors. It is unnecessary to expand further on the importance of education. Reasons to emphasize this are listed below.

(i) Improvement of skills

(ii) Awareness training for a state of emergency

(iii) Prevention of labour turnover among skilled labourers (An increase in the number of engineers would dissuade the more able, skilled workers from allowing themselves to be poached by other factories.)

Under present conditions, it is difficult to establish training institutions in each factory. The central supervisory authorities should accept the responsibility of implementing this [establishment of training institutions].

(5) Labour organizations

Most factories have just a simple labour organization such as a foreman/workshop system. Some factories set up a slightly more complicated system by appointing unit leaders under the foreman (see table 5.30). Unit leaders are not always necessary for the work to be done, but they are used so that the factories can give honour and pay bonuses to them ($7 for a foreman and $5 for a unit leader, etc.) in order to give an incentive to the rank-and-file workmen to increase productivity. (Factory H [Nippon Nitrogen] is a good example.)

Generally, the factories in this area have only simple labour organizations because industrialization and the factory system are still at an early stage of development. But the so-called Mandore system remains strongly entrenched, and in those factories where it is used there are lower rates of absenteeism and turnover of labour (see factories D, F, Q [Gokō Shipyard, Kurosaki Ceramics and Tajima Construction]). In locally run industries labour turnover is kept to a minimum—not only because the number of workers is small and they live near their places of work, but additionally because in such factories the traditional relationship between a boss and his workforce persists, and this influences the situation (see table 5.14).

As discussed in detail below, under the present system factories in this locality have only a limited number of engineers who can fill leadership positions. It is important to study further the way to extract the full potential of the Mandore/foreman system and to raise productivity.

The ratios of engineers to workmen are set out in table 5.34. Compared to table 5.35 on Japan, the ratio of engineers to workers in the 20 Syonan factories is extremely low. In the sample from Japan's metalworking industry, the ratio of engineers to workers is around 3.7 per cent, which is about one engineer to every 25–30 workers. Among the total workforce, one out of ten would have a secondary school education. Additionally, most of the workers [in Japan] are educated at least to an advanced elementary level. There is a wide gulf in this respect between this locality and Japan. Although industries here may not on the whole require much of a skilled workforce, it is highly important to prepare for the future by training a semi-skilled workforce.

Table 5.34 Syonan Municipality percentage of engineers to workers, end of April 1944

Industry	Number of workers	Japanese engineers	Local engineers	Total engineers	%
Metalworking	1,835	18	5	23	1.3
Shipbuilding	962	19	0	19	1.9
Ceramics	659	8	5	13	2.0
Chemicals	1858	31	69	100	5.4
Woodworking	648	14	0	14	2.2
Food	625	4	3	7	1.1
Electrical engineering	817	20	15	35	4.3
Civil engineering and construction	2,353	15	0	15	0.6
Smelting	271	-	10	-	-
Spinning	441	-	-	-	-
Miscellaneous (bleaching)	262	1	0	1	0.4

Factory Statistics, Department of Commerce and Industry.

Cited from Minoguchi Tokijiro, *Nihon Kōgyō Rōdōryoku Ron* [The Labour Force Theory of Industry in Japan] (Osaka: Kobundo Shoten, 1943).

Table 5.35 Japan percentage of engineers and workers, 1938

Industry	Number of engineers	Number of workers	%
Total workers and engineers	119,284	3,215,421	3.7
Heavy industries	80,162	1,675,846	4.8
Metal	13,106	177,398	3.5
Machinery	45,570	60,431	5.3
Chemicals	16,061	12,205	5.0
Ceramics	3,331	106,345	3.2
Gas and electrical	2,092	10,517	19.9
Light industries	39,122	17,539,525	2.5
Spinning	16,857	976,953	1.7
Woodworking	2,364	113,823	2.1
Printing and bookbinding	1,681	63,568	2.6
Food	7,083	190,697	3.7
Other industries	3,828	194,484	2.0

Factory Statistics, Department of Commerce and Industry.

Cited from Minoguchi Tokijiro, *Nihon Kōgyō Rōdōryoku Ron.*

6. Conclusion: Appropriate Action

As stated above, our conclusion is unavoidably an interim report because it is based on insufficient data with regard to overall economic conditions in Syonan Municipality. On this basis, we set out our findings below.

- There is a greater imbalance in the demand and supply of labour than might be expected.
- Labour conditions and administration vary among workplaces directly managed by the military, Japanese-managed factories and locally managed factories. There are, for example, differences in the interpretation of the Labour Book rules. This kind of inconsistency creates disruption and a scramble for workers, especially for skilled workmen. These factors increase rates of labour turnover and absenteeism, with a consequent knock-on effect on productivity in the affected factories.
- Incentive schemes are almost non-existent to accomplish the mission of ensuring a large enough labour force through maintaining and nurturing existing workers.

- Little consideration is given to improving workers' skills and abilities.
- Little consideration is given to labour strategies in view of the state of emergency [that is to say, war].

Appropriate countermeasures are not easy to devise in the current local confusion of managerial styles between Japanese and local managers. Ultimately, however, all these problems arise from labour shortages. Individual factories have given too much time to this problem, leaving no time to resolve other difficulties. Therefore, this is the area that must be addressed and thoroughly reflected upon. Some of our own suggestions are set out below.

First, taking an overall view, the labour force shortfall (section 3-[1]) by the end of 1944 will be:

- Industry (Japanese-managed only), about 21,000
- Transportation (maritime, dock and land transport), about 10,000
- Military (army and navy), about 40,000
- Total 71,000

In addition, estimates show that about 33,000 labourers will be required for food production (Agriculture and Forestry Group of the Chōsabu [see chapter 9, sections 3-A-(1) and 3-B-(1)]). Locally managed industries will also require more workers. Overall, we think we will need well in excess of 100,000 labourers. Evidently, current labour supplies do not satisfy these requirements. Current labour demands would therefore, unavoidably, have to be suppressed. However, the size of the labour demand should be borne in mind when any corrective measures are introduced.

(1) Direct countermeasures
  (i) Introduction of outside labour
  (ii) Mobilization of potential labour force by:
    a. enhancement of the Special Rations scheme [aimed at labourers in priority industries]
    b. establishment of a labour exchange
  (iii) Maintaining and nurturing the existing labour force by:
    a. prevention of absenteeism
    b. prevention of high labour turnover
    c. increase of food rations
    d. expansion of welfare facilities
(2) Indirect countermeasures
  (i) Training and improving labour sources [by encouraging young people and women]
  (ii) Establishment of a labour management institution for research and guidance
(3) Establishment of a central administrative department to administer labour management [for both military-managed and civilian-run workplaces]

(1) Direct countermeasures

(i) Introduction of outside labour

The introduction of labour from areas such as Java and Sumatra would unnecessarily increase the population, and might also lead to food shortages and problems in the defence and transport systems. Additionally, it would be inconsistent with the policy of evacuation. Therefore, this countermeasure should, if possible, be avoided.

(ii) Mobilization of potential sources of labour

We have already indicated (section 2-[1]-[B]) the sources of labour that could directly address ongoing labour shortages. If appropriate measures were introduced, these sources could be turned into an available labour force.

Workers currently in inessential and unnecessary occupations should therefore be encouraged as far as possible to switch jobs, so long as this does not impact negatively on the civilian economy. The range of occupations in which the employment of males is prohibited should be expanded, and these workers should be replaced by females, older workers and children. Male workers in this range of occupations should be able to transfer to other sectors with little effect on the day-to-day civilian economy. This measure would also satisfy the initial required target (see report on Reorganizing Commercial Businesses in Syonan Municipality [chapter 4]).

There are about 162,000 women of working age in the unemployed female population [table 5.6 and chapter 3 table A.3.3]. Although there is disagreement on what percentage should be assigned to the actual labour force, it would be better first to consider unmarried women, who could take up jobs more easily. According to the 1931 census, there were about 27,100 unmarried women, or 28 per cent of the female working-age population of about 95,600. While not all unmarried woman can be expected to work, some portion even of married women may join the labour force. Thus, taking into consideration the above 28 per cent, it may not be impossible to mobilize around 30 per cent of women of working age.[22] In addition, if the female population between the ages of 45 and 50 and 13- and 14-year olds, who are close to working age, also worked, the female labour force participation rate would be even higher. If 30 per cent of working-age women in the female unoccupied population can be mobilized, this will produce about 48,600[23] new labour recruits, who, when added to the

[22] Here the figure refers to women aged 15 to 44, whereas elsewhere in this report and chapter 3 the working age usually refers to men aged 15 to 50.

[23] That is, 162,000 x 0.30 = 48,600.

30,000 currently employed females[24] would total about 78,600 female workers. This total would be 30 per cent of the whole working population of about 250,000. In international wartime labour conditions, the percentages of females in the labour force are reported to be 46 per cent in Britain, 47 per cent in Germany, 50 per cent in Italy, 30 per cent in the United States and 50 per cent in the Soviet Union (*The Diamond* [weekly magazine] 31, 18). Compared to these percentages, 30 per cent of local female labour force is not low, particularly when local customs and conditions are taken into account.

From the viewpoint of employers' demand for labour, the percentage of females in the workforce, as already pointed out, could be raised in the industrial sector to 30 per cent (see section 3-[3]). In addition, females could comprise more than 30 per cent of the labour force in agriculture (see the Chōsabu report by the agriculture and forestry group). In the current climate of particularly stringent labour shortages, businesses must abandon the view that females cannot be employed, and actively consider how to mobilize the female labour force.

Turning to the unemployed male population, it is difficult to establish what percentage can realistically be mobilized as new recruits, as some are in poor health. Additionally, the custom is that where a man can make a living without having a job, he does not work. However, in view of the low rate of male employment (60.4 per cent),[25] a certain percentage of the male population can be mobilized into the labour force. Therefore, it is not impossible to raise the employment rate by a further 2–3 per cent. (Raising the male employment rate by a further 2.5 per cent, for example, would provide an additional 13,000 workers. This is about 50 per cent of the 27,000 unoccupied males of working age.[26])

Countermeasures to turn the potential labour force as stated above into an actual labour force are as follows:

A. Direct mobilization

B. Indirect mobilization

The current critical situation is close to the level that necessitates direct mobilization. But indirect and gradual mobilization would be more appropriate and acceptable to the locals. (However, there might have to be some mandatory occupational changes implemented systematically on a well-designed plan.) This aim might be achieved in several ways:

---

24 From table 5.6, 33,819.

25 From table 5.3 and chapter 3, table A.3.3, employed males 307,454 / total males 509,032 = 60.4 per cent.

26 Chapter 3, table A.3.3, unemployed males 15–50 = 27,091.

a. Enhancement of the Special Rations scheme [for labourers in priority industries]

b. Establishment of a labour exchange

With regard to the Special Rations scheme, we would propose the following:

Step 1. Increase the ration of non-essential food, tobacco and textiles.

Step 2. Increase the ration of staple foods. (It would be necessary simultaneously somewhat to decrease the ration for ordinary citizens. The ration for ordinary labourers, and secretaries in administration offices, factories and trading companies should be increased. But allowance should be made for the fact that some families may contain fewer working-age adults and more older people and children.)

If step 1 does not achieve sufficient indirect labour mobilization, it would be necessary to proceed to step 2. But step 2 should be taken only when the situation becomes more urgent.

These two steps could give ordinary citizens an indirect incentive to work. An institution would then be required to encourage them to seek or change employment. Such an institution would advise job applicants and facilitate changes of job or employment. It would then provide appropriate work placements with regard to gender, ethnicity and age.

It would also train labourers and teach them skills if necessary. Consequently there should be an institution to provide both labour exchange and training services. We believe that these two services would allow the smooth supply of a new source of labour.

(iii) Maintaining and improving the existing labour force

Although turning a potential into an actual labour force would increase the absolute number of labourers, productivity improvements cannot be expected unless the existing labour force is maintained and improved. The quality of labour is particularly likely to decline if it comes from a new source of supply. Therefore, retaining and training the current labour force is a very important issue that should not be ignored.

Labour efficiency is currently diminished for the following reasons:

- High absenteeism
- High labour turnover
- Food shortages
- Insufficient welfare facilities

a. Prevention of absenteeism

The average rate of absenteeism in workplaces is 15 per cent, which is very high. Direct measures to prevent this situation would be to pay an allowance for good attendance, to distribute rations according to the rate of attendance, and to give prizes for good attendance.

Indirect measures would be to establish new accommodation, to improve the transport system (more municipal bus and railway services), to improve workers' nutrition by increasing rations, to provide simple medical treatment, to distribute (to factories and businesses) medical supplies, and to give advice on health problems. Feasible measures should be introduced as soon as possible.

b. Prevention of high labour turnover

In terms of labour turnover, the average rate of discharge for the 14 selected factories is 10 per cent (data for April 1944). Even if we disregard this percentage, it implies a high potential incentive to change jobs. The actual rate of labour turnover is probably higher than our estimate, for the following reasons:

- Workers employed by the military are provided with large payments in kind (rice 15–20 catties).
- Labour conditions are better in locally managed industries (table 5.24).

Although the Labour Book sets out an existing scheme to prohibit job switching to deal with these problems, it does not seem to have had a practical effect. However, in our view the Labour Book is still the best way to control workers. Therefore, the range of workplaces in which workers are required always to have their Labour Book with them should be expanded. Moreover, Labour Books and Ration Cards should be integrated, so that those labourers with good attendance records over a given period in each workplace would be rewarded with higher rations. (It would only be necessary to add a section recording work performance to the current Labour Book.)

Furthermore, the Ordinance on Wages and Salaries should be expanded to cover the whole labour force. The regulations to prevent job switching, which are at present only nominal, will be made effective by the implementation of these measures and should prevent labour turnover caused by wage differentials.

c. Increase in food supply

While our proposal above [6-(1)-(ii)-a] to increase rations for workers should be implemented and will ease the problem to a certain extent, we did witness during our survey factory workers who were unable to work hard because of hunger, and these were not merely a small minority of the workforce. However, in present circumstances this is a persistent problem in all the surveyed factories, about which nothing can be done by the factories themselves. Workers' productivity is likely to improve if they have an adequate diet, and it might be possible to extend the working day (now eight and a half hours) by an hour or two. From the viewpoint of finding new sources of labour as well as improving work efficiency and maintaining health standards, it is urgent to increase food rations. However, it should be noted that productivity will not necessarily improve if the rice ration alone is increased. [If the ration was increased,] some workers would provide for other family members and some would sell the rationed rice on the black market at higher prices. Workers in the employ of the military in particular receive higher rations, and in a few cases they sell their rations to street hawkers. Consequently, in these cases food rations have provided no direct nourishment to the workers themselves. A solution to this problem would be to replace part of the rations with cooked rice. While it would be difficult to implement this measure for the whole ration, it would at least be feasible to provide cooked rice for lunch in factories.

d. Expansion of welfare facilities

– Educational provisions

The role of education in improving labour quality and promoting labour efficiency need hardly be emphasized. Particularly in local conditions, it is very important to supplement low skill levels with technological training to prevent the poaching of workers, especially skilled workers, with the prospect of higher wages. Moreover, in order to prepare for a military emergency, it is important to train workplace leaders who would be psychologically prepared and capable of keeping workplaces secure while maintaining existing levels of productivity. Education in itself is an urgent problem, as we have already mentioned. Training workplace leaders is an important matter to which priority should be given.

– Health facilities

In the course of our research we found almost no health facilities, and accommodation was provided in only a few of the factories surveyed. These facilities play an important part in improving and retaining the labour force. They should be established as far as circumstances permit. For example, if the introduction of these measures improved current efficiency by 5 per cent, this would be equivalent to recruiting about 12,000 new labourers (estimating the current number of labourers as about 250,000). If a 10 per cent efficiency gain were achieved, this would be equivalent to employing 25,000 new labourers. Therefore, the focus should not be just on an increase in the number of workers; the importance of focusing on the improvement and retention of the current labour force should not be forgotten.

(2) Indirect countermeasures

(i) Improving the sources of labour supply

A programme to increase the labour force could not be achieved without setting up training schemes for the future labour force, together with nurturing and maintaining the existing labour force. This, in a broad sense, is another aspect of the importance of education. It is unnecessary to dwell on the value of children's education here, since its great importance is universally recognized. We nevertheless wish to stress the importance of teaching children adequately to realize the value of industriousness.

(ii) Establishing an institution for research and training in labour management

The scientific study of labour management is significant to the maintenance and training of the labour force, and to improving the efficiency of the current labour force. However, neither the military nor the civilian sector regards this as important. They have focused solely on unnecessarily increasing the number of workers.

Research should be conducted on labour management from the viewpoints of ethnicity, culture and climate. We need to establish a research institution where scientific research and reorganization of all the existing statistics are conducted, and also where guidance and supervision are provided in order to apply research results to the actual situation.

(3) Establishing a centralized administrative department for labour management [for both military and civilian sectors]

As already mentioned, the main source of turbulence in the current labour management system is competition for labour between the military, civilian and local factories.

The payment of wages in cash or kind was used to secure workers, which not only caused labour management disorder but also had a detrimental effect more generally on the economic situation. Furthermore, viewed overall, the major problem is that this situation impedes production efficiency. The establishment of a strong, centralized organization capable of controlling the whole labour problem in both the military and private sectors is needed to resolve the situation. It is very important to draw up the implementation plan for the countermeasures suggested above. It is also very important to maintain a correct balance of labour supply and demand and to plan and distribute labour appropriately.

CHAPTER 6

An Overview of Important Industrial Factories in Syonan Municipality

Military Administration, Department of General Affairs, Research Office, March 1943

This report was prepared as reference material for the Committee for Resource Utilization based on an inspection of factories and a survey of current bottlenecks.[1]

Contents

[1] This report was not written by the Chōsabu, and the approach to the issues on industrial factories may be different from that of the Chōsabu members. This report may be compared with chapter 5.

12. Mitsui Chemical Laboratory
13. Shiraki Trading Company, Miscellaneous Factories
14. Alexandra Brick Factory
15. Syonan Paint Factory
16. Opium Factory Managed by the Department of Finance

1. Syonan Steam Power Plant

Location: Telok Blangah Road, Syonan Municipality (tel. 3574)

Inspection date: 26 February 1943

Interviewee: Akagi Kuninori

(a) Main equipment

Table 6.1 Syonan Steam Power Plant equipment

Type of machine	Output	Manufacturer	Number of machines
Turbine generator	2,000kw	6,600V 50 cycle Metropolitan-Vickers	1 machine
Turbine generator	5,000kw	Same as above	2
Turbine generator	10,000kw	Same as above	2
Total amount of electric power	32,000kw		
Boiler evaporation	23 tons per hour	Pressure of 13 atmospheres Babcock & Wilcox	8 boilers
Transformer	2,000KVA	22,000V/ 6,000V Metropolitan-Vickers	2

All boilers have stokers, and two of them are heavy oil burners. The building is an impressive brick construction. It has room for a further generator and two more boilers. The main electric distribution switchboard is a Metrovick vertical engine. The switch is a Layrole metal-clad style with double generating lines. Coal is transferred from external coal storage (storage capacity is 18,000 tons) by dump car to each side of the boiler. Buckets and elevators are used to lift the coal to the two storage areas on both sides above the boiler. The [eight] boilers are installed in two parallel lines. The coal feeder is placed between and above the parallel boilers, and it moves from side to side to feed coal into each boiler's stoker. Ashes are removed from the boilers by the parallel conveyors and the gutters, collected in two ash hoppers, and transported to lorries for disposal. There is a fenced wharf for coal in the south of the grounds, but it does not have a good connection to the plant. The coal is transported by lorry.

Near the Syonan (Tanjong Pagar) Station there are six tanks for heavy oil, of 7,000 tons capacity each. These connect to the electricity-generating plant by pipe. An oil storage tank inside the plant has a capacity of 1,000 tons. During the period of British occupation, heavy oil was often used.

(b) Air raid precautions

To ensure that the building is blacked out, the windows are fitted with shutters, and transoms that separate doors from the windows above and provide ventilation are fitted with plywood. To protect against bomb blasts and splinters, 40mm steel plates have been installed between the turbine generators and sandbags placed between the switchboard and the main machine room. Air raid shelters were constructed with four 6mm steel plates for walls. Externally, protective walls were built for the 2,000KVA transformer by packing soil between two boards.

Table 6.2 Specification of operations

Current load	Maximum	14,200kw	8–9pm
	Daytime	9,500kw	
	Minimum	3,500kw	

(c) Coal

Coal is shipped from Sumatra Ombilin by a 3,000-ton class vessel.[2] Mitsui Trading Co. is in charge of this operation. The coal costs $20 per ton. A lorry shuttle is used to transport the coal from vessel to plant, at a cost of $4 to $5 per ton. The current coal storage capacity is 12,000 tons. The ash content of this type of coal is low. However, this causes too much air to enter into the front part of the stoker, which makes it difficult to burn the coal.

(d) The workforce

The workforce includes 70 Indians, 35 Chinese and 30 Malays. Among them are four clerks, four engineers and four Japanese engineers. Two British former employees are also employed. A mechanical engineer and an electrical engineer are employed at $50 a month.

[2] Sumatra Ombilin is located near Padang on Sumatra Island.

(e) The current situation

The factory is in a difficult situation because of the increasing price of repair materials. For example, if the factory requested a Chinese ironmaster to estimate for the cost of long bolts of 1.25 inches diameter and 8 inches length, he would quote $24. This is because the Chinese anticipate a shortage of iron and conceal it with a consequent increase in black market dealing. When the plant needs bolts it now asks the nearby Harbour Dock, which is run by the navy, to make them. Under the British administration, spare parts were sent from Britain in response to a mere telegram. There is thus only a small stock of spare parts.

2. Syonan Municipality Gas Factory

Location: Klang Road, Syonan Municipality (tel. 5988-89)

Inspection date: 25 February 1943

Interviewee: A.V. Erulappan, Indian engineer

The gas factory has been operated as a municipal concern for 42 years. It was formerly called the Singapore Gas Co.

Table 6.3 shows the factory's main equipment.

Table 6.3 Syonan Municipality gas factory equipment

Retort furnace: Hudson	6 furnaces	Daily full ability 900,000 cubic feet
Water gas generator: Humphrey	1	Daily ability 200,000 cubic feet
Unknown make	1	Daily ability 500,000 cubic feet
Gas washout device	1	Currently not working
Desulfurizing device	1	
Booster exhauster	2	Volume 6,000 cubic feet
	2	4,000
	2	2,000
	2	1,500
Water pipe boiler: Babcock	4	Pressure of 100 pounds
Gas tank	4	

(a) Gas generation

Coal is transported by lorry from the coal yard and dumped into a hopper at the retort house of the gasworks. A crusher beneath the hopper reduces the coal to nut size. Crushed coal is loaded by bucket conveyor into an overhead coal tank. To one side of the generator a charging machine receives coal from the tank and pours it into the retorts. There are eight retorts for one generator. Gas is generated for two hours, and the coal is transformed into coke. The charging machine pushes out the coke from the other side of the generator into a bucket. The coke is hosed down with water to cool. The bucket is hung on a monorail hoist by which it is moved out of the factory. As it is moved through a cooler, the coke is completely cooled by water and then dumped into a coke tank.

A trapdoor beneath the coke tank opens when coke is needed. There is a water gas generator next to the boiler room. The bucket of coke is hung on a reeled rope with a steam-powered hoist and poured into the water gas generator when the bottom of the bucket opens. The city is supplied with a mixture of coal and water gas.

(b) The current situation

Currently working gas generators are the three retort generators and the two water gas generators with a capacity of 200,000 cubic feet each.

Each day about 30 tons of coal is consumed and 500,000 cubic feet of gas generated (the pre-war level was 1,200,000 cubic feet). The coal currently used is from India, but stockpiles are shrinking (they are about 11,000 tons), and investigation is now being made into using coal from Sumatra. Coal costs $26 a ton (the pre-war price was about $16). The by-products of coal are coke and tar. Seven hundred tons of coke are produced a month, and 6,000–7,000 gallons of tar. The selling price of tar is $10 a tin (which holds 40 gallons); for coke it is $45 a ton. At present there are 840 gas lamps in the city (before the war there were 4,050). The selling price of gas, $2.50 per 1,000 cubic feet, is the same as it was in the pre-war period.

3. General Army Arsenal, Factory No. 1

Location: River Valley Road, Syonan Municipality (tel. 5971)

Inspection date: 13 February 1943

Interviewee: Lieutenant Shintani Takeshirō

The munitions factory is not under the control of the Military Administration, and because it is relevant to military matters this interview does not include any details of its operations.

The factory was originally the British-owned United Engineering Ltd. (with a paid-up capital of $3,190,000) and had branch factories in Ipoh, Penang and Malacca. It was the largest machine factory in the Malay Peninsula for the maintenance and repair of imported machines and manufacture of spare parts.

The factory has now been converted to the General Army Arsenal, Factory No. 1. Apart from repairing heavy and light weapons for operational troops, it manufactures items for railway construction, including fishplates,[3] shovels, pickaxes, axes and nails. The manufacturing complex comprises an iron foundry, a forge, a machine factory, an assembly plant, a saddle factory that includes woodworking facilities, and a nail workshop. There are also repair workshops for communications equipment and electrical equipment. The facilities have in general deteriorated and seem disorganized, but the factory has an electric furnace, a melting pot furnace and a cupola. The machine factory has at least 50 machine tools such as large lathes. The forge has two steam hammers. Technical guidance is provided by engineers from Tokyo Shibaura Electric Co.,[4] and hundreds of workers are employed. It is intended to extend the factory's woodworking facilities and to build capacity to handle special steel.

4. Osaka Steel Plates Manufacturing Co., Syonan Can Manufactory

Location of Factory No. 1: Bukit Timah Road, 5¾ mile (tel. 3202)

Location of Factory No. 2: Tanjong Pagar Road, Centre Pier (tel. 4192)

Inspection date: 10 February 1943

Interviewee: Mōri Kazuo, factory manager

(a) Factory No. 1

The factory was built as part of an enterprise originally called Eclipse Manufacturing Co. (a concrete manufacturer). A drum-can-making machine was installed, which has been seized and stored by the military. Osaka Steel Plates Manufacturing Co. was appointed to take over the business of the factory and began operations last August [1942]. The appraised property value of the factory is about $400,000, which breaks down as $200,000 for equipment, $100,000 for the machinery that has been relocated, and $100,000 for other machinery. The factory began by manufacturing 50,000–60,000 drum cans, using reserved material, of which there was then enough to make 70,000 drum cans. Further materials necessary for production are now being requested from the Logistics Department [to be shipped from other parts of the East Asia Co-prosperity Sphere]. For the moment, the factory has to rely on military provision of materials for repairs and manufacturing. The factory has the capacity to produce 30,000 drum cans a month, for which it needs 1,000 tons of thin steel plate of 1.6mm thickness, 30 tons of thick steel plate, 30 tons of casting iron and 30 tons of coke. Other materials necessary to manufacture one drum can include: a kilo of cast

[3] Railway term for a metal bar bolted to the ends of two rails to construct a track.

[4] Now known as Toshiba.

iron (for making caps), 180 grams of carbide (for repair), 600 grams of welding rod and a kilo of thick steel plates for washers. Electrically powered welding is used for manufacturing and acetylene for repairing.

The plant's principal machinery is a stamper, a hoist, an electric welding machine and four lathes. Three hundred and forty operatives are regularly employed and 80 coolies. Fifty per cent of the regular operatives are Chinese; the rest are Indians and Malays. The average daily wage is $1.20, and coolies are paid 80 cents daily. The Indian and Malay workers are generally lazy, and their skills are inferior to those of the Chinese, with the consequence that most are coolies. Present manufacture of drum cans is limited by shortages of additional materials. The factory is therefore quiet, but the repairing section still gets some work (the daily repairing capacity is 800 cans, but currently 300 cans are being repaired a day). To keep workers busy, the factory manufactures simple tools such as screwdrivers and punches.

Drum cans are used to hold petrol, heavy oil, kerosene, latex and other vegetable oils. A standard drum holds 45 gallons, and its manufacture costs $1.39.

(b) Factory No. 2

This factory was originally the former Standard Oil Company's Can Making Factory. It has a daily manufacturing capacity of 460 drums. Current production is limited to 200 drum cans. A single drum takes 15 minutes to make. The number of operatives is 45.

5. Japan Outfitting Industry Company, Syonan Factory

Location: 472 Beach Road, Syonan Municipality (tel. 2853)

Inspection date: 20 February 1943

Interviewee: Itō Toshio, principal administrative director of the shipyard

The shipyard was started on 25 October 1942. It is currently constructing 25 150-ton wooden boats. The boats' maximum loading capacity is 300 tons. The boats are fitted with 115-horsepower hot-bulb [heavy oil] engines. They can navigate continuously for 2,000 knots, at 7 knots an hour. Each boat costs $90,000 to build the body and $150,000 for the engine and outfitting. A 150-ton class wooden boat requires 350 tons of teakwood (as material) and 10 tons of iron. Their construction takes four months. At present the main factory has 995 shipbuilding workers. The construction of each ship requires two builders from Japan and 40 local builders. Shipbuilding needs to be speeded up, but the local builders are unskilled, and not all tools have been issued. Efficiency is also low because only one sawing machine has been installed. Only 50 per cent of necessary materials such as teakwood from Burma have arrived. These factors slow down the speed of shipbuilding.

Factory facilities are also inadequate: there is no provision for protection against bad weather or any drainage. There is also a shortage of tools. Most of the local shipbuilders are Chinese, and their average wage is $1.50 a day.

6. Yokohama Rubber Manufacturing Company, Factory Nos. 1, 2 and 3

Location of Office: Room 15, 6th floor KPM Building, Robinson Road, Syonan Municipality (tel. 2877-79)

Location of Factory No. 1: 805 Pasir Panjang Road, Syonan Municipality (tel. 7907)

Location of Factory No. 2: Bukit Timah Road 10 mile, Syonan Municipality (tel. 3805)

Inspection date: 8 February 1943

Interviewees: Matsumura Senzō, product manager, and Kubota Takeo, factory manager, Factory No. 1

The first of these Yokohama Rubber factories was formerly the Dutch-owned Singapore Rubber Works Ltd. (paid-up capital of $1,200,000). The second is a Chinese-managed factory called the Nanyang Manufacturing Co., Ltd. (paid-up capital of about $80,000). The third factory, an automobile tyre factory in Syonan Municipality, is now under construction. The fourth factory, in Kuala Lumpur, is the former British-owned Wilkinson Process Rubber Co., Ltd.

At present the first and second factories are working, the first since 23 June 1942. It produces about 1,700 items of various descriptions. Its main products are rubber hoses, belts, rubber shoes, pneumatic tyres [i.e., tyres for automobiles and bicycles], hygienic sacks [condoms] and Bakelite [thermosetting resin] goods. Of the production materials required other than rubber, a year's supply of chemicals is available from pre-war stocks and from other stock collected from the city, but cotton textiles are in short supply. The possibilities of obtaining raw materials are now being examined: brimstone can be secured from Sumatra, carbon black from the Southern Regions Fuel Depot, and there are plans to manufacture zinc oxide in Syonan using zinc imported from Burma (for details, see the inspection report for the Syonan Paint Factory). With regard to textiles such as cotton, studies are being conducted on the feasibility of substituting pineapple and hemp fibres. All products are delivered for use by the military, for example in the arsenal, cargo warehouses, shipyards, hospitals and aviation headquarters.

Factory No. 2 was established by the acquisition of the Nanyang Manufacturing Company (which had a pre-war debt of $210,000). The factory produces rubber shoes, of which 1,000 are manufactured daily, and diving suits, of which 150 are made a month. The factory also produces slippers. Factory No. 3 is now under construction as an automobile tyre factory. It has a site of 99 sq. km. at Pasir Panjang. Machinery has been acquired from the (overseas Chinese-managed) Feng Kiong [馮强] Rubber Factory in Klang, Selangor; it had not been installed in this factory in Klang. The machinery is capable of manufacturing enough rubber for 100,000 automobile tyres.

Annual pre-war consumption of crude rubber in Malaya was 1,000 long tons. The purchase price for smoked rubber sheet at Malayan factories is 32 cents a pound. Feng Kiong Rubber Factory in Klang, Selangor, seems to buy rubber sheet for 20 to 25 cents.

7. Six Oil-related Factories in Syonan

Locations:

Ho Hong [和豊] Soap Factory Co., Ltd.

Commissioned by Japan Nitrogen Fertilizer Ltd., 23 Peng Siang Quay, Syonan Municipality (tel. 7045)

Ho Hong Oil Mill Co., Ltd.

Commissioned by Japan Nitrogen Fertilizer Ltd., Havelock Road, Syonan Municipality (tel. 3139)

Si Sian [時鮮] Soap Factory

Commissioned by Asahi Electronic Industry Co., Ltd., 555 Havelock Road, Municipality (no telephone)

Kian Guan [建源] Oil Factory Company

Commissioned by Asahi Electronic Industry Co., Ltd., 1 Tai Gin Road, Syonan Municipality (tel. 4187)

Khiu Tsong Ting [丘宗庭] Company

Commissioned by the Marumiya Store Company, 5 Tai Gin Road, Syonan Municipality (tel. 2295)

Ban Hok Liong [萬福隆] Oil Factory

Commissioned by the Marumiya Store Company, 491 Macpherson Road, Syonan Municipality (tel. 84751)

Inspection date: 12 February 1943

Interviewees: Yoshida Shinsaku, employee of Asahi Electronic Industry (as a guide), and Kinugasa Shizuo, employee of Marumiya Store Company

Six factories were inspected, but there was not enough time for all the interviewees to provide full information. This report therefore sets out outlines below.

(a) Soap

There are 53 soap factories in Malaya, with an annual production of 22,580 tons. Of this, 22,000 tons are detergent and 580 tons toilet soap. A total of 3,450 tons of soap was imported in 1940; therefore, the total demand was 26,030 tons (without subtracting exports/re-exports from the total). Soap demand in Sumatra is 26,350 tons of detergent and 1,500 tons of toilet soap, a total of 27,850 tons. At present all the factories have difficulty in obtaining caustic soda, and the substitute use of wood ash (which contains potassium, the ash being sawdust burnt at the sawmill) is now being examined. It has been suggested that coconut shell ash contains the highest percentage of potassium.

(i) Ho Hong Soap Factory (formerly managed by overseas Chinese, with a paid-up capital of $450,000) is the largest-scale enterprise. It produces 100 tons of detergent and 20 tons of toilet soap a month. The factory has a machine capable of producing 2.5 to 3 tons of glycerine monthly [as a by-product of soap]. This factory does not perform the process of 'salting out' in the solidification process. Eighteen or 19 parts of caustic soda are used to every 100 parts of oil. Theoretically, glycerine as 5 per cent solid from the undiluted liquid can be collected, but poor facilities in this factory mean that only 2 per cent is collected. The factory also has machinery, not currently used, to make margarine.

(ii) Si Sian Soap Factory (under an overseas Chinese management) produces 100 tons of detergent a month. It has four soap-building pots, but there is no churning machine. Nor is there a cutting machine. The soap is cut with a simple wire device. The factory does not use electric power, only manpower and firewood. Nineteen parts of caustic soda are required per 100 parts of oil. Ho Hong supplies coconut oil [to Si Sian].

(b) Oil extraction

There are 30 oil mills in Malaya that extract oil from copra. Every month 11,000 tons of oil is extracted, which is 70 per cent to 80 per cent of capacity. The mills prioritize exports to Japan and Germany. However, the shortage of storage tanks has limited the amount of oil that can be extracted, as has the shortage of oil tankers. Current storage capacity is 4,000 tons in tanks, and in factories a total of 6,500 tons. The overall total stored is 10,500 tons. Of this total, Syonan has storage capacity of 5,100 tons and Penang 5,400 tons. Oil storage capacity must be increased to 20,000 tons.

Figure 6.1 Coconut oil extraction flowchart

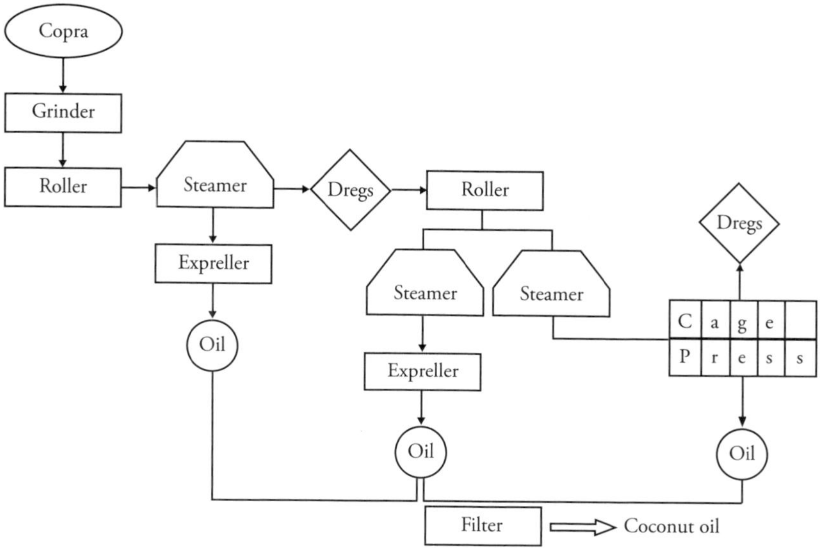

8. Dai-Nippon Beer Company, Syonan Factory

Location: 365 Alexandra Road, Syonan Municipality (tel. 5996 and 80338)
Inspection date: 9 February 1943
Interviewee: Wakaizumi Hisayasu, factory manager

The factory was originally managed by Archipelago Breweries Ltd., a German company established in 1932. As a result of the war between England and Germany, Fraser & Neave Ltd. took over its management as an enemy property, and Malayan Breweries Ltd. used it as an auxiliary factory. Its assets are valued at about $1,000,000, and it has a monthly maximum production capacity of 700,000 large bottles. It currently produces 480,000 bottles a month, all of which are purchased by the military and delivered to the Supply Regiment Depot. Because collection of the empty bottles tends to be delayed, the factory occasionally has to halt production. The reason for the collection difficulties is because the price that the factory pays for empty bottles is 5 cents a bottle, while the black market price is more than 8 cents. Factory facilities are excellent for the first part of the process of brewing but not so good for the latter stages of production such as storage. Nor is the bottling section good. Nine thousand litres are brewed at a time. This is a very small quantity compared to brewing facilities in Japan, and the brewing tanks are made of wood. If I may speak ill of this factory, there seems to be a jumble of facilities.

Malt, used as a raw material, has been obtained from the pre-war stock, imported from Australia. This stock will soon be depleted, and malt will be imported from Japan. Hops have been imported from Tasmania, and although they are of poor quality there is sufficient stock for two years. There is a two-year stock of bottle caps at a soda pop factory managed by an affiliated company. In the pre-war period cork was imported from Spain, but the use of balsa as a substitute is now being examined. Balsa grows to a 30–40cm diameter in four years. Plywood caps can be made by using three sheets of balsa and covering it with tin sheet. One hundred and fifty tons of coal a month are used. As part of a self-sufficiency programme, if 200 hectares of land for growing barley could be obtained, at current production the factory would be able to increase production by 50 per cent. A study is now being made of the suitability for this purpose of arable land in Berastagi, in the Sumatra highlands, which is 1,300 to 1,500 metres above sea level. Filtered tap water is used, but its quality is poor. One hundred and twelve kilograms of malt can be brewed to produce about 200 gallons of beer. Four per cent of the ingredients are extracts, and alcohol content is 4 per cent.

9. Kirin Beer Company, Syonan Factory

Location: 948 Alexandra Road, Syonan Municipality (tel. 3640 and 3641)

Inspection date: 24 February 1943

Interviewee: Tsuruta Masao

The factory was formerly known as Malayan Breweries Ltd. and was established in 1931 with a capital of $1,500,000 (paid-up capital of $1,000,000). Kirin was commissioned for management by the Military Administration in November and began business in December.

Annual production capacity is 200,000 boxes of large bottles, there being four bottles per box, but this depends on the condition of the bottling machine. Using smaller bottles does not greatly alter this. Smaller bottles would allow an annual production of 250,000 boxes. Malt from stock has been used for production, but almost all the stock has now been used. For the present, arrangements are being made to import malt from Japan for military use. The annual amount required for beer is 1,000 long tons. There is still a year's stock of Australian hops. A shortage of bottles is not a concern, since there are 1.2 million. The collection price of old bottles is 3 cents.

This factory's buildings and machinery are new and up-to-date. For example, the factory uses an air-transfer system to move the malt from storage to the tank. An entirely automated system is used to wash, bottle and label. One hundred male and 50 female workers are employed. Many of the engineers are Indian, and Eurasians are employed as clerks.

(a) Outline of the manufacturing process

Malt is delivered by pipeline to the highest point of the factory and temporarily stored in a storage tank. Having then been passed through a meter and crushed in a roller crusher, the malt is poured into the brewing pot. One brewing produces 9,000 litres of beer and requires 1,000kg of malt, 300kg of crushed rice and 100kg of sugar. These ingredients are heated to 80 degrees in the brewing pot and become a syrup. This process is conducted twice a day. Heated syrup is first poured into a shallow tank called a cooling down tank and is cooled by fan. The syrup then passes through a cooler to bring its temperature down to 6 degrees. The cooler is encased in copper pipes through which cold water runs to cool the syrup. Brewer's yeast is added to the syrup when it is 6 degrees, and the syrup is stored in tanks for ten days, until 90 per cent of the sugar has been converted into alcohol. This process is called the primary fermentation. The alcohol is then poured into the secondary fermentation tank and kept at a temperature of around 0 degrees for two or three months to allow further fermentation. The carbon dioxide generated in the tank is siphoned off and used. One hundred litres of yeast are required to brew 9,000 litres of beer. The yeast increases in volume to 200 litres during the brewing process. Having finished secondary fermentation, the beer is passed twice through a filter of 4cm thick cotton to complete the production of draught beer. The beer is then bottled by bottling machine and warmed to a temperature of 60 degrees to disperse the remaining yeast and produce bottled beer. Empty bottles are washed with hot caustic soda.

The working room [i.e., malt house] is cooled by cool liquid ammonia passed through pipes installed around the room. In Japan brine cooled by liquid ammonia is often used, which differs from the present factory's cooling method. The factory has two ammonia compressors of 50 horsepower each, but at present only one of the compressors is used. Germinated from barley, the malt's yield is about 80 per cent.

(b) Differences between beer and stout brewing

There are differences in the degree of fermentation and the varieties of yeast used. Yeast known as bottom fermentation yeast [Saccharomyces carlsbergensis] is used for brewing beer [lager]. Yeast known as surface fermentation yeast [Saccharomyces cerevisiae] is used to brew stout. Stout has a dark colour because it contains well-roasted barley malt. Primary fermentation is at 17 to 18 degrees and secondary fermentation at 6 degrees. Two thousand kilograms of malt are required to brew 9,000 litres of stout. The alcohol content is usually 8 per cent, which is higher than the 4 per cent of beer.

(c) Plan for bottle manufacture

It is planned to build a bottle-making factory near the Syonan River, using a facility near the old Ford factory on Bukit Timah Road. The annual output capacity will be 10 million bottles. This factory will have a bottle-making machine, a melting furnace, a cooler and a conveyor. Machines such as a motor, a blower and a tank will be reinstalled. Sand with silica is available on Syonan Island, and the factory has a large store of soda ash.

10. Ting Bian Huat-tsiu Tsong Liquor Company [鄭綿発酒莊]

Location: 75 Alexandra Road, Syonan Municipality (tel. 6813)

Inspection date: 24 February 1943

Interviewees: Ting Tsik Kong [鄭則光], Ōga Yuichirō

The company is owned by Mr Ting from Taiwan, and its capital is $140,000. It has a monthly brewing capacity for Chinese herbal alcohol of 5,000 beer bottles. At the end of November the company was contracted by the Supply Regiment Depot to produce pine brandy for three months, at a monthly production of 30,000 bottles. Currently it brews Ngoo Ka Pi wine [五加皮酒] ('five orange peel wine').[5] It also brews Mui Kui Lok wine [玫瑰露酒],[6] Ban Siu Lok wine [萬壽葯酒] ('10,000-year-old herbal wine'), Ban Kin Tong wine [萬金堂酒] ('10,000 golden temples wine') and Peh Lok Tsiu wine [白鹿酒] ('1,000-year-old white deer wine'). Its raw ingredients are sugar, Indian corn and padi, but it is becoming difficult to get sugar. With the support of the Military Administration's tax office the company is occasionally able to buy 100kg of sugar at $14, but the black market price is $80. Indian corn is purchased from the military at $8 per 100 catties [60kg], but its black market price is $18. The company employs 65 workers, of whom the men earn 80 cents (including a meal) and the women 70 cents a day.

The factory's manufacturing facilities include two boilers, one copper distiller for rice wine, one wooden distiller for Kaoliang wine [sorghum wine] and one distiller for wine lees,[7] three tin coolers, one distiller for Mui Kui Lok wine,

---

[5] This wine contains 30 different kinds of leaves, dried peel, tree bark and roots.

[6] Rose syrup is developed from a mixture of sorghum liquor, clear syrup and extract of fresh roses.

[7] Lees are the deposits of dead or residual yeast and other particles that precipitate, or are carried by the action of fining, to the bottom of a vat of wine after fermentation and ageing.

nine wine tanks, four wine pumps, three streamers, two filters, one sterilizer, one motor, four flour mills, a stirrer and a compressor. Table 6.4 sets out taxation on Chinese wines, their factory prices and retail prices.

Table 6.4 Chinese wine tax and prices

	Tax (dollars)	Factory price (dollars)	Retail price (dollars)
Five Orange Peel Wine 五加皮酒	2.125	2.475	5.600
Great White Deer Wine 大白鹿酒	1.575	2.117	2.700
Great Ten Thousand Year Old Temple 大萬壽堂	1.375	1.633	3.000
Great Blood Transfusion 大補血液	0.875	1.475	2.300
Great Red Brandy 大紅色白蘭酒	1.025	1.000	2.000
Great Overseas Philosophers 大百家済	1.000	1.466	2.500

11. Japan Physics and Chemistry Industry, Syonan Oxygen Factory

Location: 851 Pasir Panjang Road, Syonan Municipality

Ground area: 3,200 square metres

Inspection date: 23 February 1943

Interviewee: Obara Naoyuki, chief engineer

This factory was formerly the Far East Oxygen & Acetylene Co. It has a branch factory in Penang.

(a) The oxygen factory

The factory in Syonan is capable of producing 150 bottles of oxygen a day and the Penang factory 60 bottles. Between them, the two factories could supply all the oxygen demanded in Malaya, Sumatra and Thailand before the war. The oxygen is 99 per cent pure. Currently only 2,000 cylinders for use as containers are in stock, which is insufficient for full capacity production. The Syonan factory started production at the beginning of last June and the Penang factory at the end of last September. It would, ideally, be best to operate the machines for 25 days every month. In fact, the factory has to halt production for six days every month, because of the need to repair and adjust the machines. The machinery was manufactured in France, but it is old and needs a complete overhaul.

With machinery in good repair and an abundant supply of containers, monthly production would be 150 bottles per day over 25 days, a total of 3,750 bottles. Oxygen is used for welding and cutting. Seventy per cent of it is used in shipbuilding, 20 per cent in the aviation industry, and 10 per cent for research. Most oxygen is used by the military. The raw material of oxygen is air, but in the process of decomposition [of O_2 from N_2, CO_2, Ar, H_2, etc.] after the air has been compressed and turned into liquid, a small amount of caustic soda is required to absorb moisture. Every month 100–200kg caustic soda is used. The waste fluid it produces is sold to soap-making factories.

(b) The acetylene factory

This factory produces 30 bottles of acetylene a day. Carbide is provided by the military, to whom the products are supplied. Acetylene is used in the repair of airplanes belonging to the aviation corps. The factory works for eight-hour stretches.

(c) The carbonic acid gas factory

This factory burns coal to produce 35 bottles of carbonic acid gas a day. The raw material is anthracite coal, which is imported from Hong Gai in French Indochina, although volatile coal such as Fushun coal from China is more suitable. Theoretically, 1kg of coal can produce 1kg of carbonic acid gas, but currently 2kg of coal is required. The factory started operations at the end of last August, and it now supplies beverage factories in town.

The main factory employs 52 workers, including, in order of their share of the workforce, Indians, Chinese and Malays. The Indian workers are the most numerous, but the Chinese work hardest. Daily wages range from $2.50 at the top to 30 cents at the bottom. Over 700kWh of electricity a day is used. Oxygen is contained in iron bottles with a volume of 7 square metres. Acetylene gas containers are 4 square metres, and carbonic acid gas containers are 20kg.

12. Mitsui Chemical Laboratory

Inspection date: 19 February 1943

Interviewee: Hiro'oka Naosuke

The purpose of the laboratory is to conduct experiments with intermediate industries into ways to achieve local self-sufficiency. The following possibilities are currently under examination:

(a) Calcium carbonate powder

This is used as a filling material for rubber. It is made from limestone that comes from near Kuala Lumpur. Limestone is calcined into a powder of 80 mesh.

(b) Lubricating grease substitute

Mitsui Mine has requested this lubrication for the roller of the dredger conveyor. The volume requested at present is 60 tons a month. Lubricating grease substitute is made by boiling palm oil or coconut oil with lime. Yellow grease is made from palm oil and white grease from coconut oil. This grease substitute is to be used where high-quality grease is not needed.

(c) Potassium soap

Potassium liquid soaked from wood ash is used as a substitute for soda. It is made into bar soap. One hundred pounds of this product have been produced. Burnt ash is collected by burning sawdust from the local sawmill in the boiler; burnt coconut shell ash is rich in potassium.

(d) Pineapple fibre

This is used for fishing nets, belt conveyor hoses and tyres. It is too expensive to use as a substitute for jute bags and not profitable. Pineapple fibre is made by soaking pineapple leaves in water and then rolling them. Female workers then pare off the flesh with small knives and clean it with water. The fibre is then dried and twined to make string. Pineapple fibre is water-resistant.

Pineapple leaves yielding a pound of fibre cost $1. Two grams of fibre can be made from a leaf.[8] Fibre currently costs $7 a pound to produce, but this cost can be reduced to $5. Daily production per female worker is four to five ounces. At present daily production of pineapple fibre is 12 to 13 pounds, and over the whole peninsula it is possible to produce 2,000 tons.[9]

(e) Carbon black

Carbon black is produced by incomplete combustion of crude rubber in a special furnace. The current yield rate is 3.5 per cent of the pure rubber, but it would be possible to achieve a yield of 5 per cent. The principal use of carbon black is to fill rubber.

---

[8] It therefore required about 225 leaves to manufacture a pound of pineapple fibre, which implies that $1 would buy 225 leaves.

[9] Two thousand tons presumably relates to yearly production and would require 36,000 female workers and approximately 0.25 million pineapples a day.

(f) Waste oil collection

At present, the military wastes good-quality oil. It is necessary to collect, heat and filter waste oil so that it can be recycled.

13. Shiraki Trading Company, Miscellaneous Factories

Location: This enterprise manages Chinese factories that it bought out.

Inspection date: 18 February 1943

(a) Paper recycling factory, Jalan Besar Road

The factory's raw material is waste paper which is boiled with caustic soda to produce low-quality paper such as tissue paper. The manufacturing processes resemble a handicraft. Current daily output is 1,000 sheets. Each sheet is cut into eight equal smaller sheets and bundled in 50-sheet bundles. Bundles are sold for 25 cents each. This factory will soon be scheduled to double its production capacity.

(b) Tannery (a factory appointed by Yasuda Unit)

The tannery can at present tan 250 oxhides, 500 square inches of crocodile skin and 500 sheepskins a month. The products are used for belts and as oil strainers. The tanning process for oxhide is to soak rawhides first in water for a month and then in tanning extracts for three months. The hides are then moved to a less concentrated liquid. After drying, they are buffed and polished. Tannin is made from the liquid derived from soaking mangrove bark. Stored bark is dry and needs to be soaked in water for three to four days. Crocodile rawhide costs between $1.80 and $1.30 a square inch. The price of the finished product is $2.80. The factory employs 45 operatives: 25 Chinese and 20 Malays.

(c) Cigarette factory

Current production is practically a handicraft. Cigarettes are made from Virginia tobacco leaves from Ipoh. Daily production is 2,000 boxes (each box contains 20 cigarettes). A female worker can make between 600 and 1,200 cigarettes a day. The factory has a stock of six months' worth of rice papers.[10] But the rice papers are of such low quality that the sheets have to be pieced together. The machinery currently installed is old and needs maintenance, leading to a production rate

[10] Rice paper was made from rice straw and often used for cigarette paper, lampshades and partition screens.

of 300 cigarettes a minute. The cigarettes have not yet been sold, but there is a timetable to sell after Syonan Wings Blue Brand has been registered as a trademark.

(d) Soy sauce and miso factory

It is planned to buy out a Chinese factory and use it as a Japanese soy sauce and miso factory.

14. Alexandra Brick factory

Location: 947 Pasir Panjang Road, Syonan Municipality

Inspection date: 23 February 1943

Interviewee: Tanaka Masato

This was formerly Alexandra Brickworks Ltd., established in 1928. It has a paid-up capital of $1,400,000. There are branch factories in Ipoh, Kuala Lumpur and Perai [or Prai in Penang]. At present the factory is managed by Syonan Municipality's Department of Commerce and Industry. Apart from general bricks, it produces firebricks, drainpipes, roofing tiles (French and Indian tiles) and ceramics. A current concern is to improve the quality of the firebricks. On a 40-acre site, the factory buildings cover about one-third of the site and comprise three brick kilns, two kilns for pipes, and one kiln for firebricks. The crushing-moulding machine is excellent, and it offers an integrated production process from clay digging to putting bricks into the kiln. Two hundred and fifty workers are employed (before the war there were 200), 90 per cent of them Indians. The raw material of clay is dug from the factory site and conveyed on a trolley to the factory. The reserves of clay on the site are expected to last 10 to 15 years. Every month 350 tons of coal from Bukit Asam, Sumatra, are used, at a factory gate price of $27 a ton. All factory products are delivered to the military.

This factory will be dedicated to improving the quality of firebricks in response to the demand from a smelting furnace for charcoal pig iron (now being constructed), a tin-refining plant, a thermal power plant and a glass manufacturer. To achieve these aims, the municipality and the military want to introduce techniques from the best companies in Japan. At present, clay for firebricks is brought from Johore state. Firebricks now being manufactured can be used at temperatures of up to 1,400 degrees but need to be capable of withstanding 2,400 degrees.

Table 6.5 provides an analysis of the composition of Johore clay.

Table 6.5 Composition of Johore clay

CHINA CLAY
SRI MEDAN MINE JOHORE

$A1_2O_3$	S_1O_2	F_2O_3	T_1O_2	NGO	IGLOSS
37.99	41.02	4.08	1.92	0.06	14.52
39.58	39.82	3.93	1.75		14.90
40.68	39.25	2.82	1.44		16.42

SG. PERPAT PENDAS JOHORE

$A1_2O_3$	S_1O_2	Fe_2O_3	T_1O_2	IGLOSS
37.99	41.02	4.08	1.92	14.52
39.58	39.82	3.93	1.75	14.90
40.68	39.25	2.82	1.44	16.42

15. Syonan Paint Factory

Location: 610 Telok Blangah Road, Syonan Municipality

Inspection date: 22 February 1943

Interviewee: Soga Masami

This was formerly the Dutch factory of P.A.R. Malayan Paint Works Ltd. It had a paid-up capital of $500,000. The factory is now managed by Syonan Municipality's Department of Commerce and Industry, with technical guidance from two experts sent from Dai-Nippon Paint Company. Daily production before the war was 90 tons of normal paint and 90 tons of water-based paint, boiled [linseed] oil, enamel and varnish, a total of 180 tons. After the outbreak of war, the machinery needed repairs for six months. Having been put back into working order, the factory has followed a request from the military and produced normal paint using stored materials. There have recently been shortages in pigments such as linseed oil, and production has had to be reduced. The factory initially imported semi-manufactured or finished products from Europe or Java, and simply prepared them for sale. There is thus no plan for self-sufficiency in raw materials. The technical manager is now examining the use of rubber seed oil as a substitute for linseed oil. It is intended to build a zinc oxide factory capable of producing 100 tons annually, using zinc plate imported from Burma.[11]

[11] See also 6. Yokohama Rubber above.

In view of the shortage of goods in the city, the factory has also been producing toothpaste, using stores of calcium carbonate,[12] and is also considering the production of shoe polish.

16. Opium Factory Managed by the Department of Finance

Inspection date: 24 February 1943

Guide: Head of Monopoly Section, Department of Finance

(a) Branch factory

Location: Telok Blangah Road, Syonan Municipality

This factory, which employs 27 people, boils and refines opium to produce opium resin. It was destroyed during military action but has been restored and started working again last August [1942]. Current production has fallen to a third of pre-war levels, and daily output is 4,680 tahil.[13] The only equipment in the factory is a pot for boiling the opium. The raw opium derives from seized goods brought from Afghanistan, Burma and Persia. Cultivation of opium poppies in Malaya and Sumatra would be difficult, so future supplies of opium are expected to be imported from Mengjaiang.[14] There are 70,000 opium smokers in Malaya and Sumatra, and a current supply of three million tubes (the pre-war supply was seven million tubes).

(b) Main factory

Location: Pasir Panjang Road, Syonan Municipality

This factory packages the opium resin in tubes and boxes the tubes. It began packaging seized opium resin on 1 May 1942. Currently the factory is working at one-third of pre-war capacity, and daily output has risen to 150,000 tubes of 0.45g each. The factory is very well equipped. The machinery in the main workshops is as follows.

---

[12] See also 12. Mitsui Chemical Laboratory above.

[13] In Southeast Asia a tahil or tael is equivalent to 1/16 of a catty.

[14] Autonomous area in Inner Mongolia.

A. *Tube-making factory*

Two melting furnaces (these melt one part of lead to ten of tin), two casting machines, two rolling machines, six punching machines (with a punching capacity of 68,000 pellets a day), and 28 tube machines (producing 43 tubes a minute).

B. *Injection workshop*

Four water pressure machines, 17 water pressure delivery machines, 33 injecting machines (producing 43 tubes a minute), 33 wrapping machines (to cap the tubes, wrapping capacity 43 tubes a minute), six tube weighing machines.

C. *Wood workshop*

Five sawmills, nine cutters, ten box-making machines, three checking machines.

D. *Machine repair shop*

12 machine tools.

There are 185 employees, 115 of them female who work mainly at tube manufacture (20) and injecting (65). Most of the employees are Cantonese. The average daily wage is 70 cents, and the maximum wage does not exceed $1.

Note on Tahil:
1 tahil = 10 chee [mace] = 100 hoon [candareen] = 10000 li.

Prices, Inflation and Rationing

CHAPTER 7

Countermeasures for Prices for Syonan Municipality

Compiled for the Committee for the Problem of Prices, Data Compilation by Kirita Naosaku, March 1944

This report is a study of price rises, their cause, and countermeasures in Malaya, especially Syonan Municipality. The Chōsabu organized an in-house Committee for the Problem of Prices and had Civilian Administrator Kirita Naosaku integrate data from various fields for the report. Owing to the speed with which data were collected and analyzed, the report may not be comprehensive enough. Despite its status as an interim report, however, this survey on countermeasures for prices can be regarded as a reference point.

The report's main focus is on measures for collecting and rationing necessities [including food, clothing and other daily necessaries], which is a problem that needs to be dealt with immediately in Malaya.

Contents

Specific Measure 2: Securing Collateral Goods to Barter for Food

Specific Measure 3: Measures in Relation to Currency, Notably Techniques to Absorb Purchasing Power

4. **Conclusion**

Appendix Tables

1. Causes and Characteristics of Price Rises

Malaya has been occupied by the Imperial Army for about two years. Prices are now much higher than before the war. The reasons for this are as follows.

(1) Shortages of commodities caused by the cessation of imports

Malaya's economy was largely reliant on importing commodities. Consumer goods comprised 75 per cent of imports, and 65 per cent of consumer goods imported were food, which met over two-thirds of food demand in Malaya. Fifteen per cent of consumer goods imports were clothing and the remaining 20 per cent miscellaneous daily necessities. These imports meet almost all demand for such items.

The outbreak of war and cessation of imports therefore caused severe disruption to the Malayan consumer economy. Transactions of non-food consumer goods can be characterized as a 'stock' economy owing to Malaya's reliance on pre-war stocks. Decreases in food supply have also resulted from falls in imports due to the shortage of vessels and from the failure to increase food production in the region. This is the basic cause of price rises in Malaya.

(2) The unbalanced expansion of circulating currency

The amount of currency was originally kept in balance by exports, which release currency into circulation, and imports, which remove currency from circulation. Therefore, the amount of circulating currency adjusts automatically. After the occupation, however, currency released into circulation through payment of military expenditure and the costs of buying goods and materials to be shipped to Japan could no longer be removed from circulation through the purchase of imports.[1] When all issued currency is in circulation, most of it is diffused towards the merchant class in the urban areas, who have stockpiles of goods imported before the war. Large quantities of currency are used to buy goods, the supply of which is diminishing daily. [Because of merchant hoarding,] Prices rise faster than they would if there were only an imbalance between goods and money. This is the second fundamental cause of price rises in Malaya.

These two causes arise from structural changes to the Malayan economy from the pre-war period to the present day. Several other causes should also be mentioned.

---

[1] Because Malaya was not regarded as an independent entity, the Japanese originally uses the term 'shipped' instead of 'exported' from Malaya.

(3) Failure to increase local production

The shortage of commodities arising from the cessation of imports should be ameliorated by increasing local production. However, production levels have not improved. The main reasons for this are as follows.

(i) Shortages of materials and ancillary producer goods

Malaya originally depended on imports for all materials and ancillary goods, and the depletion of stockpiled materials has made it difficult to increase production.

(ii) Shortages of collateral goods

Originally, imported commodities such as food, clothing and other daily necessities were given to producers in exchange for the produce collected. The shortage of imported goods therefore lessens the incentive to increase production levels. A knock-on effect is that less progress than anticipated has been made towards meeting quotas for production.

(iii) Smaller labour force to meet quotas for production

Farmers now concentrate mainly on producing food for immediate family consumption, because there is a shortage of collateral goods to stimulate production. This creates a labour shortage to meet production quotas.

(4) Decline in transport capacity

The shortage of vessels is reducing the level of imports from overseas, and shortages in railway carriages and lorries also reduce the transport of goods to consumers within Malaya and Syonan. As a result, an obvious imbalance in the distribution of goods is emerging. Lack of transport capacity has particularly affected the flow of goods to the city. Compared to the pre-war period, when annual imports via rail and road averaged 800 railway carriages and 1,400 lorries full of cargoes, and there was a good supply of imported rubber tyres and spare parts, the current transport shortages associated with the cessation of the imports [particularly of tyres and spare parts] have had a devastating impact.[2]

---

[2] There were two or three railway carriages and three or four lorries a day carrying cargoes to Singapore before the war.

(5) Competition between military and civilian organizations in obtaining produce

Military and civilian organizations collect cargoes independently of each other and without any liaison. This leads to spiralling price rises and impairs planned cargo collection and the distribution of rations for civilian use. The problems created for collection and distribution are the most damaging consequence of price rises.

(6) The emergence of autarky in each state

Falls in transport capacity are one cause of the uneven distribution of goods. In addition, there is no inter-state communication, and a tendency for each state to have an autarkic economy. This further enhances uneven goods distribution. The consequence is that each state ceases to produce goods for export, and instead it produces only for local demand within the state. This encourages a general decline in the fulfilment of production quotas.

(7) Relative urban overpopulation

Before the war, most of the urban population in places such as Syonan or Penang engaged in commerce because these were commercial port cities. Since the outbreak of war, however, as the necessity for the regional production of goods has increased, most of the urban population has become a surplus, nonproductive population. The distribution of goods is correspondingly severely uneven, with a consequent remarkable price rise in urban areas.

Clearly these causes do not operate singly; rather, they interact with each other and together exert upward pressure on prices. Price rises in Malaya therefore have several characteristics that arise from the causes described above.

(i) Regional price differences

In consequence of falls in transport capacity and urban overpopulation, together with speculation by overseas Chinese traders—who take advantage of current shortages—price rises in urban areas such as Syonan Municipality are higher than in agricultural producing areas or in surrounding areas. Analysis of price structures in urban areas shows price rises many times higher than suggested by costs in producing regions because they are augmented by the cost of rationing (see table A.7.1).

(ii) General and specific prices

If price rises were caused only by currency problems, the result would be a general rise in prices. Because the primary reason for price rises is commodity shortages due to the cessation of imports, however, the rate at which prices have risen has varied according to commodity. The real problem is therefore price increases for individual commodities, rather than a general price rise. The speed with which separate prices have risen depends on the degree of dependence on imports during the pre-war period, the price elasticity of demand, and the extent to which production has been encouraged. Therefore, price rises are highest for materials for industrial production and clothing, followed by daily necessaries and food (see table A.7.2).

(iii) The influence of black market prices

Although black market prices initially depended on activity by the affluent, their influence has spread through the wider population. Black market prices are most felt in small-scale retailing and therefore threaten general daily life. The extent of black market activity compared with official transactions differs according to goods. For those goods with demand significantly higher than the quantities officially on offer, the black market operates. For example, if the official rice supply is set at 4,800 tons,[3] and if special trade through import—'smuggling'—by licensed overseas Chinese traders was, as estimated last December, at least 2,000 tons,[4] then the ratio of the official rice supply to the special trade rice should be 7:3. Forty per cent of vegetables are derived from official channels of distribution, and 60 per cent on the black market.[5]

Overall, urban prices, especially those in Syonan Municipality, are becoming markedly higher than in other states of Malaya. Because Syonan Municipality is the focal point for the military, and for the economy of the whole Southern Military Administration, prices there impact directly on prices in Malaya and indirectly on every occupied area under the Southern Military Administration. The mere fact of price rises in Syonan Municipality spreads upwards price pressure

---

[3] This is a recommended level. Table A.7.4 in fact shows smaller actual deliveries.

[4] Table A.7.6 shows the total to be 2,939 tons of parboiled and dehydrated rice permitted. If 70 per cent was actually imported that would be 2,057 tons.

[5] Special trade was carried out by overseas Chinese traders using private boats with permits from the authorities. Official rice imports were carried out by Mitsubishi Shoji Corporation. The original text refers to 'smuggling', but this was in fact the same as 'special trade', which was opened up in March 1944 with the Alor Setar trade agreement with Thailand. After June 1944, subsequent to this report, 'smuggling' activity was merged with the main rice collection and became official as described in chapter 11. Because 'smuggling' was semi-legal, we put the term in quotes, as does the original Japanese text.

to the entire occupied area. In every respect, therefore, this shows how important it is to take countermeasures against price rises in Syonan Municipality.

2. Aims and Policies to Combat Price Rises

(1) The aim of price measures

The fundamental goals of price measures are to sustain minimum standards of living for the local people, to secure the supply of materials and labour for the military in preparation for the Imperial Army's final battle, and to maintain public order by safeguarding the lives of the population. Measures should thus focus on the general population, especially on those who engage in productive work. Daily necessities, particularly staple foods, should also be targeted.

(2) Basic policies to combat price rises

The basic policies to combat price rises, considering the aim of price measures as stated above, are: first, to increase productivity in the supply of daily necessities and the collection of freight; second, to establish a strong rationing system that can reliably distribute goods to end consumers. As far as the currency is concerned, policies are required, as far as possible, to soak up purchasing power possessed by merchants' accumulated currency. In implementing these policies in practice, the following points should be kept in mind.

(i) Increasing production and using overseas Chinese businesses

The aim of increased production of supplementary foods and vegetables should be self-sufficiency for the island. At present, the island has an estimated 7,000 acres of farmland. More unused land needs to be brought under cultivation to grow food crops.[6] The reasons for the failure to increase production quota contributions in other nearby states or islands have already been noted. Attention must be focused on how to secure materials and ancillary goods for production, collateral goods to barter and labour, for which shortages exist.

Overseas Chinese capital and labour should be used for food production. One approach would be to require overseas Chinese businesses to set up a company to produce food and to use government-owned land without charge for a stated period. As in the production of daily necessities, unused production facilities owned by overseas Chinese businesses might be used.

---

[6] See chapter 9 on the implementation of this policy.

(ii) Establishment of a centralized freight collection system

To prevent the harmful consequences of inconsistent military and civilian cargo systems, it goes without saying that the two parties should maintain close contact. If possible, a centralized and unitary freight-collecting system that integrates both military and civilian systems should be established. If this cannot be done, a committee should be set up comprising the army, navy and civilians, to allow the different parties to keep in close contact. Currently, some of the army cargo collection subcontractors are an impediment to what is supposed to be a smooth collection process. The employment of such subcontractors should be curtailed immediately.[7]

(iii) Efficient use of transport facilities

Shortages in transport facilities, especially lorries, lead to problems in transporting commodities from the place of production to trading centres or the place of consumption. In view of this situation, transport substitutes such as oxcarts or other forms of transportation should where possible be found to transport commodities that do not perish rapidly. The available lorries should be used only to transport perishable foods. Furthermore, in order to avoid wasting transport facilities, daily necessities should be produced around Syonan City.

(iv) Rationing priorities and out-migration

At present, the current availability of necessities [including food] is insufficient for minimum requirements. We must therefore put in place a more intensive priority rationing system. This would cause nonproductive urban labourers to migrate to the countryside or change occupations.[8] Existing rationing agencies should be tightened to promote a universal priority rationing system.

(v) Increasing imports by overseas Chinese traders

As goods are in insufficient supply to meet minimum requirements, shortages will continue for some time, even with a stimulus to production. This problem should be solved by promoting imports, particularly of Thai rice, through those overseas Chinese merchants who have traded with Thailand, Sumatra and Java since the pre-war period. This kind of trade has always been done in the past, and

---

7 See chapter 9.

8 See chapter 4.

always on a completely laissez-faire basis.[9] Because of the shortage of collateral goods, in particular, import trades are settled in Southern Development Bank notes.[10] The exchange rate in March [1944] was $100 to 35 baht. This payment method therefore worsens the situation. It is not possible to cover the balance except by selling imports at higher prices. In these circumstances, the Military Administration should devise an easier way for overseas Chinese merchants to purchase commodities [including parboiled and dehydrated rice] in Thailand, particularly in Southern Thailand. Further, if appropriate collateral goods are available, they should be supplied to these merchants. The resulting imports should be sold under the Military Administration's supervision. These measures would to some extent prevent the harmful consequences of the black market pricing attendant on 'smuggling'. Hopefully the measures would also end commodity shortages.

Furthermore, commodities other than controlled goods [i.e., rice, salt and sugar] imported by overseas Chinese traders should be left to the free market, so that shortages of these commodities will ease in a while. If supply of standard rations eventually exceeds demand, the activity will cease in the natural course of time, or can easily be terminated.

(vi) Price controls and their limits

Once controlled goods [i.e., rice, salt and sugar] are secured in Syonan, their prices should be set by the appropriate cost accounting method. However, once a supply of rice, salt and sugar sufficient to meet quotas has been secured from identified collection agents, the prices for the balance of these commodities available should be left to find their own level. This will increase the amount supplied to the market. Apart from price-controlled commodities, prices for non-essential goods should also be left to find their own market level for the time being.

(vii) Absorption of purchasing power

In determining currency policy, this report regards the absorption of excess liquidity as of secondary importance. Monetary policy should be used together with market controls. The amount of currency in circulation is just over three times as large as in the pre-war period, but we should not be optimistic, because

---

9 Just as 'rice-smuggling' was being conducted by the permit-holding traders (and presumably also by unlicensed traders) at the time when this report was written, around March–April 1944. See chapter 11 for the out-of-control state of trade with which the Japanese authorities were faced in early 1944.

10 *Nanhatsuken* was the currency of the occupied area and was similar to military scrip.

currency in circulation will continue to increase in the future. Measures must be put in place to absorb excess currency.

Before the war, overseas Chinese residents in Malaya deposited money in British banks or purchased British government bonds. Measures taken by the Imperial Army deprived these capital sums of value. It is unlikely that the overseas Chinese will absorb currency voluntarily [i.e., deposit money in the bank or buy bonds], since their expectations will largely be influenced by the view they take of the outcome of the war. Taking this into consideration, appropriate measures should be put in place.

3. Specific Measures

Specific Measure 1: Measures for Individual Commodities

Before describing measures for individual commodities, it is necessary to compare pre-war and present food consumption. As table A.7.3 shows, current food consumption is around 32 per cent of pre-war levels for staple foods, 29 per cent for vegetables and fruit, and 59 per cent for fish and meat.[11] Although these levels are inadequate, if they are used as the basis for the standard ration, the following measures should be adopted.

Rice

I. Measures to be taken if 4,400 tons of rice were set as the standard monthly quota from the Military Administration to Syonan Municipality

(1) Monthly ration (based on current adjusted ration levels)

(i) General ration (distribution stations)

Table 7.1 Syonan Municipality monthly rice rations[12]

	Persons	Ration per person (catties)
Adult males	360,000	8
Adult females	270,000	6
Children	230,000	4
Total	860,000	3,330 tons

[11] The source for the pre-war data is not indicated, but it may be the Colonial Office, Food and Nutrition Survey.

[12] Tables 7.1–7.7 show the level of planned official rationing for fiscal year 1944.

(ii) Rations for special areas

Table 7.2 Syonan Municipality special area rice rations[13]

	Persons	Ration
Adult males	39,700	
Adult females	6,700	
Children	5,200	
Total	51,600	230 tons

(iii) Ration for adjacent islands [i.e., Bintan, Riau Islands, etc.]

Average ration: 5 catties per person
Population: 160,000
Total: 490 tons

(iv) Extra ration for labourers

Two allocations: 9 or 5 catties per person monthly
70,000 currently selected labourers entitled to extra rations: 360 tons
60,000 additional labourers to be given extra rations: 308 tons (9 catties per person) (see note below)

(v) Temporary ration

Schools, hospitals, training institutes: 30 tons

(vi) Ration for Japanese

Civilians and Japanese-only hotels: 70 tons

(vii) Other rations

Rice for charity, rice for marine supplies, rice for food manufacturing such as soy sauce and vinegar: 30 tons

[13] Special Areas may denote jails and concentration camps for Allied POWs and civilians. Ration amounts on a par with general rations for the local population, calculated at the individual level, were set aside at the discretion of officials.

(viii) Rations for public canteens

The 35-ton ration allocation to local restaurants is redirected: 35 tons
This includes 15 tons of rations arising from the closure of Japanese restaurants.[14]

Total ration: 4,883 tons

Note: Currently 70,000 labourers are employed by the navy and by Japanese companies. In addition, local clerks working for Japanese companies and factory labourers working for local companies should receive extra rations (see table A.7.4).

(2) Ensuring supply

- Quota from Military Administration: 4,400 tons a month
- Additional supplies to be secured: 483 tons a month

Plans to secure additional supplies

(i) Overseas Chinese traders should be allowed to import rice from Thailand for the Military Administration to purchase and ration at the standard ration price. (The difference between the purchasing and selling prices should be managed by the Military Administration accounts [*Ringun Kaikei*].) Table A.7.6 gives the amount and value of Thai rice imports. The rice was imported by those issued a permit by Syonan Municipality from January to December last year [1943]. Even on the assumption that actual rice imports were 60 per cent of the face value shown in the table, imports of about 1,200 tons in November and 1,800 tons in December would easily make up the shortage of 483 tons.[15]

Most of the 'smuggled' rice comes from Southern Thailand, especially from Kedah.[16] There is therefore some hindrance to rice collections by Mitsubishi Shōji Corporation. Where overseas Chinese traders buy rice from producers, the Military Administration should facilitate its easy purchase at a low price. We should also consider how, as soon as possible, we might channel rice collected by overseas Chinese into official systems by using overseas Chinese organizations. It would also be advisable for

[14] Ordinary local restaurants were closed and public canteens were opened, and the rice originally rationed to the restaurants was reallocated to the public canteens.

[15] Table A.7.6 shows the total of permitted parboiled and dehydrated rice imports to be 2,089 and 2,939 tons for November and December. If 60 per cent was actually imported, that would be 1,253 and 1,763 tons respectively.

[16] Kedah was transferred to Thailand on 18 October 1943.

Mitsubishi to change the collecting centre from Kedah to an alternative location such as central Thailand. Furthermore, it would be preferable to provide collateral goods such as petrol to merchants, since accounts can be settled easily with these goods.

(ii) As has already been done in Perak, states must stop rice rationing to agricultural villages as a matter of principle. The surplus rice available from this policy (estimated at 1,200 tons) can be allotted [to Syonan Municipality] (see table A.7.6).

(iii) Labourers in the employ of the army are granted a monthly rice ration of 8 catties by the municipality, and also a direct supply of 15 catties from the army. This amounts to 23 catties, which is over-rationing in comparison to labourers in navy employment, as well as those who are given priority rationing by Syonan Municipality, which has a maximum amount of 17 catties. Labourers working for the army get 6 catties more than others. The army should stop these excess rice rations and allocate them [to Syonan Municipality] (see note below).

(iv) The monthly quota for Japanese soldiers living in Syonan and civilian administrators in military service is 37 to 38 catties. This seems too large considering actual consumption levels. The ration should therefore be reduced to a reasonable amount and the surplus rice allocated [to Syonan Municipality].

(v) The policy of out-migration serves as a passive measure to secure food. The target of this policy is to remove Syonan Municipality's unproductive population to estates, mines and factories in Malaya, and compel them to change their jobs.

Note: If the 23 catties a month ration received by labourers in army employ is considered 'appropriate', then the ration would have to be increased from 17 to 23 catties for labourers in the navy and labourers granted priority rations by Syonan Municipality. Such a course of action would increase shortages by a further 464 tons, to 957 tons. This gap may be filled by enforcing measures (i), (ii) or (iv) set out above, but if these approaches are not effective, measure (iii) should be applied.[17]

---

[17] Table 7.9 shows the comparison between the estimated food intake of those on priority rations and that of the army (combatants) standard. The priority ration shown in table 7.9 is 21 catties, a value intermediate between the priority rations for army employees (23 catties) and the navy and municipality priority rations (17 catties). The army standard, in contrast, presumably related to Japanese soldiers and is shown as 33 catties (660g a day), which is less than the actual amount allotted to the soldiers stationed in Singapore (37–38 catties) as (iv) above.

(3) Rationing measures

Rationing stations were originally set up under the Food Supply Office [*Shokuryō Kanri Sho*] of Syonan Municipality. They comprise 43 wholesalers and about 1,007 retailers (1 retailer per 200 households).

The current adverse effects of rationing are as follows:

- Some retailers arbitrarily change the rationing day and adulterate rations with other ingredients to make up the volume and sell rice on the black market.
- Some wholesalers give short measures of rice when they sell it to the retailers. The result is reduced rations for consumers.

These malfunctions should be reduced by the following actions.

(i) Rationing dates should be fixed to prevent retailers from varying them. Additionally, ration distributions should be supervised by police officers.

(ii) Where violations occur, wholesalers and retailers should be punished severely.

(iii) If it were possible for neighbourhood associations of consumers [*tonarigumi*] to operate the rationing system, such an arrangement might be effective.

(4) Transport measures

The current transport system for rice is the use of lorries from the warehouse to wholesalers and retailers. Because of future shortages of lorries, it is necessary to consider using oxcarts for transport as soon as possible.

II. Measures to be taken if the 4,400-ton quota from the Military Administration to Syonan Municipality is reduced

The current military situation suggests that the current standard quota of 4,400 tons will in the future be reduced. The following measures should be taken.

(i) The rations of those receiving general rations should be reduced where they do not make increased contributions to the war effort.

(ii) In view of likely military developments, the out-migration policy should be implemented as soon as possible within reasonably achievable limits.

(iii) Looking forward, supplementary foods as well as staple foods such as rice will be important. Their production should therefore urgently be increased, utilizing unused land on the island or in nearby areas.

(iv) There will be an increasing need to import rice through overseas Chinese traders.

III. Other matters to be taken into account

(i) Public canteens

Public canteens should be opened for labourers employed in priority industries who need to eat out. The canteens should be supplied with 35 tons of rice a month that can be saved with the cessation of rations to ordinary restaurants. Canteen facilities could be set up in former restaurant premises, or at any other suitable places that still operate as restaurants.

(ii) Provision of substitute foods

Currently, 80,000 loaves of tapioca bread are produced. This must be increased to 140,000 loaves, together with the additional supply of 50,000 catties of fresh tapioca noodles. These foods should not be distributed at market prices but sold only to workers in priority industries.

Supplementary Foods

(1) Monthly rations

The current level of rations should be retained but apply only to the old town and not the new town.[18]

(i) General ration (distribution stations)

Table 7.3 Syonan Municipality monthly supplementary food rations through distribution stations[19]

	Persons	Ration per person (catties)
Adult males	180,000	4
Adult females	132,000	3
Children	110,000	2
Total	422,000	820 tons

[18] The two Chinatowns on either side of the Singapore River. Police precincts A. South Bridge Road, B. Kandang Kerbau, and C. Tanjong Pagar accommodated 408,679 residents in November 1943.

[19] Rations of supplementary food were distributed only to the old town. The ration amount corresponds to the weight in dried form. Four catties of tapioca flour is equivalent to 16 catties of unprocessed tapioca.

(ii) Rations for special areas

Table 7.4 Syonan Municipality special area supplementary food rations, March 1944

	Persons	Ration
Adult males	39,700	
Adult females	6,700	
Children	5,200	
Total	51,600	120 tons

Total: 940 tons (See table A.7.5)

(2) Ensuring supply

At present, tapioca flour, soybeans, cassava roots [i.e., (dried) cassava root imported mainly from Thailand], maize, sago flour, sago pearl and black soybeans have to be imported from elsewhere. In the future, increasingly acute shortages of vessels will make it particularly difficult to import tapioca flour, cassava roots, soybeans and maize. Implementation of the local self-sufficiency policy should therefore focus mainly on [unprocessed] tapioca and sweet potatoes.

Amounts supplied:

- Tapioca and sweet potatoes from Johore: 3,000 tons (about 750 tons as dried flour)
- Shortfall: 760 tons (190 tons as dried flour)

The shortfall should be made up by the following measures.

(i) Production of tapioca and sweet potatoes should be increased on Syonan Island as much as possible. At present, 3,000 acres are used for supplementary foods on Syonan Island and produce 1,250 tons a month, consumed mainly in the new town. An increase in the production of supplementary foods for the old town, utilizing unused land on Syonan Island, is therefore urgent. To achieve this, 50,000 acres should be converted from rubber plantations if possible.

(ii) A surplus production of sweet potatoes in Selangor can be shipped to Syonan if necessary. Deliveries to Syonan Municipality should be made as soon as possible.

(3) Freight collection arrangements

Freight collection arrangements should take into account the following factors.

(i) The collecting agency

In Johore, members of the Overseas Chinese Commission Agents Association collect freights, supervised by Japanese personnel from the Higashiyama Agriculture Corporation.[20] The management of the transport of freight from Johore to Syonan Municipality is handled by the Syonan Vegetable and Fruit Association. However, the importance of supplementary foods is now increasing, and these must be considered as a staple food on par with rice. Mitsubishi Corporation, which already deals in rice, should take over the transport of supplementary foods from the Syonan Vegetable and Fruit Association.

(ii) Transport

Although 12 lorries are allocated for the transport of goods from the areas of production in Johore to the railway stations in Johore, deliveries of fruit and vegetables from Johore are also increasing, and lorries should as far as possible be used to transport fruit and vegetables. Supplementary foods should, where possible, be transported by oxcart within Johore. Transport from loading stations in Johore to Syonan Municipality should principally be by rail. If possible, within Syonan Island, transport should be by oxcart.

(iii) Methods of freight collection

Purchasing prices at the cargo exchange in Johore are currently fixed at 14.5 cents per catty for sweet potatoes and 8 cents for cassava. It would be better to use daily necessities as collateral goods instead of money to increase the amounts collected. If no collateral goods are available, purchasing prices must be raised in accordance with local conditions to allow for current difficulties in making collections.

(4) Rationing arrangements

Rationing arrangements for supplementary foods should be the same as for rice and should be carried out through the same agencies.

---

[20] Higashiyama Agriculture Corporation was part of the Mitsubishi conglomerate. In this passage, the members of the Association for the Overseas Chinese Commission Agents are collecting the rice. The Japanese personnel sent from the Higashiyama Agriculture Corporation supervise the agents.

Vegetables

(1) Ensuring supply

It is estimated that 50 tons of vegetables a day are supplied from Syonan Island sources. Assuming that 15 tons are taken for military use, 35 tons are available for civilian consumption. But the actual level of average daily consumption is 90 tons, and most of these vegetables are freely delivered by overseas Chinese merchants from within and outside the island. This is because, in contrast to fish and meat, it is difficult to collect vegetables centrally in a single wholesale market. The control of fish and meat is easy, because fish supplies depend on ice and fuel, while meat can be collected from the slaughterhouse. The target amount to be supplied through the Syonan Vegetable and Fruit Association daily should be set at 60 tons of vegetables. To achieve this as soon as possible, vegetables should be diverted from Chinese merchants, who are importing them without hindrance, and put under the control of the association. On the supply side, production in the island and nearby areas must be promoted, together with delivery from Perak and Negeri Sembilan.

(2) Freight collection policies

Individual vegetable collections by overseas Chinese do not enter official channels, because the trade is with hawkers outside the market. Therefore, in order to bring these goods into official channels, the overseas Chinese wholesale merchants should, as an urgent and pressing matter, join the association. A unified collection system under the control of the Syonan Vegetable and Fruit Association would thereby be achieved. It might, however, remain difficult for wholesalers to collect produce, owing to the low purchase prices paid by the association. The approach to this difficult situation should be as follows.

(i) Purchasing prices should be raised and profits to the association reduced. (At present the association makes a very substantial commission income, which seems inappropriate.)

(ii) Collateral goods such as rice, agricultural tools, seeds, fertilizer and daily necessities should be provided to facilitate deals.

(iii) Collection agencies should be reorganized. Overseas Chinese wholesale merchants should be allowed to join the Syonan Vegetable and Fruit Association. In a reorganized association these merchants, as experts in the collection of fruits and vegetables, should be central to the association's deliberations. Reorganization should be through the merchants' own initiative.

(iv) Transport of rice, tapioca and sweet potatoes should be changed from lorry to oxcart. The lorries made surplus by this measure can then be used to transport perishable vegetables.

(3) Rationing arrangements

(i) Monthly rations

The daily supply of 60 tons of vegetables (1,800 tons a month) is to be ensured. Priority rationing should be as in table 7.5.

Table 7.5 Syonan Municipality monthly vegetable rations, March 1944

	Persons	Ration per person (catties)	Total amount (tons)
Priority ration*	130,000	6	462
General ration	730,000	3	1,304
Total			1,766

*About 50% of average pre-war consumption

(ii) Rationing arrangements

Rations should be purchased, on production of a purchasing card, from the association or appointed retailers. Those with priority rationing should be given precedence over those on general rationing. Additionally, rationing dates and frequency should be made clear.

(iii) Rationing stations

There are at present 330 retailers in the market and 400 outside, a total of 730 retailers (274 households per retailer). These retailers should be made rationing stations and should distribute vegetables to consumers under the customer registration system.[21]

(iv) Ration prices

Official rations should be sold at appropriate prices.

[21] Chapter 4 shows that in September 1944, 556 traders formed themselves into corporations [kong-si] in the 25 rationing stations inside the market, while 22 stores operated outside the market.

Fruit

(1) Ensuring supply

There is a monthly demand for fruit of 900 tons. Fruit is purchased from Negeri Sembilan, Pahang, Perak, Johore, nearby islands, and Syonan Island. If more transport were available, imports in excess of 900 tons could be expected.

(2) Rationing arrangements

The present free market policy towards the distribution of fruit should be maintained.

Fish and Meat

(1) Ensuring supply

Fresh fish, salted dried fish and meat are all protein foods. The current reduction in the supply of meat is being made up with fresh and dried fish. Total supply of fish and meat is at 60 per cent of the pre-war level. The pre-war demand was 2,574 tons (which breaks down into 900 tons of fresh fish, 660 tons of dried and salted fish, 220 tons of beef, 710 tons of pork, and 84 tons of mutton and goat meat). Sixty per cent of the pre-war level, which is 1,544 tons, should be taken as the present level of demand. The detailed amounts are as in table 7.6.

Table 7.6 Syonan Municipality monthly demand for fish and meat, March 1944

	Total amount (tons)
Fresh fish	510
Dried and salted fish	620
Beef	80
Pork	324
Mutton and goat meat	10
Total	1,544

(2) Collection arrangements

(i) Fresh fish

Areas that supply fresh fish are the Riau Islands, Johore and Syonan Island. Fresh fish is collected and bought onshore by the Syonan Fresh Fish Association, overseas Chinese shipping agents or commission agents, and sold wholesale to retailers at six collection points. Collection and retail prices have been fixed at an approved level since 23 November 1942. Little comment is necessary on collection agencies or prices. However, to stimulate the collection of fish, attention ought to be given to the provision of collateral goods such as ice, fuel, fishing nets and daily necessities. Moreover, to encourage shipping agents and commission agents to send fish, a new kickback system should be applied. In addition, some trading companies take advantage of the name of the military in collecting fresh fish, in the purchase of which they exceed its authorized amounts of fish. They forcibly purchase the fishnet full of catch at low prices from local fishermen, or engage in offshore transactions at black market prices. These activities generally put grit in the mechanism of official collections. These companies must be strictly controlled and severely punished (see table A.7.8).

(ii) Dried and salted fish

Dried and salted fish is supplied by Terengganu, Kedah, Perak and the Riau Islands. Salt and rice are needed as collateral goods for the collection of fish (the Riau Islands require rice). The manufacture of dried and salted fish requires 40 catties of salt to 100 catties of fresh fish to produce 40 catties of dried and salted fish. However, rations in Pangkor Island now allow 36 tons of salt for the production of 100 tons of dried and salted fish, a ratio of only 15 tons of salt to 100 tons of fresh fish. Shortages in the supply of salt have consequently led to black market pricing. Salt is brought in from Thailand and priced at $70–80 a picul (the official ration price is $8 per 100 catties).

For the collection of dried and salted fish, salt should as far as possible be offered as a collateral good. The military [i.e., Mitsui Bussan & Co. as its commission agent for salt] should also buy salt in French Indochina or Thailand, and overseas Chinese should handle its transportation.

(iii) Beef, goat meat and mutton

This kind of meat is imported. It is obtained in Pahang and Kedah. Animal feed must be offered as a collateral good to maintain supplies.

(iv) Pork

About 1,600 pigs a month are imported from nearby islands, Pahang, Sumatra and Johore. Apart from these imports, 75,000 pigs are currently raised on Syonan Island. The current shortage of livestock feed requires the consumption of these pigs in the next three years.

(3) Rationing arrangements

Meat is at present distributed through quota rationing. However, the system is not working properly. There is a need for adequate priority rationing of all fish and meat.

(i) Rations

Table 7.7 Syonan Municipality monthly fish and meat rations, March 1944

	Persons	Ration per person (catties)	Total amount (tons)
Priority ration*	130,000	5	387
General ration**	730,000	2.6	1,130
Total			1,517

* Slightly over 80% of pre-war consumption.
** Slightly over 40% of pre-war consumption.

(ii) Rationing arrangements

Purchasing cards should be used to purchase rations. Those on priority rations should be given precedence over those on general rations.

(iii) Rationing agencies

The sale of fresh fish is structured so that fish from the Syonan Fresh Fish Association is sold wholesale to retailers in each market, who in turn sell the fish in rations in that market. The number of markets must be increased, as there are only 17 markets in Syonan.

Dried and salted fish is sold wholesale by the Syonan Salted Dried Fish Association to retailers within and outside the market for resale to customers. It would be convenient for policing purposes to merge the distribution of salted and fresh fish. Meat is sold to retailers by the Meat Section of the Food Supply Office for resale as rations to consumers. The distributing stations should be reorganized.

(iv) Ration prices

Fresh and salted fish are sold at the recommended price, meat at the official price. These prices should all be changed to official prices, based on the appropriate pricing calculation. Black market sale of fish and meat should be strictly controlled and violators severely punished.

Specific Measure 2: Securing Collateral Goods to Barter for Food

Collateral goods are the key element in measures to produce and collect products. The goods most in demand among producers are rice, materials for production and ancillary goods, clothing, and daily necessities.

(1) Rice

The best way to ensure the availability of rice as a collateral good is to stop rationing in agricultural villages. At present the standard rice quota, given to each state including Syonan Municipality, amounts to a total of 10,000 tons (table A.7.7). Approximately 1,200 additional tons would be gained by a cessation of rationing in the states except in large and medium-sized cities. The rice saved in this way could, as already suggested, furnish a collateral good to vegetable farmers who produce for delivery and to fishermen in the Riau Islands. Even if rationing to these villages ceased, however, a surplus supply of rice could hardly be expected, in view of the fall in rice imports due to the shortage of vessels [in the near future]. This consideration would make it impossible to provide rice as a collateral good.

(2) Clothing

About 130 million yards of cotton textiles were imported in the pre-war period. This volume averaged 20 yards a person a year. Syonan Municipality has a stockpile of 1.6 million yards of cotton textiles. Following the enforcement of the Essential Goods and Materials Control Ordinance [*Jūyō Busshi Tōsei Rei*], the general ration for cotton textiles was set at only 1 yard per person per year. This rationed amount is so small that it is virtually useless. It might be better to stop the general ration and instead use the 1.6 million yards of textile thereby available as collateral goods, after excluding a portion for priority rationing. The textiles should be used as collateral for producers of rice, supplementary foods and perishable foods.

(3) Daily necessities

The main daily necessities are tobacco, matches, soap, paper, candles, towels and thread. Most in demand as collateral goods are, particularly, tobacco and soap. The production of these goods should therefore be encouraged, and strict rationing should be enforced, as before on a priority basis. Furthermore, in the case of tobacco, it must be borne in mind that production of cigarettes, cigars and cut tobacco for the local population should also be increased.

(4) Materials of production and ancillary goods

The main materials of production and ancillary goods are farming tools, fishing equipment (especially nets), fuel for fishing boats, seed, fertilizer, salt for salted dried fish, and ice. If more of these items can be produced locally, an attempt should be made to do so. Further, if it is possible to import goods such as salt, as previously discussed, overseas Chinese traders should be encouraged to do so.

Specific Measure 3: Measures in Relation to Currency, Notably Techniques to Absorb Purchasing Power

(1) Reduction of currency issue by centralized purchasing

As already discussed, competition between the military and civilians in the collection of goods raises prices with no other result. The consequent currency in circulation rises with the cost of collecting goods. Establishment of centralized collections will facilitate a mechanism to prevent price rises and reduce the release of currency.

(2) Measures to absorb purchasing power

It is important to ensure that measures to absorb purchasing power target only people with large incomes. To some extent, absorption through levying taxes or issuing bonds or through coercion will be necessary. However, other tactics that take advantage of the mentality of the overseas Chinese must also be taken into account. Specific methods are described below.

(i) Reassessment and collection of taxes

Taxes collected by the Malayan Military Administration are based on taxes that have not been changed since the pre-war period. These are inheritance tax, breweries tax and stamp duties. Following the occupation, the Imperial Army introduced taxes on mining assets, soft drinks and trading. There are plans to introduce taxes on eating out, tobacco and luxuries. Income tax, which had been levied as a wartime tax [by the British], might be reapplied in the same way as before the occupation. As for local authority taxes, similar taxes carry over from the pre-war period. Moreover, real estate acquisition taxation has been newly introduced. Taxes should also be levied on gambling and amusements, and taxes gradually raised, or indirect taxes should be increased in line with the financial ability of the local population to bear them.

(ii) Public bonds

– A further issue of the Southern Dream Lottery[22]

It would be better to increase the highest lottery prize with a larger issue in a one-off lottery and reduce the odds of winning a prize. To appeal to the Chinese mentality, the lottery should be an irregular event, to avoid the dullness of regular repetition.

– Compulsory bonds

Under Imperial Army occupation, donations from overseas Chinese businessmen have, for them, been a considerable burden. However, in view of the continued price rises, it is necessary to allocate further compulsory bonds of a value appropriate to overseas Chinese organizations and other ethnic group organizations. Bonds should also be allocated to, and held by, Japanese and overseas Chinese banks. The bonds should be either government or Southern Development Bank bonds. The number of subscribers can be increased by granting the bondholders favourable conditions and special privileges.

(iii) Disposal of enemy property at premium prices

Enemy property has usually been sold only to Japanese at low prices. From now on, there should also be disposal of enemy property by public auction open to the local population, to achieve the highest possible prices. Sales should be held in a special luxury department store, as set out in the next section.

(iv) Establishing a special luxury department store

A special luxury department store must be established to absorb the purchasing power of the rich. It can be assumed that currency in circulation would be absorbed if all available luxury goods were sold freely to the local population at near-black market prices. The marginal profits should be added to public funds. The luxury goods sold in the special department store are, as already mentioned, enemy property or surplus goods left unsold due to priority rationing. For example, general rationing of tobacco could be stopped, and its irrational purchase by the local population ended, with the result that they would not need to earn more than the daily wages of general labourers merely in order to buy tobacco. Tobacco should be rationed on a priority basis among the approximately 100,000-strong population.[23] Surplus tobacco could then be sold at a premium price in the special department store.

---

[22] Kōnan Saiken was a lottery organized by the military.

[23] That is, 130,000 people receiving priority rations, see table 7.7.

(v) *Encouraging saving*

The absorption of currency through savings is now being extensively pursued and is yielding favourable results. The policy should be continued by advertising its success, and the beneficial results maintained.

4. Conclusion

As already discussed, the two instruments of control over goods and currency should be used as countermeasures. Priority should be on control over goods. The key objectives of such measures are to guarantee the availability of official standard rations of necessities, particularly food, and to facilitate rationing arrangements. Guaranteed rations should be raised to allow the local population minimum standards of living. Until countermeasures are rigorously implemented, action should not be taken to enforce overall price controls or to suppress black market activities. Table 7.8 shows the amount of food that needs to be guaranteed in comparison to the amount that would allow the maintenance of minimum standards of living (see table A.7.3).

If comments were permitted on the level of minimum standards of living, shown in table 7.8, we would make the point that for the local population in receipt of priority rations, the minimum standard of living should be at the level at which the labour force can just be maintained; for those on general rations, it should be the level at which death from starvation can just be avoided. Table 7.9 shows the nutritional benefits of priority rations to the local population.

Table 7.9 shows that even those granted priority rationing get insufficient calories. When supplementary and other foods are included, the estimated calorie intake is 2,000 for those on priority rations[24] and 1,400 for those who receive only general rations.[25] In point of fact, the table does not show actual nutritional levels; it is a calculation aimed at ensuring minimum standards of living. Dietary levels should urgently be improved to Level B (table 7.8). Overall price controls should be imposed only after living standards have been raised to Level B.[26] In current conditions, there would be no harm in strictly controlling the black market in supplementary foods, fresh fish, salted dried fish and meat. A crackdown on black market activity must be accompanied by the provision of collateral goods to facilitate the active collection of these foods.

---

[24] Table 7.9 shows 1,922kcal in total, aggregated from priority rations currently guaranteed with the elevated level of priority rice rations at two-thirds of the army combatant level.

[25] A desired amount corresponding to 'Desirable plan' in table A.7.3 and 'Level (B) amount required for minimum standards of living' in table 7.8.

[26] 1,400kcal level.

Table 7.8 Syonan Municipality comparison of guaranteed food and requirement for minimum living standards[27]

	Pre-war consumption (tons)	Amount to be guaranteed on the current plan (Level A) (tons)	Amount required for minimum standards of living (Level B) (tons)
Rice	12,000	4,883	6,694
Supplementary foods	5,990	940	1,880
Vegetables	5,000	1,800	2,900
Fish	1,560	1,130	1,130
Meat	930	414	414

Rice supplies depend on the production of 15,000 tons a year within Malaya, the import of 30,000 tons from Kedah and, in addition, imports from Thailand. Rice imports should be increased as a matter of priority, and the supply of at least 100,000 tons a year for the Malayan Area [i.e., seven states and Syonan Municipality] ensured. Meanwhile, supplies of supplementary foods should also be increased in a much more vigorous effort to counteract dwindling rice imports. While official rations of vegetables would be increased by merging the different sources of supply, hawkers and pedlars should also be reorganized. All these measures should be taken under full supervision and surveillance. The present economic police should support and reinforce such effort. Even in the case of civil servants, transgressors should be severely punished. A speedy application of countermeasures is as necessary as a speedy execution of military operations. This constitutes an illustration of the saying 'A stitch in time saves nine'. Political power should be fully exerted.

[27] Level A indicates adult male rice rations of 8 catties (544kcal) daily, supplementary food rations of 4 catties (273kcal), and vegetables 3 catties (36kcal), which amounts to 905kcal daily. That is well below a life-sustaining level. If Level B, the minimum required standard, were to be achieved, the daily caloric intake for an adult male on general rations would be 1,469kcal. To illustrate what this would have required, suppose that rice rations had been 50 per cent higher for both general rations and special area rations, and so 12 catties for an adult male, 8 catties for a female and 6 catties for a child. The increase would mean daily rice rations of 240g (816kcal) for adult males. Suppose, too, an increase in supplementary food by 100 per cent to 8 catties, that is, to 160g daily (547kcal). Other increases would be a 50 per cent increase in vegetables, equivalent to 4.5 catties monthly, or 90g and 54kcal daily; there was no increase in fish and meat, which remained at 2.6 catties, equivalent to 52g and 52kcal daily.

Table 7.9 Nutritional values of priority rations[28]

	Monthly amount (catties)	Daily intake (g)	Caloric quantity to 1g (kcal)	Caloric intake (kcal)	Daily intake (Army standard) (g)	Caloric intake (Army standard) (kcal)
White rice	21	420	3.40	1,428	660	2,244
Supplementary foods	4	80	3.42	274	210	718
Fish	3	60	1.00	60	210	210
Meat	2	40	1.30	52		
Vegetables	9	180	0.60	108	600	360
	[Total caloric intake			1,922		3,532]

[28] The original report shows the daily rice ration of army (combatants) standard to be '870' and caloric intake to be '1244', which clearly do not add up and may have been intentionally miswritten.

Appendix Tables

Table A.7.1 Malaya regional price differences, February 1944

(dollars per catty)

		Syonan		Kuala Lumpur		Penang		Ipoh		Bangor Island	Perak	Pahang	
		Market price	Official price	Market price	Official price	Market price	Official price	Market price	Official price	Official price	Official price	Market price	Official price
Fish	Prawn	5.40	1.60			1.31						3.90	
	Ikan kurau [mullet]		4.00	2.60								3.90	1.50
	Prawn (salted)	6.00		4.00				1.25	1.25	1.00			
	Ikan bilis (salted and dried)	5.00		3.60				1.20	1.20	0.96		2.40	1.00
	Harvest fish		2.20	3.20		1.92		1.00	1.00	0.80		3.60	1.40
	Red sea bream		3.60	3.50					1.20	0.96			
	Hardtail scads			1.70					0.52	0.40			
	Ikan dori	1.50	1.20	1.70					0.49	0.37		1.70	0.60
	Ray	1.50	1.20	1.70					0.64	0.50		2.60	1.10
	Ikan yu [shark]	1.60	1.30						0.59	0.45			

(cont'd overleaf)

Table A.7.1 (cont'd)

		Syonan		Kuala Lumpur		Penang		Ipoh		Bangor Island	Perak	Pahang	
		Market price	Official price	Market price	Official price	Market price	Official price	Market price	Official price	Official price	Official price	Market price	Official price
Vegetables	Salted vegetable	2.90				0.80		0.48					
	Spinach	0.60				0.36					0.30		
	Cabbage	1.20		0.46		0.35							
	Cabbage (Cameron Highlands)	4.00									0.30		
	White cucumber	0.75		0.20				0.14	0.08				
	Cucumber	0.85		0.35		0.32						0.51	0.20
	Aubergine	0.80						0.10	0.10			0.38	0.15
	Leek	2.20									0.30		
	Onion	4.20		2.40		2.30					0.30	3.47	0.40
	Bamboo shoot	1.20						0.06	0.06				
	Turnip	0.60									0.15		
	Pumpkin	0.34						0.10	0.10			0.17	0.10
	Bottle gourd	0.75						0.05	0.08				
	Katra	1.00				0.35						0.53	0.15
	Tomato	4.30		1.80				0.40	0.40			0.80	0.55

Table A.7.1 (cont'd)

		Syonan		Kuala Lumpur		Penang		Ipoh		Bangor Island	Perak	Pahang	
		Market price	Official price	Market price	Official price	Market price	Official price	Market price	Official price	Official price	Official price	Market price	Official price
	White radish	1.50		0.55		0.35					0.12	0.70	0.20
	Bean sprouts	0.65		0.30		0.20						0.40	0.15
	Ladies' finger	1.50							0.10			0.70	0.20
	Kidney beans	1.50		0.50		0.48						0.58	0.20
	Peas	2.30		0.80							0.30		
	Red chili	4.70				2.13		0.20	0.20				
	Dried chili	6.30				3.04							
	Ginger	3.40						0.63	0.25				
	Yam bean	1.10				0.50						0.18	0.10
Fruit	Pineapple (per piece)	0.40		0.35								0.14	0.07
Meat	Beef	4.50	3.00	4.20			1.47					2.48	1.10
	Pork	6.90	3.80	4.00		2.58							
	Chicken	7.80		4.50		2.89						3.30	1.20
	Chicken egg (per piece)	0.50		0.35		0.26		0.30					

(cont'd overleaf)

Table A.7.1 (cont'd)

		Syonan		Kuala Lumpur		Penang		Ipoh		Bangor Island	Perak	Pahang	
		Market price	Official price	Market price	Official price	Market price	Official price	Market price	Official price	Official price	Official price	Market price	Official price
Other	Maize	0.33	0.06	0.75		0.67		0.15	0.15				
	White pepper	0.90		0.85									
	Tapioca flour			0.11		0.67						0.88	0.40
	Rice flour	5.70						0.53	0.53			2.15	0.80
	Palm oil	4.25	0.70		0.22	2.56	0.24	0.24	0.24			1.55	0.50
	Sago flour	1.40				0.66		0.15	0.15				

Surveyed by the Military Administration Chōsabu.

Table A.7.2 Syonan Municipality price index, July 1942–February 1944

(pre-war=100)

	1942						1943												1944					
	July	Aug.	Sept.	Oct.	Nov.	Dec.	Jan.	Feb.	Mar.	Apr.	May	June	July	Aug.	Sept.	Oct.	Nov.	Dec.	Jan.	Feb.	Mar.	Apr.	May	June
Foods	265	-	337	279	305	342	350	367	345	377	410	459	522	609	645	712	766	869	1069	1462				
Household necessities	146	-	136	319	408	402	429	381	530	472	527	852	1040	1078	835	829	1172	1193	1269	1403				
Clothing (a) Fabrics	125	-	155	152	302	279	252	291	287	381	561	836	1081	1426	373	373	373	371	373	373				
(b) Garments	131	-	-	-	-	-	200	286	330	359	450	642	711	801	404	404	404	404	404	404				
Other clothing	147	-	136	159	282	195	217	216	216	220	233	303	423	552	512	585	702	714	747	792				
Drugs (a) Medical	277	-	273	-	944	1031	-	1249	-	1515	-	2880	-	-	-	-	-	-	-	-				
(b) Patent medicine	124	-	117	250	353	341							815	817	995	1004	1136	1152	1241	1833				

Compiled by the Military Administration Chōsabu.

Table A.7.3 Syonan Municipality comparison of pre-war consumption and current monthly food consumption plan, 10 January 1944

	Pre-war consumption		Current plan		Ratio of pre-war consumption (%)	Desirable plan	
	Total amount (tons)	Per person (catties)	Total amount (tons)	Per person (catties)		Total amount (tons)	Per person (catties)
Rice	12,000	29	4,883	◎ 17 ○ 8	38	6,694	◎ 21 ○ 12
Flour	4,400	24	-		16	-	
Atta flour	150		-			-	
Supplementary food	1,440		940	⊕ 4		1,880	8
Total	17,990		5,823		32	8,574	
Sugar	3,000	7.1	870	⊕ 1	29	3,000	1
Salt	800	1.9	590	⊕ 1/3	74	800	1/3
Vegetable	5,000	12	1,800	◎ 6 ○ 3	32	2,900	◎ 9 ○ 5
Fruit	3,200	7.7	900	1.8	28	900	
Fresh fish	900	6.2	510	◎ 5 ○ 2.6	57	510	◎ 5 ○ 2.6
Salted dried fish	660		620		94	620	
Beef	220		80		36	80	
Pork	710		224		27	324	
Goat meat	84		10		12	10	

◎: Priority ration

○: General ration

⊕: Both priority and general rations

Table A.7.4 Syonan Municipality quantity of rice received and distributed, August 1942–February 1944

(bags; 1 bag = 100kg)

	Quota allotted by Military Administration	Actually received by municipality	Surplus or deficit	Cumulative deficit	Additional rice received to stockpile	Cumulative deficit – stockpile rice	Crushed rice and other	Adjusted quota for municipality	Actual ration distributed by municipality	Note
Aug. 1942	110,000	70,507	-39,493				9,043	110,000	67,503	1 Aug.: carried-over 30,674 tons, 20 catties per person
September	110,000	93,425	-16,575				484	110,000	93,960	
October	110,000	151,677	41,677				397	107,000	130,291	
November	110,000	112,005	2,005				2,769	104,627	97,899	16 Nov.: 17 catties per person
Subtotal	440,000	427,614	-12,386	-12,386				431,627	389,653	
December	105,000	72,359	-32,641					100,000	95,720	
Jan. 1943	105,000	79,323	-25,677					101,100	93,470	
February	105,000	84,524	-20,476				1,872	85,980	72,610	1 Feb.: 14 catties per person
March	105,000	113,004	8,004					85,980	87,139	
Subtotal	420,000	349,210	-70,790	-83,176				373,060	348,939	
April	90,000	96,197	6,197				3,277	85,980	81,577	
May	90,000	85,126	-4,874				251	89,000	88,110	
June	90,000	81,367	-8,633		48,974		170	89,000	89,615	

(cont'd overleaf)

Table A.7.4 (cont'd)

	Quota allotted by Military Administration	Actually received by municipality	Surplus or deficit	Cumulative deficit	Additional rice received to stockpile	Cumulative deficit – stockpile rice	Crushed rice and other	Adjusted quota for municipality	Actual ration distributed by municipality	Note
July	90,000	88,983	-1,017		16,000		560	89,000	77,629	
Subtotal	360,000	351,675	-8,325	-91,501	65,474	-26,027		352,980	336,931	
August	76,000	95,117	19,117				383	89,000	85,310	
September	76,000	44,560	-31,440				7	79,400	115,558	1 Sept.: 12 catties per person
Subtotal	152,000	139,677	-12,323			-38,350		168,400	200,868	
October	55,000	40,170	-14,830				752	79,400	60,620	
November	55,000	39,900	-15,100				1,337	61,400	41,660	1 Nov.: male 12 catties; female 9 catties; child 6 catties
December	55,000	40,850	-14,150				229	61,400	59,896	
Jan. 1944	55,000	57,311	2,311				370	61,400	60,415	
Subtotal	220,000	178,231	-41,769			-80,119		263,600	222,591	
February	(44,000)									11 Feb.: male 8 catties; female 6 catties; child 4 catties
Total	1,592,000	1,446,407	-145,593			-80,119	21,901	1,589,667	1,498,982	

Surveyed by the Department of Rice and Grains, Syonan Municipality.

Table A.7.6 Thai rice imports permitted as special trade by overseas Chinese traders, January–December 1943

	Parboiled rice		Dehydrated rice		Total	
	Tons	Dollars	Tons	Dollars	Tons	Dollars
January	42.26	4,600.00			42.26	4,600.00
February	429.18	116,950.00			429.18	116,950.00
March	1,002.00	255,484.00	48.21	4,200.00	1,050.21	259,684.00
April	1,188.34	292,108.00	249.05	42,659.00	1,437.39	334,767.00
May	483.00	149,339.00			483.00	149,339.00
June	908.00	318,539.00			908.00	318,539.00
July	1,391.00	509,977.00			1,391.00	509,977.00
August	1,220.00	650,640.00			1,220.00	650,640.00
September	1,158.00	761,550.00			1,158.00	761,550.00
October	2,233.00	1,606,302.00	14.00	16,100.00	2,247.00	1,622,402.00
November	1,253.00	1,348,647.00	836.00	898,766.00	2,089.00	2,247,413.00
December	1,176.00	1,940,621.00	1,763.00	1,910,931.00	2,939.00	4,851,552.00
Total	12,483.78	7,954,757.00	2,910.26	3,872,656.00	15,394.04	11,827,413.00

Note: The table shows the estimated imports permitted as special trade by Syonan Municipality, Department of Trade and Industry. Actual rice imported under permission would be 60% to 70% of the permitted amount of imports (Surveyed by Department of Trade and Industry, Syonan Municipality).

Table A.7.7 Malaya monthly standard rice quotas allotted to each state and municipality, March 1944

	Ration quota (tons)	Note
Syonan Municipality	4,400	
Johore	1,050	
Malacca	535	
Negeri Sembilan	300	Planning self-sufficiency
Selangor	1,450	
Pahang	80	Self-sufficient since September
Perak	900	Planning self-sufficiency
Penang	1,287	
Total	10,000	

Surveyed by Department of Agriculture, Malayan Military Administration.

Table A.7.8 Syonan Municipality fish catch, February 1944[30]

Syonan Fresh Fish Association	Catties	Average price per catty (dollars)	tons	Average price per ton (dollars)
Main fishery zone	1,321,568.00	1.51	792,952	2,517.17
Fishery zone 1	108,540.50	1.15	65,124	1,917.05
Fishery zone 2	127,512.50	1.25	76,508	2,083.75
Fishery zone 3	128,527.00	1.21	77,116	2,183.77
Fishery zone 4	Fishery zone 4 does not have its own office, and its catches are included in the main fishery zone.			
Fishery zone 5	21,704.30	1.67	13,023	2,783.89
Total	1,707,852.30	1.45	1,024,723	1,417.15

Fishery companies	Catties	Average price per catty (dollars)	tons	Average price per ton (dollars)
Eifuku Industry & Co.	246,166.63	0.96	149,191	1,600.32
Hayashikane & Co.	66,718.33	0.85	40,031	1,416.95
Taiyō Fishery & Co.	33,853.33	0.90	20,312	1,500.30
Total	346,738.29	0.93	209,534	1,550.31

Surveyed by Syonan Fresh Fish Association.

[30] Taiyō Fishery is the forerunner of Maruha Corporation, one of the largest fishing companies in Japan, famous for whale fishing before the war. It branched out from Hayashikane Company during the war. Eifuku Industry was established in Singapore before the war by Eifuku Tora, which employed fishermen from Okinawa to operate longline fishing, trawler fishing and so forth. The firm diversified into ice production, refrigeration, fishing tools and shipbuilding.

CHAPTER 8

Conditions of Economic Security in Syonan Municipality and Johore

Department of Police Administration, March 1943

Report by the staff of the Department of Police Administration [of the Southern Military Administration] arising from their survey of the real state of economic surveillance in Syonan and Johore.[1]

Contents

[1] This report was not written by the Chōsabu, and the views of the authors may be different from those of the members of the Chōsabu. The report (1943) may be compared with chapter 7 to help gauge the state of rationing in 1944.

Appendix Tables

Supplementary Material 1: Rice

1. **Rationing Organizations and Distribution Methods**
   (1) Pre-war system
   (2) Current system
2. **Levels of Rations**
   (1) Pre-war amounts
   (2) Current amounts
3. **Prices**
   (1) Pre-war prices
   (2) Current prices
4. **Specific Measures Relating to the Collection and Rationing of Rice**
5. **Specific Measures to Control Consumption (Including Measures to Encourage the Consumption of Rice Substitutes)**
6. **Number of Rice Mills**
7. **Number of Warehouses**

Supplementary Material 2: Salt and Sugar

1. **Rationing Organizations and Distribution Methods**
   (1) Pre-war system
   (2) Current system
2. **Levels of Rations**
   (1) Pre-war amounts
   (2) Current amounts

3. Retail Prices

(1) Pre-war prices

(2) Current prices

4. Specific Measures Relating to the Collection and Rationing of Salt and Sugar

5. Specific Measures to Control Consumption

6. Number of Mills

1. Summary

Under the Exchange of Goods Scheme,[2] sugar and salt are among the daily necessities imported under military control from Java, Thailand and recently from the Philippines.[3] Stocks are now stable and are about 10,000 tons. For rice, which has in the past been imported from Burma, there has been an unanticipated deterioration in transport. Because of this, only about 30,000 tons of rations have been received instead of the 33,000 tons required for the monthly average standard rations for the Malayan states.[4] Moreover, each state and municipality is required by order to stock 10 per cent of military-controlled rice [sold by Mitsubishi].[5]

In view of the amounts required for standard rations, the rice situation is not encouraging despite the fact that it is intended to switch rice imports from Burma to Thailand beginning in April [1943]. Standard rice quotas for each state and municipality are currently determined by the assessed amount of military-controlled rice that will be imported, an amount less than pre-war levels.[6] Quotas for each state are set according to the assessed amount of total rice imports, divided in proportion to pre-war [quantities of import, calculated in order to supplement the] levels of output in each state, from which have been subtracted the amount consumed (estimated at 33 catties per person [per month; 660g per person per day] multiplied by the 1941 population) in each state.[7] However, in view of the estimated quotas of rice calculated in this way and also in view of the absolute amount of military-controlled rice imported, we admit that the available amounts for each state are not really appropriate.[8]

---

[2] Busshi Kōryū Keikaku was a scheme planned by the Southern Military Administration, in association with the army's accounting department and the land and seaborne transportation units, to exchange goods among the areas of the Greater East Asia Co-prosperity Sphere. At Imperial Headquarters, the Planning Board (Kikaku-in) drew up the overall annual scheme for trade between the territories and mainland Japan.

[3] Salt and sugar were imported by the main ships (Japanese flag-flying cargo vessels) and distributed by Mitsui Bussan & Co. commissioned by the Military Administration. See *Senji Geppō* (Wartime Monthly), June 1942.

[4] The rice from Burma came on the main ships and was distributed by Mitsubishi Shōji Corporation, together with other grains from Thailand and Indochina. The initial target in 1942 for Burma rice was 40,000 tons. See *Senji Geppō*, June 1942.

[5] From January 1943, each state and municipality encouraged setting aside one month's stock of rice to counterbalance fluctuations in rice imports. See *Senji Geppō*, January 1943.

[6] Pre-war refers to the British colonial period before the start of Japanese occupation.

[7] That is, 36 catties per male, 27 catties per female and 18 catties per child under the British administration; see table A.8.4 and Supplementary Material 1 below; see also Kratoska, *Japanese Occupation*, p. 255.

[8] See tables A.8.1 and A.8.3.

Information on the precise number in the population who are rice eaters was inadequate for the revision of consumption levels.[9] Therefore, only a superficial and general assessment has been done. This revision of consumption levels has worked against either any saving of rice or fair distribution. Although distributing organizations for rations are being established, it is still necessary to rely on overseas Chinese or Indian wholesalers and retailers who only seek to maximize their own profits.[10] This system sometimes allows the illicit[11] distribution of rice among these traders.

Regions other than Syonan Municipality have an insufficient police force dedicated to the eradication of economic crimes. When inspectors were assigned to the Department of Industry to police economic crimes in parallel with the Department of Police Administration, the result was a failure to pursue a consistent policy. There should be a single policy, under the supervision of the Department of Police Administration. The police force of Syonan Municipality is now working towards a clear target, despite its lack of a sufficiently thorough approach, whereas in Johore and other states it is still not possible even to establish a policing target. Therefore, in these states (but not Syonan Municipality), in view of the current situation, at least a few officers should be allocated to the maintenance of economic security.

2. Market Situation of Military-Controlled Goods

(1) Rice

The 1941 survey showed for Malaya a monthly average of about 50,000 tons of net rice imports. However, the monthly standard chart of the intra-regional Exchange of Goods Scheme within the Southern Area, issued by the Military Administration, which was established last May [1942], shows the monthly average to be 42,000 tons. Current imports have fallen to 34,000 tons because of the shortage of shipping tonnage. About 4,000 tons of rice substitutes are

---

9 Subsequently, a household expenditures survey was carried out to address this information gap; see chapter 12.

10 Distributing organizations would include the Rice and Padi Distributing Association; rationing associations for salt and sugar, etc.; and Busshi Haikyū Kumiai (Goods and Materials Rationing Association). In Singapore, the Syonan Padi and Rice Distributing Association was established in March 1942 (National Archives, Kew WO203/4499, 'Rice S.E.A.C. Territories') and the Syonan Goods and Materials Rationing Association was established in October 1942 to coordinate distribution of imports and other goods (*Senji Geppō*, October 1942). The Syonan Rice Distributing Association and associations for salt, sugar, etc., were merged into the Food Supply Office, which was established in July 1943 and so after this report.

11 In this context, 'illicit' refers to the black market.

imported monthly to make up the shortfall in rice.[12] Until rice production can be increased, it must be said that if the standard amount of rice supply [at 1942 levels] is taken as the norm, conditions are admittedly deteriorating.

Table A.8.1 shows the supply and demand of rice, the proportion that is rationed, and the import situation. The import difficulties could be solved by diverting Thai rice intended for Japan to the Malay area, starting this April (see table A.8.2). In view of the limited shipping tonnage available, however, optimism with regard to rice imports is not possible.

(2) Sugar and salt

The monthly import scheme is to import 5,000 tons each of sugar and salt. Sugar imports were:

February 1943	7,290 tons
March 1943	11,000 tons

Salt imports were:

February 1943	5,110 tons
March 1943	10,000 tons

The balance of demand and supply was helped by diversion to Malaya of 3,700 tons of salt destined for Burma. There is a current stock of about 10,000 tons.

3. Recommended Adjustments to Rice Rations

As indicated above, the amount of planned rice ration for each state, shown in table A.8.4, is only an estimate based on assumptions about total imports, divided in proportion to the amount of production in each state from which has been subtracted the amount of consumption in each state. It is, of course, necessary to review the absolute total amount of imports, as we ought also to consider how to reduce the burden of military operations.[13] However, the way that rations are calculated also needs to be reconsidered, and the size of the rice-eating population must be surveyed to achieve something more reliable than a temporary policy. It is incorrect to consider the entire Malayan population as rice eaters; at present, many of the lower classes do not eat rice. They keep back the rationed rice and sell it on the black market. A considerable number of lower-class people thus live on rice substitutes alone. According to the departmental officer who visited

[12] Rice substitutes included maize, soybeans, tapioca flour, cassava roots (dried tapioca roots imported from Thailand) and other related products. These were also called 'other grains' or 'supplementary foods'.

[13] To allow for enough shipping space for the military.

Terengganu, only about 20 per cent (40,000) of the Terengganu population of 200,000 are rice eaters. Taking the monthly rice ration at 20 catties,[14] this would require a supply of about 500 tons. The current supply of 1,000 tons could be halved. The situation is the same in other states.

[Recommended adjustments are as below.]

(1) Generally speaking, provincial labourers, particularly rubber plantation coolies, who grow rice or rice substitutes should be given reduced rations.

(2) There should be a significant price gap between rice substitutes and rice.

(3) Canteens should be set up for coolies.

(4) Illicit double or ghost rationing should be eliminated.

(5) There should be different ration levels in the city and rural villages.

(1) Labourers should certainly be given priority rationing in order to maintain the labour force in vital industries. However, general labourers such as rubber plantation coolies are able to grow rice or rice substitutes. Rations at a reduced level should be given to those who have not achieved self-sufficiency.

(2) The retail price of rice is lower than general prices. For example, the price of rice in Syonan, 10 cents a catty, is lower than comparable prices of rice substitutes such as tapioca flour, which is 13 cents a catty. Maize sells for 6 cents a catty and soybeans for 8.5. It is therefore understandable that people are inclined to consume more rice. Black market rice is currently priced at $30 to $70 per sack. People tend to sell their rice rations to restaurants at black market prices. It would be preferable to create an appropriate price gap between rice and rice substitutes.

(3) Canteens should be set up for coolies because some coolies do not get rice rations, while others do not have cooking facilities and have no alternative but to sell rice to street vendors. Canteens would reduce surplus rice consumption and give coolies the opportunity to eat rice when they want to.

(4) Reducing excess rice consumption requires the elimination of forged or double ration cards. For rice rationing, each state (or municipality) uses ration cards.[15] But because the population survey is not yet adequate, people obtain rations by using forged or double certificates of residence [*ankyoshō*] or ration cards. Since the Police Department of Syonan Municipality has made arrests in these cases, an accurate population census is the first necessity. A door-to-door population survey will be conducted over one month in April in Syonan Municipality [see chapter 3] and over six months in Johore state [as it will take longer to survey the whole state].

[14] That is, 400g per person per day.

[15] The design of the ration card is based on the pre-war ration card issued by the British administration.

(5) It is necessary when surveying the rice-eating population to distinguish urban from rural residents. When rice ration levels are considered for each state (or municipality), the basic quantitative level of rations and the qualitative adjustments necessary for local circumstances must be taken into account. This will allow an accurate estimate of the rice-eating population.

4. Revision of Consumption Levels: The Present Situation

Table A.8.4 shows the extent to which consumption is controlled in each state (or municipality). The rice ration in Syonan Municipality is 14 catties. In states with the lowest rice ration, only 7 to 8 catties are rationed. Tightening conditions of rice supply have led Syonan Municipality to issue rations of 3 catties of miscellaneous grains as rice substitutes to ease the rice shortage. Observations of the proposals, set out below, will further allow a more substantial and higher level of priority rationing.

(1) Rice saved by the measures set out above should be diverted.

(2) The current rationing levels in Syonan Municipality, where a uniform rate is given irrespective of gender or age, should be corrected.

(3) A distinction must be made between urban and rural areas and between occupations.

Although it will be difficult to conduct the survey recommended above, this exercise is necessary to promote the current policy.

5. Distributor Problems

The municipality and state councils have used wholesalers and retailers to distribute rations of military-controlled goods[16] to supply the end consumer. The problems that this rationing system creates can be resolved by the following measures.

(1) Rationing associations[17] should place Japanese as the chief administrative managers.

(2) Racial discrimination in rationing should be removed.

(3) An appropriate level of management should be maintained at the rationing stations.

(4) The appropriate distributor should be selected for other officially priced goods and irregularly rationed items.

---

[16] That is, rice, salt and sugar.

[17] For example, the Syonan Padi and Rice Distributing Association.

(1) Separate rationing associations exist for military-controlled goods, such as rice, sugar, salt and other grains. The associations decide the quantity of rationed goods sent to each retailer or wholesaler, and appoint the retailers who deal in rationed goods. At the associations' offices, the head of office and office staff are almost all Chinese.[18] Since this work is of a public nature, current conditions will be improved by placing a Japanese as chief manager and eliminating favouritism or unfairness in rationing.

(2) Existing rationing stations in Syonan Municipality are all dominated by Chinese distributors. In Johore state, half the distributors are Indian and half Chinese. But racial discrimination at rationing stations causes inappropriate rationing and/or encourages fraud, as it is assumed that consumers are illiterate and unable to read the words on rationing cards. Racial issues therefore need to be considered in selecting appropriate distributors.

(3) Taking rice as an example, there are 50 wholesale dealers and 1,971 retailers in Syonan Municipality.[19] In Johore, there were 65 wholesale dealers and 400 retailers. As Supplementary Material 1 shows, there are 548 small-scale retailers in Syonan Municipality who deal in only 1 to 15 sacks of rice per month. Because the handling charge is set as low as 78 cents to $1.30 per sack of rice, it is not surprising that misconduct occurs, even if the retailers claim to be carrying on other businesses at the same time. In order to maintain appropriate management it is necessary to adjust the number of retailers taking into account location and transport availability.

(4) Although in Syonan Municipality about 206 locally produced goods have official prices, these prices have not been properly observed. This situation deprives the official prices of credibility, and irregularly rationed goods such as tobacco are rapidly sold out if they appear in the market. Their unavailability leads to speculative buying and excessive profits when they are sold at street stalls. This situation arises because the system of rationing is not properly organized. Further consideration of the system of selling is necessary in order to wipe out such illicit behaviour, particularly through carefully selecting the shops that deal in such items.

---

[18] For example, the head of the Syonan Padi and Rice Distributing Association was Tan Keng Kow of Tan Guan Lee & Co., a Teochew trader who was the president of the Thailand Traders Association; see chapter 11.

[19] The number of rice distribution stations was subsequently reduced to 1,007 retailers, but including the traders of unregulated staple foods there were still 2,191 traders who dealt in grain distribution in May 1944; see chapter 4.

6. Current Regulations

(1) The police system

In conjunction with surveillance of food prices by the Department of Police Administration, the Food Division of the Department of Industry appointed about 30 inspectors to supervise food prices in Syonan Municipality. Difficulties with these arrangements led to the reorganization of the system last November [1942], when control was handed over to the police force and the inspectors were made redundant. The organization of the police was also changed to allow the Criminal Investigation Division to take the lead. It is headed by a Japanese and has six full-time local officers to police economic crimes.

In Johore, the Security Division has taken charge of this sort of crime. The division did not, however, appoint special officers, and these crimes have been policed by the Criminal Investigation Division or the Special Higher Police Division. These arrangements reveal the confusion in roles between the divisions, and, in addition, the Department of Industry still uses inspectors to police food prices. Each division's authority is unclear, and the existing system is inevitably inconsistent.

(2) Policing targets

According to interviews with local police officers in Johore, targets are:

- To maintain low prices for principal foods such as rice and grains;
- To police the export of unlicensed articles from the state.

There are no clear police targets apart from the above two, although excessive profiteering occurs everywhere with regard to other articles.

In addition to the target of price stability of daily necessities, Syonan Municipality regulates such violations as profiteering, speculative buying, withholding goods from the market, and smuggling goods from the city to rural areas. Regulation consists of setting upper price limits based on current supply and demand, and the policing of prices that rise above their limits. Surveillance policies are as follows:

(i) Disruption of control of, and black market dealings in, military-controlled goods will be stopped, irrespective of the reason.

(ii) To balance supply and demand, other daily necessities will not be subject to surveillance.

(iii) Outward smuggling of goods [from Syonan] will be strictly controlled.

(iv) Profiteering will be strictly controlled, irrespective of the goods.

(v) Violation of upper price limits by large merchant warehouses will be clamped down upon, even if in the absence of excessive profiteering.

(vi) Brokers will be shut down.

(vii) General articles of textiles such as white and khaki clothing will be subject to surveillance.

(viii) Minor violations of upper price limits by smaller retailers will occasionally be regulated as a discouragement to widespread illicit pricing.

As described above, policing of economic crimes with a clear goal is under way in Syonan Municipality. The common feature between Syonan and Johore is that there must be strict control of smuggling out but lenient treatment of in-smuggling. The same applies to other states.

(3) Regulatory weaknesses

In the regulatory organizations of both Syonan and Johore there is little understanding of economic realities, and in consequence regulation is on an ad hoc basis. It is therefore difficult to devise a systematic policy. Moreover, ties with the Department of Industry are so weak that the Department of Police Administration has been unable to focus police efforts on cracking down on violations. This focus would require knowledge of the realities of distribution of goods, which could be gained through surveys conducted by the Industry Department. One such area would be in the diversion of temporary rations away from the predetermined areas [i.e., urban areas] towards the outer regions. There has not been enough effort to crack down on this diversion.

Furthermore, the Industry Department usually pays little attention to maintaining official prices or organizations of rationing and makes no effort to check such violations. Current conditions require improved communication between the Department of Industry and the Department of Police Administration on the latter's initiative.

Appendix Tables

Table A.8.1 Malaya monthly rice demand and supply, November 1942–March 1943

(tons)

<table>
<tr><th rowspan="2">State (city)</th><th rowspan="2">Standard quota from 1941 survey</th><th rowspan="2">Planned quota for April 1943</th><th colspan="5">Imported amount</th></tr>
<tr><th>November</th><th>December</th><th>January</th><th>February</th><th>March</th></tr>
<tr><td>Syonan (incl. Riau Islands)</td><td>11,000</td><td>15,000</td><td rowspan="12">Rice 58,136
Other grains 1,000</td><td rowspan="12">Rice 11,164
Other grains 1,304</td><td rowspan="12">Rice 29,506
Other grains 5,217</td><td rowspan="12">Rice 30,885
Other grains 4,000</td><td rowspan="12">Rice 33,000
Other grains 4,000</td></tr>
<tr><td>Penang</td><td>3,000</td><td>2,800</td></tr>
<tr><td>Malacca</td><td>2,000</td><td>1,800</td></tr>
<tr><td>Perah</td><td>7,000</td><td>4,800</td></tr>
<tr><td>Selangor</td><td>8,000</td><td>6,000</td></tr>
<tr><td>Negeri Sembilan</td><td>2,000</td><td>1,800</td></tr>
<tr><td>Pahang</td><td>1,500</td><td>800</td></tr>
<tr><td>Johore</td><td>7,000</td><td>4,500</td></tr>
<tr><td>Kedah</td><td>-</td><td>-</td></tr>
<tr><td>Kelantan</td><td>197</td><td>-</td></tr>
<tr><td>Terengganu</td><td>2,500</td><td>1,000</td></tr>
<tr><td>Total</td><td>44,197</td><td>34,000</td></tr>
</table>

Table A.8.2 Malaya monthly rice imports, November 1942–March 1943

(tons)

	Burma	Java	Thailand	Indochina	Total
November	52,299	4,000	1,829	-	58,136
December	5,041	5,537	586	-	11,160
January	23,474	2,508	1,610	914	29,506
February	19,514	4,766	4,982	2,623	30,885
March	500	-	32,500	-	33,000

Table A.8.3 Malaya plan of monthly rice imports, April–December 1943[20]
(000 tons)

Month	Rice		Other grains			
	Thailand	Burma	Maize	Tapioca flour	Cassava root[20]	Soybeans
April	34	1	1	3	1	-
May	34	1	1	2	1	-
June	15	20	1	2	1	-
July	15	20	1	2	1	-
August	15	15	1	2	1	-
September	15	15	1	2	1	-
October	19	11	1	2	1	-
November	19	11	1	2	1	-
December	19	11	1	2	1	-

[20] Cassava root denotes dried tapioca root. It was imported from Thailand and some other sources. Tapioca flour is the processed root.

Table A.8.4 Malaya monthly rice ration, March 1943[21]

(gantangs; 1 gantang = 6 catties)

State (city)	Current standard amount				Pre-war standard amount		
	Male	Female	Child		Male	Female	Child
Syonan	2.83 (until January) 17 catties 2.33 (from February) 14 catties			Both male and female	6	4.5	3
Johore	2	1.5	0.5				
Pahang	2	1.5	0.5		6	4	2
Malacca	5	4	3	Until March 1942	6	5	3
	4	3	2	From April 1942			
Negeri Sembilan	2	1	1		6	4.5	3
Selangor	1.5	1.6	0.17		6	4	3
Perah	4	3	2		6	6	4
Penang	3	3	2.5				
Kedah	4	3	2				
Terengganu	3	2	1	Until December 1942			
	2.5	1.5	0.75	From January 1943			

Note: The actual standard amounts were 37.5% of the standard amount in Perak; and 50% of it before October and 40% after December in Malacca. The situation is the same in other states.

[21] For rice, the conversion rate of 1 gantang = 6 catties was the standard used by the British colonial government. *Straits Times*, 16 Aug. 1921, p. 10.

Supplementary Material 1: Rice

1. Rationing Organizations and Distribution Methods

(1) *Pre-war system* [British Administration]

Organization of rationing:

Importer ⟶ Wholesaler ⟶ Retailer ⟶ Customer

Method of distribution:

General consumers (red cards)

Restaurants and hawkers (blue cards)

Institutions, food manufacturers and cattle breeders (yellow cards)

There were three categories of rationing. General consumers were required to register with nearby local retailers and received standard rations. There were different rationing limits for businesses. Retailers and wholesalers were ordered to keep a one-month stock of rice, but this was subsequently changed to 60 per cent of a month's stock.

(2) *Current system*

Rationing is organized as follows:

Distributing association ⟶ Wholesaler ⟶ Retailer ⟶ Customer

The organization of rationing is as above. There are about 50 wholesalers and 2,000 retailers. The amount of supply to the wholesalers is determined by their capital, personality and character, warehouse capacity, and previous business results. Wholesalers also have a role in supervising retailers, through administering control and giving advice on rationing, to ensure that instructions from higher offices reach the rank and file. For the rationing organization to reach its full potential, wholesalers and retailers would need to be both dealers and sources of advice.

Method of distribution:

Current total rice distributions to retailers are as follows:

Warehousing capacity (sacks of rice)	Number of retailers
1–15	548
16–30	514
31–40	234
41–70	403
Over 71	274
Total retailers	1,971

In view of government stocks and the warehousing capacity of retailers, the frequency with which rations are supplied should be as follows:

Warehousing capacity (sacks of rice)	Frequency of delivery (per month)
1–40	Once
41–70	Twice
Over 71	Three times

General consumers are allowed to purchase rations up to three times a month, but the frequency with which institutions, food manufacturers, etc., receive rations should be determined by their individual circumstances. Under the rationing scheme, the Military Administration supplies a standard amount of rations at the beginning of each month. The scheme works in the following ways:

(i) Rice for general consumption

A purchasing card is issued following registration with the nearest retailer on production of a certificate of residence.

(ii) Rice for institutions

A purchasing card is issued for institutional workers and their families who are employed in key areas such as the military and police.

(iii) Rice for charity

To aid social welfare, purchasing cards are issued through the Department of Welfare to the poor who cannot afford to purchase daily necessities.

(iv) Rice for marine supplies

Purchasing cards are issued to vessels that undertake long voyages.

(v) Rice for food manufacturers

Purchasing cards are issued to manufacturers of daily necessaries.

(vi) Rice for restaurants and hotels

(vii) Rice for the Japanese

(viii) Rice for the islands

(ix) Rice reserved for adjustment[22]

Suggested Future Approaches

There are only a few Japanese appointed to the organizations of food rationing, so new staff should be recruited immediately to improve the system. Additionally, there is insufficient warehouse capacity because of warfare and military operations. New warehouses should be built or existing warehouses refurbished.

2. Levels of Rations

(1) Pre-war amounts [British Administration]

Catties per capita per month	
Males	36
Females	27
Children under 12	18

Rations were issued following registration at the nearest retailer.

(2) Current amounts

From 1 February [1943] monthly rations have been set at 14 catties [8.4kg; 280g daily] per capita, with a further 3 catties of rice substitutes for those who want them. Up to an extra 20 catties [12kg; 400g daily] is provided specifically for labourers in certain occupations.

3. Prices

(1) Pre-war prices

See appendix.[23]

[22] The one-month stock of rice.

[23] This appendix was omitted from the original report.

(2) Current prices

Retail price per catty

White rice	10 cents
Crushed rice	8 cents

Wholesale prices for business-to-business traders per sack of white rice

White rice [see table A.8.5 for prices]
Crushed rice [see table A.8.6 for prices]

Table A.8.5 Syonan Municipality white rice wholesale prices, March 1943

(dollars)

Amount	Municipality to rationing association	Rationing association to wholesaler	Wholesaler to retailer
100kg	14.00	14.50	15.30
73kg	10.22	10.72	12.22
120kg	16.80	17.30	18.20

Table A.8.6 Syonan Municipality crushed rice wholesale prices, March 1943

(dollars)

Amount	Municipality to rationing association	Rationing association to wholesaler	Wholesaler to retailer
100kg	11.50	11.50	12.20
73kg	8.40	8.40	8.90
120kg	13.80	13.80	14.50

4. Specific Measures Relating to the Collection and Rationing of Rice

No measures.

5. Specific Measures to Control Consumption (Including Measures to Encourage the Consumption of Rice Substitutes)

As already indicated in the section on 'distribution methods', consumption levels will be revised and surveillance will be carried out. Each retailer should stock rice substitutes and sell up to 3 catties per person to anyone wishing to purchase them. Furthermore, as a substitute food, bread made of tapioca and sago flour will soon be available for distribution as special rations.

6. Number of Rice Mills

One mill, daily production capability 2,000 sacks.

7. Number of Warehouses

See appendix.[24]

[24] This appendix was omitted from the original report.

Supplementary Material 2: Salt and Sugar

1. Rationing Organizations and Distribution Methods

(1) Pre-war system

Organization of rationing:

Import merchant ⟶ Wholesaler ⟶ Retailer ⟶ Consumer

Method of distribution:

Goods were sold freely without any restriction on quantity.

(2) Current system

Organization of rationing:

(i) Rationing association ⟶ Wholesaler ⟶ Retailer ⟶ Consumer
(ii) Rationing association ⟶Wholesaler ⟶ Special retailer ⟶ Institutions ⟶ Food manufacturer

Method of distribution:

(i) As in the case of rice for households, purchasing cards are issued on production of a certificate of residence, and goods are purchased from registered retailers.
(ii) In the case of rice rations for institutions and food manufacturers, etc., purchasing cards are issued on production of an operating licence, and goods are purchased from special retailers.

2. Levels of Rations

(1) Pre-war amounts

No limit.

(2) Current amounts

Sugar: 1 catty per person a month
Salt: 1/3 catty per person a month
For businesses, rationing levels depend on individual circumstances.

3. Retail Prices

(1) Pre-war prices

Sugar: 8 cents a catty
Salt: From Thailand (unrefined) 2.5 cents a catty
From Egypt (unrefined) 2.75 cents a catty
From Egypt (refined) 3 cents a catty

(2) Current prices

Sugar: 9 cents a catty
Salt: (Unrefined) 3 cents a catty
(Refined) 4 cents a catty

4. Specific Measures Relating to the Collection and Rationing of Salt and Sugar

No relevant measures.

5. Specific Measures to Control Consumption

Essentially, the same measures as for rice are to be adopted.

6. Number of Mills

Not applicable.

Rice and Food Supplies

CHAPTER 9

Methods of Increasing Food Production on Syonan Island

Yamada Isamu, October 1944

This report on increasing food production in Syonan Municipality was prepared by Isamu Yamada, assistant professor at the Tokyo University of Commerce, assisted by the administration of Syonan Municipality. Although the proposals cannot easily be implemented, as they relate to military-managed farms, they might have some implications for increasing food production. This report is mimeographed for reference purposes.

Contents

Supplementary Material 1. Supply and Demand of Vegetables on Syonan Island

1. Outline

2. Consumption Levels

(1) Pre-war consumption

(2) Current conditions

A. Collection by Syonan Vegetable and Fruit Association for the Military

B. Collection by the Syonan Rationing Association, Department of Vegetables and Fruit for Civilians

Supplementary Material 2. Method Used to Estimate the Acreage of Crops of Sweet Potatoes, Tapioca and Other Vegetables

Verdict

A. Farms Directly Managed by the Military Sector

(1) The farms managed by the Supply Regiment of the Seventh Area Army, the *Tsukasa* and *Akatsuki* military units[1] and a few other productive military farms that are currently managed either directly by the military or by military-appointed subcontractors should all be transferred to the direct management of the military. The Supply Regiment and Tsukasa and Akatsuki military units should allocate the transferred farmland between themselves. The Supply Regiment should be responsible for distributing food rations to military units other than Tsukasa and Akatsuki, while Tsukasa and Akatsuki should be responsible for food self-sufficiency in their own units.

(2) Use of sufficient fertilizer, equipment, seeds and seedlings, and the most appropriate amount of labour (5 coolies or 1.7 farming families[2] per acre) on the total of 4,000 acres of land would make possible the application of intensive farming methods. These farms, by March 1945, should be able to produce 7 tons per acre. This would meet the requirement of self-sufficiency in rice substitutes and vegetables for military units on Syonan Island. This policy requires a maximum of 5,049 farming families (14,629 coolies), and the settlement of these farmers must be implemented as soon as possible.

(3) The former agents who were in charge of collecting produce should be removed from the position as managers of subcontracting farms. The distribution of fertilizer and farming equipment and setting of purchasing prices will be carried out centrally by the Department of Agriculture and Forestry in Syonan Municipality.

B. Farms Managed by Syonan Municipality

(1) With the exception of farms under direct military management, all the rest of the farms should be brought under the control of Syonan Municipality's Department of Agriculture and Forestry. The current farm acreage is 7,260 acres, and it is anticipated that farmland will be increased to 15,000 acres by March 1945. A steady supply of farming tools, seeds and seedlings will be required. An annual production target until March 1945 should be set

---

[1] *Tsukasa* = office; *Akatsuki* = dawn; within the army the Akatsuki unit usually engaged in seaborne transport.

[2] *Nōka* = farming families = farmhouses.

at 3 tons per acre of sweet potatoes and tapioca, which are rice substitutes, and 6 tons per acre of vegetables. A maximum of 6,130 farming families (18,390 coolies) are required to fulfil the need of self-sufficiency for the entire population of ordinary citizens on Syonan Island.

(2) The management methods should be as indicated below. If there is an agent in charge of collecting produce, he should be dismissed, unless he is good at this task, and replaced by an overseas Chinese, who will work extremely hard. In other cases, the decision of whether or not to appoint an agent depends on each local situation.

(3) Produce delivery measures should be as below.

(i) The extent of farm acreage will determine output quotas of principal produce for each family. The standard annual output quotas per acre to be achieved by the end of 1944 are 2 tons of sweet potatoes and tapioca and 4 tons of vegetables. By March 1945 this should be increased to 3 tons of sweet potatoes and tapioca and 6 tons of vegetables. Quotas will be set by the heads of local Auxiliary Police Assistant Organizations [*Keisatsu Kyōjo Kyōkai*], who will take into consideration the circumstances of each farming family.

(ii) If standard quotas are not met, the purchasing price will be set as follows (here 'standard price' refers to the purchasing price for standard quotas):

- If over 90 per cent and less than 100 per cent of the standard quota is achieved, 90 per cent of the standard price will be paid;
- If over 80 per cent and less than 90 per cent of the standard quota is achieved, 80 per cent of the standard price will be paid;
- Where less than 80 per cent of the standard quota is met, the purchasing price will be 70 per cent of the standard price;
- If the deficiency is supplemented by delivery on the next day, all the produce will be purchased at standard prices.

(iii) Where the quota is exceeded, the sale will be left to the discretion of the producer.

(iv) Official standard prices will be determined by the living and administration costs of farming families; 43 per cent profit should be added to the cost.

(4) The Syonan Municipality Department of Agriculture and Forestry is to undertake the distribution of fertilizer, farming equipment, seeds and seedlings.

(5) The Syonan Municipality Department of Food is to purchase the agricultural produce and distribute it to the citizens of Syonan via the Department of Vegetables and Fruit of the Syonan Rationing Association [*Syonan Busshi Haikyū Kumiai*].

Report

1. Overview of Syonan Island

The island of Syonan can be divided, on the basis of the 1940 statistics, into the geographical areas shown in table 9.1.

Table 9.1 Syonan Island land use, 1940

Land use	Acres	%
Urban area	20,000	14.2
Rubber	51,700	36.7
Oil palm	8,250	5.9
Forest	15,400	10.9
Farmland	5,200	3.7
Pineapples	800	0.6
Orchards	3,300	2.3
Reservoirs	7,600	5.4
Cemeteries	320	0.2
Marshland	14,000	9.9
Roads and other	14,230	10.2
Total	140,800	100.0

Sources: *Malayan Agricultural Statistics*, 1940. Data on reservoirs are from Singapore, *Administration Report of Singapore Municipality* 1939 (Singapore, 1940), p. 2. Data on cemeteries and 'roads and other' are calculated for the current research.

Under the British administration unused land and rubber estates were turned to agricultural use, and in 1940 cultivated farmland extended to 5,200 acres. After the fall of Singapore, this grew to 6,662 acres by May 1943, as more land was used as farmland (survey by the Overseas Chinese Association, which excludes some of the militarily managed farms). By June 1944 farmland was estimated to have reached 11,260 acres (excluding orchards and land under pineapple cultivation).

The breakdown of the current extent of land under farm cultivation with the total of 11,260 acres is shown in table 9.2.

Table 9.2 Syonan Municipality farm acreage, June 1944[3]

Farm type	Acres	% of farmland on Syonan Island
Farms managed by military	7,000	62.2
Farms managed by public administration	530	4.7
Farms managed by trading companies	450	4.0
General farms:	3,280	29.1
ordinary farms	500	
urban area farms	500	
farmland within rubber plantations	2,280	

Sources: Data on farmland within rubber plantations is based on a survey by the Syonan Rubber Association at the end of June 1944.

This year's Plan to Increase Food Production, presented [by the military] at the Conference of District Officers in March 1944, sets out a plan to cultivate 10,000 acres on Syonan Island and 5,000 acres on other islands. Clearing for cultivation has now [end of July 1944] started on land of over 15,000 acres, including the effort to extend by approximately 400 acres cultivated land at the edges of roads. Together with all other efforts, it is quite possible that this will add about 7,740 acres.[4] And with these further efforts, a total of 19,000 acres of farmland will therefore definitely be worked in the present fiscal year.[5] Any further cultivation, however, would be impossible due to defence considerations and a lack of appropriate technology.

[3] Syonan Municipality under the Japanese Military Administration covered all areas of Syonan Island and adjunct islands, all of which were included in the eight police precincts. The total size of the island was 140,800 acres in 1940 (table 9.1), of which farmland was only 5,200 acres. As explained in the text, the farmland doubled under the Japanese.

[4] See section 3-B-(i) for derivation of this number.

[5] That is, the existing 11,260 acres plus the newly cultivated 7,740 acres, which becomes smaller than the addition of 11,260 acres and 10,000 acres planned by the military.

2. Military-Managed Farms

Militarily managed farms currently encompass 62.2 per cent[7] of all cultivated land.[8] These farms include most of those worked prior to the war. They are far better than other farms. Farms under military management are therefore a key element in increasing food production on Syonan Island.

The present survey focuses mainly on current working practices of military-managed farms. Several farms were selected for the survey. The interviews took place in three different locations within each military-managed farm: the Military Accounting Department, the agent in charge of collecting produce, and the farmer who managed the farmland. A list of military-managed farms is set out below:

> Oka 10354; Oka 1615; Tsukasa Accounting Department [9813]; Oka 9923; Oka 15847; Oka 15847 Syonan branch; Oka 10355; Malaya POW concentration camp; Oka 10412; Oka 4834; Oka 6091; Oka 10414; Oka 15801; Oka 9285; Oka 10356; Oka 10345; Oka 9323; Oka Mass Prison; Syonan Dormitory group; Oka 2944; Oka 2944 Morishita unit; Oka 2949; Oka 1615 Syonan branch. (Survey by the Seventh Area Army, June 1944 to the present.)[9]

This survey further divides farms into excellent and other farms. A sample list of farms is given below:

- A+ Excellent farms: Oka 10356 (Supply Regiment, Seventh Area Army), Tsukasa 9813, Oka 2944 (Third Shipping unit), Oka 9323 (Yasuda unit)
- A– Poor-performing farms: Oka 2949 (Shipping and Armoury Regiment), Oka 9923 (Tsukasa unit)

The following points relating to table 9.3 should be noted:

(i) As column 2, 'Management organization', shows, there are two types of farm management. (A+) There are farms that are directly managed by the military, including: (a+) farms to which coolies are brought and required to perform farm work (e.g., Oka 10356's Tengah farm and Oka 10356's Bukit Timah farm); (b+) farms established by farmers who later came to be employed as wage-earning coolies (e.g., Oka 9323's Paya Lebar farm); and (c+) farms run by established farmers, and not by coolies, to which the military directly supplies fertilizers, etc., and from which it purchases

---

[7] 7,000 acres.

[8] 11,260 acres, from table 9.2.

[9] *Oka* (meaning 'hill') is a code name for the Seventh Area Army, which was formed on 19 March 1944 (stationed in Singapore as an Area Army, combining the former 25th Army, which came to be assigned solely to Sumatra, the 29th Army assigned to Malaya, the 16th Army in Java and the Borneo Defence Army).

produce at a fixed price (e.g., Oka 10356's Lim Chu Kang farm and Tsukasa 9813's Geylang farm). (A–) Poor-performing farms are managed by a subcontractor appointed by the military. The military appoints the agents in charge of collecting produce to ensure the provision of fertilizers, farming tools, seeds and seedlings; to be responsible for collecting produce and payment to the farmers; and to see to a variety of administrative matters. Here the agents in charge of collecting produce are usually paid a commission of between 10 per cent and 20 per cent. The farms of this type include: (a–) farmers who can self-provide fertilizers and other items necessary for farming; and (b–) farms who cannot self-provide. This is shown in column 11 of the table, 'Source of fertilizers, tools and seeds'. The difference between farmers [of the military-managed farms] who make do by themselves without receiving fertilizers, etc., and general farmers who are not part of the farms managed by the military is whether they can sell produce on the open market or whether they have to hand it over to the military for between 10 per cent and 30 per cent of the market price (e.g., Oka 9923's Yio Chu Kang farm and Oka 2949's Paya Lebar farm).

(ii) In column 4, 'Acreage', figures in brackets show acreage including land at the planning stage. Figures without brackets are for acreage already planted as part of total planned acreage.

(iii) In column 5, 'Daily production' for Oka 10356's Tanpines farm, the figure in brackets of 4,800kg is for tapioca and sweet potatoes used for pig feed. Total production will therefore be 5,700kg: 4,800kg plus 900kg. (The bracketed figures in columns 6 and 10 indicate the respective amount for pig feed.) However, total production figures do not indicate the total amount actually produced. A proportion of the produce is consumed by the farmers themselves. The figures represent total production for farms that employ coolies.

(iv) In column 6, 'Annual production per acre', the figures are calculated from daily production of cultivated acreage.

(v) In column 7, 'Number of farmhouses', the figures in brackets are calculated from column 8, 'Number of agricultural workers', on the basis of three workers per farming family.

(vi) In column 9, 'Number of farmhouses per acre', the figures are calculated by dividing the number of farming families by the acres planned under the acreage extension programme.

The table shows the following:

(1) The large per acre disparities between farms in annual production (column 6) are to some extent caused by the nature of the soil [which depends largely

on effort] after cultivating. Other factors are the very uneven distribution of farming equipment, fertilizer, seeds, seedlings and labour. Divergences between directly managed farms that use coolies and farms managed by subcontractors also arise from the fact that directly managed farms can supply their entire production without any deduction.

(2) As figures for the number of farmhouses per acre (column 9) show, the deployment of the labour force is not even (e.g., more farming families should be allocated to Oka 10356's Tanpines farm, and Oka 2944 unit's Jurong No. 1 and No. 2 farms). These farms will need more farm labour.

(3) As column 10, 'Daily production per farmhouse', shows, the most efficient farms are those that are directly managed. Examples are Oka 10356's Tengah farm, Oka 9323's Paya Lebar farm and Tsukasa 9813's Geylang farm. These farms get higher purchasing prices than other farms. It must be noted that they receive fertilizer, etc., as military rations.

(4) In general, a higher 'percentage of purchasing price to market price' (column 13) leads to a larger daily production per farming family (column 10). The most difficult issue that came up through our interviews with the farming families was pricing. While noting that these workers are urban dwellers and mostly overseas Chinese, it is essential to add that price is the most important factor in maintaining and increasing food production. When purchasing prices are low and fertilizer cannot be obtained from the military agent who is in charge of produce collection, the efficiency of the affected farming families is very low. Examples are Oka 9923's Yio Chu Kang farm, Oka 9923's Changi farm and Oka 2949's Paya Lebar farm. These farms could not afford to buy expensive fertilizers. The response of farming families to want and hardship is that the majority of the family members seek different occupations that offer better earnings, or they sell produce through illegal channels to the black market. It is clear that the imposition of control over these farming families caused their morale to wane (e.g., Oka 2949's Paya Lebar farm).

(5) Directly managed farms are more efficient than farms managed by subcontractors. The reason behind this is that the agents in charge of collecting produce engage in profit-making activities. The actual prices paid to farming families by the agents are lower than the purchasing prices the agents said that they had paid. Such intermediary agents are vicious operators whose sacrifice of general farming families for their own benefit alienates the opinion of the farming families. There must be stricter surveillance by the military of these private operators, or they should be removed and replaced with better individuals. Direct military management would be the most effective way of avoiding such harmful activities.

Note:
The only instance of the employment of an overseas Chinese as an intermediary agent in this survey is Oka 2944's Jurong No. 1 farm.[10] At this farm there is no difference between the prices that the agents reported and actual selling prices. Although we cannot rule out the possibility that the amount of delivery may be dishonestly reported, it is extremely difficult to establish the actual amounts supplied, and impossible to verify the figures. The agent does not give the impression of being dishonest, and the affected farming families told us they were extremely satisfied with the existing arrangements.[11]

3. Reorganization of Farms

To assess this problem, it is necessary to consider the relationship between military-managed and general farms. At present, food self-sufficiency is difficult to achieve within Syonan Island. Rice, sweet potatoes and tapioca have to be imported from Thailand, the Malay Peninsula and the islands around Syonan. About 108 tons of these three foods are produced daily. This divides into military use of about 48 tons and 60 tons for civilian use. As already noted, military-managed farms have an acreage of around 7,000 acres, and other farms 4,260 acres. However, about 20 tons of food a day are derived [through legal and illegal channels] from military-managed farms for civilian consumption. Complete self-sufficiency in tapioca, sweet potatoes and vegetables for Syonan Island and southern Johore can only be achieved by the redistribution of farmland. This is necessary to supply civilian consumption of sweet potatoes, tapioca and vegetables to a level that would ensure the maintenance of minimum living standards for the local population, while reserving the same share as now of these products for military consumption. Specific policies must be implemented in order to maintain support from the farmers and encourage food production [by raising the purchasing price] while also ensuring a supply of cheap vegetables, etc., for civilian consumption. The course that should be followed is now set out.

---

10 The author preferred to use 'overseas Chinese' (華僑) or 'ethnic Chinese' instead of 'Chinese' (支那人), which had pejorative connotations in the wartime context; see also chapter 12.

11 From table 9.3, the land productivity rates in the Jurong area were quite low, probably due to poor soil conditions. Later in this report, the author takes this into consideration as he formulates his productivity figures for the farmland managed by Syonan Municipality.

A. Farms under Direct Military Management

(1) Acreage

Military farms that are managed by the Supply Regiment and Tsukasa and Akatsuki units (with total farm acreage of 3,194 acres[12], of which 1,345 acres[13] are under existing cultivation as explained below) and other selected military-managed farms (with a total acreage of the 806 acres)[14] should all be under direct military management, whether or not they have previously been managed directly or by subcontractors. The Supply Regiment and Tsukasa and Akatsuki units should determine among themselves the allotment of the directly managed farms.

[Here the total acreage of farms managed by the Supply Regiment and Tsukasa and Akatsuki units refers to the total of] the farms managed by military units as indicated in table 9.3 (column 4), including Oka 10356 unit's Thompson farm (now under development, with a total acreage of 80 acres), but subtracting Oka 9323's [= Yasuda unit's] Tanah Merah farm and Paya Lebar farm in exchange for a total acreage of 15 acres, of which 5 acres are under existing cultivated land. If this is implemented, the Supply Regiment should be responsible for providing food rations for each unit apart from the Tsukasa and Akatsuki units. The Tsukasa and Akatsuki units should be self-supporting in food supplies.

It would be possible to supply 7 tons of produce annually per acre by March 1945 if on the total 4,000 acres[15] intensive farming methods were introduced through the supply of fertilizers, farming equipment, seeds and seedlings, together with the settlement of an appropriate agricultural labour force of 5 coolies or 1.7 farming families per acre. These measures would have to be adopted to achieve complete self-sufficiency in staple food substitutes and vegetables for all units on Syonan Island. It is necessary to resettle a maximum of 5,049 farming families (with a minimum of three workers per farming family) or 14,629 coolies[16] as soon as possible if complete self-sufficiency of the military units is to be achieved.

---

[12] From table 9.3, column 4, total planned acreage (3,224), minus Oka 9323's Paya Lebar farm (25) and Tanah Merah farm (100), plus new farmland in exchange (15) and Oka 10356's Thompson farm (80), 3,224 – 25 – 100 + 15 + 80 = 3,194.

[13] That is, total cultivated acreage (1,410), minus Oka 9323's Paya Lebar farm (25) and Tanah Merah farm (45), plus new farmland already cultivated (5), 1,410 – 25 – 45 + 5 = 1,345.

[14] No breakdown of 806 acres, which are from outside the surveyed farms, is provided in this report. The author's recommendation is that the military should give up 3,000 acres.

[15] That is, from footnote 12 above, 3,194 + 806 = 4,000.

[16] That is, the total number of farming families necessary to intensively cultivate (1.7 / acre) the total planned acreage under military management (4,000), minus the total number of existing farming families from table 9.3, column 7 (1,751), 4,000 x 1.7 – 1,751 = 5,049; likewise, workers (5 / acre) for total farmland (4,000), minus existing workers from table 9.3, column 8 (5,371), 4,000 x 5 – 5,371 = 14,629.

Notes:

(i) It has been shown above that directly managed farms are the most efficient of the military-managed farms.

(ii) Seven thousand acres on military-managed farms can produce 2.5 tons per acre annually of staple substitutes and vegetables. (On normal farms the annual production per acre is about 10 tons of sweet potatoes and tapioca, and about 6 tons of vegetables. However, data relating to military-managed farms, as shown in the survey results table, yield a total annual supply of sweet potatoes, tapioca and vegetables of 2.6 tons [per acre]. Here, following the table, the total daily delivery is 9.53 tons and total acreage is 1,345 acres.[17] By considering these factors, the annual supply is calculated to be 2.5 tons [per acre].) Total daily consumption of military units [if this equals total production of military-managed farms] in Syonan is 48 tons.[18] From this total, if we assume that about 20 tons a day that derive from military-managed farms are sold to the black market, production on military-managed farms of only 28 tons would actually be necessary to meet military consumption. Adding to this, around 40 tons delivered daily by the Syonan Vegetable and Fruit Association to the military (including about 20 tons of tapioca transferred from the Syonan Rationing Association, Department of Vegetables and Fruit, to the military), the daily consumption of the Syonan-stationed military units would be about 68 tons.

(iii) The application of intensive farming to the 4,000 acres under military management would increase production to 6 tons per acre annually by the end of the present fiscal year. If this approach were adopted by all the military-managed farms, total daily supply would be 66 tons.[19] Therefore, if the current military consumption level (estimated to be 68 tons) is cut as far as possible without compromising military operations, it could possibly approach the new level of production [66 tons]. Any shortages that persist despite all efforts made at the military-managed farms could also be made up in the usual way by the Syonan Vegetable and Fruit Association. Additionally, it may be desirable to attempt full military food

---

[17] That is, from table 9.3, column 5, average daily production (9.53) for one year (365) divided by total cultivated farmland (1,345), 9.53 x 365 / 1,345 = 2.58.

[18] That is, applying the above 2.5 tons as the average annual productivity per acre for the total current acreage of military-managed farms (7,000) for one year (365), 2.5 x 7,000 / 365 = 47.94.

[19] That is, from table 9.3, column 6, applying the second highest productivity rate (6.1), after the abolished Oka 9323's Paya Lebar farm, which was run by established farmers who later came to be employed as coolies, 6 x 4,000 / 365 = 65.7.

self-sufficiency by increasing food production to 7 tons per acre annually, and achieving 77 tons daily by the end of next March.[20]

(iv) As indicated above, the highest level of production is achieved by allocating 1.7 farming families (or 5 coolies) per acre. This is clearly demonstrated at Oka 9323's Paya Lebar farm, as shown in table 9.3. Six thousand eight hundred farming families (20,000 coolies) are required for 4,000 acres of farmland.[21] There are already [from table 9.3, column 7] at least 1,751 farming families (at least 5,371 coolies) in these 4,000 acres of farmland. Therefore, an additional maximum 5,049 farming families (14,629 coolies) are required.[22]

(2) Management

Among the military units managing their own farms, included in the 4,000 acres above, those that employ agents to collect produce should eliminate these intermediaries. Decisions relating to the rationing of fertilizers, farming equipment and seeds, and the level of purchasing prices for farms should be made centrally by the Syonan Municipality Department of Agriculture and Forestry. The military, however, should bear the administrative cost of implementing these recommendations.

Note:
As already observed, the actions of the agents in charge of collecting produce have lowered the farmers' motivation to increase food production. Therefore, the agents should be removed and all activity put under direct military control, and rationing of goods such as fertilizers, and other administrative activities that were performed by those agents, should now be performed by the Syonan Municipality Department of Agriculture and Forestry. This department should also take on the redistribution of fertilizers and administrative activities by re-assessing conditions at each unit farm and make decisions based on civilian demand and needs.[23] This will decrease the burden on the Accounting Department of the military. The Syonan Municipality Department of Agriculture and Forestry should also maintain close liaison with the Seventh Area Army Accounting Department, and conduct negotiations with each Accounting Department of each army unit.

---

[20] That is, 7 x 4,000 / 365 = 76.7.

[21] 4,000 x 1.7 = 6,800.

[22] 1,751 + 5,049 = 6,800 farming families; 5,371 + 14,629 = 20,000 coolies.

[23] Meaning that fertilizers should be reallocated to local general farms for civilian use.

(3) *Imports*

Until self-sufficiency is fully achieved, shortages of vegetables for military consumption will be made up by imports from Pahang or Perak through the Syonan Vegetable and Fruit Association.

B. Farms Managed by Syonan Municipality

(1) *Acreage*

With the exception of farms managed by the military, general farms should all be under the control of Syonan Municipality's Department of Agriculture and Forestry. Current acreage is 7,260 acres (derived from 4,260 acres[24] at present farmed and 3,000 acres that are intended to be returned by the army through the recommendation of this report). A steady supply of fertilizers, farming equipment and tools will be required if farmland is to be expanded to 15,000 acres [as targeted by the Military Administration] by the end of March 1945 to achieve self-sufficiency for the population of Syonan Island. The production of staple substitutes and vegetables should be increased to an annual production per acre of 3 and 6 tons respectively, and the number of farming families (housing at least three people available for work) should be increased to 6,130, or 18,390 coolies.[25] However, 7,740 acres[26] of newly developed farmland should only be used to grow staple food substitutes [i.e., tapioca and sweet potatoes] before the end of March 1945.

Notes:

(i) There are farms outside both the military-managed farms and Syonan Municipality Department of Agriculture and Forestry. These free farms impede price regulation. All farms should be under military or Syonan Municipality control. However, if a few farms remain under public administration or trading company control, this will not hinder proper regulation. These farms should be considered the same as those under Syonan Municipality management.

(ii) In this case [if all the farms outside military control are transferred to Syonan Municipality], the existing acreage of farms under Department of Agriculture and Forestry control is 7,260 acres. This figure is derived by subtracting from the total acreage of 11,260 acres 4,000 acres of land

---

[24] From table 9.2, farms managed by public administration (530), trading companies (450) and general farms (3,280), 530 + 450 + 3,280 = 4,260.

[25] See note (iv) below.

[26] 15,000 – 7,260 = 7,740.

that should be directly managed by the military.[27] The maximum extension of cultivation will result in 15,000 acres [as planned by the Military Administration] by the end of March 1945.

(iii) The current daily consumption of sweet potatoes and tapioca is about 48 tons,[28] of vegetables 57.5 tons,[29] and of other fruit 24.5 tons.[30] Of these quantities, 55 tons of sweet potatoes and tapioca, 0.5 tons of other vegetables, and 14.5 tons of fruit are imported daily from Johore and Negeri Sembilan, through the Syonan Rationing Association.[31] (From this, 20 tons[32] daily of sweet potatoes and tapioca are allocated to the military. See supplementary material 1 for details.) Local daily general trade [excluding imports] in sweet potatoes and tapioca is about 13 tons.[33] In other vegetables, it is 57 tons,[34] and for fruit 10 tons[35] (see supplementary material 2 [tables 9.12 and 9.13] for details). Daily consumption per person [i.e., divided by the current population of Syonan Municipality, as calculated below] should therefore be 0.09 catties[36] of sweet potatoes and tapioca, 0.11 catties[37] of other vegetables and 0.05 kins[38] of fruit, a total of 0.25 catties.[39] However, these figures derive from an estimated current consuming population of 875,000, calculated from a total population in Syonan Municipality of

---

27 The author implies here again that 3,000 acres are to be returned to the citizens.

28 From table 9.5, consumption of supplementary food, that is staple food substitutes 17,280 / 365 = 47.3; also, calculation below, local trade (13), plus imports (55), minus those allocated to the military (20), 13 + 55 – 20 = 48.

29 Vegetables produced on the island (20,800) plus daily imports (0.5), 20,800 / 365 + 0.5 = 57.5; also, derived from the hawker trade survey in table 9.13 (93,607) plus imports (0.5), 93,607 x 0.6 + 0.5 = 56.7.

30 Imports from Johore and Negeri Sembilan (14.5) plus local trade (10) as explained below, 14.5 + 10 = 24.5; but this is much less than the pre-war production level of 45 tons and consumption level of 30 tons in January 1944; see supplementary material 1 below. Fruit was a luxury item that rarely reached ordinary urban households with low levels of living; see chapter 12.

31 *Syonan Busshi Haikyū Kumiai*; see supplementary material 1. From table 9.8, average daily imports of sweet potatoes and tapioca, minus commission charge (56.4), vegetables (0.59), fruit (14.1).

32 That is, local trade (13) plus import (55), minus local consumption (48), 13 + 55 – 48 = 20.

33 That is, assuming daily trade by hawkers, as in table 9.12, to be 85 per cent of total trade, 18,161 / 0.85 / 1,000 x 0.6 = 12.8.

34 79,566 / 0.85 / 1,000 x 0.6 = 56.2.

35 14,125 / 0.85 / 1,000 x 0.6 = 9.9.

36 54g, 48 x 10^6 / 875,000 = 54.8.

37 66g, 57.5 x 10^6 / 875,000 = 65.7.

38 30g, 24.5 x 10^6 / 875,000 = 28.

39 150g, 54 + 66 + 30 = 150.

900,000,[40] from which has been subtracted an agricultural population of about 25,000 (according to the 1943 census survey, the agricultural population is 24,734).

(iv) [Future daily consumption of sweet potatoes and tapioca, other vegetables and fruit is calculated below.] Of the 7,260 acres[41] of farmland [which are to be] managed by the department, 2,218 acres[42] are estimated to produce sweet potatoes and tapioca. (Of this farmland, at present 1,660 acres[43] are outside the military-managed farms. When new policies based on this current report recommendation have been implemented, 558 acres[44] now under direct military management will be transferred to Syonan Municipality farms.) A total of 5,042 acres are estimated to produce other vegetables and fruit. (At present, 2,600 of these acres[45] are outside direct military management. Implementation of a new policy based on this current report recommendation will transfer 2,442 acres[46] from direct military management to Syonan Municipality farms.) The projected daily production of sweet potatoes, tapioca, and other vegetables and fruit is 12.2 tons[47], 80 tons[48] and 10 tons[49] respectively, a total production of 102.2 tons. Daily production of 63.6 tons[50] of sweet potatoes and tapioca could be achieved with a production of 3 tons an acre annually on 7,740 acres[51] of newly developed farmland.[52] These figures indicate that, adding to the former,[53] a total of 165.8 tons[54] of staple substitutes, vegetables and

---

40 See chapter 3, 2-(1), total population from census of November 1943 (855,679), plus those in Seletar port, lodgers in police dormitories and prisoners (about 35,000).

41 That is, current 4,260 acres plus 3,000 returned from the military.

42 See below, 2,218 = 1,660 + 558.

43 See supplementary material 2, 1,660 + 2,660 = 4,260.

44 See supplementary material 2. From table 9.14, 3.7 tons of sweet potatoes and tapioca from the military-managed farms are channelled to the black market. If these are to be produced at the rate of 2.43 tons per acre per year, the farmland required would be 558 acres, 3.7 x 365 / 2.43 = 558.

45 From supplementary material 2, 2,600 = 4,260 – 1,660.

46 From the above calculation, 2,442 = 3,000 – 558.

47 See supplementary material 2 (5), that is, production from existing civilian-managed farms (9.1) and from farms returned by the army (3.1), 9.1 + 3.1 = 12.2.

48 Likewise, 39.9 + 40.1 = 80.

49 As table 9.12 and calculation above (iii).

50 7,740 x 3 / 365 = 63.6.

51 15,000 – 7,260 = 7,740.

52 Following the plan laid out at the Conference of the District Officers, total target acreage (15,000), minus existing farmlands (4,260 + 3,000).

53 = total production of 102.2 tons from the existing 7,260 acres of farmland.

54 63.6 + 102.2 = 165.8.

fruit can be produced locally. Assuming the consuming population to be about 850,000 by the end of next March, daily consumption per person would be 0.15 catties[55] of sweet potatoes and tapioca, 0.16 catties[56] of other vegetables, and 0.02 catties[57] of fruit. This would total 0.33 catties (198g) and represents a consumption of 166.7 per cent[58] of sweet potatoes and tapioca compared to current consumption, 145.5 per cent[59] of other vegetables, and 40 per cent[60] of fruit. The total equivalent is 132 per cent (see supplementary materials 1 and 2 for details).

(v) Therefore, local self-sufficiency in vegetables is possible. However, in the near future, rice imports for local consumption will present difficulties. To make up the shortfall, it would be necessary to facilitate the daily import of around 50 tons[61] of sweet potatoes and tapioca and some vegetables from the southern state of Johore. This together with local production [of 165.8 tons] will secure a daily food consumption of more than 200 tons as laid out [by the Military Administration] in the intra-Syonan production plan.[62]

(vi) The 7,740 acres of farmland to be developed by the end of next March should be used solely to produce sweet potatoes and tapioca. Since around 80 per cent of vegetable and fruit imports from Johore and Negeri Sembilan comprise sweet potatoes and tapioca, the level of self-sufficiency is currently low. Extrapolation to 7,740 acres of the number of farming families required to cultivate, i.e., 2 acres per family [0.5 families per acre] of sweet potatoes and tapioca, gives 3,870 farming families. This implies that 11,610 coolies are needed, on the basis that each farm family is equivalent to three available workers. If the method of intensive cultivation is applied to 7,260 acres of established farmland, it will require one farming family per acre,[63] and 7,260 farming families or 21,780 coolies in total for those on established farmland. According to the May 1943 survey by the

---

55 90g, $(63.6 + 12.2) \times 10^6 / 850{,}000 = 89.1$.

56 96g, $80 \times 10^6 / 850{,}000 = 94.1$.

57 12g, $10 \times 10^6 / 850{,}000 = 11.7$.

58 0.15 / 0.09 x 100 = 166.66.

59 0.16 / 0.11 x 100 = 145.5.

60 0.02 / 0.05 x 100 = 40.

61 From table 9.8, average daily import from Johore of 49.9 tons.

62 That is, imports 50 + local production 165.8 = 215.8. If the 15,000 acres are supposed to produce 200 tons daily, the assumed annual productivity rate here would be 4.8 tons per acre.

63 That is lower than the recommended 1.7 farming families per acre on military-managed farms.

Overseas Chinese Society, there are 6,707 farming families.[64] If about 5,000 of these existing farming families[65] are working on the farms[66] which are to be under the management of Syonan Municipality, only the remaining 2,260 families (6,780 coolies) will still need to be resettled to supply the necessary farming labour. Thus, a total additional 6,130 farming families will be required.[67]

(2) Management

In appointing the agents in charge of produce collection, the most efficient agents may be retained, but it would be preferable to make replacements by more efficient overseas Chinese or to make appointments according to the local situation. Syonan Municipality's Department of Agriculture and Forestry should be put in charge of overall supervision of farming families.

Notes:

(i) As already noted, some Japanese agents in charge of collecting produce have employed illicit practices. The Military Administration will never achieve acceptance unless such illicit conduct is completely eliminated. It is recommended that Japanese be replaced with overseas Chinese agents. Japanese agents cannot act as a channel of communication between farmers and the municipality. Where overseas Chinese are agents, there will be an easier channel of communication. Moreover, as agents, overseas Chinese would also be capable of facilitating the smooth running of the office work required for the cultivation and supply of products. This system is also in accord with the general policy of employing overseas Chinese companies.

(ii) Management inconsistencies will be detrimental to the efficiency of all the farms. The Department of Agriculture and Forestry should therefore comprehensively supervise all of these farms.

(3) Delivery quota of farm produce

(i) The delivery quota of principal farm produce should be determined by the cultivated acreage of each farm family. Annual production per acre will be

---

[64] See chapter 3, table 3.6, population of farmers at 24,375 implies 8,124 farming families, assuming three workers per family.

[65] That is, total farming families (6,707), minus farming families working on the military farms (1,751) as in table 9.3, 6,707 – 1,751 = 4,956.

[66] Total 7,260 acres.

[67] That is, intensive farming requirement 7,260 – existing farmers 5,000 = 2,260 and 2,260 + tapioca-only new farmers 3,870 = 6,130.

Figure 9.1 Locations of vegetable collection points

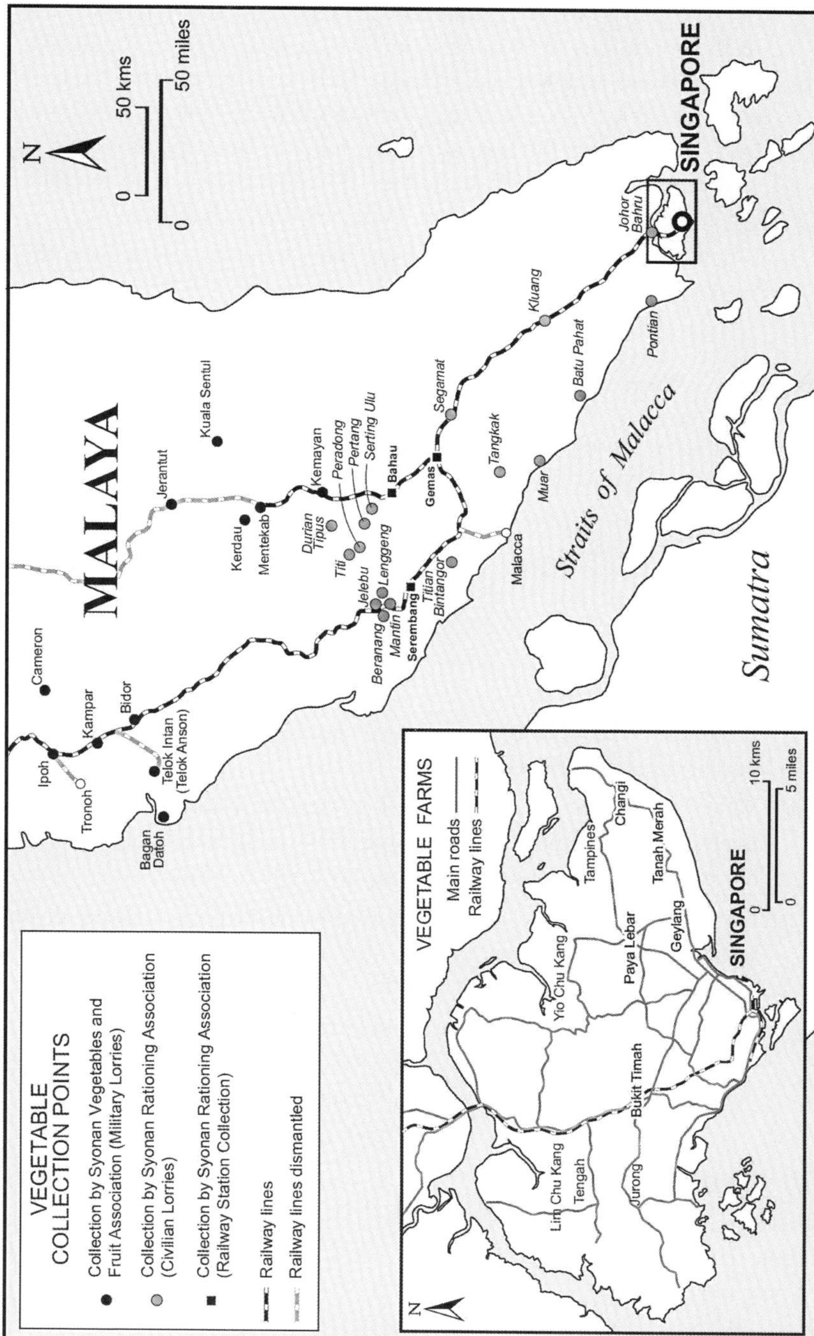

2 tons of sweet potatoes and tapioca per acre and 4 tons of other vegetables by the end of 1944. The farm produce supply quota should be set according to the conditions of farming families with the production guideline of 3 tons of sweet potatoes and tapioca and 6 tons of other vegetables by the end of March 1945. However, where farmland has been newly transferred from the military, the annual supply quota of sweet potatoes and tapioca should be set at 2 tons by the end of 1944. Quotas are to be determined by the leader of each local Auxiliary Police Assistant Organization.

(ii) If delivery falls short of the level set, the purchasing prices from the farm family will be as in table 9.4.

Table 9.4 Prices paid according to production levels

Ratio of set production level to actual production level	Price paid as % of standard price
Less than 100 and over 90%	90%
Less than 90 and over 80%	80%
Less than 80%	70%

The 'standard price' is the purchasing price for the prescribed delivery quota.

If daily shortfalls can be made up the next day, the whole amount will be purchased at the standard price.

(iii) When production exceeds prescribed delivery quotas, it may be traded freely. However, where previous supply shortfalls exist, shortages must first be covered before the remaining surplus can be sold freely.

Note: The minimum amount required for local needs will be secured by setting prescribed delivery quotas. Free trading of surpluses will provide an incentive to increase food production.

(iv) A standard price should be based on farmers' total living costs and running costs. A profit of 43 per cent of aggregate living costs and running costs (30 per cent of standard prices) should be budgeted in the present price.

(4) Fertilizers

The Syonan Municipality section of Agriculture and Forestry should centrally ration fertilizers, farming equipment, seeds and seedlings. Farming families are to bear the costs.

Note:

The Department of Agriculture and Forestry should take into account the relationship between military and local needs. Priority should be given to local demand for fertilizers, farming equipment, seeds and seedlings, and the remainder should be allotted subsequently to the farms directly run by the Department of Agriculture and Forestry. Costs should be borne by each farm family. This system differs from that employed by military-managed farms [where the cost of fertilizers, etc., is borne by the military]. Its adoption is to encourage farmers to voluntarily use fertilizers efficiently. [The farmers themselves must take the initiative] because surveillance over municipality-managed farms [which cannot resort to illicit means] can be less effective than for military-managed farms.

(5) Purchase of farm produce

Farm produce will be purchased by the Syonan Municipality Department of Food. The purchased vegetables will be used for local rations through the Syonan Rationing Association Department of Fruit and Vegetables. The department will employ the same existing rationing organizations as previously used [i.e., Syonan's distribution stations, etc.]. Service charges [paid to the retailers at the rationing stations] will be determined jointly by the Syonan Municipality Department of Food and the Department of Agriculture and Forestry.

(6) Imports

When production of vegetables falls short of local self-sufficiency on Syonan Island, the shortfall should be made up by imports from Johore and Negeri Sembilan. As usual, this will be the responsibility of the Syonan Rationing Association's Department of Vegetables and Fruit.

Supplementary Material 1. Supply and Demand of Vegetables on Syonan Island

1. Outline

The farmland on Syonan Island should be used wholly to produce principal foods such as sweet potatoes, tapioca, vegetables and fruit. The target of increased food production on Syonan Island means nothing except increased production of these vegetables and fruit. The following material describes the current conditions of import and consumption of vegetables, etc., directly relevant to the policy of increasing consumption.

2. Consumption levels

(1) Pre-war consumption

Table 9.5 shows the annual consumption of vegetables, etc., on Syonan Island, calculated from data relating to the six-month period before the war.

Table 9.5 Annual pre-war consumption of supplementary foods and vegetables

(tons)

Consumption of supplementary foods	17,280
Consumption of vegetables	34,600
In details, volume of net imports	13,800
Production within the isle	20,800
Total consumption of vegetables	51,880

Sources: Supplementary foods, from chapter 7, table A.7.3; vegetables (production within the isle) from table 9.1;[68] vegetables (net imports), Singapore, *Report of Singapore Municipality 1939.*

Table note:

The data for supplementary foods is from *Report 35*,[69] Nampō Gunsei Sōkanbu Research Reports.[70] Production of green vegetables on Singapore Island is calculated by assuming that 5,200 acres of farmland produced 4 tons of food annually.[71]

The population at the end of June 1941 was 770,000 (S.S., *Government Gazette*, 28 Feb. 1941, p. 501). The average daily consumption of vegetables, etc., per person was 0.31 catties.[72] Adding to this, the average daily fruit consumption of 0.20 catties,[73] pre-war consumption of fruit and vegetables, etc., was about 0.51 catties.[74]

---

[68] Farmland 5,200 x production of 4 tons per acre.

[69] Chapter 7, 'Countermeasures for Prices for Syonan Municipality' ('Syonan Tokubetsushi wo chūshin to seru Bukka Taisaku').

[70] Chapter 7, appendix 3 gives pre-war monthly 'Supplementary Food' consumption as 1,440 tons. Supplementary Food includes tapioca and sago products, corn and soybeans, but not wheat flour or atta flour (used for chapati); 1,440 x 12 = 17,280 tons.

[71] That is, 5,200 x 4 = 20,800.

[72] 186g, that is, total vegetable consumption (table 9.5) per person per day, 51,880 x 10^6 / 770,000 / 365 = 184.5.

[73] 120g, that is, total fruit consumption (from below) per person per day, 33,360 x 10^6 / 770,000 / 365 = 118.6.

[74] 306g, 186 + 120 = 306.

When the planned daily consumption per person of 0.33 catties (198g) is achieved by the end of March 1945, per head consumption will be about 65 per cent of pre-war levels. However, here, total fruit consumption[75] is calculated as below:

> Total fruit consumption is an aggregation of 16,860 tons of net imports[76] and 16,500 tons of island production (calculated assuming annual production of 5 tons per acre over 3,300 acres),[77] giving a total of 33,360 tons.

(2) Current conditions

The better farms on Syonan Island are almost exclusively those managed by the military. The vegetables, etc., produced by these farms are consequently destined for military consumption. However, price rises have caused a small quantity of vegetables, etc. (about 20 tons a day) to be supplied to the market for consumption by local people. But this supply cannot meet the food demands of local people. Substantial imports from the Malay Peninsula are therefore necessary. Two means of importing have been employed. One is to import vegetables, etc., designated for military consumption from Pahang and Perak through the Syonan Vegetable and Fruit Association, as has been done since 1 May 1944. The other is to import for local consumption from Johore and Negeri Sembilan through the Syonan Rationing Association's Department of Vegetables and Fruit, as has also been done since 1 May 1944. In addition, the Department of Vegetables and Fruit has engaged in the collection of produce, and the Syonan Municipality Department of Food has handled its rationing.

The report now turns to the current situation of import of vegetables, etc., for military and local consumption.

A. Collection by the Syonan Vegetable and Fruit Association for the Military

Initially, the Southern Army's Field Supply Regiment, Section of Food and Clothing was in charge of collecting vegetables for military consumption. This duty was taken over by the present association on 15 August 1943. For a brief period from 1 February 1944 the association also collected vegetables, etc., for local consumption. But since 1 May 1944 the association has again dealt solely

---

[75] 33,360 tons.

[76] Imports excluding re-exports. Source: Administrative Report of Singapore Municipality, 1939.

[77] From table 9.1 Orchards.

with military consumption. The military requires 80 tons of vegetables, etc., daily to be collected. Performance is set out in the table below.

As table 9.6 shows, collection was steady until February 1944 but fell in March and further deteriorated in May.

Amounts collected reached their lowest point of 14,251kg on 3 May. The main reasons for this decline are as follows:

- Newly developed military brigade camps in Kuala Lumpur and Ipoh increased their consumption of vegetables, etc.
- Consumption of staple food substitutes increased as a consequence of reduced rice rations throughout the Malay Peninsula.
- There is a shortage of lorries, particularly because of a shortage of tyres (for details, see below).
- Irregular railway services, resulting from military operations in Burma and the defence of Malaya, have spread to disruptions in general cargo transportation. Some vegetables, etc., especially white radishes, bananas and pineapples, rot during such disruption to transportation.

With such a low level of imports, it is impossible to meet military requirements. Consequently, the daily supply of 20 tons of vegetables earmarked for local use is now channelled to the military.

Table 9.6 Syonan Vegetable and Fruit Association average daily collection, December 1943–July 1944

(kg)

	Total[78]	Sweet potatoes and tapioca
Dec. 1943	61,860	17,924
Jan. 1944	54,853	11,804
Feb. 1944	60,256	18,164
Mar. 1944	51,797	12,024
Apr. 1944	42,839	15,568
May 1944	35,831	12,690
June 1944	41,361	22,090
July 1944	43,271	22,098

Sources: Syonan Vegetable and Fruit Association, Department of Sales, 'Daily Reports by Items'.

[78] Total includes all vegetables, sweet potatoes and tapioca.

(i) Military delivery price

The delivery price is made up of the purchase price, [Pahang and Perak] State Council's commission of 10 per cent of the purchase price, a transport tariff for the lorries, miscellaneous expenses such as transporting sacks and baskets, a 10–30 per cent depreciation rate during transport, and a commission charged by the [Syonan Vegetable and Fruit] Association of 10 per cent of the total cost. This price changes monthly but remains fixed for a month. Purchasing prices from military-managed farms are usually determined by this method.

Table 9.7 Syonan Vegetable and Fruit Association prices, May–July 1944
(cents per kg)

	May	June	July
Highland white radishes	49	49	49
Carrots	110	110	110
Cabbages	86	86	86
Dried soybeans, sugar-coated	94	163	131
Lotus roots	117	160	167
Cucumbers	58	83	86
Aubergines	39	72	92
Taro	52	80	85
Eddoes	52	-	-
Yams	52	-	-
Pumpkins	33	69	76
Wax gourds	32	63	69
Sweet potatoes	63	78	84
Ginger	228	228	257
South Sea white radishes	33	50	57
White cucumbers	32	50	50
Agar-agar	22	-	29
Papaya	78	78	82
Bananas, first grade	58	58	64
Bananas, second grade	50	50	57
Pineapples, first grade	54	54	66

(cont'd overleaf)

Table 9.7 (cont'd)

	May	June	July
Pineapples, second grade	39	39	52
Oranges	350	350	-
Pomelo	200	200	400
Kangkong	29	24	29
Mustard leaves	-	-	-
Red cabbages	-	24	-
Long beans	225	225	230
Bok choy	40	43	46
Chinese cabbages	83	91	-
Tomatoes	110	110	110
Small hairy gourds	-	82	82
Spring onions	147	147	147
Lettuces	83	91	90
Bamboo shoots	43	-	62
White radishes with leaves	54	54	54
Chinese quinces	23	33	32
Bean sprouts	-	-	-
Tapioca	36	54	56
Watermelons	150	-	-
Chilli, red	564	450	-
Chilli, green	238	248	237
Chinese chives	72	86	-
Choy sum	44	53	53
Leeks	160	160	172

Prices are a fifth of market prices. The association made a total profit between September and December 1943 of $118,000.

(ii) Transport conditions

Pahang—There are collection points at Kuala Sentul, Jerantut, Kerdau, Mentekab and Kemayan. There are at present seven transport lorries, one of them small. (Five of the lorries are out of use because they have no tyres.) When all the lorries are available, and if each lorry has a maximum load, it would be possible to dispatch 60 tons per day [8.5 tons per vehicle]. In May, however, the average daily collection was 15 tons.[79] At production points, tapioca is left behind. Transport requires 1,200 gallons of petrol a month, which the association claimed; but only 1,000 gallons of petrol were rationed (surveyed in June).

Perak—There are collection points at Bagan Datuk, Teluk Anson [Teluk Intan], Bidor, Cameron, Kampar and Ipoh. There are at present 13 transport lorries, and a maximum of 60 tons [4.6 tons per vehicle] a day can be dispatched. In May, however, many of the lorries broke down, and the quantity dispatched was only 20 tons a day.[80] On average, 800 gallons of petrol are required, all of it from rations (surveyed in May).

Apart from road transport, there are no obstacles at present in either state to transporting cargoes by railway.

(iii) Storage capacity

A stockpile [in deep freeze] of 100 tons of sweet potatoes, tapioca and green vegetables existed at the end of December 1943. However, capacity is only available to freeze up to 200 tons, and storage of large amounts for extended periods is not possible now or in the future.

(iv) Future prospects

If daily collections are increased to 100 tons, a small proportion of the produce could be diverted to the local civilian market. To achieve this, all lorries would have to be repaired and new tyres supplied immediately. These possibilities are advanced with the caveat that the railways are not destroyed. But preparations for an emergency require that vegetable production on Syonan Island [become a substitute for this effort to collect enough vegetables from Pahang and Perak]. Further, any surplus farmland should be diverted to producing dried sweet potatoes and dried tapioca, which should be stored in large quantities in the Syonan uplands as soon as possible.

B. Collection by the Syonan Rationing Association, Department of Vegetables and Fruit for Civilians

On 1 May 1944 the Department of Vegetables and Fruit was set up to handle collection for local civilian consumption on Syonan Island. Table 9.8 shows the results that have been achieved for the collection of vegetables and fruit (including pineapples).

---

[79] That is somewhat less than for the two functioning lorries, 8.5 x 2 = 17.

[80] Therefore, Pahang 15 tons + Perak 20 tons = 35 tons, while a maximum of 120 tons would be possible if all the vehicles were functioning.

Table 9.8 Vegetable and fruit collection, Negeri Sembilan and Johore, 1944
(catties)

		Sweet potatoes and tapioca	Other vegetables	Fruit	Total
Early June	Johore	937,780	12,492	119,872	1,070,144
	Negeri Sembilan	79,309	-	138,520	217,829
	Total	1,017,089	12,492	258,392	1,287,973
Mid-June	Johore	994,566	9,529	79,896	1,083,991
	Negeri Sembilan	108,855	-	128,821	237,767
	Total	1,103,421	9,529	208,717	1,321,667
End June	Johore	658,563	10,701	95,521	764,785
	Negeri Sembilan	101,573	-	89,483	191,056
	Total	760,136	10,701	185,004	955,841
Early July	Johore	879,685	15,670	100,943	996,298
	Negeri Sembilan	92,615	-	127,025	219,640
	Total	972,300	15,670	227,968	1,215,938
Mid-July	Johore	975,971	6,916	102,851	1,085,738
	Negeri Sembilan	78,082	-	188,621	266,703
	Total	1,054,053	6,916	291,472	1,352,441
End July	Johore	850,567	4,137	29,604	884,308
	Negeri Sembilan	27,695	-	215,240	242,935
	Total	818,261	4,137	244,844	1,127,242

Table note: Figures are for the total amount of each item for each ten-day period. To calculate the actual rations for sweet potatoes and tapioca 3,300 catties (2,000kg) must be subtracted from the figures.[81]

A daily collection of vegetables and fruit of 147.56 tons (about 150 tons) is expected for the future.[82] The anticipated amount of collection and fixed prices are as in table 9.9.

[81] Subtracted as commission charges by the Syonan Rationing Association, as explained below. From table 9.8, 3,300 catties would make 3.3 per cent of average total 60.4 tons.

[82] At present, it is 60.4 tons.

Table 9.9 Syonan Rationing Association vegetable and banana anticipated monthly collection and fixed prices after July 1944[83]

(piculs and dollars per picul)

	Anticipated amount	Rationing Association price	Wholesale price	Retail price
Tapioca	40,796	25.00	27.50	32.00
Bananas	15,965	20.00	25.50	30.00
Sweet potatoes	11,873	36.00	39.50	45.00
Dried tapioca	5,146	46.80	51.50	60.00
Dried sweet potatoes	-	69.70	76.70	88.00
Total	73,780			

Calculation methods for these prices are as follows:

– Rationing [Association] price. Cost price at place of production + loss to Syonan Station (about 15%) + tariff and other fees (7%) + commission charged by association (2% – 5%).

– Wholesale price. Rationing [Association] price + tariff between the station and market and commission paid to loader (10%).

– Retail price. Wholesale price + retail mark-up (15%).

These prices are only a fifth of the market price. The Syonan Rationing Association, Department of Vegetables and Fruit made a loss of $77,637 in May, because it did not take into account spoilage of vegetables and because of the rise in cost prices at the points of production. The department decided to change fixed prices as below. Here, the association's commission fee was fixed at 2 per cent of the association's profit and 4 per cent of rationing cost and 2 per cent of retail prices.

[83] Data may be compared with table 9.7, for example, the Tapioca Rationing Association price of $25 per picul = 41 cents per kg.

Table 9.10 Vegetable and banana fixed prices after May 1944

(cents per catty)

	Average price in production area	Rationing Association price	Wholesale price	Retail price
Tapioca present (previous)	22.1 (19.0)	33.5 (25.0)	36.5 (27.5)	42.0 (32.0)
Sweet potatoes present (previous)	33.0 (27.5)	51.0 (36.0)	56.0 (39.5)	59.0 (43.0)
Bananas present (previous)	15.37 (14.36)	21.0 (20.0)	25.5 (25.5)	30.0 (30.0)
Dried tapioca present (previous)	40.0 (40.0)	51.0 (46.8)	56.0 (51.5)	64.0 (60.0)

Apart from these foods, durians and mangosteens are also collected.

(i) Rationing

Paperwork relating to rationing is handled by Syonan Municipality's Department of Food. The department sells vegetables and fruit collected by the Syonan Rationing Association's Department of Vegetables and Fruit to locals at markets at over 42 distribution points. At each point locals buy daily rations per person of 2 catties (1.2kg) of tapioca, 1 catty (600g) of sweet potatoes per person twice weekly, and 2 catties (1.2kg) of bananas (about six bananas) per person daily. Other rationed foods include green chillies, papaya, pineapples and spring onions. Locals buy these vegetables at retail prices set by the Department of Vegetables and Fruit. However, insufficient quantities of the foods are available, so that locals form long queues to buy from as early as 2am when the market opens between 8am and 12am.

Because prices as indicated above are set so low, the general market price of sweet potatoes and tapioca is falling.

Table 9.11 Tapioca and sweet potato market prices, April–July 1944

(dollars per catty)

	April	May	June	July
Tapioca	1.50	1.40	1.10	1.00
Sweet potatoes	2.20	2.10	1.70	1.50

Table note:
Source: Chōsabu, Malay Military Administration, 'Outline of the Retail Price of Necessities in Syonan'.

Future reductions in staple food substitute prices can be achieved by increases in supply. The prices of other vegetables and fruit may also fall in step with those of staple food substitutes. The prospect of low prices may be anticipated.

(ii) Transport

Negeri Sembilan—There are collection points at Titi, Pertang, Mantin, Lenggeng, Durian Tipus, Serting Ulu, Beranang, Peradong, Titian Bintongor and Jelebu. Collections are made at Seremban, Gemas and Bahau railway stations. At present four vehicles are used for dispatches, but they frequently break down. Thirteen other vehicles were offered by the Special Cargo Regiment [of the army] to help transport vegetables. If the lorries are in a good state of repair, food deliveries of 50 tons [that is, 3 tons per vehicle] can be expected in the future.

Johore—There are collection points at Tangkak, Muar, Kluang, Batu Pahat, Pontian, Johore Bahru and Segamat. Thirty lorries should be used for transport, but the actual dispensing fleet is 11, of which three have broken down. The shortage of lorries is thus a bottleneck. If this can be overcome, collections of 100 tons [that is, 9 tons per vehicle] can be expected in the future.[84]

[84] Therefore, Negeri Sembilan 50 tons + Johore 100 tons = total of 150 tons. At present, it is 60.4 tons.

Supplementary Material 2. Method Used to Estimate the Acreage for Sweet Potatoes, Tapioca and Other Vegetables

(1) Survey of street hawkers selling vegetables throughout the city

On 2 August, a survey of vegetable street hawkers was conducted all over the municipality. The results are set out in table 9.12.

Table 9.12 Survey of vegetable street hawkers, 2 August 1944[85]

(catties)

Total number of hawkers	2,038 (hawkers)
Total volume of vegetables sold (estimate)	111,852
Breakdown of hawker transactions:	
Sweet potatoes and tapioca	18,161
Other vegetables	79,566
Fruits	14,125

It is unknown whether these figures could be used to calculate an annual average. Since there are no reliable local data, these figures may be regarded as base data. (It is necessary to conduct periodic surveys to establish whether or not the figures are representative.)

(2) Estimated volume of vegetable sales in the municipality

Vegetables, etc., for local civilian consumption except supplies from the Syonan Rationing Association, Department of Vegetables and Fruit [i.e., imports from Negeri Sembilan and Johore], and vegetables for military supplies, are sold by street hawkers as well as at appointed markets by shop traders. Taking this distribution system into account, the transactions of street hawkers, estimated at 111,852 catties, should be regarded as 85 per cent of the total (except for fruit).[86] The total amounts traded can be estimated as in table 9.13.

85 According to Syonan Municipality Department of Security, there were 2,746 hawkers in the vegetable and fruit trade, see chapter 4. Hawkers sold a little over half a picul (32kg) per hawker per day.

86 That is, 114,973 catties as indicated in table 9.13.

Table 9.13 Estimates of vegetables sold by hawkers and shops on Syonan Island, August 1944

(catties)

Total volume of vegetables (except fruit) distributed through Syonan Island	114,973
Sweet potatoes and tapioca	21,366
Other vegetables	93,607

(3) Drainage of 20 tons from military-managed farms

The total amount distributed includes the supply of 20 tons from military-managed farms [channelled] to the local [black] market. If this supply has the same proportions of sweet potatoes, tapioca and other vegetables as was found in the survey of street hawkers, the breakdown for this 20 tons would be as follows:

Table 9.14 Estimated breakdown of daily supplied vegetables (20 tons) from military-managed farms (based on the hawker survey)

(kg)

Sweet potatoes and tapioca	3,717
Other vegetables	16,283

(4) The equation

[In order to determine how much farmland of the total of 4,260 acres[87] should be allocated to produce enough vegetables for local consumption,] The following equation can be written, where:

a kg = annual supply of tapioca and sweet potatoes per acre

x acres = acreage of land farmed for a year

b kg = annual supply of other vegetables per acre

y acres = acreage of land farmed for b

0.6 = conversion rate from catties to kg

4,260 = cultivated acreage apart from military managed farms:

ax = (21,366 x 0.6 – 3,717) x 365 =3,322,449[88]

[87] From table 9.2, 530 + 450 + 3,280 = 4,260.

[88] 9.1 tons daily; that is, estimated total trade of tapioca and sweet potatoes (21,366) from table 9.13, minus the transfer from the military (3,717) from table 9.14.

by = (93,607 x 0.6 – 16,283) x 365 = 14,556,565[89]
x + y = 4,260

Suppose that a = 2,000 and b = 5,600
x = 3,322,595 / 2,000 = 1,660 acres
y = 14,556,565 / 5,600 = 2,600 acres

This yields the results shown in table 9.15.

Table 9.15 Suggested breakdown of 4,260 acres of cultivated farmland and production of vegetables per acre

(acres and tons per acre)

	Acreage under cultivation	Annual production per acre
Sweet potatoes and tapioca	1,660	2.0
Other vegetables	2,600	5.6

(5) Estimated acreage necessary to yield sufficient crop

Data from the hawker survey show that the current daily supply of sweet potatoes and tapioca is 9.1 tons (without making allowance for drainage into the black market from the military-managed farms).[90] Production before the end of March next year of 3 tons annually per acre from 7,740 acres of newly developed farmland would yield 63.6 tons daily. However, following the policy as recommended by this report 3,000 acres should be transferred to the municipality. And if 558 acres from this 3,000 acres were allocated to sweet potatoes and tapioca (and 2,442 acres to other vegetables) and cultivated to yield 2 tons per acre annually, due to the quality of the soil[91] this would result in 3.1 tons a day and would ensure an overall total 75.8 tons of sweet potatoes and tapioca.[92] (At present it is 48 tons.)

[89] 39.9 tons daily; that is, estimated total trade of vegetables (93,607) from table 9.13, minus the transfer from the military (16,283) from table 9.14.

[90] That is, from tables 9.13 and 9.14, 21.3 x 0.6 – 3.7 = 9.1.

[91] The author uses a lower estimate for annual production per acre.

[92] That is, production from existing civilian-managed farms (9.1) plus from newly cleared land (63.6) plus farms returned by the military (3.1), 9.1 + 63.6 + 3.1 = 75.8.

(6) Acreage to be returned to the municipality

The hawker survey shows that 39.9 tons of general vegetables are supplied daily (without making allowance for drainage into the black market from the military-managed farms).[93] If the policies proposed here are followed, 2,442 acres of farmland due to be transferred from the military to the municipality should yield 6 tons per acre annually, and therefore a daily supply of 40.1 tons can be anticipated. This will result in an overall total supply of 80 tons a day.[94] (At present it is 57.5 tons.)

[93] That is, from tables 9.13 and 9.14, 93.6 x 0.6 – 16.2 = 39.9.

[94] That is, production from existing civilian-managed farms (39.9), plus farms returned by the military (40.1), 39.9 + 40.1 = 80.

CHAPTER 10

Food Problems and Cultivation of the Sweet Potato

Unknown author, c. early 1943

In the blessed climate of the Southern Regions, the only immediate measure suitable to address the food self-sufficiency problem is to cultivate sweet potatoes. This option has often been emphasized elsewhere.

It is well known that sweet potatoes have ten times the yield of rice, have a short growing period, and are relatively easy to cultivate. However, when we think about planning for mass production to achieve increased food output, it is necessary to prioritize securing the labour force and land. These issues have been difficult to address. So, it has simply been asserted in general terms that 'because sweet potatoes have a ten times higher yield than rice, their cultivation should be promoted'.

Research in our spare time has resolved the problem of cultivating sweet potatoes without the need to tackle the obstacles of labour force and land shortage. Our methods are as follows:

1. Plant sweet potato runners horizontally.
2. Use fallow fields of minimum area.

As a rule, learn to use a grab hoe to cultivate the fields by yourself.

1. We need to plant sweet potato runners not vertically but horizontally. This idea derives from the observation of leaves and roots growing from the nodes on runners at intervals of 4 or 5cm. If a half metre of sweet potato runners are planted horizontally, 2 to 5kg of sweet potatoes can be harvested after three months. (The yield will be two to five times higher than previously.) The minimum yield will be 2kg per half metre of sweet potato runners. Six runners will yield 12kg. This would be equivalent to one month's food for a person. For six runners the planting area required is 3 square metres.

2. Because 3 square metres is such a small area, one day's cultivation a month is enough even for an inexperienced amateur. An experienced professional farmer will cultivate 300 square metres per day. Cultivation on one Sunday a month will suffice. After cultivating fields of the same size once a month over four months, the first field will then be ready to [harvest and] cultivate again. So after cultivating the land four times over four months, a rotation cycle of four months is set [and it is no longer necessary to cultivate new land].[1]

   The aggregate area for four months is 12 square metres. It is not so large an area as to prevent anyone from finding this amount of fallow land at or near their homes. Those who have no access to fallow land because they live in stores or terraced houses can easily find such land just outside the cities.
3. A fallow field of 3 square metres is just 1/100 that of a professional farmer. Anyone can manage to cultivate this much land. Everyone should therefore be required to grow their own food in this way.

Medan [in Sumatra], which is a busy city, has a population of 160,000. The area required for cultivation is 117.6 acres for one month, and 470.4 acres for four months, which is only 12 per cent of the city's total area of 3,920 acres. The city surely has plenty of fallow land suitable for cultivation.

Needless to say, people who live in villages and are either public servants or farmers have ample cultivable land around their house. Even woodcutters who live deep in the mountains can easily find as small an area as 2 square metres anywhere in the locality. The method proposed not only obviates the need for labour force and land but also makes producing and consuming area identical. That saves transport. Quite literally, this is food self-sufficiency.

Since one month's yield is at least 12kg, in a year this amounts to 144kg per person. Applying this method to the whole population in the East Coast Residencies results in an annual yield of 288,000 tons, and for the whole of Sumatra 1.5 million tons yearly. Increased production on this scale will solve the food problem.

As discussed above, if sweet potatoes are the food for self-sufficiency, no one will have to buy them in the market, and the price of grains and other foods will decline. Food self-sufficiency will therefore inevitably function to readjust prices.

Because of similar climates in Sumatra, Malaya, Borneo and New Guinea, they are all appropriate for sweet potato cultivation. Adoption of this method will resolve their food problems. Everybody, including soldiers, military employees and all other Japanese—who will without doubt voluntarily serve society—and also the Chinese and Indian locals, everyone, regardless of class or occupational

[1] Sweet potatoes can be cropped continuously without fallowing.

or racial differences, is recommended to carry out this cultivation method. This is my sincere and humble wish.[2]

Finally, we turn to methods of large-scale cultivation. As indicated above, small fallow fields require cultivation only once a month. But large fields are preferably cultivated professionally and daily. Even with careful, deep cultivation, one farm labourer can work at least 30 square metres a day. Thus, each day a single labourer is able to cultivate as much as ten amateurs can, and in a month as much as 250 amateurs can (assuming that there are 25 cultivation days per month). Accordingly, a yield of 3,000kg can be estimated.[3]

Table 10.1 demonstrates that by increasing the number of full-time farmers, mass production will be achieved.

Guidelines for the horizontal cultivation of sweet potatoes:

1. Partition land into strips 1m wide and 3m long. Cultivate deeply [using a grab hoe], then form a trench on each side to a depth of 20 to 30cm. Use sandy earth to raise the centre half a metre high (like a mountain range). At the top of the centre, form a gutter 5cm deep (figure 10.1).
2. Use the runners that are available[4] two to two and a half months after a previous planting. Select and pick well-grown runners for your own seedlings [see step 7 below]. Cut the runners into 50cm lengths and plant them horizontally in the 5cm deep gutter. The mound should be 3m long for planting six runners of 50cm each (figure 10.2).
3. When seedlings are planted horizontally, the leaves should be visible on the ground. Cut the runner if it has grown over 30cm.
4. After two and a half to three months, when the colour of the leaves turns to yellow and milky liquid appears, the plants are ready to harvest. Dig up the sweet potatoes. If buds have appeared on the potatoes, harvest has been delayed too long. Since sweet potatoes enlarge 50 per cent in the last half month, be careful not to harvest too quickly.
5. Water the seedlings [once or twice a day] for one or two weeks after planting.
6. Although manuring depends on soil conditions, it is necessary to manure just once after cultivation, and only in small amounts. Use either compost manure or horse or human faeces.
7. Well-grown runners shall be cut and distributed to others by their owners after two to three months of planting [see step 2 above].

---

[2] The author of this report speaks to the reader in an elaborately modest manner.

[3] 250 x 12 = 3,000 for 750m^2 of land.

[4] Supplied by others to start with.

Table 10.1 Estimated sweet potato yields

Number of workers	Cultivation Harvest	October January	December March	February May	April July	June September	August November	Total
1	Area (m^2)	750	750	750	750	750	750	4500 [1.11 acres]
	Yield (tons)	3	3	3	3	3	3	18
10	Area (m^2)	7,500	7,500	7,500	7,500	7,500	7,500	4.5 hectares
	Yield (tons)	30	30	30	30	30	30	180
100	Area (m^2)	75,000	75,000	75,000	75,000	75,000	75,000	45
	Yield (tons)	300	300	300	300	300	300	1,800
1,000	Area (hectares)	75	75	75	75	75	75	450
	Yield (tons)	3,000	3,000	3,000	3,000	3,000	3,000	18,000
10,000	Area (hectares)	750	750	750	750	750	750	4,500
	Yield (tons)	30,000	30,000	30,000	30,000	30,000	30,000	180,000
20,000	Area (hectares)	1,500	1,500	1,500	1,500	1,500	1,500	9,000
	Yield (tons)	60,000	60,000	60,000	60,000	60,000	60,000	360,000

Notes:

1. Selection of the land, its acreage, and its planting season and frequency will be determined by taking into account the availability of workers, land, irrigation water levels in the dry season, and storage and transport facilities for sweet potatoes.
2. Assuming monthly consumption per head of 12kg, a farm worker who cultivates for 25 days in a month can harvest sweet potatoes for 250 people.
3. For a group of 1,000 residents, four workers can therefore be employed to cultivate land of 3,000 square metres, which will supply enough sweet potatoes for all [12 tons per month]. If the farm workers cultivated new land every month [for 12 months], only 3.6 hectares would be required to supply sufficient acreage for one year [and 144 tons of sweet potatoes]. Bearing in mind storage and transport, if we consider a group of 1,000 people living communally, then the appropriate amount of land should be found in the vicinity of the community.[5]

[5] Four workers per 3.6ha = 8.88 acres (0.45 workers per acre), annually 16 tons per acre (36 tons per worker). Compare these figures with the best practice farm's numbers in chapter 9: 5.1 workers per acre, annually 11 tons per acre (2 tons per worker).

8. The cultivation procedure will be the same as in step 1 above on large-scale fields. However, 50cm runners for the horizontal planting as in step 2 above should be planted in the ratio of 18,000 runners to one hectare.[6]
9. The major types of sweet potatoes sold in Medan market are shown in table 10.2.

Table 10.2 Sweet potato varieties sold in Medan market

Type[7]	Outer colour	Inner colour	Cultivation period	Harvest per hectare
Ubi Setela (Ubi Kangkong)	Red, yellow	Yellow	3 months	15 tons
Ubi Cina (Ubi Bubur)	Red	White	3	15
Ubi Padang	White	White	3	10
Ubi Kentang	White	Pale yellow	2	10
Ubi Torak (Alu Hantu)	White	White	5	18

Figure 10.1 Sweet potato ridge, depth and width

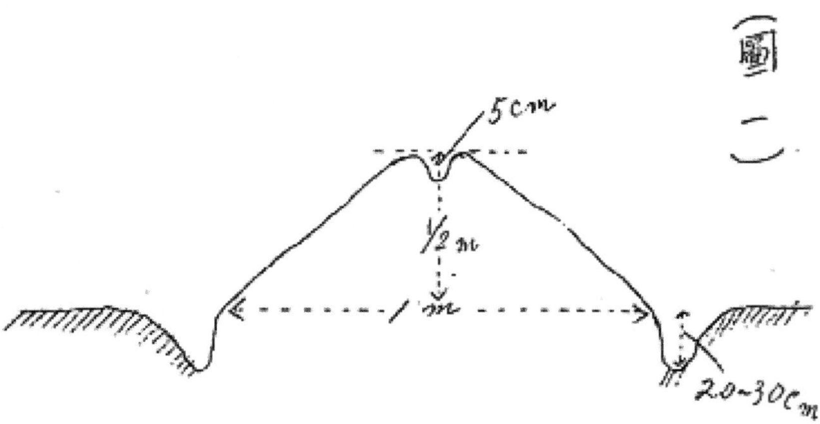

[6] Step 2 confers the ratio of 20,000 runners to one hectare.
[7] Ubi = potato or tuber in Bahasa Melayu.

Figure 10.2 Sweet potato ridge, length

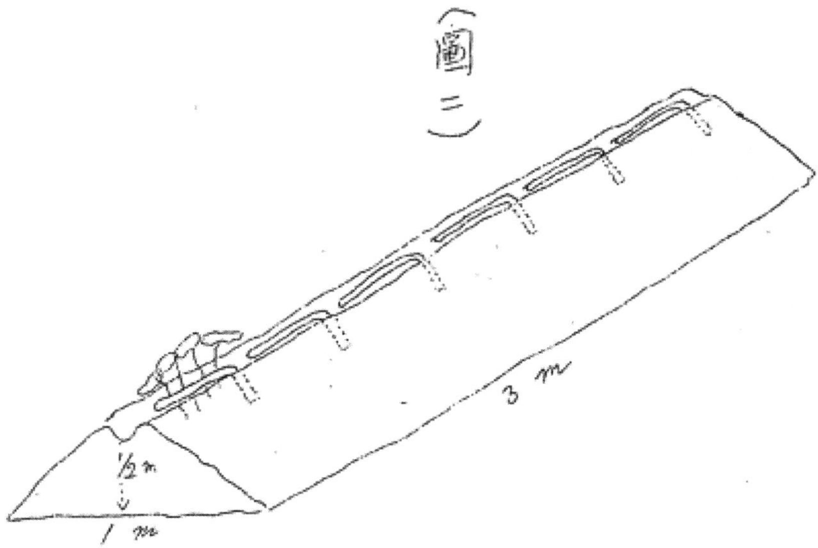

A Song Recommended for Sweet Potato Cultivation

1. In the South Sea where natural resources abound/ Who would speak of food shortage/ It is our shame, backlash of easy-going life/ Stir yourself, see the situation
2. Immediate resolution of the food problem/ No discrimination by class or race/ No distinction of occupation/ Let us plant potatoes now together
3. Fallow land only 3 meter length/ A Sunday for a month/ Plant runners horizontally/ A harvest will be 12kg
4. Literally this is food self-sufficiency/ No worry of land and labour/ Grab a hoe and use a lot/ Let us make sweet potatoes
5. No one buys potatoes, lower prices of potatoes/ This is what is called killing two birds with one stone/ Let us move on to sweet potato cultivation

CHAPTER 11

Rice Imports to Malaya, with Special Reference to Syonan Municipality

Matsu'ura Shigeharu, Surveys by Kirita Naosaku and Nagamori Masaji, September 1944

This report is based on research carried out by Matsuura Shigeharu, a civilian associate, and supported by results of a survey conducted by Kirita Naosaku and Nagamori Seiji, civilian administrators [all affiliated with the Chōsabu of Southern Military Administration]. The report is mimeographed and circulated for reference purposes.

Contents

[1] *Jōnō-mai*, levy rice. For a definition, see Appendix A.4 below. The words that were used in the report, i.e., *Jōnō-mai* and *Jiyū-mai*, were literally 'levy rice', and 'tax rice delivered to the Military Administration', and literally 'freedom rice', and 'unregulated rice'. These descriptions explain the difference between these two Japanese administrative arrangements, since if rice was unregulated or 'free' it could be sold on the open market.

(2) Membership
(3) Registered vessels
(4) Collateral goods[2]
(5) Import channels

4. Rice Imports by the Nami Kikan[3]

5. Conclusion

Appendices

A.1 The Rules of the Syonan Rice Import Association

A.2 Syonan Rice Import Association Business Regulations

A.3 Implementation Guidelines for Desirably Obtained Rice Transport Cooperation for Syonan

A.4 Tei Kan San[4] No. 614: Implementation Guidelines for the Use of Motorsailers and Junks to Transport Thai Rice and Java Salt and Sugar

A.5 Total Rice Imports of the Syonan Rice Import Association

[2] Collateral goods, sometimes also called exchange goods, were consumer goods and manufactured materials that, in the Southeast Asian wartime environment of extreme shortages and high inflation, were often necessary items to be able to sell in exchange for food, especially rice. Principal collateral goods included items of clothing, rubber oil, matches, soap and other daily necessities.

[3] The Nami Kikan was a military intelligence unit set up in late 1943 after the Allied bombing of Seletar Port; see chapter 2, section on 'Asking Overseas Chinese Businesses for Help'.

[4] Tei Kan San is an abbreviation for Malayan (Tei = code name) Military Administration (Gunsei Kanbu) Department of Industry (Sangyō-bu) Directive.

1. Estimate of Surplus Thai Rice Available for Export

Because Malayan rice imports are drawn mainly from Thailand, it is necessary first to consider available surpluses. Before the war, annual rice production in Burma was 7 million tons and local consumption 3 million tons. The exportable surplus was thus 4 million tons. Since the beginning of the Burma Operation, rice production is said to have declined to a quarter of its former level. There is now a very small rice surplus, and export to Malaya is difficult. Surplus rice in Indochina available for export is estimated to be between 1 million and 1.2 million tons, and in Java 100,000 tons. Exportable rice in Thailand has been put at 1 million tons. This point is now discussed.

(1) Estimated Thai rice production between December 1943 and November 1944

Table 11.1 shows the amount of padi produced in recent years. (Data for 1931/32–1940/41 are derived from the Thai census and for 1941/42–1942/43 from a Mitsubishi estimate.[5])

Table 11.1 Thailand padi production, 1931/32–1942/43

(000 piculs)

1931/32	Water shortage, below average crop	67,829
1932/33	Good harvest	85,273
1933/34	Good harvest	83,462
1934/35	Average crop	76,630
1935/36	Average crop	78,783
1936/37	Drought, bad harvest	56,331
1937/38	Average crop	75,928
1938/39	Excessive water, below average crop	75,394
1939/40	Average crop	76,607
1940/41	Average crop	82,056
1941/42	Water shortage, below average crop	78,200
1942/43	Flood, bad harvest	63,470
1943/44*	Water shortage, below average crop	74,450

Note: * Estimate for this year [1943–44] (old Thai territory [not including Perlis, Kedah, Kelantan, Terengganu]).

[5] From May 1940 Mitsubishi Shōji Corporation was commissioned to deal with the Thai rice trade by the Thai government.

The estimate in table 11.1 for rice production over the fiscal year 1943–44 is calculated taking into account the following considerations:

(i) Floods in the last fiscal year (which made farmers anxious and led to problems in seed padi supply and the fertilization of farmland)

(ii) Government encouragement to convert rice land to other uses (for example, to produce textiles, food and military necessities)

(iii) The weather in the current fiscal year (a delayed rainy season, a little less than usual rainfall)

Newly acquired territory (including the four Malay states and Shan states) contribute 3.4 million piculs to estimated padi production in this fiscal year of 77.85 million piculs.

(2) Estimate of the quantity of rice available for export

Estimates of the quantity of rice available for export in the present fiscal year must take into account the following considerations:

(i) The quantity of rice carried over from the previous fiscal year

(ii) Domestic consumption and the surplus available in the present fiscal year

(iii) Methods and costs of domestic transport

(iv) Availability of warehouses and coolies in Bangkok

(v) Availability of materials for rice-milling facilities

(vi) Gunnies [jute bags] or other substitute bags for packaging

Transporting rice to Bangkok is difficult by both land and sea, because of developing shortages in railway transport and rising maritime costs as a result of shortages of fuel, lubricating oil, fittings and labour. There is limited warehouse capacity in Bangkok, making it difficult to store large amounts of rice at any one time. The availability of coolies and vessels is decreasing, while there are extremely limited supplies of magnesium oxide, cement and emery for rice milling. Furthermore, too few gunnies are produced and imported. Bearing all this in mind, tables 11.2 and 11.3 show that rice available for export can, in terms of white rice, with reasonable confidence be estimated as 900,000 tons.

Note: Zones 1 and 2 are located on the plains between the Menam, Tha Chin, Mae Klong and Bang Pakong Rivers around Bangkok and in the central plain of Thailand and are the country's rice granary. All the padi and some white rice are brought to Bangkok in vessels known as 'padi boats' and transported along a far-reaching network of creeks (klongs) that connect the rivers above.

Table 11.2 Thailand rice surplus, 1943–44

Output in 1943/44 (000 piculs)	As seeds for next year (000 piculs)	As food for local people (000 piculs)	Balance (000 piculs)		Estimated in padi (000 tons)	Estimated in white rice (000 tons)
77,850	4,700	46,000	27,150		1,642	1,100
Carried over from fiscal year 1942–43				Scattered in various parts of Thailand (difficult to send to Bangkok)	580	390
				Bangkok and its surrounding areas	230	150
Total 2,452						1,640

Estimates based on data relating to Mitsubishi Shōji Corporation's Bangkok branch.

Note: Unexportable surplus rice due to increasing difficulties in domestic transport is also included.

Table 11.3 Thailand exportable surplus rice in 1943–44

(000 tons)

Exportable surplus in/around Bangkok	Padi	White rice
Zone 1 and 2 (by padi boats):	1,020	
Other regions (excl. Southern Thailand):	70	
Total:	1,090	730
Carried over from last year[6]		150
Total		880
Exportable rice from Southern Thailand		20
Thailand total exportable rice		900

Estimates based on data relating to Mitsubishi Shōji Corporation's Bangkok branch.

Two hundred thousand to 300,000 tons of Thai rice is thus available for export to Japan this fiscal year. One hundred and fifty thousand tons of rice are to be shipped to China. The total amount of Thai rice to be procured this fiscal

[6] 'Carried over from last year … 150 (000 tons)' corresponds to 'Carried over from fiscal year 1942–43, Bangkok and its surrounding areas, estimated in white rice … 150 (000 tons)' in table 11.2.

year should be set at 680,000 to 780,000 tons, including rice for consumption by the military stationed in Malaya. When Councillor Niino [Katsumi] and Mr. Wanit [Pananon] met at the beginning of last October, Mr. Wanit said that exportable rice available to Japan this fiscal year would be between 800,000 and 1 million tons.

2. Imports of Levy Rice

This study does not consider all of the rice controlled by the military but only considers the rice intended for civilian consumption.

(1) Three channels for rice imports

Since its appointment in November 1942, Mitsubishi Shōji Corporation has been in charge of levy rice imported by the Military Administration, paid for by Special Yen under the Japan-Thai Agreement, which follows the Plan for Exchange of Goods.[7] However, the current general shortage of rice must be approached in the context of the present deterioration in maritime and overland transport; it also should be viewed as a temporary phase until food self-sufficiency schemes become operational. Rice shortages are especially severe in Syonan Municipality. The Syonan Rice Import Association was established on 16 May 1944 to address this problem, based on the framework of 'Private Vessels B' (note 1) in 'Implementation Guideline for the Use of Motorsailers and Junks to Transport Thai Rice and Java Salt and Sugar' (Tei Kan San No. 614), and took charge of imports of levy rice. On the same day, 16 May 1944, the intelligence unit, known as the Nami Kikan of the Seventh Area Army, informed the association that it would also begin commercial activity and make unregulated purchases in Southern Thailand[8] for import. In this way, three channels for rice imports were established (see note 2).

---

[7] Busshi Kōryū Keikaku, plan of imports and exports within the Greater East Asia Co-prosperity Sphere; see chapter 8. The Military Administration depended on the monopoly supplier Mitsubishi Shōji Corporation for public distribution. Special Yen were paper credits to the Bank of Siam given in exchange for Thai baht. The latter could be used to purchase goods in Thailand, but Special Yen could not be spent in Japan or used to pay for imports from it.

[8] That is, without official assignment.

Note 1:
See appendix 4, Tei Kan San No. 614: Implementation Guidelines for the Use of Motorsailers and Junks to Transport Thai Rice and Java Salt and Sugar, for the definition of 'Private Vessels B'.[9]

Note 2:
The cooperative relationship between the Nami Kikan and the Syonan Rice Import Association has been an outstanding matter; however, since 6 August this year, all rice sales have been transferred to the Syonan Rice Import Association (see Appendix A.5).

On 20 June the merger of 13 major rice traders into four corporations [*kong-si*] established the Penang Rice Import Public Bureau[10] to provide leadership as the liaising and controlling organization. The Public Bureau took over the import of levy and unregulated rice.[11] Up to the end of August, the Public Bureau had imported about 60,000 piculs of unregulated rice. Apart from the use of the rice for rations in Penang State, arrangements for the sale of rice are described below.

Tei Kan San No. 401 (17 August 1944) 'Implementation Guidelines for the Purchase and Sale of Imported Rice by Private Vessels' stipulates that rice (special rice) imported by the Syonan Rice Import Association, Penang Rice Import Public Bureau, and other private vessels appointed by the Military Administration should partly be distributed to each state [other than Syonan and Penang] through traders appointed by the Military Administration (Appointed Traders), who buy it from private vessels.

---

[9] However, such a clear-cut definition of 'Private Vessels of Category B' in opposition to 'Category A' as in Tei Kan San No. 614 (issue date unknown, but probably issued sometime in September 1944, immediately before this current chapter was published in October as Report No. 51) and detailed procedures for imports were not prescribed ex ante, but ex post facto as a product of a compromise between the official line (A) and the Chōsabu's recommendation (B). It is probable that Import Association vessels were engaged in uncontrolled rice imports from the start of the association's business on 16 May 1944 until the issue of Tei Kan San No. 401 on 17 August 1944; see below.

[10] *Kong-kiok*, administrative bureau run voluntarily by the local elites.

[11] The Penang Rice Import Public Bureau was established by the young elites of Penang who gathered around the Eppōsho (reading room). Akashi Yōji explains that the Eppōsho cooperated with the Nami Kikan and imported unregulated Thai rice from Bangkok through Singgora to Penang using junks. Akashi Yōji, ed., Nanpōgun Gunsei Sōkanbu Chōsabu, Malai Gunsei Kanbu Chōsabu Hōkokusho [Research Reports by the Southern Military Administration Chōsabu and the Malaya Military Administration Chōsabu], 1943–1945, Vol. 1 (Tokyo: Ryūkei Shosha, 2006).

On the same day, 17 August 1944, the directive 'Implementation Guidelines for Rationing the First Round of Special Rice', Tei Kan San No. 402, was published, governing the purchase and sale of white and dehydrated rice by the Penang Rice Import Public Bureau. For information on the Penang Rice Import Public Bureau, a separate report will be written.[12]

Apart from this, uncontrolled rice (rice purchased from Southern Thailand, Kedah State and other locations) was purchased and imported freely by overseas Chinese traders, acting on permission gained from each state council, until the prohibition on 20 March this year [1944] of those imports. It is estimated, on the basis of annual imports in fiscal year 1943, that a total of 16,500 tons of rice, valued at $12,469,409, came from Thailand to Malaya—including the four states of Kedah, Perlis, Kelantan and Terengganu—as uncontrolled rice. Thailand accounted for 14,940 tons (90.5 per cent) of these imports, at a cost of $10,936,691 (87.7 per cent of the total). This indicates the high dependence on Thai rice.

(2) Channels for levy rice imports

Mitsubishi Shōji Corporation's rice imports were initially planned to proceed in the following order of procedure. The Malayan Military Administration was to first submit plans for the import scheme [from the point of view of demand] to the Logistics Unit, the Shipping Unit and the Railway Unit through the Seventh Area Army's Department of Agriculture and Forestry. Then, taking into account the situation in Thailand, Indochina and Burma, they were to make plans to allocate transport such as marine and railway resources. In reality, however, the procedure was the opposite of this. The first consideration was available transport, after which the Military Administration was informed of arrangements [from the point of view of supply]. Railways have been the main form of transport to the peninsular states, and marine transport by the main ships[13] (2,000–8,000 tons) has been used for Syonan.

Imports from November 1942 to July 1944 from rice-exporting countries are given in Table 11.4.

[12] If this report—no. 84—was ever written, it now appears to be missing. See chapter 2, appendix A.2.

[13] Japanese flag-flying cargo vessels in military employ.

Table 11.4 Syonan sources of rice imports, November 1942–July 1944

(tons)

Thailand (including Kedah)	193,678
Burma	180,023
Java	28,421
Saigon	42,162
Total	444,284

Thailand is the largest source of rice imports. Falling rice production in Burma and transport difficulties have led to lower rice imports from Burma, which have been replaced by imports from Thailand. Additionally, the shortfall in rice from Burma, and the intervals between imports from Thailand, have been filled by rice imported from Java, Saigon and Kedah, responding to emerging circumstances (see figure 11.1). Measures to promote self-sufficiency and shortages of transport capacity have since April [1944] reduced the initial monthly import of over 40,000 tons [planned for August–November 1942] shown in table 11.5 to 10,500 tons. Marine transport [by the main ships] is still the principal mode of rice transport; railways do not carry very large amounts of rice. Junks are used to make up for the shortage of vessels (see figure 11.2[i]). Figure 11.2 (ii) charts the different types of transport used to carry rice to Syonan. There are three different categories of vessel: the main ships (2,000–8,000 tons), Thai Navigation Company ships (150–500 tons) and motorsailers.

As shown in the recent reports on rice transport channels, monthly imports vary according to circumstances (see figure 11.3 and tables 11.6 and 11.7). Over the last four months, most imports to Syonan were by the main ships. More rice was imported from Saigon than from Thailand (see figure 11.2[ii]).

Thai rice reached Selangor and Negeri Sembilan mainly by rail; Perak's rice deliveries were chiefly from Burma, via Khao Fa Chi (where vessels offloaded to lorries), and Thai rice was transported by rail. The rice for Penang was carried from Burma in junks and the main ships, using an interchange between vessels and lorries at Khao Fa Chi, and also by motorsailers. Penang also receives rice from Kedah by rail. Johore, Malacca and Pahang receive rice forwarded from Syonan (see table 11.7). (Khao Fa Chi is a seaport located on the west coast of the Kra Isthmus. It connects via a 90km branch line to Chumphon on the East Coast Line, to Burma along the northwest coast [see figure 11.3].)

Figure 11.1 Monthly rice imports by country of origin, January 1943–July 1944

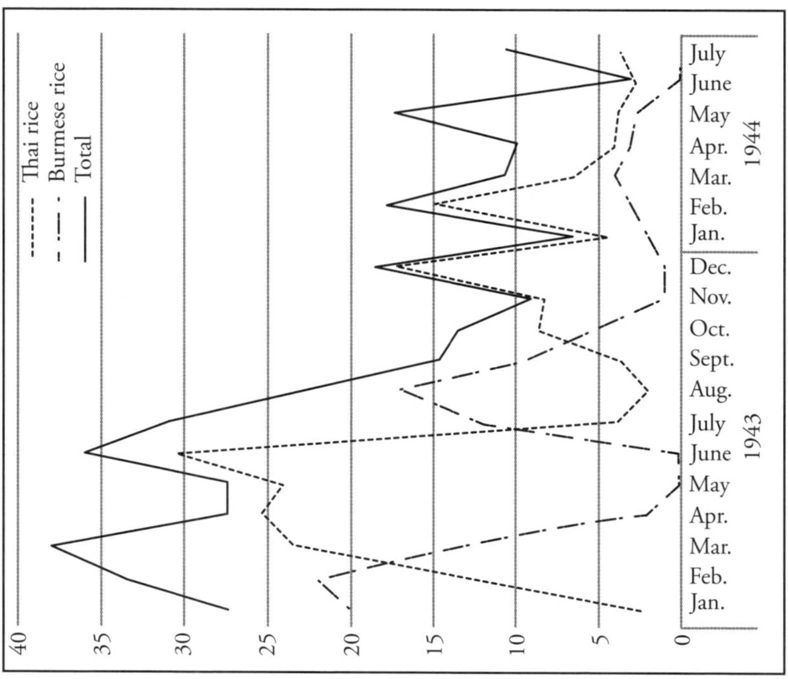

Figure 11.2 (i) Monthly rice imports by transportation means, January 1943–July 1944

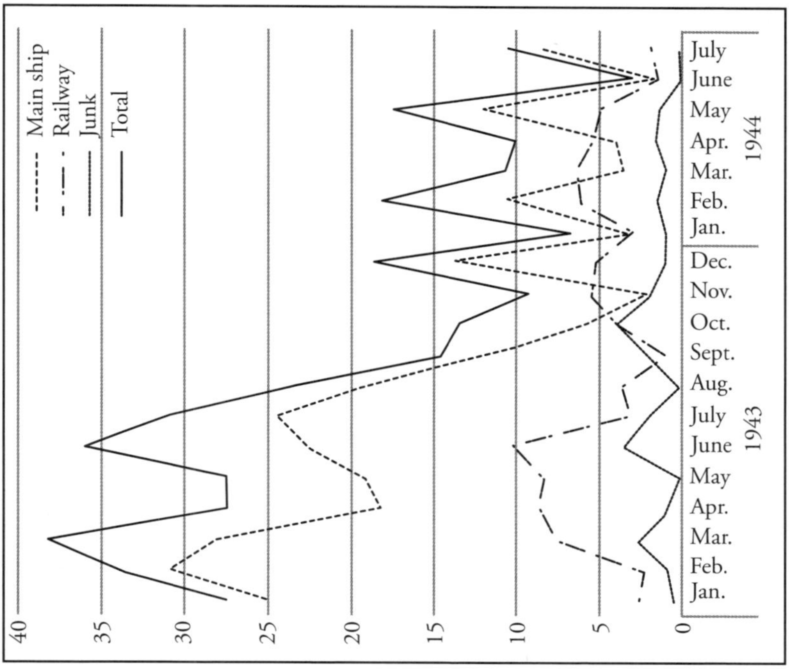

Figure 11.2 (ii) Classification of rice unloaded at Syonan, April–July 1944

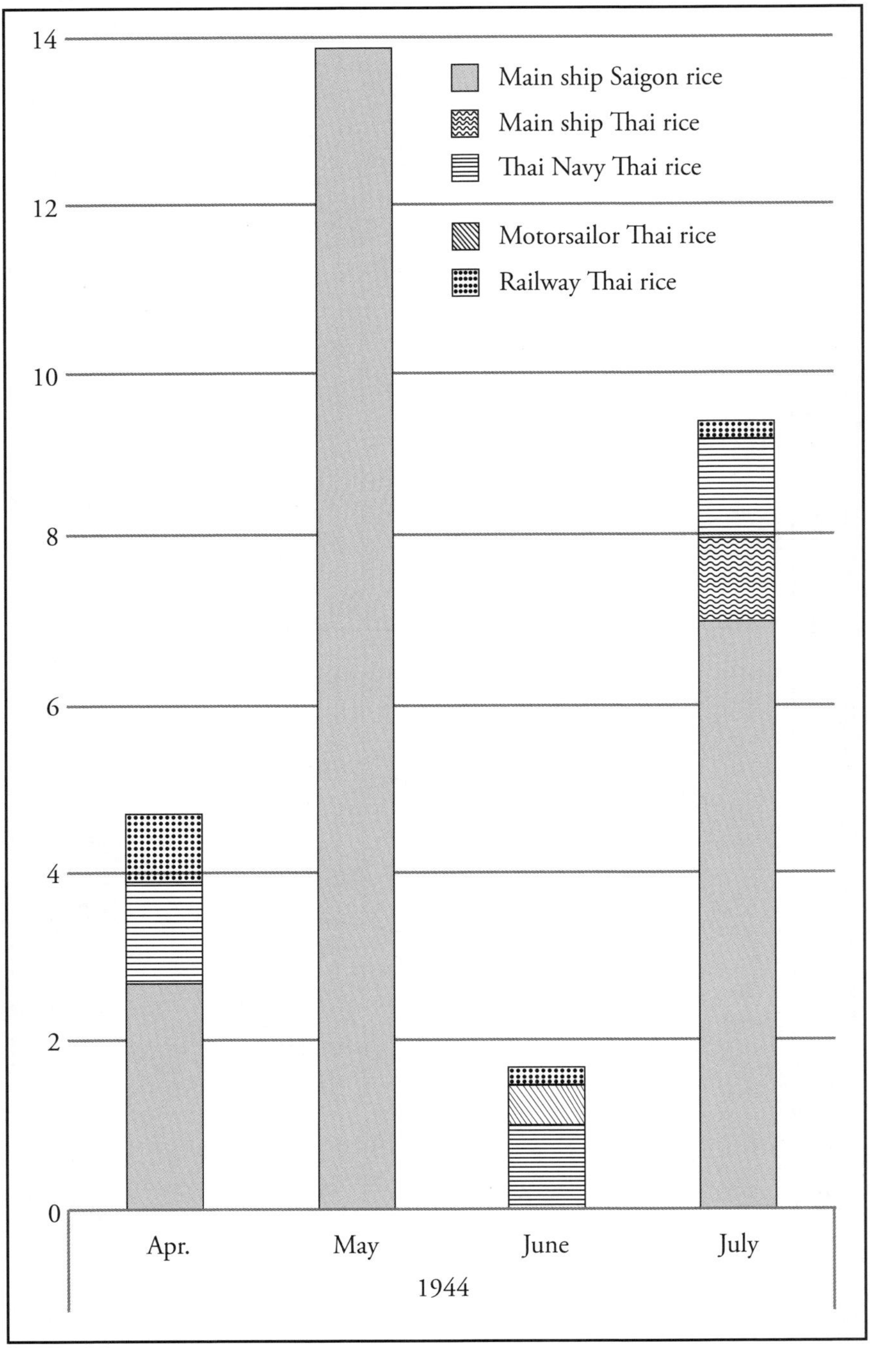

Figure 11.3 Railway network map

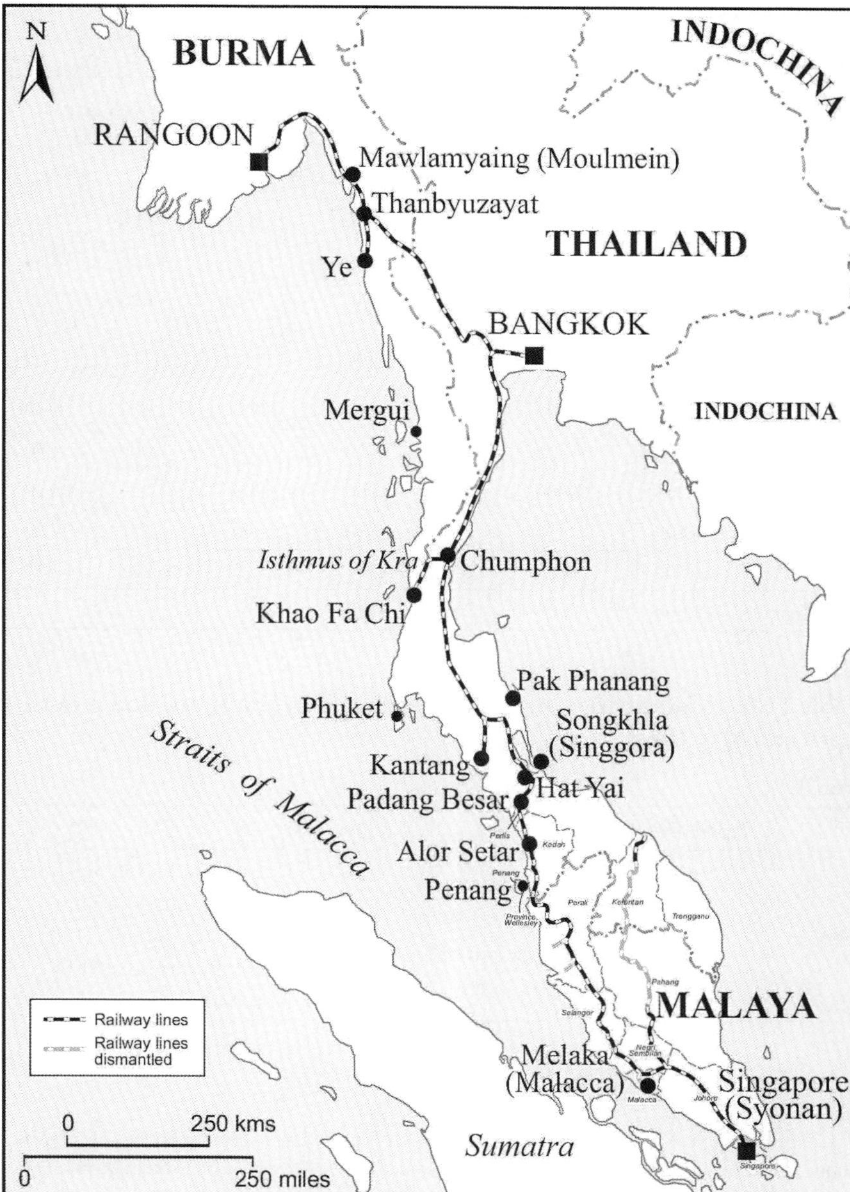

Table 11.5 Monthly rice quota supplied by Mitsubishi Shōji Corporation to Malayan states, August 1942–April 1944[14]

(tons)

	August–November 1942	December–March 1943	April–May 1943	June–September 1943	October–January 1943/44	February–March 1944	April–[July] 1944
Syonan	11,000	10,500	9,000	7,600	5,500	4,400	5,000
Johore	7,000	4,500	3,700	2,700	1,420	5,136	1,050
Malacca	2,000	1,800	1,400	950	780	624	560
Negeri Sembilan	2,000	1,800	1,400	900	630	504	300
Selangor	8,000	6,000	4,800	3,500	2,040	1,687	1,430
Perak	7,000	4,800	4,000	3,400	2,500	2,000	850
Penang	3,000	2,800	1,800	2,000	1,900	1,520	1,220
Pahang	1,500	800	750	650	440	352	90
Total	41,500	33,000	26,850	21,700	15,210	16,223	10,500
Terengganu	2,500	1,000	752	180			

Table 11.6 Monthly rice imports by states and by transportation means, April and May 1944[15]

(tons)

	April 1944		May 1944	
Syonan	(4,174) 4,174	(Saigon rice 2,587 by main ship; Thai rice 970 by Thai Navigation, 617 by rail)	(13,924) 13,924	(Saigon rice 11,150 by main ship; Thai rice 510 by Thai Navigation, 2,113 by rail; Burma rice 151 by motorsailer)

[14] Chapter 7, table A.7.4 shows the same figures for August 1942–February 1944 on monthly quota allocations for Syonan Municipality. The actual amounts received by Syonan Municipality were smaller than those quotas. For other states, chapter 8, table A.8.1 and chapter 7, table A.7.7 show the monthly quotas allocated for March 1943 and 1944. These figures are slightly different, but the overall variation and long-term decline in quota allocations can be noted.

[15] Although it is not clear from this table, the text indicates that Johore, Malacca and Pahang received rice forwarded from Syonan (or from its previous stock) and Negeri Sembilan may have received rice forwarded from Selangor.

Table 11.6 (cont'd)

	April 1944		May 1944	
Johore	(0) 181	[Forwarded from Syonan]	(605) 949	(Thai rice by rail)
Malacca	(0) 285	[Forwarded from Syonan]	(0) 777	[Forwarded from Syonan]
Negeri Sembilan	(0) 85	[Forwarded from Selangor]	(0) 571	[Forwarded from Selangor]
Selangor	(2,599) 2,599	(Thai rice by rail)	(583) 0	(Thai rice by rail)
Perak	(1,405) 1,405	(Burma rice by junk boats connecting to lorries via Khao Fa Chi)	(828) 828	(Burma rice by junk boats connecting to lorries via Khao Fa Chi)
Penang	(1,975) 1,975	(Burma rice 1,143 junk boat, 332 by main ship; Kedah rice 500 by rail)	(1,645) 1,645	(Burma rice 940 by junk boat, 506 by junk boats connecting to lorries via Khao Fa Chi, 199 by motorsailer)
Pahang	(0) 38	[Forwarded from Syonan]	(0) 90	[Forwarded from Syonan]
Total	(10,153) 10,942		(17,585) 19,367	

Note: The brackets above show [the amount] unloaded [in the states or municipality where the rice imports were first unloaded]; the figures below show the amount of rice received in each state and municipality.

Table 11.7 Monthly rice imports by states and by transportation means, June and July 1944

(tons)

	June 1944		July 1944	
Syonan	1,370	(Thai rice 970 by Thai Navigation, 390 by motorsailer, 10 by rail)	8802	(Saigon rice 6,338; Thai rice 880 by main ship, 1,500 by Thai Navigation, 84 by rail)
Johore	738	(By rail from Syonan)	817	(By rail from Syonan)
Malacca	552	(By rail from Syonan)	751	(By rail from Syonan)
Negeri Sembilan	1,271	(Thai rice by rail)	0	

(cont'd overleaf)

Table 11.7 (cont'd)

	June 1944		July 1944	
Selangor	-10	(Transferred to Syonan)	148	(Thai rice by rail)
Perak	257	(Thai rice 202 and Burma rice 55 by rail)	0	
Penang	128	(Burma rice 121 by motorsailer and 7 by rail)	1,660	(Thai rice by rail)
Pahang	92	(By rail from Syonan)	0	

(3) Conflict between levy and unregulated rice imports

Levy rice unloaded at Malayan ports and designated stations is priced at $12.13 per 100kg for white rice and $9.685 for crushed rice. This is the f.o.b. price at ports and stations. Mitsubishi obtains rice at this price and distributes it as rations to the Food Supply Office[16] and associations of wholesale traders in each state. At this point prices increase to $14 for white rice and $11.50 for crushed rice. This sets a reference price for rationed rice of 10 cents per catty,[17] which is very low compared to black market prices for unregulated rice. Rice collections are therefore frequently disrupted because buyers made unregulated purchases. In particular, there were frequent activities to import uncontrolled rice from Southern Thailand and Kedah.[18] Because of these smuggled imports it became difficult for both the military and the local population to import rice from Kedah to Malaya. That was the reason for the sudden announcement on 20 March this year of the prohibition on the import of unregulated rice. The prohibition order was so sudden that the Department of Commerce and Industry had to issue permits to traders who still wished to import rice. The details of the prohibition order were as follows:

(i) Rice in traders' warehouses bought before 20 March could be sold as usual.

(ii) Rice stored in junks in port was not to be moved, pending further instructions.

(iii) Rice still in transit at sea was to be treated as (ii) on reaching the next port of call or Syonan.

In response to the prohibition, traders who were transporting rice to Syonan moved junks with stores of rice to nearby islands and sold the rice or hid the

[16] Shokuryō Kanri Sho was a bureau formed by the merger of the Syonan Rice and Padi Distributing Association and separate associations for salt, sugar and other grains in July 1943.

[17] That is, $16 per 100kg; the price of rationed rice was meant to be two thirds that of the unregulated price. Syonan retails prices. Ration prices can vary in each state.

[18] In other words, rice smuggled into Syonan and sold on the unregulated market.

junks there. Although the price of rice in Alor Setar has declined, in Syonan rice shortages and other influences and speculations led to a black market price of $1,800 per 100kg ($1,090 per picul [60kg]). This caused public anxiety. Consideration was given to purchasing confiscated rice at the official price, but it was instead decided to buy rice at $100 per picul. The Military Administration provided collateral goods to traders to allow them to make good their losses as quickly as possible. At the same time, a rice collection company was set up in Alor Setar, backed by Mitsubishi, Taitaku [the Taiwan Development Company], Totaku [the Oriental Development Company] and Daimaru Co.[19] The estimate of 45,000 tons annually of surplus rice in Kedah State is divided into 10,000 tons for military use and 35,000 tons for civilian rations. The company applies a purchasing price of $27 per 100kg of white rice ($16.33 per picul) and $10 per 100kg of padi. (Padi is bought for $13 per picul in the Malay states, which includes a subsidy of $2–4.) The price of $200 per picul of rice charged in Alor Setar's black market is certainly very high. Clearly, therefore, it is not easy to control how rice is collected.

One reason underlying the prohibition of the import of unregulated rice was the sharp increase in dollars sent to Alor Setar from Malaya. This January $3 million were remitted, and in March the amount peaked at $14 million. This produced a ratio of black market dollar prices of $100 to 33 baht.[20] The estimates are set out in table 11.8. Although the ratio improved slightly in April, it again widened in May and June, because the purchase of unregulated rice began again in Southern Thailand. In August the ratio was down to 28 baht. Since early March, money transfers to Southern Thailand have been limited to a monthly allowance of $1,000 per person. But the transfer of bullion is still permitted. This is indicated in table 11.9, which shows remittances of exchange to Alor Setar from Kuala Lumpur and Ipoh.

Table 11.8 Alor Setar black market price of baht per $100, 1944

Month	Maximum	Minimum
January	50	-
February	50	40
March	50	33

(cont'd overleaf)

[19] These companies also owned large rice mills in Kedah, Perlis, Perak and Penang that could produce 20–60 tons of white rice daily; National Archives, Kew, WO203/4499, 'Rice SEAC Territories', p. 13.

[20] The official exchange rate determined by Japan at the outset of occupation was that one Straits dollar equated one Thai baht and was equal to a yen.

Table 11.8 (cont'd)

Month	Maximum	Minimum
April	50	40
May	40	35
June	35	31*

Note: * Rate for 6 June 1944.

Table 11.9 Remitted payments for rice from Kuala Lumpur and Ipoh to Alor Setar, 1944

Remitted payments for rice, dollars			% of all remittance	% of all turnover
From Kuala Lumpur	January	412,652	83.87	72.73
	February	2,411,117	98.80	93.94
	March	190,000	85.31	28.00
From Ipoh	January	133,140	55.49	48.00
	February	236,500	49.97	41.86
	March	45,000	71.77	26.67
Remitted payments, dollars				
From Syonan	January	2,148,356	Remittances for rice imports are estimated to be 50% of these totals.	
	February	4,744,608		
	March	1,366,431		

Note: Survey conducted by Yokohama Specie Bank.

As already indicated, prohibiting the uncontrolled import of rice slightly pushed down the black market price, which had been over $200 per picul in Kedah State. Prices rose above $200 again in June and July. Rice collections were also unsuccessful. Even in the March to June trading season, collections were poor.

Table 11.10 Kedah State rice collections, 1944

(1 sack = 100kg)

January	2,634
February	18,319
March	21,589
April	16,149
May	12,449

3. Rice Imports by the Syonan Rice Import Association

(1) Preparations to set up the association

The prohibition on the import of unregulated rice has made the rice shortage more acute, with no prospect of future improvement, which has caused the local civilian population to become anxious. The plan to import Thai rice [through alternative channels] to deal with this problem was starting to be implemented when a preparatory committee for the Syonan Rice Import Association was set up on 13 April. The committee held meetings at the Syonan Municipality hall with government officials and local rice traders and wholesalers with strong connections to the Thai trade. Discussion took place on the import of surplus levy rice paid for with Special Yen and still stored in Thailand.

In the summary of the minutes, the overseas Chinese traders felt that transport should be by junk and railway from Bangkok to the transfer point in Southern Thailand. However, a transport agreement with the Thai[21] is in force that does not permit this suggested use of the railway but allows the use of Thai junks.

Detailed arrangements for transport were to be settled after conditions in Thailand were surveyed. The survey was to be carried out by the branch liaison office in Southern Thailand [at Singgora], which was set up when the association was established. The government officials promised to consider how to provide collateral goods to use as payment for the charter of junks between Bangkok and Southern Thailand, and agreement was reached so that traders' profits were set at 30 per cent of total transport costs. To begin with, the feasible amount of rice to be transported in the first month was set as 10,000 bags (1 bag = 100 catties), which was to be increased to 20,000 to 30,000 bags from the second month (30,000 bags = about 1,800 tons). The authorities [i.e., the high officials of the Military Administration] declared that imported rice should be rationed as Special [Heavy-duty] Rations to local citizens employed in building war capacity or in construction, and to avoid diverting excessive rations to people who were voluntarily unemployed.[22] With mayoral approval, the association was officially established on 16 May and its inaugural meeting held on 27 May.

(2) Membership

The association began with 162 members. By the end of July the number had increased to 181, of whom 115 were Hokkien, 47 Teochew, 7 Cantonese, 2

[21] Reference here to 'the Thai side' refers to the decision makers in Bangkok, including Wanit Pananon, Ban Hong & Co. and Fujishima Ken'ichi.

[22] Literally, those who 'idle their time away'. Apparently, the Chōsabu authors and Syonan Municipality did not agree with this suggestion and decided to distribute the imported rice to all citizens. See note for (5) Import channels.

Hainanese, 1 Shanghainese, 7 Indian and 2 Malay. For details of the board members, see table 11.11. The two major groups of Syonan traders are Teochew and Hokkien. We can see that the board membership was drawn particularly from these two groups while maintaining the power balance between the two. The two groups [Teochew and Hokkien] have individual characteristics as sketched in the note following table 11.11.

Table 11.11 List of board members of the Syonan Rice Import Association

Principal President of the Association:

Tan Guan Lee Limited Company 陳元利有限公司 Tan Keng Kow (T) 陳肯構（潮）

Vice Presidents of the Association:

Tong Yah Trading Company 東營貿易商行 Ng Khian Teck (H) 黃建德（福）

Chng Kee Chiang 曾啓昌 Chng Kee Chiang (H) 曾啓昌（福）

Finance Directors:

Tai Seng Company 大成公司 Chew Kee Din (H) 周起鎮（福）

Loong Hin 隆興 Law Kong Peng (T) 盧光平

Managing Directors (General Department):

Lee Sit Tong (C) 李実東（広）

Kim Leng Thye 金龍泰 Chng Chi Sang (H) 曾智生（福）

Directors:

Khian Guan Malay Limited Company 建源馬来有限公司 Lim Liat Boon (H) 林烈文（福）

Nam Yang Trading Limited Company 南洋貿易有限公司 Tan Sun Ye (H) 陳三餘（福）

Ik Chng Chin Chan Kee 億中桟振記 Lee Kan Bin (T) 李幹民（潮）

Tan Soon Seng 陳順成 Tan Yun Siang (T) 陳雲翔（潮）

Sin Eik Bee 新益美 Koh Dun Kow (H) 高敦厚（福）

Thong Ah 通亜 Sim Beng Tee (H) 沈明池（福）

Chuan Hin Company 泉興公司 Teo Tat Kim (H) 張達金（福）

Auditors:

Sin Hiap Hoe Company 新協和公司 Tan Hock Sin (H) 陳福星（福）

Khiaw Thong Hung 僑通行 Lim Chiu Chan (H) 林樹産（福）

Table 11.11 (cont'd)

Advisers:
Malayan Maritime Navigation Association 馬来海運組合
Mitsubishi Shōji Corporation 三菱商事株式会社
Syonan Goods and Material Rationing Association 昭南物資配給組合
Syonan Overseas Chinese Commerce Association 昭南華僑商業組合
Indian Commerce Association 印度商業組合
President of the Overseas Chinese Society 華僑協会会長 Lim Boon Keng (H) 林文慶（福）
Vice President of the Overseas Chinese Society 華僑協会副会長 Wong Siew Qui [better known as 'SQ Wong'] (C) 黄兆桂（広）
Director of the Overseas Chinese Society 華僑協会理事 Lim Khian Beng (T) 林建明（潮）
President of Su Hai Tong Bank 四海通銀行総理 Lee Wee Nam (T) 李偉南 （潮）
Manager of Chia Hin Hung 正興行支配人 Khomei Ye 何茗余
Malayan 馬来人 Nash Arif 那査阿利夫

Note: (T) Teochew; (H) Hokkien; (C) Cantonese

Teochew: Before the war this group had influence over the Thai trade and held assets, but now they assume the stance of onlookers. They are unwilling to act publicly and are not actively engaged in this Thai rice trade.

Hokkien: Before the war this group were only second- or third-grade traders in the Thai trade. Since the outbreak of war, they have hoped to get rich quickly and have made aggressive advances in this risky sector, many of them successfully.

(3) Registered vessels

There were 138 registered vessels at the end of July with a total tonnage of 4,533.88 tons. Small vessels are in the 5-ton class and large vessels in the 100-ton class. The number of vessels by registered port is shown in table 11.12.[23]

Table 11.12 Number of vessels by registered port, July 1944

Syonan	76
Penang	13

(cont'd overleaf)

[23] Apparently these vessels were wooden boats.

Table 11.12 (cont'd)

Terengganu	9
Perak	6
Johore	5
Sumatra	2
Thailand	2
Lombok	2
Jakarta	2
Other	1

For the moment the monthly load has been set at a target of 3,000 tons, with the following transport plan. The east coast route along the Malay Peninsula will be used from the period after the monsoon season from April to September. A return journey will take 40 days, with transfers at the Port of Singgora [Songkhla]. For the first round of transport between Syonan and Singgora, the boats set off from Syonan on 27 March. (The west coast route during the monsoon season [November to March] has not yet been confirmed.)

(4) Collateral goods

Table 11.13 shows the collateral goods provided up to 20 July for the import of (i) levy rice and (ii) unregulated rice. As will be seen from the table, in the case of goods provided to the association by the Malayan Military Administration, through Syonan Municipality, there is a large discrepancy between official provision prices to the association and the association's loading prices for each association member. The difference is used to control the sale price of the association's imported rice. However, the association importers are at a disadvantage compared to Nami Kikan importers, who are provided with collateral goods at quite low prices at the time of loading. This explains why the association's business has not been very active.

Table 11.13 (i) Collateral goods provided for the Import Association for levy rice, 20 July 1944

	Amount (picul) otherwise stated	Price at loading (dollars) Association → Members	Official price (dollars) Municipality → Association
Coffee WIB	33,024	148,608.00	24,705.25
Coffee 30%	41,250	74,250.00	21,813.00

Table 11.13 (i) (cont'd)

	Amount (picul) otherwise stated	Price at loading (dollars) Association → Members	Official price (dollars) Municipality → Association
Pepper	33,024	26,419.20	8,833.92
Tiger Balm	3,000 dozen	45,000.00	2,880.00
Eight trigrams board[24]	3,000 dozen	22,500.00	2,880.00
Headache powder	3,000 dozen	22,500.00	2,880.00
Sanitary sacks	6,000 items	72,000.00	7,880.00
Enemy cosmetics	102 dozen	94,227.00	12,113.50
Palm oil	330	33,000.00	3,356.10
Coffee B 30%	321	41,580.00	12,215.28
Coffee WIB 2	398	139,300.00	119,400.00
	Total for (i)	719,384.20	213,877.05

Table 11.13 (ii) Collateral goods provided for the Import Association for unregulated rice, 20 July 1944

	Amount (picul) unless otherwise stated	Price at loading (dollars) Association → Members	Official price[25] (dollars) Municipality → Association
Sugar	3,310 bags	1,884,227.50	81,922.50
Coffee WIB	1,219.56	548,802.00	91,235.28
Coffee 30%	1,187.29	213,712.20	62,783.89
Singapore matches	1,490 boxes	327,600.00	110,260.00
Candles	248.70	124,350.00	19,589.90
Pepper	379.63	30,370.00	10,155.10
Palm oil	112	13,440.00	5,924.80
Bicycle tyres	500 items	22,500.00	6,750.00
Bicycle tubes	3,000 items	21,000.00	10,500.00

(cont'd overleaf)

[24] An eight trigrams board is a fortune-telling board.

[25] The difference between the 'official price' and the 'price at loading' was used to adjust the difference between rice prices.

Table 11.13 (ii) (cont'd)

	Amount (picul) unless otherwise stated	Price at loading (dollars) Association → Members	Official price (dollars) Municipality → Association
Wax	3,300 catties	16,500.00	2,441.00
Grease	148.50	66,875.00	-
Palm oil	1,380	165,600.00	73,002.00
	Total for (ii)	3,434,976.70	474,564.47
	Total collateral goods (i)	719,384.20	213,877.05
	Total collateral goods (i & ii)	4,084,360.90	688,441.52

(5) Import channels

Ban Hong & Co. is in charge of transportation between Bangkok and Singgora, and transport to Syonan is undertaken by the Syonan Rice Import Association. Ban Hong & Co. is an organization newly created to transport levy rice, using 'Private Vessels B'. The company was set up with the permission of the embassy in Bangkok and the Gi unit[26] and is headed by Mr. Fujishima [Ken'ichi] of *Tiong Guan Po*[27] in Bangkok. Ban Hong & Co. incorporates important overseas Chinese traders there. (For details, see Appendix A.3.) Levy rice is transported according to the implementation guidelines set out in Appendix A.3.[28] This was the outcome of negotiations between Ban Hong & Co. and the Import Association. The outline sets the standard sea fare between Bangkok and Singgora at 26 baht a picul. The current cost of these imports is estimated in figure 11.4. But the sea fare of private vessels is increasing. Conversely, the black market rate of the dollar to the baht is decreasing. The cost estimate in figure 11.4 may therefore be too low. The initial selling price in Syonan was $100 per picul, but the price was around $300 for rice provided by the Nami Kikan. The price of rice from the association therefore had to be raised to the same level as that from the Nami Kikan.

Nevertheless, the quantities of levy rice imported for [civilian consumption] by the Import Association have been unsatisfactory. They are far lower than the quantities of unregulated rice imported by the Nami Kikan. Even the association

[26] Gi (meaning 'righteousness') was a Japanese military unit code name.
[27] An overseas Chinese newspaper, owned by Fujishima.
[28] The Implementation Guidelines have no issue date.

Figure 11.4 Cost of Syonan Rice Import Association rice imports

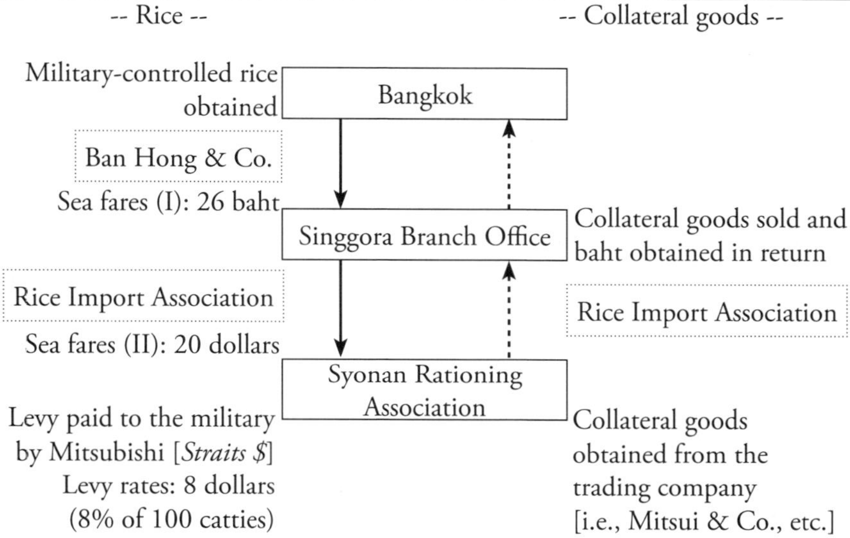

Estimation of the cost required to import 100 catties (1 picul) of levy rice

78--- sea fares (I) (33 baht = $100)

20--- sea fares (II)

8--- handling fees to Mitsubishi for delivery

7--- profit for the association members (30% of sea fares (II))

Total cost --- $113

members themselves purchase unregulated rice at Singgora [to sell on the unregulated market] and make this their main business.[29]

In Thailand there are overseas Chinese traders such as Yu Lee & Co., which export unregulated rice from Bangkok. These Thai traders have close connections with overseas Chinese traders from Penang and Syonan. Consequently, overseas Chinese exporters in Thailand pay around 20 baht or less per picul as sea fares when using private vessels, while Ban Hong & Co. pays a sea fare of 26 baht per picul (of which 6 baht are handling charges taken by Ban Hong & Co.). Private vessel owners are eager to export unregulated rice, as it offers them higher profits through access to collateral goods. It can therefore be assumed that owners of private vessels (who are, in many cases, themselves the exporters) can also gain extra

[29] It appears that the Import Association members came back only with unregulated rice in June and July (see table 11.14). This was an expected result for the first trials and was permitted, as the rice transported by private vessels was to be 'principally treated as freedom rice'; see Appendix 4.2(3)(ii).

income apart from the transport of rice.[30] Therefore, table 11.14 shows the total amount of unregulated rice and other grains imported [by the Syonan Rice Import Association] before 20 July. A total of 17,260 piculs (1,040 tons) of unregulated rice were imported, and the total of rice and other grains was 20,728 piculs (1,260 tons) (see Appendix 5 for details).

Note: Some of the imported rice, including rice imported after 20 September—and also what the Nami Kikan imported after it officially ceased rice transactions—is used to provide 3 catties per capita as the first round of one-off special rations for the entire civilian population in Syonan.[31] This was the first extraordinary special ration provided to the whole civilian population of Syonan Island.[32]

Table 11.14 Imports of unregulated rice and other grains up to 20 July 1944

	Amount (picul)[33]
White rice	9,230
Glutinous rice	481
Dehydrated rice	1,666
Wholegrain rice	119
Padi	264
Rice flour	5,765
Total freedom rice	17,525
Peanuts	715
Black soybeans	430
White beans	73
Mung beans	1,139
White sesame seeds	13
Black sesame seeds	233

[30] Here the authors shift the blame for the failure to transport levy rice back to Singapore onto Thai traders.

[31] '3 catties extra rice to public from Private Importers Stock in September 1944'; National Archives, Kew, WO203/4499, 'Rice SEAC territories', p. 7. This may amount to a total of 1,440 tons, or 24,000 piculs, while the total of levy rice imported by the Import Association and the rice received from the Nami Kikan by the end of September was 71,755 piculs.

[32] This implies that levy rice imported by the Syonanese Chinese traders was not always or totally sold as special rations.

[33] Figure A.11.1 also shows the amount of unregulated imports in June and July.

Table 11.14 (cont'd)

	Amount (picul)
Yellow beans	337
Green beans	508
Red beans	20
Total	20,993

4. Rice Imports by the Nami Kikan

On 16 May, in addition to the official inauguration of the Syonan Rice Import Association, which was given authority by Syonan Municipality, the Nami Kikan also began to import freedom rice from Southern Thailand. The overseas Chinese were said to be aware of the establishment of the Nami Kikan by the end of April.[34] Owing to the prohibition on the import of uncontrolled Kedah rice, many junks had not entered the port at Syonan but anchored nearby. The Nami Kikan used these junks to import rice. The Nami Kikan also handled the sale of rice. It sold rice at $285–300 a picul. This price level is much higher than the $170 selling price expected by the Rice Import Association for its first scheduled sales. Moreover, association members were made uneasy by the sudden introduction of the Nami Kikan, which also started to operate at exactly the same time as the Import Association. This confusion had some influence on Syonan prices. The Nami Kikan seems to have begun operations for the following reasons.

(1) The recall for other military use of private vessels that, due to the prohibition on the import of uncontrolled Kedah rice in March, used anchorage around the Riau Islands, Sumatra and elsewhere.[35]

(2) A successful operation requires the support of overseas Chinese, which would be difficult to gain without the prospect of adequate economic profits. The aim of importing rice is to secure support from these junk boat owners. The Nami Kikan's real purpose arose from military necessity. The import of rice was a means to gain control over these private vessels.

It should also be noted that if the amount of sugar can be increased as a collateral good, this will allow a large reduction in the selling price. There are currently 200 vessels, with a total tonnage of 6,000 tons. Therefore, there is good transport of rice from Southern Thailand at the moment. The cost of the Nami Kikan's rice imports is given in table 11.15 below (see also figure 11.5).

---

[34] The Nami Kikan was set up as an intelligence agency after the bombing of seven ships in September 1943 to maintain vigilance for intruders in the sea around Singapore.

[35] The boats anchored around these islands and Sumatra had traded illegally in rice brought from Kedah and elsewhere before March 1944.

Figure 11.5 Organization of Nami Kikan

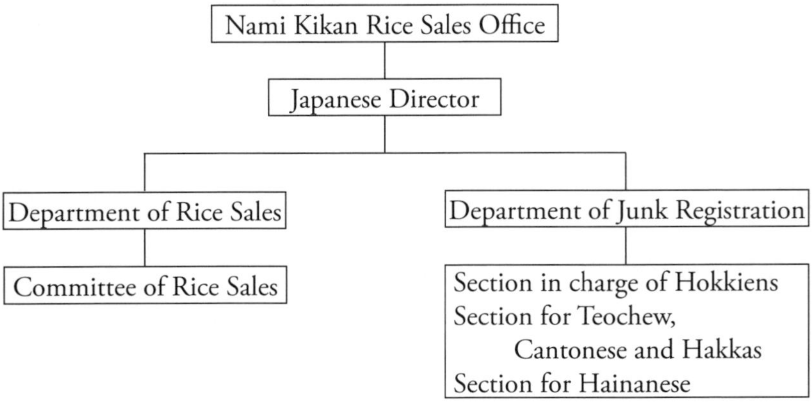

Table 11.15 Cost of Nami Kikan's rice imports

Per picul

15 baht	– Market price in Bangkok
20	– Sea fare to Singgora
5	– Other handling fee
15	– Sea fare from Singgora to Alor Setar via Hat Yai or Padang Besar
55 baht	
$165	– 55 baht [as above, cost from Bangkok to Alor Setar] with exchange of currency around Hat Yai or Padang Besar, where $100 = 33 baht is the black market exchange rate.[36]
$100*	– Total sea fare [from Alor Setar] to Syonan along west coast line, including profits.
$265	– Total cost

* Between Alor Setar and Syonan, using 100-ton class junk boats the transport cost including profits per picul would be $100, which would be about $165 for 100kg. For 100 tons it would be $165,000. (1)

However, currently the estimated charge for the monthly-chartered ships of the Nami Kikan is $64 per picul, which would be $1,060 for 1 ton, and for 100 tons it would be $106,000.

The charge for the chartered ships might be $124,000 to cover 35 days for the round trip between Syonan and Alor Setar. (2)

[36] Because of this exchange rate the cost of 55 baht becomes $165.

Table 11.15 (cont'd)

The balance of (1) – (2) = $41,000 could be expected as profits [for the Nami Kikan if the rice was sold at this price level].

In this connection, the standard charges for chartered ships are:

1 ton monthly;	Ships owned by Southern Navigation Company	– $18
	Ships supplied by Japanese trading companies	– $36
	Ships owned by the overseas Chinese traders	– $300–500

It can be assumed that charter charges for the ships owned by the Nami Kikan would be much higher than those above.

Charter charges for ships owned by overseas Chinese traders and paid for by the Nami Kikan before April 1944 had been $20 to $100.

Note: The recent price of white rice in Kedah has risen to $220 per picul. And the black market rate of baht against $100 has been reported as 28. Because of this the total cost might become considerably higher.

Collateral goods have been provided on four occasions to the registered rice traders. On three occasions the traders were supplied with 6,000 bags of sugar, each of which contained 165 catties, at a value of $160 per bag.[37] On the remaining occasion, about 35,000 gallons of petroleum oil were supplied, at a value of $1.50 per gallon. To begin with, traders imported rice at a rate of 2 catties of rice for a catty of sugar. This subsequently increased to 3 catties, and then to 3.5 catties. In the case of petroleum oil, 1 picul of rice was first valued at 3 gallons and later at 6 gallons.

In mid-May, initially, rice loaded in junks concealed in nearby islands could be sold at $295 per picul. This price benefited locals, and it also cut the price of black market rice to $900, from a previous maximum of $1,090. On 29 May the Department of Sales was established, and the Committee for Sales was also set up [at the Nami Kikan]. The committee had regular twice-weekly sales (on Wednesdays and Saturdays) in the city and suburbs, helped by local volunteers, until the sale of rice was suspended on 6 August. A total of 200,000 piculs (12,200 tons) of rice were sold. The price of white rice was first $310 and then $285 a picul. Parboiled rice was sold first at $280 and then $260 a picul. The price of rice flour started at $230, then was reduced to $225. The effect of the sales was not only to reduce black market rice prices to $550 a picul in July, but also to reduce other black market food prices. When the committee stopped rice sales, however, the price of black market rice briefly jumped from $500 to $2,800.

[37] Syonan Rice Import Association members had to pay $570 per bag (100kg) of sugar used for unregulated rice imports; table 11.13 (ii).

5. Conclusion

The import of Thai rice has given rise to the following problems:

(1) There has been no progress in importing levy rice using private vessels. Activity has, instead, concentrated on the import of unregulated rice.

(2) The Syonan Rice Import Association, Nami Kikan, Penang Rice Import Public Bureau and other importers in each state have not been cooperating in the import of rice via private vessels. This has pushed up the price of imported Thai rice.

(3) The black market exchange rate of dollars against baht has fallen, which has created difficulties for those in Malaya.

(4) Charter charges for private vessels have also increased.

(5) In this circumstance it has been necessary in places such as Syonan at the end of the import chain to increase purchase prices.

Resolution of the first problem—the lack of progress in using private vessels to import levy rice—requires the supply of attractive collateral goods at reasonable prices. The trade must be as profitable to the overseas Chinese traders as the import of unregulated rice. These aims can be secured, for example, by not allowing a large discrepancy between prices for collateral goods applied by the Import Association and Nami Kikan on the one hand, and black market prices on the other. Furthermore, it would be necessary for Ban Hong & Co. to liaise with unregulated rice exporters such as Yu Lee & Co. on the Thai side to work collaboratively and establish an organization in which their profits are the same, irrespective of whether they carry unregulated rice or levy rice.

The second problem could be resolved by establishing a central organization to coordinate the various rice-importing institutions that will be, or are already, established in each state in Malaya. It would be necessary to bring them all under a treaty, and together establish policies aimed at eliminating regional profit disparities in sea fares and boat charter charges, and the supply and selling prices of collateral goods.

The establishment of a centralized import organization would stop rapid increases in the charter fees of chartered ships, which comprises the fourth problem and also resolves the fifth problem of disparities in purchasing prices paid by different importing areas. It would, moreover, prevent declines in the black market exchange rate of the dollar for baht, which is the third problem. An avoidance of falling black market dollar exchange rates requires, insofar as possible, the elimination of rivalry in purchasing rice (as indicated above) and a rapid increase in the supply of desirable collateral goods.

In view of the export prices of collateral goods, an extensive integration of all the rice-importing concerns would be beneficial to traders in Malaya making payment to Thai traders through allowing them to set prices in their own favour.

Appendices

A.1 The Rules of the Syonan Rice Import Association

Chapter 1. General rules

Article 1. This Association is named the Syonan Rice Import Association.

Article 2. The aim of the Association is extensively to integrate those rice importers wishing to work under Malayan Military Administration control, to allow them to cooperate with the Military Administration policy on rice imports between Thailand and Malaya.

Article 3. To achieve this aim, the Association shall control members' activities as indicated below, and direct and support them.

(1) The import of rice from Thailand, Malaya, and the areas appointed by the Military Administration.

(2) Other activities related to (1).

(3) Business regulations applying to (1) and (2) are to be prescribed separately.

Article 4. Costs of Association membership are an admission fee, a membership fee and a share of expenses. These shares are to be determined separately.

Article 5. The Head Office of the Association is to be in Syonan Municipality. Branch offices are to be located in Malaya, Thailand and elsewhere as required.

Chapter 2. Members of the Association

Article 6. Members of the Association are persons engaged in the import of rice at their own risk from the southern areas who have been given permission by the executive committee, regardless of whether or not they own means of transport such as junks.

Article 7. Members of the Association are controlled and directed by the Association.

Article 8. A member who wishes to transfer a part or all of his right to trade shall require the permission of the executive committee. A member who wishes to leave the Association must follow the same procedure.

Article 9. Omitted.

Chapter 3. Business of the Association

Article 10. Members must be registered with the Association if they wish to engage in the business defined in Article 3 (1). Members must also obtain advance authorization from the Maritime Bureau on necessary matters. These include the number and tonnage of junks used, and registration details are to be given to the Maritime Bureau together with the owner's name, the name of the employer, charter fees earned, sailing areas, scheduled dates of sailing and other associated matters.

Article 11. Where a member needs to make a voyage for the purpose identified in Article 3 (1), the Association must obtain advance permission from the Military Administration's Maritime Bureau for the use of registered vessels.

Article 12. Where a member as identified in Article 11 needs to undertake a voyage and engage in business as defined by Article 3 (1), the vessel must carry the certificate issued by the Military Administration and fly the ship's prescribed flag during the voyage.

Article 13. When a member cancels a ship's charter, or transfers, rents or changes the use of the vessel registered with the Association, he must gain advance permission from the executive committee.

Article 14. Damage and loss to cargoes caused by accidents at sea shall be the responsibility of the traders in charge, who are to pay for the damages arising from activity identified in Article 3.

Chapter 4. Executive Committee members

Articles 15, 16, 17, 18, 19, 20, 21. Omitted.

Chapter 5. Meetings

Articles 22, 23. Omitted.

Chapter 6. Accounts of the Association

Article 24. The Association's accounting year, divided into half-yearly periods, is from 1 April to 31 March.

Article 25. Policies relating to the treatment of surplus funds and defrayment of deficits shall be determined by a general meeting.

Article 26. The Association does not accept responsibility for losses to third parties caused by members making transactions without the permission of the Association.

Article 27. The president of the Association is required to report on the accounts as indicated below by the end of the fiscal year, and to submit the material, as below, to the auditor-secretary for inspection one week before the date of the general meeting:

1. Inventory of property
2. Balance sheet showing assets and liabilities
3. Business report
4. Budget and final statement balance sheets showing income and expenditure

Article 28. The secretary is to prepare the papers listed above and then pass them to the president of the Association. The president must submit the papers for approval to the mayor of Syonan Municipality.

Article 29. The president of the Association is required to report on the papers itemized in Article 27 at regular general meetings.

Article 30. The president must keep in the head office the papers on which he reports at regular general meetings as defined in Article 29.

Chapter 7. Penal Rules

Article 31. Where a member's actions are contrary to the policies of the Military Administration and violate the Association's rules, that member shall be excluded from the Association by decision of the executive committee.

Article 32. In the event of Article 31 being implemented, or if any violation is committed, the member concerned shall be requested to pay a fine for negligence and may be deprived of any of his membership rights. Fines and punishments shall be decided by the executive committee.

A.2 Syonan Rice Import Association Business Regulations

Business regulations arising from the activities set out in Article 2 of the Rules of the Association are set out below.

Article 1. Collection of money

A share of the costs incurred by the Association is to be collected from members.

Admission fee per member: $100

Monthly membership fee: $50

Administration fee: 10 per cent of profits earned from selling imported goods as regulated by Article 3.

Article 2. Marine insurance

The Syonan Rice Import Association shall take out marine insurance for the import of goods as regulated by Article 3.

Article 3. Sea fares

The Association pays sea fares as follows to members of the Association who transport the goods appointed by the Association:

(i) The official sea fare determined for transport between the designated areas, or a commission of 30 per cent of the official price of the loaded goods as indicated on the invoice, whichever is higher, shall be paid to the Association member [in advance to their voyage].

(ii) However, 50 per cent of the sea fare paid is to be shared with other members. The payment is shared only with those who own vessels that have been ordered to sail without cargo [i.e., collateral goods].

(iii) Commissions will be paid only when the amount of the commission exceeds the official sea fare [paid in advance]. However, 50 per cent of the commission paid is to be shared with other members. The payment is shared only with those who own vessels that have been ordered to sail without cargo.

(iv) Payment for the cargoes to be transported [i.e., collateral goods]: The Association is to pay for the costs of the goods to be transported, overhead expenses of marine insurance, storage fees, loading costs at the branch office [i.e., at Singgora] and other expenses.

(v) It is the business of the Association to receive the cargoes [i.e., collateral goods] disposed of by the military or appropriate authorities in Thailand and to allow members to engage in the marine transport of these goods.

Article 4. Branch offices

(i) A branch office is to be opened in Singgora, in Southern Thailand, to deal with the business of the Association at transfer points.

Representatives to handle branch business are sent: one branch office manager, two deputy managers and a few clerks.

(ii) The branch manager and deputy managers shall be appointed and dismissed by the board of trustees.

(iii) Clerks shall be appointed and dismissed by the branch manager.

(iv) The branch manager shall control the business at branch level, following the instructions of the Syonan Head Office. The assistant managers are to support the branch manager and carry out the daily business of the office.

(v) The branch manager, following Syonan Head Office instructions, is to report in detail in the areas indicated below.

a. Detailed information on the cargoes [i.e., rice and other grains] carried from Bangkok to Singgora: the sea fare, the total amount of cargo, and the date of port entry on the Bangkok-Singgora route.

b. Detailed information on the cargoes [i.e., collateral goods]: amounts, names of vessels and their registration numbers, the date of port entry, and the market price and clearing price of the cargoes carried from Syonan to Singgora.

c. The order in which cargoes from Singgora to Syonan should be loaded on the boats is the same as the order in which the boats from Syonan to Singgora have entered the port. If changes in loading order are made they must be reported.

d. The names of vessels bound for Syonan, their registered numbers, details of cargoes [i.e., rice and other grains], amounts and departure dates.

Article 5. Selling prices

(i) For the business regulated by Article 3, selling prices of imported goods [i.e., rice and other grains] shall be determined by the sum of charter fees for the transport routes between the designated areas [i.e., Singgora and Syonan] and the cost of losses at sea, together with profits. The executive committee will determine an appropriate level that is equal to the above-stated sum.

a. Charter fees and overheads are to cover the cost of the return voyages.

b. Charter fees depend on the fee rates approved by the executive committee.

Article 6. Sale of imported goods

Sales of goods, imported under Article 3, will be directed by Syonan Municipality. Free market sales will be barred to all including the importers.

(i) List of rice importers immediately prior to issue of the order prohibiting the import of uncontrolled rice

Hokkien merchants

*1. Ban Thye Guan 萬泰源
*2. Tai Kee 大記
*3. Sin Hiap Hoe 新協和
*4. Tai Tong Yah 大東営
*5. Nam Kong Seong Hung 南光商行
*6. Tai Seng 大成
*7. Yah Kee Chuan 営記栈
*8. Ban Hoe Joo 萬和裕
*9. Hiap Teck 協徳
*10. Siang Guan祥源
*11. Kim Soon Hin 金順興
*12. Thong Ah 通亜
*13. Thong Yah Hung 東営行
14. Hock Hin 福興
15. Nam Chun 南春
16. Yah Kai 営凱
17. Hock Yah 福営
18. Chng Kee Chiang 曽啓昌
19. Yah Cheong Chiang Kee 営昌炳記
20. Khian Chuan 建川
21. Leng 龍

22. Joo Seng 裕成
23. Guan Huat Seng 源発成
24. Heng Joo 恒裕
25. Cheng Moh 振茂
26. Joo Bee 裕美
27. Bee Tat 美達
28. Hiap Lee 協利
29. Hock Tong Hin 福同興
30. Hiap Lian Hock 協联福
31. Bee Huat 美発
32. Chia Hin 正興
33. Heng & Co., 恒公司
34. Hock Hin Bee 福興美

Teochew merchants

*35. Tan Soon Seng 陳順成

*36. Tsu Hing Siang 聚豊祥

*37. Soon Lee 順利

Note 1. This name list includes only the important merchants among all the importers.

Note 2. Those with an asterisk before the number had their rice confiscated by the order of prohibition.

(ii) Committee members who drew up the rules of the Association

Khiaw Thong Hung 僑通行

Kim Leng Thye 金龍泰

Nam Yang Trading Limited Co., 南洋貿易有限会社

Tan Soon Seng 陳順成

Chng Kee Chiang 曽啓昌

A.3 Implementation Guidelines for Rice Transport Cooperation for Syonan

Determined by the Syonan Goods and Material Rationing Association Syonan Rice Import Association and representatives of Ban Hong & Co.

1. Purpose

To obtain rice for Syonan (Malaya), where rice is the staple food, this agreement aims to streamline the transport of rice that had been earmarked for consumption by the military through the use of vessels owned by overseas Chinese to distribute rice [mostly through the unregulated market] to fulfil the Syonan people's hopes and desires.

2. Plan

Levy rice is to be carried to Singgora by vessels owned by overseas Chinese in Bangkok, and transferred to vessels owned by Syonanese overseas Chinese. The cargoes will be carried from Singgora to Syonan by Syonanese overseas Chinese. Ban Hong & Co. is to organize the transport from Bangkok to Singgora.

3. Measures

(1) Rice deliveries

The rice to be transported is levy rice. Mitsubishi will receive this rice [from the warehouse in Bangkok where rice for the Japanese military is stored] and transfer it to Ban Hong & Co., which will be responsible for its transport to Singgora.

(2) Transport of rice

The rice to be carried to Syonan is designated as levy rice, and the vessels used to carry the rice are designated [not as military vessels but] as private vessels.

(3) Methods of delivery and responsibility for transport

When the rice is transferred by Mitsubishi, Ban Hong & Co. will assume responsibility for its transport until the point of delivery for Syonan vessels at Singgora has been completed. In principle, transfer shall be done at sea [and straight into junks]. In principle, vessels from Syonan will be waiting for the arrival of vessels from Bangkok in order to begin transferring the rice cargo. When there are no vessels waiting at Singgora, the Bangkok vessels are to wait as necessary for the arrival of junks from Syonan. However, if there is a gap of a few days between the timing of delivery and collection, the rice should be temporarily warehoused. The Syonanese side is to be responsible for preparing the warehouse and the miscellaneous expenses related to reception of the goods.

(4) Settlement of accounts

Because there are no funds in baht in Malaya, transport costs [between Bangkok and Singgora] should be met by the carriage of collateral goods by Syonanese Chinese importers, allocated for meeting transport funds. The collateral goods are to be handed on to Ban Hong & Co., at Singgora prices. Ban Hong & Co. is to sell the goods in the open market to settle the sea fares [Bangkok and Singorra] in baht. Settlement of accounts can then be changed by case-by-case negotiation between the Bangkok and Syonan sides based on the prior agreement [see ▲ Guidelines below].

(5) Special Rice Transport Accounts

Special Rice Transport Accounts are to be established by Ban Hong & Co., which is to settle accounts for the transport of rice and for the sales of collateral goods. Ban Hong & Co. shall maintain a balance between the two in order to avoid large deficits.

(6) Setting sea fares

Taking into account measures (1) to (5), the c.i.f. sea fare from Bangkok to Singgora is to be set and agreed with the Syonan side. The standard sea fare between Bangkok and Singgora is to be 26 baht per picul.

Breakdown of the sea fare: Sea fare of 20 baht net of any commissions and 6 baht (30 per cent) are to be paid as commission to Ban Hong & Co.

Note: The sea fares should cover risk incurred not only by vessels but also by their rice cargoes.

▲ *Guidelines for the marketing of collateral goods*

Plan 1.

Initially, the Syonanese Chinese importers are to obtain baht funds by selling goods sent to Singgora to the Syonan side [Syonan Rice Import Association's branch office]. Transport costs can then be paid to Ban Hong & Co. in baht cash.

Note: This method should be used to begin with for ease in the first round [of this Private Importers' rice transport operation].

Plan 2.

[From the second round onwards] at Singgora, the Syonanese Chinese importers are to transfer goods to Ban Hong & Co. immediately. Ban Hong & Co. can then sell goods in the open market (selling on commission) without waiting for the bid prices set by the Syonan side [Syonan Rice Import Association's branch office] and add the proceeds to their Special Rice Transport Account. When dealing with transport payments, Ban Hong & Co. can earn a certain commission from the proceeds of sales.

Plan 3.

[Alternatively] collateral goods shall be designated as under the control of the military. They are to be carried in military vessels (there is, however, a problem of identification flags on the Syonan side,[38] and cargoes are to be unloaded at the military warehouse in Bangkok. Ban Hong & Co. will then receive goods in exchange at a low (actual cost) price and sell them appropriately (at market prices [in Bangkok]). Ban Hong & Co. will add the profit from these sales to the Special Rice Transport Account and be given, in return, a certain commission determined by the selling price.

Note: For the present, the procedure in Plan 1 is to be followed, but in future the procedure of Plan 2, with a few alterations, will be used, with exchange goods sold at the market value in Singgora.

[38] On the Syonan side, trading vessels are designated as private vessels; see also Syonan Rice Import Association's 'Private Vessels B', appendix 11.4.

A.4 Tei Kan San No. 614: Implementation Guidelines for the Use of Motorsailers and Junks to Transport Thai Rice and Java Salt and Sugar

1. *Policy*

The aim is to relieve severe shortages in the quantities of rice, salt and sugar available for consumption by civilians in Malaya by transporting rice from Thailand and salt and sugar from either Java or Thailand by means of motorsailers and junks using the guidelines set out below.

2. *Procedure to be followed*

(1) *Imports under this scheme are separate from the general Plan for Exchange of Goods*[39]

(2) *Method of imports*

(i) The director of the Marine Bureau is to make a trial consignment by the Southern Navigation Company (Nanpō Unkō Gaisha), using about seven motorsailers (1,050-ton class) due to be built after April.[40] The Southern Navigation Company is to engage in the transport of rice from Bangkok to Syonan and of salt and sugar from Jakarta to Syonan.

(ii) The Military Administration, state councils and Syonan Municipality are to cooperate to mobilize private vessels for the transport of rice, sugar and salt under the control of the Marine Bureau and the Malayan Marine Transport Association.

(3) *Procedures*

(i) Under this scheme, procedures for the import of rice, sugar and salt shall be governed by Nan Sō Kei Shu [Southern General Army Department of Finance Directive] No. 10. Procedures in relation to the military are to be carried out by Mitsubishi Shōji Corporation [for rice and other grains] and Mitsui Bussan & Co. [for sugar and salt].

(ii) Rice imported using motorsailers and private vessels (called A) procured by Japanese trading companies [i.e., Mitsubishi and Mitsui] are to be designated as rations controlled by the Military Administration. Rice transported by other general private vessels [i.e., junks owned by Syonan

---

39 In the Greater East Asia Co-prosperity Sphere.

40 Nanpō Unkō Gaisha was established on 21 March 1943; *Senji Geppō*, March 1943.

people] (called B) is principally treated as freedom rice. In principle, all sugar and salt are to be controlled rations under Military Administration surveillance.

(iii) Prices of rice, salt and sugar are to be the military disposal price in Malaya. These are kept at the same level as prices for regular rice, salt and sugar disposed of by the military, which were imported under the Plan for Exchange of Goods. However, the price of rice transported by private vessels B ([ii] above) is to be set by the price of levy rice delivered to Bangkok.

(iv) The sea fare for motorsailers and private vessels is set by the Military Administration, except where the Southern General Army has set and approved a sea fare, for which it shall take responsibility. However, rice defined as carried by private vessels B ([ii] above) does not fall into this category.

(v) Risks incurred during transportation will be borne by the Military Administration. However, those incurred for the rice carried by private vessels B ([ii] above) do not fall into this category.

3. Details

(1) Means of transport

(i) The Military Administration determines the private vessels to be mobilized for each item [rice, salt or sugar], through negotiating with the Marine Bureau, the Department of Industry and the Malayan Marine Transport Association. The Military Association takes into account the volume of cargo requested by the state councils and Syonan Municipality for each item, and the capacity of the exporters to ship each item.

(ii) The import of Thai rice by private vessels is divided into categories A and B.[41]

A. Category A comprises local ships (owned by Japanese trading companies and other private vessels that can work a direct route between Malaya and Bangkok).

These vessels are procured by the states and municipality and authorized by the Military Administration. This transport will be managed by Mitsubishi Shōji Corporation in association with the Malayan Marine Transport Association.

B. Category B comprises local private vessels mobilized by Syonan Municipality and approved by the Military Administration.

The group appointed by the Military Administration (hereafter, the overseas Chinese group [i.e., Syonan Rice Import Association]) is to

[41] Category A and Category B refer to the kind of vessels used; see 2(3)(ii).

handle the day-to-day business of the transport of Bangkok rice from Southern Thailand in association with the Malayan Marine Transport Association.

(iii) The private vessels for the transport of salt and sugar are to be the local vessels procured by the states and municipality and authorized by the Military Administration. This transport will be directed by Mitsui Bussan & Co. in association with the Malayan Marine Transport Association.

(iv) Based on this implementation guideline, the Military Administration will issue certificates to vessels engaging in the transport of rice, sugar and salt for the Military Administration, which are to fly the identification flag. The issue of certificates and flags by the Syonan Liaison Office or the Marine Bureau will confer on private vessels the approval of the Military Administration to navigate in the waters to and from Syonan. However, for those ships under special conditions, the person in charge will report to the Syonan Liaison Office and follow various formalities.

(2) Procedures

(i) Goods carried by motorsailers will be under the direction of Mitsui Bussan & Co. (salt and sugar) and Mitsubishi Shōji Corporation (rice) according to the rules for Exchange of Goods.

(ii) Procedures for Thai rice carried by private vessels will be as follows.

A. Mitsubishi Shōji Corporation will be in charge of traffic relating to category A as follows.

a. Mitsubishi Shōji Corporation is to control the reception of the cargo and allocation of the unloaded rice. Forty-five per cent of unloaded rice will be allocated to the control of the Military Administration [to be distributed as general rations]. The rest (50 per cent) will be left to the discretion of the states and municipality from which the private vessels came [to be distributed as Special Heavy-duty Rations; *see 3. (1) Preparations to set up the association*], and 5 per cent to the owners of the vessels who will be allowed to purchase ex vessel at the military disposal price [and to sell the uncontrolled rice in the free market].[42]

b. To cover the sea fare set by the Military Administration and risks in transit, Mitsubishi Shōji Corporation will make a payment to be reimbursed on application to the Military Administration

[42] Category A vessels were larger motorsailers, and the owners (probably Mitsubishi-related) were paid sea fares of $70 per ton, and thus $70,000 for a maximum load on a motorsailer, in addition to the 5 per cent allocation; see table A.11.1.

(sea fares paid by the Southern General Army will be handled by the Southern General Army).

c. Losses incurred in transit will be the responsibility of shipowners. Damages arising from special circumstances not chargeable to the transporters (marine accidents or acts of war) will be chargeable to Mitsubishi Shōji Corporation.

B. The overseas Chinese group will be in charge of traffic relating to category B as follows.

a. The amount of cargo unloaded is to be checked against the bill of lading for levy rice and reported to the Military Administration through Syonan Municipality.

b. Mitsubishi Shōji Corporation is to be paid for rice [that it received in Bangkok and commissioned to Ban Hong Co.] in Malayan [Straits] dollars according to the amount (as levy rice) and the price (levy rice) as designated in the bill of lading for levy rice.

c. Unloaded rice is to be sold under the direction of Syonan Municipality [to be distributed occasionally as Special One-off Rations to all citizens and/or mostly through the open market].[43]

(iii) Salt and sugar shipped by private vessel from Java (or Thailand) are to be in the charge of Mitsui Bussan & Co.

a. Mitsui Bussan & Co. is to facilitate the reception of these items. Fifty per cent of the salt and 45 per cent of the sugar are to be put under the control of the Military Administration. Fifty per cent of the salt and sugar are to be allocated to the states and municipality that procured the private vessels, and 5 per cent of the sugar is to be sold to the vessels' owners at the military disposal prices ex vessel.[44]

b. Other matters [i.e., responsibility of risks, etc.] are to be handled [by Mitsui Bussan & Co.] in the same way as applies to rice by Mitsubishi Shōji Corporation.

---

[43] It is implied that much of the unloaded 'levy' rice was sold by the overseas Chinese importers of category B on the open market, and the proceeds of the sales were paid to Mitsubishi at a fixed price ($8 per picul), and then paid as a levy to the Military Administration by Mitsubishi; see table A.11.3.

[44] In other words, 50 per cent of salt and 45 per cent of sugar went to the Military Administration to be used as collateral goods for the Private Importers' rice transport operation, while 50 per cent of the salt and 50 per cent of the sugar went to the state that offered the boats. The remaining 5 per cent of the sugar (but no salt) went to the boat owner.

(iv) Sea fares that do not fall on the Southern General Army are to be paid by the Military Administration. However, expenses arising from the transport of rice, as in (1)(ii)B [by the overseas Chinese group] above will not be borne by the Military Administration.

Table A.11.1 Allocation of sea fares and shares

	Allocation of sea fares (dollars per ton)			Allocation of cargoes paid by Military Administration as supplement to the sea fare
	Share paid by Military Administration	Share paid by General Army	Total fares set by Military Administration	
Rice between Bangkok and Malaya	46.50	23.50	70.00	5% of the weight of unloaded rice. Loss of cargo during the voyage will not be taken into account.
Salt and sugar between Java and Malaya	22.50	17.50	40.00	5% of the weight of unloaded sugar. Same condition as for rice.

If any transportation needs arise apart from these two routes, they will be considered on a case-by-case basis.

(v) Risks incurred in the course of transport are defined as sinking, damage to the vessel recognized by the Director of Marine Bureau, and the death of sailors. In the event of an accident, the Military Administration will pay compensation to the amount estimated by the director of the Marine Bureau. However, no payment will be made by the Military Administration in the case of cargoes as defined by (1)(ii)B.

(vi) Rice from Thailand carried by vessels in category A, and salt and sugar from Java, which are the cargo allocated to the states and municipality as defined in (2)(ii)A and (iii), are used as the general ration. Furthermore, if any additional surplus arises, it is to be used for Special [Heavy-duty] Rations or to build up stocks.

(vii) Transportation of Thai rice by private vessel in category B is in practice limited to Syonan Municipality. However, private vessels that wish to join the scheme should be approved by the Military Administration before contacting Syonan Municipality directly through each state council. These vessels would operate under the control of the overseas Chinese group [i.e., Syonan Rice Import Association].

(viii) If Syonan Municipality is contacted by another state council with regard to the operation as in (vii) above, Syonan Municipality will advise the owners of private vessels (category B vessels) with regard to the sales of Thai rice, to sell rice in the state from which they originate.[45]

[45] The unregulated market price would have been higher in Singapore, but with a view to reducing the rice shortage in peninsular states, access to the Singapore market was understandably restricted.

A.5 Total Rice Imports of the Syonan Rice Import Association

The total amounts of rice seized, freedom rice, levy rice, and rice received from the Nami Kikan from the start of business of the Syonan Rice Import Association to 15 October are set out in table A.11.2.

Table A.11.2 Rice and other grains, start of business–15 October 1944[46]

(piculs)

(1) Total purchases of seized rice	14, 584
(2) Total imports of freedom rice	91,851
(3) Total imports of levy rice	23,872
(4) Total rice received from Nami Kikan after 15 August	83,621
(5) Total imports of other grains after 30 September	7,738

The total of (2), (3) and (5), 123,461 piculs (7,470 tons) of rice and other grains, was transported by the association's vessels from Southern Thailand. The total from (1) to (5) was 221,672 piculs (13,411 tons).

(1) Total purchases of seized rice

This is rice that was imported as uncontrolled rice from Southern Thailand prior to the establishment of the association but seized by the administration when rice imports were prohibited as of March 20, and purchased by the association. Although the purchasing price for this rice [paid to the rice traders] was $100 a picul,[47] 200 catties of sugar and 100 catties of salt were additionally given [to the rice traders through the association as collateral goods] for each 900 catties of seized rice. Details are as in table A.11.3 (1).

[46] Start of business probably means 27 May 1944, when the first round of the private importers' transportation missions left the Port of Singapore. However, according to figure A.11.1, the starting date for '(3) Total imports of levy rice' seems to have been August 1944, when the regulations and guidelines for levy rice and freedom rice imports by private vessels were issued ex post facto.

[47] The market price for rice imported by the Syonan Rice Import Association of $100 per picul was much higher than the official price and much lower than the Nami Kikan's market price; see 3. (5) Import channels. The seized rice was presumably sold in the open market to try to limit price inflation.

Table A.11.3 (1) Total purchases of seized rice, June–August 1944[48]

(piculs)

White rice	5,054
Dehydrated rice	3,303
Glutinous rice	1,880
Wholegrain rice	71
Dehydrated glutinous rice	168
Glutinous rice flour	178
Rice flour	3,507
Rice flour bar	181
Broken white rice	26
Broken dehydrated rice	22
Broken rice flour	128
Broken glutinous rice	66
Total June–August	14,584

(2) Details of unregulated rice imports

Table A.11.3 (2) Unregulated rice imports, start of business [June]–15 October 1944[49]

(piculs)

White rice	46,702
Rice flour	18,297
Dehydrated rice	11,720
Glutinous rice	303
Padi	4
Wholegrain rice	197
Glutinous rice flour	597
Rice flour bar	135
Broken white rice	358
Broken rice flour	388
Broken dehydrated rice	377
Broken wholegrain rice	1

[48] Prohibition of rice smuggling began on 20 March 1944. The total may include rice seized and stored by the authorities since March.

[49] Start of business may mean the date that the first vessel returned from Singgora at the end of June 1944; see figure A.11.1.

Table A.11.3 (2) (cont'd)

Broken glutinous rice	4
Dehydrated rice bar	103
White rice bar	151
Total from start of business to 30 September	79,337
Total 1–15 October	12,513
Total	91,850

(3) Details of levy rice imports

Table A.11.3 (3) Levy rice imports, start of business [August]–15 October 1944[50]

(piculs)

White rice	10,332
Broken white rice	85
Total to 30 September	10,417
1–15 October	13,465
Total	23,882

(4) Rice received from the Nami Kikan after 15 August

The Nami Kikan ceased sales of rice on 6 August. Since 15 August, the association has purchased rice imported by the Nami Kikan. The aims of the Nami Kikan are now deemed to have been met; vessels belonging to the Nami Kikan were transferred to the Syonan Rice Import Association as of 30 September. Details of rice received are as in table A.11.3 (4).

Table A.11.3 (4) Rice received from Nami Kikan, 15 August–15 October 1944

(piculs)

White rice	40,694
Dehydrated rice	7,852
Rice flour	11,650
Glutinous rice	148

(cont'd overleaf)

[50] Start of business may mean the date that the regulations were issued ex post facto, separating the responsibilities of levy rice and freedom rice imports. See figure A.11.1.

Table A.11.3 (4) (cont'd)

Glutinous rice flour	248
Rice bar	121
Broken rice	302
Broken dried rice	69
Broken rice flour	225
Broken glutinous rice flour	34
Broken rice flour bar	5
Total 15 August–30 September	61,348
Total 1–15 October	22,279
Total	83,627

It should be noted that from the start of business up to 6 August the Nami Kikan is estimated to have sold a total of about 200,000 piculs of rice, as stated above.[51]

(5) Total imports of other grains

Table A.11.3 (5) Beans and other non-rice grain imports, start of business [June]–30 September 1944[52]

(piculs)

Green beans	3,490
Yellow beans	842
Red beans	221
White beans	192
Black beans	438
Peanuts	2,215
White sesame seeds	13
Black sesame seeds	294
Broken peanuts	17
Broken green beans	9
Broken yellow beans	5
Broken black beans	1
Mixed beans and sesame seeds	1
Total from start of business to 30 September	7,738

51 See 4. Rice Imports by the Nami Kikan.

52 The start date of business may be the same as for freedom rice imports.

(6) Monthly imports

Monthly imports of unregulated rice, levy rice, and other grains imported by the association are shown in figure A.11.1.

(7) Reallocation of import operations

From 1 October, the process of importing rice by private vessel will be further improved through a reallocation of rice import operations among the organizations as described below.

i. The purchase in Thailand of rice for import and its carriage between Southern Thailand and Syonan: the Import Association
ii. Unloading and warehousing the imported rice in Syonan: Mitsubishi Shōji Corporation
iii. Paying for purchased rice, stocking and rationing rice in Syonan: Food Supply Office of Syonan Municipality
iv. Buying collateral goods and other activities to promote the Rice Import Association: Syonan Goods and Material Rationing Association

(8) Purchasing price of unregulated rice and other grains

The Import Association's purchasing prices for unregulated rice and other grains are as in table A.11.3 (6).

Table A.11.3 (6) Purchasing price of unregulated rice and other grains

(unit: 100 catties; place of purchase: Syonan Goods and Material Rationing Association Warehouse)

White rice – $295
Dehydrated rice – $270
Rice flour – $270 (if shipped after 15 August, $150)
Rice flour bar – $490
Dehydrated rice bar – $450
Glutinous rice flour – $295
Glutinous rice – $295
Dehydrated glutinous rice – $285
Wholegrain rice – $270
Peanuts – $350
Green, yellow, red, white beans – $300
Black beans – $350
Black sesame seeds – $300
White sesame seeds – $420

Figure A.11.1 Monthly imports of unregulated rice, levy rice and other grains imported by the association, June–September 1944

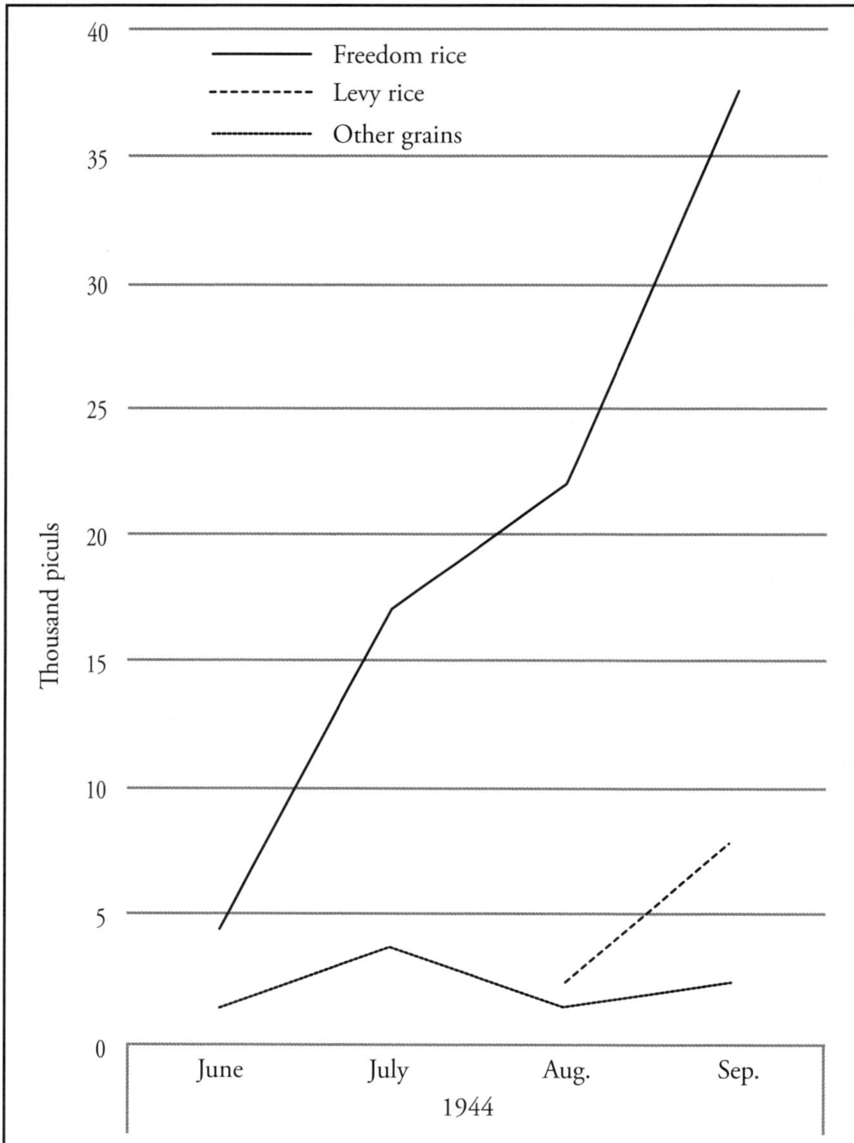

Living Standards

CHAPTER 12

A Study of Lowest Levels of Living by Ethnic Group in Syonan Municipality

Price, Quantity and the Relative Importance of Daily Necessities, by Ethnic Group

Surveyed by Yamada Isamu and Kawai Mikio, October 1943

The survey for this report was conducted over four months from April to July 1943 by Yamada Isamu, assistant professor at Tokyo University of Commerce,[1] and Kawai Mikio, civilian associate,[2] both of whom are affiliated with the Chōsabu of the Southern Military Administration. This report is mimeographed and circulated for reference purposes.[3]

Contents

[1] Yamada's characteristic handwriting appears in sections 1–3 and in the conclusion of this chapter.

[2] The author of sections 4 and 5.

[3] This report is written in hiragana, a Japanese writing system used by women, literati and academics to indicate academic autonomy in the face of military rule. Other reports are written in katakana, a writing system used by the pre-war and wartime government and the military.

4. **Research Results**

5. **Family Budgets in Households Surveyed**

Appendices

1. Objectives of the Study

As is widely acknowledged, the three objectives of military administration are to acquire resources for military demand, to ensure that local forces are self-sufficient, and to restore public order. Without securing public order, none of these objectives—even to produce and transport military materials or supply local forces—can easily be achieved.

Communist agitation and disruption arising from the daily stresses of life in the current economic circumstances are destabilizing influences on public order. These two forces are linked. Were the ordinary Malayan population to be faced with starvation, there would be a risk of expanding Communist Party influence.

Rising prices following the occupation of Malaya have led to considerable hardship and, as already indicated, will eventually lead to public unrest. The best approach to this problem is to guarantee a minimum standard of living. This would provide an effective solution, although other courses of action are possible.

Consequently, the minimum standard of living in the Southern Regions cannot be considered without accounting for differences among all ethnic groups. Because manners and customs vary according to ethnicity, there is also variation in what each group considers the minimum standard of living. It is impossible to apply a single measure in this regard, since ordinary Malayans live in a primitive manner in the countryside, while overseas Chinese traders enjoy high standards of living in the city. Therefore, in setting minimum living standards guaranteed by the Military Administration, each ethnic group should be separately considered.

What, then, is the lowest living found for each ethnic group?[4] Unfortunately, we do not have overall data for the Southern Regions. Therefore, we decided at the Southern Military Administration to undertake a project called 'A Study of Price and Quantity of Daily Necessities by Ethnic Group' in order to make a systematic estimation of the minimum cost of living by region and ethnic group

[4] In the text, the term 'minimum standard of living' is not actually used, but 'lowest living' in general, without 'standard' or 'level'. In contexts where a descriptive term is more appropriate we use 'lowest living'; and in contexts where a prescriptive term is more appropriate we use 'minimum standard of living' or 'minimum cost of living'.

to encompass the entire Southern Regions.[5] Pre-war sources are used to select an appropriate basket of goods to calculate minimum costs of living. However, such a pre-war basket of goods would not yield sufficiently reliable results, since living conditions are now said to be completely different. Use of pre-war sources would require a significant level of estimation and assumption. As it happens, some data have been collected on a local level relating to prices or living expenses since the Japanese occupation [see sections 3(i)–(iv) below]. While these provide a useful guide, the lack of information on ethnic groups rules out their direct use in the present study.

Therefore, before embarking on a systematic estimation of minimum living standards by region and ethnic group for the entire Southern Regions, we determined to carry out a pilot survey of prices, quantities and variations in baskets of goods that constitute daily necessities for various ethnic groups in Syonan Municipality. Our principal purpose was to establish appropriate baskets of goods, in order to identify daily necessities for each ethnic group. Of course, applying the results of a survey of Syonan Municipality alone to the whole Southern Regions requires a high level of assumption. But urgent action was needed to put in place policies to guarantee minimum living standards. By aggregating available data in Syonan Municipality on ethnic variations in what constitute necessities, we hoped to arrive at a more generally applicable minimum living standard. Any significant differences in other regions from the Syonan findings can be addressed by later supplementary research.

In summary, the present survey is intended as a pilot study of price and quantity of daily necessities for various ethnic groups in the entire Southern Regions, as well as an independent study of the lowest living in Syonan Municipality. We hope that the study proves useful for future policy determination.

2. Groups Surveyed

The results of this year's door-to-door census survey [conducted by the Department of Police Administration] are shown in table 12.1.

[5] Yamada tried to convince other Chōsashitsu (research offices) allotted to the Java Military Administration and elsewhere to establish a standardized format of a household expenditure survey, but he could not gain consent. Nevertheless, he conducted a methodologically sound household expenditure survey for Malaya on the basis of this pilot study (Chōsabu Report 12, this chapter) and produced a thoroughly comprehensive report (Chōsabu Report 50: A Report on the Household Expenditures Survey in Malaya, Taiping: Military Administration Chōsabu, October 1944) not included in this book. See chapter 2 for the results of the household expenditure survey.

Table 12.1 Syonan Municipality population, April 1943[6]

	Number	Percent
Chinese	679,420	78.7
Malay	95,524	11.1
Indian	76,987	8.9
Eurasian	8,031	0.9
Other	3,753	0.4
Total	863,715	100.0

The majority of the population is Chinese, followed by Malays and Indians.[7] Eurasians and other ethnic groups are such a small proportion of the population that it is unnecessary to consider them in our current discussion. Moreover, since the purpose of the present survey is to determine minimum living standards, discussion of the condition of groups such as Eurasians can be left aside, as they had a preferential status under the British government. Therefore, this survey mainly considers Chinese, Malay and Indian populations.

With regard to household occupational structure, selection of respondent households has to be considered with some care in light of the present study's focus on the lowest level of living. It is necessary to select those occupations that are particularly related to a low standard of living. In practice, a typical household is hard to find. It is particularly difficult to make householders in different ethnic groups fully understand the purpose of the survey. Furthermore, the time pressures associated with this survey made some inconsistencies in household selection unavoidable, although every effort has been made to achieve the best combination of households to fit with the purpose of this survey. The following section describes the households surveyed by ethnic group.

(1) The Chinese

As is well known, the Chinese live in the centre of the city and concentrate their activities in commerce and industry. That section with the worst living standards—the object of the present survey—also live in the city centre and are affected by price rises. By occupation, those with the worst living standards are

[6] See chapter 3, table A.3.2.

[7] The authors of this report prefer to use 'overseas Chinese' (華僑) to indicate the ethnic Chinese population in Singapore, while other reports use 'Chinese' (支那人), though the latter carries pejorative connotations in the wartime context. However, because the word 'Chinese' in English does not bear any such meaning, we simply use 'Chinese' for translation.

poorly paid factory workers, coolies, street vendors, called hawkers, and rickshaw pullers. There are Chinese miners who have very low standards of living, but they do not live in Syonan Municipality and consequently are not considered here.

In Syonan Municipality street vendors sell food and sundry goods, whether or not they hold a permit, and this is how they make a living. Some people say that there are ten times more street vendors than there were in the pre-war period.[8] Street vendors buy goods from the market or purchase controlled goods such as tobacco on a retail basis to resell. Because street vending is an occupation that requires a very small capital outlay and no previous experience, it provides a last resort for people with the worst living standards and for the unemployed. We chose four households to represent this group.

Next, we chose for factory workers three coolie households from a rubber company and one family from a mechanical engineering factory. They all receive low payment. We regard them as among the households with the lowest standard of living.

With respect to harbour coolies, we selected two households headed by offshore coolies [those who work on dinghies], one household headed by a coalman and one headed by a dock coolie. All four fall into the group with the lowest living standards, and work in transportation, which at present is a crucial sector. Consequently, establishing the real living standards of these workers must take priority in view of the need to secure important natural resources [for the military].

Others, such as overseas Chinese farmers who live in the suburbs, tend to have higher cash flows than in the pre-war period, due to the increasing prices of agricultural products, livestock and poultry. Moreover, they are self-sufficient in vegetables and fruit. Thus, farmers in the agricultural areas seem to have better living conditions than other Chinese living in the city. Since the reason for this is evident from our simple prior survey, overseas Chinese farmers were not included in any of the groups surveyed.

(2) The Malays

The Malays live in the fringe area around the city, and in far lower conditions than the overseas Chinese who live in the urban areas. The occupations

[8] The 1931 census enumerated 20,499 persons employed in hawking and street selling. This suggests that the numerical increase was less than double, and bearing in mind population growth between 1931 and 1943, the number of hawkers on a per capita basis was much less than some people apparently thought; see chapter 3, table 3.7. The number of hawkers was 38,402 in April 1943. Just after the war those returning to Singapore commented on the great increase in hawkers (O.W. Gilmour, *With Freedom to Singapore*, London: Ernest Benn, 1950, pp. 112, 157).

associated with the lowest standard of living are fishermen, farmers and coolies in the rubber plantations. The fishermen concentrate in the northeast of Syonan (around Bedok, Changi and Pasir Panjang). The farmers live in the northern part of Syonan town (mainly in Geylang Road and Bukit Timah Road). In this survey we chose two households of fishermen and three households of farmers to form the survey group. Those employed as plantation workers are generally unmarried Javanese and therefore do not fulfil the conditions of our survey. There are also some Malay drivers and police officers, who are the envy of other Malays. Also, their housing is provided by their employer or the government. This group may reasonably be excluded from our survey. We were aware of the need to include in our survey households drawn from coolies employed on rubber plantations. However, it proved difficult to find such Malay households on Syonan Island. Therefore, we substituted households from the Senai rubber plantation in the state of Johore. The same rubber plantation provided Indian coolie households for our survey.

(3) The Indians

The poorest group among the Indians are Tamils, who work as road coolies and live in the built-up area. Although they are hired by the city council and are housed in the coolie lines established by the municipality, they live desperate lives at bare subsistence levels. Three such households were chosen for the present survey.

We judged coolies employed on rubber plantations to be the poorest occupational group, and surveyed living conditions of Indian coolies in Johore's Senai rubber plantation.

For the selection of targets, the survey owes much to the assistance of Toyoda Kaoru, director of the General Affairs Department of Syonan Municipality,[9] and Shinozaki Mamoru, the chief manager of the Welfare Section of Syonan Municipality.[10] A summary of the above information is shown in figure 12.1, which indicates the distribution of Syonan Island households surveyed.

3. Research Methods

As already stated, the main aim of this research is to establish, by ethnic group, what constitute daily necessities and to survey their price and quantity. A survey of distribution systems such as retailers alone would not provide adequate data for a proper survey of differences between ethnic groups. In other words, analysis

---

[9] The Japanese consul before the war.

[10] After the war Shinozaki published *Syonan, My Story: The Japanese Occupation of Singapore* (Singapore: Times Books International, 1975), which describes his wartime experiences.

Figure 12.1 Locations of households surveyed

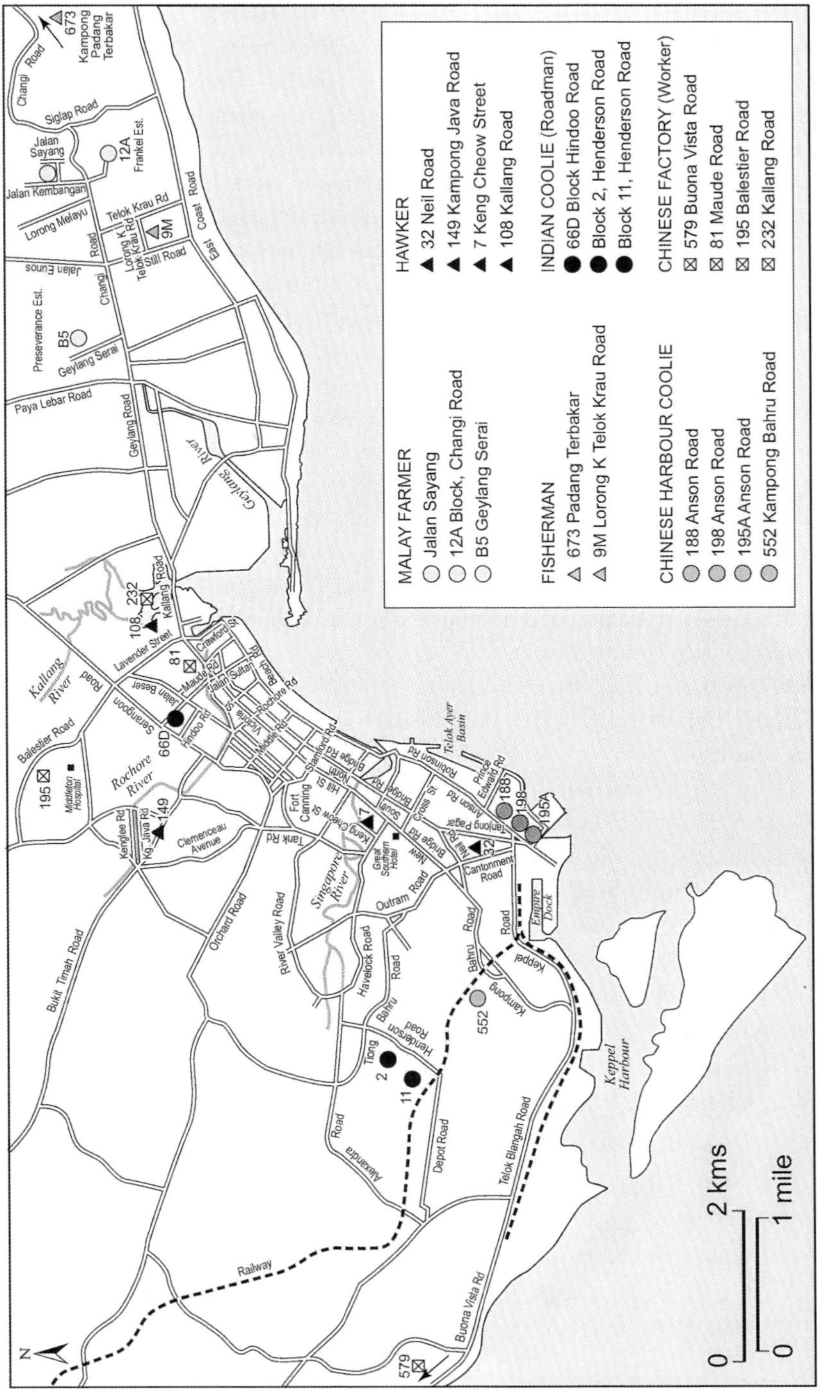

of retail data [i.e., retail prices survey data] would not identify consumption variations between ethnic groups or allow us to survey the price and quantity of daily necessities at the level of ethnic groups. Consequently, the present survey employs the method of a household expenditures survey and uses direct interviews at the household level. An additional advantage of this method is that it could yield some information on the city's black market prices. Of course, these prices could also be surveyed through having researchers from each selected ethnic group purchase goods from retailers while pretending to be end consumers. While reliance on this method alone would allow the compilation of data on price, it would provide insufficient data on quantity. Such a study would be limited to an examination of prices. Moreover, individual researchers would risk influencing data by becoming acquainted with the shop owners they dealt with, creating the need for frequent and inconvenient changes in personnel employed. For these reasons, this survey employs solely the method of a household expenditure survey. The best method would be to prepare household expenditure diaries in advance, which researchers instruct each household to complete. There was, however, insufficient time for this preparation, and instead this pilot survey was conducted by interview. It should therefore be noted that this survey has not adopted standard methodology. (Formatted household expenditure diaries completed by householders will be used, when we at the Southern Military Administration Chōsabu conduct the planned survey of 'Price, Quantity and the Relative Importance of Daily Necessities, by Ethnic Group' [covering all areas of the South].)

Our survey was conducted by Japanese researchers accompanied by local research assistants, both to act as interpreters and to reassure the surveyed households about the purpose of the survey visit.

Classifications for the major daily necessities adopted in this pilot survey are listed in the 'Sample questionnaire on major items of food and clothing, their degree of importance, quantity per month, and prices' [figure 12.3]. Our choice of classification was guided by a small number of published studies listed below, supplemented by the findings of our own small prior survey.

(i) 'A survey of retail price of daily necessaries' by the Department of General Affairs, Malay Military Administration.

(ii) 'General price levels in the Southern Regions' by the Department of Finance, Southern Military Administration.

(iii) 'Report of prices survey' by the Association of Labour Management of Malaya and Sumatra.

(iv) 'A survey of factories producing important daily necessaries' by the Java Military Administration.

Figure 12.2 Sample questionnaire on respondent's household characteristics

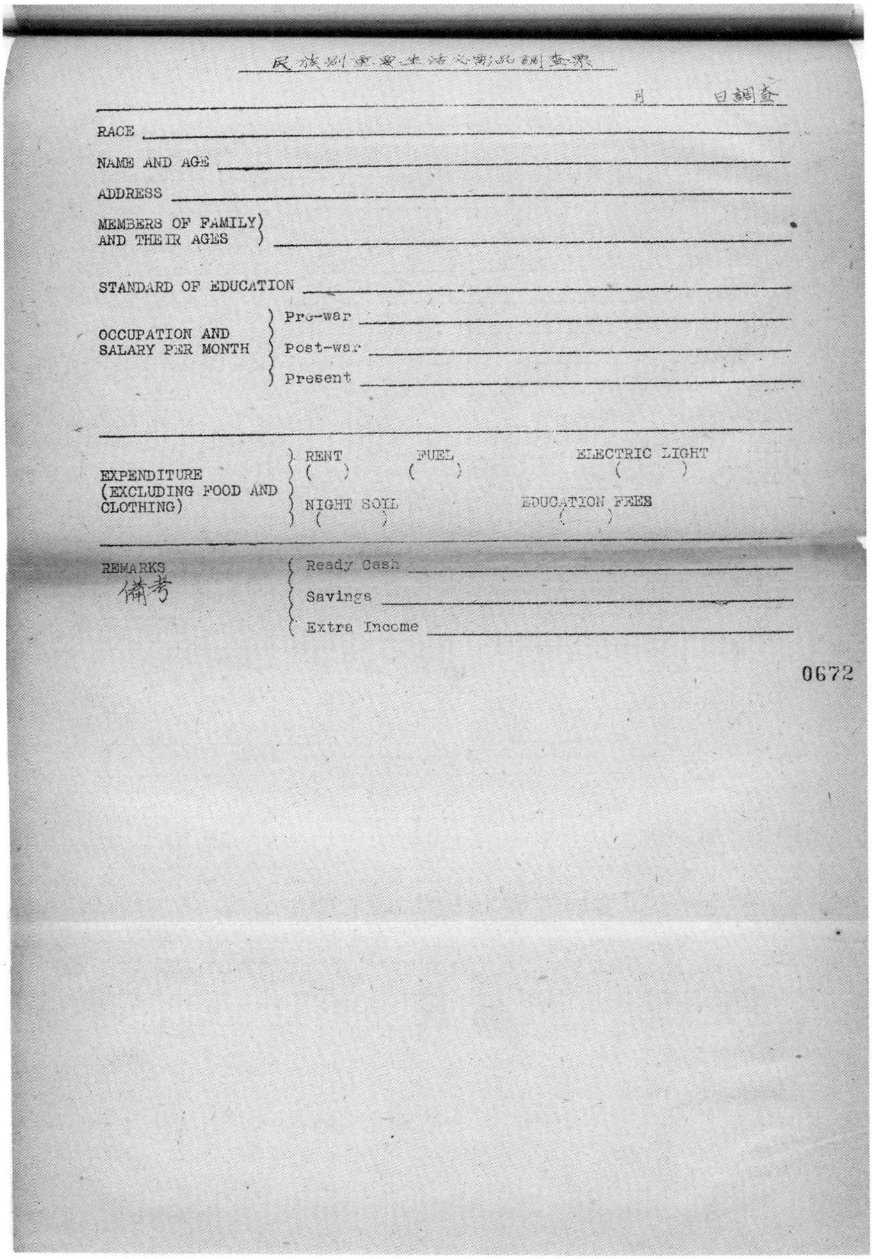

民族別重要生活必需品調査票

月 日調査

RACE ____

NAME AND AGE ____

ADDRESS ____

MEMBERS OF FAMILY AND THEIR AGES ____

STANDARD OF EDUCATION ____

OCCUPATION AND SALARY PER MONTH
- Pre-war ____
- Post-war ____
- Present ____

EXPENDITURE (EXCLUDING FOOD AND CLOTHING)
- RENT ( )
- FUEL ( )
- ELECTRIC LIGHT ( )
- NIGHT SOIL ( )
- EDUCATION FEES ( )

REMARKS 備考
- Ready Cash ____
- Savings ____
- Extra Income ____

0672

Figure 12.3 Sample questionnaire on major items of food and clothing, their degree of importance, quantity per month, and prices

主要食料・衣料品名	必要ノ程度	月當リ消費量	價額
MEATS AND EGGS			
201. Beef			
202. Cow's Lungs			
203. Mutton			
204. Goat's head			
205. Goat's lungs			
206. Goat's stomach			
207. Goat's legs			
208. Pork, lean			
209. Pork, thigh flesh			
210. Pork, stomach flesh			
211. Pork, ribs and flesh			
212. Pork, salted			
213. Pork, lard fat			
214. Fowls			
215. Ducks			
216. Eggs, fresh hens'			
217. Eggs, fresh ducks'			
218. Eggs, fresh turtles'			
FISH			
301. Sepat			
302. Bawal Puteh			
303. Bawal Hitam			
304. Tengiri			
305. Tengiri Papan			
306. Parang			
307. Selah			
308. Kurau			
309. Ikan Merah			
310. Tamban			
311. Billis			
312. Gulamah			

0674

We acknowledge the advice of the Department of Food, Syonan Municipality, in identifying essential food categories for each ethnic group and are particularly grateful to Kitagawa Harutomi for his assistance.

Our survey sought to establish, for each household, the quantity, amount paid, and relative importance of food and beverages purchased over an entire month and the same information for clothes in the course of a year. It was necessary to survey by ethnic group the value attached to various items, since it was possible that the importance accorded to the same item might vary according to ethnic group. We classified items into three groups, as follows: 1. goods indispensable to survival; 2. goods necessary to secure and maintain labour efficiency; 3. other goods. These three groups were coded as A, B and C. Goods other than those initially chosen, which subsequently proved to be necessities in light of the interviews, were included in the survey results.

4. Research Results

As mentioned above, the primary purpose of this research is to determine, by ethnic group, the principal necessities consumed on a daily basis. To this end, the present section sets out the results of our detailed survey of the items of food and clothing as chosen in advance [figure 12.3]. This section aims to indicate what goods are considered necessary by each ethnic group and to estimate their importance. The items of food and clothing in the table [table 12.2] are the same as those in the section above [section 3] as are the codes A, B and C. The superscript numbers attached to these codes indicate the number of households that answered in the affirmative.

Table 12.2 Daily necessities, food and clothing, April–July 1943

	Commodity	Malays, seven households	Chinese, twelve households	Indians, five households
Cereals	Rice, white	A^7	A^{12}	A^5
	Glutinous rice	-	-	-
	Wheat flour	C	-	-
	Barley	C	-	-
	Oats	-	-	-
	Maize	C^2	B, C	A^2, B
	Black soybeans	C	-	-

(cont'd overleaf)

Table 12.2 (cont'd)

	Commodity	Malays, seven households	Chinese, twelve households	Indians, five households
Cereals	Red [aduki] beans	-	-	-
	White beans	-	B	-
	Soybeans	-	-	-
	Kidney beans	C	-	-
	Long beans [haricot]	A, B^2	A^6, B^3	A^2, C
	Sword beans	-	-	-
	Kachang botol [winged beans]	B	-	-
	Green peas	B, C	C^3	A^2, B
	Ragi	-	-	A^2
	Mee-hoon [noodle flour]	-	B^3, C	-
	Mee-kuah [noodles, dried]	-	-	-
	Mee [noodles]	-	C	B, C
	Bean stick	-	B, C	-
	Kway-tiow [rice noodles]	-	B, C	-
	Chinese bean curd	-	C	-
	Chinese tofu [tow-kuah] (white and yellow)	C^2	A^4, B^5, C^2	C^2
	Tofu [tow-hoe] (soft)	-	A, B^3, C^2	C^2
	Sago flour	B^2, C	A, C^8	C
	Sago pearl	-	C^2	C
	Tapioca flour	C	B, C^3	-
Meat and eggs	Beef	-	C	-
	Beef lungs	-	C	-

Table 12.2 (cont'd)

	Commodity	Malays, seven households	Chinese, twelve households	Indians, five households
Meat and eggs	Mutton	-	-	
	Goat, head	-	-	C (Goat, head; lung; gut; leg)
	Goat, lung	-	-	
	Goat, gut	-	-	
	Goat, leg	-	B^2	
	Pork, lean	-	A^2, B^4, C	-
	Pork, thigh	-	A^2, B^3, C^2	-
	Pork, stomach	-	A^2, B^2, C^2	-
	Pork, ribs	-	A, B^2	-
	Pork, salted	-	A, B^2	-
	Pork, lard	-	-	-
	Chickens	-	-	B, C
	Ducks	-	-	B
	Eggs, fresh hen	-	C	-
	Eggs, fresh duck	-	C^2	-
	Eggs, stored duck	-	C	-
	Eggs, fresh turtle	-	-	-
Fish	Sepat	A^2, B^2	B	A^2, C
	Bawal puteh [white harvest fish]	-	A	-
	Bawal hitam [black harvest fish]	-	-	-
	Tengiri [Spanish mackerel]	A, B	A, B	A, B
	Tengiri papan [South Seas sardines]	A	-	-
	Parang [cutlassfish]	A, C^2	A^2, C	A, B

(cont'd overleaf)

Table 12.2 (cont'd)

	Commodity	Malays, seven households	Chinese, twelve households	Indians, five households
Fish	Selah	A^3, B	A^2, B	A
	Kurau	-	-	A, B
	Ikan merah [red sea bream]	-	-	-
	Tamban [sardines]	A^2, C	A^2	A
	Bilis	A^2, B^2	A^7, B^3	A^4, C
	Gulamah [white croaker]	A^2	-	-
	Pari [lobster]	B	C	A, B
	Terubok [gizzard shad]	B	B	-
	Yu [shark]	B	B, C	A
	Kembong	A^2, B	A^3	-
	Prawns	A, B	B, C^2	A, B
	Blachan	A^5	C	-
	Squid	A	-	-
	Crab	-	C^2	-
	Oysters	-	-	C^2
	Clams, Kerang	C	C	-
	Lokar [clams, common orient]	-	-	-
	Kurang [mussels]	C	-	-
	Sea cucumber	-	-	-
Vegetables	Kuchair [Chinese chives]	-	B, C^2	-
	Ginger	B, C	B^2, C	-
	Tomatoes	-	B	-
	Potatoes	-	-	B, C

Table 12.2 (cont'd)

	Commodity	Malays, seven households	Chinese, twelve households	Indians, five households
Vegetables	Leakuas [turmeric]	-	-	-
	Choy sum	-	A^4, B^4, C^2	-
	Yam	B^3	B^2	B, C
	Ladies' fingers	C	-	A^5
	Priya	C	B^4, C^4	A, C
	White radish	-	C	-
	Bamboo shoots	-	-	-
	Serai [lemongrass]	C	-	-
	Limes	C^2	C	A
	Brinjal	A^4	A, B^4, C	A^5
	Tuah chye [leaf mustard]	-	A, B	-
	Snake gourd	-	-	A^2, B, C
	Meh kuay [yellow cucumbers]	-	-	-
	Tapioca	A^3, B^2	-	A^2
	Sweet potatoes	A^3, B^2	A^{12}	A^2, B
	Cucumbers	-	A, B^3	A, C
	Pumpkins	-	B	B
	Spinach	B	B	-
	Turnips	-	B	A, C
	Bean sprouts	C	A^3, B^2, C	A^2, C
	Kangkong	A^2, B	A^7, B^3	A^2
	Tamarind	A^7	C^2	A^5
	Salted vegetables	C	A^2, B^2, C^2	-
	Salted white radish	-	-	-
	Onions	A^2, B, C	B, C^7	A^5
	Garlic	A, B, C	B, C^4	A^5

(cont'd overleaf)

Table 12.2 (cont'd)

	Commodity	Malays, seven households	Chinese, twelve households	Indians, five households
Fruits	Pineapples	B, C	C^2	C
	Papaya	C	C	-
	Watermelons	C^2	-	-
	Bananas, green			
	Bananas, gold	C^3 (Bananas, green; gold; tandok)	C^3	B
	Bananas, tandok			
	Coconuts, fresh	A, B^2, C^2	C	A^4, B
Condiments and relishes	Sugar, white	A^7	A^{12}	A^5
	Sugar, brown	-	-	-
	Sugar, Malacca brown	A, C^2	-	-
	Coconut sugar	C	-	-
	Coarse salt	A^7	A^{12}	A^5
	Salt, fine	-	-	-
	Sauces	B^2	A^9	A^2
	Coriander seeds	-	A	A^5
	Cumin seeds	-	-	A^4
	Methi seeds	-	-	A^4
	Pepper, black	C	-	A^3
	Pepper, white	A, C	-	A^3
	Chillies, red	A^6, B	A, B^3, C^3	A^4
	Chillies, green	A^6, B	A, B, C	A^3
	Chillies, dried	A^5	A, B, C^3	A^5
	Buah keras [candlenuts]	A	C	-
	Lankuas [galangal]	C	-	-
	Vinegar	-	C^2	-
	Chuka manis [sweet vinegar]	-	-	-

Table 12.2 (cont'd)

	Commodity	Malays, seven households	Chinese, twelve households	Indians, five households
Miscellaneous	Coffee, fresh	-	-	-
	Coffee, powdered	A^4, B^2	A^4, B^2, C	A^4, B
	Tea, black	B, C^3	A, B^2, C	A, B
	Cocoa	-	-	-
	Milk, fresh	-	-	C
	Milk, condensed	-	-	-
	Milk, powdered	-	-	-
	Butter	-	-	-
	Jam	-	-	-
	Gambier, round	A, C	-	B^2
	Groundnuts, shelled	-		-
	Groundnuts, boiled	-	C^3	-
	Groundnuts, nut	-		-
	Pickles, garlic	-	-	-
	Pickles, mango	-	-	-
	Aerated orange punch	-	-	-
	Aerated water, sweet	-	-	-
	Cigars	B^2, C	B^2, C	A^3
	Cigarettes	-	A^5, B, C	A^2
	Manufactured tobacco	A^2, B	B	-
	Ginger oil	-	-	A, C
	Coconut oil	A^7	A^7, C	A^3
	Cooking oil	-	A^9	-

(cont'd overleaf)

Table 12.2 (cont'd)

	Commodity	Malays, seven households	Chinese, twelve households	Indians, five households
Wearing apparel	White cloth for shrouds	A^7	-	-
	Cotton cloth for daily use	A^6	A^{11}	A^5
	Rayon cloth	-	-	-
	Silk	-	-	-
	Bed sheets	A	A^2	A
	Shirts	A^5	-	A
	Sarongs	A^7	-	A^5
	Towels	A^3, C^2	A^{12}	A^3
	Trousers	A^6	A^{11}	A^4
	Coats	A^7	A^{10}	A^3
	Hats or caps	A^7	A^7	A
	Socks or stockings	A^2, C	-	-
	Shoes	A^6	A^{10}	-
	Mosquito nets	A^3	A^2	A

We now give further information on the data in table 12.2.

(1) Food

(i) The Malays

The main staple food of Malays is white rice.[11] When rice is in short supply, Malays will eat tapioca and sweet potato to supplement their diet. For accompanying dishes, Malays eat fish (sepat, selah and bilis)[12] and vegetables (kangkong and brinjal).[13]

Obviously, seasonings such as sugar and salt are important, and for the Malays chillies are an essential seasoning. Onions and garlic are also used as seasonings.

---

[11] See chapter 2 for the significance of this statement in relation to rations.

[12] Ikan sepat is a kind of gourami, selah is yellowtail scad, and bilis is anchovy.

[13] Kangkong is a long-stalked leaf vegetable, and brinjal is aubergine.

As is generally known, blachan[14] is a favoured Malay side dish. Tamarind, cooked as soup, is also a highly relished food.

Among fruits, we found that the only favoured ones are coconuts (A), (B^2) and pineapples (B). All other fruits rated at C. This result indicates that although this land is abundant in fruits, fruits are still luxury goods for the poorest class of Malays. This finding is true not only of Malays; it recurred throughout our research. However, the research area was confined to the city area, and suppressed demand caused by price rises may have affected the survey result.

The market prices of fruit at the time of the survey are set out in table 12.3.

Their religion forbids Malays from eating pork. This gives the Malay diet its most distinct feature. Moreover, the Malay demand for coffee is so strong that this item ranks as a daily necessity alongside foodstuffs such as rice, sugar and salt.

Table 12.3 Market fruit prices, April 1943

	Price (cents per catty)
Pineapple	6
Papaya	47
Watermelon	22
Banana	3–8 (piece, depending on size)
Fresh coconut	14 (piece)

(ii) The Chinese

As in the case of Malays, rice is the staple food for Chinese. However, they only substitute sweet potato [and not tapioca] for rice. Their main accompanying dishes are long beans, Chinese tofu, bilis, choy sum, bean sprouts and kangkong.

Like the Malays, the Chinese favour bilis among fish and kangkong among vegetables. This arises partly from similar tastes. However, the effect of relatively cheap market prices and better distribution around Syonan Municipality cannot be overlooked.

For comparison, table 12.4 shows market prices of various foods at the time of this survey.

The high consumption of pork confirms what we know about the Chinese diet. What was unexpected was the high consumption of coffee, which appears in table 12.2 as A^4, B^2 and C. Chinese respondents told us that they could not obtain enough sugar through rationing to make coffee at home. Being desperate for coffee, they therefore had to buy it at a coffee house. No doubt the habit

[14] A dried shrimp paste.

of drinking coffee has been acquired as they have slowly assimilated the local custom since the Chinese immigrated to Syonan Island.

Table 12.4 Market food prices, April 1943

	Price (cents per catty)
Bilis	90
Selah	190
Cutlassfish	174
South Seas sardine	242
Kangkong	11
Choy sum	37
Brinjal	21

All ethnic groups requested, above all, an increase in the white rice ration. Chinese engaged in heavy labour, such as harbour coolies, particularly complained that the ration of 14 catties per person per month was insufficient. At work, the harbour coolies are provided with 0.5 to 0.3 catties of meal by their subcontracting employers, so the real total amount of their food ration is more than 14 catties. But considering the nature of their work, their demand is, of course, reasonable. There are two reasons why a higher ration is demanded. One is that the ration does not meet consumption demand, particularly since the current high price of vegetables has changed dietary patterns by increasing consumption of cheap rationed rice to substitute for vegetables. The second reason is that rationed rice is sold on the black market for cash, and the Chinese then complain about insufficient rations; this, however, is a consequence of their own actions.

Therefore it may be necessary to re-examine the uniform rationing system for rice, to allow higher rations for a selected group of workers (for details, see 'Report on Retail Prices in April' by the Department of Planning, Military Administration). We only mention these issues since the rationing problem is not the prime purpose of this research.

(iii) The Indians (Tamils)

As in the case of the first two groups, white rice is the staple food for Indians. Maize, tapioca and sweet potato are accepted as substitutes.

Among southern Indians, ragi[15] is a staple food. This is difficult to obtain in Syonan owing to the present closure of transport routes. The information on ragi

[15] Finger millet.

(A[2] in the table) is derived from rubber plantation coolies, who produced a small amount of ragi for their own household consumption.

The main accompanying dishes are green peas, long beans, sepat, bilis, ladies' fingers, brinjal, snake gourd and bean sprouts.

Onions, garlic and tamarind are used as seasonings, while coriander seeds, cumin seeds, methi seeds,[16] pepper and chillies are indispensable constituents of what they call curry stuff.

Coriander, cumin and methi are imported from India. Because it is hard to obtain them nowadays, prices have risen. The dependence of southern Indians on imports has made their situation desperate. Owing to their distinct diet, the complaint that there is insufficient salt in the ration is particular to them, and not expressed by the other two ethnic groups. Southern Indians also complain strongly about inadequate sugar rations, owing to their use of sugar in coffee. This is also a frequent complaint among the other two ethnic groups.

(2) Wearing apparel

All ethnic groups complain that in current market conditions the price of wearing apparel is too high to allow them to buy clothes within their household budgets.

No survey respondent had been able to buy new clothes since the start of the occupation.

As soon as we raised the question of purchasing clothes, the survey respondents replied so universally and so bitterly that they were unable to buy anything at all that it was as if their response had been agreed in advance. We were shown tattered and mended shirts and outer garments of their own and their family members, and heard complaints that this desperate state of affairs was becoming the norm.

At present, they are still managing with clothes bought in the pre-war period. Since this is a tropical zone, an optimistic interpretation is that the need for clothing is not great. But because it is a tropical zone, shirts have to be washed frequently. However, washing soap is now in short supply and very expensive. Shirts washed without soap spoil quickly. The assertion of respondents that shirts last for only between six months and a year has validity.

The same situation prevails for Malays with respect to white cloth for shrouds. Before the war, 9 yards of cloth was used for an adult and 4 yards for a child. This has now had to be reduced to 3 yards for adults. We were told that when white cloth could not be obtained, it was necessary to use instead an already well-worn sarong belonging to a deceased person. Since these customs have a religious origin, we consider that the problem cannot be overlooked.

---

16 Methi seeds are seeds of fenugreek.

Moreover, washing soap is difficult to buy because of price increases, as mentioned above. In current conditions, people have no option but to wash clothes without soap or to use ash as a substitute.

5. Family Budgets in Households Surveyed

While conducting research into daily necessities, we also asked subjects for overall incomes and expenditures. This section sets out our findings for household budgets among our survey subjects [see also tables 12.5–12.9 and 12.11].

(1) The Malays

As mentioned above, Malays live in fringe areas of Syonan and because of this, farmers and fishermen build their own houses. These are very basic structures. The coolies on rubber plantations live on the plantation in lines of housing. They can therefore easily obtain wood for fuel from the surrounding area without payment.

Consequently, their main expenditure (over 90 per cent) is on food. In both of the rubber plantation coolie households, the householder's wife also works for 45 cents daily. Rubber plantation coolies work 20 days a month, and for the remaining 10 days they grow food for themselves. As a result [adding together the earnings of husband and wife], they earn $18 per month.

Food production on the rubber plantation is encouraged by the plantation's managers. This, combined with the coolies' own efforts, has resulted in a recent rise in food production on the estate which seems to have markedly improved living conditions for coolie households.

(2) The Chinese

(i) Hawkers

In order to select the respondent households, the local research assistant first visited the streets where hawkers trade and sought cooperation in the research. A date was then set to complete the questionnaire at hawker households (table 12.6). Hawkers live in Chinatown, in second- or third-floor flats in low-cost buildings. There are generally four or five households on each floor, and individual households therefore occupy very small flats.

Because they live in the centre of the city, expenditure on fuel is high, being between 10 per cent and 20 per cent of total expenditure.

The third sample householder was a hawker, who since the pre-war period has also earned $20 per month as a coolie in a Chinese trading company. He pays $3 for his eldest daughter's school fees.

Table 12.5 Malay household monthly incomes and expenditures, April–July 1943

Occupation and monthly wages, dollars			Family members	Level of education	Monthly expenditure, dollars					
Present	Before Feb. 1942	Just after Feb. 1942			House rent	Fuel	Lighting	Education	Food	Total
Farmer, 30	Sailor, 26	Farmer	Wife and child	None	0.00 (Own house)	0.00	1.60	0.00	26.60	28.20
Farmer, 30 (Syonan Municipality farm)	Janitor, 18 and tailor, 24	Tailor, 24	Wife and child	Malay primary school, third grade	0.00 (Rent-free council house)	0.00	2.00	0.00	13.90	15.90
Farmer, 15	Driver, 40	Farmer, 9	Wife and child	None	0.00	0.00	2.00	0.00	17.70	19.70
Fisherman, 40	Fisherman, 40	Fisherman, 40	Father, wife, 6 children, nephew	None	0.50 (Land rent)	0.00	3.00	0.30	32.80	36.60
Fisherman, 30	Doorkeeper, 25	Fisherman, 30	Wife, 2 children, 2 grand-children	None	4.00	0.00	0.00	0.00	25.80	29.80
Occupation and daily wages, dollars										
Rubber plantation coolie, 0.45	Rubber plantation coolie, 0.70		Wife and 2 children	Third grade	0.00	0.00	0.70	0.00	9.20	9.90
Rubber plantation coolie, 0.45	Rubber plantation coolie, 0.80		Wife and child	None	0.00	0.00	2.10	0.00	11.20	13.30

Note: Lighting expenses were for the lamp oil.

Table 12.6 Chinese household monthly incomes and expenditures, hawkers, April–July 1943

Occupation and monthly wages, dollars			Family members	Level of education (ethnic group)	Monthly expenditure, dollars					
Present	Before Feb. 1942	Just after Feb. 1942			House rent*	Fuel	Lighting	Education	Food	Total
Fruit hawker, 70	Building coolie, 50	Hawker, 70	Mother, wife, 2 children, 2 younger sisters	None (Cantonese)	5.00	15.00	0.00	0.00	49.10	69.10
Vegetable and dried fish hawker, 50	Hawker, 50	Hawker, 50	Wife, 2 children	None (Teochew)	7.50	3.50	0.00	0.00	46.70	57.70
Sweet potato hawker,[17] 60 (incl. income as coolie, 20)	Coolie, 20		Wife, 3 children	None (Teochew)	6.00	7.00	1.00 lamp oil	3.00	39.50	56.50
Rice noodle hawker, 50	Rice noodle hawker, 50	Rice noodle hawker, 50	Wife	None (Teochew)	4.50	6.00	0.40 lamp oil	0.00	22.40	33.30

Note: * House rent includes lighting and water.

[17] The blank entry for the wage of the sweet potato hawker may mean that he was temporarily unemployed just after February 1942.

Table 12.7 Chinese household daily incomes and monthly expenditures, harbour coolies, April–July 1943

Occupation and daily wages, dollars			Family members	Level of education (ethnic group)	Monthly expenditure, dollars					
Present	Before Feb. 1942	Just after Feb. 1942			House rent	Fuel	Lighting	Education	Food	Total
Off-shore coolie, 1.50	Off-shore coolie, 1.40	Off-shore coolie, 1.40	Wife and 2 children	None (Hockchia/ Hokkien)	5.00 (incl. lighting)	10.00	0.00	0.00	52.70	67.70
Off-shore coolie, 1.50	Off-shore coolie, 1.20	Off-shore coolie, 1.20	Wife and child	None (Hockchia/ Hokkien)	7.00	6.00	0.00	0.00	62.20	75.20
Coal coolie, 1.50	Coal coolie, 50 monthly	Coal coolie, 50 monthly	Mother, wife and child	None (Hokkien)	5.50	8.00	0.00	0.00	45.70	59.20
Dock coolie, 1.80	Dock coolie, 1.60	Cock coolie, 1.60	Wife and child	None (Hokkien)	2.75	14.00	0.00	20.00 remitted to mother	64.25	101.00

Table 12.8 Chinese household daily incomes and monthly expenditures, factory workers, April–July 1943

Occupation and daily wages, dollars			Family members	Level of education (ethnic group)	Monthly expenditure, dollars					
Present	Before Feb. 1942	Just after Feb. 1942			House rent	Fuel	Lighting	Education	Food	Total
Rubber company coolie, 0.65	Rubber company coolie, 0.80	Rubber company coolie, 0.80	Grandmother, father, mother, wife, 2 children, younger brother, 5 younger sisters	None (Teochew)	4.00	4.00	6.00 (lamp oil)	1.00	78.80	93.80
Rubber company coolie, 0.70	Unemployed	Unemployed	Husband and 3 children	None (Hokkien)	4.00	8.00	3.00 (lamp oil)	0.00	33.70	48.70
Rubber company coolie, 0.70	Rubber company coolie, 0.70	Rubber company coolie, 0.70	4 children	None (Cantonese)	5.50	7.00	0.00	0.00	69.00	81.50
Machinery factory worker, 2.70	Machinery factory worker, 2.75	Machinery factory worker, 2.75	Wife and 6 children	None (Cantonese)	10.00	6.00	2.20 (lamp oil)	0.00	96.50	114.70

The fourth sample householder used to remit $5 a month to his mother in China before the war. He said that he wanted to resume these remittances as soon as possible through money transfer services now made available by the Military Administration.

(ii) Harbour coolies

We identified harbour coolies for this study at the Syonan Harbour Company, with the assistance of the company's Personnel Department. Harbour coolies can be separated into four different occupational categories: offshore [dinghy] coolies, dock coolies, coal coolies and general ancillary coolies. Within these four distinct groups, general coolies do not specialize in harbour work, and they are omitted from the table.

Harbour coolies' daily wages are between $1.50 and $1.80. The monthly wages may increase considerably in the future because the amount of cargo work is greater, the length of the working day has increased, and there is a rise in the number of night shifts. In our first sample household of an offshore coolie, the householder's wife earned about $6 per month for rope making. The wife of the coal coolie in our sample earned $13 per month as a general ancillary coolie, and her income augmented the household budget. Whether or not coincidentally, all four coolies smoked opium. The hard physical work performed by coolies, such as loading and unloading, seems to make opium an indispensable source of stimulus.

The legally controlled price of opium amounts to $1.50 for four days' supply. Coolies spend $12 per month on opium, which, remarkably, is more than 10 per cent of their income.

Data provided by the Syonan Harbour Company show that of 1,601 Chinese coolies, 933 (58 per cent) smoked opium.

(iii) Factory workers

The householder in the first sample household worked as a coolie at Yokohama Rubber Company but had additional income of $30 from his father, who worked as a vegetable hawker, and $8 from his younger brother, employed as a kitchen boy for one of the army units. The household's total income was $56, but there were outgoings of nearly $94, which was unusually high. When we asked why there was such a large discrepancy, we were told that the younger brother, who works as a kitchen boy for the army, brought home 12 catties of leftovers every day. Since rice rations are a half-catty per person per day, 12 catties a day is not a negligible quantity. It was therefore likely that the surplus rice from 12 catties of leftovers was sold on the black market, and the income derived from this must have contributed to the household economy.

Table 12.9 Indian household daily incomes and monthly expenditures, rubber plantation coolies, April–July 1943[18]

Occupation and daily wages, dollars			Family members	Level of education	Monthly expenditure, dollars					
Present	Before Feb. 1942	Just after Feb. 1942			House rent	Fuel	Lighting	Education	Food	Total
Rubber plantation coolie, 0.40	Rubber plantation coolie, 0.50		Wife, 4 children	None	0.00	0.00	0.00	0.00	27.41	27.41
Rubber plantation coolie, 0.40	Rubber plantation coolie, 0.80		Wife, 5 children	None	0.00	0.00	0.00	0.00	33.30	33.30

[18] The report leaves the entry blank for post-war wages. This may mean that the workers were temporarily unemployed just after the start of Japanese occupation.

In both the second and third sample households, the principal worker was a woman employed as a rubber company coolie at Tōshin Kōgyō Company. In the second sample the female coolie was temporarily employed, because her husband was out of work. In the third sample the coolie was a widow who tried to scrape together a household income with her eldest son, who earned $1.60 daily. Both households also received economic help from their relatives. The worker in the fourth sample was an assembly worker at Suen An (順安) Company. As a skilled worker, his monthly salary was over $100 due to the current increase in the number of night shifts. When an additional income of $20 per month from his two daughters was added to this, the family, although large, could afford a comfortable lifestyle. The householder also formerly sent $20 to his father in China, and when asked he said he would like to start sending money again now that remittances are permitted.

(3) The Indians

(i) Rubber plantation coolies

The householder in the first sample, his wife and his 14-year-old eldest son all worked at the rubber plantation [Senai plantation in Johore], earning 40 and 20 cents each. In the second sample, too, the wife worked for 40 cents. Their monthly income was therefore $20 and $16 respectively [working for 20 days]. As with the Malays, Indians grow food for themselves, which is of considerable help to the household budget. In addition, to meet expenditure in excess of income, the householder in the second sample sold his wife's jewellery (table 12.9).

As indicated below, rubber plantation coolies are meant to receive rations of rice, salt and sugar from the plantation. It should be noted that in July [1943] 80 per cent of the stipulated rice ration was distributed, and 50 per cent of the salt and sugar rations.

Table 12.10 Rubber plantation coolie stipulated monthly rations, April–July 1943

Rice	Male	3 gantang [18 catties]
	Female	2 gantang [12 catties]
	Child	0.8 gantang [4.8 catties]
	Dependant, male	1.5 gantang [9 catties]
	Dependant, female	1 gantang [6 catties]
Sugar		1 catty per person
Salt		1 catty per person

Table 12.11 Indian household daily incomes and monthly expenditures, road construction workers, April–July 1943[19]

Occupation and daily wages, dollars			Family members	Level of education	Monthly expenditure, dollars					
Present	Before Feb. 1942	Just after Feb. 1942			House rent	Fuel	Lighting	Education	Food	Total
Road construction worker, 1.02	Road construction worker, 0.94		Wife and child	Tamil education, fifth grade	0.00	0.00	2.50	0.00	47.30	49.80
Road construction worker, 0.80	Road construction worker, 0.56		Wife, 3 children	Tamil education, a little	0.00	6.00	2.50	0.00	32.20	40.70
Road construction worker, 0.62	Road construction worker, 0.54		Wife, 5 children	None	0.00	3.00	2.50	0.00	36.00	41.50

Note: Lighting expenses were for the lamp oil.

[19] The report leaves the entry blank for post-war wages. This may mean that the workers were temporarily unemployed just after the start of Japanese occupation.

(ii) Road construction workers

In researching road construction workers, we were helped by staff of the Labour Office of Syonan Municipality's Department of Welfare. These road construction workers lived in tenements owned by Syonan Municipality. Therefore, they did not pay rent or for water or for the daily latrine exchange service. However, the tenement is not provided with lighting, obliging residents to buy coconut oil to use for lighting. The tenements are constructed out of concrete, and there are around ten rooms in each. There are a few similar buildings built in a row, which comprise the residential area. Each building has a communal kitchen, bathroom and toilet. A married man has a room to himself, while single men share one room with two others. All three sample households spent considerably more than they earned. It is possible that they were over-optimistic in planning their budgets, but it must also be recognized that recent price increases have particularly affected curry seasonings (a daily necessity) and raised living costs. Of all the groups surveyed, Indian road construction workers, whose earnings are in any case very low, were the group with the worst conditions.

In conclusion, on the basis of the findings presented above, we selected for each ethnic group the most important goods in daily consumption. The list titled 'Itemized list of goods of importance in daily consumption by ethnic group' is shown in table A.12.1.

Our selection criteria, for the items shown in table A.12.1 as the final list,[20] are:

1. All the items categorized as 'A' in table 12.2; however, there were more Malay and Chinese households than Indian households, so we did not list the items that received only one A [as the important daily necessity] for Malay and Chinese households.
2. Even when none of the households categorized an item as A, when the total number of B's and C's for the item exceeded half the total number of households, we included the item in the final list.
3. Several items that had not been included in the pilot survey, such as matches, soap, fuel, opium and alcohol, were added to the final list, because during the course of our research we recognized them as necessities.
4. In the case of clothing, some respondents chose all the items in the questionnaire as necessities. We narrowed down the selection[21] as appropriate, as shown in table A.12.1. In doing so, we bore in mind our emphasis on identifying the lowest standard of living.

[20] This final list of itemized goods of daily necessities by ethnic group was used for the forthcoming main survey of household expenditures, c.f. Chōsabu Report 50.

[21] 8 out of the initial 14 in figure 12.3.

5. We also added to the final list several types of food and clothing that were found in the price survey conducted by the Department of Finance of Southern Military Administration (previously mentioned [section 3, (ii)]) and the food survey by the Department of Food, Syonan Municipality (previously mentioned [section 3, but the survey title is not mentioned]).

Appendices

Table A.12.1 Itemized list of goods of importance in daily consumption by ethnic group

Indonesians [Malays]	Chinese	Indians
Cereals		
(101) Rice, white	(101) Rice, white	(101) Rice, white
(102) Maize		(102) Maize
(103) Haricots	(103) Haricots	(103) Haricots
	(104) Green peas	(104) Green peas
	(105) Mee	
		(106) Ragi
	(107) Tofu (white / yellow)	
	(108) Tofu (soft)	
(109) Sago flour	(109) Sago flour	
Meat and eggs		
(201) Beef	(201) Beef	
(202) Mutton		(202) Mutton
	(203) Pork, lean	
	(204) Pork, thigh	
	(205) Pork, stomach	
	(206) Pork, ribs	
	(207) Pork, salted	
	(208) Pork, lard	
(209) Chickens	(209) Chickens	(209) Chickens
		(210) Ducks
(211) Eggs, fresh hen	(211) Eggs, fresh hen	
	(212) Eggs, fresh duck	
Fish		
(301) Sepat		(301) Sepat
(302) Spanish mackerel	(302) Spanish mackerel	(302) Spanish mackerel

(cont'd overleaf)

Table A.12.1 (cont'd)

Indonesians [Malays]	Chinese	Indians
(303) Cutlassfish	(303) Cutlassfish	(303) Cutlassfish
(304) Selah	(304) Selah	(304) Selah
		(305) Kurau
(306) Sardines	(306) Sardines	(306) Sardines
(307) Bilis	(307) Bilis	(307) Bilis
(308) White croaker		
		(309) Lobster
(310) Kembong	(310) Kembong	
(311) Prawns	(311) Prawns	(311) Prawns
Vegetables		
	(401) Choy sum	
(402) Yam		(402) Yam
		(403) Ladies' fingers
	(404) Priya	(404) Priya
(405) Brinjal	(405) Brinjal	(405) Brinjal
		(406) Snake gourd
(407) Tapioca		(407) Tapioca
(408) Sweet potatoes	(408) Sweet potatoes	(408) Sweet potatoes
	(409) Cucumber	(409) Cucumber
		(410) Turnips
	(411) Bean sprouts	(411) Bean sprouts
(412) Kangkong	(412) Kangkong	(412) Kangkong
(413) Salted vegetables	(413) Salted vegetables	
(414) Onions	(414) Onions	(414) Onions
(415) Garlic	(415) Garlic	(415) Garlic
Fruit		
(501) Pineapples	(501) Pineapples	(501) Pineapples
(502) Bananas	(502) Bananas	(502) Bananas
(503) Coconuts, fresh	(503) Coconuts, fresh	(503) Coconuts, fresh
Condiments and relishes		
(601) Sugar, white	(601) Sugar, white	(601) Sugar, white

Table A.12.1 (cont'd)

Indonesians [Malays]	Chinese	Indians
(602) Sugar, brown	(602) Sugar, brown	(602) Sugar, brown
(603) Coarse salt	(603) Coarse salt	(603) Coarse salt
(604) Sauces	(604) Sauces	(604) Sauces
		(605) Coriander seeds
		(606) Cumin seeds
		(607) Methi seeds
(608) Curry powder		(608) Curry powder
(609) Pepper, black		(609) Pepper, black
(610) Pepper, white		(610) Pepper, white
(611) Chillies, red	(611) Chillies, red	(611) Chillies, red
(612) Chillies, green	(612) Chillies, green	(612) Chillies, green
(613) Chillies, dried	(613) Chillies, dried	(613) Chillies, dried
Miscellaneous		
(701) Coffee, powdered	(701) Coffee, powdered	(701) Coffee, powdered
(702) Tea, black	(702) Tea, black	(702) Tea, black
(703) Gambier, round		(703) Gambier, round
(704) Tamarind		(704) Tamarind
(705) Blachan		
(706) Cigars	(706) Cigars	(706) Cigars
	(707) Cigarettes	(707) Cigarettes
(708) Manufactured tobacco		
	(709) Opium	
	(710) Chinese wine	
		(711) Toddy
(712) Matches	(712) Matches	(712) Matches
(713) Soap	(713) Soap	(713) Soap
		(714) Gingelly oil
(715) Coconut oil	(715) Coconut oil	(715) Coconut oil
(716) Charcoal	(716) Charcoal	(716) Charcoal
(717) Firewood	(717) Firewood	(717) Firewood

(cont'd overleaf)

Indonesians [Malays]	Chinese	Indians
Wearing apparel		
(801) Cotton cloth	(801) Cotton cloth	(801) Cotton cloth
(802) Rayon cloth	(802) Rayon cloth	(802) Rayon cloth
(803) Shirts	(803) Shirts	(803) Shirts
(804) Cotton sarongs		(804) Cotton sarongs
(805) Rayon sarongs		(805) Rayon sarongs
(806) Towels	(806) Towels	(806) Towels
(807) Trousers	(807) Trousers	(807) Trousers
(808) Hats and caps	(808) Hats and caps	(808) Hats and caps

Figure A.12.1 Major daily necessities in five languages

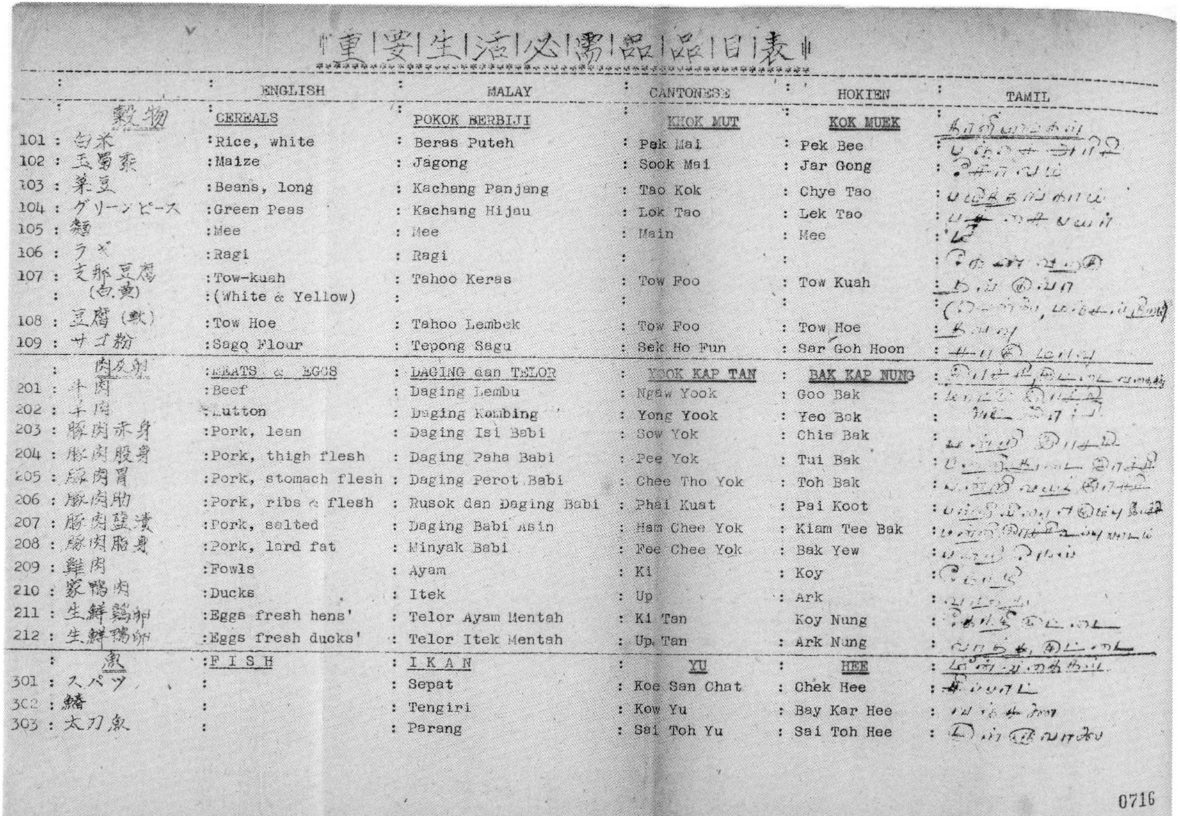

重要生活必需品品目表

		ENGLISH	MALAY	CANTONESE	HOKIEN	TAMIL
	穀物	CEREALS	POKOK BERBIJI	KHOK MUT	KOK MUEK	[illegible]
101	白米	Rice, white	Beras Puteh	Pek Mai	Pek Bee	[illegible]
102	玉蜀黍	Maize	Jagong	Sook Mai	Jar Gong	[illegible]
103	菜豆	Beans, long	Kachang Panjang	Tao Kok	Chye Tao	[illegible]
104	グリーンピース	Green Peas	Kachang Hijau	Lok Tao	Lek Tao	[illegible]
105	麺	Mee	Mee	Main	Mee	[illegible]
106	ラギ	Ragi	Ragi			[illegible]
107	支那豆腐 (白.黄)	Tow-kuah (White & Yellow)	Tahoo Keras	Tow Foo	Tow Kuah	[illegible]
108	豆腐 (軟)	Tow Hoe	Tahoo Lembek	Tow Foo	Tow Hoe	[illegible]
109	サゴ粉	Sago Flour	Tepong Sagu	Sek Ho Fun	Sar Goh Hoon	[illegible]
	肉及卵	MEATS & EGGS	DAGING dan TELOR	YOOK KAP TAN	BAK KAP NUNG	[illegible]
201	牛肉	Beef	Daging Lembu	Ngaw Yook	Goo Bak	[illegible]
202	羊肉	Mutton	Daging Kambing	Yong Yook	Yeo Bak	[illegible]
203	豚肉赤身	Pork, lean	Daging Isi Babi	Sow Yok	Chis Bak	[illegible]
204	豚肉股身	Pork, thigh flesh	Daging Paha Babi	Pee Yok	Tui Bak	[illegible]
205	豚肉胃	Pork, stomach flesh	Daging Perot Babi	Chee Tho Yok	Toh Bak	[illegible]
206	豚肉肋	Pork, ribs & flesh	Rusok dan Daging Babi	Phai Kuat	Pai Koot	[illegible]
207	豚肉塩漬	Pork, salted	Daging Babi Asin	Ham Chee Yok	Kiam Tee Bak	[illegible]
208	豚肉脂身	Pork, lard fat	Minyak Babi	Fee Chee Yok	Bak Yew	[illegible]
209	鶏肉	Fowls	Ayam	Ki	Koy	[illegible]
210	家鴨肉	Ducks	Itek	Up	Ark	[illegible]
211	生鮮鶏卵	Eggs fresh hens'	Telor Ayam Mentah	Ki Tan	Koy Nung	[illegible]
212	生鮮鴨卵	Eggs fresh ducks'	Telor Itek Mentah	Up Tan	Ark Nung	[illegible]
	魚	FISH	IKAN	YU	HEE	[illegible]
301	スパツ		Sepat	Koe San Chat	Chek Hee	[illegible]
302	鰆		Tengiri	Kow Yu	Bay Kar Hee	[illegible]
303	太刀魚		Parang	Sai Toh Yu	Sai Toh Hee	[illegible]

0716

Bibliography

Archives

Japan

Center for Asian Historical Resource, National Archives of Japan (JACAR).
Hitotsubashi University, Institute of Economic Research Library (IER).
Kishi Koichi Collection, Institute of Developing Economies, Japan External Trade Organization (IDE-JETRO) (KKC).
National Institute for Defense Studies, Military History Research Centre (NIDS).
Nishijima Collection, Waseda University, Tokyo (NC).
Hitotsubashi University College History Archive (CHA).

Malaysia

Arkib Negara Malaysia (National Archives of Malaysia) (ANM).

Singapore

National Archives of Singapore (NAS).

United Kingdom

National Archives, Kew (NA).
CO273 Straits Settlements Original Correspondence.
CO852 Colonial Office Economic General Department.
WO203 War of 1939–45; Military Headquarters Papers, Far East.

Official Publications

Japan

Japan, Army. 'Nanpō Gunsei Chōsa Keikaku An [Southern Military Administration Research Plan], 16 August 1942', based on Riku-A-Mitsu Order No. 2772. In *Sakakibara-ke Shozō Nanpōgun Gunsei Sōkanbu Kankei Bunsho* [Documents of Sakakibara Family Related to Southern Military Administration Superintendent General's Office], Vol. 7, ed. Yōji Akashi. Tokyo: Ryūkei Shosha, 2004.

Japan, Cabinet Planning Board, *Gendai Shi Shiryō (43) Kokka Sōdōin (1) Keizai* [Materials on Recent History, Vol. 43 National Total Mobilization, Part 1 Economy]. Tokyo: Misuzu Shobō, 1970.

Japan, Cabinet Statistical Office. *Kakei Chōsa Kekka no Gaiyō* [A Summary of Household Expenditure Survey Results], *October 1941–September 1942*. Tokyo: Cabinet Statistical Office, 1977.

Japan, Imperial Headquarters. *Gozen Kaigi Shidai* [Minutes of Imperial Conference] 5 Nov. 1941, 'Tai Ei-Bei-Ran Sensō ni tomonau Zaisei Kin'yu no Jikyuryoku Handan ni kansuru Setsumei Yōshi (Ōkura Daijin)' [Summary of Explanation (by Finance Minister) on Financial Durability in Relation to the War against Britain, America and the Netherlands], in Institute of Developing Economies, Japan External Trade Organization (IDE-JETRO), Kishi Collection File No. B1-209.

———. Nampo Senryōchi Gyōsei Jisshi Yōkō, presented at the Liaison Conference, 20 Nov. 1941, in Kishi Collection B1-224.

Japan, Southern Military Administration Superintendent General's Office. 'Gunsei Sōkanbu Sōmu-buchō Kōen Yōshi [Lieutenant General Tanakahashi Tan: Summary of a Speech by the Director of General Affairs Department, Southern Military Administration Superintendent General's Office], 8 February 1943'. In *Sakakibara-ke Shozō Nanpōgun Gunsei Sōkanbu Kankei Bunsho* [Documents of Sakakibara Family Related to Southern Military Administration Superintendent General's Office], Vol. 7, ed. Yōji Akashi. Tokyo: Ryūkei Shosha, 2004.

———. 'Shōkō-ren Meibo Kōtōkan-ren Meibo [List of Officers' Names, List of Higher Civil Administrators' Names] 21 March 1943'. In *Sakakibara-ke Shozō Nanpōgun Gunsei Sōkanbu Kankei Bunsho* [Documents of Sakakibara Family Related to Southern Military Administration Superintendent General's Office], Vol. 7, ed. Yōji Akashi. Tokyo: Ryūkei Shosha, 2004.

Japan, Statistical Office of the General Administrative Agency of the Cabinet. *Kakei Chōsa Kekka no Gaiyō* [Summary of Household Expenditure Survey], *October 1941–September 1942*. Tokyo: Statistical Office of the General Administrative Agency of the Cabinet, 1977.

Institute of East Asian Economis (IER)

Institute of East Asian Economies. *Tokyo Sangyō Daigaku Tōa Kenkyūjo Gaiyō* [A Summary of the Institute of East Asian Economies at Tokyo University of Industry]. Tokyo: Tokyo Sangyō Daigaku Tōa Kenkyūjo, 1943.

IER, Azb: 1. *Chōsabu Report No. 36: Malaya ni okeru Inflation no Jōkyō to Sono Taisaku* [Inflationary Situation in Malaya and Its Countermeasures]. Taiping: Malayan Military Administration Chōsabu, Apr. 1944.

IER, Azb: 3. *Chōsabu Report No. 44: Syonan tōnai Shokuryō Zōsan Saku ni tsuite* [Methods of Increasing Food Production on Syonan Island]. Taiping: Malayan Military Administration Chōsabu, Oct. 1944.

IER, Azb: 4. *Chōsabu Report No. 45: Syonan Tokubetsushi Syōgyō Seibi ni tsuite* [Reorganizing Commercial Businesses in Syonan Municipality]. Taiping: Malayan Military Administration Chōsabu, Sept. 1944.

IER, Azb: 5. *Chōsabu Report No. 47: Syonan Tokubetsushi Rōmu Jijō Chōsa: Hōjin Keiei Kōgyō wo chūshin to shite* [A Study of the Labour Situation in Syonan Municipality Focusing on Factories Managed by Japanese]. Taiping: Malayan Military Administration Chōsabu, Oct. 1944.

IER, Azb: 7. *Chōsabu Report No. 50: Malaya-chiku Kakei Chōsa Hōkoku* [A Report on the Household Expenditure Survey in Malaya]. Taiping: Malayan Military Administration Chōsabu, Oct. 1944.

IER, Azb: 8. *Chōsabu Report No. 51: Malaya tokuni Syonan Tokubetsushi ni okeru Beikoku Yu'nyu ni tsuite* [Rice Imports to Malaya, with special reference to Syonan Municipality]. Taiping: Malayan Military Administration Chōsabu, Oct. 1944.

IER, Azb: 10. *Chōsabu Report No. 55: Malacca Shū Shokuryō Tōsei Mondai tokuni Kōtei Kakaku-sei Haishi ni tsuite* [On the Issue of Food Control in Malacca Region, Particularly the Repeal of the System of Official Pricing]. Taiping: Malayan Military Administration Chōsabu, Nov. 1944.

IER, Azb: 13. *Chōsabu Report No. 61: Malaya ni okeru Seisen Shokuhin Tōsei Hōshiki to Nijū Kakaku-sei Mondai ni tsuite* [On the System of Controlling Perishable Foods and the Issue of Double Pricing in Malaya]. Taiping: Malayan Military Administration Chōsabu, Jan. 1945.

IER Azb: 27A. *Chōsa Kikan Shunin Kaidō Hōkokusho* [Report on the Heads of Research Conference], 11–12 Oct. 1943. Singapore: Military Administration Chōsabu, 1943.

IER, Azb: 48. 'Malaya ni okeru Inflation no Jōkyō to Taisaku' [Inflationary Situation in Malaya and Its Countermeasures]. *Chōsabu News* 2 (25 May 1944): 23.

IER, Azb: 48. 'Syonan Seikatsu Hitsujuhin Kouri Kakaku Shirabe [Survey of Retail Prices of Everyday Necessities in Singapore], April 1943–April 1944'. *Chōsabu News* 2 (25 May 1944).

IER, Azb: 48. 'Chōsabu Nisshi [Chōsabu Diary]'. *Chōsabu News* 3 (5 June 1944): 35–6.

IER, Azb: 48. 'Penang Eppōsho no Kaisetsu' [Establishment of a Reading Room in Penang]. *Chōsabu News* 4 (20 June 1944): 19.

IER, Azb: 48. *Syonan Seikatsu Hitsujyuhin Kouri Kakaku Gaiyō* [Summary of Retail Prices of Daily Necessities in Singapore] *May 1944*. Taiping: Malaya Military Administration Chōsabu, June 1944.

IER, Azb: 48. 'Syonan Bukka no Dōkō [Movement of Prices in Singapore], June 1944'. *Chōsabu News* 6 (20 July 1944): 15–8.

IER, Azb: 48. 'Syonan Haikyū Kikō' [Rationing Organization in Singapore]. *Chōsabu News* 6 (20 July 1944): 1–7.

IER, Azb: 48. 'Syonan Tokubetsushi Shuyō Shokuryō Haikyū Kikō ni tsuite' [Syonan Municipality Major Food Rationing Organizations]. *Chōsabu News* 6 (20 July 1944): 7.

IER, Azb: 48. 'Syonan-tō Hatasaku Nōka Jittai Chōsa Kanken' [A Survey of Syonan Island's Vegetable Farmers]. *Chōsabu News* 6 (20 July 1944): 8–11.

IER, Azb: 50. *Chōsabu Report No. 23: Zairai Tsūka Kaishū Mondai ni tsuite* [On Issues Related to Withdrawal of Local Currency]. Singapore: Southern Military Administration Chōsabu, Dec. 1943.

IER, Azb: 50. *Chōsabu Report No. 26: Syonan Tokubetsushi no Shokugyō betsu Jinkō* [Syonan Municipality Population by Occupation]. Singapore: Southern Military Administration Chōsabu, Dec. 1943.

IER, Bn: 4. *Gench Jikatsu Gokanen Keikaku (An)* [A (Draft) Five-Year Plan for a Local Self-sufficient Economy]. Singapore: Southern Military Administration, Department of General Staff, September 1943.

National Institute for Defense Studies (NIDS)

NIDS, Nansei Gunsei 16. *Chōsabu Report No. 12: Syonan-shi ni okeru Minzoku-betsu Seitei Seikatsu Jittai Chōsa: Minzoku-betsu Jūyō Seikatsu Hitsujuhin ni kansuru Kakaku, Sūryō oyobi Hitsuju no Teido no Chōsa wo chūshin to shite* [A Study of Lowest Levels of Living by Ethnic Group in Syonan Municipality: Price, Quantity and the Relative Importance of Daily Necessities, by Ethnic Group]. Singapore: Southern Military Administration Chōsabu, Oct. 1943.

NIDS, Nansei Gunsei 18. *Chōsabu Report No. 35: Syonan Tokubetsushi wo chūshin to seru Bukka Taisaku* [Countermeasures on Price, Especially in Syonan Municipality]. Singapore: Southern Military Administration Chōsabu, Mar. 1944.

NIDS, Nansei Gunsei 18. *Chōsabu Report No. 41: Dokō Kankei Shūkyō Gyōsei Sankō Shiryō* [Reference Materials on Sultan's Religious Administration]. Singapore: Southern Military Administration Chōsabu, July 1944.

NIDS, Nansei Gunsei 27. *Showa 19 nendo Malaya-Chiku Chōsa Keikaku* [A (Draft) Research Plan for the Malaya Region in 1943]. Singapore: Southern Military Administration, Chōsabu, June 1943.

NIDS, Nansei Gunsei 29, *Keizai Hoan ni kansuru Jōkyō Shirabe, Syonan Tokubetsushi oyobi Johore shū* [Conditions of Economic Security in Syonan Municipality and Johore]. Singapore: Southern Military Administration, Department of Police Administration, Mar. 1943.

NIDS, Nansei Gunsei 29. *Syonan Tokubetsushi Jūyō Kōjō Genjō Gaikyō* [Important Industrial Factories in Syonan Municipality]. Singapore: Southern Military Administration, Department of General Affairs, Research Office, Mar. 1943.

NIDS, Nansei Gunsei 30, *Shokuryō Mondai to Kansho Saibai* [Food Problems and Cultivation of the Sweet Potato]. Publication place unknown [probably Medan, Sumatra], n.d. [probably spring 1943].

NIDS, Nansei Gunsei 47. 'Perak Dokō Jijō ni tsuite' [Matters Related to the Sultan of Perak], *Chōsabu News* 4 (21 June 1944): 3–6.

NIDS, Nansei Malaya/Java 412. *Syonan Seikatsu Hitsujuhin Kouri Kakaku Gaikyō* [Summary Report on Retail Prices of Everyday Necessities in Singapore]. Singapore: Southern Military Administration, June 1944.

NIDS, Nansei Malaya/Java 412. *Malaya Tōkei* [Malayan Statistics], *No. 3 Penang*. Penang: Penang State Government, Jan.–June 1944.

Malaya and Singapore

Straits Settlements. 'Commission on Profiteering, Straits Settlements (Second Interim Report)', *Straits Settlements Legislative Council Proceedings, 1920*. Singapore: Government Printing Office, 1920.

Federated Malay States, *Report of the Rice Cultivation Committee*, 2 vols. Kuala Lumpur: Government Press, 1931.

'Report on the Straits Settlements Police Force and on the State of Crime', *Straits Settlements Annual Reports 1930*. Singapore: Government Printing Office, 1931.

Malaya. *British Malaya, a Report on the 1931 Census* by C.A. Vlieland. Singapore: Government Printing Office, 1932.

Straits Settlements. 'Committee to Investigate the Hawker Question', *Straits Settlements Legislative Council Proceedings 1932*.

———. *Report of the Commission to Enquire into and Report on the Trade of the Colony*, 5 vols. Singapore: Government Printing Office, 1934.

British Military Administration. *Final Report Nutrition Unit*. April 1946.

Malayan Union. *Report of the Medical Department 1946* by R.B. MacGregor. Kuala Lumpur: Malayan Union Government Press, 1947.

Singapore Department of Social Welfare. *First Report of the Singapore Department of Social Welfare, June to December 1946*. Singapore: G.H. Kiatt, 1947.

Singapore. *Annual Report of the Medical Department 1946*. Singapore: Government Printing Office, 1947.

Singapore Department of Social Welfare. *A Social Survey of Singapore*. Singapore: Department of Social Welfare, 1947.

Malayan Union. *Report on the Registration of Births and Deaths for the Years 1941 to 1946*. Kuala Lumpur: Malayan Union Government Press, 1948.

Singapore. *Annual Report on the Registration of Births and Deaths for the Years 1940–47*, by E.J. Phillips. Singapore: Government Printing Office, 1948.

Malaya. *A Report on the 1947 Census of Population*, by M.V. Del Tufo. London: Crown Agents, 1949.

United States

Office of Strategic Services, Research and Analysis Branch: Assemblages and Reports (published in Washington, DC, or Honolulu)

United States Strategic Bombing Survey. *The Effects of Strategic Bombing on Japan's War Economy*. Washington, DC: Overall Economic Effects Division, United States Strategic Bombing Survey, 1946.

———. *The War against Japanese Transportation 1941–1945*. Washington, DC: Transportation Division, United States Strategic Bombing Survey, 1947.

R&A 34 *Singapore*. 12 Dec. 1941.

R&A 1433 *Political and Economic Changes Effected by the Japanese in Malaya*. 1 Dec. 1943.

R&A 1791 *Implementation Study of Malaya, Part 1 Moral Objectives*. 15 Mar. 1944.

R&A 2137 *Industrial Facilities in Malaya*. 15 May 1944.

R&A 2072 *Japanese Administration in Malaya*. 8 June 1944.
R&A 2423 *Singapore under Japanese Domination*. 8 Sept. 1944.
R&A 2589 *The Rubber Industry of Southeast Asia: An Estimate of Present Conditions and Anticipated Capabilities*. 16 Dec. 1944.

United Kingdom

NA, WO203/4499, 'Rice—S.E.A.C. Territories'.

International Organizations

League of Nations, *World Economic Survey, 1941/42*. Geneva: League of Nations, 1942.

Books and Articles

Adachi Hiroaki. *'Dai Tōa Kyōei Ken' no Keizai Kōsō: Ikinai Sangyō to Dai Tōa Kensetsu Shingikai* [Economic Design of the 'Greater East Asia Co-prosperity Sphere': Intra-sphere Industrial Development and the Council for the Greater East Asia Co-prosperity Sphere]. Tokyo: Yoshikawa Kōbunkan, 2013.

Akamatsu Kaname. 'Wagakuni Yōmō Kōgyōhin no Sūsei' [Trend of Japan's Woollen Goods Industry]. *Shōgyō Keizai Ronsō* 13 (1935): 129–212.

———. 'Ueda Sensei to Shōdai Tōa Keizai Kenkyūjo' [Professor Ueda and the Research Institute for East Asian Economies at Tokyo University of Commerce]. *Ikkyō Ronsō* 7, 1 (1941): 112.

———. 'Dai Tōa bōeki no Rekishiteki Ruikei' [Historical Patterns of Great East Asian Trade]. In *Tōa Keizai Kenkyūjo Nenpō*, Vol. 1. Tokyo: Nihon Hyōron Sha, 1942.

———. *Keizai Shin Chitsujo no Keisei Genri* [Theory of the Formation of New Economic Order]. Tokyo: Risōsha, 1944.

———. 'A Theory of Unbalanced Growth in the World Economy'. *Welwirtschaftliches Archiv* 86, 2 (1961): 192–215.

———. 'A Historical Pattern of Economic Growth in Developing Countries'. *Developing Economies* 1 (1962): 1–23.

Akamatsu Kaname, Nakayama Ichirō and Ōkuma Nobuyuki. *Kokubō Keizai Sōron* [Theory of National Defence Economy]. Tokyo: Ganshōdō, 1942.

Akashi Yoji. 'Japanese Policy towards the Malayan Chinese 1941–1945'. *Journal of Southeast Asian Studies* 1, 2 (1970): 61–89.

———, ed. *Sakakibara-ke Shozō Nanpōgun Gunsei Sōkanbu Kankei Bunsho* [Documents of Sakakibara Family Related to Southern Military Administration Superintendent General's Office], Vol. 7. Tokyo: Ryūkei Shosha, 2004.

———, ed. *Nanpōgun Gunsei Sōkanbu Chōsabu, Malaya Gunsei Kanbu Chōsabu Hōkokusho* [Research Reports by the Southern Military Administration Chōsabu and the Malayan Military Administration Chōsabu], 1943–1945, Vol. 1. Tokyo: Ryūkei Shosha, 2006.

———. 'Colonel Watanabe Wataru: The Architect of the Malayan Military Administration, December 1941–March 1943'. In *New Perspectives on the Japanese*

Occupation in Malaya and Singapore, 1941–1945, ed. Akashi Yoji and Yoshimura Mako. Singapore: NUS Press, 2008, pp. 33–64.

Akashi Yōji and Nippon no Eiryō Malaya/Singapore Senryō Shiryō Chōsa Forum, ed. *Interview Kiroku: Nippon no Eiryō Malaya/Singapore Senryō 1941–1945* [Interview Records: Japan's Occupation of British Malaya and Singapore 1941–1945]. Tokyo: Ryūkei Shosha, 1998.

Akashi Yōji and Tokyo Daigaku Kyōyō Gakubu Kokusai Kankeiron Kenkyūshitsu, ed. *Interview Kiroku D: Nihon no Gunsei 6* [Interview Record D: Japanese Military Administration 6]. Tokyo: Tokyo Daigaku Kyōyō Gakubu Kokusai Kankei Ron Kenkyūshitsu, 1981.

Akashi Yoji and Yoshimura Mako. *New Perspectives on the Japanese Occupation in Malaya and Singapore, 1941–1945*. Singapore: NUS Press, 2008.

Allen, Louis. 'Japan as Occupying Power: The Revision of History'. In *Rethinking Japan: Social Sciences, Ideology and Thought*, ed. Adriana Boscaro, Franco Gatti and Massimo Raveri. London: Routledge, 1995.

Atcherley, Harold. *Prisoners of Japan*. Cirencester: Memoirs, 2012.

Bourne, Geoffrey H. 'Nutrition Work in Malaya under the British Military Administration'. *International Review of Vitamin Research* 21 (1949): 265–307.

Cagan, Philip. 'The Monetary Dynamics of Hyperinflation'. In *Studies in the Quantity Theory of Money*, ed. Milton Friedman. Chicago: University of Chicago Press, 1956, pp. 25–117.

Chapman, Sydney J. *The Lancashire Cotton Industry: A Study in Economic Development*. Reprint. Clifton: A.M. Kelley, 1973.

Cheah Boon Kheng. 'The Japanese Occupation of Malaya, 1941–1945: Ibrahim Yaacob and the Struggle for Indonesia Raya'. *Indonesia* 28 (Oct. 1979).

———. *Red Star over Malaya: Resistance and Conflict during and after the Japanese Occupation, 1941–1946*. 3rd ed. Singapore: Singapore University Press, 2003.

Chin Kee Onn. *Malaya Upside Down*. Singapore: Jitts & Co., 1946.

———. *Bushidō ni Naku: Nihon Saiken wo Kigansuru Ichi Gaijin yori* [Crying for Samurai Spirit: By a Foreigner Who Prays for Reconstruction in Japan]. Tokyo: Shintai Sha, 1949.

Collingham, Lizzie. *The Taste of War: World War II and the Battle for Food*. London: Allen Lane, 2011.

Corner, Edred John. *The Marquis: A Tale of Syonan-to*. Singapore: Heinemann Asia, 1981.

Dunn, C.L. and D.D. Pandya. *Indian Hygiene and Public Health*. Calcutta: Butterworth & Co., 1925.

Fryer, D.W. 'The "Million City" in Southeast Asia'. *Geographical Review* 43, 4 (1953): 474–94.

Fukami Sumio. 'Tōnan Asia ni okeru Nihon Gunsei no Chōsa' [Research by the Southern Military Administration in Southeast Asia]. *Nan'yō Bunka* 15 (Nov. 1988): 119–41.

Furuta Moto'o. 'A Survey of Village Conditions during the 1945 Famine in Vietnam'. In *Food Supply and the Japanese Occupation*, ed. Paul H. Kratoska. Houndmills: Macmillan, 1998.

Gaus Mahjudin. *M. Gaus Kaisō Roku* [Memoir of M. Gaus]. Tokyo: Waseda University Asia Pacific Research Centre, 2012.

Gilmour, O.W. *With Freedom to Singapore*. London: Ernest Benn, 1950.
Hara Kakuten. *Gendai Asia Kenkyū Seiritsushi Ron* [A Study of the History of Modern Asian Studies]. Tokyo: Keisō Shōbō, 1984.
Hara Yōnosuke. 'Hitotsubashi Daigaku no Asia-gaku: Akamatsu Kaname no Asia Keizai Ron wo chushin toshite' [Asian Studies at Hitotsubashi: Theory of Asian Economics by Akamatsu Kaname]. *Japanese Asian Studies: Booklet Series Middle East within Japan*, 8 (Mar. 2011). Available at http://www2.econ.hit-u.ac.jp.
He Wen-Lit. *Syonan Interlude*. Singapore: Mandarin Paperbacks, 1991.
Higuchi Gorō. *Sengo Zaisei Seisaku to Kokumin Keizai Kanjō* [Post-war Financial Policy and National Income Calculation]. Tokyo: Tōyō Keizai Shinpō Sha, 1950.
———. *Ginkō Riron* [Theory of Banking]. Tokyo: Tōyō Keizai Shinpō Sha, 1963.
———. *Kin'yū Shinron* [New Theory of Finance]. Tokyo: Kin'yū Journal Sha, 1964.
———. *Kokusai Kin'yū Ron* [International Monetary Theory]. Tokyo: Tōyō Keizai Shinpō Sha, 1967.
———. 'Kikeika shita Nihon no Kin'yū Seisaku' [Deformation of Japan's Monetary Policy]. *Keizai Ōrai* 20, 3 (Mar. 1968): 42–51.
Hikita Yasuyuki. *Nanpō Kyōeiken: Senji Nihon no Tōnan Asia Keizai Shihai* [Southern Co-prosperity Sphere: Japanese Economic Control in South East Asia during the War]. Tokyo: Taga Shuppan, 1995.
Hionidou, Violetta. 'The Demography of a Greek Famine: Mykonos, 1941–1942'. *Continuity and Change* 10, 2 (1995): 279–99.
Hirayama Tsutomu, 'Kokusaku Gaisha ni okeru Shain Dantai no Bunseki: Mantetsu no Middle Management wo megutte [An Analysis of an Employee Association in a Statutory Corporation: On the Middle Management of Manchurian Railway]', *Journal of Oriental Cultures* 18 (Mar. 2016): 67–104.
Hitotsubashi Daigaku Gakuenshi Hensan Jigyō Iinkai, ed. *Dainiji Taisen to Hitotsubashi* [World War II and Hitotsubashi]. Tokyo: Hitotsubashi Daigaku Gakuenshi Hensan Jigyō Iinkai, 1983.
———. *Hitotsubashi no Seminar* [Seminars at Hitotsubashi]. Tokyo: Hitotsubashi Daigaku Gakuenshi Hensan Jigyō Iinkai, 1983.
Hitotsubashi Daigaku Gakuseishi Senmon Iinkai. *Hitotsubashi Daigaku Gakusei Shi Shiryō* [Historical Material on the Academic Organization of Hitotsubashi University], Vol. 8. Tokyo: Hitotsubashi Daigaku Gakuen Shi Henshū Iinkai, 1986.
Huff, Gregg. *The Economic Growth of Singapore: Trade and Development in the Twentieth Century*. Cambridge: Cambridge University Press, 1994.
———. 'Finance for War in Asia and Its Aftermath'. In *The Cambridge History of the Second World War*, Vol. 3, ed. Michael Geyer and Adam Tooze. Cambridge: Cambridge University Press, 2015, pp. 56–93.
Huff, Gregg and Shinobu Majima. 'Financing Japan's World War II Occupation of Southeast Asia'. *Journal of Economic History* 73, 4 (2013): 938–78.
Ikema, Makoto, Yoshio Inoue, Tamotsu Nishizawa and Susumu Yamauchi, eds. *Hitotsubashi University, 1875–2000: A Hundred and Twenty-five Years of Higher Education in Japan*. London: Palgrave, 2000.
Ikeo Aiko. *Hyōden Nihon no Keizai Shisō: Akamatsu Kaname* [Biographies of Japanese Economic Thoughts: Akamatsu Kaname]. Tokyo: Nihon Keizai Hyōron Sha, 2008.

Institute of East Asian Economies. *Tōa Keizai Nenpō* [Annual Report on East Asian Economy], Vol. 1. Tokyo: Nihon Hyōron Sha, 1942.

Ishii Kanji, Hara Akira and Takeda Haruhito, eds. *Nihon Keizai Shi <4> Senji, Sengo-ki* [Japanese Economic History Vol. 4 Wartime and Postwar Periods]. Tokyo: Tokyo University Press, 2007.

Isono Osamu and Emi Kōichi. 'Tōkeigaku, Keiryō Keizaigaku' [Statistics and Quantitative Economics]. In *Hitotsubashi Daigaku Gakumonshi* [Intellectual History of Hitotsubashi], ed. Hitotsubashi Daigaku Gakuenshi Kankō Iinkai. Tokyo: Hitotsubashi Daigaku Gakuenshi Kankō Iinkai, 1986.

Itagaki Yoichi. 'Malaya Fukugō Shakai ni okeru Nationalism no Hatten' [The Development of Nationalism in Malayan Plural Society]. *Hitotsubashi University Research Annual: Economic Research*, Departmental Bulletin Paper No. 6, Mar. 1962.

Iwatake Teruhiko. *Nanpō Gunsei-ka no Keizai Shisaku: Malaya, Sumatra, Java no Kiroku* [The Economic Policies in the Southern Regions under the Military Administration: Record of Malaya, Sumatra and Java], 2 vols. Tokyo: Kunko Shoin, 1981.

———. *Nanpō Gunsei Ronshū* [Essays on Southern Military Administration]. Tokyo: Gan'nandō Shoten, 1989.

———. *Nanpō Gunsei-ka no Keizai Shisaku: Malai, Sumatora, Jawa no Kiroku* [Economic Policy under the Southern Military Administration]. Tokyo: Ryukei Shosha, 1995.

Kaneko Takanosuke. 'Dai Tōa Kensetsu no Rekishiteki Hitsuzensei' [Historical Inevitability of the Greater East Asia Co-prosperity Sphere]. In *Tōa Keizai Kenkyūjo Nenpō*, Vol. 1. Tokyo: Nihon Hyōron Sha, 1942.

Karashima Masato. *Teikoku Nihon no Asia Kenkyū* [Research on Asia by Imperial Japan]. Tokyo: Akashi Shoten, 2015.

Ko Yamada Isamu Sensei Tsuitō Bunshū Kankō Sewanin Kai. *Riron to Keiryō ni Tesshite: Yamada Isamu Sensei Tsuitō Bunshū* [Devoted to Theory and Quantification: Anthology in Memory of Professor Yamada Isamu]. Tokyo: Ronsōsha, 1987.

Kojima Kiyoshi, ed. *Akamatsu Kaname Hakase Kanreki Kinen Ronshū: Keizai Seisaku to Kokusai Bōeki* [Anthology Commemorating the Sixtieth Birthday of Dr Akamatsu Kaname: Economic Policy and International Trade]. Tokyo: Shunjyūsha, 1958.

———. 'Bōeki Seisaku, Keizai Kaihatsu Ron' [Trade Policy and Economic Development]. In *Hitotsubashi Daigaku Gakumonshi* [Intellectual History of Hitotsubashi], ed. Hitotsubashi Daigaku Gakuenshi Kankō Iinkai. Tokyo: Hitotsubashi Daigaku Gakuenshi Kankō Iinkai, 1986.

Kratoska, Paul H. 'The Post-1945 Food Shortage in British Malaya'. *Journal of Southeast Asian Studies* 19, 1 (1988): 27–47.

———. 'Banana Money: Consequences of the Demonetization of Wartime Japanese Currency in British Malaya'. *Journal of Southeast Asian Studies* 23, 1 (1992): 322–45.

———. *The Japanese Occupation of Malaya: A Social and Economic History*. London: Hurst & Company, 1998.

Kurasawa Aiko. 'Forced Delivery of Paddy and Peasant Uprisings in Indramayu, Indonesia: Japanese Occupation and Social Change'. *Developing Economies* 21, 1 (1983): 52–72.

———. 'Transportation and Rice Distribution in Southeast Asia during the Second World War'. In *Food Supplies and the Japanese Occupation*, ed. Paul H. Kratoska. Houndmills: Macmillan, 1998, pp. 32–66.

———. 'Senjiki Malaya Singapore ni okeru Beikoku Haikyū Seido' [Rice Rationing System in Wartime Malaya and Singapore]. *Mita Gakkai Zasshi* 104, 4 (Jan. 2012): 623–49.

Lee Kuan Yew. *The Singapore Story*. Singapore: Times Editions, 1998.

Lee Say Lee. 'A Study of the Rice Trade in Kedah before and during the Japanese Occupation'. *Malaysia in History* 24 (1981): 109–16.

Lee Ting Hui. 'Singapore under the Japanese, 1942–1945'. *Journal of the South Seas Society* 17, 1 (1961): 31–69.

Low, N.I. *When Singapore Was Syonan-to*. Singapore: Eastern Universities Press, 1973.

Low, N.I. and H.M. Cheng. *This Singapore (Our City of Dreadful Night)*. Singapore: Ngai Seong Press, 1946.

MacGregor, R.B. 'Medical History of the War in Malaya'. *Medical Journal of Malaya* 3, 3 (1949): 146–72.

Majima Shinobu. 'The Japanese Military Administration Department of Research Reports on Singapore's Wartime Economy'. *Journal of Asian Cultures* 18 (Mar. 2016).

Matsumura Takao. *'ABC' Mondai wa Kaiketsu dekirunoka?* [Can We Solve the 'ABC' Problem?]. Tokyo: ABC Kikaku Iinkai, 2014.

Mazower, Mark. *Inside Hitler's Greece: The Experience of Occupation, 1941–44*. New Haven: Yale University Press, 1993.

Milward, Alan S. *War, Economy and Society, 1939–1945*. London: Allen Lane, 1977.

Morris-Suzuki, Tessa. *Shōwa: An Inside History of Hirohito's Japan*. London: Athlone Press, 1984.

Nakano Satoshi. *Hishima Chōsa Hōkokusho* [Philippines Research Reports], Vols 1–4, Sept. 1943. Reprint published by Ryūkei Shosha, 1993.

Nicholls, Lucius. 'Nutrition in Singapore during Japanese Occupation'. *British Medical Journal* 1, 4548 (1948): 37–9.

Nishizawa Tamotsu. 'Ueda Teijirō no Keizai Shisō: Shakaikaizō to Kigyōsha wo chūshin ni' [Ideas of Ueda Teijirō: On Social Reform and Entrepreneurship]. In *Kindai Nihon to Igirisu Shisō* [Modern Japan and British Philosophy], ed. Sugihara Shirō. Tokyo: Nihon Keizai Hyōron Sha, 1995.

———. 'Fukuda Tokuzō no Keizai Shisō: Kōsei Keizai, Shakai Seisaku wo chūshin ni' [Ideas of Fukuda Tokuzō: On Welfare Economics and Social Policy]. *Ikkyō Ronsō* 132, 4 (2004): 357–85.

———. 'Fukuda Tokuzō no Keizai Shisō: Kōsei Keizai, Shakai Seisaku wo chūshin ni' [Ideas of Fukuda Tokuzō: On Welfare Economics and Social Policy]. *Hitotsubashi Forum* 21, 59 (public lecture, 28 June 2005). Available at http://jfn.josuikai.net.

Odabe Yūji. *Tokugawa Yoshichika no Jūgonen Sensō* [Tokugawa Yoshichika's 15-Year War]. Tokyo: Aoki Shoten, 1988.

Odaka Kōnosuke. 'Senji-ka no Gakumon to Kenkyū' [Scholarship and Education during the War]. Josuikai Forum: 7/8, uploaded on 1 Apr. 2008. Available at https://www.josuikai.net.

Okazaki Tetsuji. 'Development and Management of the Manchurian Economy under Japan's Empire'. In *Economies under Occupation: The Hegemony of Nazi Germany and Imperial Japan*, ed. Marcel Boldorf and Tetsuji Okazaki. London: Routledge, 2015, pp. 178–90.

Ōkōchi Kazuo. *Senji Shakai Seisaku* [The Theory of Wartime Social Policy]. Tokyo: Jichō Sha, 1940.

Ooi Keat Gin. 'The Japanese Occupation and the Peoples of Sarawak'. In *Southeast Asian Minorities in the Wartime Japanese Empire*, ed. Paul H. Kratoska. London: Routledge, 2002, pp. 133–52.

Ōtsuka Kin'nosuke. *Ōtsuka Kin'nosuke Chosaku Shū* [Writings of Ōtsuka Kin'nosuke], Vols 1–9. Tokyo: Iwanami Shoten, 1980.

Pluvier, Jan M. *South-East Asia from Colonialism to Independence*. Kuala Lumpur: Oxford University Press, 1974.

Satō Ryūzō and Martin J. Beckmann, eds. *Technology, Organization and Economic Structure: Essays in Honour of Prof. Isamu Yamada*, Lecture notes in economics and mathematical systems. New York: Springer-Verlag, 1983.

Sato Shigeru. 'Oppression and Romanticism: The Food Supply of Java during the Japanese Occupation'. In *Food Supply and the Japanese Occupation*, ed. Paul H. Kratoska. Houndmills: Macmillan, 1998.

Scott, James C. 'An Approach to the Problems of Food Supply in Southeast Asia during World War Two'. In *Food Supply in the Second World War*, ed. Bernd Martin and Alan S. Milward. Ostfildern: Scripta Mercaturae, 1985, pp. 269–82.

Shibata Yoshimasa. *Senryōchi Tsūka Kin'yū Seisaku no Tenkai* [Japan's Monetary Policy in the Occupied Territories]. Tokyo: Nihon Keizai Shinbun Sha, 1999.

Shinozaki Mamoru. *Syonan, My Story: The Japanese Occupation of Singapore*. Singapore: Times Books International, 1975.

———. *Singapore Senryō Hiwa: Sensō to sono Ningenzō* [Secret Stories of the Occupation of Singapore]. Tokyo: Hara Shobō, 1976.

Singapore Shisei Kai, ed. *Syonan Tokubetsushi Shi: Senji chū no Singapore* [Syonan Municipality during the war]. Tokyo: Nihon Singapore Kyōkai, 1987.

Su Fang Ng. 'Chin Kee Onn's Ma-rai-ee and the Narration of the Malayan Nationalist Subject in the Aftermath of the Pacific War'. *Journal of Commonwealth Literature* 34, 1 (1999): 87.

Sugimoto Ei'ichi. *Beikoku Juyō Hōsoku no Kenkyū* [A Study of Patterns of Rice Demand]. Tokyo: Iwanami Shoten, 1925.

———. 'Keizai Tōsei to Ryūdōsei Genri [Economic Control and the Principle of Liquidity]'. *Ikkyō Ronsō* 6, 1 (1940).

Takase Sōtarō Sensei Kinen Jigyōkai, ed. *Takase Sōtarō*. Tokyo: Takase Sōtarō Sensei Kinen Jogyōkai, 1970.

Tan Yeok Seong. *The Extortion by the Japanese Military Administration of $50,000,000 from the Chinese in Malaya*. Singapore: Nanyang Book Co., 1947.

Tarling, Nicholas. '"An Attempt to Fly in the Face of the Ordinary Laws of Supply and Demand": The British and Siamese Rice 1945–7'. *Journal of the Siam Society* 75 (1987): 140–86.

Thompson, Virginia. *Labor Problems in Southeast Asia*. New Haven: Yale University Press, 1947.

Tokugawa Yoshichika. *Saigo no Tonosama* [The Last Samurai Lord]. Tokyo: Kodansha, 1973.

Tooze, Adam. *The Wages of Destruction: The Making and Breaking of the Nazi Economy*. London: Allen Lane, 2006.

Totani, Yuma. *The Tokyo War Crimes Trial: The Pursuit of Justice in the Wake of World War II*. Cambridge: Harvard University Asia Center, 2008.

Twang Peck Yang. *The Chinese Business Élite in Indonesia and the Transition to Independence*. Kuala Lumpur: Oxford University Press, 1998.

Ueda Teijirō. *Ueda Teijirō Nikki* [Diary of Ueda Teijirō]. Tokyo: Keiō Tsūshin, 1963.

Valaoras, V.G. 'Some Effects of Famine on the Population of Greece'. *Milbank Memorial Fund Quarterly* 24, 3 (1946): 215–34.

Yamada Isamu. *Tōa Nōgyō Seisan Shisū no Kenkyū: Naichi, Chōsen, Taiwan no bu* [A Study of East Asian Agricultural Production Indices], Institute of East Asian Economies Monograph No. 1. Tokyo: Nihon Hyōron Sha, 1942.

———. *Theory and Application of Interindustry Analysis*, Economic Research Series No. 4. Institute of Economic Research, Hitotsubashi University. Tokyo: Kinokuniya, 1961.

———. 'Measuring Changes in Economic Structure with Special Reference to the Industrial Population in Malaya'. *Kajian Ekonomi Malaysia: Journal of the Malaysian Economic Association* 1, 1 (June 1964): 59–69.

———. 'Input-Output Model of a Dual Economy'. *Kajian Ekonomi Malaysia: Journal of the Malaysian Economic Association* 3, 2 (Dec. 1966): 59–70.

Yamaguchi Shigeru and Higuchi Gorō. *Nihon Inflation no Bunseki* [Analysis of Inflation in Japan], Monographs in Modern Economics No. 12. Tokyo: Tōyō Keizai Shinpō Sha, 1948.

Yamamoto Yūzō. '*Dai Tōa Kyōei Ken no Keizai Shi Kenkyū* [An Economic History of the Greater East Asia Co-prosperity Sphere]'. Nagoya: Nagoya University Press, 2011.

Yamashita Kunio. 'Kin'yū Ron [Money Theory]'. In *Hitotsubashi Daigaku Gakumonshi* [Intellectual History of Hitotsubashi], ed. Hitotsubashi Daigaku Gakuenshi Kankō Iinkai. Tokyo: Hitotsubashi Daigaku Gakuenshi Kankō Iinkai, 1986.

Yap Pheng Geck. *Scholar, Banker, Gentleman Soldier: The Reminiscences of Dr. Yap Pheng Geck*. Singapore: Times Books, 1982.

Index

References to figures are shown in *italics*. References to tables are shown in **bold**. References to footnotes consist of the page number followed by the letter 'n' followed by the number of the note, e.g. 62n58 refers to note no. 58 on page 62.